AMERICAN GOVERNMENT

Horydczak

★
★

MAGRUDER'S

AMERICAN
GOVERNMENT

★
1954
★
★

REVISED BY

WILLIAM A. McCLENAGHAN

DEPARTMENT OF POLITICAL SCIENCE
OREGON STATE COLLEGE

★
★
★
★
★

BOSTON
ALLYN AND BACON, INC.
NEW YORK   CHICAGO   ATLANTA   DALLAS   SAN FRANCISCO

★
★
★

American Government, first published in 1917, is an enduring symbol of its author's faith in American ideals and American institutions. The life of Frank Abbott Magruder (1882–1949) was an outstanding example of Americanism at its very best. His career as teacher, author, and tireless worker in civic and religious undertakings remains an inspiring memory to all who knew him.

During the last years of Dr. Magruder's life, his former student and close friend, Mr. William A. McClenaghan, assisted him in preparing the annual editions of *American Government* and will carry on the work of revision. Thus teachers in high schools everywhere may be sure that *American Government* will continue those features which have made it the leader in its field.

PREFACE

Magruder's *American Government*, 1954, revised by McClenaghan, is the thirty-seventh edition of this national leader. This favorite in its field combines an excellent description of the basic structure of government with an up-to-date annual report of our government at work.

These annual revisions are needed to show the functional nature of our government. Indeed, only by such annual revisions, which present new legislation as it results from popular demand, can a book give us a true picture of our government as a living and growing thing.

Among the new topics presented are those dealing with the first Republican administration in twenty years, the reorganization of the Defense Department, the new Cabinet Department of Health, Education and Welfare, our $53,000,000,000 Congress of the past year, the "Fair Trade Acts" controversy pro and con, the appointment of a new Chief Justice of the United States, municipal problems today, the Korean Truce, the 1953 Treaty with Spain, and consideration of the position of the United States in World Affairs in 1954.

Supplementary materials have been revised in keeping with changes in the subject matter. In this way the new edition presents recent developments in local government, new statistics on expenditures and taxes, new illustrations, new references, and new problems for discussion.

Loyal Americans, as in years past, feel that there must be no let-up in our attack on threats to our American way of life. Eternal vigilance is still a necessary safeguard to our liberty. All of us must keep in our minds and hearts a knowledge and love of the documents that set forth our rights, our privileges, our duties. We should know our Declaration of Independence (page vii) and the American's Creed (page xi). We should be thoroughly familiar with our Constitution (pages 731–754). Students, teachers, everyone, must be helped to know our government, to take a constant interest in it, and be a part of it. Thus can our liberty be preserved and the blessings of our republic be assured to future generations.

iii

Class Activities and Study Aids

The subject of American government is especially rich in resource materials for class projects and supplementary reading programs. The following suggestions have been carefully developed to aid the teacher in discovering and selecting those activities which are particularly suited to the needs and interests of the class.

Field trips are always an incentive to interest. They should be made a specific part of the year's activities and should be definitely scheduled. Plan surely for trips to local and county agencies of government and, if possible, to the State and National capitals. Plan, likewise, to invite local, State, and National legislators to discuss their work before the class or school assembly, or even before a community group if that is necessary in order to justify taking the officials' time. Plan, also, to publicize community lectures and forums on subjects closely related to the work of the class.

To conserve time in study activities, the author has prepared a workbook to accompany this textbook. The workbook, *Our Government at Work*, contains exercise materials that include class activities, summary and thought questions, and information tests. A special set of achievement tests, also expressly designed to accompany this textbook, is Erbe and Denny's *American Government Tests*. These tests are easy to administer and are easily scored by special scoring methods.

The reading program is an important part of the course in American government no matter how limited the local facilities for research may be. Before the year's study begins, every student should *read* and remember for quick reference THE CONSTITUTION OF THE UNITED STATES, reprinted with annotations as Appendix I in this book.

The Select Bibliographies, the General Bibliography (Appendix III), and the discussion of Government publications (Appendix IV) provide guidance to excellent resource materials. Every effort should be made to use them to the fullest extent possible.

CONTENTS

CONTENTS

Painting by John Trumbull

PRESENTING THE DECLARATION OF INDEPENDENCE TO CONGRESS

The Committee, through its chairman, Thomas Jefferson, is presenting the written sheets to John Hancock, president of the Congress. We do well to read anew the words of this document before we take up the study of our Constitution and the principles of citizenship it supports.

DECLARATION OF INDEPENDENCE

In Congress, July 4, 1776

THE UNANIMOUS DECLARATION OF THE THIRTEEN UNITED STATES OF AMERICA

WHEN in the Course of human events, it becomes necessary for one people to dissolve the political bands which have connected them with another, and to assume among the Powers of the earth, the separate and equal station to which the Laws of Nature and of Nature's God entitle them, a decent respect to the opinions of mankind requires that they should declare the causes which impel them to the separation.

We hold these truths to be self-evident: that all men are created equal; that they are endowed by their Creator with certain unalienable Rights; that among these are Life, Liberty and the pursuit of Happiness. That to secure these rights, Governments are instituted among Men, deriving their just powers from the consent of the governed; That whenever any Form of Government becomes destructive of these ends it is the Right of the People to alter or to abolish it, and to institute a new Government, laying its foundation on such principles and organizing its powers in such form, as to them shall seem most likely to effect their Safety and Happiness. Prudence, indeed, will dictate that Governments long established should not be changed for light and transient causes; and accordingly all experience hath shown, that mankind are more disposed to suffer, while evils are sufferable, than to right themselves by abolishing the forms to which they are accustomed. But when a long train of abuses and usurpations, pursuing invariably the same Object evinces a design to reduce them under absolute Despotism, it is their right, it is their duty, to throw off such Government, and to provide new Guards for their future security. — Such has been the patient sufferance of these Colonies; and such is now the necessity which constrains them to alter their former Systems of Government. The history of the present King of Great Britain is a history of repeated injuries and usurpations, all having in direct object the establishment of an absolute Tyranny over these States. To prove this, let Facts be submitted to a candid world.

He has refused his Assent to Laws, the most wholesome and necessary for the public good.

He has forbidden his Governors to pass Laws of immediate and pressing importance, unless suspended in their operation till his Assent should be obtained; and when so suspended, he has utterly neglected to attend to them.

He has refused to pass other Laws for the accommodation of large districts of people, unless those people would relinquish the right of Representation in the Legislature, a right inestimable to them and formidable to tyrants only.

He has called together legislative bodies at places unusual, uncomfortable, and distant from the depository of their Public Records, for the sole purpose of fatiguing them into compliance with his measures.

He has dissolved Representative Houses repeatedly, for opposing with manly firmness his invasions on the rights of the people.

He has refused, for a long time after such dissolutions, to cause others to be elected, whereby the Legislative Powers, incapable of Annihilation, have returned to the People at large for their exercise; the State remaining, in the meantime, exposed to all the dangers of invasions from without, and convulsions within.

He has endeavored to prevent the population of these States; for that purpose obstructing the Laws for the Naturalization of Foreigners; refusing to pass others to encourage their migration hither, and raising the conditions of new Appropriations of Lands.

He has obstructed the Administration of Justice, by refusing his Assent to Laws for establishing Judiciary Powers.

He has made Judges dependent on his will alone for the tenure of their offices, and the amount and payment of their salaries.

He has erected a multitude of New Offices, and sent hither swarms of Officers to harass our People and eat out their substance.

He has kept among us in times of peace, Standing Armies, without the Consent of our Legislatures.

He has affected to render the Military independent of, and superior to, the Civil Power.

He has combined with others to subject us to a jurisdiction foreign to our constitutions, and unacknowledged by our laws; giving his Assent to their acts of pretended legislation:

For quartering large bodies of armed troops among us;

For protecting them, by a mock Trial, from Punishment for any Murders which they should commit on the Inhabitants of these States;

For cutting off our Trade with all parts of the world;

For imposing taxes on us without our Consent;

For depriving us, in many cases, of the benefits of a Trial by Jury;

For transporting us beyond Seas, to be tried for pretended offenses;

For abolishing the free System of English Laws in a neighboring Province, establishing therein an Arbitrary government, and enlarging its Boundaries, so as to render it at once an example and fit instrument for introducing the same absolute rule into these Colonies;

For taking away our Charters, abolishing our most valuable Laws, and altering, fundamentally, the Forms of our Governments;

For suspending our own Legislatures, and declaring themselves invested with Power to legislate for us in all cases whatsoever.

He has abdicated Government here, by declaring us out of his Protection, and waging War against us.

He has plundered our seas, ravaged our Coasts, burned our towns, and destroyed the lives of our people.

He is at this time transporting large armies of foreign mercenaries to complete the works of death, desolation and tyranny, already begun with circumstances of Cruelty and perfidy scarcely paralleled in the most barbarous ages, and totally unworthy the Head of a civilized nation.

He has constrained our fellow-citizens, taken captive on the high seas, to bear Arms against their Country, to become the executioners of their friends and Brethren, or to fall themselves by their Hands.

He has excited domestic insurrection among us, and has endeavored to bring on the inhabitants of our frontiers the merciless Indian Savages whose known rule of warfare is an undistinguished destruction of all ages, sexes, and conditions.

In every stage of these Oppressions We have Petitioned for Redress in the most humble terms. Our repeated Petitions have been answered only by repeated injury. A Prince whose character is thus marked by every act which may define a Tyrant, is unfit to be the ruler of a free people.

Nor have we been wanting in our attentions to our British brethren. We have warned them, from time to time, of attempts by their legislature to extend an unwarrantable jurisdiction over us. We have reminded them of the circumstances of our emigration and settlement here. We have appealed to their native justice and magnanimity and we have conjured them by the ties of our common kindred to disavow these usurpations, which would inevitably interrupt our connections and correspondence. They, too, have been deaf to the voice of justice and of consanguinity. We must, therefore, acquiesce in the necessity which denounces our Separation, and hold them as we hold the rest of mankind — Enemies in War; in Peace, Friends.

We, therefore, the Representatives of the **United States of America** in General Congress Assembled, appealing to the Supreme Judge of the world for the rectitude of our intentions, do, in the Name and by the Authority of the good People of these Colonies, solemnly publish and declare that these united colonies are, and of right ought to be, **Free and Independent States;** that they are Absolved from all Allegiance to the British Crown, and that all political connection between them and the state of Great Britain is, and ought to be, totally dissolved, and that, as **Free and Independent States,** they have full Power to levy War, conclude Peace, contract Alliances, establish Commerce, and do all other Acts and Things which INDEPENDENT STATES may of right do. And for the support of this Declaration, with a firm reliance on the protection of Divine Providence, we mutually pledge to each other our Lives, our Fortunes, and our sacred Honor.

JOHN HANCOCK

New Hampshire
JOSIAH BARTLETT
WILLIAM WHIPPLE
MATTHEW THORNTON

Massachusetts Bay
SAMUEL ADAMS
JOHN ADAMS
ROBERT TREAT PAINE
ELBRIDGE GERRY

Rhode Island
STEPHEN HOPKINS
WILLIAM ELLERY

Connecticut
ROGER SHERMAN
SAMUEL HUNTINGTON
WILLIAM WILLIAMS
OLIVER WOLCOTT

New York
WILLIAM FLOYD
PHILIP LIVINGSTON
FRANCIS LEWIS
LEWIS MORRIS

New Jersey
RICHARD STOCKTON
JOHN WITHERSPOON
FRANCIS HOPKINSON
JOHN HART
ABRAHAM CLARK

Pennsylvania
ROBERT MORRIS
BENJAMIN RUSH
BENJAMIN FRANKLIN
JOHN MORTON
GEORGE CLYMER
JAMES SMITH
GEORGE TAYLOR
JAMES WILSON
GEORGE ROSS

Delaware
CÆSAR RODNEY
GEORGE READ
THOMAS M'KEAN

Maryland
SAMUEL CHASE
WILLIAM PACA
THOMAS STONE
CHARLES CARROLL of Carrollton

Virginia
GEORGE WYTHE
RICHARD HENRY LEE
THOMAS JEFFERSON
BENJAMIN HARRISON
THOMAS NELSON, JR.
FRANCIS LIGHTFOOT LEE
CARTER BRAXTON

North Carolina
WILLIAM HOOPER
JOSEPH HEWES
JOHN PENN

South Carolina
EDWARD RUTLEDGE
THOMAS HEYWARD, JR.
THOMAS LYNCH, JR.
ARTHUR MIDDLETON

Georgia
BUTTON GWINNETT
LYMAN HALL
GEORGE WALTON

THE AMERICAN'S CREED

I believe in the United States of America as a government of the people, by the people, for the people, whose just powers are derived from the consent of the governed; a democracy in a republic; a sovereign Nation of many sovereign States; a perfect Union, one and inseparable, established upon those principles of freedom, equality, justice, and humanity for which American patriots sacrificed their lives and fortunes.

I therefore believe it is my duty to my country to love it; to support its Constitution; to obey its laws; to respect its flag; and to defend it against all enemies.

WILLIAM TYLER PAGE

LEADERS OF THE PAST

Mount Rushmore Memorial is famous throughout the world for these massive
carvings of Washington, Jefferson, Theodore Roosevelt, and Lincoln.

AMERICAN GOVERNMENT

CHAPTER I

STRENGTH THROUGH UNION

THE FRUITS OF FREEDOM: PEACE, JUSTICE, AND SECURITY

Our American Heritage. — "We hold these truths to be self-evident: that all men are created equal; that they are endowed by their Creator with certain unalienable Rights; that among these are Life, Liberty, and the pursuit of Happiness. . . ." With these bold words our forefathers founded this nation — the United States of America. This faith in individualism, in freedom, in equality, which gave it birth, has made it the greatest nation on earth. This faith is our American heritage.

Ours is a nation with the highest standard of living ever known to man. Look about you; it is easy to see the material things that make it so: automobiles, skyscrapers, radios, busy factories, airplanes, mighty dams, electric lights, and fertile farms; the list is endless. But these things are only the material evidences of America's greatness. They may *show* that we are great, but in themselves they do not *make* us great.

We are a great nation and a great people today because we have carried forward the spirit of the Declaration of Independence; we have maintained what is truly "a government of the people, by the people, for the people."

"Peace, Good Will toward Men." — The increasing horrors and waste of war make world peace and security more vital now than ever before. As the leader of the free nations of the world, the United States is working for a lasting peace among all nations. But at the same time we know that the only sure guarantee of peace in today's strife-torn world lies in our own strength and in that of our Allies. We oppose the Soviet-led communist dictatorships because we love liberty even more than we prize peace. We agree with Patrick Henry that peace is not to be bought at the price of chains and slavery.

"To Form a More Perfect Union"

(From the Preamble to the Constitution of the United States)

In Union There Is Strength. — In these days of world tensions, thoughtful students of government realize more keenly than ever before that Federal Union is America's contribution to nation-building.

Courtesy Philadelphia Chamber of Commerce

INDEPENDENCE HALL

The Declaration of Independence was signed here July 4, 1776; and the Constitution September 17, 1787.

Here, on this continent, our forefathers created the United States,

"to form a more perfect Union, establish justice, insure domestic tranquillity, provide for the common defense, promote the general welfare, and secure the blessings of liberty to ourselves and our posterity."

Thus the makers of the Constitution of the United States of America showed mankind that independent states could, through peaceful agreement, form a Federal Union in which powers of general concern were vested in the Union, while authority in local matters was retained by the States.

Our struggle as a nation for closer union and common justice has not been easy. Occasionally political strife and sometimes physical violence have marred our progress. Yet these growing pains have not kept us from moving ahead toward a standard of living unequaled by any other nation.

The Union Has Given Us a Land of Abundance. — We are fortunate in having a climate that varies from semi-tropical to arctic, and produces everything from tropical oranges to arctic furs. We have iron, coal, oil, and timber in abundance. Because our forty-eight States are united in one great nation, we have a vast domestic market containing 160,000,000 people and stretching across the continent. And within this market are none of the trade barriers and petty international jealousies that plague other areas of the world.

A Closer Union through Transportation and Communication. — The formation of a Federal Union created a tool with which to build a stronger Nation. This tool, the Constitution, has made possible the co-operation of our present forty-eight States in the common interest. Because we were united we were able to build our railroads over almost

A CATERPILLAR COMBINE

This machine will harvest forty acres of wheat in ten hours in the famous hilly Palouse Wheat Belt near Spokane, Washington. Here forty bushels to the acre are not unusual.

uninhabited plains to connect the West with the more populous East. We joined our highways into a network from the Atlantic to the Pacific and from Canada to Mexico. We have also connected all parts of the country with airways.

Telegraph and telephone lines were built so that we might talk from New York to New Orleans or from Washington to Walla Walla with the same ease that we call the neighborhood grocer. Radio and television have given every American a ringside seat at the important events of the world — an address by the President, United Nations proceedings, political party conventions, or on-the-scene broadcasts from the

DOUGLAS F4D SKYRAY

In October, 1953, this carrier-based jet interceptor achieved an official world speed record at an average speed of 753.4 miles per hour.

S.S. UNITED STATES

This 51,500 ton passenger liner now holds the records for both east and west crossings of the Atlantic — the first time in 100 years that an American-built liner has held these records.

trouble-spots of the world.   Press, radio, and television coverage of
the 1952 presidential campaign was the most extensive in our history.
Some 60,000,000 people witnessed the national conventions on television and millions more followed the proceedings by radio.   The
whole world is seemingly smaller — almost a neighborhood — because
time and space have been conquered by man's ingenuity.

"To Establish Justice"
(From the Preamble to the Constitution)

Justice and the American Heritage. — We have defined the American
heritage as a faith in individualism, in freedom, and in equality.   It
is a belief in the dignity and worth of every human being.

The Framers of our Constitution recognized that an ordered system
of justice is essential to the maintenance of this belief.   They agreed
with Thomas Jefferson that the establishing and maintaining of justice
is "the most sacred of the duties of a government."

Federal Courts Provided. — Until the Constitution was established,
we had only State courts to decide disputes between States or between
citizens of different States.   The Constitution provided for a Supreme
Court and also authorized Congress to establish other Federal courts.
The first bill to be considered in the Senate of the new Congress of
the United States in 1789 was a measure which set the basic pattern
of our national court system.   Since that beginning, the national
judiciary has acted as the guardian of the rights and liberties of our
people.   It is the duty of all the branches and agencies of the National
Government to operate within the limits of the Constitution.   But
it is the special function of the courts to safeguard the people against
arbitrary action by the Government.

The Bill of Rights was added to the Constitution in 1791 to guarantee
the people freedom from injustices by the National Government such
as those they had suffered under George III of England.   For instance,
a man cannot be haled into a Federal court and forced to stand trial
until a grand jury composed of his fellow citizens decides that there is
enough evidence against him to justify a trial.

At times the Government finds it desirable to take over certain
property for its own use, such as the right of way for a street or highway.   Under the Bill of Rights this cannot be done without paying
the owner a fair price for the property.

1—10 amend.

JUDGMENT BY HYSTERIA

Old common-law practices like this seventeenth century trial for witchcraft have long since been dropped from our statute books.

Our Idea of Justice Becoming More Humane. — We inherited from the English many common-law rules which were developed by their courts, but in recent years we have replaced some of these rules by more humane statutes. For instance, under the old law, a young woman, whose hair was disheveled because of the heat, and whose scalp was torn off by a laundry mangle, could not obtain damages because the employer showed that she had contributed to the accident. A workman injured in a quarry by a runaway car could not obtain damages because a drunken fellow workman had released the car.

State after State has abolished these old common-law defenses, and today in all States the injured in designated industries are paid damages even though they have been careless. This compensation is paid from workmen's compensation insurance funds maintained by taxing employers and employees. Thus the cost of all injuries is placed upon the entire industry rather than upon the individual.

In the earlier years of our industrial development factory shutdowns might last for weeks or even months, leaving the head of a family without income to meet his grocery bills and rent. Today unemployment compensation relieves this hardship. An unemployment compensation fund is raised by taxing employers a percentage of the payroll. When employees are laid off they receive a small weekly check from the fund for a limited number of weeks.

"To Insure Domestic Tranquillity"
(From the Preamble to the Constitution)

The Government Guarantees Order. — Order is essential to the well-being of any society, and keeping the peace at home has always been one of the major functions of government. This responsibility was very much in the minds of the men who framed the Constitution.

As we shall see, the economic difficulties of the 1780's in the United States was one of the reasons for the drafting of the new Constitution. The strained conditions of the period (known as the Critical Period in American history) even led to open violence in some instances.

One of the most spectacular of these incidents, Shays' Rebellion, took place in Massachusetts. As in most States at that time, the farmers and merchants were ranged against one another over the question of "hard" or "soft" money. For six months (1786–1787) an armed band of several hundred farmers and debtors under the command of Daniel Shays defied the State Government. They prevented many of the county courts from sitting in debt cases and even threatened to lay siege to Boston. Their attempt to capture the arsenal at Springfield had to be repulsed with grape-shot. Only when the State militia took the field were the "rebels" finally dispersed.

If rebellion or riots occur in any State today, the President can use his power as Commander-in-Chief of the armed forces to send troops to restore order. When the trouble is purely local, the President will furnish protection if asked to do so by the State legislature or the governor.

Man-made violence is much less disruptive than the rampages of nature. Here, too, the Government stands ready to come to the aid of the stricken areas. For example, the Missouri River flood in the spring of 1952 was the most disastrous one since 1844. The armed forces were used to aid flood victims and protect their property. Medical supplies, food, clothing, temporary shelter and other necessities were rushed to the critical areas.

"To Provide for the Common Defense"
(From the Preamble to the Constitution)

National Defense. — In addition to keeping the peace at home, defense against foreign enemies has always been one of the major functions of government.   The men who drafted the Constitution well understood this fact.   George Washington was President of the Constitutional Convention and many of its members had served in his Revolutionary armies.

THE JEFFERSON MEMORIAL IN WASHINGTON   © *Harris & Ewing*

This memorial on the Tidal Basin in Washington is in honor of the author of the Declaration of Independence, founder of the University of Virginia, promoter of the Louisiana Purchase, and the third President of the United States.

Two World Wars and the threat of a third have sharply emphasized the importance of national defense.   No sooner had Hitler's war-making dictatorship been defeated than the Soviet Union, through its military and political expansion, became another threat to the democracies of the world.   Today Congress appropriates some $40,000,000,000 a year for national defense.   Since World War II we have sent $45,000,000,000 in military and economic aid to our Allies in the Cold War against world communism.   Our armed forces are larger than ever before in our peacetime history.

But We Are a Non-Militaristic People. — As a people, we hate war. We have a strong non-militaristic tradition.   The armed forces are controlled by civilian authorities — the President and Congress. The law even requires that the Secretary of Defense must not have served in the armed forces for at least ten years before his appointment. Control by militarists has usually gone hand-in-hand with dictatorship, as it did in Germany and Japan.

Increasing Cost of Wars. — It is said that in earlier wars it cost 50 cents to kill an enemy; now it costs $75,000. The First World War cost the United States about $25,000,000,000; but the second one cost us about $300,000,000,000. Interest on the Second World War debt costs the United States almost $6,000,000,000 a year — one-and-one-half times the cost of public school education. National defense and foreign aid in the Cold War have cost us some $200,000,000,000. Much more important than the cost in dollars and resources were the deaths of 300,000 youth of our land and the disabling of nearly twice that number in World War II. To that sad total we must now add our dead and wounded in the Korean War.

Increasing Destructiveness of Wars. — The mere mention of atomic weapons, the hydrogen bomb, rockets, and bacteriological warfare emphasizes the fact that war today means *total* war. The atomic ruins of Hiroshima and Nagasaki, the war-scarred face of Europe, and the awesome destruction wrought in Korea, all bear eloquent testimony to the increasing destructiveness of war. The world now knows that no nation can possibly "win" a Third World War — the entire world would be the loser.

Military Defense. — To say that no nation can possibly "win" a Third World War does not mean that one may not come. To guard against that possibility, and to be so strong as to discourage any attack, is the basic pattern of our military policy. In a world as unsettled as ours, we must be prepared to meet any eventuality. We work for peace, but we keep our powder dry.

The Army, Navy, Marines, and Air Force are stationed around the globe. In addition to the billions now being spent on our own arms and on aid to our Allies, we are forging a system of *defensive* alliances in both Europe and Asia.

Industrial Defense. — The tremendous productive capacity of American industry is a trump card in our defense hand. A modern war can be won or lost in the factory, on the farm, or in the laboratory just as assuredly as on the battlefield.

"Oh, Boy! What I Could Do With All That Stuff!"

NEA Service, Inc.

The war against Japan was shortened by the perfection of the atomic bomb — a laboratory product of Allied scientists. Since the end of the war scientific research has continued at a rapid pace — indeed, many claim that American industrial and scientific achievements have been the major reason that World War III has not come.

But we cannot rest on past laurels. Scientific research, industrial development, agricultural improvements must continue if we are to maintain our superiority. For example, food for ourselves and for our Allies is of first importance to defense. Yet, for lack of adequate flood control, much of our rich soil is rapidly being washed into the Gulf of Mexico and the oceans. Because some strategic items are not available in quantity in the United States, the Government stockpiles such items against the day when our foreign sources of supply might be cut off.

SHASTA DAM

This powerful new dam, near Redding, California, is the second largest in the world — 602 feet high, with a crest length of 3500 feet. It supplies power for the great San Francisco industrial area and water for the rich San Joaquin Valley.

Physical Welfare for Defense. — Millions of Americans were rejected from service in the Second World War because they were physically unfit. Today many men are being rejected for the same reason. Local, State, and National Governments, through Departments of Health and otherwise, contribute in many ways to the good health of our citizens. Periodic physical examinations are today an important part of every school program.

Educational Defense. — The United States spends ten times as much on military defense as we spend on education. Yet in modern warfare educated scientists are as important as soldiers. A highly educated nation has the advantage in diplomacy and in propaganda. Today the communists are trying to give the rest of the world a false and distorted picture of the United States, to turn our allies away from us, and even to make the American people lose faith in themselves and in the Government. In order to prevent this we must know the facts and present them to the world.

Patriotic Defense. — Many people thought Great Britain was doomed when in 1940 the Germans bottled the British Army at Dunkirk; but intangible patriotism plus an abhorrence of dictators caused sturdy British civilians to swarm to the rescue. In little gasoline launches they braved the waves of the rough Channel, the bombs from the German planes that swarmed over them, and even the flaming seas, because of this intangible something called patriotism.

Patriotism can be aroused by patriotic teachers, editors, radio news interpreters, film producers, and Government propaganda; but patriotism whose roots grow deepest comes from a just Government that creates equal opportunities for all — a Government of, for, and by the people. Such a Government is our own, "established upon those principles of freedom, equality, justice, and humanity for which American patriots have sacrificed their lives and fortunes." Thus it is our privilege as well as our duty to love our country, support its Constitution, obey its laws, respect its flag, and defend it against all its enemies.

All Types of Defense Depend upon High Moral Standards. — The shocking report of the Senate Crime (Kefauver) Committee indicates that organized crime operates on a large scale in the United States today. Illegal gambling, narcotics, political bribery, labor and business racketeering, and gangsterism in all forms can undermine the moral strength of the nation. Yet, according to F.B.I. Director J. Edgar Hoover, most crime could be eliminated in forty-eight hours by vigorous action at the local level all over the country.

Religion as a Foundation of Strength. — As the dignity and worth of the individual lies at the very heart of the American heritage, so it lies at the very heart of religion. Over a century ago, Alexis de Tocqueville said that he sought for the greatness and genius of America in her harbors and her ample rivers; in her fertile fields and boundless forests; in her rich mines and her vast world commerce; in her public schools and institutions of learning; in her

Courtesy Middlebury College, Vermont

America's Strength

All over the United States are college and university chapels like this one where American students learn the lessons which will help keep our country great.

13

democratic congress and her matchless constitution; and it was in none of these.

Not until he went to the churches of America and heard her pulpits flame with righteousness did he understand the secret of her genius and power. He said:

"America is great because America is good, and if America ever ceases to be good, America will cease to be great."

The Good-Neighbor Policy as a Source of Strength. — The greatest law in the world is the Golden Rule; and if a Government adopts this rule in its foreign policy most countries will respond and be neighborly. The United States applied the good-neighbor policy to Canada and Latin America, and when we became involved in war they became our Allies. We are now applying the good-neighbor policy to Western Europe, and in case of war these countries would almost certainly be our Allies.

PHILLIPS BROOKS

As rector of Trinity Church, Boston, this eloquent speaker made his pulpit a flame of righteousness. He was the author of "O Little Town of Bethlehem."

How to bring about peaceful and neighborly relations between the free nations led by the United States and the communist nations led by Russia (if, indeed, it can be done) is the big question today. As we have said before, so long as Russia has powder we must keep our own powder dry; but this should not mean that war is inevitable. The only *sure* way to win World War III is to prevent its ever breaking out.

Defense through Co-operation with the United Nations. — The United Nations was founded "to save succeeding generations from the scourge of war." Its Charter was approved by the United States Senate by a vote of 89 to 2. In some ways, and especially because of obstructions by Russia, it has not accomplished all that we hoped it might. But we support it as a genuine and in many ways an effective international organization for peace.

Armed forces of the United States fought aggression in Korea with other United Nations troops as their allies. Thus, for the first time in the history of man, an international organization met aggression with armed force.

Lambert in "The Chicago Sun"

WILL THE NATIONS USE ATOMIC ENERGY FOR PEACE OR FOR WAR?

We have peace in our cities because we have agreed to local laws and have police to enforce them. We have peace in our States because we have agreed to State laws and have State police to enforce them. We have peace in the United States because we have agreed to Federal laws and have an army to enforce them. If we could have definite international laws and means to enforce them, perhaps we might then have international peace, as well.

"To Promote the General Welfare"

(From the Preamble to the Constitution)

Government as Servant. — Centuries ago the chief task of government was felt to be that of defending the people against foreign invasion and domestic violence. Defense is still one of the main functions of government, but gradually through the years government has assumed a much broader role. Especially in democratic countries, such as the United States, it has become the *servant* as well as the protector of the people.

Few people realize the many and varied ways in which government — National, State, Local — serves them, providing them with services they could hardly live without.

All through life the citizen is served by his Local, State, and National governments. The food that he eats is inspected to guarantee its purity and protect his health. He may receive much of his education at public expense. The hours and conditions under which he works, the quality of the clothing he wears, and the home he lives in, all are protected in one way or another by governmental regulations meant for his safety and well-being.

His automobile must be licensed and must meet certain safety standards set by government, and he must pass a driving test to secure an operator's license. The public roads that he drives on are built, maintained, and protected by the government. Employment service, on-the-job training, unemployment compensation, injury benefits, collective bargaining rights, and social security for old-age are a few among the many ways in which government serves its citizens.

Government regulates public utilities such as electric power companies, bus, railway, and air lines in order to insure safe and adequate service. It guarantees bank deposits and, in periods of national emergency, it may regulate wages and prices. Dope peddlers, gamblers, criminals of all sorts are hunted down and prosecuted by government. Property is protected by fire departments against fire, by police agencies against theft, and by various other services against the ravages of nature. In these and countless other ways, government serves the people — "to promote the general welfare."

"To Secure the Blessings of Liberty to Ourselves and Our Posterity"

(From the Preamble to the Constitution)

Liberty versus Authority. — This country was founded by men who loved liberty and prized it above all earthly possessions. For it they pledged their lives, their fortunes, and their sacred honor. Patrick Henry electrified the colonists with his stirring cry "Give me liberty or give me death!" Thomas Jefferson declared that "The God who gave us life, gave us liberty at the same time." Benjamin Franklin wrote "They that can give up essential liberty to obtain a little temporary safety deserve neither liberty nor safety." The desire for liberty for their country and for the individual was the prime force governing the leaders of our Revolution, and these objectives have remained our goal throughout our history. We are opposing communist aggression in the world today in order "to secure the blessings of liberty to ourselves and our posterity."

For us liberty is *relative*, not absolute. We recognize that absolute liberty is impossible in an ordered society. Each individual cannot do exactly as he pleases because in so doing he would inevitably interfere with the rights of his neighbors. So liberty by its very nature is a mutual privilege. Justice Oliver Wendell Holmes once emphasized the fact that liberty is relative and not absolute in a case in which he remarked that "the most stringent protection of free speech will not protect a man in falsely shouting 'Fire!' in a theatre and causing a panic."

While liberty must be exercised with due regard for others, authority must be limited also. If a government is able to do anything it pleases, individual liberty cannot exist at all. The Soviet Union and her satellites ruthlessly suppress individual freedom because they fear popular revolt. It is estimated that there are between twelve and twenty million so-called "political prisoners" in Russian slave-labor camps. Only those things which are "acceptable" to the Soviet government may be thought, spoken, or written in Russia today.

By sharp contrast, our government is subject to the will of the people. In other words, we have taken the middle ground between absolute liberty and absolute authority and strive for a just balance between the interests of the individual and those of society as a whole.

"Proclaim Liberty Throughout All the Land Unto All the Inhabitants Thereof."

In brief, liberty is a thing of the spirit — to be free to worship, to think, and to speak without fear — free to challenge wrong and oppression with surety of justice. Liberty conceives that the mind and the spirit of men can be free only if the individual is free to choose his own calling, to develop his talents, to win and to keep a home sacred from intrusion, to rear children in an orderly society. It holds that man must be free to earn, to spend, to save, and to accumulate property that may give protection and security to himself and to his loved ones.

Our Task. — Because America has been the melting pot of all the nations of the world, our national thought represents the hopes and the aspirations of liberty-loving people everywhere. These people are our close neighbors today because modern communication and travel have made them so. They have the right to take the same steps that we have taken as a nation "to secure the blessings of liberty to ourselves and our posterity." So we have fought, and will fight again if need be, "for the things which we have always carried nearest our hearts — for a democracy, for the right of those who submit to authority to have a voice in their own governments, for the rights and liberties of small nations, for a universal dominion of right by such a concert of free peoples as shall bring peace and safety to all nations and make the world itself at last free." Thus Woodrow Wilson phrased the goal which only the good citizenship of every American can safeguard.

More than two thousand years ago, Aristotle wrote that "If liberty and equality are chiefly to be found in democracy, they will be best attained when all persons alike share in the government to the utmost." So you, your teachers, and all of us who have America's welfare at heart must study to know our government in order that we may protect it from all its enemies both at home and abroad. "Eternal vigilance is the price of liberty."

QUESTIONS ON THE TEXT

1. What is the American heritage?
2. What are the purposes of our Government as stated in the Preamble to our Constitution?
3. How have transportation and communication strengthened the Federal Union?

Berg in "The Christian Science Monitor"

UNCLE SAM NEEDS OUR PROTECTION

The United States faces a grave threat from abroad, but there are serious problems at home, too. "A democracy can recover quickly from physical or economic disaster, but when its moral convictions weaken, it becomes easy prey for the demagogue and the charlatan. Tyranny and oppression then become the order of the day." — Senator J. William Fulbright.

4. How is our idea of justice becoming more humane?

5. What is our basic military policy? Why must we keep our powder dry?

6. How much did the Second World War cost in lives? Resources? Dollars? How much interest do we pay on the war debt? How does this compare with the cost of public school education?

7. Explain the following kinds of national defense:

1. Military	6. Moral
2. Industrial	7. Religious
3. Physical Welfare	8. Good-Neighbor Policy
4. Educational	9. Through United Nations
5. Patriotic	

8. Explain what is meant when we say that our Government is our servant. How many examples of governmental service at all levels can you list?

9. Explain the distinction between governmental regulation and governmental protection. Illustrate with examples.

10. Why, in a democracy such as ours, must liberty be relative and not absolute? Why must authority be limited?

11. Why is eternal vigilance the price of liberty?

12. What is liberty?

PROBLEMS FOR DISCUSSION

1. A century and a half ago a young English economist named Malthus figured that the population was increasing more rapidly than the food supply, and that an overcrowded world would soon be stricken with famine unless large numbers of the people died from plagues or were killed off by wars. What has science done toward preventing starvation from overpopulation? How has the formation of a strong Union helped to prevent it in the United States? How might science and an international organization prevent it on a world-wide scale?

2. What new inventions made the Second World War more destructive than the First? In what ways could another war be even more destructive than the Second World War?

3. Congressman Herter of Massachusetts has stated: "Eighty-five cents out of every dollar spent by the Federal Government since the beginning of this Republic has been spent on wars, or preparation for wars, or repairing the damages caused by wars." The Second World War cost the world about $1,000,000,000,000. If this had been borne equally by each of the two and a half billion people in the world, how much would each man, woman, and child have paid?

4. How would you express the following statement of the American heritage in your own words?

"The central theme in our American heritage is the importance of the individual person. From the earliest moment of our history we have believed that every human being has an essential dignity and integrity which must be respected and safeguarded. Moreover, we believe that the welfare of the individual is the final goal of group life. Our American heritage further teaches that to be secure in the rights he wishes for himself, each man must be willing to respect the rights of other men. This is the conscious recognition of a basic principle: all men are created equal as well as free. Stemming from this principle is the obligation to build our social institutions so that they will guarantee equality of opportunity to all men. Without this equality, freedom becomes an illusion. Thus the only aristocracy that is consistent with the free way of life is an aristocracy of talent and achievement. The grounds on which our society accords respect, influence, or reward to each of its citizens must be limited to the quality of his personal character and of his social contribution.

"This concept of equality, which is so vital a part of the American heritage, knows no kinship with notions of human uniformity or regimentation. We abhor the totalitarian arrogance which makes one man say that he will respect another man as his equal only if he has 'my race, my religion, my political views, my social position.' In our land men are equal, but they are free to be different. From these very differences among our people has come the great human and national strength of America.

"Thus, the aspirations and achievements of each member of our society are to be limited only by the skills he brings to the opportunities equally offered to all Americans. We can tolerate no restriction upon the individual which depends upon irrelevant factors such as his race, his color, his religion, or the social position to which he is born." — Quoted from page 4 of The Report of the President's Committee on Civil Rights.

SELECT BIBLIOGRAPHY

JESSUP, JOHN K. "Western Man and the American Idea." *Life*
     November 5, 1951, pages 96–116. (Very readable.)
"Let Freedom Ring." U. S. State Department. Washington, D. C.   1953.
MOULTON, H. G. America's Wealth. The Brookings Institution. Washington, 1952. $1.00. (Illustrated story of our dynamic economy.)
Sevareid, E. "Why Did They Fight?" *Reader's Digest.* October, 1953.

THOMAS JEFFERSON

These students in the Jefferson Memorial, Washington, D. C., find inspiration from one of our greatest patriots. Jefferson believed that all men were created equal, that men should make their governments, and that men should enjoy freedom of speech, of the press, and of religion. In his sixty years of public service, Jefferson stamped his personality and ideals indelibly upon our country.

CHAPTER II

THE DEVELOPMENT OF THE STATE

Simple Beginnings. — All living organisms tend to develop from the simple to the complex; and so it has been with organized society — the state. In the beginning the state performed very few functions, but new discoveries and inventions created conditions which could be solved only through the united action of society; so the state developed to its present position along with these various social and economic changes.

Originally the ancestors of every race of people lived in a rude, uncivilized manner. The want of food and of other material comforts brought suffering; superstition brought fear; and lack of wisdom brought misunderstanding, quarreling, fighting, war. From this rude condition some peoples have advanced through many stages of social and economic progress, the most highly developed going through the following stages: hunting and fishing, pastoral, agricultural, commercial, manufacturing, and capitalistic. Each social or economic stage demanded a more extensive organization; and in turn, each extension of political organization made possible the advance to a more complex social or economic stage.

Hunting and Fishing Stage. — During the hunting and fishing stage of each race, men lived from hand to mouth in the struggle for existence. Ownership in land was unknown, but each savage horde had temporary hunting grounds beyond which its members went at their peril. These hordes had little need, and less capacity, for political organization.

Pastoral Stage. — When an ingenious horde saved the young of wild animals and domesticated them, an epoch-making step was taken. By a little foresight and self-denial, food was on hand for times of scarcity. Permanent food supplies and slaves gave leisure and opportunity for meditation.

Thus, in time, the wandering horde became a family tribe bound together by the common possession of flocks. These possessions aroused

STONE AGE MEN

Men on the rock are hurling huge stones on the entrapped elephant, which is being attacked below by spear, sling, and dogs. Our early ancestors learned to co-operate in their primitive ways.

Courtesy Milwaukee Public Museum

LAKE DWELLERS

The lake dwellers are shown merging from the hunting and fishing stage to the pastoral stage. They lived on man-made islands for protection.

the envy of neighboring tribes, and organization for defense became necessary. The patriarch of a family became leader of this organization and developed absolute authority over his wives, sons, daughters, sons' wives and children, and slaves. He was an absolute ruler over a "family state."

PRIMITIVE AGRICULTURE NEAR THE NILE IN EGYPT

When patriarchal families became strong enough in themselves, or through loose confederations, to protect their holdings, they trained their domestic animals for beasts of burden and planted seed.

Agricultural Stage.—With the ownership of flocks, the next step was the planting of seeds with the thought of reaping the harvest. For this, the possession of land became necessary, and ownership desirable. As family tribes increased, they sent out clans to establish new village communities. In these clans common blood, common religion, and common economic interests held them together in loose confederations for social and commercial intercourse and for self-defense. In this stage the necessary elements of a modern state existed: law and authority, permanence of organization, and a consciousness of political unity.

Commercial Stage. — Wealth in flocks, herds, and agriculture multiplied man's needs. Commerce met the demand; forms of money came into use as a medium of exchange; and the merchant took a place in civilization. Cities developed at convenient locations on trade routes. Co-operation against pirates and robbers and regulation of populations made city states necessary.

Manufacturing Stage. — The establishment of cities and commercial routes encouraged manufacturing, and in turn manufacturing gave a further contribution to commerce. During the manufacturing

Bettman Archive

EARLY COMMERCE

A merchant fleet departs for the East from an Italian harbor during the time of Colonial Expansion.

stage, hand implements slowly gave way to machines. For example, the hand spindle of prehistoric times was replaced by the spinning wheel in 1530; and late in the eighteenth century steam power was applied to the manufacture of cloth. This process brought people from scattered farms into growing towns and cities. City life brought experience and education to the people, and enabled them to wrest their rights from absolute monarchs or privileged nobles.

Capitalistic Stage. — One inevitable outcome of industrial and urban development was the concentration of capital, especially in large cities.

A WEAVING ESTABLISHMENT

By the 19th century steam was applied to the manufacture of cloth in England.

THE BEGINNING OF THE NEW YORK STOCK EXCHANGE

Congress issued bonds. Factories needed capital, and corporations were created to raise it. So in 1792 pioneer brokers decided to meet daily under a buttonwood tree. These men were the original members of the New York Stock Exchange.

In advanced nations expensive factory machines which make large-scale production profitable were produced. The maintenance of such factories required large capital, which modern banking provided. Nationwide and even worldwide monopolies developed which could control prices and wages of the workmen. As a protection against this danger, here in the United States, Congress enacted anti-trust laws and set up regulatory commissions to enforce these laws.

Increased Power of Labor. — Compulsory education advanced industrial workers to a position where they saw the advantages of organization, and they were able to achieve it. As unionism expanded, it was able to pay higher salaries to its leaders, sometimes comparable to those paid by capital. The votes of labor elected officials friendly to labor, and Congress enacted laws to the advantage of organized labor. Today unions have a bargaining power equal to or even greater than that of capitalists.

Equalizing Opportunity. — The first duty of the state was the protection of life and movable property; then the regulation of land was added; and now commerce and manufacturing are regulated by law. If the price of any commodity is unduly advanced by a combination of capitalists seeking unreasonable profits or by a group of laborers demanding unfair wages, the people are disposed to use their power, the state, to prevent it. In other words, government recognizes as one of its duties co-operation with all the people to look out for the best interests of all.

The government acts not only in this negative way to prevent injustices; it also acts in many positive ways. Examples of this positive action include such things as public education, loans and advice to businessmen, aid and advice to farmers, and social security.

Some have urged a further development of the co-operative stage in the form of government ownership of large businesses, which would be conducted by the National Government in the same manner that it now operates the post office and the production and distribution of electric power; or as Great Britain owns and operates the radio service, civil aviation, coal mines, railways, waterways, busses, and trucks. When co-operative action reaches this point, it becomes socialism. But the danger of developing the co-operative stage too far is that it tends toward inefficient bureaucracy and stifles the initiative of the individual.

GOVERNMENT IN THE WORLD TODAY

The State. — A *state*[1] is an organized body of people living within a defined territory and having the power to make and enforce laws without the consent of any higher authority. There are more than seventy states in the world today and they vary greatly in size and importance. But each of them meets the four basic requirements of (1) *population*, (2) a defined *territory*, (3) political organization, or *government*, acting through law, and (4) *sovereignty*, the right of the state to decide its own internal problems without interference from any outside source.

Government. — The agency through which the state exerts its will and accomplishes its ends is the *government*. It consists of the machinery and the personnel by which the state is ruled (*governed*). In effect, the government may be likened to an engine that keeps the entire machine (the state) moving.

Types of Government. — Because government is the product of human experience, human needs, and environment, no two governments are exactly alike. There are, however, several different ways in which governments may be classified:

A. *According to Distribution of Powers.* — Under this method of classification there are three types or forms of government to be considered:

(1) *Unitary,* (2) *Federal,* and (3) *Confederation.*

(1) *Unitary.* — A unitary government is one in which all *governmental* powers are concentrated in the hands of a single central government. Although local governments exist, they are really only administrative agents of the central government and derive such powers as they have from that source. Great Britain is the outstanding example of a unitary government today.

(2) *Federal.* — A federal government is one in which the powers of government have been divided between a central and several local governments. This division of powers is made by an authority superior to both and cannot be changed by either acting alone. For

---

[1] Throughout this volume the word *state* printed with a small "s" denotes an independent state belonging to the family of nations, as England, France, the United States; the word *State* printed with a capital "S" refers to one of the members of the United States of America, as Maine, Pennsylvania, Virginia.

example, in the United States certain powers of government belong to the National Government and others to the States. The sovereign people have made this division of powers through the Constitution; and that document cannot be altered unless the people, acting through both the National and the State Governments, approve such a change. Canada, Australia, and Switzerland are other examples of federal government.[1]

(3) *Confederation.* — A confederation is a very loose form of federalism with very little real power placed in the hands of the central government. A confederation is more an alliance of independent states, usually for defense purposes. The American States (1781–1788), under the Articles of Confederation, and the Confederate States of America during the Civil War afford examples. The device was most widely used among the ancient Greek city-states.

B. *According to Executive Types.* — Here there are two major forms of government to be considered: (1) *Presidential* and (2) *Parliamentary.*

(1) *Presidential Government.* — This form of government is characterized by an executive (president) elected by the voters for a fixed term of office. Hence the chief executive is independent of the legislative branch. He cannot be removed except by the cumbersome process of impeachment. Usually, as in the United States or in any of the forty-eight States, and in most Latin American countries, a written constitution provides for a separation of powers among the executive, legislative, and judicial branches. Although each branch has its own distinct set of powers, all three must work together in order that the government may function smoothly.

(2) *Parliamentary Government.* — Under this form of government the executive is composed of a prime minister and his cabinet, and they are themselves members of the legislative branch (parliament). The prime minister is the leader of the majority party in the parliament and is chosen to his office by that body. With majority approval, he in turn selects his cabinet from among the members of parliament. The prime minister and his cabinet are thus chosen by the legislative

---

[1] It is sometimes said that the 1936 Constitution of the U.S.S.R. created a federal government in Russia, but this is true only on paper. Virtually all power is concentrated in the hands of the central government in Moscow despite the provisions of the 1936 Constitution.

branch and are subordinate to it. They hold office only so long as
their policies and administration retain the confidence of at least a
majority in parliament. If they lose on an important issue ("a vote
of confidence") they must resign. Then a new "government" must
be formed or a general election held. Great Britain, most European

Courtesy British Travel Association

BRITISH PARLIAMENT HOUSE

In this beautiful brownstone Gothic capitol on the Thames, the laws of Great
Britain and the Empire are made. The Speaker of the House has an apartment
in the clock tower.

countries, and the members of the British Commonwealth have governments of this type. Indeed, Britain is often referred to as the
"Mother of Parliaments."

C. *According to How Many Rule.* — The most realistic classification
of governments is based upon the number of people participating.
Formal legal institutions are important to the successful mechanical
operation of government, but the degree of popular participation is
the vital heart of the matter. Here we consider: (1) *Dictatorship*
and (2) *Democracy.*[1] All people do not use terms like these in the same
way. We should keep that fact in mind as we study their use here.

[1] Another traditional classification, dating from Aristotle (384–322 B.C.), groups
governments as: *autocracies* — rule by one; *oligarchies* — rule by a select few
(aristocracy); or *democracies* — rule by many.

(1) *Dictatorship.* — When unlimited political authority rests with one person or with a very few persons, a dictatorship is said to exist. Examples of modern dictatorships are: Nazi Germany, Fascist Italy, and the Soviet Union. A dictatorial government is usually in the hands of a single all-powerful individual, but not always. Georgi Malenkov is a dictator yet he must rule with the aid of the small, potent Presidium of the Communist Party of the U.S.S.R. The primary characteristic of any dictatorship is that *it is not responsible to the people and cannot be limited by them.*[1] Freedom of speech, press, thought, and association, so vital in a democratic system, are not permitted in a dictatorship; the individual exists for the state, not the state for the individual. Benito Mussolini spoke for all dictators when he said, "All is in the state and for the state; nothing outside the state, nothing against the state."[2]

(2) *Democracy.* — Democracy is a form of government in which supreme power rests with the people. In other words, the people govern themselves. Democracy may be either *direct* or *indirect*. In a *direct democracy* the will of the state is formulated directly and immediately through a mass meeting of the people.[3] In the United States, we have *indirect* or *representative democracy* — *a democracy in a republic.*[4] The will of the state is formulated and expressed through a relatively small body of persons chosen by the people to act as their representatives. These representatives are responsible to the people for the day-to-day operation of government and must face periodic election. The ultimate source of all political authority is in the people; the people are sovereign. Democracy in a republic, then, is "government of the people, by the people, for the people."

---

[1] The formal elections of the Soviet Union and other communist countries do not mean that these governments are responsible to the people. The only "candidates" on the ballot are those of the communist party; the voter has no real choice.

[2] A totalitarian state is one in which *all* (total) power is held by the government. Dictatorships are usually, but not always, totalitarian dictatorships.

[3] Direct democracy is practicable only in small communities where it is physically possible for the entire citizenry to assemble in a given place and where the problems of government are few and simple. It does not exist anywhere on a national level today. However, the New England town meeting and the *Landsgemeinde* in five of the smaller Swiss cantons are excellent examples of direct democracy in action. In a limited sense, law-making by initiative petition is a form of direct democracy.

[4] A *republic* is representative government without a monarch. Great Britain has a *limited monarchy* — representative government with a queen who possesses no real powers.

Capitalism versus Socialism and Communism

Capitalism. — Our economic system, founded as it is on free enterprise and private ownership of production, distribution, and exchange, is known as capitalism (or free or private enterprise). In a capitalistic society factories, mines, stores, farms, banks, and the like, are the private property of individuals or companies formed by individuals.

Courtesy Levitt & Sons, Inc.

MASS PRODUCTION HOUSE

A company operating in New York, by building thousands of houses, has been able to sell the one shown here for $7990, including radiant heat, stove, refrigerator, and washer. It illustrates free enterprise or capitalism working at its best.

These owners run their businesses largely at their own discretion, hire labor, and compete with one another to provide goods and services at a profit.

The life-blood of the free enterprise system is competition — providing the best product at the lowest possible cost. In other words, capitalism means economic freedom and the incentive to do one's best. Generally speaking, anyone may start a business, large or small, and the risks and the rewards are his.

Most large and many small businesses in the United States are actually owned by millions of individual stockholders — people who own shares in the business itself.   The Bell Telephone Company, for example, now has more than one million stockholders.   In our system, if a company makes money, part of its earnings is paid out as dividends (interest) to the stockholders, and part is "plowed back" into the business.   Thus business expands, more jobs are created, more people buy more things, and a still higher standard of living is created.

Unregulated capitalism may result in monopolies and other injustices.   To prevent this, the National Government and the States increasingly regulate our economy by such means as anti-trust, labor-management relations, and, in times of crises, price and wage control laws.   Competition acts as an effective business regulator, too.

We have discovered that some activities are better carried on by society as a whole acting through the government.   Free public education, the postal system, and help for the aged are familiar examples of long standing in the United States.

One needs only to look at the great achievements and the standard of living in the United States to see the advantages of the free enterprise system.   Freedom of choice is inherent in a democracy — and in our economic system, too.   We view the trend toward nationalization and socialism in other countries with misgivings.   We stand for a well-regulated capitalism as the best guarantee of the better life for all mankind.

Socialism is often identified with communism, primarily because followers of Karl Marx often refer to themselves as socialists.   But socialism is really much older than Marxism.   While the socialists believe and preach many of the things that the Marxists do, most of them today reject the Marxian ideas of class struggle, the necessity of a violent revolution, and the dictatorship of the proletariat.   The "evolutionary socialists" (for example, the British Labour Party) believe that they can bring about socialism peaceably.   They feel that they can best accomplish this by working within the established framework of the government of their own particular country.

Socialists advocate government ownership of the *major* instruments of production, distribution, and exchange such as industry, transportation, and banking.   The opponents of socialism condemn it because they claim that government regimentation and bureaucracy will inevitably lead to a police state and that socialism is merely a step along the road to communism.

The complexities of modern industrial society have led to vastly expanded governmental activities. Many of these new governmental activities are attacked by opponents on the grounds that they are "socialistic."

Communism. — In 1848 Karl Marx and Friedrich Engels published the *Communist Manifesto.* In it they laid down the cardinal premises of what they called "scientific socialism" or communism. Since then a great many followers have interpreted and elaborated their theories. Chief among these have been Lenin and Stalin.

The four central ideas of communist theory are: (1) the labor theory of value, (2) the communist philosophy of history, (3) the communist theory of the nature of the state, and (4) the dictatorship of the proletariat.

(1) *The Labor Theory of Value.* — According to Marx, the value of any commodity is determined by the amount of labor necessary to produce that commodity. In other words, a pair of shoes is worth so much because it takes so much labor to produce the shoes. Because the laborer created the value of the shoes, the communists claim that he should receive that value in full. They maintain that all income should come from work. They are opposed to the free enterprise profit system of capitalism and condemn profits as "surplus value." They claim that this "surplus value" should go to the worker.

(2) *The Communist Philosophy of History.* — All of history, say the communists, has been a story of "class struggle." According to this communist theory, there have always been two opposing classes — the oppressors and the oppressed. This interpretation they call *dialectical materialism.* In feudal times, they say, the landed noblemen were the oppressor class and the serfs the oppressed. Today, they assert that capitalists (the bourgeoisie) and wage-earners (the proletariat) are the opposing classes. Workers in capitalistic countries are described by the communists as wage-slaves who are paid only enough to permit them to eke out a starvation living. The communists claim that this alleged situation must be changed by a mass revolt of the workers and the "liquidation" of the capitalists.

(3) *Communist Theory about the Nature of the State.* — To the communists the state is the instrument of the dominant class — a tool with which the bourgeoisie keeps the proletariat in bondage. Because the capitalists are so firmly entrenched, said Lenin, it is only

through "a violent and bloody revolution" that this allegedly unjust situation can be altered. (The communists claim that other institutions are used in this manner, as well. They speak of religion as "the opiate of the people" — a drug fed to the proletariat as a hoax through which the people are led to tolerate their supposed harsh lot in this life in order to gain the afterlife.)

The "violent and bloody revolution" envisioned by Lenin would wipe out the capitalist class and place all of their holdings (factories, farms, etc.) in the hands of the people collectively.

(4) *The Dictatorship of the Proletariat.* — The communists do not envisage a proletariat that will be able to govern themselves after a revolution. They will need "guidance" from the communist party. The communists would set up a "dictatorship of the proletariat" to accomplish this. The dictatorship would "educate" the people to the place where each individual would work not for himself but for the good of all. Then the state would "wither away," and the communist dream of a "free classless society" would be realized. In the new society the cardinal principle would be "From each according to his ability, to each according to his need."

Evaluation of Communism. — The Soviet Union presents the outstanding example of communism in action. Strictly speaking, the Russians do not have pure communism today, but a peculiar type of socialism.[1] After the 1917 Revolution Lenin attempted to establish communism, but it failed. The inefficient and the lazy were paid as much as the efficient and the industrious. The lazy became indifferent and the industrious disgruntled. Workers and peasants refused to work to support the ne'er-do-wells, and the government executed many for disobedience. Finally the Soviet leaders turned to socialism and now claim that they are working toward communism.

Communism and socialism destroy the individual's incentive to produce because he knows that he will get only so much, no matter

---

[1] According to Marx, the guiding economic principle of communism is "From each according to his ability, to each according to his need." Compare this with Article 12 of the Soviet Constitution of 1936: "In the U.S.S.R. work is a duty and a matter of honor for every able-bodied citizen in accordance with the principle: 'He who does not work, neither shall he eat.' The principle applied in the U.S.S.R. is that of socialism: 'From each according to his ability, to each according to his work.'"

However, the Russians still refer to themselves as communists.

how hard or how little he works.   If the state owns everything, there is no opportunity for the inventive and enterprising to strike out on their own to create new and better things.

The class-struggle theory of the communists is disproven many times over by the American way of life.   We strive to promote equality

Sovfoto

SUPREME COUNCIL BUILDING, MOSCOW

The Supreme Council, the legislative branch of the Soviet Government, meets in this building, which is within the Kremlin walls. The Council is often called a "rubber stamp" because its decisions are really those of Malenkov and the other leaders of the Communist Party.

of opportunity whereas communists and socialists argue for equality of condition.   Ours is an individualistic society.   We do not have sharp divisions of classes, and our standard of living is the highest in the history of the world.

A serious question is presented by the communist dictatorship of the proletariat.   What guarantee is there that the dictatorship (as it exists in the U.S.S.R. now) will ever end?   With all power gathered in the hands of a few at the top, what is to prevent the few from perpetuating their rule?

But man is independent by nature, and by suppressing this trait, communism is surely signing its own death warrant.

Fascism. — Yet another challenge to democracy is to be found in fascism. The defeat of Hitler's Germany and of Mussolini's Italy in World War II left fascism without a home state from which to operate on the world scene. But fascist theory remains as a danger to the free world and the possibility of the re-emergence of a fascist state cannot be overlooked.

Politically, fascism rests upon two tenets utterly contrary to those upon which democracy is based: (1) the leadership principle (the *Fuhrer prinzip*) and (2) state socialism (*etatism*). Under the leadership principle, absolute and final power is held by the leader to whom all must pay allegiance and obedience. *Etatism* is an extreme form of totalitarianism in which the state embodies everything and everybody.

In fascism, as in communism, force and terror, combined with all-out propaganda, are used to further the interests of the state as determined by the leader. A fascist state usually retains the outward forms of representative government, but inside it is a totalitarian dictatorship. No opposition groups are tolerated; the only political party allowed is composed of the "elite," the well-disciplined and privileged few.

QUESTIONS ON THE TEXT

1. Most highly developed nations have gone through what stages of social and economic development?

2. Describe the stages and explain how each developed into the other.

3. How have economic development and political development (government) depended upon each other?

4. What is a *state?* What is a *government?* Distinguish clearly between a state and a government.

5. Distinguish between *state* and *State* as used in this text.

6. Does the United States have an executive or parliamentary type of government? Is it a republic or a monarchy? Is it of the centralized or federal type? Is it constitutional or dictatorial?

7. Describe parliamentary government as it is in Great Britain.

8. What is the totalitarian theory of government?

9. Under socialism in Russia what is the form of government?

10. Distinguish between: a federal and a unitary government; presidential and parliamentary; democratic and dictatorial.

11. What is capitalism? How does it provide for incentive?

12. What is the communist theory of history? The labor theory of value? The communist theory of the nature of the state? What is meant by the dictatorship of the proletariat?

13. List as many criticisms of communism as you can.

PROBLEMS FOR DISCUSSION

1. Prepare a short essay explaining why you agree or disagree with each of the following statements: (*a*) A dictatorship is the most efficient form of government. (*b*) Parliamentary government is more responsible to the popular will than presidential government. (*c*) A unitary government is always dictatorial while a federal government is always democratic.

2. Do you think your town should own its water system? Electric power system? Gas system? Bus system? Explain your answers.

3. There was no great need of laws governing copyrights until long after the printing press began its work. The invention of the steam engine created a need for what character of laws? The automobile? The moving pictures? The wireless? The airplane?

4. What did Dwight D. Eisenhower mean when he said: "Tyrannies must feed on new conquests or wither."

5. The government of Great Britain is known as a parliamentary government, or a responsible government, because the executive branch is responsible to the legislative branch. Many governments outside of America have followed this parliamentary system. Our American system is known as a presidential or executive government because the executive branch is independent of or co-ordinate with the legislative branch. Latin-American governments have followed this executive system.

Do you agree with Professor Burgess in his defense of the American type of government? He says in part: "I think that we are upon the right line, and that those nations which have developed parliamentary government are beginning to feel, as suffrage has become more extended, the necessity of greater executive independence. Parliamentary government, *i.e.*, government in which the other departments are subject to legislative control, becomes intensely radical under universal suffrage, and will remain so until the character of the masses becomes so perfect as to make the form of government very nearly a matter of indifference. There is no doubt that we sometimes feel embarrassment from a conflict of opinion between the independent executive and the legislature, but this embarrassment must generally result in the adoption of the more conservative course, which is far less dangerous than the course of radical experimentation. . . . The feature *par excellence* of the American governmental system is the constitutional, independent, unpolitical judiciary and the supremacy of the judiciary over the other departments in all cases where private rights are concerned."

6. In 1952 Galo Plaza, who was born in New York and once played football for the University of California, completed a constitutional four-year term as President of Ecuador. He thus became the first man in 32 years to turn the trick. Prior to Plaza, Ecuador had 23 chiefs of state in 28 years. Some of them were constitutionally-elected presidents, but most were acting presidents and dictators. Each of these 23 was deposed by revolutions or military coups. The man who succeeded Plaza and is now President, Velasco Ibarra, has held the post twice before, 1934–1935 and 1944–1947. Both times he was overthrown by army officers who felt that he had become a dictator. What reasons would you give for this marked difference between Ecuador and the United States?

7. Thomas Paine wrote: "Those who expect to reap the blessings of freedom must undergo the fatigues of supporting it." Has indifference been the main reason for the rise of dictatorships? Have there been other reasons?

8. Explain why you agree or disagree with these lines from Alexander Pope's "Essay on Man":

> "For forms of government let fools contest;
> Whate'er is best administer'd is best."

SELECT BIBLIOGRAPHY

ALLEN, F. L. "The Unsystematic American System." *Reader's Digest.* August, 1952, pages 107–111.

BISHOP, H. M., and HENDEL, S. *Basic Issues of American Democracy.* Appleton-Century-Crofts. New York. 1952. Secs. 2 and 3.

WIKE, J. R., and RUBENSTEIN, A. Z. "Socialism in Post-War Europe." *Current History.* February, 1952, pages 80–85.

McCARTHY, J. "The Amazing Ford Bonanza." *Reader's Digest.* August, 1953.

ROUNDS, F. "Behind the Kremlin Walls." *Collier's.* May 2, 1953.

WALSH, W. B. "Can We Co-exist with Russia?" *New York Times Magazine.* May 24, 1953.

AMERICAN BAR ASSOCIATION. *Brief on Communism, Marxism, and Leninism.* Ave Maria Press, Notre Dame, Indiana. 1953. 15¢.

MULLIN, E. "Government by Conversation." *Reader's Digest.* August, 1953. (British Parliament in Action.)

"The Soviet Union." *Current History.* August, 1953. (Entire issue.)

CHAMBERS, W. "What Is a Communist?" *Reader's Digest.* October, 1953.

THE FIRST WOMAN ARRIVES AT JAMESTOWN

After the original men settlers in Jamestown had built homes and started farms, their wives and sweethearts were brought from England. The history of Jamestown is a violent one, for the colonists were in constant danger from disease and Indian massacres. Yet life at Jamestown had its romantic side, too, as you probably know from the story of Captain John Smith, leader of the colony, and Pocahontas. The Indian girl eventually married John Rolfe, another of the Jamestown colonists.

CHAPTER III

THE ORIGIN OF OUR FEDERAL CONSTITUTION

Government in the Colonies. — The first permanent English settlement in America was made at Jamestown, Virginia, in 1607. These colonists were sent out from England by a commercial corporation,

JAMESTOWN

Here the first representative legislature that ever sat in America met in 1619.

known as The London Company. At first the Company placed a council with a president over the colonists, but in 1609 a governor replaced the president. In 1619 the Company permitted the addition of a general assembly composed of burgesses[1] elected by the inhabitants of each settlement.

---

[1] The term "burgesses" was used because it was expected that the settlements would develop into boroughs (towns). After 1634 the "burgesses" represented counties, and in 1776 the name was changed to "assemblymen." Virginia called its colonial representatives "House of Burgesses"; South Carolina, "House of Commons"; Massachusetts, "House of Representatives."

This assembly, the first representative legislature that ever sat in America, met on the 30th day of July, 1619, in the chancel of the church at Jamestown. In 1624 The London Company surrendered its charter, and henceforth Virginia was known as a Royal Colony until it declared itself independent of England in the year 1776. The other twelve colonies were established in various ways and from time to time enjoyed different rights or degrees of self-government. According to the mode of government the colonies were divided into three classes: Royal, Proprietary, and Charter.

The Royal Colonies. — At the time of the Revolution, 1776, there were seven Royal colonies: New Hampshire, New York, New Jersey, Virginia, North Carolina, South Carolina, and Georgia. For each of these colonies a governor and a council, "upper house," were appointed by the King, and a popular assembly, "lower house," was elected by the people. The governor in conjunction with his council and assembly ruled the colony in conformity with written instructions issued from time to time by the Crown. There was no written charter between the colony and the King; nevertheless various concessions that the Crown made to the people and the customary mode of government formed a traditionary charter or constitution.

The Proprietary Colonies. — In 1776 there were three Proprietary colonies: Pennsylvania, Delaware, and Maryland. These colonies got their name, "Proprietary," from the term *proprietor*, which was applied to a "petty king" to whom the King of England had granted the land. For each of these colonies a governor and a council were appointed by the proprietor and a popular assembly was elected by the people. Hence we may think of a Proprietary colony as very similar to a Royal colony, the only material difference being that the proprietor, or "petty king," was obliged to concede more rights and privileges to the people than the King would grant. As in the case of the Royal colonies, the concessions and precedents of government formed a traditionary charter or constitution.

The Charter Colonies. — In 1776 there were three Charter colonies: Massachusetts, Rhode Island, and Connecticut. Unlike the other two classes of colonies, a real charter existed between each of these colonies and the King. This charter was a written document outlining certain rights of self-government which could be withdrawn by the King at any time he saw fit to do so. In each of these colonies, except Massachusetts, the governor was elected by the people; in two the council was elected by the assembly; and in each the assembly was elected by the people.   The charters of Connecticut and Rhode Island were so liberal that by substituting the word "people" for "King" these colonial charters served as State constitutions until 1818 and 1842 respectively.

WILLIAM PENN RECEIVING THE CHARTER OF PENNSYLVANIA FROM CHARLES II

Legislative Power. — In all the colonies except Delaware and Pennsylvania where the council had no legislative power, there were two legislative branches; and in all except Rhode Island the governor had the veto power.   Legislation was enacted on purely colonial affairs. In matters of general interest to the whole British Kingdom the British Parliament or the King exercised control.   It was often a disputed question whether a particular affair was purely colonial or a matter of general interest to the whole Kingdom.   These disputes sometimes led to feelings of injustice, and the question, whether or not a stamp tax to support a standing army in America was a tax which the British Parliament had a right to impose upon the colonies, was decided only by the Revolutionary War.

Continental Congresses. — In 1774 the Virginia House of Burgesses issued an invitation to all the colonial assemblies, calling a meeting of delegates at Philadelphia to consider what could be done to meet their common grievances. This Congress, in which all the colonies except Georgia were represented, is known as the First Continental Congress, and it met in Carpenter's Hall on September 5, 1774. It adopted a declaration of rights and grievances to be presented to the King, and adjourned.

INDEPENDENCE HALL

This Philadelphia street scene shows Independence Hall as it was when the Second Continental Congress met there in 1775.

In 1775, after the battle of Lexington, the Second Continental Congress met at Philadelphia, with representatives from all thirteen colonies. Schouler, the historian, describes this Congress (including the Confederate Congress) as follows:

"The Continental Congress . . . with its periodical sessions and frequent changes of membership bore for fifteen years the symbols of Federal power in America; which, as a single house of deputies acting by colonies or States, and blending with legislative authority imperfect executive and judicial functions, raised armies, laid taxes, contracted a common debt, negotiated foreign treaties, made war and peace; which, in the name and with the assured warrant of the thirteen colonies, declared their independence of Great Britain, and by God's blessing accomplished it; which, having

1781-1789
critical period

framed and promulgated a plan of general confederation, persuaded these
same thirteen republics to adopt it."   1775 - 1781

The Articles of Confederation. — The authority for the acts of the
Second Continental Congress rested upon no definite grant of powers
by the colonies, but was assumed by it to meet the crisis of war.   However, a plan of perpetual league and a statement of the powers which
the Continental Congress might exercise was framed and proclaimed
by the Second Continental Congress in 1777.

This scheme of union was set forth in a paper termed "The Articles
of Confederation."   These articles did not go into effect until 1781 because it was necessary for them to be ratified by all the States of the
Confederation before they could become the law of the land, and it was
not until that year that the ratification of Maryland was secured.

These articles provided that each State should be represented in this
Confederate (Continental) Congress by not less than two or more than
seven members, to be elected annually and to be subject to recall by the
legislatures of the respective States; but each State should have only
one vote, regardless of the number of representatives.   This body
had power to declare war, enter into certain treaties and alliances
with foreign nations, borrow money, coin money, establish post offices,
regulate the affairs of all Indians not members of the States, together
with a few less important duties.

The expenses of this government were to be paid by taxes raised
through the respective State legislatures, the amount to be paid by
each State being in proportion to the value of all real property within
its boundaries.   The compensation of the delegates was paid directly
by the State which they represented.

The distinctive features, which also proved to be the greatest defects,
of the Articles of Confederation were:

(1) One vote for each State, to which the larger States objected because they wanted representation in proportion to population.

(2) Want of power by the central government to act directly on individuals.   The articles bestowed upon Congress no direct power to
raise revenue other than to borrow money.   The States retained this
power and they frequently refused to collect the amount of taxes demanded of them by Congress.

(3) Want of means for enforcing obedience to the Acts of Congress.
They provided neither for an executive, except committees, nor for

WASHINGTON ENTERTAINING LAFAYETTE AT MOUNT VERNON IN 1777   *Metropolitan Museum of Art*

permanent courts.   A single State could disregard any law, or treaty, which fact was soon recognized by foreign countries, and clearly expressed by Washington, who said: "We are one nation today and thirteen tomorrow.   Who will treat with us on such terms?"

(4) Want of power by the central government to regulate commerce with foreign countries and between the several States.

(5) The requirement of unanimous consent of the thirteen States for any amendment of the Articles of Confederation.   The consent of nine of the States was required for all important ordinary laws.   Thus legislation was retarded because of the difficulty in securing the required majorities.   *1781 – 1789*

The Critical Period. — The independence of the thirteen States was recognized in 1783, but a large national debt remained unpaid, upon which the interest was not met, because only about one fourth of the revenue which Congress asked of the States was collected.   Under these circumstances even the existence of Congress was threatened. For example, some eighty drunken soldiers of the Pennsylvania line mutinied from want of pay and forced Congress to flee from Philadelphia to Princeton, where the college afforded it shelter.

In 1785 Congress made a final attempt to raise the necessary revenue by endeavoring to add an amendment to the Articles of Confederation levying a tax on imports.   New York reaped the benefit of a State tax on imports and refused to agree to this amendment, so the measure failed.   To save expense some States failed to send delegates to this Congress, and unfortunately many of those who attended were not the leading statesmen who were present during the period of the war.   The condition was so bad that the French minister was prompted to write to his country thus: "There is now no general government in America, no head, no Congress, no administrative department."

In colonial days there had been little communication between the colonies, and as soon as peace was restored after the Revolution, the States began to fall apart, and to manifest their sectional jealousies by commercial discrimination.

The following quotation from Fiske well illustrates the existing conditions:

"The city of New York with a population of 30,000 souls had long been supplied with firewood from Connecticut, and with butter and cheese, chickens and garden vegetables from the thrifty farms of New Jersey.   This

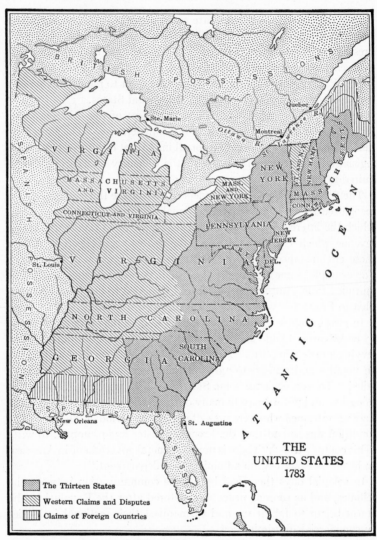

THE
UNITED STATES
1783

The Thirteen States
Western Claims and Disputes
Claims of Foreign Countries

THE CRITICAL PERIOD

The thirteen colonies had gained their independence, but without the able leadership that came forward they could have lost it through wars over the disputed claims to the unsettled interior.

trade, it was observed, carried thousands of dollars out of the city and into the pockets of the detested Yankees and despised Jerseymen. 'It was ruinous to domestic industry,' said the men of New York. 'It must be stopped by . . . a navigation act and a protective tariff.' Acts were accordingly passed, obliging every Yankee sloop which came down through Hell Gate and every Jersey market boat which was rowed across from Paulus Hook to Cortlandt Street to pay entrance fees and obtain clearances at the custom house, just as was done by ships from London and Hamburg; and not a cart-load of Connecticut firewood could be delivered at the back door of a country house in Beekman Street until it should have paid a heavy duty. Great and just was the wrath of the farmers and lumbermen. The New Jersey legislature made up its mind to retaliate. The city of New York had lately bought a small patch of ground on Sandy Hook, and had built a light-house there. This light-house was the one weak spot in the heel of Achilles where a hostile arrow could strike, and New Jersey gave vent to her indignation by laying a tax of $1800 a year on it. Connecticut was equally prompt. At a great meeting of business men, held at New London, it was unanimously agreed to suspend all commercial intercourse with New York. Every merchant signed an agreement, under a penalty of $250 for the first offence, not to send any goods whatever into the hated State for twelve months." [1]

The tariff system of Virginia imposed higher duties upon imports than those imposed by the system of Maryland, and naturally all articles which could be distributed from Maryland as well as from Virginia were brought to Maryland instead of to Virginia. Virginia retaliated by imposing a toll upon vessels entering Chesapeake Bay between the Virginia capes. Maryland disputed the right of Virginia to impose these tolls. To settle this dispute, as well as to reach an agreement upon other rules governing the Chesapeake Bay and Potomac River, commissioners from Maryland and Virginia met at Alexandria, but upon the invitation of Washington moved to Mount Vernon.

Through discussion the commercial difficulties were found to extend beyond the two States, and the commissioners recommended that Delaware and Pennsylvania be invited to meet with them the following year, 1786. Maryland did better; she invited *all* the States to meet at Annapolis. However, delegates arrived from only five States, and these delegates, after concluding that it was necessary to amend the

---

[1] *The Critical Period of American History*, page 146.

Articles of Confederation before any real commercial progress could be made, adjourned to meet at Philadelphia in 1787.

The Constitutional Convention. — Virginia was the first State to announce her delegates for the Philadelphia Convention. They were Washington, Madison, and Edmund Randolph. The name of Washington inspired confidence. In May, 1787, delegates from all the States except Rhode Island assembled, fifty-five able delegates being present. Washington was chosen President of the Convention, and it was agreed that each State should have one vote, and that the sessions should be secret.

Drafting the Federal Constitution. — Immediately the Convention divided into two factions — the one representing the smaller States and the other the larger States. Randolph of Virginia presented the Large State Plan, or the so-called "Virginia Plan," which proposed a Congress of two houses with power to legislate on all national matters and to compel obedience on the part of the States. Representation in both houses was to be based on population, thus giving the larger and more populous States the control of both branches of the legislature. Furthermore, since by this scheme the President, executive officers, and judges were to be appointed by Congress, supervision of the whole administration of the new government would be under the control of the larger States.

Paterson of New Jersey introduced the Small State Plan, or the so-called "New Jersey Plan," which provided for a Congress of one house. By this plan each State was to have equal representation.

The result was a compromise. It was agreed that there should be a legislature of two houses: a Senate, the less numerous branch, and a House of Representatives, the more numerous branch. In the Senate each State was to have an equal representation, thus putting the small States on an equal footing with the large ones; but in the House of Representatives the representation was to be according to population, thus favoring the larger States.

It was also decided by the Convention that the Constitution should be considered ratified and should go into effect as soon as accepted by nine of the thirteen States. Persons favoring the adoption of the Constitution by their respective States were called Federalists, and those opposing it were called Anti-Federalists. From this contest rose the first political parties in the United States.

SIGNING THE CONSTITUTION OF THE UNITED STATES

Washington presides and Gouverneur Morris signs. At the lower left is Madison, above him is Franklin, and at the lower right is Edmund Randolph.

NEW YORK CELEBRATING THE ADOPTION OF THE CONSTITUTION

President Washington and Congress are standing on the fort.

53

The Convention adjourned in September, having been in session a little under four months.   Gladstone, the famous English statesman, considered this Constitution "the most wonderful work ever struck off at a given time by the brain and purpose of man."

MOUNT VERNON, THE HOME OF WASHINGTON

To Washington more than any other statesman we owe our peacefully established Federal Union.

The fundamental difference between the new Constitution and the old Articles was that the Constitution provided an adequate executive and judiciary to enforce the Federal laws directly upon the individual instead of depending upon the indirect enforcement by the State governments, which had enforced only such as they individually approved.

Arguments for and against Adoption. — The Federalist Party with such leaders as Hamilton, Washington, and Madison favored the proposed Constitution because it established a strong National government which would attract outstanding statesmen and develop a great, united nation.   This party was especially strong in commercial New England, where the weakness of the old Confederation and the tariff discriminations of the States were brought forcibly home.   The arguments of the Federalists appeared in a collection of eighty-five essays, called "The Federalist," written by Alexander Hamilton, John Jay, and James Madison.   These essays contain an excellent exposition of the Constitution.

The Anti-Federalists, such as Patrick Henry and George Clinton, favored strong State governments and a comparatively weak National government.   They felt that too much power was given to the central government and that State liberty would be crushed out.   Patriotism at that time was devotion to the State.   A citizen of Virginia abroad called himself a "Virginian" and not an "American." The Anti-Federalists compared a strong National government to the English government, by which they had so recently felt oppressed, and they declared that it would be a government founded upon the destruction of the governments of the several States.

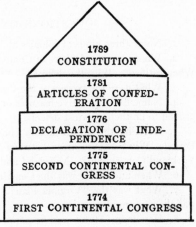

STONES IN THE MONUMENT TO UNION
Adapted from Forman's *Advanced Civics*

A further objection was that the Constitution contained no definite "bill of rights" guaranteeing to individuals such fundamental liberties as freedom of speech, liberty of the press, assurance against unjust arrest, and trial by jury.   The Federalists practically agreed to add these guarantees, which promise was fulfilled by the adoption of the first ten constitutional amendments in 1791.   It was feared that a President might become so popular as to obtain life tenure of office, and thus the government might degenerate into a monarchy.   Patrick Henry cried, "We shall have a King; the army will salute him monarch."

By June, 1788, the Federalists prevailed.   New Hampshire,[1] the ninth State, ratified.   The Continental Congress provided for the election of a President and his inauguration on March 4.   This day

---

[1] The Constitution was ratified by the several States in the following order: Delaware, December 7, 1787; Pennsylvania, December 12, 1787; New Jersey, December 18, 1787; Georgia, January 2, 1788; Connecticut, January 9, 1788; Massachusetts, February 6, 1788; Maryland, April 28, 1788; South Carolina, May 23, 1788; New Hampshire, June 21, 1788; Virginia, June 26, 1788; New York, July 26, 1788; North Carolina, November 21, 1789; and Rhode Island, May 29, 1790.

continued to be observed as the beginning of a new term of office until 1933 when it was changed to January 20 by ratification of the Twentieth Amendment. Owing to a delay in the assembling of the new Congress, which had to count the electoral vote, Washington was not inaugurated until April 30, 1789.

QUESTIONS ON THE TEXT

1. Name three kinds of colonies and describe the characteristics of each.

2. What were the Articles of Confederation? When were they framed? When ratified? Why the delay?

3. What were the powers of the Confederate (Continental) Congress?

4. Name five distinctive features of the Articles of Confederation which proved to be their greatest defects.

5. Describe the unsatisfactory conditions existing during the Critical Period. What dispute arose between New York and New Jersey? New York and Connecticut? Maryland and Virginia?

6. When and where was the Constitution drafted?

7. What was the "Virginia Plan"? The "New Jersey Plan"? What was the compromise?

8. How many States were required for the ratification of the Constitution?

9. What was the fundamental difference between the Constitution and the Articles of Confederation?

10. Who favored the adoption of the Constitution and what argument did they use for its adoption? Who opposed it and what were their arguments?

11. In what year was the required number of ratifications obtained?

12. When was Washington inaugurated as the first President of the United States?

PROBLEMS FOR DISCUSSION

1. What did the individual State gain by entering the Federal union? What did it lose?

2. If our thirteen States had not united, what nation would probably control northern New England today? Florida? Louisiana? Texas? California? Washington? Wisconsin? Minnesota?

3. The Constitutional Convention met in the old State House in Philadelphia (probably in a room directly above the one in which the Declaration of Independence had been signed eleven years before). On the first day, May 25, 1787, the delegates unanimously elected George Washington as

presiding officer. Why was this particular choice so significant? What was Washington's standing with the people of the day? Could the fact that Washington had presided at the Convention have had any effect in the ratification controversy?

4. When the thirteen States federated, there was need of much self-government within a State because there was so little communication or travel or transportation between States. Today all of New England is relatively smaller than any of the States at the time of union. Would it be more convenient for the business man and traveler and less expensive for the resident taxpayer if there should be one State government for all New England? (Assume the representation in the United States Senate unchanged.) Advance arguments for and against such a State.

5. Several of the leaders of the Revolutionary period were conspicuous by their absence at the Philadelphia Convention. Thomas Jefferson was at the time on a diplomatic mission to France and John Adams was in Holland. Samuel Adams and John Hancock declined to serve. Patrick Henry also refused to attend saying that he "smelt a rat." Richard Henry Lee, the man who had introduced in the Continental Congress the resolution proposing a Declaration of Independence and Articles of Confederation, was not appointed in Virginia. Thomas Paine was in Paris where he shortly would take a part in the French Revolution. Why has it been said that it was perhaps a fortunate thing that some of these men (especially Patrick Henry, Samuel Adams, and Thomas Paine) were not in Philadelphia?

SELECT BIBLIOGRAPHY

DeVoto, B. "The Louisiana Purchase." *Collier's*. March 21, 1953.

Ferguson, J. and McHenry, D. *The American System of Government*. McGraw-Hill. New York. 1953. Chs. 2 and 3.

Farrand, M. *The Framing of the Constitution*. Yale University Press. 1913.

Fiske, John. *The Critical Period of American History*. Houghton-Mifflin. 1888 and subsequent editions.

"Basic Principles of the Government of the United States." *Congressional Digest*. June, 1951, pages 163–192. (Texts of seven basic documents.)

"George Washington: A Man to Remember." *Time*. July 6, 1953.

Johnson, C. O. *American Government*. Crowell. New York. 1951 Ed. Chs. I–II.

Ogg, F. A. and Ray, P. O. *Essentials of American Government*. Appleton-Century-Crofts. New York. 1952 ed. Chs. I–II.

Van Doren, Carl. *The Great Rehearsal*. Viking Press. 1948. (Story of making and ratifying the Constitution.)

CHAPTER IV

OUR FEDERAL SYSTEM OF GOVERNMENT

The Fundamental Bases of American Government. — Government in the United States is firmly based upon two essential propositions: the twin doctrines of popular sovereignty and limited government.

Popular Sovereignty. — In the United States, *all* political power resides in the people. The people are sovereign and *from* them flow any and all powers of government. Through the National and State Constitutions the people have granted to the National and State Governments such powers as they enjoy. Thus, no statement in the Constitution is more significant than that in the Preamble: "We, the people of the United States, . . . do ordain and establish this Constitution for the United States of America."

Limited Government. — While *all* governmental power flows from the people, government may exercise *only* those powers that the people have seen fit to vest in government. The National Government may exercise only those powers vested in it by the National Constitution and the States may exercise only those powers vested in them by the National Constitution and their own State Constitutions.

As we shall see, there are a great many areas in which the people have not authorized government to act and many others in which government is severely restricted. In illustrating the limited character of governmental power under the Constitution, George Washington, in writing to his friend Lafayette in 1788, remarked that the proposed new document was "provided with more checks and barriers against the introduction of tyranny . . . than any government hitherto instituted among mortals hath possessed."

The United States a Federal Government. — The Philadelphia Convention was bent on creating a National Government adequate to meet the needs of the country and at the same time to preserve local self-government in the States. In order to accomplish this, our Constitution makers changed the thirteen *confederate* States into the thirteen *federated* States. In so doing they brought into being a federal system, a type of government never before tried.

58

THE CAPITOL OF THE UNITED STATES

Federalism has its roots deep in American history. Few if any of the Founding Fathers favored the creation of a strong centralized (unitary) government for all of the United States. They knew how stoutly the people had fought for and believed in their rights of local self-government. At the same time, they knew how sincerely the people would distrust a strong centralized national government.

Advantages of Our Federal Government. — The system of Federal Government in the United States has all the advantages of local self-government for the States as well as the great strength which results from union. This system of state-making is the most complicated of all methods, but is at the same time the most stable. Not only are the American people enabled to protect their liberties through representation in Congress; but in such matters as religion, suffrage, and education, which produce determined sentiments, the American Federal system gives consideration to the wishes of the people of each State.

For example, Texas can tax church property or not as it thinks best; South Carolina can have the educational test to bar illiterates from voting; and any state may provide free textbooks if it so desires. Furthermore, if the peace of Texas should be disturbed by Mexican invaders, Texas could depend upon the assistance of the remaining forty-seven States for defense; and should yellow fever in Cuba threaten the United States, the united effort of the States would be exerted to prevent it.

Division of Powers between Nation and States. — The Constitution outlines the basic scheme of the American federal system. It provides for a *division of powers* on a territorial basis; that is, a division of powers between the National Government on the one hand and the States on the other. This division of powers is most clearly stated in the Tenth Amendment:

The powers not delegated to the United States by the Constitution, nor prohibited by it to the States, are reserved to the States respectively, or to the people.

The National Government is a government of *delegated powers*. That is, the National Government possesses only those powers *expressly* delegated (granted) to it in the Constitution or those which may be reasonably *implied* from the *expressed powers*.[1]

A. The Expressed Powers include, among others, the power to:

Declare war and make peace
Maintain armed forces
Make treaties and conduct foreign relations
Regulate foreign and interstate commerce
Lay and collect taxes

Maintain post offices and post roads
Issue coins and paper money
Borrow money
Grant patents and copyrights
Maintain a Federal court system
Regulate bankruptcy and naturalization

Do anything "necessary and proper for carrying into execution the foregoing powers."

B. The Implied Powers arise from the so-called "Necessary and Proper Clause." [2] For example, the regulation of labor-management relations, the building of power dams, river and harbor improvements, flood control, punishment as a Federal crime the transporting of stolen goods across a State line — these and many other powers are exercised by the National Government because they may be

---

[1] Most of these expressed powers are to be found in Article I, Section 8.

[2] "Congress shall have power . . . to make all laws which shall be necessary and proper for carrying into execution the foregoing powers, and all other powers vested by this Constitution in the government of the United States, or in any department or officer thereof." Article I, Section 8, Clause 18. This clause is also known as the "Elastic Clause" and, through Supreme Court interpretation, the words "necessary and proper" have come to mean "convenient and appropriate." See Chapter VI.

DIVISION OF POWERS BETWEEN THE NATIONAL GOVERNMENT AND THE STATES

"The powers not delegated to the United States by the Constitution, nor prohibited by it to the States, are reserved to the States respectively, or to the people" — Amendment 10

POWERS OF GOVERNMENT

FEDERAL [1]
- Expressed [2] — (Article I, Section 8, Clauses 1-17; Amendment 16)
- Implied [3] — (Article I, Section 8, Clause 18)
- Denied — (Article I, Section 9; Amendments 1-11; 13)

CONCURRENT [4]
- (Examples: taxation, eminent domain)

STATE
- Reserved [5] — (Amendment 10) — Example: police powers — { Health, Morals, Safety, Welfare }
- Denied — (Article I, Section 10; Amendments 13-15, 18, 19)

[1] The terms "national" and "delegated" mean the same as "federal" in this connection.

[2] The term "enumerated" (numbered) means the same as "expressed" in this connection.

[3] The term "resultant power" is used when a power is not clearly implied from any one "expressed power" but results from several expressed powers. The term "inherent in sovereignty" is sometimes used for powers neither clearly expressed nor clearly implied but necessarily belonging to a sovereign state. Recognizing new sovereign states and deporting aliens are examples of powers inherent in sovereignty.

[4] The term "concurrent power" means one which may be exercised by either the Federal Government or the State Government or both.

[5] The term "residual" is often used in the sense of "reserved."

61

reasonably implied from the expressed power to regulate foreign and interstate commerce.

C. Powers Denied the National Government. — While the Constitution delegates certain expressed and implied powers to the National Government, it also denies to the National Government certain powers.[1] To illustrate, Congress may not pass any ex post facto laws or bills of attainder, nor may it levy duties on exports or grant titles of nobility.

The State Governments possess what are known as *residual* or *reserved powers.* In other words, the States may exercise any power not delegated by the Constitution to the National Government and at the same time not denied by it to the States.[2] Thus the State of Alabama, or any other State, may require police consent for the holding of religious services in the streets. She could forbid persons under age twenty-one to marry or to vote; could prohibit the carrying, or even owning, of firearms; and could charter and control corporations. She may also establish public school systems and units of local government and legislate concerning marriage and divorce.

Alabama can do all these things and more because there is nothing in the Constitution of the United States which prohibits her from doing so. The National Government cannot do these things because, as we have seen, it has not been delegated the power to do so. Thus the power to do these things is *reserved* to the States.

At the same time, Alabama, and every other State, is prevented from doing certain things by the Constitution. For example, no State may enter into any treaty, alliance, or confederation, nor may it coin money, make any law impairing the obligation of contracts, grant titles of nobility, or deprive any person of life, liberty, or property without due process of law.

Exclusive and Concurrent Powers. — Some of the powers delegated to the National Government are denied to the States by the Constitution. For example, the power to coin money is expressly granted to the National Government and expressly denied to the States. Thus, the power to coin money is an *exclusive power* of the National Govern-

---

[1] Most of these are found in Article I, Section 9, and Amendments I–X.

[2] Most of the powers denied to the States are found in Article I, Section 10. One must always remember that a State's own constitution may further restrict the powers of the State Government.

ment, as are the powers to make treaties, establish post offices, etc. But some of the delegated powers are *not* denied to the States.[1] While the National Government may lay and collect taxes, so may the States. Hence, the power to tax is a *concurrent power* (one enjoyed by both the National and State Governments).

Supremacy of Federal Law. — In our Federal system of government some powers granted to the National Government are almost certain to conflict with others which were apparently reserved for the State governments. The following passage from the Constitution shows that State laws which conflict with such National laws as Congress has constitutional authority for enacting must yield to the National laws:

"This Constitution and the laws of the United States which shall be made in pursuance thereof, and all treaties made or which shall be made under the authority of the United States, shall be the supreme law of the land." This means that California could not prohibit Chinese born in the United States from voting at regular elections, as this would violate the Fifteenth Amendment to the Constitution of the United States. Further, this also means that California could not hold regular elections for Congressmen in June because a law of the United States prescribes the month of November. Or, if the United States should make a treaty with China agreeing to guarantee to all Chinese residing in the United States all privileges of citizens of the United States, California could not place a higher license upon laundries run by alien Chinese than upon similar laundries conducted by Americans.

Supremacy of the Federal Courts — Judicial Review. — Not only is the Federal law supreme but the Federal courts decide whether a State or an individual has violated this law. If Virginia should pass a law conflicting with the Constitution, laws, or treaties of the United States,

---

[1] The Supreme Court has held that those delegated powers which are of such a character that the exercise of them by the States would be, under any circumstances, inconsistent with the general theory of a *National* Government, may be exercised only by the United States.

Those delegated powers not of this character may be exercised by the States until the United States sees fit to exercise them. To illustrate, the Constitution delegates to Congress the power to enact bankruptcy laws. From 1878 to 1898 Congress did not desire a National bankruptcy law. All States enacted them. When a new National bankruptcy act was passed in 1898 any details of State laws inconsistent therewith became void. Therefore, while the States have a certain amount of power, the National Government is in reality supreme in the field of concurrent powers.

any individual who shows injury thereby may go to court; and, if the case is finally appealed to the Supreme Court of the United States, this court would decide whether the State law really conflicts. The decisions of the Supreme Court are binding not only on private persons, but on States, and even on the Congress of the United States, if the latter passes a law contrary to the Constitution.[1]

Obligations of the National Government to the States

Guarantee of a Republican Form of Government. — The Constitution requires that the National Government "guarantee to every State in this Union a republican form of government."[2] Although the phrase "republican form of government" has never been defined by the courts, it is generally understood to mean a representative democracy.[3]

---

[1] *Judicial review*, the power of the courts to determine the constitutionality of Acts of Congress or of the State legislatures and actions of the executive agencies of National or State Governments, is not granted to the courts by the United States Constitution. It was first announced as affecting the United States Constitution in the case of *Marbury* v. *Madison* (1803). On the evening of March 3, 1801, President Adams signed and sealed a commission appointing one Marbury justice of the peace for the District of Columbia. On the next day Jefferson was inaugurated as President and immediately instructed his Secretary of State, James Madison, not to deliver the commission.

Marbury thereupon applied to the Supreme Court for a writ of *mandamus* compelling Madison to make delivery, and cited an Act of Congress, the Judiciary Act of 1789, which empowered the Court to issue such writs against officers of the United States. But a unanimous decision of the Court written by John Marshall held that the section of the Judiciary Act which authorized the Court to *mandamus* the chief executive was beyond the powers granted Congress by the Constitution and hence unconstitutional. Thus Marshall proclaimed, for the first time in any United States Supreme Court decision, the right of this tribunal to declare an Act of Congress void.

Today any State or Federal court may refuse to enforce an Act of Congress or an Act of a State legislature, if it believes it to be unconstitutional, unless and until the Act is declared constitutional by the United States Supreme Court.

[2] Article IV, Section 4.

[3] In the case of *Luther* v. *Borden* (1849) the Supreme Court declared that the question of a "republican form of government" is a political one to be decided by Congress. In seating Senators and Representatives from the questioned State, said the Court, Congress recognizes that State as republican in form. The case grew out of Dorr's Rebellion (1841–1842) in Rhode Island. The followers of Thomas W. Dorr attempted to force the conservative ruling clique to ease the suffrage requirements. They proclaimed a new constitution and named Dorr "governor." However, when Dorr attempted to put the new government in

Protection against Invasion and Domestic Violence. — In addition to guaranteeing to each State a republican form of government, the National Government is required to ". . . protect each of them against invasion; and on application of the legislature, or of the executive (when the legislature cannot be convened), against domestic violence." [1] Today, of course, an invasion of one State would be considered an attack upon the United States as a whole.

The President, as commander-in-chief of the armed forces, may use Federal troops to quell domestic violence, such as riots and looting. Normally, he sends troops only when requested to do so by the governor or legislature of the State involved. However, when a Federal question is involved, he need not wait for such a request. [2]

In recent years, domestic violence has come to mean more than man-made violence. Thus the armed forces and other Federal agencies are used to render emergency assistance in such catastrophes as the disastrous Kansas-Missouri floods of 1951 and 1952.

Respect for Geographic Identity. — The National Government is further obliged to respect the geographic identity or integrity of each of the States. Thus Congress may not create a new State from territory belonging to one or more of the existing States unless it first has the consent of the State legislatures involved. [3] Nor may a State be denied its equal representation in the Senate without its own consent. [4]

INTERSTATE RELATIONS 6

States Legally Separate. — Each State is legally separate from every other State in the Union. When the States are acting within

operation, the governor under the original State Constitution appealed to President John Tyler for assistance. When the President took steps to put down the rebellion, it subsided. But a new and more liberal constitution was adopted in 1842.

In a 1912 case (*Pacific States Tel. & Tel. Co.* v. *Oregon*) the Court repeated the earlier holding. An Oregon corporation had refused to pay a tax levied by the voters, claiming the use of the initiative and referendum (direct legislation) in Oregon meant that the State no longer had a republican (representative) government.

[1] Article IV, Section 4. Note that the States themselves are prohibited from maintaining standing armies or navies. (Article I, Section 10, Clause 3.)

[2] Indeed, when President Cleveland sent Federal troops to restore order in the railyards during the Chicago Pullman strike of 1894, he did so over the express objections of Governor Altgeld of Illinois. Because the rioters threatened United States property and impeded the flow of the mails and interstate commerce, the Supreme Court upheld his action in 1896. Since then, several Presidents have acted in similar situations without waiting for a request.

[3] Article IV, Section 3, Clause 1.   [4] Article V.

the sphere of their reserved powers they stand toward one another as independent and wholly separate. Each State has no jurisdiction outside its own boundaries.[1] But given the interwoven nature of the American scene, the States must of course have dealings with one another. In several important respects these interstate relationships are covered by the United States Constitution.

Courtesy The Port of New York Authority

THE LARGEST BUS TERMINAL IN THE WORLD

Interstate Compacts. — As we have seen, no State may enter into any treaty, alliance, or confederation. But States may enter into *compacts* or agreements among themselves and with foreign States.[2]

In the last several years an increasing number of compacts have

---

[1] "Hot pursuit" agreements are an exception here. Most States now permit police officers from an adjoining State to pursue lawbreakers across the State line, arrest them, and turn them over to local authorities. But this can be done only when the police are in actual "hot pursuit" of their quarry.

Air travel provides another exception. Washington and Minnesota, for example, now permit adjacent counties in neighboring States to acquire and operate airports within their States, provided the neighboring State does the same.

[2] Article I, Section 10, Clauses 1 and 3. The Supreme Court has ruled that Congressional consent need not be had for compacts which do not "tend to increase the political power of the States." Thus, some years ago, New York, New Jersey, and Connecticut, without going to Congress at all, settled among themselves a long-standing dispute over sewage pollution of New York harbor. As a matter of course, however, practically all agreements are submitted for Congressional action.

been concluded and today well over one hundred are in force. Oregon and Washington have protected fish in boundary waters; New York and New Jersey created the Port of New York Authority to provide wharves, tunnels, bridges, street approaches, bus terminals, and airports; nearly all the States have now entered the Parole and Probation Compact which provides for interstate supervision of parolees and probationers. In 1953 Congress approved the Connecticut River Flood Control Compact involving Connecticut, Massachusetts, New Hampshire, and Vermont. The pact aims to co-ordinate interstate action and Federal flood control along the Connecticut River.

Most compacts relate to the common use of natural resources, as the Hoover Dam Compact involving the States of the Colorado River Basin. This compact was the first great attempt to bring several of the States together as political units for the development, control, and management of a regional river in which they all are interested.

Many other compacts have been used to settle interstate disputes while still others have been instrumental in promoting interstate co-operation in the handling of common problems.

The Full Faith and Credit Clause. — Each State is required to give "full faith and credit . . . to the public acts, records, and judicial proceedings of every other State." [1]

The words "acts, records, and judicial proceedings" here refer to legislative acts, statutes, ordinances, records of births, marriages, divorces, wills, deeds, contracts, and the decisions, judgments, and decrees rendered by courts. For instance, if a man dies in Baltimore and his will disposes of property in Chicago, Illinois must give full faith and credit to the will probated under Maryland law.

One may prove age, marriage status, or title to land by obtaining a certificate from the State where the record was made. Or, suppose that A secures a judgment for $1000 against B in a New York court, in which State both parties reside. B moves to New Jersey, taking all his property with him before it can be attached for the debt. A follows him and shows the New York judgment in the proper New Jersey court. The New Jersey court, without re-examining the merits of the original claim, will give full faith and credit and have its officer collect the debt for A.

---

[1] Article IV, Section 1.

Two exceptions to the rule of full faith and credit must be noted. First, it applies only to civil matters; that is, one State will not enforce another State's criminal laws. Secondly, and for the present at least, full faith and credit need not be given, in certain cases, to a divorce granted by one State's courts to citizens of another State.

This confusing situation in the matter of "interstate divorces" came about as the result of a 1945 Supreme Court decision. The Court held that a Nevada divorce granted to *bona fide* (good faith) Nevada residents must be recognized in all other States. But a Nevada divorce granted to citizens of another State need not be. The Court felt that the forty-two days required by Nevada's divorce law is not long enough to establish *bona fide* residence. In order to become a resident of a State one must intend to reside there indefinitely. This decision and several others which have followed have cast a dark cloud of doubt over thousands of interstate divorces.

Privileges and Immunities. — The Constitution specifically provides that "the citizens of each State shall be entitled to all privileges and immunities of citizens in the several States." (Art. IV, Sec. 2.) This means that a citizen of one State may go to another State and there enjoy the same civil rights [1] that citizens of the latter State enjoy, and likewise be subject to the same restrictions. [2]

As an example of the rights a citizen of one State may enjoy in another State, the legislature of Maryland passed a law (1868) imposing a license on the privilege of selling articles not manufactured in Maryland. For citizens of Maryland the license was not to exceed $150, but for citizens of other States the license was to be $300. Mr. Ward of New Jersey refused to pay more than $150, and the Supreme Court of the United States decided that Mr. Ward could not be required to pay more than citizens of Maryland.

---

[1] *Civil rights* are those of person and property.

[2] Under the "privileges and immunities" clause a corporation is not a citizen. Therefore a State may refuse a corporation chartered in another State the privilege of conducting business in its borders. For instance, outside insurance companies may enter a State only on such conditions as the State may impose; *e.g.*, that premiums collected in a State be invested there. But a State cannot interfere with interstate commerce without the consent of Congress, and a corporation has the same privileges of interstate commerce as a natural person. It may ship commodities into a State under the same conditions as a natural person, and may likewise become an interstate common carrier.

As an illustration of a restriction upon a citizen of one State while in another State, a citizen of Washington State cannot marry in Oregon unless he is physically and mentally examined in accordance with the Oregon law.

The courts have never given a complete list of privileges and immunities, but the following are some of them: The right to pass through, or reside in any other State for the purpose of trade, agriculture, professional pursuits, or otherwise; to demand the writ of *habeas corpus;* to bring suit in the courts of the State; to make contracts; to buy, sell, and own property; to pay no higher taxes than the citizens of the State; to marry.

A State is not required to grant *public* or political privileges to nonresidents. It may require one to live in a State a specified period before voting or holding office.

A State may require a period of residence in a State before it grants licenses to practice medicine or dentistry, and may restrict the practice of law to citizens of the State. The State has the right to take time to observe the moral character of a person who desires to enter an occupation of great importance to the general public.

Wild fish and game are property of the State, therefore a nonresident may be compelled to pay a higher fee for a hunting or fishing license than a resident, who pays taxes to help maintain the State game and fish hatcheries. Likewise a State school may charge higher tuition to nonresidents than to residents.

Extradition.[1] — The Constitution provides that "a person charged in any State with treason, felony, or other crime, who shall flee from justice and be found in another State, shall on demand of the executive authority of the State from which he fled be delivered up to be removed to the State having jurisdiction of the crime." (Art. IV, Sec. 2.)

A man, and a woman who posed as his sister, operated a racket in New York in which the man made love to wealthy widows, obtained money from them, and then jilted them. The couple killed one suspicious woman to prevent her exposing them, and moved to Michigan. In Michigan they likewise killed a woman and her child to cover their tracks, and were caught. The governor of New York requested

---

[1] Extradition has been carried on between sovereign states from early times, and the word extradition has been the popular term used in the United States for what is more technically known as *interstate rendition.*

⑥ Commerce is usually carried on freely between states — no tariffs

extradition of the couple and the governor of Michigan complied because Michigan does not have capital punishment for murder but New York has. In New York the couple was sentenced to death.

The return of a fugitive is usually a routine matter. Occasionally, however, a governor will refuse to surrender a wanted man. Despite the fact that the Constitution says "shall," the Supreme Court has consistently held that the Constitution imposes only a *moral* duty on a governor. As the National Government cannot force a governor's hand, when one governor refuses the request of another, whether the reasons be good, bad, or indifferent, there the matter ends.

Several years ago, ex-Governor Taylor of Kentucky was implicated in the murder of Governor Goebel and he fled to Indiana. The governor of Indiana, feeling that Taylor, a Republican, would not receive a fair trial with the Democrats then in control in Kentucky, refused to extradite him. Recently, the governor of Oregon refused a West Virginia request based on a crime committed in 1903 because the wanted man had lived as a respected member of his Oregon community for nearly half a century.

Congress, acting under the commerce power, has made it a Federal crime to flee across a State line to avoid prosecution. This means that State police now have the invaluable assistance of the Federal Bureau of Investigation in such cases.

THE ADMISSION OF NEW STATES

Congress Admits New States. — Congress has the sole power to admit new States, but it may not create a new State by taking territory of an existing State without the consent of that State.[1] Aside from the thirteen original States, thirty-five States have been admitted by Congress.[2]

The normal admission procedure is relatively simple. The territory desiring Statehood petitions Congress for admission. If Congress is

---

[1] Article IV, Section 3, Clause 1.

[2] Although North Carolina (November 21, 1789) and Rhode Island (May 29, 1790) ratified the Constitution after the new Government had been organized (April 30, 1789), they are, of course, included among the original thirteen. Five States (Vermont, Kentucky, Tennessee, Maine, and West Virginia) were created from parts of already existing States. Texas was an independent republic before admission. California was admitted after being ceded by Mexico. The other twenty-eight States were admitted after a period as organized territories of the United States.

favorable, it passes an "enabling act" which directs the framing of a constitution. After the document is drafted, it is submitted to Congress and, if Congress is still agreeable, it passes a resolution of admission. Hawaii has already drafted a constitution to submit if and when an enabling act is passed.

Before finally admitting a new State, Congress usually imposes certain conditions. Thus, in 1896, Utah was admitted on condition that its new constitution outlaw polygamy; and, in 1802, Ohio was required not to tax for five years any public lands sold within her borders by the United States.

But each State enters the Union on an equal footing with each of her sister States. When Oklahoma was admitted in 1907, Congress required that the State capital not be moved from Guthrie prior to 1913. In 1910 the legislature moved the capital to Oklahoma City. When this step was challenged, the Supreme Court declared that Congress may impose conditions as it sees fit, but they cannot be enforced when they compromise the independence of a State to manage its own internal affairs. Again, President Taft vetoed a resolution admitting Arizona because he objected to the constitutional provision permitting the popular recall of judges. Arizona was admitted by a new resolution in 1912, but without the recall provision. Almost immediately thereafter the people of Arizona added the recall provision to their new State Constitution.

Separation of Powers of the National Government

In addition to a *division of powers* between the National Government and the States, the Constitution also provides for a *separation of powers* within the National Government. That is, the powers of the National Government are separated (distributed) among three distinct branches of the National Government — the legislative, the executive, and the judicial branches.

In defense of this unusual arrangement, James Madison, the "Father of the Constitution," wrote:

The accumulation of all powers, legislative, executive, and judiciary, in the same hands, whether of one, a few, or many, and whether hereditary, self-appointed, or elective, may justly be pronounced the very definition of tyranny.

Legislative Branch. — The Constitution vests *all* of the legislative (law-making) powers of the National Government in Congress. This body cannot authorize any other persons to legislate in its stead. But it often passes acts which outline general policies and set certain standards while leaving the actual details of day-to-day administration to some governmental agency. For instance, Congress has provided for the regulation of freight rates and created the Interstate Commerce Commission to fix the actual rates in a given case. If Congress were to fix the rates in each case, it would have no time for other business.

Executive Branch. — The Constitution provides that all executive (law-executing, law-enforcing, law-administering) powers shall be vested in the President. Of course, he is assisted by all of the departments and agencies of the vast executive branch, but he alone is personally responsible for its actions.

Judicial Branch. — The Constitution vests the judicial (law-interpreting, law-applying) powers in the Supreme Court and such inferior courts as Congress may create. The courts interpret and apply the law in actual cases as they come before the courts.

Check and Balance System. — Thus, three separate and distinct branches of the National Government exist. But these three branches are not *completely* independent of one another. While each branch has its own distinct field of powers, it is subject to a series of constitutional checks which the other branches may exercise against it. For example, the President may veto acts of Congress; Congress may override a veto by a two-thirds vote in each House. Or Congress may refuse to appropriate funds requested by the President, or may impeach the President, judges, and other civil officers. The courts have assumed the power to pass on the constitutionality of acts of Congress or actions of the President (judicial review).

As a concrete illustration, when in 1952 President Truman seized the steel industry to prevent a strike, he claimed that such a strike would endanger the nation's security and that, as Commander-in-Chief of the armed forces, he had the Constitutional authority to act. But the Supreme Court, saying that "this is a job for the Nation's lawmakers, not for its military authorities," declared that the President's seizure action exceeded his powers under the Constitution and was, therefore, unconstitutional.

The Founding Fathers intended the check and balance system to prevent "an unjust combination of the majority." And, on the whole, the system has worked well. The people have learned, however, that while mistakes or evil designs of one department may be checked by another, so also can well-planned, honest policies of one be checked by another for political reasons.

When both houses of Congress are controlled by the President's supporters the system works well. But when one or both houses are in the hands of the opposing party it is exceedingly difficult for the National Government to operate smoothly. In such instances the National Government does not fail completely, of course. But it is many times stalled over vital policy decisions.

The check and balance system makes compromise necessary, and compromise is of the essence in a democratic system. Dictatorships are based upon the usurping of power by one man or a small group. Thus the check and balance system prevents the rise of an all-powerful dictator in the National Government.

OUR CHANGING CONSTITUTION

Formal Amendment. — The methods for amending the Constitution are set forth in Article V. Of the four methods there provided, only two have thus far been used.

First, an amendment may be proposed by a two-thirds vote of each house of Congress and ratified by the legislatures of three-fourths of the States. Twenty-one amendments have been adopted in this manner.

Second, an amendment may be proposed by a two-thirds vote of each house of Congress and ratified by conventions in three-fourths of the States. The convention method has been used only once, in the case of Amendment XXI. The disadvantage of this method lies in the fact that there is only one opportunity in each State for ratification; whereas, under the first method, if a legislature refuses to ratify at one session, a subsequent one might do so. But once a legislature does ratify, it can never rescind that action. Amendment XXI was ratified by convention because Congress felt that the people would be more favorable to it than the State legislators.

Third, an amendment may be proposed by a National Convention, called by Congress at the request of two-thirds of the State legislatures, and ratified by the legislatures of three-fourths of the States.

Fourth, an amendment may be proposed by a National Convention, called by Congress when requested by the legislatures of two-thirds of the States, and ratified by conventions in three-fourths of the States. The Constitution was originally adopted in this manner.

Referendum Denied. — In 1920 the United States Supreme Court ruled that State legislatures may not refer Federal amendments to the people but must pass upon them themselves. However, a legislature may be influenced by an advisory vote of the people.

FOUR WAYS OF AMENDING THE CONSTITUTION OF THE UNITED STATES

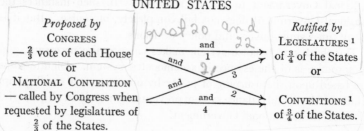

Proposed by CONGRESS — ⅔ vote of each House		Ratified by LEGISLATURES [1] of ¾ of the States
or		or
NATIONAL CONVENTION — called by Congress when requested by legislatures of ⅔ of the States.		CONVENTIONS [1] of ¾ of the States.

The Twenty-Two Amendments. — The first ten amendments, the Bill of Rights, were added to the Constitution in 1791.[2] They define most of the rights individual citizens are guaranteed by the National Government. For example, the guarantees include freedom of speech, press, religion, petition, and assembly; protection from unreasonable searches and seizures; freedom from double jeopardy and self-incrimination; protection from the depriving of life, liberty, or property without due process of law; and numerous other guarantees of fair treatment before the law. (See Chapter XXII, "Civil Rights.") But it must always be remembered that the Bill of Rights restricts *only* the National Government, and not the States. Amendment X reserves to the States those powers not granted to the National Government.

---

[1] Congress determines whether an amendment is to be ratified by State legislatures or by State conventions.

[2] Many people, including Thomas Jefferson, agreed to support the adoption of the original Constitution only on condition that a listing of the rights of the people against the National Government be added immediately. These amendments were proposed by the First Congress in 1789 and ratified in 1791. They are known as the Bill of Rights because they contain many of the rights gained by the British people in their Bill of Rights passed by Parliament in 1689.

The Eleventh Amendment (1798) provides that a State may not be sued by a citizen of another State without its consent. The twelfth (1804) deals with the election of the President and Vice-President. No more amendments were added for the next 61 years. The Civil War resulted in the adoption of the thirteenth (1865), the fourteenth (1868), and the fifteenth (1870). These so-called "Civil War Amendments" abolished slavery, defined citizenship and thus extended it to former slaves, and prohibited any voting restrictions "on account of race, color, or previous condition of servitude." The fourteenth also extended the "due process clause" to the States. (See Chapter XXII.)

After 43 more years, in 1913, both the Sixteenth Amendment, providing for a Federal income tax, and the Seventeenth, for the popular election of senators, were ratified.

The Eighteenth Amendment (1919) established national prohibition, and the Nineteenth (1920) provided for woman suffrage. The Twentieth, providing that Congress shall meet January 3d and that the President shall take office January 20th, and the Twenty-first, repealing the Eighteenth, were adopted in the same year, 1933. The Twenty-second Amendment, adopted in 1951, limits a President to two full terms or not more than ten years in office.

Thus is the Constitution formally amended. Because the formal process is so difficult, the Supreme Court has been led to give an "elastic" construction to the Constitution; in effect, informally amending it.

Informal Amendment. — In the more than 160 years the Constitution has been in force, great changes have taken place. In 1789, the young Republic was a small agricultural nation of some 4,000,000 souls scattered along the eastern edge of the continent. Today, she is the most powerful nation on earth. The nation spans the continent and has many far-flung dependents and commitments; and 160,000,000 people live within the borders of her modern, highly industrialized and technological domain.

How has the Constitution kept pace with this astounding growth and change? A glance will show that the twenty-two formal amendments, important as they are, have not been responsible for the document's adaptability and vitality.

Rather, the changes have come about through a process of what might be called "informal" amendment. That is, they are the result of developments in the day-to-day, year-to-year experience of government under the Constitution.

To understand the true nature of our government and constitutional system as it exists today, one must consider five methods whereby the Constitution has developed, aside from formal amendment — basic legislation, executive action, court decisions, party practices, and custom.

1. *Basic Legislation.* — Many portions of the Constitution are vague and skeletal in nature. The Framers purposely left it to Congress to fill in the details as circumstances required. For example, the entire Federal court system, except the Supreme Court itself, has been created by Acts of Congress. So have all of the dozens of departments and agencies of the executive branch, save the offices of President and Vice-President. The question of who shall act as President should both the Presidency and the Vice-Presidency become vacant, is answered by an Act of Congress, not by the Constitution.

2. *Executive Action.* — The manner in which the various Presidents have exercised their powers has contributed to this "informal" development of the Constitution. Although only the Congress may declare war, the armed forces have been used by various Presidents (acting as Commander-in-Chief) for military action abroad on no fewer than 127 occasions, without Congressional action in the matter.

Among the many other examples, the device of "executive agreements" is typical. Recent Presidents have made such agreements rather than use the cumbersome process of treaty-making outlined in the Constitution. Executive agreements are agreements made personally by a President with the head of a foreign state, and the courts consider them as binding as treaties.

3. *Court Decisions.* — Under the American doctrine of judicial review, as we have seen, the Supreme Court is the ultimate interpreter of the Constitution. In short, the Constitution means what the Court says it means. This is what Chief Justice Charles Evans Hughes meant when he described the Court as "a continuous Constitutional Convention."

Again, judicial review (the power of the courts to determine the constitutionality of some governmental action) is not expressly bestowed upon the courts by the Constitution. The Supreme Court established the practice in *Marbury* v. *Madison*, 1803. It is based upon logic rather than on any specific constitutional provision, and it has come to constitute one of the most notable features of the American system of government.

In expanding the Constitution through judicial interpretation, the Court has leaned most heavily on the Necessary and Proper Clause, the Commerce Power, and the Taxing Power, all to be found in Article I, Section 8.

4. *Party Practices.* — Political parties themselves have grown up *extra*-constitutionally. Not only does the Constitution not even mention parties, but most of the Founding Fathers were opposed to their growth. In his Farewell Address in 1796, George Washington warned the people against "the baneful effects of the spirit of party." Yet, in many ways today, government in the United States is government by party.

As an illustration, the electoral college system has become a "rubber stamp" for party action. The national convention system for selecting party candidates for the Presidency is not provided for in the Constitution; the device was originated by the parties. Actions and policies of the House of Representatives are largely determined by party caucuses.

5. *Custom.* — Unwritten custom may be as strong as written law. When a President dies in office the Vice-President becomes President. Read carefully the *exact* wording of Article II, Section 1, Clause 6. It is a well-established custom for the Senate to reject an appointment by the President if it is opposed by a senator of the majority party from the State where the appointee is to serve. The most recent dramatic example of the application of this custom, known as *senatorial courtesy*, occurred in 1951. President Truman had appointed two new U. S. district judges for Illinois. Senator Douglas of Illinois objected and the Senate refused to confirm the President's appointments by a vote of 89-0. This practice practically shifts the power to appoint many Federal officers from the President to the senators. The strength and importance of unwritten customs is well illustrated by the rare instance in which one of them was nullified. From the time George Washington refused a third term as President in 1796, there had existed the so-called "no-third-term tradition" in American politics. But, in 1940 and 1944, Franklin D. Roosevelt sought and won not only a third term but a fourth as well. Since then the

[handwritten: name and explain the six interstate relations?]

Twenty-Second Amendment has been added to the Constitution, thus making an unwritten custom a part of the written Constitution.

QUESTIONS ON THE TEXT

1. Define federalism. What are the advantages secured by the American Federal System? *[handwritten: Define confederation]*

2. List the powers granted by the Constitution to the National Government. What powers are prohibited to the National Government?

3. Distinguish between "delegated" and "reserved powers." "Concurrent" and "exclusive powers." Give examples of each. *[handwritten: 10th amend]*

[handwritten: last one that is made is the one considered]

4. If a State law conflicts with a National law, which must yield? A National law with a treaty of the United States? *[handwritten: One who came first]*

5. With whom does the ultimate interpretation of the Constitution rest?

6. Explain the Supreme Court's decision in *Marbury* v. *Madison*.

7. Who has the sole power to admit new States? What is the usual process of admission?

8. What is meant by the Full Faith and Credit Clause? Privileges and Immunities? Interstate Rendition?

[handwritten: writ of mandamus]

9. What relation do States bear to one another except as specifically provided in the Constitution? Under what conditions may they enter agreements among themselves? Give examples.

10. Explain the meaning of the doctrine of separation of powers. What are the three great departments? What is the check and balance system?

11. In what ways may the Constitution be formally amended? How has it been developed otherwise? *[handwritten: 12. Explain the "Unwritten" Constitution]*

PROBLEMS FOR DISCUSSION

1. Let each pupil prepare a large chart showing the powers of government under our Federal system. The accompanying figure designed by Professor Frank H. Garver can be enlarged. Circle I represents all possible powers of the National Government and circle II all possible powers of State governments. Area *A* represents powers delegated to the National Government and area *B* those reserved to the State governments; segment *C* concurrent powers; segment *D* powers prohibited to the National Government; segment *E* powers prohibited to the State governments; and segment *F* powers prohibited to both governments. Space can be economized by the use of figures. 1.8.3. in area *A* would mean Article I, Section 8, Clause 3; Am. X in area *B* would mean Amendment X.

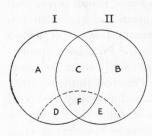

[handwritten: ⚹ a writ to compel a person to do something]

2. Give reasons why each power granted exclusively to the National Government was so granted.

3. What legal complication would arise if the Federal law and system of courts were not supreme?

4. Some people view our Constitution as a sacred document that should not be changed, but Thomas Jefferson expresses the contrary view in the following words: "Some men ascribe to the men of the preceding age a wisdom more than human, and suppose what they did to be beyond amendment. I knew that age [of the Revolution] well. I belonged to it and labored with it. It deserved well of its country. It was very like the present, but without the experience of the present; and forty years of experience is worth a century of book reading; and this they would say themselves were they to arise from the dead." Are these words more or less true today than when they were spoken?

5. Congress defeated a proposed Constitutional amendment which would have allowed the Constitution to be amended by a bare majority vote of Congress and a bare majority of popular votes at an election. The makers of the Constitution were unwilling to trust every Tom, Dick, and Harry voter with the amendment of the Constitution. Were they right or wrong?

SELECT BIBLIOGRAPHY

Constitution of the United States. (Should be read by all students at this time. See Appendix I of this text.)

BEATTY, J. "A New Trap for Runaway Husbands." *Saturday Evening Post*, April 19, 1952, page 19. (States co-operating in desertion cases.)

JOHNSON, C. O. *American Government.* Crowell. New York. 1951 edition, Chapters III and IV.

PADOVER, S. *The Living U. S. Constitution.* Frederick A. Praeger. New York. 1953.

SWARTHOUT, J. and BARTLEY, E. *Materials on American Government.* Oxford Univ. Press. New York. 1952. Pages 40–87. (Basic readings.)

SWARTHOUT, J. and BARTLEY, E. *Principles and Problems of American National Government.* Oxford University Press. New York. 1954 ed. Chapters 2–4.

"The Government of the U. S. A." *Fortune*, February, 1952. Entire issue.

CHAPTER V

THE LEGISLATIVE DEPARTMENT

Congress the Law-Making Branch. — Article I, Section 1 of the Constitution declares: "All legislative powers herein granted shall be vested in a Congress of the United States, which shall consist of a Senate and House of Representatives." Congress, then, is the law-making branch of the National Government. It is the branch which, in our representative democracy, is responsible for translating the popular will into public policy.

Bicameralism. — Congress is bicameral (composed of two houses) for several reasons: *Historically*, the British Parliament had consisted of two houses (Lords and Commons) since the 13th century; most of the colonial legislatures and all but two (in 1787) of the State legislatures were bicameral. *Practically*, the compromise between the Virginia and New Jersey Plans in the Constitutional Convention solved the most serious dispute there and dictated a two-chambered Congress. *Theoretically*, the Founding Fathers leaned toward a bicameral Congress in order that one house might act as a check on the other.

Thomas Jefferson, who possessed great faith in "the voice of the people," was in France when the Constitution was framed. Upon his return, while taking breakfast with Washington, he opposed the two-body form of legislature, and was disposed to twit Washington about it. At this time Jefferson poured his coffee from his cup into his saucer. Washington asked him why he did so. "To cool it," he replied. "So," said Washington, "we will pour legislation into the Senatorial saucer to cool it."

A bicameral Congress has worked extremely well because: (1) A bill passed in the heat of passion by one house can be submitted to the cool judgment of the other. (2) The urban and industrial Northeast controls the House and the rural and agricultural South and West control the Senate. (3) One large house elected for a short term can

CAPITOL HILL, WASHINGTON, D. C.

This airview shows (*center*) the Capitol, with House Chamber in left wing and Senate Chamber in right; (*left*) House Office Buildings; (*right*) Senate Office Building; (*foreground*) Library of Congress and Annex; (*right of Library*) Supreme Court Building.

express the wishes of the people, while the other, smaller, house elected for a long term can weigh and consider them. (4) The press and radio, groups especially affected, and the general public have a better opportunity to examine a bill and effect its fate when two houses rather than one must act on it.

It has been argued that the equal representation of the States in the Senate should be scrapped as undemocratic.[1] Some argue it is unfair, for example, that Nevada, the State with the smallest population (160,083), should have as many senators as the largest, New York (with 14,830,192). Those who argue this ignore the fact that senators were never intended to represent people as such. The Senate represents the States as co-equal members and partners in the Federal Union. Besides, had not the States been equally represented in the Senate, there might never have been a Constitution!

Terms of the Congress. — Each term of Congress, lasting two years, is numbered consecutively from the first term, which began March 4, 1789. The term of the Eighty-third Congress extends from January 3, 1953, to January 3, 1955.

Sessions of the Congress. — There are two regular sessions of each Congress. The first begins January 3 following the election of Congressmen in November of each even-numbered year; the second begins the next January 3.

Congress adjourns when it sees fit.[2] In the past, Congress met for no more than four or five months a year. But the many important issues of today have forced Congress to remain in session most of the year. The President may adjourn Congress only when the two houses cannot agree upon a date for adjournment. This has never happened.

The President may call extra sessions of Congress. President Roosevelt called such a session in 1939 at the outbreak of the Second World War; and in 1948 President Truman called a special session to consider high prices and other social legislation. Presidents have called only the Senate in special session some forty times to consider treaties and appointments.

---

[1] The prospects for any such change are so slim as to be non-existent. Article V of the Constitution provides, in part: "and that no State, without its consent, shall be deprived of its equal suffrage in the Senate." In the face of this, the physical impossibilities of securing a change are obvious.

[2] The Reorganization Act of 1946 provides that Congress shall adjourn by July 31 each year, unless it decides otherwise or a national emergency exists.

The House of Representatives. — *Membership.* — The House of Representatives is the more numerous body of Congress. The Constitution directs Congress to determine the membership after each census, and the number allotted to each State must be in proportion to

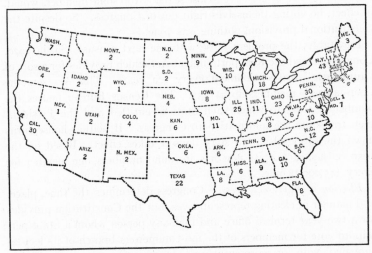

NUMBER OF REPRESENTATIVES APPORTIONED TO EACH STATE UNTIL THE
CENSUS OF 1960

Following the 1950 Census, California gained seven members, Florida two, and Maryland, Michigan, Texas, Virginia, and Washington one each; Pennsylvania lost three seats, Missouri, New York, and Oklahoma two each, and Arkansas, Illinois, Kentucky, Mississippi, and Tennessee lost one each.

its total population,[1] excluding Indians not taxed; but a State is entitled to at least one member.[2]

After the First Census in 1790 the size of the House was set at 105. As the number of States increased and as the nation's population grew,

---

[1] The Fourteenth Amendment declares that whenever a State shall limit the right of its adult male citizens to vote, except for crime, its representation in Congress shall be proportionately reduced. This provision has never been enforced, and some statesmen claim that it has been superseded by the Fifteenth Amendment.

[2] Delaware, Nevada, Vermont, and Wyoming have one vote each. A territory is represented in the House by a delegate and Puerto Rico by a Commissioner. Each receives an annual salary of $12,500 plus $2500 for expenses, but has no vote.

so did the size of the House. After the 1910 census the House stood at 435. After the 1920 census Congress did not want to add more seats; the House was already too large for effective floor action. But to reapportion the seats without increasing the total number meant that some States would have to lose seats. And some members would, in effect, be voting themselves right out of Congress. So despite the constitutional provision, nothing was done.

Inevitably, the problem arose with the next census. So, in 1929, Congress passed the Reapportionment Act which provides for a sort of "automatic" reapportionment every ten years. This Act sets the "permanent" membership at 435. The Census Bureau figures the number of seats to which each State is entitled and the President then transmits the information to Congress. If neither house turns down the proposal within sixty days it takes effect. Based on the 1950 census, each State now has, in round numbers, one member for every 345,000 people.

Election of Representatives. — Congress determines the time, place, and manner of electing representatives, but the Constitution provides for a two-year term of office and that any person whom a State permits to vote for members of the most numerous branch of its legislature may vote for representatives. In 1872 Congress enacted that congressional elections should be held on the same day throughout the country — the Tuesday following the first Monday in November of every even-numbered year.[1] In the same year it decreed that representatives should be chosen by written or printed ballots. The use of voting machines has been permitted since 1899. When a vacancy occurs, the Governor must call a special election.[2]

During the first fifty years of our Union the States were permitted to elect their representatives as they chose. The method of electing them by districts early became popular, but some States elected all members at large,[3] which made it possible, for example, for a State with a small majority of one party to elect all members of that party.

---

[1] By special act of Congress, Maine holds her congressional election in September.

[2] United States Constitution, Art. I, Sec. 2, Cl. 4. Congress has power to control State election officials in the execution of State election laws when national officials are being chosen. All corrupt practices automatically become Federal offenses.

[3] *At large* means from the entire State. Each voter votes for all in the State.

This was clearly unrepresentative, and in 1842 Congress prescribed that thenceforth all members should be chosen by districts.[1] The district system tends to give representation to the minority party; but, as the States were laid out into districts by the State legislatures, the districts were generally so arranged that the majority party continued to have a great advantage.

By an Act passed in 1872, Congress required that the congressional districts be of contiguous territory and contain as nearly equal populations as practicable.

In 1911 Congress amended the Act to read "contiguous and compact territory." But in 1932 the United States Supreme Court held that the 1929 Reapportionment Act does not require contiguity and compactness of territory or equality of population; and populations vary greatly. For example, in Michigan at the time of the 1950 census, the Twelfth Congressional District had a population of only 177,360, while the Seventeenth District in the same State had a population of 724,717.

Gerrymandering.[2] — The scheme resorted to by an unfair legislative body to lay out congressional or other districts so as to secure a majority of voters for the party in power in the greatest possible number of them is known as "gerrymandering." This can sometimes be done

---

[1] If the reapportionment following a decennial census increases the representation of a State, the additional representatives may be elected at large until the State is reapportioned. If the representation of a State is reduced, the remaining representatives must be elected at large until the districts are redrawn.

[2] The scheme of unfair apportionment of districts is called "gerrymandering" from Elbridge Gerry of Massachusetts. In 1812, when Gerry was governor of Massachusetts, the Republican legislature re-districted the State in such a manner that one district had a dragonlike appearance. It was indicated on a map of Massachusetts which hung over the desk of a Federalist editor. A celebrated painter added with his pencil a head, wings, and claws, and exclaimed, "That will do for a salamander!" "Better say Gerrymander," growled the editor.

THE ORIGINAL GERRYMANDER

by collecting as many voters of the minority party as possible into one district so as to make other bordering districts safe for the majority party.

For instance, Figure *A*, on this page, represents a State with four congressional districts, each consisting of 75,000 voters. In districts 1 and 2 the Republicans have a majority, whereas in districts 3 and 4

1 R	2 R
50,000 REP. 25,000 DEM.	60,000 REP. 15,000 DEM.
3 D	4 D
40,000 DEM. 35,000 REP.	38,000 DEM. 37,000 REP.

FIGURE A

1	2	3	4
45,000 REP. 30,000 DEM.	40,000 REP. 35,000 DEM.	50,000 REP. 25,000 DEM.	47,000 REP. 28,000 DEM.

FIGURE B

the Democrats have a majority, but in the entire State the Republicans have a majority of voters and therefore elect the majority of the members of the State legislature. This Republican State legislature redistricts the State as shown in Figure *B*, having gerrymandered it so that the Republicans have a majority of voters in districts 1, 2, 3, and 4.

The map opposite shows how the districts of South Carolina were skillfully arranged in 1890 so as to throw large blocks of the Republican Negro vote together, the populations varying from 134,000 in the first district to 217,000 in the seventh.

Qualifications of Representatives. — According to the Constitution, a member of the House must be a man or woman at least twenty-five, at least seven years a citizen of the United States,[1] and an inhabitant of the State in which he is chosen. Political custom dictates that a

---

[1] Ruth Bryan, daughter of William Jennings Bryan, married a British subject named Owen in 1910 and resided in England until 1919, when she and her husband returned to the United States and resided in Florida. In 1925 Ruth Bryan Owen became a naturalized citizen of the United States. In 1928 she was elected to Congress from Florida. Her election was contested on the ground that she had not been seven years a citizen just before her election. In 1930 the House Committee on Elections decided that she had been seven years a citizen, including her citizenship before her marriage. Hence she was allowed to retain her seat in the House.

representative should also reside in the district.[1] The Constitution adds that no member may hold any other office under the United States, *e.g.*, in the Cabinet or as a Federal judge.

The House is judge of the elections, returns, and qualifications of its members and has excluded persons for various reasons.[2] Two thirds

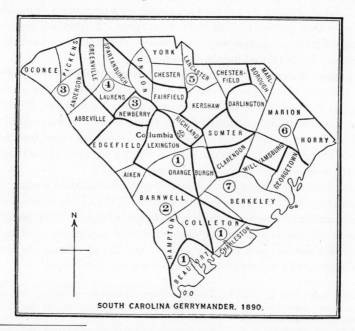

SOUTH CAROLINA GERRYMANDER. 1890.

[1] This district custom dates from colonial days and is based upon the feeling that the representative should be a man who knows the local problems. It is often criticized because it buttresses the "errand boy" concept; *i.e.*, many people look upon their representative as a man to go to for all sorts of favors. The average congressman is plagued with many requests from the time he enters until he leaves office — help in securing government contracts, appointments to West Point, free sightseeing tours in Washington, even help in settling marital disputes. To refuse such requests would mean to lose votes. Many claim that the district custom means that the voters cannot always select the best available man. In rare instances, a man from outside a district is chosen. For example, in the 81st and 82d Congresses, as well as in the present 83d, Franklin D. Roosevelt, Jr. represented New York's 20th District, but he does not live in his district.

[2] Thus the House may, in effect, add additional informal qualifications. In 1900, for example, the House refused to seat Brigham H. Roberts of Utah on grounds that he had been a polygamist. In 1919 the House excluded Victor L. Berger, a Socialist from Wisconsin, on grounds of sedition and "un-Americanism"

of the House may expel a member for any reason it thinks fit, but no
member has been expelled in recent years.

The Senate. — *Membership.* — The Senate is the smaller body of
Congress, and is composed of two members from each State.   As there
are now forty-eight States there are ninety-six senators.

Term of Senators. — Senators are chosen for a term of six years, one
third of their number retiring every second year.   By dividing senators
into three classes in this way, the presence at any time of too many
new and inexperienced members is avoided.

Election of Senators. — Until the Seventeenth Amendment was ratified in 1913 senators were elected by State legislatures.   Now at the
regular November election of every even-numbered year, one third of
the senators are elected directly by the people and are sworn into office
when the new Congress assembles.[1]   Each senator is elected from his
State at large.   All persons qualified to vote for members of the House
of Representatives may vote for senators.

Qualifications of Senators. — A senator may be a man or a woman, at
least thirty years of age, nine years a citizen of the United States, and
an inhabitant of the State which sends him to Congress.   The Senate,
like the House, is judge of the qualifications of its members and may
exclude a member by a majority vote.[2]   Also, like the House, the Senate may expel a member for any cause by a two-thirds vote.

---

during World War I.   The Supreme Court later cleared Berger of the sedition
charge and, finally, after being elected from his Milwaukee district for the third
time, the House seated him.

[1] Barring vacancies in the Senate because of death or resignation, only one
senator is elected from a State at any one election.   The Seventeenth Amendment
provides that a vacancy be filled by an election called by the governor, or that
the legislature may authorize the governor to make a temporary appointment until
the people fill the vacancy at an election.   The State legislature determines the
method to be used and most States follow the latter practice.   Thus, in 1952, the
death of Senator Brien McMahon meant that Connecticut voters elected two
senators at the November election — one to the normal six-year term and another
to fill out the remaining four years of Senator McMahon's unexpired term.

[2] In 1912 Mr. Lorimer of Illinois was excluded by a majority vote, being elected
as a result of bribes paid to Illinois legislators in behalf of his election.   He had been
seated, although under protest, and had voted on many measures before the committee on elections could investigate.   In 1928 Mr. Smith of Illinois was excluded
because $203,000 expended in his behalf in the primary election was contributed
by officials of public utility corporations whose rates were regulated by the Illinois
Commerce Commission, of which Mr. Smith was a member.   In 1947, Mr. Bilbo of
Mississippi was temporarily excluded because he urged the use of "any means" to

Special Functions of the Senate. — The Senate performs three special or nonlegislative functions, two of which are executive and the third judicial. They are as follows:

(1) As a part of the system of checks and balances, the Constitution makes the approval of the Senate necessary to all major appointments made by the President. Such nominations to office are referred to the Committee on Appropriations by the Vice-President, unless the Senate orders otherwise. The committee's report may be considered by the Senate in secret ("executive") session.

The appointments of Cabinet officers and other top officials in the President's "official family" are seldom rejected by the Senate. But the unwritten rule of "senatorial courtesy" enters the picture in the appointments of Federal officers who serve in the various States. This custom provides that the Senate will not approve appointments if a majority party senator from the State involved objects to the person named by the President. In practice, this means that the majority party senators dictate such appointments as those of postmasters, Federal judges, Federal attorneys, and customs collectors.[1]

(2) Treaties are made by the President "by and with the advice and consent of the Senate . . . provided two-thirds of the senators present concur." For a while after the adoption of the Constitution the advice of the Senate was asked before the President prepared a treaty, but now he merely consults with the Senate Committee on Foreign Relations and with influential members of both parties. The Senate may reject a treaty in full or may suggest amendments to it. Treaties may be considered in "executive session."[2] Because the House has a hold on the governmental purse-strings, influential House members are often consulted in treaty matters, too.

---

keep the Negro away from the polls and allegedly accepted illegal gifts from war contractors. Mr. Bilbo's death precluded any final Senate action in the case.

[1] See page 77. Those who criticize the practice often forget that a senator is much more likely to know more about affairs in his own State than does the President. Occasionally, however, senators have been known to block appointments for purely personal or vindictive reasons.

[2] Previous to 1929, appointments and treaties were regularly considered in closed sessions. But a Senate rule adopted that year reads, in part: "Hereafter all business in the Senate shall be transacted in open session unless the Senate in closed session by a majority vote shall determine that a particular nomination, treaty, or other matter shall be considered in closed executive session. . . . Provided that any senator may make public his vote in a closed executive session."

OUTLINE OF CONGRESS

MEMBERS	HOUSE OF REPRESENTATIVES 435	SENATE 96
Qualifications . .	25 years of age, 7 years a citizen of the United States, inhabitant of State where elected. Other qualifications determined by the House.	30 years of age, 9 years a citizen of the United States, inhabitant of State where elected. Other qualifications determined by the Senate.
Elected by . . .	Votes of Congressional Districts.	Votes of State.
Term	Two years.	Six years.
Salary	$12,500 and allowances.	$12,500 and allowances.
Sole Powers . .	(1) To impeach civil officers. (2) To originate revenue bills. (3) To elect a President if no candidate has a majority of the electoral votes.	(1) To try persons impeached. (2) To confirm appointments made by the President. (3) To approve treaties. (4) To elect a Vice-President if no candidate has a majority of the electoral votes.
Convene (in regular session) . .	Third of January every year.	Third of January every year.

PRESIDING OFFICER	SPEAKER	VICE-PRESIDENT[1] OF THE UNITED STATES CALLED "PRESIDENT OF THE SENATE"
Qualifications . .	Member of House.[2]	The same as for President.
Elected by . . .	Members of the House.	Presidential electors or Senate.
Term	Two years (often re-elected).	Four years.
Salary	$30,000 + $10,000 expenses	$30,000 + $10,000 expenses
Vote	The same as any other member of the House.	Only in case of a tie vote.

[1] A president *pro tempore* of the Senate is elected by the Senate to preside in the absence of the Vice-President.

[2] According to custom based on parliamentary and colonial precedents.

(3) The Constitution provides that the President, Vice-President, and all civil officers of the United States may be removed from office "on impeachment for, and conviction of, treason, bribery, or other high crimes and misdemeanors." [1] The House impeaches (brings charges) and the Senate sits as a court to try the case.

A two-thirds vote of the senators present is necessary for conviction and the Chief Justice presides when a President is being tried. The penalty for conviction is removal from office, and if it desires, the Senate may add a provision against the holding of any future Federal office. After removal, charges may be brought in the regular courts.

To date there have been but twelve impeachments and four convictions. On several other occasions officers have resigned under the threat of impeachment. [2] When the House impeached President Andrew Johnson in 1868 the Senate failed by only one vote to convict him.

Compensation of Congressmen. — Congressmen, unlike other officers or employees of the government, fix their own salary, and the only limit upon the amount is the President's veto and the possibility of not being re-elected. Senators and representatives have always received equal salaries. Each senator and representative receives: (1) a salary of $12,500 per annum [3] — plus $2500 "expense allowance"; (2) twenty cents a mile going and coming by the shortest route for

---

[1] Article II, Section 4. Military officers are not "civil officers" and are removed by court martial; and members of Congress are not so considered here. When the House impeached Senator Blount of Tennessee in 1798 the Senate refused to try the case on grounds that it had the power to expel its own members if it saw fit. Blount was later expelled and this precedent is followed today.

[2] The four removed were all judges. One other judge resigned after the House impeached him but just before the Senate began his trial, and the case was dropped. Four other judges were acquitted. Aside from Senator Blount and President Johnson, W. W. Belknap, who was President Grant's Secretary of War, was impeached and acquitted in 1876 on the ground that the Senate no longer had jurisdiction because Belknap had resigned.

[3] The salaries of congressmen from time to time have been as follows:

1789–1815, $6 per diem while in attendance.	1874–1907, $5000 per annum.
1815–1817, $1500 per annum.	1907–1925, $7500 per annum.
1817–1855, $8 per diem.	1925–1946, $10,000 per annum.
1855–1866, $3000 per annum.	1946– , $12,500 plus $2500
1866–1871, $5000 per annum.	per annum.
1871–1874, $7500 per annum.	

each regular session and usually for special sessions; [1] (3) publication and free distribution of speeches; [2] (4) free postage for official business, called the "franking privilege"; (5) free offices; (6) an allowance for stationery, long distance telephone calls, and telegrams; (7) an allowance for hiring clerks; (8) a pension at the age of 62 if he has served six years and is not re-elected; and (9) a $3000 tax exemption because of the need to maintain a place in Washington as well as at home.

Privileges of Congressmen. — Congressmen are free from arrest during their attendance, and in going to and returning from the sessions, in all cases except treason, felony, and breach of the peace. As persons are no longer imprisoned for debts the privilege is of little value.

Another privilege of congressmen is freedom of speech during debate in Congress. That is, they may not be sued for any statement made on the floor of Congress. This privilege includes the right to circulate copies of their speeches delivered in Congress. But a congressman is not privileged to defame any person in a newspaper article.

The reason for granting congressmen immunity from suit for anything they may say during debate in Congress, is to encourage them to state all the facts they know in regard to matters that vitally concern the people's welfare. This privilege is truly a grave responsibility.

QUESTIONS ON THE TEXT

1. What Article of the Constitution treats of Congress? (See Appendix, I.)

2. Congress consists of what two houses? Each represents what?

---

[1] When a special session of Congress merged into a regular session, Theodore Roosevelt allowed mileage for both sessions; but under like conditions Wilson denied it. Congressmen have since insured their mileage for special sessions by adjourning before the regular session.

[2] Many speeches which are not actually delivered on the floor of Congress are published in the Congressional Record, of which each congressman receives sixty copies free. He may obtain any number of reprints of his speech by paying the Government Printing Office the actual cost of reprinting.

3. What are the advantages of a two-body legislature?

4. When do regular sessions of Congress begin? Who may call extra sessions?

5. How is the membership of the House of Representatives determined? Of how many members does it now consist? Each represents approximately how many people?

6. Do any States have more senators in the Senate than representatives in the House?

7. When are congressional elections held? How long is it after the election until the members take their seats? What is the term of office?

8. Explain *gerrymandering*.

9. What are the qualifications for membership in the House?

10. Of how many members does the Senate consist? What is the term of office?

11. When are senators elected? Who may vote for them? What are the qualifications for office?

12. By what vote of either house may a member be excluded? Expelled?

13. What special functions are performed by the House? The Senate?

14. What business of the Senate is sometimes transacted behind closed doors? Why?

15. What salary do congressmen receive? What other compensation do they receive?

16. What special privileges have congressmen? May a congressman defame the character of a person in a newspaper article?

PROBLEMS FOR DISCUSSION

1. Do you favor equal representation of States in the Senate? Would your answer be the same whether you lived in New York or in Nevada?

2. The number of any Congress can be determined by subtracting 1789 (the year the 1st Congress met) from the closing year of the Congress to be identified, and dividing the remainder by 2, because a Congress lasts two years. It always ends in an odd-numbered year. What number Congress is now in session?

3. How many women are now in Congress? (See *World Almanac, Congressional Directory*, or *United States Government Manual*.) Give arguments for and against electing them.

4. How are the political parties represented at present in the Senate and in the House of Representatives?

5. Is your State gerrymandered?

6. To how many representatives is your State entitled?

7. In what congressional district do you live? Who is your representative? How long has he been in Congress? What party does he represent? (See *Congressional Directory* or *World Almanac*.) What stand has he taken in regard to important legislation recently before Congress? (See Congressional Record.)

8. Discuss in regard to your senators the same matters that you have considered in regard to your representative.

9. Many times a Congressman finds himself faced with a conflict between his own thinking on a particular piece of legislation and that of his constituents, upon whom he must depend for re-election. Do you think that Congressmen should respond to public opinion or should they investigate, debate, and decide according to their convictions? Consider the words of one of the foremost statesmen in British history, Edmund Burke, speaking in 1774:

"Certainly it ought to be the happiness and glory of a representative to live in the strictest union and the most unreserved communication with his constituents. Their wishes ought to have great weight with him, their opinion high respect, their business unremitted attention.

"But Parliament is not a congress of ambassadors from different and hostile interests; which interests each must maintain, as an agent and advocate, against other agents and advocates; Parliament is a deliberative assembly of one nation, with one interest, that of the whole; where not local purpose, not local prejudices ought to guide, but the general good. You choose a member, indeed. But when you have chosen him he is not a member of Bristol, but he is a member of Parliament."

10. Why is the "errand-boy" concept so often criticized? Consider these remarks made in the House by former Representative Luther Patrick of Alabama: "A Congressman has become an expanded messenger boy, an employment agency, getter-outer of the Navy, Army, Marines, ward heeler, wound healer, trouble shooter, law explainer, bill finder, issue translator, resolution interpreter, controversy oil pourer, gladhand extender, business promoter, convention goer, civic ills skirmisher, veterans' affairs adjuster, ex-serviceman's champion, watchdog for the underdog, sympathizer with the upper dog, namer and kisser of babies, recoverer of lost luggage, soberer of delegates, adjuster for traffic violators, voters straying into Washington and into toils of the law, binder up of broken hearts, financial wet nurse, good samaritan, contributor to good causes — there are so many good causes — cornerstone layer, public building and bridge dedicator, ship christener — to be sure he does get in a little flag waving — and a little constitutional hoisting and spread-eagle work, but it is getting harder every day to find time to properly study legislation — the very business we are primarily here to discharge, and that must be done above all things."

11. "Although there is an unmistakable glamour surrounding the job and the person of a member of Congress, the cold fact is that many statesmen spend long and melancholy evenings with the family account books, trying to balance their payables with their receivables. Like citizens of lesser stature, they are beset by debts, mortgages, installment payments and all the other vicissitudes of trying to make ends meet. For not a few it is an unequal and exasperating contest, and one that is not made any easier by the lack of popular understanding. . . . Figured either on the importance and responsibility of the job, or on what it actually costs a member of Congress to live in reasonable comfort, his pay and perquisites fall short by at least $3,000 a year." Cabell Phillips, "The High Cost of Our Low-Paid Congress," *The New York Times Magazine*, February 24, 1952.

Mr. Phillips says that "an outside income — whatever the source — is an almost indispensable requirement for Congressional service these days," and he quotes Senator Hubert Humphrey of Minnesota on that point: "To do my duty as a Senator I have to go back home at least once a month. Each trip costs me from $200 to $250. But every time I go I have to scrounge the countryside like the Russian army, making speeches and lectures along the way. I simply can't afford it out of my salary."

Most people who have considered the problem agree that members of Congress should receive higher pay. What do you think? Why are Congressmen reluctant, for political reasons, to raise their own salaries?

12. It may seem at times that popularity is the only requisite for Congressmen except citizenship, age, and residence within the State. Do you consider this a sufficient requisite for such an important position?

13. Following the death of Abraham Lincoln, Congress and Lincoln's successor, Andrew Johnson, fought almost constantly. In 1868, Johnson was impeached by the House but was not convicted by the Senate. Let one student make a report to the class on the entire episode.

SELECT BIBLIOGRAPHY

GRIFFITH, E. *Congress.* New York University Press. New York. 1951.

GROSS, B. M. *The Legislative Struggle.* McGraw-Hill. New York. 1953.

JAVITS, J. "Congress Wants to Hear from You." *American Magazine.* June, 1952, page 15. (By a Congressman from New York.)

JOHNSON, C. O. *American Government.* Crowell. New York. 1951 Edition. Chapters XII–XIII.

SWARTHOUT, J., AND BARTLEY, E. *Principles and Problems of American National Government.* Oxford University Press. New York. 1954 ed. Chs. 10 and 11.

CHAPTER VI

POWERS OF CONGRESS — EXPRESSED AND IMPLIED

Congressional Powers. — As we have seen, Congress may exercise only those powers delegated to it by the Constitution. And the Constitution gives Congress only those powers enumerated in that document, plus those "necessary and proper" to carry the expressed powers into execution.

PRESIDENT GEORGE WASHINGTON

Our first president voiced the sentiments of the Federalist Party by supporting a liberal interpretation of the Constitution. This meant a strong National Government.

Liberal vs. Strict Construction. — Hardly had the Constitution come into force when a dispute arose as to how broad the powers granted to Congress actually are. The *strict-constructionists*, led by Thomas Jefferson, favored strong State governments and a weaker National Government; hence, they favored restricting the Congress to those powers actually expressed in so many words in the Constitution.

Alexander Hamilton and the *liberal-constructionists* favored a strong National Government and, therefore, a liberal interpretation of the Constitution in order to broaden the powers of Congress. As we shall see, those who favored a liberal interpretation prevailed.

Decisions of the Supreme Court have been primarily responsible for liberal construction. But the other two branches and the people have played their part in the broadening process, too.

EXPRESSED POWERS

Interpretation of Expressed Powers. — The expressed powers of Congress are enumerated very briefly; and without courts to decide exactly what they mean and what they include, Congress would often be tempted to exceed its authority. To illustrate, the Constitution (Art. I, Sec. 8, Cl. 3) provides that "Congress shall have power to regulate commerce with foreign nations and among the several States, and with the Indian tribes." These words are very general, and Federal courts have decided thousands of cases in explanation of them, and several hundred of these cases have been appealed and decided and supported by lengthy opinions of the Supreme Court of the United States.

The power to tax and the power to regulate interstate commerce are the two most important expressed powers of Congress. In fact, they are so important and require so much space and time to do justice to them that a separate chapter is given for each of them. These chapters follow immediately after this one.

Power to Make Money. — Congress has power to coin money and to issue paper money, but the States are forbidden to do either.[1]

Before the Revolutionary War the English shilling was the recognized unit of value, and the restraining hand of the Mother Country kept issues of depreciated paper money within bounds. But with the coming of independence, the legislatures of several States printed the States' names on paper and called it money.[2] As always happens, bad money drove good money from circulation; and each State had paper money of an uncertain and declining value. This variety of money made local business uncertain and interstate business intolerable.

Because of these conditions the makers of the Constitution gave Congress the exclusive right to coin money, and the United States

---

[1] The Constitution forbids the States to coin money, emit bills of credit (paper money), or make anything but gold and silver coin a tender in the payment of debts. Congress can make coins or paper money legal tender. ("Legal tender" is any kind of money which a creditor is required by law to accept in payment of a monetary debt.)

[2] The Rhode Island Legislature of 1786 issued a large amount of paper money, and in six months a dollar was passing for 16 cents. John Fiske thus describes the situation: "The farmers from the inland towns were unanimous in support of the

Supreme Court has given it the right to issue paper money, as implied in its power to borrow.

From the beginning, the United States has issued coins — in gold (until 1933) and silver. In 1791, Congress chartered the First United States Bank with the power to issue bank notes; but this paper money was not made legal tender. During the Civil War, however, Congress did provide for a national paper currency as legal tender in payment of debts.[1]

At first, these new notes ("greenbacks") could not be redeemed for coin at the Treasury and their worth fell to less than half their face value on the open market. In 1870, the Supreme Court held the issuance of these notes to be unconstitutional. Said the Court, "to coin" meant to stamp metal and this could not be held to include paper money. But the Court soon reversed itself. In 1871 and 1884 it upheld the issuing of paper money as legal tender as a proper exercise of the Congressional powers to coin money and regulate its value, to borrow money on the credit of the United States, and to make war.

Power to Borrow Money. — The Constitution gives Congress power to "borrow money on the credit of the United States." When there are unusual undertakings, like the Panama Canal, World Wars, or relief for unemployed, the usual revenues are not adequate and Con-

---

measure. They could not see the difference between the State making a dollar out of paper and a dollar out of silver. The idea that the value did not lie in the government stamp they dismissed as an idle crotchet, a wire-drawn theory, worthy only of 'literary fellows.' What they could see was the glaring fact that they had no money, hard or soft; and they wanted something that would satisfy their creditors and buy new gowns for their wives, whose raiment was unquestionably the worse for wear. On the other hand, the merchants from Providence, Newport, and Bristol understood the difference between real money and the promissory notes of a bankrupt government, because they had to pay real money to European firms from whom they bought their stocks of goods."

The penalty for not accepting this paper money in payment for goods or debts was a fine of $500 and the loss of suffrage. When a merchant refused to accept the paper the matter came to court, and the Act was declared contrary to the State constitution and hence void. A special session of the legislature dismissed the judges, but their decision remained.

[1] Congress soon found that this paper money was being interfered with by notes issued by State-chartered private banks. When Congress placed a tax of ten per cent on the issuance of private bank notes, the latter soon disappeared from circulation.

Published by special permission of the Secretary of the Treasury

Twenty-five-Dollar United States Savings Bond

United States Savings Bonds are made out in the name of one individual, two individuals as co-owners, or one individual with another named as beneficiary in case of death. The bonds are popular in saving to provide for education, old age retirement, or purchase of a home.

99

gress borrows money. There is no constitutional limit on the amount the National Government may borrow, but the current ceiling placed by Congress is $275,000,000,000.

The most common method of governmental borrowing is through the sale of bonds. Bonds used by governments or corporations when they borrow money are like promissory notes ("I.O.U.'s") given by private persons when they borrow — a promise to pay a certain sum at a specified time.

These government bonds are purchased as investments by individuals, business concerns, and especially by insurance companies and banks. The National Government could borrow all the money it needs from banks — or it could simply print all the money it wants. But to do either of these would mean placing more money in circulation and thus contributing to inflation.

The constitutional right to borrow makes borrowing a Federal function, hence Federal bonds cannot be taxed by the States. The right to borrow also implies the right to establish National Banks to assist the Government in securing loans. It would have been very difficult to finance World War II had not the banks bought most of the bonds.

Bankruptcy. — Congress has power to pass "uniform laws on the subject of bankruptcies throughout the United States." Bankruptcy laws provide for the distribution of a debtor's assets among his creditors when he is unable to discharge his obligations in full, and for the discharge of the debtor from further legal liability for debts incurred prior to the institution of bankruptcy proceedings.

Both the States and the National Government have power in the field of bankruptcy (concurrent power). Except for three brief periods, Congress left the matter entirely under State control for more than 100 years. But in 1898 Congress passed a general bankruptcy law. Since then, the Federal laws have been so inclusive as to practically exclude the States from the field.

Under the present bankruptcy statutes, an individual or corporation (except railroads, banks, building and loan associations, insurance companies, and municipal corporations) may voluntarily institute bankruptcy proceedings. Involuntary proceedings may be instituted by creditors against individuals or corporations (except those just listed plus farmers and wage-earners).

Proceedings in bankruptcy are usually handled by the United States

District Court in the district in which the bankrupt resides. The court generally appoints a referee to handle the details of the case. A petition summarizing the facts is submitted and, after a hearing, the court determines whether the petition is to be dismissed or the party declared a bankrupt.

A bankrupt is allowed to keep certain kinds of property (depending on State law), such as tools or a certain amount of land, in order to enable him to support himself and his family.

Under certain conditions it is possible for parties to become "debtors" and have their debts adjusted downward. Thus many may legally avoid the stigma of bankruptcy. Railroads and other corporations may be forced to reorganize under a court-appointed receivership rather than be forced into bankruptcy. Such revisions in the bankruptcy laws make them less rigid and more in accord with the economic realities of today.

Naturalization. — Naturalization is the process by which citizens of one country become citizens of another, and Congress has the power "to establish a uniform rule of naturalization." Under the immigration laws certain persons are not allowed to enter the United States, and naturally such persons are not permitted to become naturalized. (For more about immigration and naturalization see Chapter XIII.)

Postal Service. — Congress has power to establish post offices and post roads.[1] The Government may condemn land for post office sites and could condemn it for post roads should it become necessary. Of course a fair price must be paid the owner for his property. A State is not permitted to establish a postal system, nor is an individual. For instance, express companies could not make a business of carrying first-class mail.

Under its power to establish post roads, Congress has made it a criminal offense to obstruct or retard the passage of mails "knowingly and willfully." Examples of this crime are beating an engineer and fireman without whose services the train could not be moved, and placing obstructions on the track of an electric railway engaged in carrying the mails. Thus the criminals have committed a Federal offense as well as a State offense. It is illegal for railroad strikers to interfere with trains carrying mail; and following the Pullman strike in Chicago,

---

[1] "Post roads" are all letter carrier routes, including railroads and the waters of the United States during the time that mail is carried thereon.

A HIGHWAY POST OFFICE

SORTING MAIL EN ROUTE AND SERVING SMALL TOWNS

in 1894, Eugene Debs was sent to the Federal penitentiary because he persuaded the strikers not to move the trains.

States are not allowed to interfere unreasonably with the mails. A State cannot require mail trains to make unreasonable stops. Neither can it require a license for cars owned by the United States Government nor tax gasoline used in its mail trucks. But those who contract to carry mail may be taxed. And the United States does not protect those who use the mails to defeat the police regulations of the State made to protect the health, morals, safety, and welfare of its citizens. Thus a State can forbid the soliciting of orders for intoxicating liquor, even through the mails. Nor does the United States protect carriers when they endanger the public. For instance, a mail carrier may be arrested, while on his route, for murder; and a city might arrest and punish a mail carrier for driving recklessly through crowded streets in such a way as to endanger the lives of pedestrians.

Copyrights and Patents. — Congress has the power "to promote the progress of science and of useful arts, by securing for limited times to authors and inventors the exclusive right to their respective writings and discoveries."

A copyright is the exclusive right of an author or his assignee to print and publish his literary or artistic work. The protection is granted by the Government for a period of twenty-eight years; renewable for another twenty-eight years. The right extends to maps, charts, engravings, sculpture, dramatic or musical compositions, and pictures, as well as books. In 1912 the Supreme Court decided that moving pictures of *Ben Hur*, a copyrighted book, was a dramatization, and hence an infringement of the copyright. (See page 163, note.)

A patent is a grant of the exclusive right to manufacture, use, or sell a new and useful invention for a period of years — seventeen at present for a patent of invention. The term may be extended only by special Act of Congress. (See page 298.)

Weights and Measures. — Congress has established the pound, gallon, bushel, yard, and their subdivisions as standards of weights and measures, and has made the metric system optional. The basic standards of these measures, by which all other measures throughout the United States are tested and corrected, are deposited in the Bureau of Standards.

In 1901 Congress established the Bureau of Standards, which has become a wonderful laboratory. (See pages 295–297.) It determines the measures for our groceries, the specifications of the doctor's thermometer, and the strength of concrete and steel. It can weigh the crossing of a "t" with a pencil mark, and it tests and corrects surveyors' instruments. It has developed a clock verified from star observations, and can send an electric impulse each second by wire to any laboratory for research time precision. It now has an atomic clock.

The Bureau does not act as an agency of compulsion, but of service. For instance, it encourages the standardization of such things as bolts that will fit machines of all makes, and of different sizes of bed springs and mattresses to make them fit the corresponding beds.

Power over Federal Territories and Other Areas. — Congress has power to acquire, govern, and dispose of various Federal areas. The importance of this power can be seen in the fact that it includes a good deal more than such areas as the District of Columbia and possessions outside the United States such as Hawaii, Alaska, and Puerto Rico. It also includes hundreds of military and naval stations, forts, arsenals, dockyards, post offices, parks and forest preserves, prisons, hospitals, asylums, agricultural experiment stations, and other holdings throughout the country.

The National Government may acquire property within a State by eminent domain.[1] If it purchases such property with the consent of the State legislature, the National Government assumes exclusive jurisdiction over the area. If, as often happens, State approval is not had, then State laws continue to operate in the area. In cases of conflict, Federal law is always supreme.

Territory may be acquired from a foreign state as the result of the power to admit new States, the war powers, and the President's treaty-making power. Under international law, any sovereign state may acquire unclaimed territory by discovery. (For more on territories see Chapter XX.)

Judicial Powers. — Congress has power to establish the inferior Federal courts under the Supreme Court and to provide for the organization and composition of the Federal judicial system. It also has the power to define and punish Federal crimes and to impeach any civil officer of the United States.

---

[1] The right of eminent domain is the right that a government exercises in taking private property for a public purpose by paying the owner a fair price for it.

Powers over Foreign Relations. — The National Government has greater power in the field of international relations than in any other field. Here Congress shares its powers with the President, who is primarily responsible for the conduct of our foreign relations. The States are not sovereign and are, hence, unrecognized in international law; and the Constitution forbids them to participate.

Authority for the powers over foreign relations arise from two sources. First, from the delegated powers which include the power to make treaties, to regulate foreign commerce, to send and receive diplomatic representatives, and to define and punish piracy and other crimes committed on the high seas and offenses against the law of nations. The war powers and the power to acquire and govern territories are also the basis for action in the field of international relations. Secondly, power to act in this field arises from the fact that the United States is a sovereign member of the world community. As such, it has the authority to deal with matters which affect the interests of the United States.

War Powers. — Several of the powers provided for in Article I, Section 8, deal exclusively with war and national defense. Although the President is Commander-in-Chief of the armed forces, Congress has power to declare war, to grant letters of marque and reprisal,[1] to make rules concerning captures on land and water, to raise and support armies, to provide and maintain a navy, to make rules governing the land and naval forces, to provide for calling out the militia, and to provide for organizing, arming, and disciplining the militia.

Congress cannot appropriate money for "armies" for longer than a two-year period. This does not apply to the Navy, but is intended to ensure that the Army will always be subordinate to the civil authorities. (For more on the armed forces, see Chapter XIII.)

IMPLIED POWERS

The Necessary and Proper Clause. — Thus far we have considered the expressed powers of Congress, most of which are found in Article I,

---

[1] Letters of marque and reprisal are commissions authorizing private citizens to fit out vessels (privateers) to capture or destroy in time of war. They are forbidden by the Declaration of Paris, 1856, of which the United States is a signatory nation. See also footnote 3 on page 736 of the Appendix.

Section 8, Clauses 1–17. The final clause in Section 8, Clause 18, is the so-called "necessary and proper" or "elastic" clause:

The Congress shall have power . . . To make all laws which shall be necessary and proper for carrying into execution the foregoing powers, and all other powers vested by this Constitution in the government of the United States, or in any department or officer thereof.

The amazing vitality and adaptability of the Constitution can be traced to this clause and the Supreme Court's interpretation of it. Indeed, the implied or "necessary and proper" powers that Congress exercises today are far more extensive than the expressed powers.

Liberal vs. Strict Construction. — The Constitution had barely come into force when the meaning of Clause 18 became the subject of one of the most famous and important disputes in American political history. Thomas Jefferson and the strict-constructionists were ranged against Alexander Hamilton and the liberal-constructionists. The central issue: Was the Constitution to be so construed that Congress could exercise only those powers *expressly* stated in so many words in that document? Or could Congress exercise additional powers which could be reasonably *implied* as necessary and proper?

The dispute came to a head almost immediately. Hamilton, as Secretary of the Treasury, proposed in 1790 that Congress create a Bank of the United States. The Jeffersonians stoutly opposed the plan, saying that the Constitution gave Congress no power which would allow the creation of such a bank. The Hamiltonians replied that such a step was necessary and proper to the execution of such powers as those to borrow, to coin money and regulate its value, and to tax.

This the Jeffersonians refuted by claiming that such reasoning would give the National Government almost unlimited powers and practically destroy the States' reserved powers.[1]

---

[1] When, in 1800, a bill was introduced in Congress to incorporate a company to mine copper, Jefferson, as Vice-President, ridiculed the proposal with this sarcastic comment: "Congress is authorized to defend the nation. Ships are necessary for defense; copper is necessary for ships; mines necessary for copper; a company necessary to work the mines; and who can doubt this reasoning who has ever played at 'This Is the House that Jack Built'?"

While Jefferson himself was President (1801–1809), he and his party were many times forced to reverse their earlier position. For example, it was only on the basis of the implied powers doctrine that the Louisiana Purchase in 1803 and the embargo on foreign trade in 1807 could be justified.

Logic and practical necessity won the dispute for Hamilton and the liberal-constructionists. In 1791 Congress chartered the First Bank of the United States. The Bank's charter expired in 1811 with the Bank's constitutionality and the basis upon which it was created (the implied powers doctrine) unchallenged in the courts.

McCulloch v. Maryland. — In 1816 Congress issued a charter to the Second Bank of the United States. This action was taken only after another struggle over the extent of the powers of Congress.

Several States attempted to limit the new Bank's authority in various ways. In 1818 Maryland imposed a tax upon all notes issued by any bank doing business in that State but not chartered by the State legislature. This tax was aimed directly at the Bank's branch in Baltimore. McCulloch, the Bank's cashier, purposely issued notes on which no tax had been paid in order to challenge the Maryland law. Maryland brought suit to collect the tax and the United States, in McCulloch's behalf, carried the case to the Supreme Court in 1819.

Maryland based its case on the argument that Congress had no constitutional authority to incorporate a bank. The United States, represented by such able men as the great Daniel Webster, defended the doctrine of implied powers and further argued that Maryland had no right to tax an instrumentality of the United States.

Chief Justice Marshall [1] delivered one of the Court's most important and far-reaching decisions in this case. Here, for the first time, the Court was squarely faced with the thirty-year-old question of the constitutionality of the implied powers doctrine.

The Court upheld the constitutionality of the Bank as a necessary and proper step in the execution of such expressed powers as to borrow, to coin and regulate the value of money, and to tax. But, far more important, the Court thereby upheld the doctrine of implied powers. The decision is so important that we quote its central passage:

"We admit, as all must admit, that the powers of the Government are limited, and its limits are not to be transcended. But we think the sound construction of the Constitution must allow to the national legislature that discretion, with respect to the means by which the powers it confers are

---

[1] John Marshall was Chief Justice of the United States for a longer period of time than any other man, 1800–1835. His decisions during these crucial and formative years for the United States make him largely responsible for the enduring strength and vitality of our constitutional system.

to be carried into execution, which will enable that body to perform the high duties assigned to it, in the manner most beneficial to the people. Let the end be legitimate, let it be within the scope of the Constitution, and all means which are appropriate, which are plainly adapted to that end, which are not prohibited, but consist with the letter and spirit of the Constitution, are constitutional." [1]

This broad interpretation of the Constitution has become firmly fixed in our constitutional system and it is difficult to see how the nation could have developed as it has under the Constitution without it.

Examples of Implied Powers. — Subsequent Court decisions have continued this liberal construction of the "necessary and proper" clause. Today the words "necessary and proper" really read "convenient or useful," especially when applied to the commerce or tax powers.

The original Constitution gave the United States express power to punish only four specific crimes — counterfeiting, felonies committed on the high seas, offenses against the law of nations, and treason; but other laws that Congress has express power to enact would be worthless if it could not punish the breaking of them. Therefore, Congress has the *implied* right to punish all crimes against the United States.

The Constitution does not expressly provide for river and harbor improvements or the building of canals, but the power is *implied* from the expressed power to maintain a navy and regulate commerce.

The words *Air Force* are not in the Constitution; but should the constitutionality of the Air Force be questioned, the courts could imply it from the right to raise armies.

The power of eminent domain is not expressly granted to the United States, but is implied. The expressed powers to establish post offices and to establish courts *imply* the necessity of post office buildings and court houses, therefore the United States can condemn land for these purposes by the right of eminent domain.

If our Constitution could be more easily amended, the meaning of its clauses need not be "stretched" to meet new conditions, but most of the *implied* powers would become *expressed* powers through Constitutional amendments.

---

[1] The decision also invalidated the Maryland tax law. Because the power to tax involves the power to destroy (tax out of existence), said the Court, Maryland could not be permitted to tax the United States. The problem of intergovernmental taxation is treated later.

OUTLINE OF THE EIGHTEEN POWERS VESTED IN CONGRESS
BY ARTICLE I, SECTION 8 *Clause 1-18*

Expressed Powers:

I. PEACE POWERS:

1. To lay taxes.
   a. Direct (not used since the Civil War, except income tax).
   b. Indirect.
      Customs = Tariff.
      Excises = Internal revenue.
2. To borrow money.
3. To regulate foreign and interstate commerce.
4. To establish naturalization and bankruptcy laws.
5. To coin money and regulate its value; to regulate weights and measures.
6. To punish counterfeiters of Federal money and securities.   *Judicial*
7. To establish post offices and post roads.   *Power*
8. To grant patents and copyrights.
9. To create courts inferior to the Supreme Court.
10. To define and punish piracies and felonies on the high seas; to define and punish offenses against the law of nations.   *Impeach fed officials*
11. To exercise exclusive jurisdiction over the District of Columbia; to exercise exclusive jurisdiction over forts, dockyards, National parks, Federal buildings, etc.

II. WAR POWERS:

12. To declare war; to grant letters of marque and reprisal; to make rules concerning captures on land and water.
13. To raise and support armies.
14. To provide and maintain a navy.
15. To make laws governing land and naval forces.
16. To provide for calling forth the militia to execute Federal laws, suppress insurrections, and repel invasions.
17. To provide for organizing, arming, and disciplining the militia, and for governing it when in the service of the Union.

Implied Powers: ✳ *powers by Elastic clause*

18. To make all laws necessary and proper for carrying into execution the foregoing powers.
    For example — To punish the breaking of Federal law.
    To establish National banks.
    To improve rivers, harbors, and canals.
    To condemn property by eminent domain.

✳ ④ *borrow money*
✳ ③ *gives Congress the right to make laws necess + proper to the land those laws*

Dark — truns — bloons

QUESTIONS ON THE TEXT

1. Where in the Constitution are most of the expressed powers to be found? *Art 1 section 8 — 1 — 17*

18 — and the power to e.

2. Upon what clause is the theory of *implied* powers based?

3. What was the nature of the dispute between the liberal- and the strict-constructionists? Who were the leaders on each side?

4. What are the two most important expressed powers of Congress?

5. Why was Congress given the exclusive power to coin money?

6. What experience did Rhode Island have with paper money in the 1780's? How did Congress get its right to issue paper money?

7. What is meant by *bankruptcy? Naturalization?* What are post roads? How may the United States acquire sites for post offices?

8. What is a copyright? A patent? What is the Bureau of Standards?

9. What powers does Congress have in the field of foreign relations? What are its war powers? Why are they so important?

10. Under what authority may Congress acquire and govern territory? Does the United States own much territory? Illustrate.

11. What is meant by *implied powers?* Give examples. Give the facts in the case in which the Court upheld the doctrine of implied powers.

PROBLEMS FOR DISCUSSION

1. The English Parliament has power to do "anything but make a man a woman or a woman a man." Why has Congress only those powers enumerated in the Constitution plus those necessary and proper to carry the enumerated powers into execution?

2. Would commercial progress in the United States be promoted if each of the States had its own monetary system? Weights and measures?

3. A century ago in Pennsylvania it was found that the annual cost of keeping debtors in prison was more than the total debts they owed. Which is the more just, debtors' prisons or bankruptcy? Why?

4. Explain why Congress was given each of the expressed powers it possesses. Each of the powers might be the subject of a short class report.

5. Have one student prepare a biographical report on John Marshall. Another student might report on the extent of implied powers today.

SELECT BIBLIOGRAPHY

BINKLEY, W. and MOOS, M. *A Grammar of American Politics.* Knopf. New York. 1952 ed. Ch. 24.

FAIRMAN, CHARLES. *American Constitutional Decisions*, pages 119–135, 179–292. Henry Holt and Company. 1950 ed.

Congress can make laws necessary for the foregoing laws

CHAPTER VII

THE POWERS OF CONGRESS TO TAX

Introduction. — The power which the Constitution confers upon Congress to levy and collect its own revenues is almost absolute. However, as the chart on the next page shows, there are four not very important *expressed* limitations and two *implied* limitations.

Taxes Must Be for Public Purposes. — According to the Constitution, taxes may be levied only "to pay the debts and provide for the common defense and general welfare of the United States." This means that taxes may be used only for *public* purposes, not private benefit. Thus one of the reasons the Supreme Court invalidated the first Agricultural Adjustment Act in 1936 was because the proceeds from processing taxes under the Act were earmarked to benefit farmers who agreed to reduce production. The Court held that one group was being taxed to benefit another and, hence, the tax was invalid as not levied for a public purpose.

What is meant by "public purposes" is something for Congress and the Court to decide. The power to tax (*i.e.*, to raise money for public purposes) is much broader than the general legislative powers. For example, Congress has no power to establish colleges across the country, but it does give Federal money to the States for the support of land-grant colleges.

Export Taxes Are Prohibited. — The reason for the Constitutional prohibition against the export tax is plain. American farmers did not want to be handicapped in competing with farmers of other countries. For instance, suppose Congress could levy an export tax of five cents a pound on cotton. The English buyers of cotton would pay to the American growers no more than to those of other countries. Therefore, in order to compete, the American grower would have to pay the tax.

Direct Taxes, except the Income Tax, Must Be Apportioned among the States on the Basis of Population. — Taxes which are actually borne by the person upon whom they are imposed, such as capitation (poll) taxes and taxes on land and buildings, are direct taxes. Such

TAXING POWER OF THE FEDERAL GOVERNMENT

"The Congress shall have power to lay and collect taxes, duties, imposts, and excises, to pay the debts and provide for the common defense and general welfare of the United States." — Art. I, Sec. 8, clause 1.

Congress Has Power "to Lay and Collect Taxes," Subject to

{ 4 Expressed Limitations

1. Taxes must be "to pay the debts, provide for the common defense or the general welfare."[1]
2. No taxes may be laid on exports.
3. Direct taxes (except the income tax)[2] must be apportioned among the several States on the basis of population.
   { Head tax
     Land tax
     Property tax }
4. Indirect taxes must be uniform throughout the United States.
   { Excise tax
     Tariffs
     Estate tax
     Corporation tax }

and

2 Implied Limitations

1. The National Government may not tax the instrumentalities of States or their subdivisions — cities, counties, districts.[3]
2. Congress may be denied the power to tax purely for the purpose of social regulation, if the tax act clearly shows on its face that it is not intended for the purpose of raising revenue.[4]

---

[1] The Supreme Court has held that Congress has very extensive discretion, however, in determining what expenditures are for the "general welfare."

[2] The Sixteenth Amendment gives the National Government the right to tax incomes without apportioning such taxes among the States on the basis of population.

[3] Congress can neither tax real estate belonging to a State or its subdivision, nor State or City bonds or the income therefrom.

[4] Thus, in 1922, the Supreme Court held unconstitutional a 10% tax on the profits of concerns employing child labor and a special tax on liquor dealers operating in violation of State law. But, in 1904, it upheld a prohibitive tax on colored oleomargarine (repealed in 1950); on traffic in narcotics (1919); on sale of sawed-off shotguns (1937); on professional gambling (1953).

taxes have been levied by the United States Government only in case of war emergency — five times in all. The United States Government has not levied a direct tax outside the District of Columbia since the Civil War, except an income tax which, since the adoption of the Sixteenth Amendment to the Constitution of the United States, needs not be in proportion to population. Since wealth is not equally distributed among the States, a direct tax which must be levied in proportion to population would be unjust to certain States.

The Federal Income Tax is a direct tax expressly permitted by the Sixteenth Amendment without being apportioned among the States on the basis of population. Congress varies the rate according to the needs of the Government.[1] The tax has always been progressive; that is, the higher one's net income, the higher the rate.

The tax on individual incomes is today the largest single source of Federal revenue. The first year's take under the 16th Amendment came to only $28,000,000. Under the current 1954 rates, the tax yields some $30,000,000,000.[2] The income tax rate effective in 1954 varies from about 18 per cent on the first $2000 of net income to about 80 per cent on the amount of income over $200,000. Payment is made on "net income" (gross income minus certain allowed deductions and exemptions).[3]

---

[1] Federal taxes are close to the highest level in our peacetime history. In commenting on high taxes, Congressman Doughton of North Carolina once said: "You can shear a sheep once a year; you can skin him only once."

[2] Justice Oliver Wendell Holmes once philosophically remarked, "Taxes are what we pay for civilized society." To this, *Time* replied in 1952: "In 1927, when Holmes made this remark, he had a salary of $25,000; tax: $600. Present tax on that income: $5,456. Either there is more civilization around, which is not noticeable, or the price of civilization has increased ninefold." Reprinted from TIME, March 10 Issue, Copyright Time Inc., 1952.

Many economists maintain that taxes are a deflationary influence (draining off "excess purchasing power") up to the rate of 25 per cent of the national income. Beyond that, it is held, they become inflationary, especially if taxes do not fully cover governmental spending. Federal, State, and local taxes today take about 32 per cent of the national income.

[3] The law in effect in 1954 gives exemptions of $600 for a single person, $600 for the spouse, and $600 for each dependent son, daughter, or other close relative who has not earned more than $600 and at least half of whose support has been paid by the taxpayer. An additional $600 is allowed for each person 65 or older, or blind. Deductions are allowed for business expenses, interest on debts, most State and local taxes, medical expenses above 5 per cent of net income, loss from theft, storm, fire, etc., contributions up to 15 per cent of net income to religious, charitable, scientific, literary, or educational institutions, etc.

INFLATION

Seibel in Richmond Times-Dispatch

Will high taxes on wealth used for the reduction of the national debt, or low taxes to release capital for more production, reduce prices?

A person with less than $5000 income from wages (and no other income above $100) is taxed on the "pay-as-you-go" basis. That is, his tax is "paid at the source" — withheld from his pay by his employer and forwarded to the Treasury to be credited to the taxpayer's account. Most other income (except that of farmers) is estimated and the tax is paid quarterly beginning March 15. Farmers are allowed to file a return and pay the tax due by January 15, after having had time to harvest and market their crops.

By March 15 everyone with $600 or more gross income, except farmers, must file a return (unless included in husband's or wife's report).[1] This return is delivered or mailed to the nearest Director of Internal Revenue together with the tax due or a claim for refund because of overpayment.

Income Tax of Corporations. — A corporation organized for profit is a company owned by stockholders; and all earned above the expenses of the business is known as net income. On this net income a progressive tax runs as high as 52 per cent on all earnings above $25,000.

Nonprofit organizations, such as churches, colleges, lodges, co-operatives, and labor unions, are exempted from the income tax.

Although an "excess profits" tax on corporations expired January 1, 1954, taxes on corporations are still quite high.

Enforcement of the Income Tax Laws. — Penalties for intentional failure to report all taxable income may be imprisonment, fine, or a penalty of fifty per cent of the amount not reported, or all three. The Treasury Department has six years in which to catch a man who makes a false return and to recommend criminal action against him. But additional taxes may be assessed at any time a deficiency due to fraud is found, no matter how long after the filing of the return — even when an estate is being settled after death. Income tax evasion charges have sent many known criminals to Federal prison when State and

---

[1] The Southwestern States, first settled by the Spaniards, adopted the community property principle from Spanish law, which entitles the wife to half of her husband's property. Thus under the income tax law, each was taxed upon one half of the combined income. The Revenue Act of 1948 extended this tax advantage to married couples in all States, but not the community property principle.

ιocal police have been unable to secure sufficient evidence against them for their other crimes.

The Treasury Department has access to bank account records (and to a limited extent to safety deposit boxes) in the United States and in countries with which we have treaties which permit it, like Canada. For instance, about twenty years ago $2,000,000 was deposited in a Canadian bank to illegally avoid the United States income tax; but due to a recent treaty with Canada we were able to discover the fraud.

A New York racketeer who was known to have about $1,000,000 in safety deposit boxes under assumed names to avoid the income tax, died suddenly, and even his wife doesn't know where the money is. If detectives should locate it most of it would be taken for tax evasions.

One man brought to the Redemption Division of the Bureau of Engraving and Printing a stack of bills that had rotted underground. The examiners redeemed $53,000 — but $48,000 had to go to the Collector of Internal Revenue. The man was a gambler who had never reported his winnings.

Indirect Taxes Must Be Uniform throughout the United States. — Indirect taxes are those that can be shifted from the person who pays them to other persons, and are therefore indirectly paid by the consumers as a part of the market price. The excise tax on cigarettes and the customs tax on imports are two good examples of indirect taxes.

The constitutional requirement that indirect taxes must be uniform throughout the United States means that these taxes must be the same on the same commodities in all parts of the country. To illustrate, the Federal excise tax on the manufacture of tobacco, playing cards, or alcoholic beverages must be the same in New York as it is in New Mexico. The import duty on cut diamonds, which is now 10 per cent *ad valorem*, must be the same at the port of New York as it is at the port of New Orleans.

Excises, popularly known as internal revenue duties, are taxes on commodities produced or services performed in the United States. The producer pays the tax, but usually passes it on to the consumer. As evidence of payment a revenue stamp is placed on such commodities as cigarettes, playing cards, and alcoholic drinks. The Federal Government taxes many nonessentials, but not food, housing, or basic clothes.

Customs, popularly known as tariff duties, are taxes on commodities imported from foreign countries. The most recent tariff act is that of 1930, but it has been amended frequently. The rates vary on different articles, now being as high as 80 per cent on some. Articles entering the United States without tariff are said to be on the "free list" — *e.g.*,

CUSTOMS INSPECTION

United States Customs Inspectors examine the baggage of persons entering the country to exclude forbidden articles and to collect the duty on those taxable.

Bibles, raw silk, coffee, bananas, and agricultural implements. All articles imported solely for display at the International Trade Fair to be held at New Orleans beginning November, 1953, are permitted to enter the country duty free. Articles taxed at a low rate are said to be taxed "for revenue only" — *e.g.*, diamonds, chamois skins, and raw hair. Articles taxed at a high rate are said to be taxed "for protection" — *e.g.*, sugar at $\frac{1}{2}$ cent a pound, tomatoes at $1\frac{1}{2}$ cents a pound, beef at 3 cents a pound, eggs at $3\frac{1}{2}$ cents a dozen, wool at from 11 to 28 cents a pound, wheat at 21 cents a bushel, shoes at 20 per cent of their value, silk at 25 per cent, articles of knit rayon at 25 cents per pound plus 65 per cent of their value, and jewelry at 30 to 55 per cent.

The tax is often so high that certain articles are not shipped into this country at all. Then, of course, no revenue is collected, but the manufacturer of the articles in this country can charge more for these articles than otherwise, since foreign competition is removed. The tax is "for protection" to home industry.

Free Foreign Trade Zones may be established by cities, where importers can hold imports for reshipment to foreign countries without the payment of tariff to the United States Government.

A United States resident returning from a short trip abroad is allowed to bring home duty free $200 worth of goods for personal or household use once within 31 days; or $500 on 12-day trips once in six months. Only one gallon of an alcoholic beverage and 100 cigars are exempt.

The United States Tariff Commission[1] was created in 1916 to investigate the difference in cost of production here and abroad so as to determine the effects of the customs laws of the United States on industry. This information was supposed to prevent the log-rolling method of framing tariff laws; but when the last general tariff law was enacted in 1930 the old methods of log-rolling were not greatly modified. However, the information collected by the Commission is of value to Congress, to the President, and during time of war to the various war agencies. (See "Tariff Reciprocity" in Chapter XI.)

The Estate (Inheritance) Tax[2] varies from 3 per cent on a net estate not exceeding $5000 to 77 per cent on that portion of a net estate in excess of $10,000,000. "Net estate" means what remains after the payment of debts, bequests to governmental, religious, charitable, and educational institutions, the cost of settling the estate, and an exemption of $60,000. The exemption does not apply if the deceased was not a resident or citizen of the United States at the time of death.[3]

The community property provisions of the Revenue Act of 1948 make the net estate left by a husband to his wife or a wife to her hus-

---

[1] The Commission is composed of six members appointed by the President and Senate.   Not more than three of the six may be of the same political party.

[2] The tax upon the estate of one who dies might be levied upon the entire net estate before it is divided, and that is an "estate tax"; or the tax might be levied upon the portion inherited by each heir, and that is an "inheritance tax."   The present Federal tax is an *estate tax*.   Most States have *inheritance taxes*.   Some States have both an estate tax and an inheritance tax.

[3] If a nonresident alien dies owning property in the United States, the exemption allowed is only $2000.

band subject to the tax upon only half of its net value. But upon the death of the survivor the estate taxes apply to all of the estate that has not been spent — the community property tax advantage not benefiting the second generation. (See note on p. 115.)

An estate or inheritance tax (or both) is usually paid to a State, and for this a partial credit is allowed on the Federal estate tax, usually amounting to less than one third of the Federal tax. The estate tax has been held by the Supreme Court to be an indirect excise tax because it is a tax on the *privilege* of bequesting.

A Gift Tax (about $\frac{3}{4}$ as high as the estate tax) prevents evasion of the estate tax by gifts before death; but gifts to governmental, religious, charitable, and educational institutions are not taxed. And total gifts of $30,000, plus $3000 annually to each individual, are exempt.

The community property provisions of the Revenue Act of 1948 provide that when a husband or wife makes a gift to the other, the gift tax applies to only one half of the value of the gift because under the community property principle only half of the gift is considered as coming from the giver — the other half being considered as already belonging to the spouse.

Congress Does Not Tax the Instrumentalities of States unless Engaged in Nongovernmental Functions. — Because the power to tax is the power to destroy, the Supreme Court forbade the United States to tax the real estate, bonds, or other governmental machinery of the States, counties, districts, cities, or towns; and likewise forbade the States and local governments to tax the United States.

However, the Federal Government may tax State activities of a nongovernmental character, that is, activities which are not necessarily or ordinarily engaged in by a State or its subdivisions. Such activities are considered in competition with private businesses. For example, in 1893 South Carolina set up a liquor monopoly selling liquor at government dispensaries and claiming exemption from the Federal saloon license tax. But the United States Supreme Court required the State to pay the tax for each dispensary because the sale of liquor is not a necessary or usual government activity.[1]

---

[1] It has not as yet been judicially determined whether the States can tax those activities of the Federal Government which may be classed as nongovernmental. See Chapter XXXI, "State Finance," and the discussion of *McCulloch v. Maryland*, pages 107–108.

Congress May Sometimes Exercise the Right to Tax Merely for the Purpose of Regulation. — During the Civil War Congress established a National banking system, and desired to get rid of paper money issued by State banks. So it imposed an annual tax of 10 per cent on the circulation of such money, a rate so high as to drive it out of circulation.[1]

In 1902 Congress levied a tax of ten cents a pound on oleomargarine artificially colored to look like butter. When the manufacturers of oleomargarine protested that it was not a tax but was practically destroying an industry over which Congress did not constitutionally have control, the Supreme Court upheld the constitutionality of the law. The court refused to go into the motives behind the law, but upheld it as a valid exercise of the taxing power. The tax was repealed in 1950. (See page 161.)

DIPPING AND DRYING MATCHES

The match sticks are dipped in red phosphorus or sulfide a million at a time.

The white or yellow phosphorus used in the manufacture of the old-fashioned match is very poisonous. Workmen in match factories often had their teeth fall out or their jaw bones decay, and many died from the poison. Matches made from other materials were a little more expensive. The Constitution does not give Congress power to regulate labor conditions directly; therefore, in 1912 Congress imposed a stamp tax of two cents a hundred on

---

[1] In upholding the constitutionality of this law the Supreme Court said: "Having, in the exercise of undisputed constitutional powers, undertaken to provide a currency for the whole country, it cannot be questioned that Congress may, constitutionally, secure the benefits of it to the people by appropriate legislation." — Veazie Bank v. Fenno (1869).

matches made of white or yellow phosphorus, which is injurious to workmen. As matches sold for one cent a hundred the phosphorus match industry was of course destroyed.

In 1941 Congress laid a tax of $300 a pound on the manufacture of opium used for smoking and thus destroyed the industry by taxation.

It looked as though there was no limit on the power of Congress to regulate through taxation those industries which fall under State control and could not otherwise be regulated by Congress. So, in 1919, Congress passed a law imposing a ten-per-cent tax on any person or corporation employing child labor. But this was encroaching too far upon States' rights, and in the Child Labor Case decided in 1922 the Supreme Court said: "Taxes do not lose their character as taxes because of the incidental motive. But there comes a time in the extension of the penalizing feature of the so-called tax when it loses its character as such and becomes a mere penalty with the characteristics of regulation and punishment. Such is the case in the law before us." The court declared this law unconstitutional.

In 1934 Congress imposed a tax of $200 on the transfer of each sawed-off shotgun. The purpose of the statute is not revenue but a record of criminals who buy such guns. The Court upheld the Act in 1937; and in 1953 it also upheld a $50 stamp tax imposed on gamblers.

High tariff is largely for protection of American industries; high estate taxes are intended to destroy large estates; yet they are legal.

In recent years, Congress has used the interstate commerce clause more than its power to tax for regulatory purposes. This practice is discussed more fully in the following chapter.

QUESTIONS ON THE TEXT

1. What restrictions are placed upon Congress as to its power of taxation?

2. What is the reason for prohibiting export taxes?

3. Does the constitutional requirement that taxes must be for the general welfare really impose much of a restriction upon Congress?

4. Why has not the United States levied any direct tax, except the income tax, since the Civil War?

5. Why is the income tax, which is direct, constitutional even though it is not apportioned among the States?

6. How much income does a single person have to earn before he is taxed? How much exemption is there for each dependent?

7. What are indirect taxes? What kinds of indirect taxes are there?

8. What is meant by the requirement that indirect taxes must be uniform throughout the United States?

9. Give some examples of the *excise tax*.

10. Name an article that enters the United States free of duty. One on which tariff for revenue is imposed. One on which tariff for protection is imposed.

11. Why is the Federal inheritance tax constitutionally considered an indirect tax? Why is it called an *estate tax?*

12. Explain to what extent Congress may tax for the purpose of regulation.

PROBLEMS FOR DISCUSSION

1. The United States pays subsidies to certain American steamship lines running between the United States and countries that otherwise would not have American lines. Is this money spent for the "general welfare"?

2. Would any constitutional question be raised if Congress should appropriate $5,000,000 for a library in Chicago? Would the constitutional question be different if a library appropriation were made for every State in proportion to population?

3. Are direct taxes or indirect taxes more just? Which are easier to collect?

4. When a high internal revenue tax was placed on tobacco, the people of Virginia, who manufactured large quantities of tobacco, felt that they were being unjustly taxed. The tax has not been reduced, but complaints are no longer heard. Why?

5. Even at today's high rate of taxation, the National Government does not live within its current income. Why? How does the Government secure the additional money necessary to finance its operations? Suggest various ways in which Federal expenditures might be reduced. Discuss and evaluate each of these suggestions.

6. In November, 1951, Congress required all professional gamblers to purchase a $50 Federal tax stamp or face possible fine and imprisonment. By January, 1952, the Internal Revenue Bureau estimated that 90 per cent of the nation's illegal gambling business had been choked off. (After "the heat was off," many gamblers were back at the same old stand, but with a wary eye peeled for Federal agents.) The stamp tax does not provide much in revenue, but is intended as a regulatory measure. In purchasing the tax stamp, gamblers are forced to reveal their illegal operations to State

and local police, the general public, and the press. If they do not buy the stamp, they face Federal action.

During 1952 the tax was declared unconstitutional by two United States District Courts and upheld in another. The cases were appealed by the Justice Department and, in 1953, the Supreme Court upheld the tax as a proper exercise of the congressional power to tax. If you were on the Supreme Court, how would you have ruled? Explain your answer.

7. The power to tax is a concurrent one enjoyed by both the National and State (and local) Governments. Many items, such as individual and corporation incomes, gasoline, liquor, and tobacco are taxed by the United States and by all or most of the States, too. A steadily increasing number of local governments also tax these items. Approximately 90 per cent of all National and State tax collections come from the same sources. Why have authorities in the field of public finance repeatedly urged the development of a co-ordinated tax policy for the nation? What particular problem does the high rate of Federal taxation create for the States?

8. Explain what Alexander Hamilton meant when he wrote in *The Federalist*, No. 30: "Money is, with propriety, considered as the vital principle of the body politic; as that which sustains its life and motion, and enables it to sustain its most essential functions. A complete power, therefore, to procure a regular and adequate supply of it, as far as the resources of the community will permit, may be regarded as an indispensable ingredient in every constitution. From a deficiency in this particular, one of two evils must ensue: either the people must be subjected to continual plunder, as a substitute for a more eligible mode of supplying the public wants, or the government must sink into a fatal atrophy, and, in a short course of time, perish."

9. Explain how married couples, under the Revenue Act of 1948, are able to save taxes: (1) Income; (2) Estate; (3) Gift.

10. Is a protective tariff a tax in proportion to ability to pay?

11. When the tariff on luxuries, *e.g.*, 110 per cent *ad valorem* on cigar lighters, is so high that scarcely any are imported, is it a tax on luxuries or merely a bounty to those who produce them in this country?

12. If Congress had not been given the power to regulate interstate commerce and each of the States had imposed tariffs against the others, about how many miles of tariff walls would we have? Would automobiles be cheaper or more expensive?

13. The 1930 Tariff Act placed farm machinery on the free list. Therefore Mr. Ford manufactured tractors in Ireland and shipped them to the United States. Is this an argument for or against protective tariff?

14. John D. Rockefeller, Sr., America's first "billionaire," died in 1937

at the age of 97. Besides gifts to his children he had given over half a billion dollars in benefactions. At death he left an estate of $26,410,837. From this estate the Federal Government collected an estate tax of $12,245,000 and New York State about $4,385,000 — making $16,630,000 in taxes. Should all estate taxes go to the State? To the United States? Should the National Government collect all and return to each State a certain percentage?

15. The gift tax rates are ¾ as high as those of the estate tax. The donor, if a citizen of the United States, is not taxed on certain gifts for the welfare of society, or upon total gifts of $30,000 to any one individual, plus $3000 a year beyond the total of $30,000. For gifts in excess of these deductions the donor pays a Federal tax equal to three fourths of the estate tax. Do you favor the gift tax? Do you favor the three-fourth rates for the gift tax?

16. Should Congress be given power to tax State, county, and city bonds? As these bonds are exempt from the Federal income tax and from most or all State and local taxes, they are issued at a very low interest rate. Learn what rate of interest your State, county, or city pays on bonds it has issued in recent years.

17. If Congress should pass an Act imposing a tax of 10 per cent of the net receipts of any chain store which works any employees more than eight hours a day, do you think the Act would be constitutional?

18. The University of Georgia and Georgia Tech claimed that taxing admissions to the football games played by their schools was taxing the State and hence was unconstitutional. In 1938 the Supreme Court of the United States decided that the taxes can be collected. Why?

SELECT BIBLIOGRAPHY

CLARK, N. "They're Death on Dope Runners." *Saturday Evening Post.* July 26, 1952, page 36.

GRISWOLD, E. "Can We Limit Taxes to 25 Per Cent?" *Atlantic Monthly.* August, 1952, pages 76–78.

LASSER, J. K. *Your Income Tax.* Simon and Schuster (annual). $1.50.

PORTER, S. "Where Your Income Taxes Are Unfair." *Collier's.* March 14, 1953.

STARR, J. "Big-Time Bootlegging Is Back." *Collier's.* June 13, 1953.

"Taxes: the Big Bite." *Time.* March 10, 1952, pages 25–27.

U. S. GOVERNMENT. *Helpful Information on How to Prepare Your Income Tax* (annual). Free.

(In this text, see Chapter XII, "The Treasury Department," and Chapter XXXI, "State Finance.")

CHAPTER VIII

COMMERCIAL POWERS OF CONGRESS

(See outline on page 317.)

The Commerce Clause. — The weak Congress under the Articles of Confederation had no power to regulate commerce among the States. It had very little authority over foreign commerce. Hence, the "Critical Period" (1781–1787) was marked by intense commercial rivalries and jealousies among the newly-independent States. High trade barriers and spiteful State laws created confusion and chaos in both interstate and foreign commerce. Indeed, the situation was such that George Washington was moved to remark: "We are one nation today and thirteen tomorrow. Who will treat with us on such a basis?"

Because of this, no group was more responsible for the calling of the Philadelphia Convention in 1787 than the merchant-creditor class. They had an obvious interest in a stabilized economy. And, to accomplish it, they favored the creation of a National Government with adequate powers over foreign and interstate commerce.

The Constitution, then, gives Congress power to "regulate commerce with foreign nations, among the several States, and with the Indian tribes."[1] This "Commerce Clause" has done more to develop a loose confederation into a strong Union than any other part of the Constitution. And, together with the taxing power, it has contributed most to the tremendous growth of the power of the National Government since 1789.

---

[1] Article I, Section 8, Clause 3. The Constitution's framers viewed the Indian tribes very much as they did foreign nations, and so they gave Congress power to regulate trade with them. They also realized the importance of keeping "firearms" and "fire water" from them. Later, when the railroads were built, Congress had the power to grant rights of way through Indian lands for the construction of the railroads.

A Free Market at Home. — In parts of Europe a traveler is annoyed every few hundred miles at a national boundary, where the train is long delayed, and where he must show his passport (the visa of which may have cost several dollars), and where his baggage is gone through — and maybe taxed. When he returns to America and passes the Statue of Liberty and "goes through customs" he can travel by train in forty-eight States without delay, passport, or inspection or taxation of his baggage.

If an American wants to sell automobiles in Europe he must pay a high tariff duty, of different rates, in more than a dozen countries; and he must fight all sorts of annoying regulations imposed to give advantage to homemade cars. In our United States, an automobile dealer finds a public with a purchasing power superior to that of all Europe, without a cent of tariff to pay, and without other discriminatory regulations.

In brief, this commerce clause has given the citizens of the United States the greatest unrestricted market in the world. For whatever you have to sell you should thank your forefathers for this enormous market they have built for you.

I. FOREIGN COMMERCE

Exclusion of Imports. — Congress has "power to regulate commerce with foreign nations." Under this power Congress has prohibited the importation of numerous articles — e.g., diseased animals and plants, opium except for medical purposes, obscene literature or literature advocating the forceful resistance to any law of the United States, lottery tickets, adulterated and misbranded foods, articles having names or emblems simulating domestic trade marks, convict-made articles, white or yellow phosphorus matches, firearms except to licensed dealers, and sugar beyond the quotas assigned by the Secretary of Agriculture.

Embargo on Exports. — Congress also has power under this commerce clause to forbid the export of commodities. Thus, since the end of World War II, the exportation of war materials and certain heavy machinery has been controlled by a strict licensing system.

In trying to keep out of World War II Congress at first forbade the export of munitions to belligerent countries. Later, belligerents were allowed to buy munitions here on a cash and carry basis, but the Act

forbade our ships to enter belligerent zones.   As this Act worked to
the advantage of the Axis powers we reversed our policy by the Lend-
Lease Act.

Protection against State Interference. — In 1827 the Supreme
Court announced the Original Package Doctrine, which forbids
a State to tax or exercise police power [1] over imports from foreign

Courtesy Moore-McCormack Lines, Inc.

COASTWISE COMMERCE

This scene at Charlotte Amalie, St. Thomas in the Virgin Islands, typifies the important part that ocean traffic plays in the trade of the world.   The large liner is
the *S. S. Brazil.*

countries until the original package is once sold, broken open, or used.
That means that a State cannot tax or interfere with the sale of Havana
cigars from Cuba until the regular shipping packages are opened or
sold.   If a State could tax or otherwise interfere with commodities in
their original packages, coast States could collect revenue or otherwise
forbid imports to reach interior States.

Regulation of Navigation. — Congress regulates shipping;   determines numerous conditions under which vessels may fly the American

------

[1] The *police power* is the power of a State to protect, promote, and regulate the
public health, safety, morals, or the general welfare of its citizens.

Congress has many Impeia
"powers" which are derived from
"Commerce Clause"

128   AMERICAN GOVERNMENT

flag, such as requiring wireless equipment, life-preservers, life-boats, a
definite limit to the number of passengers, and inspection of the ships;
and prescribes how ships must enter and leave ports. In 1950 to
protect our seaports from possible atom bomb attacks, Congress provided that all foreign ships entering American waters may be boarded
and searched.

(3) **Regulation of Foreign** and interstate **Communication.** — The courts have interpreted "commerce" to include the communication of ideas as well as
the exchange or transportation of commodities. Therefore Congress
regulates cables, telegraph, and telephone wires extending to foreign
countries, all kinds of foreign wireless communications, and the importation of printed matter.

(4) **Regulation of Immigration.** — The Constitution does not in so many
words give Congress power to regulate immigration except under the
power to regulate foreign commerce. But since the courts consider the
movement of people to be commerce, Congress excludes certain classes
of aliens altogether, prescribes conditions under which others may
enter, and provides for the deportation of undesirable aliens.

II. INTERSTATE COMMERCE

Introduction. — Congress has power to regulate commerce among
the several States. The strongest motive that led to the formation of
our Union was the annoying taxes which each State placed upon the
commerce of the others, hence the Constitutional Convention was prepared to give a liberal regulation of commerce to the central government.

When the Constitution was framed, wagons or stagecoaches naturally needed very little regulation, and slow sailboats did not present
many interstate problems. The chief and perhaps the only purpose of
this clause in the minds of the Constitution makers was to prevent the
States from interfering with the freedom of commercial intercourse
among themselves: it referred to the articles to be transported rather
than to the means of transporting them.

The Supreme Court, however, has interpreted very liberally the
power of Congress to regulate commerce. Today, under the Commerce Power, Congress regulates not only the articles of commerce
and the means of transportation, but also such things as the labor
that produces them and the stocks and bonds that finance them.

Commerce Includes Navigation — Gibbons v. Ogden. — In 1807 Robert Fulton's steamboat made its first successful trip from New York to Albany; and the New York legislature gave Fulton and his partner, Robert Livingston, an exclusive long-term grant to navigate the waters of the State by steamboat. From this monopoly, Aaron Ogden secured a permit for steam navigation between New York City and the Jersey shore.

Thomas Gibbons, operating under the authority of a coasting license obtained from the United States Government, began a competing line. Upon Ogden's petition, the New York courts enjoined Gibbons from continuing his business. Gibbons appealed to the United States Supreme Court, claiming that the New York grant conflicted with the Constitution's grant to Congress of the power to regulate commerce.

The decision in this case was bound to have far-reaching effect.[1] It was the first case involving the Commerce Clause to come before the Court. And even Congress itself could not agree upon the extent of its powers over commerce.

The Supreme Court unanimously ruled in favor of Gibbons and held the New York law in conflict with the Federal Constitution. In reply to Ogden's argument that "commerce" should be narrowly defined as "traffic" or the mere buying and selling of goods, Chief Justice Marshall wrote:

Commerce, undoubtedly, is traffic, but it is something more — it is intercourse. It describes the commercial intercourse between nations, and parts of nations, in all its branches, and is regulated by prescribing rules for carrying on that intercourse.

This decision was immensly popular because it dealt a death blow to the steamboat monopolies. But its broader significance became apparent only with the passage of time. Freed from restrictive State regulation, steam navigation increased at an amazing rate throughout the country. And, in a few years, steam railroads, freed from similar restrictions revolutionized the nation's domestic transportation.

---

[1] Other States, like Massachusetts, New Hampshire, Pennsylvania, Georgia, Tennessee, and Louisiana, had made exclusive grants similar to New York's. This decision would affect them, too. And New York's neighbors, New Jersey and Connecticut, had passed retaliatory measures against New York's steamboat monopoly laws. In closing his argument against the monopoly, United States Attorney General William Wirt said: "It is a momentous decision which this Court is called on to make. Here are three States almost on the eve of war."

SAN FRANCISCO BAY BRIDGE

It was built during the depression of the thirties with a loan from the Reconstruction Finance Corporation, and is being paid for by tolls. Because it was to cross over navigable water, the consent of Congress was necessary before it could be built. (Since 1946, such consent has been obtained from the Chief of Engineers and the Secretary of the Army.)

The lower level of the bridge is for electric trains, busses, and trucks.

Under this definition of commerce as including navigation, Congress has power to regulate vessels plying from State to State and also the waters in which they navigate. Thus Congress requires vessels to be inspected, requires them to carry life-preservers, limits the number of passengers, and prescribes working conditions for the crews.

Congress appropriates money for dredging rivers and harbors, constructing canals, marking channels, and operating lighthouses. It forbids obstructions in navigable streams; and a bridge, causeway, or dam cannot be built across navigable streams without the consent of the Secretary of the Army.

Without the express permission of Congress, foreign vessels cannot carry freight or passengers from one port in the United States to another. In this way Congress protects Americans engaged in interstate shipping against the competition of foreign vessels.

The regulatory power of Congress extends to all navigable waters which are used or are susceptible of being used for interstate commerce. Congress has authority over navigable streams running through two or more States, and also over those located wholly within one State but connecting with other navigable waters so as to form a continuous channel of communication with other States.[1]

The authority of Congress has also been extended to navigable waters wholly within a State and connected with no exterior water if these waters are actually navigated by boats which connect with interstate common carriers. Thus, a box of fish shipped across a lake wholly within a State is interstate commerce if consigned to a party outside the State and delivered by an interstate railroad. Therefore

---

[1] Streams that are not navigable were not originally considered within the power of Congress. However, in 1893 Congress created the California Débris Commission to prevent such hydraulic mining in nonnavigable streams as would cause débris to float into navigable streams and fill their channels. The United States Circuit Court of Appeals sustained this Act.

Power plants built on nonnavigable streams at first came under State authority and not Federal. But a 1935 Act of Congress gives the Federal Power Commission power to refuse licenses for dams on navigable streams, and on nonnavigable streams if they affect interstate commerce.

In 1931 the Federal Power Commission claimed supervision over a power plant on New River, Virginia — a nonnavigable stream which flows into a navigable stream and thus affects the flow of the navigable stream. A United States District Court sustained the Commission in its claim to Federal control over nonnavigable streams; and in 1940 the Supreme Court sustained the right of Federal control over such dams.

CHANGING CONDITIONS NEED CHANGING LAWS

the little lake boat carrying this interstate box of fish is subject to Federal regulation by Congress.

Commerce Includes Transportation on Land. — The first railroads were built about 1830. Until the Civil War their building was encouraged by the States. Subsequently, under the Granger movement in the Middle West, they were rather drastically regulated. States even interfered with interstate rates. In 1886 the Supreme Court checked this interference, and in 1887 Congress created the Interstate Commerce Commission. The courts justified the regulation of interstate railroads under the commerce clause, saying that commerce means "traffic," "intercourse," and also "transportation."

Under this power to control interstate "transportation" the Federal Government regulates rates for articles or persons carried from one State to another, limits the number of hours that employees are permitted to work, requires safety appliances, and compels roads to pay damages to employees actually engaged in carrying on interstate commerce, or their assignees, if the employees are injured or killed through the negligence of a railroad employee. Also, it is a Federal crime to wreck an interstate train.

Commerce between the States is called *interstate commerce* and includes the movement of passengers and freight from one State to another, and the agencies and facilities by which the transfer is accomplished; and commerce within a State is called *intrastate commerce*. As a general rule, the Federal Government controls interstate commerce and each State controls intrastate commerce within its borders.

The simple rule that the States have control over intrastate commerce is modified by some court decisions. In fact, there has been a tendency to narrow the power of the States and to broaden those of the Federal Government. When State regulation of intrastate commerce directly interferes with interstate commerce, the State regulation must yield to Federal law. For example, Shreveport, Louisiana, which is near the Texas border, and Dallas, Texas, competed for the trade of the Texas towns between these two cities. The freight rates from Dallas to these towns had been fixed by the Texas Railway Commission, and they were much lower per mile than the rates from Shreveport to these towns which had been fixed by the Interstate Commerce Commission. Therefore the dealers of Shreveport complained that they were discriminated against because they happened to be located across a State line and were regulated by the Federal Interstate Commerce Commission. The Interstate Commerce Commission heard their complaint and decided that the intrastate rates from Dallas were too low, and ordered them to be raised on a par with the interstate

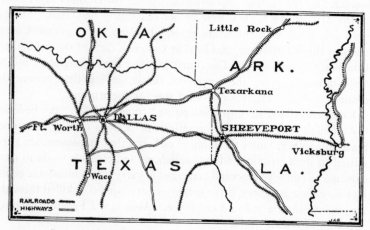

INTRASTATE RATES IN CONFLICT WITH INTERSTATE RATES

Intrastate rates from Dallas to a point midway between Dallas and Shreveport must not be less than those from Shreveport to the same point, as prescribed by the Interstate Commerce Commission.

rates from Shreveport. The case was taken to the United States Supreme Court. Here it was decided in 1914 that the order of the Interstate Commerce Commission was valid; that *the authority of the Federal Government to regulate interstate commerce carries with it the right to regulate intrastate commerce when it is necessary for the protection of interstate commerce.*

In 1935 Congress gave the Commission control of interstate common or contract carrier motor vehicles, and in 1940 of common or contract carriers by water.

Commerce Includes the Communication of Ideas. — The first telegraph line was built in 1842 and the first telephone was exhibited at the Centennial Exposition in the year 1876. Both, when extending from one State to another, are regulated by the Federal Government, inasmuch as the courts have said, "commerce includes the transmission of messages." Likewise, television and radio broadcasting are commerce, and in 1934 Congress created the Federal Communications Commission to control interstate wire and wireless communications. And it is a Federal crime to threaten to injure a person, property, or reputation, or to request a reward for the release of a kidnapped person, across a State line.

Courtesy American Air Lines

AIR TRANSPORTATION

People, as well as farm and factory products, are an important part of interstate and international commerce. Overseas air traffic is today as commonplace as that from State to State. The Boeing *Stratocruiser* shown here is typical of the fine aircraft now flying our airways.

Commerce Includes the Movement of Persons. — Vehicles carrying persons across a State line for business or pleasure are engaged in interstate commerce. Even persons walking across a State line are considered interstate commerce. In 1941 the Supreme Court held unconstitutional a California statute which forbade a nonresident indigent (poor) person to enter the State. This restriction violated the interstate commerce clause, over which the Federal Government, and not the State, has control.

Under the White Slave Act any person who knowingly transports or assists in obtaining the transportation of a female from one State to another or from a foreign country or in the District of Columbia for immoral purposes, or persuades her to come, is punishable by a fine not exceeding $5000 or imprisonment not exceeding five years or both.

Recently a movie actor was tried for paying the fare of and accompanying a single woman from Hollywood to New York. And in the District of Columbia a woman taxi driver who knowingly transported a woman four blocks to a hotel for an immoral appointment was convicted.

It is also a Federal crime to kidnap across a State line; to flee to another State to avoid State prosecution for certain crimes; or to cross a State line to avoid giving evidence in felony cases.

Commerce Includes Securities. — Many State laws give inadequate protection to investors, and billions of dollars invested in stocks and bonds have been lost through lack of information or outright fraud. In 1934 Congress created the Securities and Exchange Commission to help protect investors. (See page 333.)

Commerce Includes Insurance. — In 1944 the Supreme Court declared fire insurance (and life by inference) to be commerce.

The Right to Regulate Interstate Commerce Includes the Right to Protect It. — In interstate commerce, it is a Federal crime to obstruct trucks by violence or threatened violence, to break into a car or station or steal shipments, knowingly to receive them, or to rob passengers or steal their baggage.

The Right to Regulate Interstate Commerce Includes the Right to Prohibit It. — Congress excludes from interstate commerce such things as lottery tickets, obscene publications, game killed in violation of State laws, goods manufactured by child labor, liquor for dry States, diseased cattle, dangerous explosives, firearms shipped by unlicensed persons, disease-infected goods and persons, and impure or misbranded foods and drugs.

It had become difficult for an honest man to compete because dishonest producers indulged in every dishonest device — from misrepresenting the quantity in a package to selling fraudulent remedies for cancer. The homely squash, when doctored, flavored, colored, and attractively packed, became "canned peaches"; the apple with little seed added became "preserved strawberries"; oleomargarine dyed yellow took the name of "butter"; veal became "potted chicken"; and even mineral earths have been mixed with cheap meals to produce

FREIGHT BEING LOADED INTO AN AIR-FREIGHTER

It is a crime against the United States Government to steal from an interstate airplane or to transport prohibited articles therein.

"flour." Therefore, Congress has enacted laws prohibiting the circulation in interstate trade of foods, beverages, drugs, and cosmetics that are misbranded as to quantity, quality, or place of production, and that are injurious to health.

It is a Federal crime knowingly to transport stolen firearms, cattle, aircraft, or other vehicles of any value; stolen money, securities, or other goods of $5000 or more value; or to cause the foregoing items to be transported or to receive them across a State line. It is likewise a Federal crime to steal interstate freight, express, baggage, fares, or from passengers in a station, railroad car, aircraft, or other vehicle; or knowingly to buy, receive, or have possession of such stolen articles.

The Right to Regulate Interstate Commerce Includes the Right to Protect It against Unreasonable State Interference. — A package in interstate commerce retains Federal protection against State taxation until it is delivered to its consignee or comes to rest. Moreover, it retains Federal protection against other State regulations until the original package is once sold, broken, or used. Thus a State cannot tax cigarettes as they cross the State border but must wait until they are delivered or come to rest. Moreover, a State must wait until the package is once sold, broken, or used before regulating the sale of the cigarettes.[1]

A State may, under its police powers, require interstate commerce to comply with reasonable State regulations pertaining to health, morals, safety, and general welfare. For example, States may require proper heating of all passenger cars as well as sanitary drinking cups. They may forbid gambling on all trains, require crews of sufficient size to protect the public against accident, require all trains to slow down when going through cities, and require them to make a reasonable number of

---

[1] The original package which has Federal protection is one which the trade ordinarily uses for transportation. Thus a ten-pound package of oleomargarine was held to be an original package; but paper cartons containing a pound of oleo margarine are not original packages. The original package is the tub or box in which the pound packages are shipped. Neither is a package of twenty cigarettes an original package.

Goods brought into a State by peddlers and sold in the original package cease to have the Federal protection given to consigned commodities. Peddlers' goods are subject to State taxation and regulation as soon as brought into the State. This exception to the original package doctrine is justified because the retail transactions begin at once and the transaction is not analogous to the ordinary wholesale transaction with a jobber who stores his goods in a warehouse.

stops within the State. Of course even reasonable regulation of interstate commerce must yield to Federal regulation whenever it comes in conflict with a general Federal law.

Courtesy Chicago, Rock Island, and Pacific Railroad

"THE ROCKET," ONE OF THE ROCK ISLAND'S STREAMLINED DIESEL-ELECTRIC TRAINS

Interstate runs are subject to regulation by the Federal Government.

15. The Right to Regulate Interstate Commerce Includes the Right to Protect It against Monopolies. — By 1890 most of the major industries in the country were dominated by such combinations as the Sugar Trust, the Whisky Trust, the Beef Trust, and the Standard Oil Trust.[1] Many supposedly competing companies made agreements with one another to limit production or fix prices. Sometimes they agreed not

---

[1] The *trust* was originally a device by which several corporations engaged in the same line of business would combine to eliminate competition and regulate prices. This was done by creating a central board composed of the presidents or general managers of the different corporations and the transfer to them of a majority of stock from each of the corporations to be held "in trust" for the stockholders who thus assigned their stock. The stockholders received in return "trust certificates" showing that they were entitled to receive dividends on their assigned stock, though the voting power of it had been passed to the trustees. This enabled the trustees to elect all the directors of all the corporations, and thus prevent competition and insure better prices. Though the "trust" has been superseded by "holding companies," any monopolistic combination is today called a "trust."

to compete in certain sections of the country assigned to one or another of them. Often the same persons sat on the boards of directors of competing companies (interlocking directorates) and were thus able to regulate and restrict competition.

State regulation proved largely ineffective against these powerful interstate combinations and Federal regulation became necessary. Acting under the commerce power, Congress passed the famous Sherman Anti-Trust Act of 1890. This Act remains the basic law against monopolies today. It prohibits "every contract, combination in the form of a trust or otherwise, or conspiracy in restraint of trade or commerce among the several States, or with foreign nations." It also provides penalties for violations.

Because of the very general wording and inadequate enforcement of the law, little was accomplished until 1911. In that year the Supreme Court decided two cases involving monopoly prosecutions of the American Tobacco Company and the Standard Oil Company. In forcing the dissolution of the two monopolies, the Supreme Court announced the so-called "rule of reason." Whereas the Act prohibits *every* agreement in restraint of trade, the Court considered this to mean *every unreasonable* agreement.

In 1914 Congress passed the Clayton Act making four specific practices illegal: (1) the purchase by one corporation of the stock of another; (2) interlocking directorates; (3) "exclusive agreements" requiring a dealer to sell the products of only the one company; and (4) price discriminations in the sale of the same product to different purchasers (expanded by the Robinson-Patman Act of 1936).

Several economic groups have been specifically exempted from the provisions of the Sherman and Clayton Acts by Congress. For example, under the Transportation Act of 1920 railroads are allowed to agree to the division of traffic or earnings with the approval of the Interstate Commerce Commission. Labor unions are exempt on the grounds that "labor is not a commodity of commerce." Some utilities, farmer and dairy co-operatives, and exporters are exempted.

Examples of Anti-Trust Law Violations. — The Pullman Company, which had a practical monopoly in the manufacture of sleeping cars and which operated practically all sleeping cars throughout the country, was required either to dispose of its sleeping car factories or to dispose of its sleeping cars. It chose to dispose of the cars; and in

1902 Expedition act of T.R. administration
provided for placing cases involving
trusts in a Better position
on the court calendar

1947 fifty-seven railroad companies purchased the sleeping cars and facilities for $75,000,000.

The Associated Press was required to refrain from imposing any restrictions on the admission of new members because the papers of the applicants competed with the papers of existing members. Such restrictions were declared to be in restraint of trade.

The Ethyl Gasoline Corporation was held to be restraining trade by requiring users of its patents to sell Ethyl gasoline only to jobbers who were licensed by the Ethyl Corporation. Jobber licenses had been granted only to those who followed price policies desired by the Ethyl Corporation.

The Federal Trade Commission. — *Why Created.* — The Sherman Anti-Trust Act was indefinite, and a corporation was often uncertain as to whether it was violating the law. This was unfair to business. On the other hand, the law was not systematically enforced and the public was not protected against high prices caused by monopolistic restraint of trade. To help correct both evils the Federal Trade Commission was created (1914) to warn a business of violation without prosecution, if the business seems honestly endeavoring to obey the law; but if necessary, to proceed against the accused, impose penalties, and issue an order of "cease and desist" if found guilty of violating a law. (Appeals may be taken from the Commission to the United States Court of Appeals and in many cases may be taken from there to the Supreme Court.)

Organization. — The Commission is composed of five members appointed by the President with the approval of the Senate for seven-year terms.

The Duties of the Commission have been expanded by several Acts of Congress; but, in brief, its duty is to prevent persons, partnerships, or corporations from using unfair business practices in matters that the Federal Government can control under its interstate and foreign commerce powers,[1] and to recommend needed legislation to the President and Congress.

---

[1] It is more exact to say that the Federal Trade Commission's duty is to restrict unfair practices other than those in fields assigned to other bodies. For instance, the Interstate Commerce Commission regulates railroads and other common carriers, the Federal Reserve Board regulates banks, and the Securities and Exchange Commission regulates stocks and bonds and stock exchanges.

The Commission's work can be best illustrated by citing actual examples: In order to enhance sales, some fur dealers were in the habit of giving fancy foreign-sounding names or glamorous fictitious names to common furs. Thus rabbit furs went under at least thirty different commercial aliases — "French Chinchilla," "Electric Beaver," "Baltic Fox," etc. On the F.T.C.'s recommendation, Congress recently enacted legislation designed to end this misleading practice. Now all furs must be sold under their actual names. The F.T.C. has issued regulations requiring that rabbit be called rabbit, that skunk fur be called just that. Only furs actually produced in the Middle East may be sold as Persian Lamb. If a coat is made from ordinary cat's fur it must be labeled as Domestic Cat.

Some firms have simulated well-known trade names, labels, or slogans in attempts to capitalize on another concern's good name. Thus the F.T.C. issued a cease and desist order against the "Westinghouse Union Company" in order to protect consumers and the "Westinghouse Electric Co.", and the "Goodwear Tire and Rubber Company" was found to be too much like "Goodyear."

On several occasions the Commission has had to issue orders to forbid combinations and conspiracies in restraint of trade through price-fixing agreements to restrict competition. For instance, 45 manufacturers of book paper who produced 86 per cent of the total volume of book paper were prosecuted because of the price agreement intended to suppress competition and increase the price of paper.

The F.T.C.'s regulations forbid price discriminations where the effect is to lessen competition and promote monopoly. For instance, it forbids buying supplies at excessive prices to "freeze out" a competitor, or systematically selling below cost to suppress competition.

Manufacturers are not allowed to give discounts, rebates, and other similar allowances to chain stores if they give these large corporations undue advantages over small independent dealers. (Chain stores may still have an advantage by manufacturing their own goods, by buying the entire supply of a factory at a low price, or by buying a large supply when prices are low. Differential prices are legal when quantity buying reduces the cost of manufacturing, selling, or delivering.)

The F.T.C. holds "Trade Practices Conferences" where members of an entire industry (*e.g.*, fur, appliances, etc.) meet with the Commission to define and promote fair trade practices in that industry.

The Fair Trade Controversy

So-called "Fair Trade Acts" have produced a very interesting and most complicated problem in the regulation of interstate commerce. This problem stems from the fact that many manufacturers of nationally-advertised brand-name products attempt to set the price at which retailers may sell those products. Commonly, they require a dealer to sign a contract binding him to sell at a "fair trade" price set by the manufacturer, and making him liable for damages if he does not abide by the agreement.

However, signing all dealers is a very cumbersome, costly procedure. And many dealers refuse to sign such agreements. So, as of 1954, business groups have persuaded 45 State legislatures to pass so-called "Fair Trade Acts." These statutes legalize "fair trade pricing" by manufacturers. And most of them provide that when one or a few dealers in the State have signed "fair trade" contracts the contracts become binding on all dealers selling the particular item in the State — whether or not they themselves have actually signed such contracts.

Of course, these State laws cannot bind those who deal in *inter*state commerce — only in *intra*state commerce. But in 1937 Congress passed the Miller-Tydings amendment to the Sherman Anti-Trust Act. This amendment permits "interstate price-fixing" in those states in which such a practice is permitted in *intra*state commerce. The Miller-Tydings amendment, however, did not mention non-signers.

The question of the legality of the non-signer provisions of State laws insofar as interstate commerce was concerned reached the Supreme Court in 1950. The Calvert Corporation, a liquor concern, had signed several "fair trade" contracts with dealers in Louisiana. Louisiana's law binds both signers and non-signers. Schwegmann Brothers Giant Supermarkets, Inc., of New Orleans did not sign a contract and was selling Calvert's liquor at cut-rate prices. Calvert sued, but in 1950 the Supreme Court held that by the Miller-Tydings amendment Congress did not intend to bind non-signers.

So, in order to bind non-signers, business groups persuaded Congress to further amend the Sherman Act to that effect. In 1952 Congress passed the McGuire Act which provides that if a State's laws decree that both signers and non-signers are bound in *intra*state commerce by "fair trade" contracts, then the Federal law binds them in *inter*-state commerce, as well.

Now, with manufacturers attempting to force non-signers to comply as provided in the McGuire Act, literally dozens of court cases have been instituted across the country.

It seems probable that the Supreme Court will rule on the legality of the McGuire Act in 1954. Several cases involving the Act have been appealed to it. One of the principal cases involved Schwegmann Brothers, this time against Eli Lilly & Co. Lilly & Co. obtained an injunction against Schwegmann Brothers in the U.S. District Court in Louisiana. This injunction directed Schwegmann Brothers to halt the sale of Lilly & Co.'s products below the "fair trade" price. In 1953 the U.S. Court of Appeals upheld the injunction (and thus upheld the McGuire Act), and the Supreme Court refused to review.

In the first Schwegmann case (1950) the question was *had* Congress (in the Miller-Tydings amendment) included non-signers. The question in the second Schwegmann case (and in those cases still to be heard) is *could* Congress (in the McGuire Act) include non-signers.

The Pro Argument. — "Brand name" manufacturers, thousands of small independent merchants, the drug trade, and some department stores support "fair trade" laws. They argue that such laws prevent big department and chain stores from offering "fair-traded" items at cut-rate prices the small merchants cannot meet. They also contend that the larger stores used the reduced price on brand-name goods to lure customers into the store. These customers also buy other merchandise, it is said, and the profits lost on cut-rate items are more than offset by the overall increase in business.

Manufacturers supporting these laws claim that they protect their products and good name from being "cheapened and debased" by retail price-cutting. And they say that the manufacturer should be allowed to set the price to be charged for his product, adding that if the price is too high the customer will turn to a competitor.

The Con Argument. — The opponents of these laws argue that they violate the basic principles of free enterprise. The large retailers believe that they are in a better position than the manufacturer to determine what the retail price of any item they sell ought to be.

Macy's of New York, the world's largest department store, claims that "fair trade" is a "misleading title — the real title is 'price-fixing.' The simple truth is that no group fights for price-fixing privileges except to make prices higher than they would be under free and open competition."

QUESTIONS ON THE TEXT

1. Under the commerce clause what power has Congress over imports? Exports? What is the *original package doctrine?*

2. In what ways does Congress regulate navigation? Foreign communication? Immigration?

3. What is meant by interstate commerce? By intrastate commerce?

4. What was decided by the case of Gibbons *v.* Ogden? *navigation*

5. Does a body of water necessarily have to communicate with another State to come under the regulation of Congress?

6. Under what condition does the Federal Government regulate intrastate rates? Explain by the Shreveport case.

7. Are bus lines engaged in interstate commerce?

8. What does Congress regulate under its power to regulate interstate communication of ideas?

9. Is a person walking across an interstate bridge interstate commerce according to the commerce clause?

10. Can one caught taking a stolen car from one State to another be prosecuted in a Federal court?

11. Give some examples of the regulation of interstate commerce by States under their police power.

12. What is a monopoly? What is a "trust"?

13. What exceptions are there to the original meaning of the Sherman Anti-Trust law?

14. Why was the Federal Trade Commission created? What are some unfair practices announced by it?

15. *Name and explain 15 or more implied powers C*

PROBLEMS FOR DISCUSSION

1. A ranchman was driving his sheep from Oregon to Montana through Idaho on the day that annual property taxes were assessed in Idaho. The tax assessor in Idaho endeavored to tax these sheep but was unsuccessful because the owner appealed to the Federal courts, basing his case upon Art. I, Sec. 8, Cl. 3, of the U. S. Constitution. Explain.

2. A loaded freight truck, en route from New York to Portland, Maine, was put in a garage in Boston on the evening of March 31st. The next morning it was assessed for taxation by the Boston assessors under the provisions of the Massachusetts law which permits the levy of a tax on all

tangible personal property within the State on the first day of April each year. Why was this assessment unconstitutional?

3. Can a State tax an "original package" from a foreign country? From another State? Can it regulate it under its police power if from a foreign country? If from another State? Do you think this wise? Explain.

SELECT BIBLIOGRAPHY

CARTER, E., AND ROHLFING, C. *The American Government and its Work.* Macmillan. New York. 1952 ed. Chs. 16–21.

FERGUSON, J., AND MCHENRY, D. *The American System of Government.* McGraw-Hill. New York. 1953 ed. Chs. 25–28.

Fortune. "The Zealous Men of F.T.C." February, 1952.

SWARTHOUT, J., AND BARTLEY, E. *Materials on American Government.* Oxford University Press. New York. 1952. pp. 453–505. (Selected articles, documents, and court decisions.)

CHAPTER IX

CONGRESS IN ACTION

How the House of Representatives Is Organized. — When a new Congress assembles, the members of the majority party hold a caucus to nominate the Speaker, who is the presiding officer of the House; a clerk; a chaplain, who opens each daily session with a short prayer; a sergeant-at-arms, who preserves order;[1] a door-keeper; a postmaster; and other less important officers. The action of this caucus is considered binding upon the majority members, so the final election after the House convenes is a mere formality.

Opening of a New Congress. — The Twentieth Amendment provides that representatives who are elected in November of the even-numbered years shall succeed their predecessors the following January 3, when the previous Congress officially ends. Immediately after the expiration of a Congress at noon on the 3d of January of every odd-numbered year the House is without a Speaker and committees. It has no rules, no sworn membership, and no actual existence as an organized body. All unpassed bills of the old Congress are dead but may be reintroduced when the new Congress organizes.

When a new Congress assembles in January the members-elect are called to order by the clerk of the preceding House. The clerk reads a roll of members-elect whose credentials are in due form; the members-elect select the Speaker who has already been chosen by the caucus of the majority party; he takes his oath of office from the oldest member-elect in point of service — called "the Father of the House";

---

[1] The sergeant-at-arms also has charge of the halls and pays members their salaries, but his most interesting function is that of custodian of the mace, a representation of the Roman *fasces* surmounted by a globe and an eagle of silver, which is the symbol of authority. When the House is in session the mace is always in a stand to the right of the Speaker. If the Speaker cannot maintain order, he instructs the sergeant-at-arms to approach the unruly member with the mace and demand order in the name of the House. If the display of the mace does not restore order, the House may authorize the sergeant-at-arms to arrest the unruly member.

then the Speaker administers the oath to members-elect against whom no objections are raised by fellow members; the Democrats seat themselves to the right of the center aisle, the Republicans to the left; and, finally, the new clerk is chosen. The rules, usually those of the preceding House, are adopted. Thus the House is organized.

The Senate, a continuous body, is notified that the House is organized and ready to proceed to business. A joint committee of the two houses notify the President that they are ready to receive any communications. The following day the President's message, outlining desired legislation, is sent to the houses and read, or delivered by the President himself as Washington, Wilson, Franklin Roosevelt, and most recent Presidents have preferred to do.

Party Control in Congress. — *The Speaker of the House* presides over the House and maintains order. He may impartially use his power of recognizing members who wish to speak or he may use it to party advantage. He refers bills to the appropriate standing committees, and he appoints special and conference committees. As a member of the House he may discuss and vote on any measure, though he cannot be required to vote except to break a tie.

The President of the Senate, who is also the Vice-President of the United States, conducts himself as a rather impartial presiding officer. He is not actually a member of the Senate and votes only in case of a tie. A President *pro tempore* is elected by the Senate after nomination by the caucus, and presides over the Senate when the Vice-President is absent or when the post is vacant.

The Majority and Minority Floor Leaders, selected by their respective party caucuses in each house, are managers of their party's program on the floor; and though the positions are unofficial, each is provided with a huge desk on his party's side of the center aisle. Here they are on the alert against surprise votes that might work to their party's disadvantage. They agree upon the time to be allowed for debate on a measure, and allot portions of that time to their respective members.

The Party Whips, chosen by the Floor Leaders in each house, canvass members on issues and policies for the guidance of the Floor Leaders. They are responsible for keeping party members in line and assuring their attendance when important party measures are to be voted upon. If a party member is away from the Capital his Party

Whip sees that he is paired with a member of the opposing party who agrees not to vote on certain measures during his absence. Each Party Whip may appoint as many assistants as he needs.

The Party Caucus. — Each party in each house of Congress has a secret conference of its members, known as the caucus, for the purpose of securing party action on such matters as nominating a Speaker and electing the Floor Leader of the party. More often the work of the caucus is to determine the party attitude on pending legislation.

When important legislation is under consideration the majority caucus decides whether or not the bill will be made a party measure. Each member may speak freely; but if the majority decide to make the bill a party measure, every member of the party is expected to vote for it in his branch of the legislature. For instance, when the Tariff Bill of 1913 was under consideration, the Democratic caucus decided that the bill should pass, and that it should not be amended unless Mr. Underwood, chairman of the Ways and Means Committee, should offer the amendment. Any member may vote on any matter as he sees fit, but the party uses the caucus in an attempt to achieve party unity.

In each house of Congress there is a caucus room, and each party in each house holds secret caucuses; but the results of these caucuses are always made known.

The direct primary has tended to make Congressmen more independent of party discipline. And the leadership of President Franklin Roosevelt subordinated the importance of the caucus. However, the caucus now seems to have regained much of its lost importance.

Policy Committees are the small groups of leading members chosen by caucus to direct the party's work in each house in accordance with caucus decisions and party policies. The majority party's Policy Committee tells the official Rules Committee what to do.

Rules of Procedure. — According to the Constitution, each house may make its own rules of procedure but must keep a public journal showing how motions are disposed of and the vote for and against bills and resolutions. It also requires the votes of each member to be recorded, if one fifth of the members present demand it. This requirement enables a small number of members to put all the members on record, and thus their constituents may know how their representatives have voted on important bills.

Senate Rules are not so drastic as those of the House because the body is smaller and can proceed in a somewhat less formal manner. The President of the Senate recognizes members in the order in which they rise, and a member may speak as long as he chooses, unless the Senate resorts to the closure rule, which was adopted in 1917. According to this rule, on petition of sixteen senators, supported two days later by a full two-thirds of the Senate, no senator can speak on the measure under discussion more than one hour. Thus the old abuse of "talking a bill to death," which is known as *filibustering*,[1] may be prevented if two thirds of the members desire to do so.

House Rules are changed oftener than Senate rules, and are more drastic; otherwise the larger house would make little progress. A member may not speak more than an hour without unanimous consent; the Speaker is not obliged to recognize members in the order in which they rise; and a majority, by means of the "previous question,"[2] may limit the length of a debate at any time.

Though the rules prescribe a regular order of business for each day in the week — *e.g.*, Friday is "private bill day" — most bills are considered when the regular order of business is departed from. The regular order of business may be departed from by the unanimous consent of the members or by the adoption of a "special order" recommended by the committee on rules. On two Mondays in every month, and during the last six days of the session, rules may be suspended by a two-thirds vote, and therefore popular bills may be taken up out of their regular order.

The House Committee on Rules was originally intended to report upon desirable changes in the rules of the House. Gradually it obtained the power to determine the order of procedure and usually what measures should be considered.

Standing Committees. — The two houses of Congress have become too large for free debate and the scope of their business is now

---

[1] In ordinary use, the term "filibuster" means to act as a freebooter or buccaneer, but in the congressional sense it is applied to the obstruction of legislation by use of the technicalities of parliamentary law or privilege, such as the Senate privilege of unlimited debate (aside from Rule 22 adopted in 1917). Thus several senators with great power of endurance and a liberal supply of documents from which to read, may consume the time of the Senate and prevent it from acting on measures which they oppose. If the Senate adjourns while a member is speaking he has the floor when it meets the next day.

[2] "The previous question" means, "Shall the main question now be put?"

too great to be handled by all of the members acting together.   Neither
the House nor the Senate could work out the details of important legislation upon the floors of the houses.   Therefore each house is divided
into numerous standing committees, which are permanent throughout
a term of Congress (two years), and into other temporary committees.
These committees investigate proposed legislation and recommend for
passage the bills which they approve.

Under the Legislative Reorganization Act of 1946 there are 19
committees in the House and 15 in the Senate.   Committees vary in
size from 9 to 50 members in the House and 13 to 21 in the Senate.
Generally, representatives may serve on only one committee and
senators on only two.

House Committees	*Senate Committees*
Agriculture	Agriculture and Forestry
Appropriations	Appropriations
Armed Services	Armed Services
Banking and Currency	Banking and Currency
Post Office and Civil Service	Post Office and Civil Service
District of Columbia	District of Columbia
Education and Labor	Expenditures in the Executive De-
Expenditures in the Executive De-	partments
partments	Finance
Foreign Affairs	Foreign Relations
House Administration	Interstate and Foreign Commerce
Interstate and Foreign Commerce	Judiciary
Judiciary	Labor and Public Welfare
Merchant Marine and Fisheries	Interior and Insular Affairs
Interior and Insular Affairs	Public Works
Public Works	Rules and Administration
Rules	
Un-American Activities	
Veterans' Affairs	
Ways and Means	

The names of committees indicate the class of bills which the Speaker
of the House and the President of the Senate refer to them; for instance, the Speaker refers bills for raising revenue to the Ways and
Means Committee of the House and the President of the Senate refers
them to the Finance Committee of the Senate.

House committees are elected by the members of the House [1] and Senate committees are elected by members of the Senate.[2] The majority party of each house gives the minority party representation on each committee.

Owing to the rule of seniority,[1] committee action may not always reflect immediately current opinion as expressed in election returns. In the long run, however, a continuing national sentiment is certain to prevail.

Investigating Committees of Congress may be one of the standing committees (or sub-committees thereof), a special House Committee appointed by the Speaker, a special Senate Committee appointed by the President of the Senate, or a joint Committee from both houses. The following examples illustrate their purpose and value.

Expose Inefficiency. — The Senate Armed Services Committee saves millions of tax dollars yearly by reporting on waste in the Armed Forces. Inefficiency can have as dire results as corruption.

Expose Disloyalty. — Largely because of Nazi "fifth column" activities the House created a special Un-American Activities Committee in 1938 which investigated the actions of the members of the German-American Bund. In 1945 it was made a standing committee and its most recent and spectacular investigations have concerned Communist activities within the United States.

Uncover Fraud by Officials. — Recently a House committee reported

---

[1] Though the committees are formally elected by the members of the House, they are really chosen in a very different manner. When the Republicans gained control of the House in 1919 they created a Committee on Committees to select the Republican members. This committee consists of one Republican from each State having Republican representation in the House, and each committeeman casts as many votes as there are Republican representatives from his State. The Democratic committee members are selected by the Democratic members of the Ways and Means Committee, who are named by the Democratic caucus. These nominated members of the standing committees are then promptly elected by the House.

Members continue upon the same committees term after term unless transferred upon request of the member or for special qualifications.

The committee member longest in continuous service, if he belongs to the party in power, is usually made chairman according to the rule of seniority. The Senate has the same rule.

[2] Committees of the Senate are in reality chosen by two Committees on Committees selected by the caucuses of the two leading parties. The nominees of these committees are usually elected by the Senate without debate.

that one Congressman was "padding" his office payroll and requiring members of his staff to "kick back" part of their salaries to him. The courts sentenced him to a Federal penitentiary.

Protect the People against Large-Scale Private Frauds. — A Senate committee once uncovered a $20,000,000 fraud being committed against thousands of innocent stockholders.

United Press Photo

A SENATE APPROPRIATIONS SUBCOMMITTEE HEARING IN
WASHINGTON

Dr. James B. Conant, United States High Commissioner for Germany, seeking approval of a new budget, answers Senator McCarthy's questions regarding his policies.

There is no power like the sovereign legislative power armed with the right of subpoena [1] and search that can tear away the veil behind which powerful and unscrupulous groups operate.

Other Committees. — Besides the standing and investigating committees there are three other types of committees:

Conference Committees, composed of an equal number of senators and representatives appointed by the President of the Senate and the

---

[1] Writ compelling one to testify or produce evidence under penalty.

Speaker of the House, meet to "iron out" the differences that may occur in a bill passed by both houses.

Special Committees, whose members are appointed by the Speaker of the House or the President of the Senate are temporarily created to consider specific questions which they might be able to handle more adequately than one of the regular standing committees.

Joint Committees are composed of members of both houses acting together — *e.g.*, the Joint Committee on Atomic Energy.

The Committee of the Whole in the House (but not in the Senate because it is a smaller body) consists of all of the members of the House. For its functions see note on page 156.

Bills. — Any member of either house of Congress may prepare and introduce bills, except that a bill for raising revenue may originate in the House of Representatives only. But the most important bills are prepared by committees, or by Government agencies with further consideration by committees, and formally introduced by committee chairmen. Members introduce many bills for organizations or friends, and may disclaim responsibility for them by labeling them "by request." An average of about 15,000 bills are introduced each term, but only 10% become law.

A bill may become law by a majority vote of each house of Congress and the signature of the President. If the President vetoes a bill, it may still become a law if passed by a two-thirds vote of each house. Or, if the President takes no action within ten days, Sundays excluded, the bill becomes a law without his signature, provided Congress does not adjourn meanwhile. If Congress does adjourn within the ten-day period, the bill does not become law without the President's signature. This method of killing a bill is known as the "pocket veto."

A bill usually relates to only one subject, but sometimes a "rider" [1] dealing with a different matter is included in a bill. For instance, some years ago the barrooms in the Capitol Building were abolished by a short sentence tucked in an annual appropriation bill — a bill

---

[1] In legislation, the word "rider" refers to a measure which rides through the legislative body and past the chief executive attached to a more important and usually unrelated bill which is certain to go through.

The term "rider" probably comes from the field of music. A musical string vibrates in segments, and if you pinch a strip of paper and hang it over the string at an interval where the string vibrates least, the paper will *ride* the string; if at the wrong interval, it will bounce off.

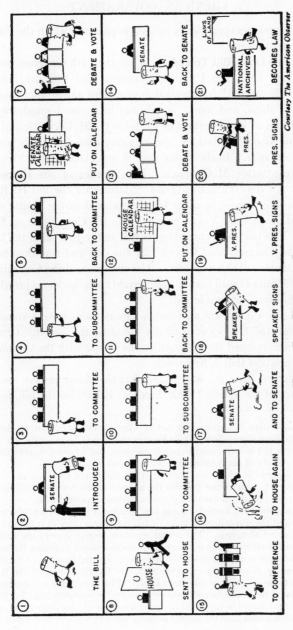

HOW A BILL BECOMES A LAW

Courtesy The American Observer

155

which Congress was practically obliged to pass and which the President was obliged to sign.[1]

The Lend-Lease Bill Traced. — When the 77th Congress convened in January, 1941, the President recommended that we become a "democratic arsenal" for invaded democracies and supply them with munitions, ships, and food. A bill was introduced simultaneously[2] in the House of Representatives by John W. McCormack and in the Senate by Alben W. Barkley, the majority leaders of each house, on January 10, 1941. In the House the bill was placed in the "hopper"[3] by Representative McCormack. The Speaker of the House, Sam Rayburn (or his "Parliamentarian"), numbered the bill H. R. 1776 (there having been 1775 other bills introduced in the House since it convened on January 3) and referred it to the Committee on Foreign Affairs. The bill was recorded by its title in the Journal of the House[4] and in the Congressional Record[5] for the day and was thus brought to the attention of the members. The chairman of the Committee on Military Affairs argued that the bill should come under its jurisdiction, but the bill was not re-referred.

The House Committee on Foreign Affairs spent a week conducting hearings on the bill before it finally voted to approve it. Chairman Bloom then reported the bill back to the House with the Committee's recommendation that it be passed.

A resolution (Res. 89) was passed that the House resolve itself into Committee of the Whole[6] for a three-day debate on the bill, followed

---

[1] The Legislative Reorganization Act of 1946 places restrictions on the use of riders in appropriation bills but these have not proved to be very effective.

[2] Usually a bill is introduced in one house only, but in order to save time in a preliminary study of the measure it was introduced in both.

[3] The "hopper" is a large box hanging at the end of the Clerk's desk.

[4] The Journal of the House contains the minutes of the daily proceedings, which are read at the opening of each daily session, unless dispensed with.

[5] The Congressional Record reports the debates of congressmen, the motions, the votes, and the disposition of bills. Each morning a copy of it is furnished to each member of Congress. The official reporters always correct the English of speeches and often give them a more elegant finish without changing the meaning.

[6] After revenue or appropriation bills have been reported from one of the standing committees, the House always resolves itself into the Committee of the Whole in order that these bills may be discussed freely. This committee is composed of all the members of the House, but only 100 are required for a quorum, therefore members who are not interested in the bill under consideration need not attend. It operates with less formal rules than the regular sessions of the House and no individual votes

by as much time as was necessary to consider any amendments, but restricting the members to five minutes each for discussion of the amendments. As the measure was considered of first importance the Rules Committee gave it priority on the House Calendar and it was debated almost at once. At the end of five and a half days Chairman Cooper of the Committee of the Whole reported the bill back to the House which passed it on February 8 by a vote of 260 yeas to 165 nays.

On February 10 a clerk of the House carried a certified copy of the bill to the Senate and announced that it had been passed by the House and asked for the Senate's concurrence. The bill was immediately referred by Vice-President Wallace to the Foreign Relations Committee of the Senate, which spent two weeks in hearings on it. One of the star witnesses for the bill was Wendell Willkie, 1940 Republican candidate for the Presidency, who had just returned from England. The chairman of the Committee on Foreign Relations reported the bill back to the Senate as amended by the Committee. The bill was then freely debated by the Senate clause by clause for nearly two weeks and passed with amendments by 60 yeas to 31 nays on the 8th of March.

As the Senate made a few amendments to the bill a Conference Committee from the two houses convened. The Speaker appointed seven representatives and the Vice-President appointed seven senators. Three days later, March 11th, the House committeemen reported back to the House, recommending the acceptance of the amendments that had been made in the Senate. The House then voted by 317 yeas to 71 nays to accept the Senate amendments.

---

are recorded — only the totals. The Speaker does not preside when the House is in Committee of the Whole but calls another member to the chair. There is no reason for his vacating the chair except that we follow the old English custom whereby the Speaker of the House of Commons was excluded from the Committee of the Whole of Parliament for fear he would report to the King what was being discussed in committee. The mace is also removed from its high pedestal at the right of the Speaker. In Committee of the Whole the bill is discussed in detail, and amendments are usually recommended when it is reported back to the House (regular session) for final vote.

Since 1930 the device of Committee of the Whole has been employed by the Senate only when treaties are being considered, and not always then. Because of the Senate's smaller size, all types of committee procedure are not so important or necessary as in the House.

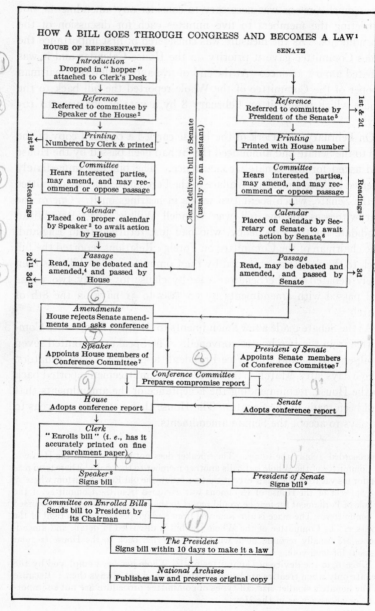

HOW A BILL GOES THROUGH CONGRESS AND BECOMES A LAW[1]

HOUSE OF REPRESENTATIVES | SENATE

Introduction
Dropped in "hopper" attached to Clerk's Desk

Reference
Referred to committee by Speaker of the House[2]

Reference
Referred to committee by President of the Senate[5]

1st & 2d

Printing
Numbered by Clerk & printed

1st[10]

Printing
Printed with House number

Committee
Hears interested parties, may amend, and may recommend or oppose passage

Committee
Hears interested parties, may amend, and may recommend or oppose passage

Readings

Readings[13]

Calendar
Placed on proper calendar by Speaker[3] to await action by House

Calendar
Placed on calendar by Secretary of Senate to await action by Senate[6]

3d

Passage
Read, may be debated and amended,[4] and passed by House

2d[11] 3d[12]

Passage
Read, may be debated and amended, and passed by Senate

3d

Clerk delivers bill to Senate
(usually by an assistant)

Amendments
House rejects Senate amendments and asks conference

Speaker
Appoints House members of Conference Committee[7]

President of Senate
Appoints Senate members of Conference Committee[7]

Conference Committee
Prepares compromise report

House
Adopts conference report

Senate
Adopts conference report

Clerk
"Enrolls bill" (i. e., has it accurately printed on fine parchment paper)

Speaker[8]
Signs bill

President of Senate
Signs bill[9]

Committee on Enrolled Bills
Sends bill to President by its Chairman

The President
Signs bill within 10 days to make it a law

National Archives
Publishes law and preserves original copy

EXPLANATION OF CHART

[1] This bill is assumed to have originated in the House of Representatives.

[2] The Clerk refers private bills; and in practice the Parliamentarian of the House acts for the Speaker in referring public bills not in controversy.

[3] The Clerk does this work for the Speaker if there is no controversy.

[4] Finance bills, and certain others, are considered item by item in Committee of the Whole. (See page 156, note.) After approval by Committee of the Whole the House proper commonly passes the bill without further debate.

[5] In practice the Parliamentarian of the Senate acts for the President of the Senate.

[6] There is only one calendar in the Senate.

[7] The House and Senate do not always appoint the same number, as the conferees of each house vote separately. Five from each house is about an average number.

[8] The Committee on House Administration finds bill accurately enrolled.

[9] The Senate Enrolling Clerk safeguards the bill in the Senate.

[10] First Reading merely means printing title in Journal and Congressional Record.

[11] Second Reading, when bill is read for amendment, is usually the only actual reading. For finance bills the real reading is in Committee of the Whole.

[12] Third Reading, just before passage, is by title unless a member demands reading.

[13] The three readings demanded by Senate Rules have become perfunctory. The third reading, just before passage, is by title unless a member demands the reading. The actual reading of the bill when it is up for amendment is not one of three historical "readings."

159

After the presiding officers had signed this final agreement, it was flown to the President, who was then cruising in the Caribbean. His signature made the bill H. R. 1776 Public Law No. 11, being the eleventh public law enacted by the 77th Congress.[1]

Types of Bills and Resolutions. — Some measures introduced in Congress take the form of bills while others are called resolutions.

Public Bills are measures of general application, such as the Selective Service Act or an income tax law.

Private Bills are those that apply to specific persons or places. For example, Congress granted the late Sister Kenny, the great Australian nurse, the right to enter and leave the United States without regard to existing immigration restrictions.

Joint Resolutions differ very little from bills, but they usually deal with a single and simple matter. They have the same force and effect as bills do when they become law. A typical joint resolution would be one setting aside a certain week as Boy Scout Week.

Concurrent Resolutions deal with matters in which joint action of the Senate and House are necessary but for which a law is not needed. The setting up of a joint committee is usually handled by this device.

Simple Resolutions are passed by only one or the other house and deal with matters relating only to that branch of Congress. For example, special committees are set up by simple resolution.

Making the National Budget. — A budget is a method of worrying before you spend instead of afterwards. The Bureau of the Budget, with a Director appointed by the President, is independent of the Treasury Department and responsible only to the President. Under the budget law the head of each department and establishment prepares an estimate of its needs for the next fiscal year and transmits it to the Bureau by September 15. Then the Bureau prepares the budget subject to the President's directions. Once, for example, President Coolidge directed that each agency reduce its requests by ten per cent. After the President has approved the budget, he sends it to Congress early in January so that Congress may enact it by the beginning of the fiscal year, July 1st.

The Ways and Means Committee of the House and the Finance Committee of the Senate consider taxes; and the Committee on

---

[1] An excellent illustrated treatment of How a Bill Becomes Law will be found under the heading "United States, Government of," in the World Book Encyclopedia.

Appropriations of each house considers expenditures. Finally, the House and Senate must agree on taxes and expenditures, and the President must accept or veto entire finance bills. He cannot veto only certain items, as most Governors may do.

The Government's fiscal year runs from July 1 to June 30. In 1953, as in most recent years, Congress had not completed action on all the budget measures by July 1. So it was forced to make "stop-gap" appropriations for certain agencies until it had completed action.

Each Congressman naturally endeavors to get as much money spent in his home district or State as possible — to use the congressional phrase, "to get pork out of the public pork-barrel." He may request appropriations for relatively unimportant river and harbor improvements, or to support higher prices on some local commodity. Such appropriations may seem important to a Congressman's constituents, even though they appear unnecessary from a national standpoint.

Each Congressman can usually get "pork" for his district because he helps every other one to get it for his own. This practice of working together in securing appropriations is known as "log-rolling" — a term from pioneer life when neighbors always lent a hand in rolling logs to the place where a settler was building his cabin.

Many committees of the House prepare bills which authorize the expenditure of money when passed by Congress. But the money is not available until the passage of an appropriation bill, prepared by the Committee on Appropriations, which contains the item authorized.

Lobbyist and Pressure Group Activities. — Practically all organized groups in the country — business, labor, agriculture, the professions, veterans, "drys," churches, and a host of other interests — maintain *lobbies* in Washington. Nearly a thousand well-paid persons are regularly employed as legislative agents or *lobbyists*. Their task is to work for or against legislation in which their groups are interested. They spend millions each year in their activities.

One of the most bitterly fought lobbying actions has lasted for almost fifty years. It was partially settled in 1950 when the oleomargarine interests overcame the opposition of the dairy interests and persuaded Congress to repeal the 1902 Federal tax of ten cents a pound on their product. However, some restrictions still remain — e.g., oleomargarine must be plainly marked as such and individual States may still exclude it or impose heavy taxes upon it.

CONGRESS IN ACTION

HOW PRESSURE GROUPS WORK

Graphics Associates for Public Affairs Committee

Some lobbyists are former Congressmen who know "the legislative ropes" and have intimate Congressional contacts. Others are lawyers or former journalists or experts in special fields. Government officials also lobby for appropriations and administrative programs.

The lobbyist employs numerous and varied methods in his work. Many times he offers expert (or biased) testimony at committee hearings or furnishes individual Congressmen with information. The so-called "social lobby" (parties, dinners, excursion trips, and the like) affords opportunities for more intimate contacts.

Wider in the scope of its activities than the lobby is the *pressure group*. Actually, lobbies are only the Washington arm of pressure groups which employ high pressure experts to wage campaigns through the press, radio, petitions, letters, and telegrams to form favorable public opinion.

The public generally regards these groups as "bad," but some are definitely "good." One such group is the Citizens Committee for the Hoover Report which works for "better government at a better price." A Congressman may call upon a lobby for valuable advice and information. All of these groups form a part of the give-and-take of compromise so necessary in representative government.

The Library of Congress — the largest in the world — now occupies two buildings with 35 acres of floor space and shelving for 20,000,000 books, pamphlets, maps, pieces of music, manuscripts, and bound volumes of papers. The two buildings are on adjoining blocks, and books are carried from the center of one building to the center of the other at the rate of 25 feet a second. The Library has 200 research rooms — many of them air-conditioned. The Library's Legislative Reference Service compiles information and makes studies to aid Congress in its deliberations. The Copyright Office is also within the Library.[1]

---

[1] Subordinate to the Librarian of Congress is the Register of Copyrights, whose office is in the annex Library of Congress building in Washington. When a book is published, the notice of copyright should be printed on the title page or the page following. Promptly after publication two copies of the best edition must be sent to the Register with an application for registration and a money order for four dollars payable to the Register of Copyrights. Application forms will be furnished upon request. For a work of art a photograph is sent. Any print or label used for an article of merchandise may be copyrighted for a fee of $6. Lectures and dramatic or musical compositions also may be copyrighted, whether published or not, for a fee of $4.

Congressional Reforms. — Much of the internal organization and rules of procedure are in sore need of streamlining. Congress itself has recognized the problem. The Legislative Reorganization Act of 1946 was passed to bring about many of the badly needed reforms. But it did not go far enough.

That Act reduced the number of standing committees in each house, furnished committees with expert professional staffs, and created the Legislative Reference Service to aid Congressmen. It further provided for the registration of lobbyists, attempted to reduce the number of private bills, and removed many petty tasks from the shoulders of Congress.

But much still remains to be done. Indeed, many Congressmen were surprised that so much was accomplished in 1946. Petty politics and vested interests have several times blocked further improvement.

The seniority rule for committee chairmanships still vexes both houses. At the end of each session a "log-jam" of unpassed bills always piles up; many of these are then passed with inadequate consideration while other more worthy bills are lost in the shuffle. Filibustering in the Senate continues to be a matter for debate (page 150).

Many Congressmen have long complained of the need for closer contact with the executive branch of the Government. Several members think that this can be accomplished by allowing members of the President's Cabinet and other officials to appear on the floor of each house at regularly scheduled times for questioning and debate.

Many constituents make unreasonable demands on their Congressman, who feels obligated to meet these demands if he is to keep good will at home. Some Congressmen spend more time with their private affairs than with the nation's business. It is up to Congress, supported by public opinion, to solve these problems.

QUESTIONS ON THE TEXT

1. What is a *caucus?*
2. When are representatives elected? How many months later do they succeed their predecessors? How many sessions do they serve? When do their terms end?
3. Who calls a new House to order? Senate?
4. How is the Speaker of the House chosen? The floor leaders?

5. A term of Congress extends over how many years? Does the Senate ever have to reorganize?

6. Who makes the rules of procedure for each house?

7. How many members of each house are necessary to demand that all votes on any measure be recorded?

8. How long may a member of the Senate speak? What is meant by a *filibuster?*

9. How long may a member of the House speak? How may a debate be brought to a close in the House?

10. How may a bill be taken up out of its regular order?

11. What committee recommends changes in the rules of the House?

12. Name several standing committees in Congress. What are their functions?

13. How are House committees chosen?

14. Who may introduce bills? About what proportion of the bills introduced become law?

15. Name the steps through which a bill must pass to become law.

16. When a term of Congress comes to an end, what becomes of all the bills which have been introduced during that term?

17. Trace the course of the Lend-Lease Bill.

18. What is the Congressional Record? How often is it issued?

19. What is the Committee of the Whole? Who presides? How many members constitute a quorum of this committee? Of the whole House?

20. Who is responsible for the preparation of the national budget?

21. Explain the party caucus; lobby; invisible government.

22. What is done by the investigating committees of Congress?

23. Suggest needed reforms in Congressional organization and procedure.

PROBLEMS FOR DISCUSSION

1. Instead of making busy people appear before the corresponding committees of the House and the Senate at different times would you favor having joint hearings of like committees?

2. The "seniority rule" for determining committee chairmen in each house has long been criticized, but no one has come up with a satisfactory alternative method. List the disadvantages of this practice. The rule also has distinct arguments in its favor. Can you list some of them?

3. Under Senate rules a Senator may speak as long as he desires, and this privilege is abused by *filibustering.* A two-thirds vote may force a vote, but there is usually a bare majority only on controversial matters. What prevents filibustering in the House? What could in the Senate?

4. For a temporary purpose Congress usually passes a *Joint Resolution* instead of an *Act*. Excepting proposed Constitutional amendments, a Joint Resolution is signed by the President and has the effect of law. A *Concurrent Resolution*, passed by the two houses, merely affects matters over which they have jurisdiction. A *Simple Resolution* is a *Senate Resolution* or *House Resolution* affecting one house. Which would the following be: declaration of war, declaration of neutrality, creating a joint committee of the two houses, creating a committee of one house, adjournment of the two houses, rules of either house, or admitting exhibition exhibits free of tariff duty?

5. The American Institute of Public Opinion uses as many as 1000 public opinion samplers in the forty-eight States to ask voters their opinion regarding questions of the day. This assists Congressmen to determine the wishes of their constituents. Should the Congressmen vote according to a public opinion poll or according to their own convictions after congressional investigations and debate? If public opinion is contrary to the results of an investigation should Congress immediately legislate their convictions or first try to educate the people?

6. The Legislative Reorganization Act of 1946 went a long way toward eliminating many of the criticisms which may be offered against the legislative procedure in Congress. But most observers, and many Congressmen, too, agree that it did not go far enough. For example, filibustering in the Senate and the so-called "seniority rule" for committee chairmanships were not dealt with in the law. What reasons can you suggest for the fact that the law "went only part way?"

SELECT BIBLIOGRAPHY

BAILEY, S. and SAMUEL, H. *Congress at Work.* Holt, New York. 1952.

DAVIDSON, B. *Why Congress Acts That Way.* Collier's. May 14, 1949. page 18.

"Eyes on Congress: Should Sessions Be Televised?" *Scholastic.* February 13, 1952, pages 7–9.

GALLOWAY, G. "To Break the Congress Log-Jam." *New York Times Magazine.* July 26, 1953.

"Has Congress Broken Down?" *Fortune.* February, 1952, page 81.

PHILLIPS, C. "The High Cost of Our Low-Paid Congress." New York Times Magazine. February 24, 1952, page 7.

SMITH, GEORGE and RIDDICK. *Congress in Action:* or *How a Bill Becomes Law.* National Capital Publishers, P.O. Box 7706, Washington 4, D. C. 1948. (In words, pictures, and staged. 87 pages. 75c.)

CHAPTER X

THE EXECUTIVE DEPARTMENT

THE PRESIDENT

The Most Important Office in the World. — On the twentieth of January, 1953, Dwight David Eisenhower placed his left hand on a Bible, raised his right hand, and solemnly swore that he would "preserve, protect and defend the Constitution of the United States." With this pledge he became the thirty-fourth President of the United States. As President, he occupies the most powerful and the most important office in the world. His powers in both domestic and foreign affairs are vast, and the manner in which they are used is of the greatest importance to people everywhere. And the problems he faces are as complex as his powers are great.

The President's Qualifications. — Whatever else he must be to gain this highest of offices, the Constitution provides that the President must: (1) be a natural-born citizen of the United States, (2) be at least thirty-five years of age, and (3) have been at least fourteen years a resident within the United States.

How the President Is Elected. — It was the intention of the framers of the Constitution to remove the office of chief magistrate so far as possible from the passions of the masses. Accordingly they arranged that the President should be chosen indirectly by a "college of electors" composed of as many members as there are representatives and senators in Congress. These electors were expected to use their own judgment and to select the best qualified person for the presidency. This system of electing the President continues, but since Washington's two terms (1789–1797), *i.e.*, since political parties became well defined, these electors have been merely honorary mouthpieces to vote as their political party directs.

Each State is entitled to as many electors as it has representatives and senators in Congress, and may select them in any manner that the

167

primaries are usually held early in the election year in many states to determine the people's choice of delegates to the national convention

State legislature desires.   At first the legislatures themselves chose the electors, and chose those who were known to favor certain candidates. This method was considered undemocratic, and gradually in each State the legislature provided for choice by the voters themselves.[1]

Today in each State the electors are chosen on a general State-wide ticket.   Thus in a State whose Democratic voters are in the majority, all the electors will be Democrats; in a State whose Republican voters are in a majority, all electors will be Republican.[2]   To illustrate, in 1884 the Democratic party in New York had a majority of only about 1000 out of a total vote of more than 1,000,000: but all of the thirty-six electors chosen were Democrats and they cast their electoral votes for the Democratic candidate, Grover Cleveland.   In the same election, the Republicans had a majority of 81,000 in a total Pennsylvania vote of 866,000; hence all thirty of Pennsylvania's electors were Republicans and cast their electoral ballots for James G. Blaine.   In other words, in these two States Blaine received some 80,000 more popular votes than Cleveland, but Cleveland received six more electoral votes.   (If Blaine had carried New York, he, not Cleveland, would have been President.)

In brief, the President is elected as follows: Each major party nominates a candidate for the presidency at a national convention held in June or July of the "presidential year."   At about the same time, the various parties in each State nominate their candidates for electors, in whatever manner is provided by State law.   The electors

---

[1] See Article II, Section 1, Clause 3 and Amendment XII.   Most of the Framers agreed with Alexander Hamilton's defense of the indirect method (in *The Federalist* No. 69): "The process of election affords a moral certainty that the office of President will never fall to the lot of any man who is not in an eminent degree endowed with the requisite qualifications.   Talents for low intrigue, and the little arts of popularity, may alone suffice to elevate a man to the first honors in a single State; but it will require other talents, and a different kind of merit, to establish him in the esteem and confidence of the whole Union."

[2] In only three States (California, Massachusetts, and Oregon) are the electors *legally* bound to vote for the candidate who carries their State.   But, because electors are themselves party men, they almost always vote for their party's candidate.   Except in the three States just noted, it is quite possible, however, for an elector to vote for some one other than the candidate of his party.   Only four have ever done so — one in 1796, one in 1824, one in 1912, and one in 1948.   In the latter case, a Tennessee elector voted for the State's Rights candidate, although the Democratic party had carried Tennessee and the other eleven Tennessee electors voted for Harry S. Truman.

are then chosen by the voters in each State on the Tuesday following the first Monday in November of every year divisible by 4. Thus the electors were chosen on November 4th in 1952. About half the States still print all the names of the various parties' candidates for elector, but some of these do not include the presidential candidates' names.

To illustrate the election process, if a Republican in Wisconsin votes for the twelve Republican electors, he places an X after the name of the Republican presidential candidate on the ballot (page 170). Then, if after the State election board has received all of the returns of the election from the various local election boards, it is found that the Republican electors have received more votes than any other set of electors, they assemble at the capital city,[1] Madison, and cast their votes the first Monday after the second Wednesday in December. The votes are signed by each elector, sealed, and sent by registered mail to the president of the United States Senate.[2] The same method is followed in all States today.

On the sixth day of January next following, the president of the Senate opens these returns and, in the presence of the two houses, counts them and declares the candidate elected who has received the majority of electoral votes. If no candidate has a majority (266) of all the electoral votes (531), the House of Representatives elects one of the three leading candidates, the representatives from each of the 48 States casting one vote. If no candidate receives a majority (25) of these votes by the twentieth of January next following, the newly elected Vice-President is inaugurated as President.[3] The election of the Vice-President is described on pages 185–186.

---

[1] The law provides that the electors shall meet "at such place in each State as the legislature of such State shall direct." All of the legislatures have designated their State capitals.

[2] Two lists of votes are sent to the State Secretary of State, two to the Archivist of the United States, one to the president of the Senate, and one to the local U. S. District Judge. If the president of the Senate, or the Archivist of the United States, does not receive the votes of any State and cannot obtain them from the State Secretary of State by the 4th Wednesday of December, he sends a special messenger for the votes filed with the District Judge.

[3] Two vital objections have been suggested against electing the President by the House: (1) a small State, like Nevada, has the same vote as a large State, like New York; and (2) if the House membership of a State divides equally, the State loses its vote. Fortunately, an election is seldom thrown into the House.

Official
Presidential Ballot

Make a cross (X) or other mark in the square opposite the names of the candidates for whose electors you desire to vote. Vote in ONE square only.

DWIGHT D. EISENHOWER--President ⎫
RICHARD M. NIXON---Vice President ⎬ Republican ☐

ADLAI E. STEVENSON------President ⎫
JOHN J. SPARKMAN----Vice President ⎬ Democrat ☐

FARRELL DOBBS----------President ⎫
(Socialist Workers Party)
MYRA TANNER WEISS-Vice President ⎬ Independent ☐
(Socialist Workers Party)

VINCENT HALLINAN-------President ⎫
(Progressive—Peace, Freedom, Security)
CHARLOTTA A. BASS---Vice President ⎬ Independent ☐
(Progressive—Peace, Freedom, Security)

ERIC HASS-----------------President ⎫
(Socialist Labor Party)
STEPHEN EMERY------Vice President ⎬ Independent ☐
(Socialist Labor Party)

DARLINGTON HOOPES-----President ⎫
(Socialist Party)
SAMUEL H. FRIEDMAN-Vice President ⎬ Independent ☐
(Socialist Party)

WISCONSIN PRESIDENTIAL BALLOT FOR THE 1952 ELECTION

Unlike most States, Wisconsin has a separate ballot for the names of presidential and vice-presidential candidates. Whereas half the States have the names of the presidential electors on the ballot, Wisconsin and Massachusetts omit them. The Constitution provides that State legislatures may determine the method of choosing presidential electors; thus a legislature may name the electors and direct them to elect the candidates who receive the most popular votes.

Criticisms of the Electoral College System have been made almost from its beginning.[1] One of the most common complaints involves so-called "minority" elections.   As we have seen, Blaine lost New York's electoral votes, and hence the election, in 1884, by only about 1000 votes out of a total New York vote of 886,000.   The most striking example occurred in the election of 1888.   Benjamin Harrison received a majority of the electoral votes even though Grover Cleveland actually received over 100,000 more popular votes.   This happened because Cleveland piled up votes in the Southern States (with less electoral votes) while Harrison carried most of the Northern States by small majorities.

In 1860 Abraham Lincoln received *more* popular votes than any of his rivals, but still had 500,000 less than a majority of all votes cast. In 1912 Woodrow Wilson received some 2,000,000 more popular votes than his nearest competitor, Theodore Roosevelt; still Wilson received only 42 per cent of all the votes cast.

In short, the record shows that the electoral votes bear only a very indirect relationship to the national preference as expressed in the total popular vote.   Note how disproportionate the electoral and popular votes were in 1952:

Eisenhower: 442 electoral votes; 33,927,549 popular votes.

Stevenson: 89 electoral votes; 27,311,316 popular votes.

The Electoral College was once criticized by Elbert Hubbard as follows: "The original argument was that the people should not vote directly for President, because the candidate might live a long way off, and the voter could not know whether he was fit or not.   So they let the citizen vote for a wise and honest elector he knew.   The result is

---

[1] On the whole, the system worked rather well in the elections of 1789 and 1792, largely because George Washington was the unanimous choice of all the electors. But difficulties arose especially with the 1800 election.   Both Thomas Jefferson and Aaron Burr received 73 electoral votes, and so the choice moved to the House. Although popular opinion clearly favored Jefferson for President and Burr for Vice-President, the House had to take 36 separate ballots before Jefferson was finally chosen.   The 73–73 tie was possible because under the original Constitution each elector cast two votes, each for a different man, the candidate with the highest number of votes to be President and the man with the second highest to be Vice-President.   To correct this situation, the Twelfth Amendment was added in 1804 It provides that each elector shall cast one ballot for his presidential choice and a second and separate one for his vice-presidential choice.

that we all now know the candidates for President, but we do not know the electors. The Electoral College in America is just about as useful as the two buttons on the back of a man's coat, put there originally to support a sword belt. We have discarded the sword, yet we cling to our buttons."

Current Proposals for Change revolve around two generally-supported moves. Both would require amendment of the Constitution:

(1) Retain the electors and continue to choose two at large in each State (*i.e.*, one for each Senator) plus one for each representative-at-large (if any) and choose all others from the Congressional districts.

(2) Discard the electors and allow the people to vote directly on the presidential and vice-presidential candidates, then apportion each State's total electoral vote among the candidates on the basis of the popular vote, with a plurality of 40 per cent the minimum for election.

Direct popular election (which would mean discarding both electors and electoral votes) would mean that a State with unrestricted suffrage requirements would have an unfair advantage over a State with higher educational requirements for voters.

Term of the President. — Upon his inauguration on January 20 following his election, the President serves a four-year term. Until the Twenty-second Amendment, there was no constitutional limitation on the number of terms a President might serve, provided he could gain the necessary votes.[1] The Twenty-second Amendment, added in 1951, now provides that no President may serve more than ten years — a maximum of two elected terms of his own plus not more than two years of a term to which he had previously succeeded from the vice-presidency.

Succession to the Presidency. — Should a President die in office, resign, be removed by impeachment, or otherwise be unable to continue in office, the Constitution says that the powers and duties of the office devolve upon the Vice-President.[2]

---

[1] Several Presidents, beginning with George Washington, refused to run for more than two terms. Soon the so-called "no-third-term tradition" became an unwritten custom. Franklin Roosevelt, however, broke with tradition when he sought and won third and fourth terms in 1940 and 1944. The Twenty-second Amendment made the old unwritten custom a part of the written Constitution.

[2] But, strictly speaking, the Constitution (Article II, Section 1, Clause 6) does not say that the Vice-President shall become President. Only tradition dictates this — beginning with John Tyler's succession in 1841.

The order of succession following the Vice-President is left for the Congress to determine. The Presidential Succession Act of 1947 provides for the succession of the Speaker of the House, followed by the President *pro tem* of the Senate, who acts until a President shall have qualified. To act only until a Speaker or President *pro tem* qualifies, the Secretary of State and other cabinet officers follow in order of precedence (page 187).

Compensation of the President. — The President's salary is set by Congress, and it cannot be changed during his term of office. He receives a salary of $100,000 yearly plus a $50,000 "expense account," both of which are taxable.

The Constitution forbids him "any other emolument from the United States or any of them." [1] But this provision is not construed to forbid such supplementary funds as are necessary to provide the White House (with its 16 acres of grounds including a swimming pool, theater, tennis courts), a large suite of offices, a large official staff, a private railway car, an airplane, a fleet of automobiles, free medical and dental care for himself and his family, a very liberal travel and entertainment fund, and similar perquisites. The total of his salary and perquisites comes to about $3,000,000 a year. Still his actual income is well below that of many persons in private life.

Duties and Powers of the President. — In order that the President may perform the various duties which the Constitution, Acts of Congress, treaties, and customs place upon him, he has to have corresponding powers. As the head of the executive branch of government it is his duty to see that the Constitution, law and treaties, and decisions of the Federal courts are enforced. To perform this duty he has been given power to appoint and dismiss thousands of officers; command the army and navy; call extra sessions of Congress, recommend proper legislation, and veto improper bills.

An aggressive President who becomes party leader or a national hero can greatly increase his powers by a loose construction of the Constitution.[2] During the Civil War Congress permitted Lincoln to

---

[1] At the Constitutional Convention Benjamin Franklin argued that, since money and power might corrupt a man, the President should receive nothing beyond his actual expenses. But Franklin's suggestion was never brought to a vote.

[2] But no President possesses unlimited authority. The Steel Seizure Case of 1952 provides a good example of the point. President Truman issued an Executive

become practically a dictator. He issued a proclamation suspending the writ of *habeas corpus*, which Congress subsequently legalized. He also issued the emancipation proclamations of 1862 and 1863, declaring

United Press Photo

THE PRESIDENT'S PRESS CONFERENCE

At these weekly White House press conferences, the President answers reporters' questions on his Administration's current plans and policies, both national and international.

all slaves in the insurgent States to be thenceforth free; and he secured the adoption of the Thirteenth Amendment in 1865 legalizing the proclamations. Though the President cannot declare war he can at

---

order in April, 1952, directing the Secretary of Commerce to seize and operate several steel plants for the Government. This action was taken, said the President, to avert a steel strike which could seriously cripple the defense effort and the war in Korea. He cited his constitutional powers as Commander-in-Chief of the Armed Forces as authority for the action. In June, 1952, the Supreme Court, in a 6–3 ruling, declared the seizure unconstitutional as beyond the powers of the President.

any time bring on war, by ordering the army into foreign territory, or by managing foreign affairs in such a manner that a foreign nation will become the aggressor.

Power of Appointment. — The Constitution provides that the President "shall nominate, and by and with the advice and consent of the Senate, shall appoint ambassadors, other public ministers and consuls, judges of the Supreme Court, and all other officers of the United States whose appointments are not herein otherwise provided for,[1] and which shall be established by law; but the Congress may by law vest the appointment of such inferior officers as they think proper in the President alone, in the courts of law,[2] or in the heads of the departments."

Excluding pensioners, reliefers, and compensated unemployed, legislative and judicial branches, the Army, Navy, Air Force, Coast Guard, and government of the District of Columbia, the United States has some 2,300,000 in the executive civil service. Of these the President unaided appoints very few; with the consent of the Senate he appoints about 26,000 of the most important; perhaps half are selected by civil service competitive examinations; and the remainder, some of whom are laborers, are appointed directly or indirectly by cabinet officers. Since cabinet officers are themselves dependent upon the President, he can influence many of these appointments if he desires.

The President alone appoints his three secretaries and six assistants. These assistants, nicknamed "Little Presidents," assist the President in publicity, public relations, personnel problems, as a go-between for the President and Congress, in foreign affairs, and the like. The President alone may appoint confidential officers for secret missions. And only twice in our history has the Senate refused to confirm Cabinet appointees of the President.

The President with the consent of the Senate appoints the most important officers.[3] For the positions to be filled within a congressional

---

[1] The officers whose appointments are "otherwise provided for" are the President, Vice-President, electors, senators, representatives, and officers of the Senate and House of Representatives.

[2] Courts of law appoint clerks, reporters, and other minor ministerial officers.

[3] This class includes such officers as ambassadors, ministers, and consuls; Federal judges; most military and naval officers; cabinet officers and their immediate subordinates; the Treasurer of the United States; the Comptroller of the Currency;

district, the President usually confers with the representative from that district if he is of the same party; for the more important ones, the senators will be consulted. When the Senate receives the names

Fabian Bachrach

DWIGHT DAVID EISENHOWER

The inauguration, on January 20, 1953, of Mr. Eisenhower as President marked a turning-point in the government of the United States.

of persons selected for positions, it refers them to the appropriate standing committee.

If the majority of the Senate is of the President's party (which is usually the case), the Senate will ratify only those appointments which are approved by the senators of the President's party from the State in which the offices in question are to be filled. This practice is known as "senatorial courtesy." It applies only to officials who serve within

superintendents of mints; commissioners of internal revenue; collectors of customs; heads of independent administrative establishments such as the interstate commerce commission; district attorneys and marshals; territorial governors; and postmasters of the first, second, and third classes (any postmaster whose postoffice has gross annual receipts of $1500 or more).

the senator's State. It does not apply to offices in the foreign service, army and navy, or those in the District of Columbia.

The Civil Service Commission examines applicants for more than a million positions, and the President and other higher officers make appointments according to civil service rules.[1]

Heads of Departments directly or indirectly appoint several hundred thousand employees without civil service examinations. Many of these are laborers.

Term of Officers. — Most of the important officials are appointed for four years.[2] The cabinet officers are appointed to serve during the pleasure of the President, and they almost always resign when a new President enters office. The terms of minor officers and laborers vary, and persons who enter the civil service through competitive examinations hold office for an indefinite term.

Power of Removal. — The President may remove without the consent of the Senate any civil executive officer whom he appoints.[3] Judges may be removed by impeachment proceedings only. The President's power to remove executive officers may not be restricted by Congress and may be used for political purposes as well as for ridding the service of incompetent and unfit persons. Those who have entered office

---

[1] This class includes most of the clerks in Washington, all postmasters, first and second class post-office clerks, railway mail clerks, letter carriers, rural free-delivery men, and employees in the Indian service, customs houses, revenue service, and the government printing office.

[2] Four years is the term for territorial judges and governors, marshals, district attorneys, customs collectors, and chiefs of many bureaus.

[3] The Constitution provides impeachment for removing civil officers, but to use this cumbersome method to remove a minor officer would be like shooting birds with artillery intended for battleships. Therefore in 1926 the United States Supreme Court sustained the right of the President to remove all civil officers appointed by the President except judges (Myers *v.* U. S.); and except quasi-legislative and quasi-judicial officers under a decision of 1935 (Humphrey's Executor *v.* U. S.). This latter decision grew out of President Roosevelt's attempt to remove a Federal Trade Commissioner on the ground that "the aims and purposes of the Administration with respect to the work of the Commission can be carried out most effectively with personnel of my own selection." The Supreme Court decided that the President can dismiss a Federal Trade Commissioner only for "inefficiency, neglect of duty, or malfeasance in office," as provided by Congress.

The President may dismiss army and navy officers in time of war; but in time of peace he dismisses them only in pursuance of a sentence of a general court-martial. He may drop an officer who has been absent from duty three months without leave. And he may, in certain cases, discharge for inefficiency on recommendation of a court of inquiry.

through competitive examinations may be removed or reduced for any cause which will promote the efficiency of the service; but the President is directed to impose like penalties for like offenses, and no political or religious discrimination is supposed to be shown.

Powers in Foreign Affairs. — In the field of foreign affairs the scope of the President's powers is well-nigh immeasurable. This is particularly evident in today's critical international situation.

Receiving Diplomatic Representatives. — The President receives ambassadors and ministers sent to the United States. Upon an appointed day the Secretary of State escorts a new minister or ambassador to the White House, where the latter delivers a short ceremonial address to which the President responds. The minister or ambassador is then recognized as the official organ of communication between the United States Government and the government represented. When the independence of a country is in doubt, or the representative is personally objectionable to the United States government, the President may refuse to receive him; and the President may request a foreign country to recall a representative, or dismiss one for conduct offensive to the Government. Recognition does not necessarily indicate favor of a particular regime; and the withdrawing or withholding of diplomatic recognition has been used on several occasions to indicate official United States displeasure.

Treaty Power. — If the United States desires to enter into commercial compacts, define its boundaries, make peace, or enter into any other compacts appropriate for international agreements, the President, with the assistance of the State Department, may negotiate a treaty with the other state or states concerned. Given Congressional approval, it is then signed by his representative, usually the Secretary of State. The Constitution provides that a vote of two thirds of the Senate present is necessary before the treaty may be signed by the President and become binding.[1]

---

[1] As a treaty is merely a law, Congress may repeal it by passing a law contrary to its provisions; or an existing law may be repealed by the terms of a treaty. In other words, when a treaty and a law of Congress conflict, a court will consider the one last enacted to be the law. A treaty which is contrary to the Constitution is void, but the courts have, as yet, never declared one to be contrary to the Constitution.

Money cannot be appropriated by a treaty, but in practice whenever the Senate has agreed to a treaty providing for the payment of money, the House has concurred on a bill appropriating it.

The small original Senate of twenty-six members was considered a suitable council to advise the President as to foreign relations. Secrecy was then considered necessary in debating foreign relations, and it was not believed that secrecy could be maintained in a group as large as the House; and the two-thirds requirement compensated the House for exclusion from treaty-making deliberations.

Turn the two-thirds rule around and it becomes a one-third rule. In other words, one third of the members plus one is all that is necessary to defeat a treaty — no matter how popular it might be with the people generally. Because of this, many have criticized the rule and suggested change to a simple majority.

John Hay, one of our greatest Secretaries of State, once remarked: "The irreparable mistake of our Constitution puts it into the power of one third plus one of the Senate to meet with a categorical veto any treaty negotiated by the President, even though it might have the hearty approval of nine tenths of the people of the nation."

After World War I, the Treaty of Versailles, which included the creation of the League

FORMER SECRETARY OF STATE BYRNES SIGNING PEACE TREATIES WITH AXIS SATELLITE NATIONS

of Nations, was rejected by our Senate even though 49 senators voted for it and only 35 against it. This was 7 votes short of the necessary two thirds. More than once, the President has been forced to bow to a small minority in the Senate in order to secure passage of a treaty — even when this involved concessions opposed by the majority.

On other occasions, Presidents have had to resort to round-about methods. When a Senate minority rejected a treaty to annex Texas, President Polk accomplished annexation by a *joint resolution* of both houses — a move which required only a majority in each. Hawaii was likewise annexed by a joint resolution after a treaty had failed.

Executive Agreements. — Agreements entered into with a foreign state do not always take the form of treaties. More and more, our international agreements, especially routine ones, are made as *executive agreements*. These agreements are concluded between the President and the chief executive of the foreign state or states involved — but do not require senatorial approval. Such agreements are some-

THE ARENA

"A treaty entering the Senate is like a bull going into the arena. No one can say just how or when the final blow will fall. But one thing is certain — it will never leave the arena alive." — John Hay, former Secretary of State.

times submitted, however, for approval (by simple majority) by *both houses* of Congress. But this is not the common practice — usually being done only when appropriations are needed to implement the agreement.

The Supreme Court has held executive agreements to be as legally binding as treaties, and a part of the supreme law of the land. Indeed, some argue that executive agreements can be used instead of treaties in any and all cases.

One of the most notable of executive agreements came in 1940.

Then, President Roosevelt gave 50 over-age destroyers to Great Britain in exchange for 99-year leases to several island bases extending from Newfoundland to South America.

Among the 1953 executive agreements was one providing for mutual military assistance between this country and the Dominican Republic.

The President's Military Powers. — The Constitution makes the President Commander-in-Chief of the Armed Forces. His military powers are shared with the Congress because that body makes rules for the governance of the Armed Forces, must appropriate the funds for defense as well as for all other purposes, and has the power to declare war. The Senate must confirm the appointments (commissions) of military officers.

But the President's position here is as dominant as in the related field of foreign affairs. He may literally force Congress to act. Thus, in 1907, President Theodore Roosevelt sent the Navy around the world in order that the men might gain experience and that other nations might be impressed with its strength. Some congressmen objected to the cost and threatened to withhold the necessary appropriation. Mr. Roosevelt is said to have replied: "Very well, the existing appropriation will carry the Navy half-way around the world and if Congress chooses to leave it on the other side, all right." President Polk brought on the Mexican War by ordering troops across the Nueces River, and President Truman, acting in support of the United Nations, sent elements of the Army, Navy, Marines, and Air Force to Korea in 1950.

The President directs campaigns and could take personal command of the Army or Navy if he wished. So long as he acts within the rules of international law he may do anything to weaken the power of the enemy. In the exercise of this power President Lincoln issued the Emancipation Proclamation during the Civil War, freeing the slaves in certain Southern States.

Whenever the enforcement of Federal laws is prevented by combinations too strong to be suppressed by the courts with their marshals, the President may send United States regular troops to protect the mails and interstate commerce, as Cleveland did in 1894 during the Pullman strike at Chicago; or he may call out State militia, as Roosevelt did in 1940. When the army occupies the enemy's territory, the President, as commander-in-chief, may assume control of the enemy government, as

President McKinley did in Puerto Rico and in the Philippines, or as Truman did in Japan, in a part of Germany, and elsewhere.

In case of domestic violence, the legislature of a State, or the governor, if the legislature is not in session, may request the President to send regular troops into the State to restore order.

President's Advisory Bodies. — *The National Security Council* advises the President in respect to the integration of domestic, foreign, and military policies relating to national security. The President is chairman, and the other members include the Vice-President, the Secretaries of State and Defense, the director of the Office of Defense Mobilization, and certain other officers, including the Secretaries of the Army, Navy, and Air Force, whom the President may choose to appoint with Senate consent. The Central Intelligence Agency, under the Council, makes recommendations to that body and correlates and evaluates security information from all branches of the Government.

The Office of Defense Mobilization was created by a presidential reorganization order in 1953. It is responsible for planning the emergency steps this nation must take in the event of war. For example, the Office has blueprinted a price and wage control program and, if such controls become necessary again, will administer them. The Office also has charge of stockpiling scarce strategic materials.

The Council of Economic Advisers assists the President in economic matters, and reports to him on the condition of the nation's economy.

President's Part in Legislation. — The President is primarily an executive officer, but the Constitution bestows upon him many powers which enable him to influence legislation.

 Presidential Messages. — When Congress meets in January, the President sends his annual message to Congress, and from time to time during the term he sends special messages. In these messages he recommends the enactment of certain laws. They may be laws which the platform pledged the party to enact, laws recommended by heads of the departments of administration, or possibly a personal hobby. Most presidents have had their messages read in each house by a clerk, but some presidents read their messages to the two houses assembled in one of the chambers. Different parts of the messages are referred to appropriate committees. Full reports from the heads of departments usually accompany the annual message. The consideration of the recommendations depends upon the influence of the President. The message is at least valuable to form public opinion. It is broadcast by television and radio, and newspapers usually publish it in full.

(2) *The Budget.*— When Congress meets, the President presents the annual budget with estimates of receipts and proposed expenditures. This is compiled from the requests of the spending agencies of the Government by the Director of the Budget whom the President appoints to head the Budget Bureau.

(3) *Extraordinary Sessions.* — A President may call an extra session of Congress whenever he deems it proper. For instance, in 1948 President Truman called an extra session to consider relief from high prices and to consider other social legislation. Special sessions were much more numerous before the adoption of the Twentieth ("Lame-Duck") Amendment in 1933 than they are today. On some forty occasions the Senate has been called alone to consider treaties.

The President may adjourn Congress only when the two houses cannot agree upon a date for adjournment. No President has yet had reason to exercise this power.

The Direction of Administration. — The President might be called the "Chief Administrator" as well as the Chief Executive. He heads the vast executive branch and is responsible for the execution and the administration of the laws passed by Congress.

Congress plays a part with the President in the control of the administrative agencies and the operations of the executive branch. All of the vast executive branch below the President and Vice-President has been created by Congressional action. Through investigations and its control of the purse strings, Congress exerts considerable influence on administration. And, of course, Congress is the policy-making branch of the Government.

(4) *Executive Ordinances.* — Congress makes the laws and the President is responsible for executing them. But in making laws, Congress sets out the broad policies to be followed and leaves the details of administration to the executive branch.

These details are spelled out by the President (or his subordinates acting for him) in the form of executive ordinances or orders. For example, the Immigration and Nationality Act of 1952 lists certain grounds upon which an alien may be refused admission to the United States. The procedures to be followed in examining immigrants and in actually determining which aliens are to be denied admission under the law must, for practical reasons, be established by the executive branch — specifically in this case by the Bureau of Immigration and Naturalization within the Department of Justice.   Reductions under the Tariff Reciprocity Acts are accomplished by executive orders, and many reforms urged by the Hoover Commission (page 191) have been brought about by executive ordinance.   The President issues these orders under constitutional or congressional authority.   They are printed in the daily Federal Register.

(5)   **The Veto.** — Every bill or joint resolution[1] passed by Congress must be presented to the President for his signature.   When a bill is presented to the President, he sends a copy of it to the administrative department that will have it to enforce, for an opinion.   If he signs, it becomes a law; if he disapproves, he must return the bill to the house which originated it, giving his reason for his veto (page 154).

The veto power enables the President, who is the only representative of *all* the people, to act as a check upon the legislative branch.   The President must sign or veto a bill in its entirety.   He cannot veto certain items in appropriations bills, as many governors may do.   If he could, needless and wasteful projects might be eliminated.   But, then, he might also use the "item veto" as a political weapon.

(6)   **Extra-Legal Methods.** — The President cannot introduce a bill into Congress;[2] but if he is party leader he co-operates with any committee of Congress that is preparing an important bill.   For instance, when the Currency Bill was being prepared during the summer of 1913, Congressman Glass, Chairman of the Banking and Currency Committee, was continually conferring with President Wilson, and relying upon his influence as party leader to secure the passage of the measure.

There are many indirect methods by which a President can persuade congressmen to support his measures.   Abraham Lincoln allowed a congressman to name the appointee to a $20,000 position in the Custom House of New York in consideration of a vote which was necessary to admit Nevada into the Union, for without Nevada's vote the Thirteenth Amendment to the Constitution of the United States could not

---

[1] Joint resolutions proposing amendments to the Constitution are not sent to the President.   This is the only exception.

[2] At least one bill sent to the Speaker of the House by Franklin Roosevelt was referred to a committee without bearing the name of a Congressman.   But this is unusual.

Coolegeges White House Brefasts

have been ratified. Presidents often withhold appointments until important bills are passed by congressmen who wish appointment for self or friend. In 1938 Franklin Roosevelt unsuccessfully "took the stump" against congressmen who had not supported his measures.

Pardoning Power. — The pardoning power of the President is absolute for all offenses against the United States, except in cases of impeachment, where a pardon may never be granted. Of course he cannot pardon offenses against State laws; but for crimes committed in territories or the District of Columbia, or offenses against Federal laws such as the postal, revenue, or banking laws, the accused may be pardoned either before or after conviction.

If an individual is involved, a pardon is seldom granted before conviction. But in 1889 President Harrison issued a proclamation known as *amnesty*, which pardoned the Mormons who had violated the antipolygamy laws applying to the territories of the United States. The President may pardon conditionally provided the condition is reasonable, or he may *commute* a sentence by decreasing the penalty. He may reduce a fine or cancel it before it is paid.

A central Board of Parole, created by Congress in 1930, has authority to release Federal prisoners on parole with the assent of the Attorney-General.

Independence of the President. — The President, as head of one of the three branches of government, must have a degree of independence of the other two branches, else he would not remain a check upon them. So long as the President is in office — and he may be removed only by impeachment — he may not be arrested. But as soon as he is out of office he may be punished for any crime committed by him while in office. The courts can neither restrain nor compel him to perform any act. When Aaron Burr was being tried for treason, Chief Justice Marshall issued a subpoena requiring President Jefferson to produce a certain paper relating to Burr's acts. Jefferson refused to obey. He reasoned that the duties of a President could not be performed if he could be compelled to obey court writs.

THE VICE-PRESIDENT

The Vice-President is elected by the same electors and in the same manner as the President, except that when no Vice-Presidential candidate receives a majority of the electoral votes the Vice-President is chosen by the Senate from the two candidates receiving the highest number of electoral votes.

The qualifications for the Vice-President are the same as for the President because he succeeds to the Presidency in case of the death or disability of the President. His salary is $30,000 a year plus $10,000 for "personal expenses." His only Constitutional duty, unless he succeeds to the Presidency, is to preside over the Senate. As he is not a member of the Senate, does not appoint standing committees, and has no vote except in case of a tie, he usually has little influence.

Sometimes a candidate for the Vice-Presidency may be nominated to carry a doubtful State, to appease a defeated faction in the nominating convention, to replenish the party treasury, or to reward a faithful party worker.

Upon being elected to the Vice-Presidency in 1796 Thomas Jefferson wrote: "It will give me philosophical evenings in the winter and rural days in the summer. The second office of the Government is honorable and easy." The office has been criticized throughout our history; yet it is not right to call the Vice-President the "spare tire."

It has often been suggested that the Vice-President be given more responsibility in the executive branch. In this manner he would be more aware of the problems of the office should the President die. Too, he could be used to relieve the President of some of the heavy burden of the office. Usually the Vice-President is a man with years of legislative experience; as such, he is often a very valuable link between the two branches.

THE CABINET

In order that the President may have assistance in executing the laws, Congress has authorized him to appoint ten chiefs.[1] Washington was authorized to appoint only three: a Secretary of State, a Secretary of the Treasury, and a Secretary of War.[2] As governmental duties increased, however, the work of administration was further divided and Congress created new departments with secretaries. There are now ten chief assistants:

---

[1] The statutes creating these offices provide for the assent of the Senate, but in practice the Senate seldom interferes with the President's choice.

[2] The Attorney-General was also considered a member of Washington's Cabinet, but he was not the head of a department until 1870.

NAME OF OFFICE	OFFICE CREATED IN
1. The Secretary of State	1789
2. The Secretary of the Treasury	1789
3. The Secretary of Defense	1947
a. Secretary of War[1]	1789
b. Secretary of Navy[1]	1798
c. Secretary of the Air Force[1]	1947
4. The Attorney-General	1789
5. The Postmaster-General	1794
6. The Secretary of the Interior	1849
7. The Secretary of Agriculture	1889
8. The Secretary of Commerce	1903
9. The Secretary of Labor	1913
10. The Secretary of Health, Education and Welfare	1953

These ten secretaries are appointed by the President for indefinite terms, and as he alone is responsible for the official action of any secre-

OUR FIRST PRESIDENT AND HIS FIRST CABINET

The group is small by comparison with today's Cabinet. For his first advisers Washington had (left to right) Henry Knox, Secretary of War; Thomas Jefferson, Secretary of State; Edmund Randolph, Attorney-General; and Alexander Hamilton, Secretary of the Treasury.

---

[1] Now Secretaries of the Army, Navy, and Air Force, respectively, are without Cabinet rank; and under a 1949 Act of Congress must be civilians.

tary he may dismiss him at any time. A new President always selects some new Cabinet officers, and a President of a different party from his predecessor selects an entirely new Cabinet. The Cabinet meets twice a week, or as often as the President desires, in the executive offices, which adjoin the White House. Although the meetings are secret, officials may attend by invitation. The President meets the chiefs of each executive department alone to discuss the less important affairs, and he meets advisory groups for special matters.

There is no provision for the Cabinet either in the Constitution or in the Statutes of Congress. The Constitution says, "The President may require the opinion in writing of the principal officers in each of the executive departments upon any subject relating to the duties of their respective offices." (Art. II, Sec. 2.) At first Washington requested written opinions, but by his second term he held secret meetings, which were called "cabinet meetings."

The President is not compelled to take the advice of the Cabinet contrary to his own judgment. This is illustrated by an incident told of President Lincoln. He brought before his Cabinet a proposition which he favored, but every member of his Cabinet voted against it. He announced the vote, "Seven nays, one aye; the ayes have it."

OUTLINE FOR REVIEW

The Executive Department

I. PRESIDENT.

    (A) Qualifications:
- (1) Natural born citizen of the United States.
- (2) Thirty-five years of age.
- (3) Fourteen years a resident of the United States.

    (B) Elected:
- (1) By Electoral College, or
- (2) By House of Representatives.

    (C) Oath: Taken when inaugurated.

    (D) Term: Four years.

    (E) Vacancy:
- (1) Filled by Vice-President, or
- (2) By Speaker of the House or by President *pro tem* of the Senate, according to law of succession.

(F) Salary: (1) $100,000 + $50,000 "expenses" and allowances for traveling and official entertainment.

   (2) White House, servants, autos, etc.

(G) Powers and Duties: (1) Executes the laws of the nation.

   (2) Appoints ambassadors, consuls, judges, postmasters, and other officers.

   (3) May remove officers and fill vacancies.

   (4) Receives foreign ministers, etc.

   (5) May make treaties with consent of two thirds of Senate.

   (6) Commander-in-chief of the Army, Navy, and Air Force.

   (7) Delivers a message to Congress each January and at other times.

   (8) May call special session of Congress or of either House.

   (9) Signs or vetoes bills passed by Congress.

   (10) May grant reprieves and pardons.

(H) Removal: (1) May be impeached by majority of House.

   (2) May be tried and convicted by two thirds of Senate.

II. VICE-PRESIDENT.

(A) Qualifications: The same as required for the President.

(B) Elected: (1) By the Electoral College, or

   (2) By the Senate.

(C) Term: Four years.

(D) Vacancy: Not filled until next presidential election.

(E) Salary: $30,000 + $10,000 "expenses."

(F) Duty: Presides over Senate and votes only in case of tie. Becomes President if President dies or is in any way disqualified.

III. CABINET MEMBERS (nonofficial).

(A) Qualifications:	None prescribed.
(B) Appointed:	By President, with consent of Senate.
(C) Term:	Indefinite.
(D) Salary:	$22,500.
(E) Duty:	To advise President and administer their respective departments according to the will of the President and statutes.

REORGANIZATION OF THE EXECUTIVE BRANCH

Beginning with President Taft in 1911, every President has asked Congress to grant him authority to reorganize the Executive Branch. The need for such reorganization became especially acute with the rapid expansion of the Government in the 1930's. It became even more acute with the tremendous expansion brought on by World War II.

The First Hoover Commission. — Congress made some attempts to meet the problem (especially with the Reorganization Act of 1939), but little concrete progress was made up to 1947. In that year Congress created the Commission on Organization of the Executive Branch of the Government. Its purpose was to study the organization of the Executive Branch and to recommend ways in which waste and inefficiency could be eliminated and efficiency and economy could be secured.

This "Hoover Commission" (named for its chairman, former President Herbert Hoover) worked through twenty-four "task forces" employing some 300 of the nation's ablest authorities in the various fields of governmental activity. It took a year and a half to complete the job.

Some indication of the problems the Commission faced can be seen in the fact that it found that there were 1,816 component parts of the Executive Branch, employing well over 2,000,000 people in 9 departments, 104 bureaus, 12 sections, 108 services, 51 branches, 460 offices, 631 divisions, 19 administrations, 6 agencies, 16 areas, 40 boards, 6 commands, 20 commissions, 19 corporations, 5 groups, 10 headquarters, 20 units, 3 authorities, and 263 miscellaneous parts.

The Underwood Tariff

Contrary to party pledge

WILSON

ADMINISTRATION

President sent a message

The Senate decided to go

along with the house

The Commission found that it could not even be certain just how many agencies reported directly to the President, but that there were at least 65. Obviously, no President could handle so many sub-ordinates adequately — even if he spent only one hour a week on each and neglected all his other duties.

In 1949 the Hoover Commission reported to Congress. Its studies revealed a vast amount of waste, duplication, confusion, and in-efficiency — arising from causes within the Executive Branch, from the haphazard way in which Congress had created the various agencies, and from the greatly expanded functions of the National Government. As typical examples of duplication, the Commission found 75 agencies dealing in the field of transportation, 93 in govern-ment lending, 37 in foreign trade, and 64 in business relations.

The Reorganization Act of 1949 gave the President authority to reorganize the Executive Branch provided neither house of Congress rejects his plans within 60 days. So far, about three-fourths of the Hoover recommendations have become fact, some by executive orders not rejected within the statutory 60 days, some by direct Congressional legislation. Most of the Executive Branch has been reorganized at least to some extent, but much remains to be done.

The Second Hoover Commission was created by Congress in 1953 and the President's powers were extended under the 1949 Act until April, 1955. The new Commission is carrying on from where its predecessor stopped.

QUESTIONS ON THE TEXT

1. Explain in detail how the President is elected.
2. What are the qualifications for the presidency? Compensation?
3. What is the term of office? May he succeed himself?
4. Explain the President's powers of appointment and removal.
5. Who makes treaties? If a treaty and statute conflict, which will the courts enforce? Who appoints diplomatic officers? Receives them?
6. What are the President's powers as Commander-in-Chief?
7. Explain the President's power over legislation by means of messages; special sessions; ordinances; the veto; informal methods.
8. What is the President's pardoning power?
9. Can a court compel the President to perform a duty? Can he be punished after he is out of office for a crime committed while in office?

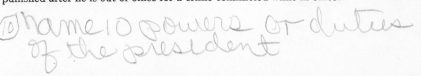

10. How is the Vice-President chosen? Term? Qualifications? Salary?
Duties?

11. Name the Cabinet offices. Term? Salary?

PROBLEMS FOR DISCUSSION

1. What Article of the Constitution treats of the President?

2. Explain how Mr. Harrison was elected President in 1888 although
Mr. Cleveland received more popular votes.

3. Following the Presidential election of 1912 the House had a majority
of Democrats from 24 States and a majority of Republicans from 24 States.
Had the election been thrown into the House as was probable because of
the three candidates, what would have happened?

4. Would a State with a large population or one with a small population
gain influence by the popular direct election of the President? Would you
vote *for* or *against* it if you lived in Nevada? In New York?

5. Would the popular direct election of the President be an incentive for
honest or dishonest elections in a one-party State? In the direct election every
vote would count. Would it be to the advantage of urban or rural States?

6. How could the President's term be increased to six years?

7. Enlarge on the following statement: "The Presidency involves the
most grinding administrative work in the world. Every major decision,
every major squabble comes inexorably to the big Presidential desk. Whenever that desk gets cluttered up, trouble ensues. The man who sits at that
desk cannot pass the time of day swapping stories, snatching catnaps,
whittling sticks or dreaming mystical dreams. It is a place for decisiveness,
clear thinking, efficiency and dispatch." — Raymond Moley. *27 Masters of
Politics*, page 82. Funk & Wagnalls. New York. 1949.

8. Name five characteristics that a President should have.

9. What Federal officers or employees reside or have duties in your city
or county? How are they appointed?

SELECT BIBLIOGRAPHY

HEALY, P. "Busiest Vice-President We Ever Had!" *Saturday Evening
Post*. September 19, 1953.

OGG, F. A., AND RAY, P. O. *Essentials of American Government*. Appleton-
Century-Crofts. New York. 1952 ed. Chs. 17, 19, 20, 21, 31, 33.

STEVENSON, ADLAI. "A Candidate's Story." *Life*. March 2, 1953.

STIMPSON, G. "What You *Don't* Know About Our Presidents." *Collier's*.
March 8, 1952, page 24.

"The Presidency." *Current History*. September, 1953. (Entire issue.)

TROUT, R. "Conventions: Party Time for Politicians." *Collier's*. July 12,
1952, page 20.

CHAPTER XI

THE DEPARTMENT OF STATE

ORGANIZATION AND FUNCTIONS

What the State Department Does. — The President is primarily responsible for the conduct of American foreign relations; but he cannot do the job single-handed. The Department of State is his "right-hand" in the conduct of foreign affairs.

The Secretary of State, appointed by the President and Senate, ranks first among the Cabinet officers because the improper handling of foreign affairs may lead to war.

Several Secretaries of State later became President: Jefferson, Madison, Monroe, John Quincy Adams, Van Buren, and Buchanan. Recent Secretaries have been Cordell Hull (1933-1944), Stettinius (1944-1945), Byrnes (1945-1947), Marshall (1947-1949), Acheson (1949-1953), John Foster Dulles (1953-   ).

Some presidents entrust foreign affairs largely to the Secretary of State, while others take foreign affairs into their own hands.

The duties of the Secretary of State are partly connected with domestic affairs, but to a much greater extent with foreign affairs.

Domestic Duties of the Secretary. — The Secretary attends to all correspondence between the President and the governors of the several States. Thus, if the President calls for a State's national guard for war, or if a governor requests the extradition [1] of a criminal who has taken refuge in a foreign country, the correspondence takes place

---

[1] Extradition means the handing over by one State to another of fugitives from justice. The United States has extradition treaties with the leading nations of the world. When a person accused of crime flees from an American State to a foreign country, the governor of the State applies to the Secretary of State for the return of the fugitive, furnishing evidence of probable guilt. The governor also names a person who will go for the fugitive. The proper papers are sent to our diplomatic representative, and he is instructed to request the extradition of the fugitive. The "President's Warrant" is given the agent whom the governor has designated to bring back the accused. Frequently an application is made by telegraph for the provisional arrest and detention of the fugitive in advance of the presentation of formal evidence.

through the Secretary of State. He also affixes the Great Seal of the United States to all commissions, executive proclamations, and warrants for extradition. Many of his former domestic functions have now been transferred to the Archivist of the United States.

THE NEW STATE DEPARTMENT BUILDING © *Harris & Ewing*

The Foreign Duties of the Secretary. — He is the President's chief aid in the conduct of American foreign relations and the "caretaker" of American interests abroad. Merely to mention such matters as Korea, Berlin and West Germany, the United Nations, the North Atlantic Treaty Organization (NATO), threats of international aggression, the seething and oil-rich Middle East, foreign economic and military aid, international control of atomic energy, the Point IV policy (aid to backward areas of the world), hemispheric solidarity and the Good Neighbor Policy, the protection of American property abroad, aid and advice to American importers and exporters, passports and visas, shipping, and tariffs, is to suggest the wide range of activities and interests of the Department of State.

Departmental Organization. — The Secretary's chief assistant and principal adviser is the Under Secretary of State, who takes over as Acting Secretary of State in the absence of the Secretary. One Deputy Under Secretary is the Under Secretary's principal aide; the other supervises the internal administration of the Department and the Foreign Service. The Counsellor, who ranks as an Assistant Secretary, is an intimate adviser to the Secretary.

Eight Assistant Secretaries are responsible for particular areas of departmental action: United Nations Affairs; Economic Affairs; Inter-American Affairs; European Affairs; Near East, South Asian, and African Affairs; Far Eastern Affairs; Public Affairs; and Congressional Relations. The Legal Adviser, who corresponds in rank with the Assistant Secretaries, handles departmental and Foreign Service legal matters.

The major officers of the Department constitute the Policy Planning Staff to assist the Secretary in the formulation of long-range policies. Under the Assistant Secretaries there are several "Offices," such as the Office of Chinese Affairs under the Assistant Secretary for Far Eastern Affairs. Each of the Offices is in turn divided into "Divisions," as the Division of Historical Policy Research in the Office of Public Affairs.

It is to this organizational structure that our diplomatic agents abroad must look for instructions and information. And it is here that (with the President) the heavy responsibilities for formulating and implementing our foreign policy belong.

The Foreign Service. — The Foreign Service of the United States represents this nation abroad. Included within its ranks are positions ranging from that of ambassador down to the lowliest alien clerk or employee in some distant outpost.

Under international law every nation has the "right of legation" (the sending and receiving of diplomatic representatives); and the severing of diplomatic relations is usually a step towards war. We send such representatives to nearly all states, and most states have representatives in Washington. The practice is ancient, history indicating that the Egyptians followed it over 6000 years ago. Benjamin Franklin is said to have been our first professional Foreign Service officer, having been elected Minister to France by the Continental Congress in 1778.

Ambassadors are sent to most foreign capitals and ministers to some of the lesser ones.[1]

---

[1] The exact titles are *Ambassador Extraordinary and Plenipotentiary* or *Envoy Extraordinary and Minister Plenipotentiary*.

When there is a vacancy in the office of ambassador or minister, or during his

Ambassadors are appointed by the President with the consent of the Senate, and they serve "at his pleasure." In the past many of them were retired business men with inadequate knowledge of foreign affairs — mere amateur diplomats. Today more than half of our ministers have risen through the ranks of the Foreign Service, and many ambassadors are now being promoted from that Service.

The term of office of an ambassador is not prescribed by law; hence there are numerous changes whenever a new party comes into power, as an ambassadorship is considered a much-to-be-desired political plum. There are no prescribed qualifications, though it is an advantage to know the language and history of the country to which an ambassador goes. Both Presidents Roosevelt and Truman appointed women as ministers, and the latter appointed the first woman ambassador as envoy to Denmark.

The chief executive to whom the ambassador is accredited may refuse to receive in a diplomatic way any person who is for any reason objectionable (*persona non grata*). In order to avoid unpleasant occurrences of this kind, our State Department makes a practice of inquiring beforehand as to the acceptability of the person we propose sending. Any country may demand the recall of an ambassador who is obnoxious to it. When war breaks out between two countries, the ambassadors and their staffs are given safe conduct home, though other "alien enemies" may be detained.

The duties of an ambassador are to (1) transmit official communications; (2) give information to foreigners concerning American institutions, laws, and customs; (3) keep his government advised of the progress of events in the country where he lives; (4) protect American citizens; (5) negotiate treaties and other agreements if requested to do so by the President; and (6) promote American interests in every way.[1]

---

absence, the position is usually filled by a secretary of the embassy or legation. This officer temporarily in charge of his country's affairs is called *chargé d'affaires*.

[1] The following extracts from a letter written by Walter H. Page, when he was ambassador to Great Britain, give us a close-up view of the daily routine of an ambassador·

If you think it's all play, you fool yourself; I mean this job. There's no end of the work. It consists of these parts: Receiving people for two hours every day, some on some sort of business, some merely to "pay respects"; attending to a large (and exceedingly miscellaneous) mail; going to the Foreign Office on all sorts of errands; looking up the oddest sort of information that you ever heard of; making reports to Washington on all sorts of things; then the so-called social duties —

To perform these duties efficiently the ambassador must be on terms of friendly intimacy with leading men in the country to which he is sent. Newspaper editors in particular may be most helpful.

THE AMBASSADOR AND THE PRIME MINISTER MEET

Here at the home of Bernard Baruch, Winthrop W. Aldrich, our Ambassador to Britain, talks with Secretary of State John Foster Dulles, Prime Minister Winston Churchill, and Mr. Baruch.

Ambassadors, and their families and servants to a great extent, are exempt from arrest and from taxation of personal belongings. Within their embassies (official residence) they may do within reason anything

---

giving dinners, receptions, etc., and attending them. I hear the most important news I get at so-called social functions. Then the court functions; and the meetings and speeches! The American Ambassador must go all over England and explain every American thing. You'd never recover from the shock if you could hear me speaking about Education, Agriculture, the observance of Christmas, the Navy, the Anglo-Saxon, Mexico, the Monroe Doctrine, Co-education, Woman Suffrage, Medicine, Law, Radio-Activity, Flying, the Supreme Court, the President as a Man of Letters, the Hookworm, the Negro — just get down the Encyclopædia and continue the list!

I forgot, there are a dozen other kinds of activities, such as American marriages, which they always want the Ambassador to attend; getting them out of jail when

not prohibited by the laws of the nation which has sent them. These privileges are associated with a legal fiction known as *exterritoriality*, which term means that the ambassador has carried a portion of the territory of his home country with its laws to the foreign country.

Special Diplomats. — Besides the men regularly stationed in major foreign capitals, there is one Ambassador-at-Large who acts as a sort of "international trouble-shooter" for the Secretary. On various occasions, men are appointed to the *personal* rank of ambassador to undertake special assignments. The chief American delegates to the United Nations also rank as ambassadors.

Ministers are sent to the governments of the less important countries. Ministers are officially outranked by ambassadors, and the official residence is called a legation. Today the United States is gradually elevating most of its legations to embassies as a gesture of international friendship and co-operation.

Until recently, *Chiefs of Missions* (Ambassadors or Ministers) received salaries much smaller than those paid by other great nations. It was impossible for someone without a private fortune to represent us, for example, in London. But the salaries now range from $15,000 to $25,000 plus liberal allowances.

---

they are jugged (I have an American woman on my hands now, whose four children come to see me every day); looking after the American insane; helping Americans move the bones of their ancestors; interpreting the income-tax law; receiving medals for Americans; hearing American fiddlers, pianists, players; sitting for American sculptors and photographers; sending telegrams for property owners in Mexico; reading letters from thousands of people who have shares in estates here; writing letters of introduction; getting tickets to the House Gallery; getting seats in the Abbey; going with people to this, that and t'other; getting tickets to the races, the art-galleries, the House of Lords; answering fool questions about the United States put by Englishmen. With a military attaché, a naval attaché, three secretaries, a private secretary, two automobiles, Alice's private secretary, a veterinarian, an immigration agent, consuls everywhere, a despatch agent, lawyers, doctors, messengers — they keep us all busy. A woman turned up dying the other day. I sent for a big doctor. She got well. As if that wasn't enough, both the woman and the doctor had to come and thank me (fifteen minutes each). Then each wrote a letter!

Then there are . . . Rhodes Scholars from Oxford . . . women who wish to go to court . . . Negroes from Liberia . . . passports, passports to sign . . . opera singers going to the United States; artists who have painted some American portraits, — don't you see?

(*Life and Letters of Walter Hines Page,* Vol. I, page 159.)

Assistants. — At most embassies and at some legations there is a counselor who gives technical advice in matters of international law and diplomatic practice. Embassies and legations have technical experts, secretaries, clerks, and interpreters. The more responsible of these are drawn from the Foreign Service of the United States, but some are alien employees recruited on the scene. Most embassies and legations have one or more military attachés assigned from the Army Department, and in those nations which are naval powers, there are naval attachés assigned from the Navy Department. These attachés and those from other departments, as from the Commerce Department, are subject to the orders of their own departments.

Let us take a military attaché to illustrate the duties performed by a departmental attaché. He is military adviser to the ambassador or minister, he collects military information on the military situation in the country to which he is accredited, he is constantly on the alert for new ideas which can be applied to his own army, and he makes confidential reports, through secret diplomatic mail bags, to the Army Department where Information Digests of world conditions are kept.

While ambassadors and ministers are sometimes political appointees of the President, more than ten thousand highly trained career men assist these diplomats and man the consulates. It is from this group of Foreign Service officers that the candidates for the top positions are increasingly being drawn. Many are now serving as ambassadors and ministers. Entrance examinations for the Foreign Service are difficult, but promotion is on the merit basis. Salaries range as high as $13,500, plus generous allowances, leaves, and contributory retirement and disability annuities.

It might be added that the diplomatic staffs of the Great Powers have increased in size because secret service work and propaganda have been carried on under the protection of diplomatic immunity.

Consular Service. — The Consular Service is a part of the Foreign Service. Its agents are appointed by the President, with the consent of the Senate, from those who have passed civil service examinations. They are commercial agents, or "America's lookouts on the watchtowers of international trade." The United States maintains some two hundred consular offices in cities through the world.

Consular Duties. — Consuls perform a great variety of duties, primarily commercial in nature. Their chief task lies in the promotion of American trade and commerce abroad by discovering new promised lands of commercial opportunity. They answer inquiries addressed to them by American exporters and importers, and send reports regarding foreign markets for American products to the State Department.[1] This information includes the special demands of local markets due to prevailing customs or prejudices or to unusual shortage of crops; includes changes in foreign laws bearing on commerce, such as customs regulations, patent laws, and food laws; and includes foreign methods of doing business.

Consuls also enforce customs regulations of the United States, assist in excluding prohibited classes of immigrants, and aid stranded or wrecked vessels and shipwrecked American seamen. They visa (approve) passports for aliens coming to the United States, and some may issue passports to Americans abroad. They assist American citizens in legal transactions of all sorts, taking oaths and depositions, and even acting as witnesses to marriages.

Consular Jurisdiction. — The consul has some jurisdiction over whatever relates to the internal economy of American vessels. He settles disputes among masters, officers, and men.

Consular officials are not entitled to diplomatic immunity, but treaties usually exempt them from arrest in civil cases and also guarantee the protection of their archives. An American consulate in a weak state is a fairly safe place in times of disturbances. An embassy or legation is almost always a place of safety (*asylum*).

Foreign Service Institute. — In 1946 Congress established the Foreign Service Institute to provide further training for the Service officers. This has tended to break down the "old school" concept of diplomacy. For instance, Ambassador Dodd had to contend with the stiff formalities of his staff in Berlin. They wanted him to travel by special train, and not in his own Chevrolet; they could not see why it was necessary for him to be in his office at nine o'clock rather than coming leisurely in at noon; and they thought he should pretend to admire Nazism.

---

[1] The weekly Commerce Report is published by the Bureau of Foreign and Domestic Commerce for American producers who subscribe for it. Items like the following are published in it:

No. 16363. Agency wanted for spark plugs for airplanes. Madrid.

(Names are not published because foreign competitors might use them.)

Passports. — The Passports Division regulates the issuance of passports, and determines questions relating to the citizenship of Americans in foreign countries. A passport is a certificate used to identify a citizen of one country when traveling or residing in another country, in order that the citizen may enjoy all the privileges that international law, treaties, or the prestige of his native country can insure.

An American citizen who desires to travel abroad may make a written application [1] to the Secretary of State for a passport. The application contains a detailed description of the person and information as to his age, residence, and occupation. It must be signed by the person applying, and an affidavit must be attested by a clerk of a Federal court, or any State court which has the authority to naturalize aliens (see page 252). It must be accompanied by a certificate from a creditable witness that the applicant is the person he professes to be, by two photographs, and by a $9 fee (clerk's fee $1 additional). A passport is valid for two years and may be renewed by an American consul for two more years.

In certain cities State Department agents perform passport duties, and in emergencies procure passports without delay.

A passport for most countries must be visaed (approved) by a consul of the country to be visited, and a fee is usually charged.

The Emergency Fund for the State Department, which has been greatly expanded in the last few years, is one of the few administration funds for which no original accounts or vouchers to the Treasury Department are required. The Secretary of State gives a certificate of such expenditure. This fund enables the President and Secretary of State to meet unforeseen emergencies in the diplomatic and consular service, to track aliens or citizens under suspicion, and to keep a watch on other countries through secret agents. It can also be used for entertaining distinguished guests.

Reciprocal Tariff Agreements Negotiated by the State Department. *Introduction.* — During the First World War, we exported commodities worth fifteen billion dollars more than those that we imported; and between that war and the panic of 1929 Americans lent ten billion

---

[1] A blank form may be obtained from the Secretary of State or from the clerks of Federal courts, or of State courts which attest passports.

dollars to the outside world.   The only way they could have paid us
all of this debt was in goods.   This was made impossible by the high

①

TRADE IS A TWO-WAY PROPOSITION

②

IF WE DON'T BUY FOREIGN PRODUCTS

③

FOREIGNERS WILL HAVE NO DOLLARS TO BUY OUR PRODUCTS

④

AND EVERYONE WILL HAVE TO CUT DOWN HIS PRODUCTION

Courtesy Graphics Associates for Public Affairs

THE ABC OF FOREIGN TRADE

tariff of 1930.   They had to stop
buying, and our exports fell from
more than five billions in 1929 to
less than two billions in 1932.

Tariff Reciprocity Act of 1934.
— Even if our high tariff was
interfering with foreign trade, a
sudden reduction would have
injured our protected industries,
because laborers in many countries work longer hours for less
pay. Also foreign countries were
raising their tariff walls against
our goods.

Congress therefore took a middle ground. It authorized the
President to lower our tariff as
much as 50 per cent on certain
commodities for any country
that would reduce its tariff on
a similar amount of commodities
that we want to sell to them.

The State Department, acting for the President, entered tariff-reduc-
tion agreements with 20-odd countries.   In 1945 Congress authorized
the President to cut these new rates (or any rates existing in 1945) by
as much as one half again for reciprocal concessions, making possible
a maximum cut of 75% of the rates in the Tariff Act of 1930.

Importance of Foreign Trade. — Each country exports the things
of which it has a surplus, or those commodities which it can make best
and cheapest. This exchange results in more necessities, comforts,
and luxuries for all nations; and when people have plenty they are
less likely to go to war.

AMERICAN FOREIGN POLICIES AND PROBLEMS

Our Foreign Policy of the Past. — Until recent years, American
foreign policy was characterized by its unconcern for other nations

and their problems. This "policy of isolationism," as it has been called, dates from Washington's administration and found expression in the Monroe Doctrine.

The Monroe Doctrine opposes any non-American encroachment upon the independence of American nations. President Monroe announced it in his message to Congress in 1823. It is not a law. Rather it is a self-defense policy used by our Presidents, and backed by public opinion, and by the British navy until we had a powerful fleet of our own. In addition to the sympathetic interest in the young South American republics, we wanted to keep powerful monarchs or dictators out of our neighboring countries; and the British as well as we wanted to keep the American republics independent in order to share their lucrative trade that Spain had formerly monopolized.

At first most Latin Americans did not pay much attention to the Monroe Doctrine. They knew that it was the British fleet and not the paper pronouncement of Monroe that protected them. Later they considered it a selfish doctrine: that Monroe was not primarily concerned with preserving Latin-American independence, but was concerned about protecting the United States. Theodore Roosevelt's imperialism and Taft's "dollar diplomacy" embittered them; but Franklin Roosevelt's "good-neighbor policy" won them for a policy of hemispheric solidarity and co-operation against the dictators of his day.

The Good-Neighbor Policy. — President Hoover withdrew the Marines from Nicaragua, and acted as a good neighbor to Latin America. Franklin Roosevelt withdrew the Marines from Haiti; terminated the hated Platt Amendment which had imposed restrictions on Cuba and had offended the other Latin-American nations; negotiated a more equitable treaty with Panama; ended the long-standing Dominican customs receivership; and coined the phrase, "Good-Neighbor Policy." Because of this friendliness, nearly all the Latin-American countries favored the Allies in the Second World War, and our investment in friendship paid enormous dividends of good will and co-operation during the war.

Two World Wars. — Germany's submarine campaign against American shipping forced the United States out of its isolationist cocoon in 1917. We entered the First World War to "make the world safe for democracy." But, after the defeat of Germany and the Central Powers, we returned to our former isolationist policy. Europe's problems and those of the rest of the world, we thought, were no concern of ours.

The rise of Mussolini in Italy, of Hitler in Germany, and of the militarists in Japan cast a dark cloud on the horizon. But in the twenty years between wars we continued to try to remain aloof from Europe's "internal problems." It took the coming of the Second World War in 1939 to awaken us to the fallacies of isolationism. We

MUTUAL SECURITY AT WORK

Wide World Photos

Specially wrapped for shipment abroad, these speedy U. S. fighter jets are moving through a Copenhagen street on their way to a Danish airfield.

know now that we cannot, if we wanted to, shut ourselves away from the rest of the world.

Most Americans were pro-Ally at the start of World War II, but our policy was to stay out of the war if at all possible. While the Government assumed an official position of neutrality, we aided the Allies through such policies as the Lend-Lease Act. Under that act the President was authorized to "sell, transfer title to, exchange, lease, lend, or otherwise dispose of defense articles" to the government of any country vital to our own security.

With the sudden Japanese attack on Pearl Harbor, December 7, 1941, all thoughts of neutrality vanished. From then until World War II ended in 1945, the United States fought side-by-side with her United Nations allies in Europe and the Pacific. American armed forces fought and defeated the Axis Powers, Germany, Italy, and Japan, on battlefronts around the world. And the United States was also the arsenal of democracy. Through Lend-Lease we gave nearly $50,000,000,000 in food, munitions, planes, tanks, and other vital war supplies to our allies.

American Foreign Policy Today is intended (as it has always been) to insure the freedom and security of the United States. It is directed toward the preventing of a Third World War and toward the forging of a lasting peace out of today's troubled world.

Peace through Collective Security and the United Nations. — We live in "one world" in the sense that no nation can live in peace and prosperity while others are at war or in want. Hence, so-called collective security, that is the preserving of international order through united efforts of free nations, has become a cornerstone in our foreign policy. Thus at the end of World War II we helped to form the United Nations to "save succeeding generations from the scourge of war . . . and to maintain international peace and security." Today we support and work through the UN because, as President Eisenhower has said, it is "the living sign of all people's hope for peace."

Resistance to Communist Aggression is another pillar of American policy. Since the end of World War II the Soviet Union has brought more than 500,000,000 people and 7,500,000 square miles of territory under its control. Today the U.S.S.R. and international communism present a serious threat to the free world. The President stated clearly the basic reason for our opposition to communism when he said in his inaugural address: "Americans, indeed all free men, remember that in the final choice a soldier's pack is not so heavy a burden as a prisoner's chains."

Foreign Aid to our friends abroad is another vital part of our foreign policy. Since the end of World War II we have given nearly $50,000,000,000 in economic and military aid to other nations. At first this aid was primarily economic. Under the Marshall Plan we sent food, fuel, farm machinery, and the like to help rebuild war-devastated nations. Now because of the successes achieved through economic aid, we are concentrating on military aid.   For example, over 90 per cent of American aid for 1954 is military.   Still, economic aid is important.   Thus in 1953 we sent 1,000,000 tons of wheat to relieve famine in Pakistan and, over Russian objections, $15,000,000 in foodstuffs to feed the hungry of East Germany.   The Point IV Program is another form of economic aid.   Under it we are providing technical, industrial, and scientific "know-how" to underdeveloped and backward areas of the world.   In this way we are helping people to help themselves to produce more and better food, clothing, and shelter, and to develop their own natural and industrial resources.

Regional Security Treaties help to spell out collective security and our resistance to communism.   They are based on the realization that distance and the oceans are no longer guarantees against foreign attack.   Atomic and hydrogen bombs and other modern weapons of mass destruction have pushed our defensive frontiers to the far corners of the earth.   Because of this the United States has concluded six "regional security" treaties with 37 nations.   Each of these is defensive in nature.   They pledge the parties to aid one another in case of attack.   The objective of each treaty is clear — security for us and for the rest of the free world.   And each bolsters and implements the UN Charter and the principle of collective security.

(1) *The North Atlantic Treaty*, signed in 1949, now includes the United States, Canada, Great Britain, France, Italy, Portugal, Belgium, the Netherlands, Luxembourg, Denmark, Norway, Iceland, Greece, and Turkey.   The member nations have agreed that "an armed attack against one or more of them in Europe or North America shall be considered an attack against them all."   The North Atlantic Treaty Organization (NATO), set up under the treaty, is building a unified armed force to discourage aggression — but prepared to fight in case of attack.   In addition to the billions of dollars in aid we have given the pact members, several U. S. Army, Navy, and Air Force units are stationed in Europe as part of the NATO forces.

(2) *The Rio Pact*, signed in 1947, binds the United States and the 20 Latin American Republics.   Our neighbors to the south are essential to our own defense.   They are, in effect, our own back yard.   For years the Latin Americans looked upon the United States as the "Colossus of the North" — and the title was not intended as a compliment.   But today a general spirit of trust and confidence prevails.

We are helping the Latin Americans along the road to economic and social betterment. We try to promote friendly co-operation through the Organization of American States and through the Inter-American (Rio) Treaty of Reciprocal Assistance which pledges each member to aid any other in case of attack.

(3) *The Anzus Pact*, signed in 1951, unites Australia, New Zealand, and the United States in a defensive alliance. If any of the three nations is attacked in the Pacific Area the others agree to come to its assistance.

(4) *The Japanese Pact*, signed in 1951, involves Japan and the United States. After seven years of American occupation, we and our World War II allies (but not Russia) concluded a peace treaty with Japan. At the same time we also signed a mutual defense pact with the Japanese. In return for American protection, we are permitted to maintain land, sea, and air forces in and about Japan. In converting Japan from a vicious enemy to a helpful friend we have enhanced our own security many times over.

(5) *The Philippines Pact*, signed in 1951, serves notice on any potential aggressor that the United States and the Philippines will stand together in the Pacific Area.

(6) *The Korean Pact*, signed in 1953, pledges the United States to come to the aid of South Korea should war break out again. (In addition to this pact, the 16 UN members whose troops fought in Korea have promised prompt action if the communists renew the war.) Congress appropriated $200,000,000 to help rebuild war-shattered South Korea.

Our Most Important Ally is Great Britain. Without her we should find our task of world leadership considerably more difficult.

Our Most Powerful Foe is the Soviet Union. If World War III is to be averted Russia must be made, in one way or another, to seek the paths of peace.

Every Nation in the World is important to us. Germany, for example, is the key to much of the future of all Europe. Thus we are working for a strong, peaceable, and united Germany. India, with its resources and teeming millions, is the key to much of the future of Asia. Thus we are striving to co-operate with her for the peaceful, non-communist development of that whole vast region. The Middle East is the land bridge connecting Europe, Africa, and Asia and is

(7) the Southern southeastern asia Security agreement 1954 Manila

immensely rich in oil. Thus we are helping those peoples to resist Soviet pressures and to co-operate with the West.

As a nation, we lead the free world in the search for lasting peace. But in this search physical power alone is not enough. Our might "is as the strength of ten" *only because we fight for the right.*

The *Voice of America*, under the United States Information Agency, combats the Soviet campaign of hate and propaganda against the United States. In co-operation with the State Department it broadcasts the official views of our Government, presents news and feature programs on the American way of life, and attempts to promote our friendship with other peoples. Its short-wave broadcasts go out from New York in 20-odd languages through transmitters in the United States and relay stations in Manila, Honolulu, and Munich. It also operates a floating transmitter to help broadcast behind the Iron Curtain.

Motion pictures, libraries, and the exchange of persons also are used to promote international understanding and good will. For example, we are engaged in a vast international student exchange program. Thousands of foreign students are now studying in American colleges and observing various phases of our national life. At the same time, thousands of Americans are studying abroad. This exchange program is intended to widen the contacts and spread understanding between the United States and our world neighbors.

QUESTIONS ON THE TEXT

1. Who is considered the most important cabinet officer?
2. What are the duties of the Secretary of State?
3. What are the duties of ambassadors and ministers? What special privileges do they enjoy?
4. What is meant by *exterritoriality?*
5. How do ambassadors differ from ministers?
6. Name some duties performed in Great Britain by Walter H. Page.
7. What are the duties of military attachés?
8. What are consuls, and how does the consular service differ from the diplomatic service? Name six important duties of consuls.
9. What is meant by consular jurisdiction?
10. What compensations are paid to Chiefs of Missions? Consuls?
11. How is a passport obtained and what is its value?
12. What is the *Emergency Fund?* How does it differ from all others?

13. Explain the importance of foreign trade.
14. Explain our reciprocal tariff agreements.
15. Why is foreign trade important?
16. What are the American foreign policies as to the UN? Russia? Germany? Japan? Great Britain? Free peoples? Latin America? Asia and the Pacific? Near East?

PROBLEMS FOR DISCUSSION

1. For training diplomatic officers to promote peace should we have an academy similar to the military and naval academies? If so, should the students admitted be high school graduates or college graduates?

2. An Executive Order issued in 1936 provides that before marriage with a person of foreign nationality each Foreign Service officer (but not an ambassador or minister) must obtain permission to do so from the Secretary of State. Each request for permission to marry an alien must be accompanied by a resignation, to be acted upon as the Secretary of State deems advisable. Why does our Government thus interfere with the domestic affairs of a Foreign Service officer?

3. A diplomatic officer cannot be arrested for exceeding the speed limit in an automobile, but he can be warned, and if he habitually violates the law in this respect complaint may be made to his government. Why is this courtesy to foreign countries necessary?

4. The communist party, directed from Moscow, is organized on an international basis. The various communist parties in countries around the world act as agents of Soviet foreign policy. In what ways has this complicated our fight against communism? In what ways do communist parties attempt to aid Russia?

SELECT BIBLIOGRAPHY

BOLLES, B., AND WILCOX, F. *The Armed Road to Peace: NATO.* No. 92. 1952. (Foreign Policy Association, New York.)

DEAN, V., AND BREBNER, J. *How to Make Friends for the U. S.* No. 93. 1952. (Foreign Policy Association, New York.)

PADOVER, S. *Steps toward European Integration.* No. 94. 1952.

BAILEY, T. A. *A Diplomatic History of the American People.* Appleton-Century-Crofts. New York. 1950 ed.

MAGRUDER, F. A. *National Governments and International Relations,* Chapters 1, 2, 9, 18, 21, 23, 27. Allyn and Bacon. 1950.

"The Case for Free Trade." *Time.* May 25, 1953.

SCHUBERT, P. "Uncle Sam's Overseas Watchdogs." *Saturday Evening Post.* July 4, 1953. (The Foreign Service.)

and Latin America outline

CHAPTER XII

THE TREASURY DEPARTMENT *Humphrey*

The Secretary of the Treasury has charge of a large number of bureaus, services, and other divisions which perform the various functions of the Department. To assist in the collection of Federal taxes are the Internal Revenue Service, the Bureau of Customs, and

Photo by David Robbins, reprinted by special permission of The Saturday Evening Post, © 1949, Curtis Publishing Company

SUPPOSE HE HAD A MILLION

Actually this man is a worker at the Bureau of Engraving, but if he really had a yearly income of a million, he would receive less than $120,000 after Federal income tax deduction. If a man is in a low income group, he pays proportionately less, because the Government uses a graduated tax system.

the Secret Service. For supervising United States money, the Secretary is aided by the Bureau of the Mint to provide the metallic money, the Bureau of Engraving and Printing to print paper money, and the Comptroller of the Currency to supervise national banks.

The Treasury Department issues public securities, including U. S.

Savings Bonds, and is generally responsible for the borrowing operations of the Government. (See pages 98–100.)

The Secretary has under his jurisdiction the Commissioner of the Public Debt, and the Bureau of Federal Supply for purchase, storage, and distribution of public property. He also has charge of the Bureau of Narcotics which enforces the criminal and tax laws relating to narcotic drugs and marihuana. The Coast Guard also is within the Treasury Department (except in wartime when it is under the Navy).

The Collection of the Revenue. — The Internal Revenue Service operates through an Income Tax Unit, an Alcohol Tax Unit, a Miscellaneous Tax Unit, and Directors of Internal Revenue at central cities throughout the country. The Bureau of Customs also has its Collectors of Customs at each important port where tariff taxes are collected.

The Income Tax, from individuals and corporations, produces about three-fourths of our Federal revenue. (See pages 113–116; 212.)

The Government has various methods of checking upon the honesty of those who should pay income taxes. It requires the keeping of records of business; it requires employers to withhold and turn in the tax due from employees; it requires corporations to report dividends and interest, and those paying royalties on patents and copyrights to report the sums of money paid; it exchanges information with State income tax collectors; it compels witnesses to testify; and it employs secret service agents. The Government can inspect bank accounts and records and, to some extent, safety deposit boxes. It even has treaties with other countries granting inspection privileges.

Those who fail to report all of their taxable income may be imprisoned, may be fined, and may have a penalty added equal to 50 per cent of the amount not reported. For example, it was discovered that a movie star had short-changed the Government $118,364. For this fraud he was required to pay the $118,364, plus a penalty of 50 per cent of the $118,364, plus a $3000 fine; or a total of $180,546. In 1931 "Scarface Al" Capone was indicted for evading an income tax on $1,000,000 obtained over a period of six years. He was given an eleven-year prison sentence, fined $50,000, and his property was seized for the taxes and penalty. Evasions may be detected even after death. Recently half of a $102,000 estate was paid as back income taxes.

Information often comes through competitors or rivals. For in-

RECEIPTS OF THE UNITED STATES GOVERNMENT FOR THE FISCAL YEAR 1952, EXCLUDING BORROWING

(Figures for 1953 were not available at time of printing.)

	1952	1951
Corporation income and profit taxes	$21,466,910,019	$14,387,569,403
Individual income and employment taxes (paid directly by individuals: $11,545,060,075; income, old-age insurance, and railroad retirement taxes withheld: $21,933,693,736; unemployment insurance: $259,616,432)	33,738,370,243	26,624,787,948
Other Internal Revenue:		
Liquor, wine, and spirits	$2,549,119,620	
Cigarettes ($1,474,071,818), cigars, tobacco, snuff, etc.	1,565,162,382	
Autos, trucks, motorcycles, and accessories	1,951,991,619	
Estate tax ($750,590,517), gift tax ($82,556,471)	833,146,988	
Gasoline and lubricating oils	808,460,257	
Telephone, telegraph, radio, etc.	705,770,284	
Transportation of property and persons (15% on tickets, berths)	663,763,004	
Admission to theaters, games, etc. (1 cent on each 5 cents)	376,370,970	
Retailers' excise taxes on jewelry, furs, toilet articles, etc.	475,529,924	
Stamp taxes on playing cards, deeds, bonds, capital stock, etc.	84,995,421	
Sugar tax (about ½ cent a pound)	78,473,191	
Club dues and initiation fees (20%, lodges and fraternities exempt)	33,591,630	
Coin-operated devices (pinball, slot machines, etc.)	18,823,167	
Miscellaneous (appliances, narcotics, firearms, etc.)	560,006,841	
TOTAL INTERNAL REVENUE	9,804,305,298	9,433,328,964
	$65,009,585,560	$50,445,686,315
Customs (tariff) principally alcoholic beverages and wool	550,696,379	624,008,052
Surplus Property sales	192,905,308	214,160,436
Proceeds from Government-owned securities	284,279,115	428,349,356
Mineral, oil, and forest leases; profit on coins, Panama Canal tolls; etc.	1,961,903,196	1,656,467,733
TOTAL BUDGET RECEIPTS [1] (not including Postal receipts, etc.[2])	$67,999,369,558	$53,368,671,892

[1] *Net* Budget Receipts (Total Budget Receipts minus tax and customs refunds, transfers to trust accounts, etc.) were $62,128,606,580 (see page 215).   [2] Government corporations, like TVA, have budgets of their own.

stance, a shoe merchant informs the collector that a rival merchant did not report all of his business. In another interesting case a man told the woman to whom he was engaged how cleverly he had defrauded the Government. After some years he jilted this woman. She then reported him for spite. So years after he thought he had "got by," he had to pay the price of dishonesty.

Other Internal Revenue is derived from inheritances, liquors, cigarettes, tobaccos, autos, gasoline, etc. The Commissioner of Internal Revenue and his deputies collect these taxes through Directors of Internal Revenue in charge of the various districts into which the country is divided. So far as feasible, these taxes are collected by means of stamps which are pasted upon packages in such a way that the stamp will be broken when the package is opened.

There are enough dishonest taxpayers to necessitate an extensive secret service department. Even some manufacturers have been guilty of counterfeiting revenue stamps.

Customs are taxes (tariff) on imported goods. These taxes are collected by the Secretary of the Treasury through the Bureau of Customs. The country is divided into customs districts. In each one of these districts there is a collector who is assisted by a surveyor, appraiser, examiners, inspectors, storekeepers, and clerks.

All articles brought into the country must enter at specified points where there are customs houses. At the principal point in each district the collector resides; at subordinate places, a deputy collector. Along the two oceans and the Canadian and Mexican borders are numerous "ports of entry"; and numerous interior cities, such as Chicago and St. Louis, are "ports of entry." [1] (For a discussion of Free Foreign Trade Zones see Chapter XXXIV.)

Customs on about 2000 taxable articles are of three kinds — *specific*, *ad valorem*, and *mixed*. *Specific* means so much per unit, as half a cent a pound on sugar or eggs at $3\frac{1}{2}$ cents per dozen. *Ad valorem* means in "proportion to value," as 55% on mesh bags valued at less than $5 per dozen and 35% if valued at more. *Mixed* means that both a *specific* duty and an *ad valorem* duty are imposed upon the same article.

As the determination of values is very difficult, persons exporting to the United States articles valued at over $100 are required to have

---

[1] More than half of all custom dues are collected at New York.

invoices certified by an American consul; when valued at $100 or less an oral statement is accepted. If the consul is not certain of the value he may demand three samples, one for himself, one for the United States Customs Court in New York, and one for the appraiser at the port to which the merchandise is sent.

To prevent fraud when merchandise is received at a port, ten per cent of the packages, taken at random, are opened and examined; and all personal baggage is examined. To prevent smuggling, detectives are at work here and abroad and the Treasury Department maintains a Coast Guard. Recently, customs inspectors at Long Beach, California, seized 700 bales of clothing which had been fraudulently listed as rags. Any person, except an officer of the United States, who gives original information which leads to the conviction of a smuggler may be rewarded by the Commissioner of Customs.

The Safe-Keeping of the Revenues. — *The Treasurer* of the United States may keep the revenues in the Treasury at Washington, in the Federal Reserve Banks, in the Federal Land Banks, or in National Banks or State Banks of the Federal Reserve System designated by the Secretary of the Treasury.

The Disbursement of the Revenue is regulated by Acts of Congress. No money is paid out of the Treasury unless authorized by an Act of Congress. The money is paid by the *Treasurer* upon the presentation of a warrant drawn by the Secretary of the Treasury and approved by the Comptroller General.

The General Accounting Office, created in 1921, is independent of the Treasury Department and is organized to safeguard our revenues even against mistakes or frauds of treasury officials. It is under the direction of the Comptroller General of the United States, who is appointed by the President, with the consent of the Senate, for a term of fifteen years. The Act creating the office provides that the Comptroller General shall not be removed except by a joint resolution of Congress.

This Office examines and audits the claims and accounts of most branches of the Government; and the Comptroller General prescribes the form and method of keeping accounts and passes upon the question of what are legal disbursements.

Upon the application of any disbursing office the Comptroller General is required to render his advance decision upon any question involving a payment to be made by this disbursing office.

UNITED STATES EXPENDITURES FOR THE FISCAL YEAR 1952

(Figures for 1953 were not available at time of printing.)

Defense Department: . . . . . . $ 402,173,023	
Army Department 16,222,957,519	
Air Force Department 12,349,594,005	
Navy Department 9,960,934,054	$38,935,658,601
Interest on the Public Debt	5,859,263,437
Veterans Administration.	4,901,625,984
Foreign Aid	4,761,423,357
Refunds of Taxes and Duties	2,302,538,227
Social Security and Railroad Old-age Benefits	1,997,060,807
Agriculture Department.	1,156,534,766
Other Expenditures (Atomic Energy, Export-Import Bank, Executive, Public Roads and Housing, Justice, Interior, etc.)	6,231,141,779
Total Expenditures	$66,145,246,958
Net Receipts	62,128,606,580
Budget Deficit	4,016,640,378

In 1934 when it seemed that the prairie States were becoming a dustbowl President Roosevelt ordered that $15,000,000 of the $525,-000,000 drought relief fund authorized by Congress be used for planting strips of trees to stop soil erosion. (See page 286.) The Comptroller General ruled that the drought relief fund was intended for *direct* and *immediate* relief — not for projects whose results lay so far in the future — so he allowed only $1,000,000 of the fund to get the scheme started. This was all that could be efficiently spent on those employed to plant the young trees available.

The General Accounting Office also superintends the recovery of debts owed to the United States. For example, a military officer received an extra allowance for his dependent mother. When it was discovered that his mother was worth $42,500, the Accounting Office took steps to recover the excess payment.

United States Debt. — Public debt is created by the Government, usually for public works, for relief during a depression, or for war. Our Federal Government debt is due to the First World War, to the depression during the decade from 1930 to 1940, to the Second World War, and to the present defense program.

The average interest rate on the debt is now a little over 2 per cent. With the national debt at $265,000,000,000 in 1953, the annual interest to be paid by the Government is nearly $6,000,000,000. The debt continues to rise because the Government is spending more than it takes in and has to borrow to make up the difference. Most economists deplore this "deficit spending" and urge that the debt be reduced in these prosperous days. As outstanding bonds come due today, new ones are sold to raise the needed funds.

Debt at the outbreak of the First World War	$ 1,000,000,000
Debt at the end of the First World War	26,000,000,000
Debt in 1930 after "Coolidge Economy"	16,000,000,000
Debt in 1940 after a decade of depression	45,000,000,000
Highest debt in our history February 28, 1946	$279,000,000,000
Debt June 30, 1953	$265,000,000,000

How the United States Borrows Money. — The Federal Government uses both the "short-term" and the "long-term" types of borrowing. Short-term borrowing uses notes, bills, and certificates of indebtedness, which run anywhere from thirty days to four years. Long-term borrowing is through the sale of bonds which usually run ten years or more — often for twenty or thirty years. For short-term borrowing the rate of interest is commonly about 1 per cent a year; but for long-term bonds the rate varies from 2 to 3 per cent, or a fraction more in some very exceptional cases.

The Federal Government issues both bearer bonds and registered bonds. The former may be passed around like money, and the interest is collected every six months by clipping and cashing at any bank the coupons attached to the bottom of each bond. The latter are registered at the Treasury in the name of the owner and cannot be disposed of without having ownership transferred. The interest is paid by checks from the Treasury. The bearer bonds are more convenient for quick sale, but the latter are safer because they cannot be sold if lost or stolen.

Series E Savings Bonds are the most popular issued by the Treasury. In 1952 the Treasury began issuing a new E bond which matures in 9 years, 8 months (instead of the former 10 years) and pays 3 per cent compounded semi-annually (instead of the former 2.9 per cent). These bonds may be held for an additional ten years after maturity, with the interest rate continuing. Thus, a $75 bond matures to $100 in 9 years, 8 months; if it is held for the ten-year extension, it matures to $134.68. This is an increase of 79.6 per cent on the original investment.

These bonds may be registered in the name of one person, two persons as co-owners, or one as owner and another as beneficiary (heir). If lost or stolen, the Treasury will replace them. They may be cashed at a bank any time after sixty days from date of issue. They are issued in denominations from $25 to $10,000, but no one may purchase more than $20,000 worth in any one year.

UNCLE SAM'S STRONG BOX FOR GOLD AT FORT KNOX, KENTUCKY

In 1934 the Government began to pay $35 an ounce for gold. By 1954 it had acquired about $23,000,000,000 worth, or 70% of the world's visible gold supply. Legally it belongs to the Government, economically to the Federal Reserve Banks who hold gold certificates, and practically to depositors who have money in banks. Almost half of this gold is stored at Fort Knox.

Currency. — Currency, that is, money authorized by the government, is of two kinds — metallic and paper.

Metallic Currency. — *Mints.* United States coins are stamped at the mints in Philadelphia, Denver, and San Francisco.

Gold. Until 1933 the double eagle ($20), the eagle ($10), and the half eagle ($5) were coined free for any person bringing the metal to the mints.[1] When the financial crisis came in 1933, many people

---

[1] As 10 per cent of the coin had to be alloy (copper, or nine parts copper and one part silver) to make it durable, there was a small charge for the alloy.

hoarded these gold coins, and others shipped them out of the country. To prevent these practices and to pave the way for re-valuing gold, the Government required all gold coins held by individuals or by banks to be turned into the United States Treasury in exchange for paper money. Gold coins are no longer allowed to circulate in this country, and the mere holding of them is illegal under heavy penalties. But gold may now be purchased from the Government and exported to pay trade balances.

MAKING OUR COINAGE

In the Philadelphia Mint this man is pouring a molten blend of silver and copper into coinage ingot molds. Coins are cut from the "ribbons" of hardened alloy. The "blanks" are cleaned, weighed, and stamped.

From 1834 until 1934 the gold content of the dollar was set at $25\frac{4}{5}$ grains nine-tenths fine; but in 1934 it was reduced to $15\frac{5}{21}$ grains nine-tenths fine. Thus by making a "sixty cent dollar" (or 59.06 to be exact) the Government caused prices to rise, which helped people who were in debt. Previous to the re-valuation of the dollar, gold sold for $20.67 per ounce. At present the Government is paying $35 in paper for an ounce of the metal; and at this artificially high price we had accumulated about $23,000,000,000 or 70 per cent of the gold money of the world by 1954.

In 1934 Federal Reserve Banks were required to deposit all their gold with the U. S. Treasurer, for which certificates of the re-valued (59.06) gold dollar were given. These do not circulate, but are used as security for Federal Reserve Notes.

Silver. — The mints now pay 90.5 cents an ounce for silver newly mined in the United States. No silver dollars have been minted since 1935, but they are still legal tender, as are half dollars, quarters, and dimes, which the mints continue to issue. Silver coins of the United States contain 90 per cent of silver and 10 per cent of copper.

Minor Coins. The five-cent piece is made of three parts copper and one part nickel, and the one-cent piece is made of bronze (95% copper and 5% tin or zinc). Metal for these coins is purchased from the lowest bidder by the superintendent of the mint, with the approval of the Director of the Mint. The profit on these coins is even greater than that on silver coins. Minor coins worn smooth are re-coined at Government expense. During the war substitute metals were used for minor coins.

Legal Tender. Money which the law requires a creditor to accept in payment of a debt when tendered by a debtor is known as *legal tender*. By a joint resolution of Congress passed in 1933 "all coins and currencies of the United States shall be legal tender for all debts, public and private."

Paper Currency consists of about 90% Federal Reserve Notes, 7% Silver Certificates, and 3% other issues.[1] *greenbacks*

Federal Reserve Notes are issued by the Governors of the Federal Reserve System (page 328) for any one of the twelve Federal Reserve Banks. The Notes are printed by the Comptroller of the Currency. Federal Reserve Notes are secured by 25% Gold Certificates and 75% Government bonds, or 75% commercial paper, which includes notes or drafts discounted by the Federal Reserve Banks from the local member banks.[2] The amount in circulation can be increased or decreased as needed by the local banks to supply their customers.

Silver Certificates are "warehouse receipts" given for the deposit of silver. They are rarely presented for redemption in coin.

Mutilated Paper Currency may be redeemed if its condition permits its identification by the Government experts.[3]

---

[1] Since 1934 all Gold Certificates, other than those held by Federal Reserve Banks, have been retired as deposited in banks. They were formerly "warehouse receipts" for gold dollars in the Treasury.

United States Notes ("Greenbacks") were first issued during the Civil War. They are partially backed by a gold reserve.

National Bank Notes were formerly issued by National Banks. They are backed by Government bonds; but are being retired whenever deposited in banks.

[2] Federal Reserve Notes are also obligations of the United States and a lien on all the assets of the issuing Federal Reserve Bank.

[3] The average life of paper money in the United States is less than three years; the average life of the dollar bill, which gets hard use, is only about one year. When the old is exchanged for the new, the old is burned.

Purchasing Power of the Dollar Changes. — How much a dollar will buy (or, to put it another way, how much a dollar is worth) varies from time to time. Quite obviously, when prices are low a dollar will buy more (is worth more) than when prices are high. A family with a $5000 income can maintain a higher standard of living in a period of lower prices than it can on the same income in a period of higher prices. The 1920 dollar was worth 65¢ of the 1926 dollar because of the soaring price level in the period immediately after World War I. Today's dollar (see chart, page 221) is worth about 53¢ as compared with the dollar of the 1935–1939 period.

THE HOUSEWIFE AND CURRENCY INFLATION

Inflation is a more rapid increase in the amount of money or purchasing power in the hands of the people than in the supply of goods they want to purchase. For instance, during the hard times of 1932 the income of all the people of the United States was only $40,000,000,000.[1] But when the United States entered the Second World War and all the requirements of our armed forces had to be produced, good times returned and nearly everybody got a job, usually at high wages. The necessity for devoting so much of our production to war requirements made it impossible to supply many of the things needed by civilians. As people had plenty of money the tendency was to pay almost any price for a desired article, thus bringing on inflation.

To control this condition, the Office of Price Administration (OPA) was established and it put "ceiling prices" on most commodities, thus saving the American people billions of dollars. But following the war

[1] The annual income now is about $300,000,000,000 — more than seven times that of 1932.

1 Gratuitous coinage — free coinage

2. Seigniorage — charge more than the cost

3. Brassage — charge just to cover the cost of coinage

price control was removed from most products and world-wide scarcities shot prices sky-high.

Inflation reduced the purchasing power of wages, reduced the purchasing power of savings for old age, and increased the cost of the war and the amount of the war debt.

Some of the war-time controls were re-imposed after the beginning of the Korean war; but most of these were eliminated by the new Administration in 1953.

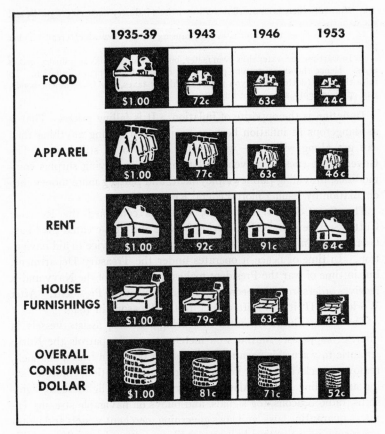

THE SHRINKING DOLLAR — 1935–1953

This chart, based on Bureau of Labor Statistics figures, shows how the purchasing power of the dollar has declined since the 1935–1939 base period.

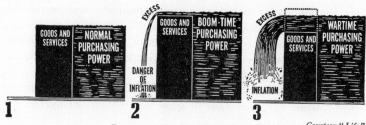

INFLATION IN ONE EASY LESSON　　　*Courtesy "Life"*

1. Normally there is no overflow; if water rises, industry makes more goods, and the dam rises.

2. In boom times the water rises fast, causing an overflow which creates higher prices.

3. In wartime the water rises even faster, but the dam shrinks as industry makes arms. Hence the excess torrent pours over, causing higher prices, inflation. To raise the dam (dotted lines) you must pay higher taxes, buy Government bonds, pay off your debts, save — not buy.

Deflation is the opposite of inflation. It is falling prices. That is as dangerous as inflation because people stop buying anything they can get along without — waiting for prices to go still lower. The Government tries to prevent deflation through buying surplus commodities, providing public employment, and putting more money into circulation by issuing more Federal Reserve Notes.

The Coast Guard. — In 1915 Congress combined the Revenue Cutter Service and the Life Saving Service and thus created the Coast Guard; and in 1939 it absorbed the Lighthouse Service to aid navigation. In time of peace it operates under the Treasury Department, but in time of war the President makes it a branch of the Navy and it receives orders from the Secretary of the Navy or the President. After World War II, it was shifted back to the Treasury in 1946.

The Coast Guard operates life-saving stations, assists vessels in distress, suppresses mutinies on merchant vessels, patrols the North Atlantic to warn ships against icebergs, breaks ice in frozen channels, removes wrecks and other floating dangers to navigation, enforces fishing and sealing laws in Alaskan waters, maintains lighthouses, lightships, radio beacons, fog signals, and buoys on navigable streams, enforces quarantine laws, and laws governing merchant vessels and motor boats such as inspecting hulls and boilers and requiring adequate life preservers, issues licenses to merchant marine personnel, and brings sick seamen or passengers to hospitals by sea-plane or fast cutter.

The Coast Guard patrols the coasts to prevent piracy and the smuggling of dutiable goods, narcotics, liquors, and undesirable persons. In time of war it escorts convoys and guards against enemy landings.

Cruisers, destroyers, patrol vessels, picket boats, lifeboats, aircraft, and other miscellaneous craft constitute the equipment of coastguardsmen; and the Coast Guard Academy at New London, Connecticut, trains officers for their duties.

Official Coast Guard Photograph

COAST GUARD LIGHTSHIP MARKING THE ENTRANCE TO NEW YORK HARBOR

This ship at the entrance to Ambrose Channel is a floating lighthouse. It provides a powerful light, a fog signal, and radiobeacon to guide vessels in all kinds of weather.

The Operation of Gambling Ships Prohibited. — It is unlawful for any citizen or resident of the United States, or any other person on an American vessel, to operate or have any interest in a gambling ship on the high seas or within the jurisdiction of the United States (*e.g.*, from low tide three miles out) and not within the jurisdiction of any State.

It is likewise illegal to operate, permit to be operated, or have anything to do with transporting passengers by water or air to a gambling ship.

QUESTIONS ON THE TEXT

1. What are the duties of the Secretary of the Treasury?

2. How much revenue does the United States Government receive annually? From what sources does this money come?

3. What is meant by *internal revenue?* income tax

4. What is meant by *customs?*

5. What is the difference between *specific* and *ad valorem* tariff?

6. How does the United States prevent fraud by importers of articles upon which a tariff is imposed?

7. Where does the United States Government keep its money?

8. For what purposes does the United States expend its money?

9. What body must authorize the expenditure of all Government money?

10. What officer sees that no money is expended except such as is authorized by Congress? What is his relationship to the Secretary of the Treasury? To the President? To Congress? For what term is he chosen?

11. What was the debt of the United States at the outbreak of the First World War? How much is it today?

12. What is meant by *currency?*

13. What metallic currency does the United States now make? Where is it made?

14. On what kinds of metallic money is a profit made?

15. What is meant by *legal tender* money?

16. What are gold certificates? Silver certificates?

17. What are Federal Reserve notes? How many may be issued? What agency guards against the issuance of too many? How are these notes secured?

18. Why is today's dollar worth less than the 1935–1939 dollar?

19. What services does the Coast Guard perform?

PROBLEMS FOR DISCUSSION

1. Some people would get all revenue from the rich (property, income, and inheritance taxes); others would get all from those who indulge in luxuries or "evils" (amusements, lotteries, tobaccos, liquors); while still others would shift taxes to the masses by taxing everything sold for consumption (tariff; severance tax on coal, oils, metals, and lumber; sales tax on gasoline or on everything). Which of these types of taxes, if used alone, would kill capital — the "goose that lays the golden egg"? Which would make it more difficult to get rid of evils? Which would be least in proportion to ability to pay?

2. If a man is saving money during a period when prices are rising, should he buy a farm or other property which will yield him 6 per cent net interest upon the amount invested, or should he lend it on a good security at 6 per cent?

3. Buying stocks is buying shares in actual property. Buying bonds is lending money. Which would you buy when prices are rising?

4. In 1896 President Cleveland received a salary of $50,000. Now the President's salary is twice that. In 1896 he did not have a high income tax to pay and prices were very low. Was he better off in 1896 or now?

5. If you buy an $18.75 Government Savings Bond from your Post Office, it increases in value each year, and if left for 9 years, 8 months you can draw out $25. What per cent interest would this be? How does owning a bond help to make you more loyal to your Government?

6. Some people propose that the Constitution be amended to limit Federal income taxes to a maximum 25 per cent, except in war-time emergencies. Assuming a continued high rate of Federal expenditures (which seems certain), what changes would be necessary in the Government's tax program if the Constitution were so amended? Why would you favor or oppose the adoption of such an amendment?

7. During periods of inflation would high or low interest rates, which banks pay on the Federal Reserve Notes they use, help to bring prices down to normal? How should interest rates be regulated to bring the country out of a period of deflation?

8. Some people, especially big-time gamblers and racketeers, conduct their operations on a strictly cash basis. They keep no records and do not deposit their profits in regular bank accounts. Thus it is very difficult for the Internal Revenue Service to check on possible tax evasions. In 1950 Congressman Sutton proposed that the United States change the color of its paper money and require that all "greenbacks" must be exchanged for the newly-colored currency within a specified time or become worthless. How would such a move be helpful in uncovering many tax-evaders who might not otherwise be caught?

9. John F. Sinclair relates the following story:

"Dr. Adolph Helfer is one of the great physicians of Vienna. He was born in America. His family lived in St. Louis. In 1912 his father died and left him $50,000, which was sent to him in Vienna. He was a careful, prudent man. He deposited the $50,000 in a savings bank in Vienna and received 3 per cent interest annually. I met Dr. Helfer in Vienna a few weeks ago. He had not taken a dollar, either principal or interest, from the original fund. He was hoping for an old age free from worry. (But Austria issued quantities of paper money without gold or silver to secure it.) Then we figured up what his $50,000 was worth in the summer of 1923. It came to exactly $3.15. The money had quickly slipped away and Dr. Helfer found himself holding an empty sack. That is what inflation does." Explain *inflation*.

10. If one defrauds the Government by not honestly paying his taxes, is he stealing from an invisible Government or from his honest taxpaying neighbors?

11. Industrial States often claim that they pay more than they get back by showing how much is collected therein as tariff duties, taxes on the manufacture of tobacco and cigarettes, etc. Is this tax really paid by the State where collected?

Suppose some wealthy States actually pay more than poorer rural States. Do they get it back indirectly? Do they get it back through profits on investments? Do people from rich centers use the roads beyond their bounds for touring, for trucking food to the city, for sending their products to purchasers? Have they any interest in the National Guards of other States? Will children educated in poor rural sections ever migrate to the cities? Is money collected in taxes from the rich States and spent in all the States charity or good business?

12. It is unconstitutional for the United States to tax State, county, or municipal bonds, or the income from them; and in practice, States do not tax their own State or local government bonds. Would you favor a constitutional amendment permitting the United States to impose the income tax upon the income from State bonds? What effect would this have upon the rate of interest the States and local governments would have to pay?

SELECT BIBLIOGRAPHY

BLOUGH, R. *The Federal Taxing Process.* Prentice-Hall. New York. 1952.

OGG, F., AND RAY, P. *Essentials of American National Government.* Appleton-Century-Crofts. New York. 1952 ed. Ch. 24.

Treasury Department. *Your Federal Income Tax, 1953.* Washington, D. C. 25¢.

Treasury Department. "Know Your Money." Washington, D. C. 1951. (32-page illustrated pamphlet. Free.)

WOLFF, H. *Look Out for the Tax Cops.* Collier's, Feb. 19, 1949, pages 16+.

ROGERS, D. "Is a Federal Sales Tax Coming?" *Collier's.* May 30, 1953. (Pro and Con)

YODER, R. "The Money Surgeons." *Saturday Evening Post.* July 4, 1953. (Recovery of mutilated currency.)

CHAPTER XIII

THE DEPARTMENTS OF DEFENSE AND OF JUSTICE

THE DEPARTMENT OF DEFENSE

According to the Constitution, national defense is the responsibility of the National Government. And, as we have seen, the Constitution grants the vast "war powers" to the President and Congress. It also makes the President Commander-in-Chief of the Armed Forces.[1]

Unification of the Armed Forces. — Until recently, the Army (including the Air Force) and the Navy operated as separate units under the Cabinet Departments of War and Navy. But two World Wars taught us the value of closer coordination in modern warfare. So, in the National Security Acts of 1947 and 1949, Congress provided for the "unification" of the armed forces under a single Cabinet Department.

These Acts created the new Department of Defense headed by a Defense Secretary. They also created the non-Cabinet Departments of Army, Navy, and Air Force, the National Security Council, the Joint Chiefs of Staff, and the Armed Forces Policy Council. The Defense Department was reorganized by President Eisenhower in 1953.

The Secretary of Defense, who must be a civilian, is appointed by the President and Senate and heads the entire Defense Department. He establishes general policies, directs the operations of the Department, and coordinates the activities of the three service departments under him. His authority over the entire Department was strengthened by the 1953 reorganization and his staff assistance is now centered around a Deputy Secretary and nine Assistant Secretaries.

The National Security Council, of which the President is chairman, has among its members the Secretary of Defense and the three service

---

[1] The States are practically excluded from the defense field. See Article I, Sections 8 and 10, Article II, Section 2, and pages 105, 181–2.

secretaries. The Council has been called "America's Cold War General Staff." (See page 182.)

The Joint Chiefs of Staff consists of a Chairman and the Chiefs of Staff of the Army and the Air Force and the Chief of Naval Operations. Under the direction of the Chairman, the Joint Chiefs are the principal military advisers to the President and the Secretary of Defense. They are assisted by a *Joint Staff* of not more than 210 officers drawn from all three of the armed services.

The Armed Forces Policy Council consists of the Defense Secretary, the Deputy Secretary, the Joint Chiefs, and the three service secretaries. It is the general policy board for the Armed Forces.

Functions of the Armed Forces. — The Armed Forces are to carry out the orders of the President as Commander-in-Chief. In brief, the Armed Forces perform the following functions: (1) Support and defend the Constitution against all enemies, foreign and domestic; (2) maintain the security of the United States, its possessions, and areas vital to its protection; (3) uphold the national policies of the United States; and (4) safeguard the internal security of the United States.

ARMY DEPARTMENT

Functions of the Army. — Of the three major services (the Army, Navy, and Air Force) the United States Army has primary interest in all military operations on land. Its main duties are to defend the United States, to defeat enemy land forces, to seize and occupy enemy territory, and to organize, train, and equip its forces. It is also charged with the administration and operation of the Panama Canal, land bases and fortifications, and river and harbor improvements in the United States and its territories.

The Secretary of the Army, the civilian chief who directs the Army, is subordinate to the Secretary of Defense.

The Chief of Staff is the chief military adviser and executive to the Secretary and commands all components of the Army. He is assisted by the General Staff and a Special Staff.

The Army Personnel. — The Army as a whole consists of the following groups:

The Regular Army is the nation's chief military force for land operations. Just before the Second World War it had an authorized strength of 375,000 officers and men. During the war it jumped to between seven and eight millions (plus a Navy of more than four millions). In 1950 we began to expand all of the Armed Forces again.

With the Korean crisis and the current remobilization program, the Armed Forces — Army, Navy and Marines, and Air Force — began expanding again. Many Reserve and National Guard units

United Press Photo

SELF-PROPELLED ARTILLERY ON THE KOREAN FRONT

These powerful 155 mm. "Long Toms" are typical of the modern equipment used by the United Nations in this front-line defense against communist aggression.

and personnel were ordered to active duty, Navy vessels were de-mothballed, and aircraft and other defense production was stepped up. Selective service (draft) calls were increased as well. There is no legal limit on the total strength of any of the services, and present plans call for the maintenance of an Army, Navy and Marines, and Air Force of about 3,000,000 men.

Enlistments, for periods ranging up to six years, and selective service (see pages 240, 242) are used to provide men for the Army. A young man may enlist at the age of 18, or at 17 with his parents' consent. Women are now able to enlist in any of the armed services, too.

Universal Military Training (UMT) for all eligible youth seems to many to be the only real solution to our military manpower problems.

Armored Force. — Smash the enemy with a fast-moving, powerful team of tanks, combat cars, trucks, "jeeps," motorcycles. There's thrilling action for gunners, drivers, radio men, and mechanics in the Army's tough armored divisions.

Cavalry. — Whether you like to ride a good horse or handle a fast armored car, motorcycle, or truck, there's a place for you in the Cavalry's mobile striking force. The rougher the going the better the Cavalry likes it.

Chemical Corps. — This Corps gives you the chance to be a combat soldier, firing chemical munitions. The 4.2-inch mortar, used for smoke screens to cover the advance of troops, will be one of your principal weapons.

Coast Artillery. — Want to fire an anti-aircraft gun — or help load and fire a giant coast defense gun? Service with the Coast Artillery will give you experience in gunnery, mechanics, electrical, and radio work.

Corps of Engineers. — In the forefront of the fighting much of the time, you'll see a lot of action with the Engineers. Building bridges, roads, air-fields, and tank-traps — planning camouflage — are all in the day's work.

Corps of Military Police. — Reliable, clear-thinking men who know how to shoulder responsibility, the Military Police speed troop movements at the front and behind the lines, guard prisoners, enforce order. They are trained fighting men.

Field Artillery. — Here's the outfit that softens up the foe with a barrage of shells, smashes his supply lines, rains fire on his reserves. The guns roll fast behind speedy trucks and tractors. Plenty of action for daring drivers, gunners, and mechanics.

Infantry. — Moving 40 miles an hour in big trucks, skiing in snowy mountains, dropping by parachute or flying into enemy territory in transport planes, today's infantry is streamlined. But still "they hike, they hike, they hike."

Medical Department. — Wherever the fighting is toughest the Medical units are on the job, saving lives. Ambulance drivers, laboratory technicians, and able young men for many other duties are needed now in this vital service.

Ordnance Department. — The supply and maintenance of all weapons are in charge of the Ordnance Department. Repairing tanks and guns under fire is a job for tough men. There's lots of room for daring drivers and good mechanics.

Quartermaster Corps. — Battle smoke and bursting shells can't stop the movement of food and supplies. Men in the front lines have to be fed. The Quartermaster Corps take care of the troops wherever they are.

Signal Corps. — In the nerve center of the Army, Signal Corps men "get the message through." Radio, telephone, and other means of swift communication are their tools. They work with "electronic sentries" and other secret weapons.

Transportation Corps. — Want to speed men and materials to the army in all parts of the world? Then join the Transportation Corps which directs the army's surface traffic and overseas shipping and operates its ports of embarkation.

The Reserves (including Women's Army Corps (WAC), Army Nurse Corps (ANC), and Women's Medical Specialists Corps (WMSC), make up a peacetime civilian army capable of being called to active duty in the event of emergency as in 1950. Reserve Officers' Training Corps (ROTC), in various colleges and universities, furnish officer personnel for the Reserve upon graduation, at which time they are commissioned in one of the several branches. Also the West Point Military Academy trains youth entirely at Government expense for commissions in the Regular Army.

The National Guard is both a State and a Federal Force. When there is no war or crisis, the National Guard of any State is subject to the command of the Governor. In time of crisis or war the President may order it into Federal service. It receives its equipment and pay for its members from the National Government. Its officers are appointed by the President, and guardsmen are trained largely by Regular Army and Air Force officers. Summer camps for two weeks intensify their training each year. Original enlistments are for a period of three years and subsequent ones are for a period of either one or three years. Both the Army and the Air Force have educational opportunities for the enlisted man, comparable to those for the Navy, described on page 234.

Effects of Recent Inventions on the Army. — The atomic bomb and long range rockets have made war a game for specialists. But the age of "push-button warfare" has not yet arrived. Though the great need now is for research and scientific development, troops are still a fundamental part of the Army.

We have always needed an army as a police force to keep the peace at home and to guard the country against foreign attack. Today the Army also mans our overseas defense posts, occupies former enemy territory, and guards against renewed war in Korea. Until we have world peace, we must maintain a large standing army to protect our freedoms and to discourage attacks by the military dictatorships of communism.

NAVY DEPARTMENT

Functions of the Navy. — The United States Navy includes naval combat and service forces, naval aviation, and the United States Marine Corps. It is organized, trained, and equipped for prompt and sustained combat at sea, and to co-operate with and support the other services.

The Secretary of the Navy, the civilian chief who directs the Navy, is subordinate to the Secretary of Defense.

Courtesy Huckins Yacht Corporation

PATROL TORPEDO BOAT (PT)

Patrol torpedo boats are the fastest naval vessels in the world, being propelled by engines of over 4000 horsepower. They are armed with torpedo tubes, machine guns, anti-aircraft cannon, and (for attack on submarines) depth charges.

The Chief of Naval Operations, who is the principal naval adviser to the President and to the Secretary of the Navy, is an admiral with supreme command of the fleets. In preparing and executing plans for naval operations in peace and war he is assisted by the General Board of the Navy.

The Navy Department comprises the United States Fleet (including naval aviation) and the Marine Corps (page 238). The basic fighting unit in the Army is the soldier who is trained to become an efficient fighter. The basic fighting unit in the Navy, on the other hand, is not the sailor but the warship. The sailor seldom fights hand to hand. His duty is to make the warship an efficient fighting machine.

Enlistments and Preliminary Training. — When a young man at least 17 years of age enlists at a recruiting station, he must pass the physical, intellectual, and moral requirements. Then he goes through an intensive eight-weeks' course of training before he sets foot upon a ship. Here he learns hospital cleanliness. Here he is taught to salute, to respect authority, and to say "aye, aye, sir," instead of "Yes, sir," or "Okay." After three weeks' training in the detention unit to safeguard against communicable diseases, he moves into the "Main Side" of the training station. The recruit is now known as a "boot" because of the leggings that he wears. He learns to handle a rifle, to drill, to signal, and the basic elements of sailing.

Educational Opportunities. — The enlisted man may take specialized courses at one of the Navy service schools. Some are held on shore and others are afloat. When the men thus become specialists they receive increased pay. In this connection, it should be noted that the Navy also accepts women for enlistment under the act already mentioned. On July 7, 1948, six women were accepted for the first enlistment of women in the Regular Navy. To give the diversified instruction needed, the Navy has schools for:

Mechanics	Torpedomen
Woodworkers	Aerographers
Electricians	Aviators
Ordnance men	Deep-sea divers
Clerical personnel	Dental technicians
Musicians	Parachute materielsmen
Hospital corpsmen	Pharmacist mates
Cooks and bakers	Photographers
Fire controlmen	Radio men
Gyrocompass electricians	Submarine personnel
Motion-picture technicians	Metalsmiths

The Navy in Action. — We have three major fleets: the Atlantic Fleet, the Eastern Atlantic and Mediterranean Fleet, and the Pacific Fleet.

Chances for Promotion. — There are seven grades of enlisted men and non-commissioned officers:

Apprentice Seaman	Petty Officer, 3d Class
Seaman, 2d Class	Petty Officer, 2d Class
Seaman, 1st Class	Petty Officer

Chief Petty Officer

OUR NAVY IN ACTION

This wartime view of an Allied convoy on the move gives little hint of the circling destroyers, always alert to safeguard the transports. One of the destroyers is seen just to the left of the line of transports.

The ranks of commissioned officers, who in peace time are usually graduates of the Annapolis Naval Academy, are the following:

Ensign	Captain
Lieutenant (Jr. Gr.)	Rear Admiral
Lieutenant	Vice Admiral
Lt. Commander	Admiral
Commander	Fleet Admiral

Ships of the Fleet. — The Navy is composed of the following types of ships:

Battleships are heavily armored and carry huge guns mounted in groups of three in turrets. Watertight compartments along the outer hulls at the water line enable them to resist torpedo attack and take and inflict severe damages in combat. Their larger guns permit them to inflict damage on the enemy from great range.

Heavy and Light Cruisers are more lightly armored and have fewer guns than battleships. But this permits greater speed.

Aircraft Carriers as large as or larger than battleships carry as many as 100 planes. Pacific action against the Japanese in the Second World War demonstrated their great value.

Destroyers or "tin cans" carry very little armor and lighter guns. Their torpedoes are deadly weapons and the ships are designed for "hit and run" attacks.

Submarines of the "silent service" operate mostly beneath the sea on long and dangerous patrols torpedoing enemy shipping.

Smaller Combat Vessels include motor torpedo boats, minelayers, sub-chasers, and patrol craft.

Non-Combat Vessels include such types as tankers, supply and ammunition ships, transports, mine sweepers, hospital ships, and destroyer, submarine, and seaplane tenders.[1]

There are also task forces for special duties — especially in time of war. These duties are to convoy our troop ships, to convoy supplies, to attack enemy convoys, or to bombard an enemy base.

When a fleet puts to sea, the largest vessels go in the center of the formation. The lighter vessels on the outer fringe protect them from torpedo attack, because the battleships are too heavy to avoid torpedoes by quick maneuvers. Ahead of the main body of heavy ships

---

[1] In 1948 the President was given authority to arm American merchant vessels in time of war or national emergencies.

go the cruisers. And there should be an outer fringe — perhaps fifty miles away — of destroyers and submarines. Aircraft carriers have been extremely important, both to molest enemy fleets, and to protect our own against the enemy's birds of the air.

Official U. S. Navy Photograph

OPERATIONAL JET FIGHTER ON AIRCRAFT CARRIER
As in conventional aircraft, the plane takes off and lands under full flaps.

"Mothballing" Surplus Ships. — At the end of World War II we found ourselves with about a thousand naval vessels not needed in time of peace. Rather than destroy them as we did at the end of World War I we "mothballed" them in a number of harbors, stripped and sealed against the effects of weather and time. Their interiors are kept so dry to prevent rust that a degree of moisture must sometimes be added to prevent dry rust. Many of these ships have now been recommissioned as part of the remobilization program.

The Atomic Bomb dropped from a bomber could destroy a $100,000,000 battleship. This may necessitate the use of smaller craft or increase the use of air craft. For instance, the United States is dependent upon sea-borne imports such as manganese, tin, lead, and zinc (and petroleum in the near future). If submarines were to cut our ocean traffic lanes, we should be in grave danger.

At the end of the Second World War the Germans had rockets which could be fired at shore targets by U-boats far beneath the sea. This could enable an enemy to deliver atomic or bacteriological warfare bombs to coastal cities.

Today Russia has a great many modern submarines built in her own yards, plus those taken from Germany following the war. We also have many submarines; but no probable enemy has a great naval or merchant fleet for us to attack, or easily accessible important ports as we have. Therefore, it seems that one of the most acute naval problems for us is the development of ever better anti-submarine devices, chiefly of an electronic nature like the radar used by the Navy and Air Forces during World War II.

The Marine Corps. — "First to Fight" is the watchword of our Marines, called the "soldiers of the sea." The Japanese learned to fear the fighting fury of the "Leathernecks" in World War II — and the communists have learned the same lesson in Korea.

The Marines act as a land force for the fleet, fortify land bases from which the fleet can operate, man anti-aircraft guns aboard capital ships, and serve as garrisons for naval establishments.

The Raider Battalion is trained for surprise attacks in rubber boats, amphibian landing boats, or other craft. The Defense Battalion is designed to protect advance bases of the Navy. The Paramarines land behind enemy lines to capture or destroy ammunition dumps, airports, railheads, and highway junctions. Garbed in heavy cloth jumpers, loose-fitting trousers tucked into leather boots, and three pieces of headgear — leather, plastic, and steel helmets — the Marines bail out from their carrier plane at the rate of two a second. Marines are also trained to operate gliders.

The Coast Guard performs all sorts of important duties along our coast in time of peace (see page 222), and in time of war the President transfers it to the Navy Department to defend our coasts and perform other tasks as part of the Navy.

Air Force Department

Functions of the Air Force. — The United States Air Force includes all military aviation not assigned to the Army and Navy. It is organ-

WOMEN IN THE ARMED FORCES

Two WAVES learn about starting engines and stand-by position, in one of the aviation technical training courses the Navy has opened to WAVE personnel.

FIGHTERS FOR DEMOCRACY

At an air base in Korea these F–84 "Thunderjets" of the U. S. Far East Air Forces prepare to battle Communism. Here, as one plane takes off with rockets and .50 calibre machine guns loaded, the other plane is gassed up, re-armed, and checked.

ized, trained, and equipped for prompt and sustained air operations in peace and war. It is responsible for preparation for war and for such peacetime duties as may be assigned to it — such as the ferrying of food and supplies to our occupation forces and German civilians in blockaded Berlin in 1948–1949. In time of war its primary functions are to repel enemy air attacks, to gain and hold air supremacy over the enemy, to support land and sea action, and to bombard enemy industrial and military centers.

The Secretary of the Air Force, the civilian chief of the Air Force, is subordinate to the Secretary of Defense. The Chief of Staff of the Air Force is the military commander, under the Secretary, of our new air arm.

Enlistments in the Air Force. — Enlistments are accepted on the same basis as for the Army and the Navy, but Air Force men must pass more rigid physical examinations. The work of our airmen demands that they be in excellent physical condition. Aviation Cadet training is open to all qualified men between the ages of 20 and $26\frac{1}{2}$ who have had two years of college training or the equivalent. As in the Army, Navy, and Marine Corps, there is a reserve force called the Air Reserve.

Air Force in Action. — The crippling blows dealt by our Air Force to the German and Japanese industrial centers during the Second World War shortened that war by untold months or even years. The atomic bombs which ended the war in the Pacific were delivered to Hiroshima and Nagasaki by the Air Force. Rockets and guided missiles have emphasized the importance of this service. Its planes include heavy and light bombers, dive bombers, attack bombers, conventional and jet fighters, transport planes, hospital ships, and observation planes.

During the military operations of the United Nations in Korea, our Air Force early demonstrated the invaluable role of aircraft in military undertakings. It is truly a first line of defense.

SELECTIVE SERVICE

The Draft. — The Second World War and world conditions since have convinced us that a small standing armed force is no longer adequate for the nation's defense. Accordingly, Congress, by Acts passed in 1948, 1950, and 1951, has authorized the induction (drafting) of eligible men for the Armed Forces.

¡Courtesy American Petroleum Institute

SCIENTIFIC RESEARCH BY U. S. ARMED SERVICES

All branches of our Armed Services contribute in many ways to new scientific developments. Here the USS PERCH tests low temperature fuels and lubricants on a run in the Bering Sea.

Those eligible include all males between the ages of $18\frac{1}{2}$ and 26, but one must register at 18. Draftees must serve for 24 months of active duty plus an additional period (up to six years) in an active reserve organization. Under the present law, which does not expire until July, 1955, any person who is deferred remains eligible for service until age 35.

Exemptions and Deferments. — Members of the Armed Forces and most reservists, those who served for one year or more during the Second World War, and ministers and theological students are exempted from (not liable to) the draft. High school students (until graduation or age 20), college students (so long as their work is satisfactory), all elected officials, and those in essential occupations or "hardship" cases are deferred under the law.

Rights and Benefits of Draftees. — All draftees receive the same pay and benefits as others in service, including the benefits of the 1952 Korean GI Bill of Rights, such as education and loan benefits. Those who held regular jobs before induction are guaranteed their same positions upon return to civilian life.

Universal Military Training. — As early as 1790 George Washington proposed a program of compulsory military training for all of the nation's able-bodied young men. Similar proposals have been heard periodically ever since. Woodrow Wilson advanced such a plan at the end of the First World War. And interest has been especially acute since the Second World War.

Congress approved U.M.T. in principle in 1951, creating a National Security Training Commission to prepare a concrete plan. The Commission's plan called for drafting all fit youths at 18. They would receive six months of basic training at camp or on shipboard and spend another six months in service schools or other training. Then they would spend several years in the reserves — ready to serve should the need arise. Altogether some 400,000 would be in training at any one time.

But Congress has not passed the legislation necessary to put the plan in operation. (Many other similar plans have been advanced by private persons and organizations.)

Many groups favor U.M.T. Most patriotic and veterans organizations and some periodicals and newspapers lead the campaign in its behalf. Basically, they argue that because of the continued possibility of another war we must be "fully prepared." The best way to do this, they say, is to maintain a large, trained "citizen reserve" rather than a large standing army. It is claimed, too, that a U.M.T. program would help to promote vigorous and effective citizenship.

Many groups oppose U.M.T. The major opponents include most religious, educational, farm, and labor groups. Basically, they argue that such a program might easily lead to the "militarization" of our society and perhaps even to military dictatorship. It is claimed, too, that U.M.T. could not provide an adequately trained reserve that could be called up at a moment's notice in this age of atomic warfare.

ATOMIC ENERGY COMMISSION

The Atomic Energy Commission, a five-man civilian body, whose members are appointed by the President and the Senate, controls atomic energy in the United States. Under the direction of the Commission, the Divisions of Research, Production, Engineering, and Military Application carry out this program using government, industrial, and educational laboratories and plants.

It is illegal to produce, possess, or transfer fissionable materials without consent of the Commission. If done to injure the United States, the penalty is death. But we are ready to use this energy to promote peace if other nations co-operate.

THE DEPARTMENT OF JUSTICE

The Attorney-General, head of the Department of Justice, is legal adviser to the President and administrative departments. He investigates crimes and enforces an increasing number of criminal laws formerly left to State enforcement or non-enforcement. He is prosecuting attorney for the Government, and directs the administration of the Federal courts and prisons.

The Federal Bureau of Investigation investigates all violations of Federal laws except those which have been assigned to other agencies — *e.g.*, counterfeiting, postal and customs violations, and internal revenue matters. The FBI is charged with guarding the internal security of the United States and has jurisdiction in cases of espionage, treason, and sabotage. It also investigates alleged violations of more than 120 Federal statutes such as: the Federal Kidnapping Statute, the National Motor Vehicle Theft Act, the White Slave Act, the Atomic Energy Act, and the National Bank Act. The G-men co-operate closely with State and local law enforcement officers and maintain a vast fingerprint and identification file that is invaluable in criminal investigations and prosecutions.

As prosecuting attorney the Attorney-General seldom appears in court in person. His numerous assistants prepare cases and represent him in court. For example, one group represents the Government in all suits brought against the United States in the Court of Claims; another has charge of cases arising out of the administration of our tax laws; while another is known as "trust busters."

As director of the Federal court system the Attorney-General is consulted by the President in the appointment of Federal district attorneys and Federal district marshals. After these officers are appointed by the President they are under the direction of the Attorney-General.

The Bureau of Prisons has charge of all non-military Federal penal and correctional institutions. At Atlanta, Georgia; Lewisburg, Pennsylvania; Leavenworth, Kansas; McNeil Island, Washington

State; Terre Haute, Indiana; and Alcatraz, California, are Federal penitentiaries. Alcatraz ("the rock"), in San Francisco Bay, is for very dangerous criminals.

Acme Photo

FEDERAL BUREAU OF INVESTIGATION (FBI) FINGERPRINT EXPERT

This investigator is checking fingerprints against card-file information. The FBI is a fact-finding agency constantly vigilant for our country's welfare.

The laboratory in Washington, along with its extensive files of fingerprints, has every modern device for scientific analysis of clues. Criminals and enemy agents are hard put to it to escape when G-Men get on their trail.

There are three reformatories for male first offenders over 17, and one reformatory for women guilty of Federal offenses. Eight correctional institutions are provided for males serving short-term sentences. Also short-term male offenders may be sent to the three Federal prison camps where they are used for roadbuilding and other construction work. Prisoners soon eligible for release are often transferred to these camps. Juvenile delinquents guilty of Federal crimes are sent to the National Training School for Boys at Washington, D. C.

The prison hospital at Springfield, Missouri, cares for prisoners who are insane, tubercular, or otherwise chronically ill.

The Federal Government contracts with county jails and State institutions for "boarding" Federal prisoners awaiting trial or serving short terms; but in such cities as New York, Detroit, New Orleans, and El Paso it operates its own jails.

The Commissioner of Prison Industries, under the Federal Prison

Industries Incorporated, uses prison labor to manufacture materials for Government use only; or he can work prisoners on Federal roads, levees, forests, lands, and the like.

A Police Academy is conducted in the Department, and is open to State and city police free.

The Board of Parole, consisting of three members appointed by the Attorney-General, was created in 1930 to replace several boards which formerly paroled Federal prisoners.

Probation Officers may be appointed by United States District Court Judges — with or without salary. These officers are to aid persons on probation and to bring about improvements in their conduct and condition. They must perform such duties for persons on parole as the Attorney-General may request.

The Criminal Division supervises criminal prosecutions under such Federal laws as those on national banking, bankruptcy, counterfeiting, postoffice frauds, customs frauds, racketeering, liquor, narcotics, and white slave traffic.

The Immigration and Naturalization Service. — The United States is a nation of immigrants. Except for American Indians, all of us have come here from abroad or are descended from those who did.

Congress Has Power to Regulate Immigration. — Under international law, all sovereign states may regulate the crossing of their borders. The Supreme Court has held that this sovereign power, although not expressed in the Constitution, is an exclusive power of Congress. In addition to this international source for the power to regulate immigration, Congress may lean on its expressed power to regulate foreign commerce — people being classed as commerce.

Congress has created the Immigration and Naturalization Service, within the Justice Department, to administer its statutes regulating immigration and naturalization. The basic statute today is the Immigration and Nationality Act of 1952.

Through the first 100 years of our national history, immigration was generally encouraged. There were vast and uninhabited stretches of the frontier West to be filled. But, by the 1880's, the open frontier was becoming a thing of the past.

Beginning with the Chinese Exclusion Act of 1882,[1] Congress began

---

[1] This law was intended to stem the flow of coolie labor to the Pacific Coast. Because of their lower standard of living the Chinese could afford to work for less

to clamp down on immigration. In the next several years Congress excluded many groups — particularly people of undesirable personal characteristics such as the feebleminded, anarchists, paupers.

But still the flood of immigration continued, running over 1,000,000 a year in the first years of this century. In 1921, Congress began limiting immigration on the basis of national origin as well as on personal grounds. Finally, the National Origins Act of 1929 set the basic pattern for the present control system.

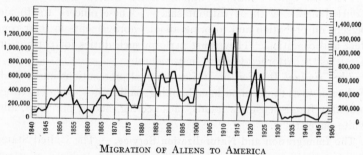

MIGRATION OF ALIENS TO AMERICA

Today no alien who is ineligible for citizenship may enter the United States, except for temporary purposes. All aliens who are permitted to enter for permanent residence, that is, to become citizens, come in as either *quota* or *non-quota immigrants*. Many *non-immigrants* are admitted each year, but only for temporary stays.

As we have seen, Congress has banned one undesirable class after another. The list of undesirables now takes up seven pages in the United States Code — such groups as feeble-minded or insane persons, epileptics, chronic alcoholics, drug addicts, vagrants, personal beggars, stowaways, paupers, tuberculars and carriers of other contagious diseases, criminals, immoral persons, polygamists, adults unable to read any language, those who advocate the forcible overthrow of government in the United States, and members or former members of communist or fascist parties.

---

than white laborers, especially in the mines and on the railroads. By 1924 all Orientals had been excluded except for temporary visits. World War II brought a slight relaxation in the Oriental exclusion policy; but up until 1952 only limited numbers of Chinese, Filipinos, and natives of India were admitted.

The Quota System. — Despite the exclusion of various groups after 1882, the number of immigrants continued to rise. So, after World War I, Congress began placing restrictions on mere numbers. Each country outside the Western Hemisphere has been assigned a *quota* — the number of immigrants that may be admitted from that country each year.[1] Quotas are allotted to each country in the same proportion to which the different nationalities contributed to the population of the United States as of the 1920 census. The grand total of all quota immigrants admitted each year is now limited to approximately 156,000, but no nation has a quota of less than 100. Under this system Great Britain naturally has the largest quota, 65,361, Germany is second with 25,814, and on down to the minimum 100 for such countries as India and Ethiopia.

Non-quota Immigrants. — In addition to the 156,000 quota immigrants, thousands of others enter the United States each year outside the quota restrictions. No quota restrictions are placed on persons born in the Western Hemisphere; but they must meet the personal standards for all aliens. Other non-quota immigrants include alien wives or husbands of American citizens, resident aliens returning from a brief visit to their native countries, ministers who intend to preach their religions here, and the alien children of American citizens.

Congress sometimes relaxes the bars for certain groups or persons. This was done for "war brides" after World War II. The Displaced Persons Acts of 1948 and 1950 allowed the admission of 415,744 refugees from war-torn Europe (but D.P.'s admitted are charged against their nationality's future quotas). In 1953 Congress authorized the admission of another 214,000 persons, mostly iron-curtain refugees.

Non-immigrants. — Each year thousands of aliens come to the United States as non-immigrants — that is, for temporary purposes. Students, tourists, businessmen, and newspapermen from other countries are examples. By special act, Congress granted the late Sister Elizabeth Kenny, the Australian nurse famed for her infantile paralysis work, the right to enter and leave the United States at will.

---

[1] An immigrant's nationality for determining under which nation's quota he enters is determined by his place of birth rather than his residence. Thus one born in Germany but entering the United States from Great Britain is admitted under the German quota. The Immigration and Nationality Act of 1952 eliminated the entire Oriental exclusion policy and extended the quota system to all parts of the Far East, as well as the rest of the world.

Aliens in the United States. — About 4,000,000 aliens now live in the United States; some 200,000 immigrants and 400,000 non-immigrants come here each year.[1] In nearly all respects these people enjoy the same great civil liberties that citizens do. In many States certain professions (such as law, medicine, and dentistry) are closed to them and in some they cannot own such weapons as rifles. In a few States their right to own property is very severely restricted and many

Photo by Ollie Atkins, reprinted by special permission of The Saturday Evening Post, © 1949, Curtis Publishing Company.

ABOARD THE *QUEEN MARY*

An Immigration Inspector checks the names of this Polish Rabbi and his family, as they arrive in this country. The Rabbi and his daughter qualify as non-quota immigrants.

defense industries will not employ aliens. They are not eligible for social security benefits. But, generally, they may attend the public schools, make contracts, use the courts, own property, enter most businesses — in short, do most of the things any citizen may do. Of course, they cannot vote or hold most public offices but they must pay taxes. When an alien becomes a citizen he gains all of the rights and assumes all of the responsibilities of that cherished status.

---

[1] Aliens of all ages must register with the Justice Department during the first thirty days in each year.

How Immigrants Enter the United States. — Every alien immigrant seeking to enter the United States must go before an American consul and obtain from him a visa establishing his apparent right to enter the United States, subject to a further examination at the port of entry.

A FAMILY OF DISPLACED PERSONS

This family, arriving from an Italian D.P. camp, gets its first look at the United States.   Such families are often sponsored by private citizens, and by civic and church groups.   More than 300,000 D.P.'s were admitted by 1954.

Consuls deny visas to aliens who are legally inadmissible to the United States.   Some few immigrants are turned back at Ellis Island and other "ports of entry" by immigration officials.

The steamship company that brings immigrants is required to return to the port of embarkation any alien that may be rejected at the port of entry.   An alien from Brazil once was rejected for insanity. Brazil would not take him back because he was not a citizen of Brazil.   The ship carried him back and forth for years, until his condition improved.

During the years indicated, the immigration to the United States and migration from the United States were as follows:

COUNTRIES	1940		1950	
	Inward	Outward	Inward	Outward
Germany	21,520	1,978	128,592	1,309
Canada	10,806	769	21,885	2,267
England	5,850	998	10,191	2,919
Italy	5,302	1,534	12,454	1,636
West Indies	2,675	1,300	6,206	3,190
France	2,575	542	4,430	1,125
Mexico	2,313	4,584	6,744	1,257
Hungary	1,902	136	190	27
Belgium	1,713	61	1,429	237
South America	1,105	1,004	3,284	2,873
Czechoslovakia	1,074	39	946	97
Greece	811	261	1,179	588
Eire	749	322	4,837	372
Poland	702	81	696	106
All others	11,659	7,852	46,124	9,595
Total Immigrant Aliens . .	70,756	21,461	249,187	27,598

Deportation. — A citizen cannot be deported. But an alien may be forced to leave for a variety of reasons. Illegal entry is the most common cause. Aliens who enter with falsified passports or sneak in by plane or ship or at night are usually persons of low moral code. Having entered illegally, they are viewed as a menace and are deported. In times like these, immigration and other Federal officers are especially concerned with foreign agents who may slip in.

"Wadies," Mexicans who wade or walk across the border, present a peculiar problem. Many are attracted by higher farm wages here and they must be rounded up periodically — sometimes hundreds of miles from the border. It is not at all uncommon for many of the very same wadies to be deported several times in the same month.

Any alien who commits a crime involving moral turpitude, or violates narcotics laws, or commits practically any other felony (not a minor crime) may be deported. Lately, the Justice Department has been moving against many alien gamblers and racketeers in order to deport them.

Any alien who teaches or advocates the forcible overthrow of the Government of the United States, or who belongs to any organization

THREE OF FORTY MEN WHO ATTEMPTED ILLEGAL ENTRY INTO THE UNITED
STATES BY HIDING IN THE FALSE BOTTOM OF THIS MELON TRUCK

which does (such as the communist party), may be deported. We
have no use for those who would come here to enjoy our liberties while
working to overthrow them.

The Alien Record is Good. — Through the years, the record of the
alien population has been quite good. According to F.B.I. records,
for example, the crime rate for aliens is well below that for citizens.
Because those who are admitted must meet the high standards set by
law, they many times become among the very best of our citizens.

Naturalization of Aliens. — One of the functions of the Immigration
and Naturalization Service is to keep records of immigration and to see
that those who desire citizenship may be naturalized according to law.

Three Ways of Becoming Citizens. — All persons born in the United
States,[1] and subject to the jurisdiction thereof,[2] are citizens of the

---

[1] Children born abroad to United States citizens who have once resided in the
United States are natural-born American citizens. Children born abroad, one of
whose parents is a citizen, must live in United States territory for at least five years
between ages 14 and 28 or lose their citizenship. See chart, page 255.

[2] See amendment XIV, note.

United States and of the State wherein they reside. Inhabitants of acquired territory are usually naturalized *en masse.* Congress determines who shall become naturalized and provides for the naturalization of individuals by the judicial process described below.

Who May Become Naturalized. — The Immigration and Nationality Act of 1952 wiped out the ban against naturalization of most Orientals. Any person who comes as a legal immigrant is now eligible to become a naturalized American citizen. The naturalization of both parents[1] naturalizes the children under sixteen if living in the United States. The naturalization of husband or wife does not automatically naturalize the other.[2]

In What Courts. — One may become naturalized in a United States District Court (and other Federal Courts) or in any State court of record having jurisdiction of cases in which the amount in controversy is unlimited.

Filing Declaration of Intention. — Although he is not required to file one, an alien at least 18 years of age may file a declaration of intention to become an American citizen with the clerk of one of the above courts. This declaration contains facts for identification, and an intention to renounce all allegiance to any foreign state and to become a United States citizen.

Filing Petition. — After five years' residence in the United States (or three years if the alien is married to an American citizen), including six months in the State, the applicant files his petition for citizenship with the clerk. He states that he is not opposed to organ-

---

[1] If one parent is naturalized before the other, the children become citizens only upon the naturalization of the latter.

[2] An alien woman or man must now become naturalized independently of husband or wife, but if the one is a natural-born or naturalized American citizen the other need not file a "declaration of intention" and need reside in the United States only three years before "filing petition."

Today American citizenship is neither acquired nor lost by marriage. Until 1922 an alien woman became an American citizen by marriage to an American citizen; and an American woman lost her citizenship by marriage to an alien. An American woman who thus lost her citizenship can regain it as soon as the naturalization examiner satisfies the judge that she was once a natural-born citizen of the United States.

Any person born in the United States who lost his or her United States citizenship by naturalization in a foreign country but was readmitted to the United States for permanent residence prior to March 3, 1931, and is eligible to citizenship, may become naturalized in the United States in as short a period as six months.

ized government, that he is not a polygamist, and that he renounces his allegiance to his former country.

Witnesses. — When the petition is filed, two credible American citizens must testify to the clerk of the court that they have known the petitioner to reside continuously in the United States during the last five years, that he has been a person of good moral character and attached to the principles of the Constitution of the United States. If part of the five years has been spent in another county, the petitioner might file depositions from other witnesses to cover that period.

ITALIAN FILM STAR APPLYING FOR CITIZENSHIP

Isa Miranda, with her husband, is taking the oath, as she files her declaration of intention to become a United States citizen.

Examination. — Formerly the judge conducted the examination. Now a United States District Judge may appoint a naturalization examiner. The examiner questions the applicant and witnesses and learns whether an applicant speaks English, has a reasonable knowledge of the Constitution and Government, and fulfills all other requirements for citizenship. He then reports what he finds with recommendations to the District Judge. The examiner may also perform this service for State judges.

Granting Citizenship. — In not less than 90 days after filing the petition the applicant comes before the judge. The judge may ask a few questions or many, and when he is satisfied that all provisions of the law are fulfilled and that the oath of allegiance is taken in good faith, he directs the clerk to issue a certificate of citizenship.

Cost. — The minimum fees for naturalization total $10, plus the cost of photographs, and legal fee if a lawyer is needed.

QUESTIONS ON THE TEXT

1. What three departments are under the Secretary of Defense?
2. Explain the organization of Army, Navy, and Air Force departments.
3. Describe the Navy, and tell something of its opportunities.
4. Who is Commander-in-chief of the Armed Forces?
5. What are the duties of the Attorney-General?
6. What undesirable classes of immigrants are excluded?
7. What racial group is excluded?
8. Explain the Quota Law.
9. For what causes may aliens be deported?
10. Who are citizens of the United States? Who have obtained citizenship collectively (*en masse*)? Give the steps by which citizenship is obtained individually.
11. Does a woman forfeit citizenship by marrying an alien unless she swears allegiance to the country of her husband?

PROBLEMS FOR DISCUSSION

1. Rockets and atomic bombs necessitate what changes in methods of defense? Are infantry and cavalry more or less important? Navy? Air Force? Distant naval bases? Distant air bases? Coast Guard? An international police force?

2. Give arguments for or against peacetime universal conscription.

3. During World War II we spent 2 billions to perfect the atomic bomb. Do you favor continued research in this big way to keep us one jump ahead of other countries?

4. Do you agree that the best way to keep out of another world war is to prevent the war? By what methods can we help prevent it?

5. "Because of its traditions and the nature of its government, it is always difficult for a true democracy to make clear to a dictator that at some point in his aggression he must face the firm resistance of free nations. Four times the democratic nations waited too long to preserve the peace. Had the Kaiser known that Britain would take the invasion of Belgium as a cause

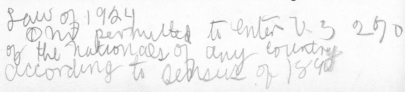

Citizenship Acquired [1]

- **By Birth**
  - Born under American jurisdiction in
    - United States
    - Hawaii
    - Alaska
    - Puerto Rico
    - Guam
    - Virgin Islands
    - United States public vessels anywhere
    - United States embassy or legation
  - Born beyond American jurisdiction to American parents who have at some time resided in U. S. A.
    - Both father and mother American citizens
    - Father or mother an American citizen [2]
- **By Naturalization**
  - Collectively by
    - Treaty — Louisiana (1803), Florida (1819), Alaska (1867)
    - Joint Resolution of Congress — Texas (1845)
    - Act of Congress — Hawaii (1900), Puerto Rico (1917), Virgin Islands (1927), American Indians (1924), Guam (1950)
    - Constitutional Amendment — Negroes by 14th Amendment
  - Courts
    - U. S. Courts of Appeals
    - U. S. District Courts
    - D. C. Municipal Court and Court of Appeals
    - District and Supreme Courts of Territories
    - State courts of record having a seal and jurisdiction of cases with amount in controversy unlimited
  - Individually by Naturalization of both parents (one parent, if other is dead or divorced) automatically naturalizes their children under 16 years of age if the children are residing permanently in the United States.

---

1 See Amendment XIV.

2 Such children (one parent being an alien) must live in the United States continuously for a period of five years between the ages of 14 and 28 years.

255

of war between herself and Germany; had the arrogance of Mussolini in invading Ethiopia been met with other than ineffective sanctions; had the Japanese entry into Manchuria been countered in 1931 with strong determination by the United States and Great Britain; had Hitler's first tentative steps in the Saar and in the Ruhr been firmly opposed—can there be doubt of the effect upon the rising tempo of their boldness?"

What bearing does this statement of the first Secretary of Defense, James Forrestal, have upon present conditions?

6. Many people object to the Immigration and Nationality Act of 1952 because it continues to limit immigration to about one-tenth of 1 per cent of our national population. Give arguments for and against increasing the number permitted to come to the United States each year.

SELECT BIBLIOGRAPHY

ANGLY, E. "Should We Open Our Doors to Immigrants?" *Saturday Evening Post*, February 8, 1947.

BALDWIN, H. "Our New Shock Troops, the Rangers." *New York Times Magazine*, April 27, 1952. pp. 8–9.

BESS, D. "Tomorrow They'll Be Famous." *Saturday Evening Post*, June 14, 1952. p. 24. (Army's future generals.)

BRUCE, J. C. "Must Liberty Bow Her Head in Shame?" *Reader's Digest*, August, 1952. pp. 4–9.

COMPTON, KARL T. "The Case for National Security Training." *Reader's Digest*. August, 1953.

"Defense Against the H-Bomb." *U. S. News*. September 4, 1953.

ELIOT, G. F. "Let's Put the A-Bomb in Macy's Window." *Collier's*. May 16, 1953.

FINLETTER, T. "Should the Navy and the Air Force Merge?" *Collier's*. May 9, 1953.

LARKIN, T. B. "New Weapons." *U. S. News*, May 21, 1952. pp. 38–43.

LAURENCE, W. L. "How Hellish Is the H-Bomb?" *Look*. April 21, 1953.

SWARTHOUT, J. and BARTLEY, E. *Principles and Problems of American National Government*. Oxford Univ. Press. New York. 1954 ed.

"Universal Military Training for U. S. A." *Congressional Digest*, October, 1947. Entire Issue.

U. S. Government Printing Office. Immigration and Naturalization Service. Pamphlet on laws, etc. 10¢.

WHITE, T. H. "The Big Red One." *The Reporter*. August 4, 1953. (The U. S. First Infantry Division in Germany.)

WALTER, F. E. "The Truth About the Immigration Act." *Reader's Digest*. May, 1953. (Defense of 1952 law by one of its authors.)

CHAPTER XIV

THE POST OFFICE AND INTERIOR DEPARTMENTS

THE POST OFFICE DEPARTMENT

The United States Postal Service serves the American people promptly and efficiently at a cost of about two billion dollars a year. Its 500,000 workers deliver nearly 50,000,000,000 pieces of mail each year through more than 40,000 post offices. Today the Post Office is the world's largest public utility.

ONE HORSEPOWER CARRYING MAIL OVER CORDUROY ROAD IN PIONEER DAYS

The Postmaster-General is the head of the Post Office Department. The work of the Department is divided among four Bureaus, each headed by an Assistant Postmaster-General. The Bureau of: (1) Post Office Operations has charge of postmasters and employees; (2) Transportation supervises the carriage of mail by land, water, and air; (3) Finance handles such matters as the sale of stamps and money orders; and (4) Facilities has charge of buildings, motor vehicles, and supplies.

257

Postmasters are graded into classes (1st, 2nd, 3rd, 4th) according to the receipts of the office. Those of the first three classes are appointed by the President and Senate.[1] The Civil Service Commission examines applicants and sends the names of the three highest to the President, who usually appoints the one recommended by the senator if a large office, or by the representative if a small office; and the appointee has indefinite tenure of office. Fourth-class postmasters, postal clerks, letter-carriers, and other minor postal employees are appointed without the ratification of the Senate, and according to civil service examinations. They enjoy permanent tenure.

Post Office Department for Service — Not Profit. — Until the middle of the last century the Post Office Department was expected to pay its own way, or even make a profit. But since 1852 service instead of profits has been our policy; and this year the postal deficit is about two thirds of a billion dollars. Moreover, government-owned post offices are paid for and serviced by general funds appropriated by Congress — and not from postal receipts.

Low Postage Rates. — Originally letter postage was determined by distance and by the number of pages, envelopes not being used. Then a four-page letter from Boston to Charleston, South Carolina, cost one dollar. In recent years such a letter has been sent all the way to Hawaii or to any remote place in this country for three cents.

Air Mail below Cost. — The 6-cent stamp on an air mail letter does not cover the cost of handling. Air mail has always been carried for less than cost; but it encouraged aviation and trained pilots for military service. The mail subsidy also hastened the development of air routes for travel and express.

Cheap air mail saves the public millions of dollars which they would otherwise have to spend for telegrams. It also speeds business and makes one dollar do the work of two. A check from New York to Chicago can be returned to New York the same night, thus saving a whole day by train. For instance, in one mail a Chicago bank returned enough checks to New York to save the bank $1700 interest in one day.

---

[1] Practically speaking, the job of postmaster most often goes to some local person as a "reward" for his support of the party in control of the national administration. The Hoover Commission has very strongly recommended "taking the post office out of politics."

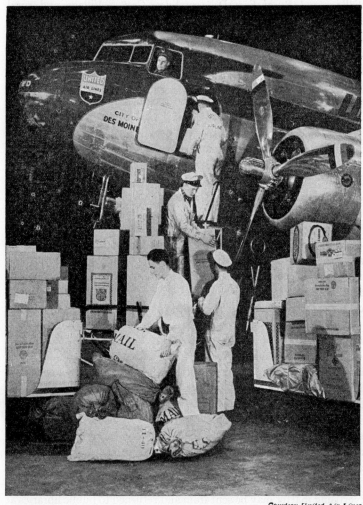

THOUSANDS OF HORSEPOWER CARRYING MAIL THROUGH THE SKY IN THIS
GASOLINE AGE

North Americans are in a hurry and do not mind expense; therefore freight
planes are growing in popularity.

Village and Rural Free Delivery below Cost. — Village and rural free delivery service is truly a service and not a self-sustaining enterprise.   Congress extended this service so that farmers and their wives might have the morning paper and the morning mail almost as soon as their city friends.   Then Congress established the parcel post with rates so low that some isolated individuals find it cheaper than bulk freight rates into inaccessible mountain regions.

Special Below-Cost Rates Are Granted Certain Periodicals Not Published for Profit. — Periodicals issued by religious, educational, scientific, fraternal, and trade union organizations, as well as health, charities, and agricultural departments of State governments, enjoy a below-cost rate of postage because they are published for the public good and not for profit.

Newspapers and Other Periodicals Are Carried at a Loss in order to encourage the spread of worth-while information.   To qualify for these below-cost rates a publication must be "published for the dissemination of information of a public character, or devoted to literature, the sciences, arts, or some special industry."   The loss on this mail reached $200,000,000 a year, so Congress authorized a gradual increase of 30 per cent over the years 1952, 1953, and 1954; but this is still below cost.   When one national magazine was denied the low rate on grounds of obscenity, the courts overruled the action.

Free Postage for County Newspapers. — Because of the difficulty of financing a newspaper in a rural community, any newspaper is distributed free within the county of origin at offices which do not have the letter carrier service.

Free Postage for Literature for the Blind. — Libraries, or other public institutions for the blind, may mail books or other non-advertising reading matter in raised type or sound records free; and the recipient may return the same free.

Reduced Postage on Books. — To encourage reading, books without advertising matter may be sent from and returned to public libraries at the low rate of 4 cents for the first pound and one cent for each additional pound.   The postage rate on books for individuals is 8 cents for the first pound and 4 cents for each additional pound, which is much less than parcel post rates.

The Franking Privilege for Government Mail. — Congressmen may send their official letters and other official mail free under what is called the "franking privilege." For instance, they can have their speeches reprinted from the Congressional Record at cost and mail them free. Before an election a congressman can have political material printed in the Congressional Record, reprints made at cost, and mailed free to post office and R.F.D. "Box Holders" without even going to the trouble of having to address them.

THE IMMORTAL CHAPLAINS   © *Harris & Ewing*

This stamp was issued as a memorial to the Jewish, Catholic, and Protestant chaplains who, in the Second World War, gave their lifebelts to others and went down with their ship.

Federal departments and agencies, agricultural colleges, experiment stations, etc., also send their official mail, such as letters and documents, free. Congress appropriates a lump sum each year to pay the Post Office for carrying this "penalty mail." Until 1954 the Post Office was not reimbursed for congressional mail, but it is now.

U. S. Savings Stamps and Bonds. — Post Offices and banks sell 10¢, 25¢, 50¢, $1, and $5 savings stamps. These may be mounted in free albums which, when filled, can be exchanged for savings bonds or cash. An album of seventy-five 25¢ stamps, having a total value of $18.75, will purchase a bond which in less than ten years will be worth $25.00. (See pages 98–100.)

Many people systematically save by buying savings bonds for self-education, the education of their children, or for old age. The scheme promotes thrift and patriotism as the ownership of a Government bond makes one more interested in the welfare and preservation of the Government.

Other Special Duties of the Postal System. — Besides its routine work the Postal System handles deposits and pays 2% interest; sells Government bonds; has registered laborers under the Social Security Act; has taken a census of the unemployed; has carried billions of dollars' worth of gold by registered mail from New York and Philadelphia to Fort Knox, Kentucky; and sells more than $2,000,000 worth of stamps through the Division of Stamps and Philately annually.

Prohibited Articles. — The following articles cannot be sent through the mails: parcels beyond a specified weight and size, poisons, explosives, intoxicating liquors, live animals and other things dangerous to the mail or the postal employees; concealable firearms except to dealers and officers; libelous, treasonable, or obscene matter, lottery tickets or other prize schemes dependent upon chance; and fraudulent schemes. Some matter is excluded except under regulations prescribed by the Postmaster-General.

Fraud Orders. — When any person or firm attempts to procure money or property through the mails by fraudulent schemes, or schemes of chance, the privileges of the mails are withdrawn from the offender.

If the Postmaster-General decides that a business is fraudulent he issues a "fraud order" to the local postmaster and to the person accused, whereupon the postmaster stamps the word "fraudulent" upon all letters addressed to the accused and returns them to the writers either direct or through a Dead Letter Office if they must be opened for the return address.

The most vicious type of frauds include the so-called work-at-home scheme and the sale of nostrums represented to be cures of disease.

Some years ago a fraudulent firm under the pretentious name of the National Mail Order Brokerage Exchange mailed letters from Minneapolis offering a $4.50 silk petticoat for ten cents in silver on condition that the purchaser notify five friends of the offer, and request each one of them to do likewise. More than 500,000 orders arrived at the Minneapolis office. The perpetrator received only about 300 dimes before a Fraud Order routed him, but it cost the Government $20,000 to return the letters.

It is illegal to use the mails in promoting any lottery scheme. A short time ago a real estate dealer advertised through the mails that he would give a chance on a house and lot to each of the first 20 people who bought a lot from him. This was construed to be a lottery and for nearly a year his incoming mail was returned to the senders with the word "fraudulent" stamped on each piece. He was also heavily fined.

THE INTERIOR DEPARTMENT

The Secretary of the Interior heads the vast Interior Department. The Department's work is especially concerned with the management, conservation, and development of the natural resources of the United States. These resources include the public lands,[1] water and power resources, oil, gas, and other mineral resources, certain forest resources, and the national park system.

The Department also has custody of 750,000,000 acres of land — in the continental United States, the Caribbean, the South Pacific, and Alaska. It promotes mine safety, the protection of fish and wildlife, the preservation of scenic and historic areas, the reclamation of arid lands in the West, and it manages hydroelectric power systems. And it is responsible for the welfare of some 3,000,000 persons in the territories and possessions and of over 430,000 Indians.

The Bureau of Land Management, the most important bureau of the department, has charge of the survey, management, and disposition of the public lands of the United States, and of the minerals therein.

Extent of and Exploitation of Public Lands. — The original States surrendered their public lands to the National Government, which assumed the State debts. Other public lands were acquired by conquest or purchase in our westward expansion. Most of this land was sold or given to settlers in 160-acre homesteads; but large tracts were given to railroads as an inducement to build into the unsettled West; much was given to States for education; but 170,000,000 acres, the worst, remains unreserved national lands (not including national forests, national parks, and Indian reservations).

Much of this public land was once well supplied with grass, but by allowing everybody to graze the land it became so overstocked that

---

[1] Soil conservation on private lands is administered through the Soil Conservation Service in the Department of Agriculture.

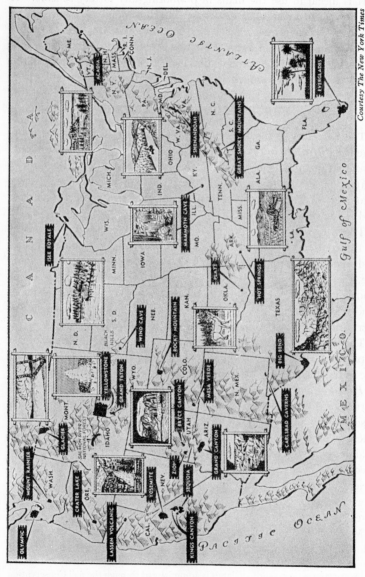

The National Parks — Where the Wilderness Makes Its Last Stand

much of it has become mere dusty plains — the water now washing gullies instead of being conserved by a heavy turf.

The following passage is self-explanatory: "In the old days cattle grazed knee-deep in verdure, rain sank into a spongy ground-covering and found its way gradually into the streams. But for a generation the range has been so overgrazed that every spear of grass has been cropped when it appeared and has been prevented from making seed for later growth. The ground has become bare, trampled down by much grazing. Rainfall runs from bleak, hard hillsides as it might from a tin roof. It cuts deep gullies in them, washes the rich humus from the surface, and exposes the underlying clay. Freshets go tearing down the Rio Grande, mud-laden, and the vegetation-producing soil finally comes to rest in the reservoir created by the Elephant Butte dam, decreasing its storage capacity. A splendid asset, neglected, has become a local menace."

Conservation of Public Lands instead of disposal is the present Government policy. Some is reserved for oil or gas or minerals, some for water power sites,[1] and over most of it grazing is now restricted. Cattle men now pay a license fee for grazing cattle on public lands.

In 1953 Congress granted the coastal States title to the submerged lands from low tide out to their "historic boundaries." In Louisiana, Texas, and California these lands contain rich oil fields. The United States has title to the rest of the Continental Shelf; these latter lands are leased and managed through the Interior Department.

The Bureau of Reclamation. — *Introduction.* — Brigham Young, traveling with his caravan to Utah, told his Indian scout that he intended to plant a farming community beyond the mountains. The scout pooh-poohed the idea and offered a thousand dollars for the first ear of corn that was grown. In July, 1847, these pioneers came from Immigration Canyon into the parched Salt Lake Valley. They unhitched their teams along the little stream now known as City Creek; and the same afternoon they unloaded their plows and began breaking this dry desert land. The next day the stream was diverted, the plowed land irrigated, and potatoes planted. This was the beginning of Anglo-Saxon irrigation in the West. Today more than 275,000 people live in this Salt Lake Valley region.

---

[1] For many years the Government has reserved power sites and sub-soil deposits even in lands disposed of for homesteads.

Reclamation Act of 1902. — In 1902, largely through the efforts of President Theodore Roosevelt, the Reclamation Act was passed. This and later Acts set aside money obtained from the sale and lease of public lands as a "revolving fund" to be applied to the reclamation of arid lands. When an irrigation project is completed, the land is sold to farmers in small tracts on easy terms, and the money collected from

Courtesy Bureau of Reclamation

YAKIMA IRRIGATION PROJECT

This young man set out 11,000 apple trees on land that was worthless until the Reclamation Service brought water to the area.

these sales goes into the revolving fund to be used in the construction of additional irrigation plants. This revolving fund amounts to about $165,000,000, but is now increasing very little because of our conservation policy. For large reclamation projects Congress has to appropriate additional funds.

Accomplishments. — The Bureau of Reclamation has built up a staff of experts on irrigation now competent to handle enormous projects like that at Grand Coulee, and its projects now water an area of more than five million acres.

As a measure of what the Federal development of irrigation lands can mean to the national economy, one project alone in the Yakima Valley of Washington has produced $76,000,000 of crops in one year, and has made it possible to furnish gainful employment for a population of 100,000, where prior to the development only sagebrush and jack rabbits were found. This project represents an investment of less than $40,000,000.

In 1952 an extensive program to discover a practical method for the converting of salt water into fresh water was begun. If it is successful, the benefits that may be realized defy the imagination.

Boulder Canyon Project and Hoover Dam. — The hot semitropical Imperial Valley at its lowest point is 300 feet below sea level. It was originally part of the Gulf of California. But the Colorado River brought down enough mud every year to cover 100,000 acres a foot deep. When in flood the river was too thick to drink and too thin to plow. So in time it filled the Gulf of California and built up a deltaic ridge, which is now over 100 feet above sea level at the international boundary.

This ridge forms the southern rim of the Imperial Valley. The Colorado River, flowing along it until it turns south to the Gulf of California, was kept out of the low valley by a levee 70 miles long; but as the river became higher each year there was danger of a break in the levee and of flooding the homes of a hundred thousand people.

Now the Hoover Dam, built by the Bureau of Reclamation, creates a navigable lake a hundred miles long which catches the silt that was raising the level of the river down at the levees; and it provides water to irrigate 50 per cent more of the Imperial Valley area than formerly.

The dam also generates 663,000 continuous horsepower of electricity, thereby saving 23,000,000 gallons of oil which otherwise would be used annually in California to generate electricity.

Moreover, the electricity pumps over the mountains an abundance of clear water to Los Angeles and neighboring communities 265 miles from the Colorado River.

This Boulder Canyon Project will pay for itself in about 50 years and will be no expense to the United States Government.

The Grand Coulee Dam, completed on the Columbia River in 1942, will provide water to irrigate 1,200,000 acres, an area larger than Rhode Island. Its power plant is the world's greatest, and has a 2,700,000 horsepower capacity. The flow of water is five times the flow at Hoover Dam, and can produce five times the power of the American Falls at Niagara.

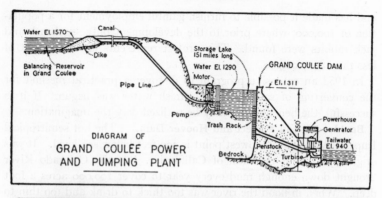

DIAGRAM OF
GRAND COULEE POWER
AND PUMPING PLANT

Courtesy "New York Times"

The project demonstrates a stream that lifts itself by its own boot-straps. During flood season surplus power will lift the water to a natural reservoir from which it will flow by gravity to a million acres. But the Northwest's rapid growth in recent years has created a severe power shortage that will not be overcome until 1957 at the earliest.

The California Central Valley Project, with its Shasta Dam near Redding, now supplements the insufficient water for the rich San

Courtesy Bureau of Reclamation

THE GRAND COULEE DAM

Joaquin Valley, and supplies power to pump the water where needed. The constant flow of fresh water protects land from salt water which may back up from San Francisco Bay.

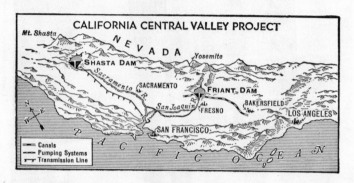

The **National Park Service**, created in 1916, is charged with the care and management of the nearly 200 national parks, monuments, and reservations (including the White House and grounds in Washington). In these areas it protects the scenery, wildlife, and historic objects, maintaining them, by law, "for the enjoyment of future generations."

The **Geological Survey** has made topographic and geologic maps of nearly half of the surface of the United States; and because of this work we not only know the height of hills and the volume of water which flows in streams, but we know where some valuable minerals are likely to occur below the surface.

As an illustration of the value of the work done by the Geological Survey, a number of years ago when the Lackawanna Railroad relocated thirty-four miles of its main line the head engineer of construction sat comfortably at his office desk and ran all the preliminary surveys, and even made the final location for the $12,000,000 improvement from the data contained on the topographic sheet. This is only one example of the many advantages we get from the Geological Survey.

Mineral Rights Reserved. — The Geological Survey makes mineral surveys and classifies the public lands, besides supervising the engineering phases of mineral leasing. Homesteaders now have only surface rights, the mineral rights still remaining with the Government. The Government then leases mining, oil, and gas rights on the homestead lands as well as on the public lands for a period of years on a royalty basis; and a certain percentage of this royalty is given to the State in which the leased land happens to be.

Petroleum and natural gas are found in underground "lakes." Hence when oil and gas are "struck" in a locality every one who owns land or has a government lease drills for oil, and the one who operates fastest makes the most money because he can drain the liquid oil or gas from his neighbors' subterranean lakes. This situation results in a wild rush, over-production, low prices, and the encouragement of waste both on the part of the producers and the consumers. As an example of this waste in production, at Kettleman Hills, California, a score of interests had sunk so many wells that the gas wasted from these wells exceeded 450,000,000 cubic feet of gas a day.

Part of the 10,800 acres of Kettleman Hills was owned by the Standard Oil Company, part by other interests, and part was leased from the Government by the same or other interests. To conserve our oil which was so wastefully being exploited, Con-

UNITED STATES GEOLOGICAL SURVEYORS AT WORK

These engineers provided maps for the Hoover Dam project, as former ones made possible our transcontinental railroads.

gress in 1930 and 1931 authorized the Secretary of the Interior to permit government lessees to pool their interests with others for unit production. Therefore, in 1931, these various interests formed the Kettleman North Dome Association — a corporation to operate the pool as a unit for the life of the field, dividing the profits on the basis of the acreage held by each interest.

A 1946 amendment to the Mineral Leasing Act provides that the lessee of public domain forfeits his lease if he does not use all reasonable precautions to prevent waste of oil and gas in his explorations and mining operations.

The Bureau of Mines has examined thousands of deposits of strategic minerals in the 48 States and Alaska — many of them by shaft-sinking, tunneling, and diamond drilling; and by experimental pilot plants, a domestic supply of such minerals as manganese and bauxite was made available.

This Bureau also supervises mine rescue training and investigates the causes of mine fires and explosions. It works to reduce the number of mine deaths, which now run to about 1000 a year. It makes thousands of coal analyses for prospective miners, and for the benefit of the Government and individuals in the selection of suitable coals.

In 1948 J. A. Krug, Secretary of the Interior, warned that the known United States petroleum reserves would be exhausted in ten years at the current rate of consumption. So Congress increased the annual appropriation for the Bureau of Mines to experiment with coals, oil shale, and agricultural and forestry products to determine which are most suitable for the manufacture of gasoline and to increase the oil resources of the United States.

In 1950 the Bureau reported the preliminary results of successful attempts to produce synthetic fuel from oil shale. The Bureau's Demonstration Plant at Rifle, Colorado, has produced gasoline from oil shale at a cost of 8.4 cents per gallon. Experiments are also being conducted with lignite and soft coal. A proposed $60,000,000 synthetic fuel industry, together with the vast reserves of shale, lignite and soft coal, are expected to make the United States independent of any foreign oil supply in time of war and to prolong indefinitely the life of our domestic oil reserve.

The Commissioner of Indian Affairs has charge of the lands, schools, moneys, supplies, and general welfare of about 337,000 Indians living on reservations. He acts as a sort of trustee to supervise the leasing of forests, mineral lands, and water power on reservations. And the Act of 1934 directs him to encourage tribal self-government and cooperative enterprises.

Old Policies. — When the white man pushed the Indians westward, he set aside portions of the public domains, called "reservations," and within these areas the Indians were allowed to practice their tribal customs. The tribes were regarded as nations and the Government made treaties with them. These treaties were sometimes violated by Acts of Congress, and in 1871 the treaty policy was abandoned and their persons and property came directly under the legislative power of Congress.

SOUTHERN NAVAJOS IN FRONT OF A HOGAN
It is warm in winter and cool in summer.

By the Act of 1887 and subsequent laws the President was given authority to divide reservations into homesteads for Indians and surplus land into homesteads for whites. After a designated period of years some Indians were allowed to sell or lease their individual lands; and since 1887 two thirds of these lands have been acquired by whites.

In 1924 Congress extended American citizenship to all Indians born in the United States. The aim was to prepare them to perform social, political, and legal duties of citizenship as any other citizen of the State in which they live. In other words, every Indian was expected to learn to hoe his own row among whites.

New Policies. — John Collier, appointed Commissioner of Indian Affairs in 1933, believed that most Indians are not trained to compete with whites in our form of civilization, and that the elimination of tribal life would leave most Indians as stranded paupers. So he secured new legislation the next year.

The 1934 Act of Congress provides that no more reservation Indian land shall be allotted to individual Indians; forbids the sale of restricted Indian lands; authorizes the Secretary of the Interior to restore to tribal ownership remaining "surplus lands" in reservations heretofore opened for sale; authorizes the appropriation of $2,000,000 a year for the acquisition of additional lands for Indians inside or outside the reservations; and authorizes new reservations on such lands.

The 1934 Act further authorizes an Indian tribe or tribes, by a majority vote, to adopt a constitution for the revival of a limited amount of self-government. It authorizes a tribe, by a majority vote, to form a commercial corporation for the co-operative holding of land or other enterprises; and the Act appropriated $10,000,000 as a revolving fund to make loans to these enterprises.

The new educational policy is to give Indians such vocational education as will prepare them for subsistence homesteads and for leadership among their own people. And the Act gives preference to Indians for positions in the Indian service without a competitive examination.

The Fish and Wildlife Service operates fish hatcheries, and investigates the best methods of cultivating and conserving the supply. It administers the Alaskan fisheries and sealeries. It also investigates birds and wild mammals for farmers and foresters, and promotes useful wildlife animals.

QUESTIONS ON THE TEXT

1. What are the duties of the Postmaster-General?
2. Explain why there is usually a deficit in the Postal Service.
3. What is meant by the *franking privilege?*
4. Explain United States Savings Bonds.
5. Name some special duties of the Postal System.
6. What articles are excluded from the mails?
7. What is a *fraud order*, and by whom is it issued?
8. What are the duties of the Bureau of Land Management?
9. Explain how we are trying to conserve our public lands.
10. Explain the Reclamation Act of 1902.
11. What are the duties of the Geological Survey?
12. What are the duties of the Bureau of Mines?
13. Explain how we are trying to conserve our petroleum.
14. Contrast the old and the new Indian policies.

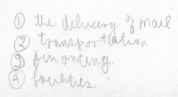

PROBLEMS FOR DISCUSSION

1. When a new post office building is erected in a small town the janitor for the new building often costs as much as the rent of the former quarters. This appears extravagant. On the other hand, a new, well-ventilated, and well-lighted building of pleasing architecture may inspire the people of the town with respect for the Government and for other civic improvements. Do you favor a Government-owned post office?

2. The general post office and 21 of the larger postal stations in New York and the general post office at Brooklyn are connected by 27 miles of double 8-inch pneumatic tubes which carry first-class mail at the rate of 30 miles an hour. Is such a system justified even if it costs more than motor bus service?

3. It is unlawful to use the mails for a fraudulent purpose. For instance, some years ago a young man from a distant State went to Maryland, married a wealthy woman, and persuaded her to send him to Philadelphia to study medicine. The young man used the allowance to support himself in idleness instead of devoting it to an education. But, inasmuch as he had used the mails to request money fraudulently from the Maryland woman, he was prosecuted by Uncle Sam.

We have seen how the United States Government has expanded its powers through its right to regulate interstate commerce and its right of taxation. Is this right to prevent fraudulent use of the mails likely greatly to increase its powers?

4. In a New Zealand post office a person can buy stamps, mail a letter or parcel, send a telegram, deposit money, collect a pension, report births and deaths, and insure his life. What new functions, if any, do you think our postmasters might economically perform?

5. In 1932, following the kidnaping of Charles Lindbergh, Jr., Congress enacted a law providing that whoever, with intent to extort money, mails matter containing any threat (1) to injure the person, property, or reputation of any person, or (2) to kidnap any person, or (3) to accuse any person of a crime, or containing any demand or request for ransom or reward for the release of any kidnaped person, shall be fined not more than $5000 or imprisoned not more than twenty years, or both. Could Congress penalize such a threat by local telephone? By long-distance telephone from another State?

6. Why does the possession of Savings Bonds by millions of people create loyalty to the Government? Why have these bonds become such a popular form of investment?

7. Some oil interests favor a protective tariff to cut off foreign oil competition. What effect would such a tariff have on the price of oil in the

United States? On the conservation of oil in the United States? The exhaustion of our oil wells would have what effect on the price of gasoline?

8. Does reclamation of arid lands increase or decrease the value of unfertile lands which are not irrigated? Increase or decrease the output of agricultural products per man? Increase or decrease national wealth? Should the Government develop reclamation projects?

9. Why are National parks more important than in times past?

SELECT BIBLIOGRAPHY

BENNETT, H. H. "Warning: the Water Problem Is National." *Saturday Evening Post*, May 13, 1950.

Facts About Oil Imports. Standard Oil of New Jersey. 1953. (Free)

FISCHER, M. "What You Don't Know About Mailing a Letter." *Collier's.* May 30, 1953.

Fortune. "Triumph of the Empire Builders." February, 1952.

HOLMAN, H. "Our Inexhaustible Resources." *Atlantic Monthly.* June, 1952. (Reprints available from Standard Oil of New Jersey, 30 Rockefeller Plaza, New York 20, N. Y.)

"Interview with Postmaster General Summerfield." *U. S. News.* July 31, 1953.

MAHONEY, J. R. "National Resources Activity of the Federal Government." *Public Affairs Bulletin No. 73*, Library of Congress, June, 1950. (Specially recommended)

Our Times, "Conserve or Perish," March 31, 1947.

SUMMERFIELD, A. "The Burden of Franking." *Newsweek.* June 22, 1953.

U. S. News, "Still Enough Gasoline, But — ," October 27, 1950.

CHAPTER XV

THE DEPARTMENT OF AGRICULTURE *Benson*

The Secretary of Agriculture is in charge of this department, which is the most scientific of the nine departments. It employs numerous experts in many lines to make studies and conduct experiments and to pass the information on to the general body of farmers.

The following are some of the divisions of the Department of Agriculture.

Animal Industry, and Dairy Industry
Plant Industry, Soils, and Agricultural Engineering
Entomology and Plant Quarantine
Agricultural and Industrial Chemistry
Human Nutrition and Home Economics

Soil Conservation	Experiment Stations
Forest Service	Extension Service
Farm Credit	Rural Electrification
Farmers Home	Crop Insurance
Commodity Credit	Commodity Exchange

AGRICULTURAL RESEARCH ACTIVITIES

The Bureau of Animal Industry studies animal diseases, enforces the National quarantine laws for livestock, and is carrying on a determined campaign to root out tubercular cattle. By experiments in the breeding and feeding of livestock and poultry, it has discovered that a large portion of the dairy cows of the United States do not pay for their feed; and if the Bureau's directions were followed as to the best breeds of chickens to keep and how to feed them, it is estimated that the increased annual value of eggs would be $100,000,000. Also the Bureau has discovered that cows fed on a good grade of alfalfa hay produce milk with five times as much vitamin A in it as do cows fed on a good grade of timothy hay.

The Federal meat inspection service is one of the Bureau's largest regulatory services. This insures the wholesomeness of meat. The Bureau is now helping to fight the foot-and-mouth disease in Mexico.

The Bureau of Dairy Industry improves the dairy cow through breeding; and determines the best feeds for growth, reproduction, and milk. It studies the nutritional properties of milk and milk products; develops better processing methods; discovers new kinds of dairy products; and finds new uses of milk in foods.

The Bureau of Plant Industry, Soils and Agricultural Engineering. — *Plant Industry.* — The Bureau studies weed control and improves the yield and quality of crops. It breeds new strains and varieties that resist disease, drought, heat, and cold. It studies methods of planting, harvesting, transportation, and storage. Also it has ransacked the world for new crops, and has brought here for trial more than 100,000 kinds of new plants and seeds many of which are an important part of our agriculture. In 1870 it brought the navel orange from Brazil and introduced this fruit in California, where it has become one of the principal crops. It has introduced the soybean from China and the pistachio nut from Western Asia. From Egypt it introduced the long fiber Pima cotton which has brought prosperity to the Salt River Valley of Arizona.

United States Department of Agriculture

MOTHER, FATHER, AND OFFSPRING

The United States Department of Agriculture breeds this high-milk-producing Jersey to a Brahman bull from India to produce cattle for hot and dry climates.

Soils. — This Bureau also maintains the soil analysis survey by which a farmer can learn from the physical and chemical analysis that the Bureau makes which of his fields are best adapted to certain crops and what fertilizers to use. In buying a new farm, this information makes it possible for him to know just what kind of soil he is getting and what crops are likely to prove most successful.

Engineering. — This Bureau investigates and improves farm machinery and equipment, including farm buildings. It has improved such appliances as harvesters, hay driers, cotton pickers, flax machines, water systems, and sanitary devices. Research is done on storages for grain and vegetables, and on temperature and humidity control in the transportation and storage of perishable fruits and vegetables.

Courtesy Bell Aircraft Corporation

CROP DUSTING

Supplementing the research of the Bureau of Entomology and Plant Quarantine, the helicopter has added immeasurably to this method of crop protection.

The Bureau of Entomology and Plant Quarantine combats insects which are a menace to crops, animals, and persons. A favorite method of fighting insect pests that come from a foreign shore is to go back to the home of the pest and discover its natural enemy. When the white scale of citrus fruits threatened this fruit industry of California, the ladybug was imported from Australia to save the industry. From California the ladybug was carried to various sections to prey upon the aphis and plant lice. One ladybug will eat about two hundred plant lice a day. The Smyrna fig trees of California did not bear until the fly which is the go-between in fertilizing the fig was imported from the Near East.

The Bureau also conducts chemical investigations to develop new insecticides and research to improve methods and equipment for their application.

The Bureau of Agricultural and Industrial Chemistry finds new uses for farm products, discovers processes for converting agricultural wastes into useful commercial articles, and carries on research in foods, feeds, and drugs. It maintains numerous experimental farms and laboratories. For instance, it has developed methods of preserving foods by freezing or dehydrating, and of manufacturing sheer cotton hose. It also is seeking a cheap substitute for gasoline from farm products.

GOAT STAND AT UNITED STATES EXPERIMENT FARM

Here is a convenient milking stand used in an experiment for getting more and better milk from the hearty goat, for babies that cannot digest cow's milk or the poor who cannot afford it.

There are four great regional laboratories for research in the use and conservation of farm products at Peoria, Illinois; New Orleans; Wyndmoor, Pennsylvania; and Albany, California.

The Bureau of Human Nutrition and Home Economics helps to raise the standard of home living through research and educational activities. It plans diets to safeguard health and to get the full return in food value from whatever supplies are available. It develops better ways of cooking foods, and works out recipes for low-cost, easy-to-prepare foods. It furnishes safe directions for home canning and food preservation. It designs functional clothes. It prepares consumer buying guides on textiles and home equipment. This research is made available through bulletins, press releases, radio talks, and exhibitions.

State Agricultural Experiment Stations are departments of State Land-Grant Colleges, and the *U. S. Office of Experiment Stations* co-operates with them in advancing experiment projects. About one fifth of the total cost is appropriated by the Federal Government.

THE FOREST SERVICE

The Forest Service has charge of the National Forest reserves — now approximating 180,000,000 acres — and co-operates in local public and private forests. We preserve the numerous large forests because they prevent floods which denude the soil, and they conserve the winter rains and snow that make rivers navigable in summer, irrigate plains, and supply pure water for our cities and towns. Besides conserving the rainfall and providing recreation for our city dwellers, the Forest Service is planting and conserving trees to help supply the lumber needs of this and coming generations.

The forests are under careful management for permanent production and wise use of their timber, water, forage, wildlife, and recreation resources. During the dry season rangers are alert to prevent or control fires. Portable, two-way radios now replace telephones and homing pigeons for communication in fire fighting.

After a forest tree reaches maturity it decays, therefore the Government sells the mature trees, which must be cut without injury to the forest. The forests may also contain minerals and water-power sites which are leased on a royalty or rental basis. The forests are also valuable for the grazing of livestock which were once allowed to graze practically unrestricted; but to prevent the destruction of herbage by over-use, a fee is now charged and the number of animals admitted is limited to the capacity of the land. In other words, forest grazing ranges as well as forests are being conserved.

The income from National forest lands is shared with the communities in which such forests are located. In this way the objection sometimes heard that Uncle Sam pays no taxes has been largely overcome.

United States Forest Service

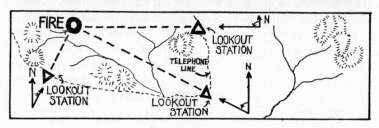

LOCATING A FIRE

The "lookouts" draw sights on the fire and phone or radio their observations to a dispatcher. He extends the various lines of sight on his own map. Intersection of the lines gives the fire's location.

RURAL ELECTRIFICATION

Rural Electrification is promoted by Federal loans up to 100% of the cost of the project at 2% interest, and paid in installments over a period as long as 35 years. They are made to individuals, corporations, States, local governments, people's utility districts, and co-operative nonprofit or limited dividend associations, for rural electric distribution systems.

Loans for Wiring, Appliances, and Plumbing. — Loans are available to help rural families to install wiring, electrical appliances, water pressure systems, and plumbing in their homes and farm buildings. No loans are made directly to the consumer, but are made to the local rural electrification co-operative which may in turn extend credit for the purchase and installation of the equipment. Loans are repaid over a period up to 5 years.

Three fourths of the farms in the United States have electricity. Electrifying these farms has provided a market for miles of electric lines, and for millions of stoves, refrigerators, motors, milking machines, water pressure systems, and radios. One farm family, for example, uses electricity in 67 ways and estimates that it saves the labor of two hired men while increasing the total output of the farm.

United States Department of Agriculture

HOMEMADE FREEZER LOCKER

This was made by William Berkheimer, farmer-mechanic, of Cumberland County, Pennsylvania, who built it in a cave dug by his ancestors beneath his farmhouse.

Rural Telephones. — The first R.E.A.-financed rural telephone system began operating in 1951. By 1954 nearly 300 such loans had been made to bring telephone service to 300,000 rural subscribers in 40 States. These loans are intended to raise further the standard of living for farm families.

STABILIZING FARM PRODUCTION AND PRICES

Wise Use of Our Land. — We Americans have a high standard of living because of the great natural resources that our ancestors found. But we cut the timber from our hills, and the resulting floods washed gulleys in our fields and carried the good soil out to sea. We overgrazed our prairies, or plowed the turf under, and the wind blew away the soil as dust, producing dunes and deserts. Or we "mined the soil" by growing the same crop year after year without putting anything back into it. If we continue to abuse our soil, it will be difficult for the next generation to eke out a living by farming.

Two Acres for Your Life. — For the more than 2,000,000,000 inhabitants of the earth there are two acres of arable land apiece. It could be enough if efficiently used and products were equally distributed. They are not, so most people don't get enough to eat. Where good methods are not used there is less for you each year. Soil erosion and depletion of fertility are working against you. Unless this trend is reversed, destructive forces will win.

ERODED FIELDS

Uncontrolled running water and intensive cultivation of steep slopes result in ill-fed, ill-clothed, and ill-housed farmers' families.

Originally everybody's two acres had perhaps an average of seven inches of topsoil; but those seven inches have been reduced by erosion and neglect to five, or three, or zero. Extend the zero area to all the productive acres of the earth and man would die. The zero acres *are* being extended.

Nearly 250,000,000 acres of crop land in the United States are being seriously damaged by erosion, and nearly 100,000,000 acres are being slowly damaged.

While the world's population is increasing, the soil fertility is decreasing. So soon man won't have two full acres of productive land unless man and science win the battle against nature and ignorance.

Soil Conservation Service. — It is estimated that 40 per cent of the soil of the United States has been lost by floods, winds, and fertility depletion. To stop this loss the Administration is endeavoring to divert about 30,000,000 acres of land from soil-depleting surplus cash crops into soil-conserving and soil-building crops. Payments are made to farmers for soil-conserving and soil-building practices.

STRIP PLANTING, TO REDUCE SOIL EROSION, IN LOS POSAS VALLEY, CALIFORNIA

The Soil Conservation Service is promoting flood control on agricultural lands. It has already aided millions of farmers in checking soil erosion on their own lands, and has purchased submarginal lands for reforestation or limited grazing.

Specific Soil Abuses.[1] — Today's soil abuses are due chiefly to old-fashioned methods of "square farming." Plowing in straight rows up-and-downhill has produced:

Sheet erosion by which the top layer of soil is skimmed off the land.

Gullies that eat away the earth in big chunks, leaving worthless subsoil.

Other abuses are:

One-crop farming which exhausts and ruins the soil.

---

[1] For these specific suggestions we are indebted to *Our Times* magazine.

Overgrazing pastures which destroys the grass and causes erosion. *Destroying forests and woodlands.*

Rescuing the Soil. — The Soil Conservation Service is teaching our farmers:

Contour plowing. — "On the level plowing" follows a contour line around sloping land. The level furrows hold the rainfall.

Courtesy Soil Conservation Service

CONTOUR STRIP FARMING AND DIVERSION TERRACES

Farmers can turn unproductive acres into productive ones by building terraces, planting legumes on contour strips, and rotating crops.

Strip farming. — Growing different kinds of crops in alternate strips blankets the soil better than large fields of a single crop, such as corn. It checks the rush of water and breaks up air currents.

Terracing. — Broad-based ridges thrown up across a sloping field on the contour slow down even the heaviest rain.

Gully control. Even badly eroded gullies can be controlled by planting shrubs, grass, and trees. Check-dams slow erosion, too.

Windbreaks and shelter belts. — Properly planted trees break the force of wind and cut down wind erosion.

Air-Conditioning the Dust Bowl. — In the drought-ridden year of 1935 the Government, under President Roosevelt, began the planting of 300,000,000 trees from the Canadian border to Texas in an effort to salvage the dust bowl area. Today the stately string of trees and shrubs stand as a growing monument to the late President who sponsored the project despite a barrage of doubts and coarse jokes.

FOREST SHELTER-BELT FROM CANADA TO MEXICO

Started in 1935, the 150-mile-wide belt has proved its worth by making the air more humid and by lessening soil erosion. Trees are still being planted.

Some 40,000 windbreaks, each with about 20 rows of trees, some of them as high as a house, cover the Shelter-Belt Area. The original planting was done by the United States Forest Service but now farmer groups have banded together in soil conservation districts. The trees are cheap, largely a Federal-State gift.

The Soil Conservation Service, which experimented with trees from all over the world, now provides machinery to speed the planting.

These windbreaks help to "condition" air by slowing down the wind; prevent valuable topsoil from blowing away; conserve needed moisture by holding winter snow; slow down evaporation from the soil; lessen the dangers from uncontrolled prairie fires; and attract insect-eating birds such as pheasant and quail.

Need for Adjusting Farm Prices to City Prices. — Following World War I there was a gradual decline in the general price level, which made the payment of debts and taxes difficult. But the decline in the price of farm commodities was greater than that of any other class of commodities. For instance, wheat dropped from the $2 war price to less than 40 cents a bushel. Cotton dropped from twenty-nine cents a pound in 1923 to $6\frac{1}{2}$ cents a pound in 1933. The farmer was unable to buy machinery and other city-made products. Therefore in 1933 the Agricultural Adjustment Administration was created to adjust farm prices to city prices. This was done by limiting production. Farmers were induced to limit their acreage a certain percent for surplus crops that were depressing the market. Acreage allotments furnish a guide for planting the right acreage of the right crop.

This program is continued under the Production and Marketing Administration which makes payments to many farmers for carrying out practices that build up and protect the soil. For instance, corn, wheat, cotton, and especially tobacco, are soil-depleting crops; but legumes like alfalfa and clover are soil-conserving and soil-building crops, so shifting from soil-depleting to soil-building crops is conservation and the development of national wealth.

The Ever-Normal Granary. — Like Joseph, who in ancient Egypt stored up grain in years of plenty to use in years of famine, we created an Ever-Normal Granary. Under this program the Commodity Credit Corporation makes loans to farmers, who co-operate in the program, to enable them to put their feed and fiber in storage until needed for use on the farm or until sold.

Achieving agriculture's wartime production goals would not have been possible without the crops previously stored under loan in the Ever-Normal Granary. Ever-Normal Granary feed grains were used to produce the urgently needed meats, eggs, milk, cheese, and other high-protein foods for our wartime demand.

Early in the Second World War Congress found it necessary to regulate agricultural and other prices by putting a price floor under producers and a price ceiling over consumers. During the First World War farm prices rose sky-high. However, at the end of that war farm prices fell so low that farmers who had purchased high-priced land and equipment went broke.

United States Department of Agriculture

EVER-NORMAL GRANARY BINS

Corn is being loaded and sold from 2700-bushel bins near Ames, Iowa, by the Commodity Credit Corporation. Bins can be dismantled and used for surplus corn or wheat crops where needed.

To prevent a recurrence of a similar price slump following World War II the Government, through the Commodity Credit Corporation, "supports" the prices of many of the major farm products. Prices of wheat, corn, cotton, tobacco, milk, butterfat, eggs, wool, tung nuts, peanuts, potatoes, and the like, have been supported through loans, purchase agreements, and direct purchases.

The general level of support has been 90 percent of "parity." Parity is the price at which a commodity must be sold to provide the producer with the same amount of purchasing power he would have had for the same commodity (on the average) during the years 1910–1914.

The Commodity Credit Corporation acts as a financing agency when it comes to price-support operations. Through its authority to borrow large sums of money from the U. S. Treasury, the Commodity Credit Corporation is able to stabilize prices of farm products. Many of the perishable commodities acquired by the C.C.C. are turned over to other Department of Agriculture agencies, through a transfer of funds, and channeled to school lunch programs, to needy persons on relief rolls, to institutions, and to foreign relief.

FARM CREDIT ADMINISTRATION

The Farm Credit Administration administers many agencies that make loans to farmers or farm groups. (See page 329.)

FARMERS HOME ADMINISTRATION

Background. — By 1935 some 42 per cent of our farmers had slipped from ownership to tenancy, but today only 27 per cent are tenants. The Farmers Home Administration is helping to save the independent farmer and to assist tenants in buying farms. By the three following methods the F.H.A. helps to finance competent tenants, share-croppers, and farm laborers who are carefully selected by a committee of three, at least two of whom are farmers in each county.

Tenant Purchase Loans are made to the above classes who are worthy but lack assets sufficient to enable them to borrow from private lenders at the usual rates of interest. Loans are made for as long as 40 years at 4% interest, hence the annual payment of interest and principal is less than the interest ordinarily charged by commercial banks. Veterans are given preference, and disabled veterans are given special consideration and advice as to what is practical for them.

Private loans to the above classes at not more than 3% interest are insured by the F.H.A. for an additional 1%. If the borrower defaults, the F.H.A. pays and takes the mortgage.

Production and Subsistence Loans are made for the purchase of livestock, seed, fertilizer, feed, supplies, equipment, or adjustment of debts, at 5% interest for a term not to exceed 7 years. Not more than $10,000 will be lent to any one person, and that only to those who do not have credit elsewhere.

MARKETING FARM PRODUCTS

The Department of Agriculture maintains a Nation-wide daily market news service by press and radio. It has established standard grading and standard containers for uniformity in marketing. The Department regulates commodity exchanges and tries to protect the farmer against fraudulent practices. It also inspects meats and other farm products. And it helps to provide nourishing hot lunches for school children.

EXTENSION SERVICE

The Extension Service co-operates with the State Agricultural Colleges in the conduct of extension work in agriculture and home economics. County Agricultural Agents bring the latest scientific and other valuable agricultural information to the farmers. County Home Demonstration Agents bring helpful suggestions to rural women. The Service is also responsible for 4–H club work with farm boys and girls.

QUESTIONS ON THE TEXT

1. What important functions are performed by the Bureau of Animal Industry? Bureau of Plant Industry, Soils, and Agricultural Engineering? Bureau of Entomology and Plant Quarantine? Bureau of Agricultural and Industrial Chemistry? Bureau of Human Nutrition and Home Economics? Experiment Stations? Forest Service? Rural Electrification?

2. How does the Government encourage soil conservation practices?

3. Explain why farm prices need to be adjusted to city prices.

4. How does the Farmers Home Administration aid the farmer?

5. How has the Government aided the farmer in marketing his products?

PROBLEMS FOR DISCUSSION

1. Erosion removes half a billion tons of our rich topsoil each year. Does this fact concern the farmer alone, or is it a national problem?

2. In your community do you have grasshoppers, Mormon crickets, black stem rust of grains, white pine blister rust, citrus canker, peach mosaic disease, pink bollworm, gypsy moths, Japanese beetles, or Mexican fruit flies? What is the Government doing to eradicate and control these pests?

3. The Government has, by various methods, maintained a price for cotton higher than in other countries. A surplus of cotton has developed because we could not sell it abroad. Is this a wise long-term practice?

4. In cities, industrial workers have been better organized to maintain high wages than farmers, who are largely individualists and scattered. What would happen to farmers if the Government did not give them numerous financial aids? What would happen to city industries that depend upon farm products or farm customers?

5. Does the money spent on agricultural research benefit the farmers more than the consumers of farm products who live in cities? In what ways does the city dweller benefit?

6. Electricity on the modern farm not only gives the farmer's wife the conveniences of the city dweller, but it also can help the farmer grind his feeds, milk his cows, and heat and light his poultry houses. For what else could a farmer use electricity?

7. Except in case of specialty farms it is difficult for a small farm to compete with a large mechanized farm, which in many cases is owned by a corporation and backed by capital and efficient management. Do you think the Government should try to conserve the independent farmer or should it accept large corporate farms as economically desirable? What are some of the advantages of each type of farm?

8. "The United States has had an economic deficit for more than three hundred years," states a conservationist. By what conservation and constructive measures could we end this practice of wasting more than we replace?

9. Thomas Malthus (1766–1834), an English clergyman, wrote in his famous "Essay on Population" that under normal conditions population increases faster than food and that human suffering was therefore inevitable because, unchecked, it would outrun the food supply. He said that in the past the natural increase of people had been held back by war and disease. Without these two "natural" checks, according to Malthus, the world would soon be so over-populated that everyone would starve.

What do you think of this idea? What can you suggest as answers to this problem?

SELECT BIBLIOGRAPHY

Congressional Digest, "Farm Legislation 1796–1950." March, 1950.

DAVIS, K. S. "Hired Man, a Vanishing American." *New York Times Magazine*, July 23, 1950.

MATHEWS, S. and FLETCHER, J. "Beltsville Brings Science to the Farm." *National Geographic*. August, 1953.

U. S. Year-Book of the Department of Agriculture.

CHAPTER XVI

COMMERCE AND LABOR DEPARTMENTS *Mitchell*

DEPARTMENT OF COMMERCE *Weeks*

The Secretary of Commerce heads the following services:

Census Bureau
Bureau of Standards
Patent Office
Civil Aeronautics Administration

Weather Bureau
Foreign and Domestic Commerce
Coast and Geodetic Survey
Foreign-Trade Zones Board

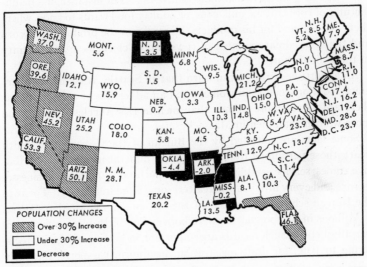

PERCENTAGE CHANGES IN POPULATION, 1940–1950

The Census Bureau. — Progress grows out of knowledge and knowledge is based on facts. The United States Census Bureau is constantly gathering facts and is therefore an important factor in progress.

The Decennial Census, taken every decade since 1790, enables Congress to apportion representatives in Congress among the States on the basis of population; it shows our military chiefs how many adults there are of military age; educators, the educational attainment of our population; [1] school boards, how many children will soon be of school age; employers and social workers, how many are unemployed; sociologists, the ages at which different racial and economic groups marry, the number of children reared, and how many families own their homes; legislators, whether more or fewer farmers than formerly own their homes; advertisers and the Federal Communications Commission, how many radio receiving sets are in each locality; and economists, the annual income of the people of the States.

Beginning in 1954, and in every tenth year thereafter, the Census Bureau will conduct a census of agriculture within the United States.

The volumes on manufactures and agriculture are especially valuable to persons interested in these industries. For instance, if a manufacturer of corn cutters, milk cans, or poultry food wants to know where there is a demand for his products, he can learn the production of corn and the approximate number of cows and of chickens in each county in the United States.

An advertiser of razors can learn that in Seattle, Washington, there are 2,600 more men than women; and an advertiser of cosmetics that there are 84,100 more women than men in Los Angeles, and 106,000 more women than men in Massachusetts.

Some facts are collected by the Bureau of the Census every tenth year; those pertaining to manufacturers, mineral industries, distributive trades, service establishments, transportation, and other businesses in 1954 and every fifth year thereafter; some more frequently. For 1954 the Bureau scheduled a census of the nation's agricultural resources.

Millions of our population were born before birth records were universally kept. Such records are important in getting a job, for registering to vote, for draft registration, insurance, passports, establish-

---

[1] Educational attainment of the population 25 years old and over, 1940

No school years completed		3.8%
Grade school:	1–6 Years	21.5
	7–8 Years	35.1
High school:	1–3 Years	15.2
	4 Years	14.3
College:	1–3 Years	5.5
	4 Years or more	4.6
	Total	100.0%

ing citizenship, etc.   As many as 600,000 American-born people have asked for a birth search in a single year.   It costs $1 and evidence is provided from census records.

The Decennial Census of 1950, taken by 140,000 enumerators at a cost of about $100,000,000, showed a population of 150,697,361, or an increase of 14% — double the 7% increase from 1930 to 1940.   This increase was due to higher standards of living and a consequently higher birth rate.   The Pacific Coast is the fastest-growing section in the country.   The 106 cities with more than 100,000 residents contain nearly three-tenths of the nation's population.   And the suburbs of the twelve largest cities outgrew the cities themselves as improved transportation facilities enabled more families to live outside the congested cities.

The Bureau of Standards. — As a uniform set of standards is needed for business practice, the Constitution gives Congress power "to fix the standard of weights and measures."   Under this authority Congress has legalized the cumbersome English system with which everybody is familiar, and also the simple metric system which the student uses in laboratories and sometimes sees applied to industry.   (See pages 103–104.)

The Bureau of Standards with a staff of more than 3000 is housed in a group of buildings on a 68-acre plot in Washington which resembles a scientific college campus.   Here the original units of weights and measures are kept;   here States get copies for local testing;   and here research and standardization centers.

Here everything is tested, from filling-station meters to brick;   from steel bridge girders to cups and saucers.   Here the Government has developed a system of tests for various materials purchased by the Government, and more than two thousand purchase specifications are continuously revised on the basis of laboratory investigations.   Like any thrifty housewife, the Government wants to get good value for its money when it buys things.   Hence, the Bureau tests the various articles bought by Government purchasing agents.   If it is an automobile tire, how long can it be used?   If it is a building material, how strong is it and how well will it resist fire?

To help in designing modern skyscrapers, a model of the Empire State Building in New York was built at the Bureau.   The model was placed in a wind tunnel and a gale of wind blown against it.   Thus engineers were able to know what strains could be placed on this highest building in the world before it was actually constructed.

Tests show that sole leathers first tanned with chromium salts and then retanned with vegetable materials wear from 25 to 75 per cent longer than the ordinary vegetable-tanned sole leathers. The durability of leathers was tested on the actual feet of policemen, postmen, soldiers, and others. Then sole leather tests in a resistance-to-abrasion measuring machine were compared with service durability by the volunteers who had worn shoes with soles of the same kind of leather. Such laboratory tests enabled manufacturers to make accelerated tests in 24 hours equivalent to several months' actual wear of shoes.

What mixture of air and gas gives most car miles? The answer becomes a standard for designers of gasoline engines. A thousand industries need such basic data, and to furnish this information is one purpose of the Bureau of Standards.

The United States bought a number of airplanes. When part were delivered the propeller of one broke. The Bureau of Standards was asked to investigate and safeguard aviators and the Government against future accidents.

Within the 20 major and 50 minor buildings of the Bureau, worth $25,000,000, are found such facilities as a three-story 1.5-million-volt X-ray, an experimental paper mill, a mathematics computation laboratory, and excellent machine shops. The Bureau co-operates with 775 scientific and technical bodies, including the American Petroleum Institute and the Society of Automotive Engineers.

Standard sizing of young girls' clothes on the basis of body measurements has been developed by the Bureau to replace the primitive age basis. When the age basis was used, different garment makers used different measurements for the same age. Height is now the primary guide to size. Weight and girth measurements are secondary guides.

The Bureau contends that adherence to the standard reduces the large volume of returns made by customers for incorrect size and also increases sales of ready-made garments. To arrive at the measurements which provide the best fit for the most persons in each size range, the Bureau followed a study made by the Department of Agriculture in which 150,000 youths were measured.

The Patent Office is administered by the Commissioner of Patents who is responsible for granting patents and registering trademarks.

STANDARDIZED SIZES FOR READY-TO-WEAR CLOTHING

The National Bureau of Standards has been working on a program to standardize all sizes on the basis of pattern grading. Standards for children's clothing are now complete.

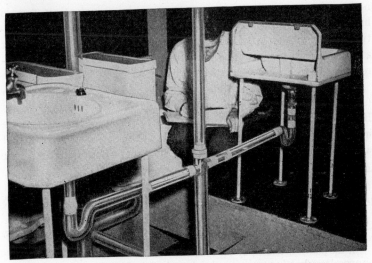

TRANSPARENT-PIPE PLUMBING SYSTEM

Another and very different service of the Bureau is seen here. This man is studying flow of water conditions to provide data needed in preparing plumbing codes.

A Patent [1] *of Invention* is an exclusive right granted by the Government to make, use, and sell any new and useful process, machine, manufacture, or composition of matter, or any new and useful improvements thereto, for a limited period — now 17 years by Act of Congress.[2] Patents are also granted for new varieties of certain living plants.

Any American and any foreigner may file an application for a patent by paying $30. An additional $30 is paid if the patent is granted. The applicant for the patent must declare to the Commissioner of Patents that he believes himself to be the original inventor; and he must submit with his application a full description of the invention, a drawing in cases that can be illustrated, and a model if the Commissioner requests it. If the examiner approves the application,[3] the patent is valid for 17 years, and it cannot be renewed except by special Act of Congress — something that rarely happens.

If by error the Patent Office grants a second patent for the same invention, the owner of the first patent can have the Federal courts declare the second patent void. In obtaining a patent an inventor is not required to employ a patent attorney; but a patent attorney is highly desirable, because without skillful preparation of the specifications and claims an application is likely to be rejected. Also a patent attorney knows how to obtain patents in all other countries that reciprocate with us. Of course a fee must be paid to each country.

Among the early important patents are Eli Whitney's cotton gin (1793) and Robert Fulton's steamboat (1809). When the Wright Brothers invented the biplane airship, they specified every phase of the invention to be protected by the patent. Thomas Edison is credited with more than a thousand patents, including the incandescent light

---

[1] A certificate issued to a patentee is called a "letters patent," meaning an open letter. (Latin: pateo, patens, *be open;* French: patent.)

[2] The right may be assigned to another person or inherited as other property. If another infringes upon a patent right the holder of the patent may apply for an injunction to restrain the infringer, and may sue him for damages as well.

[3] If the patent is refused by the examiner who examines the applicant's claims, an appeal may be taken to the Board of Appeals of the Patent Office, which includes the Commissioner of Patents. If this board also decides against the patent, an appeal may be taken to the Court of Customs and Patent Appeals. If a Constitutional question is involved, the Supreme Court may have the case certified to it for review and determination.

bulb, the phonograph, the carbon transmitter which made the telephone commercially possible, the motion picture camera, and the talking motion picture.

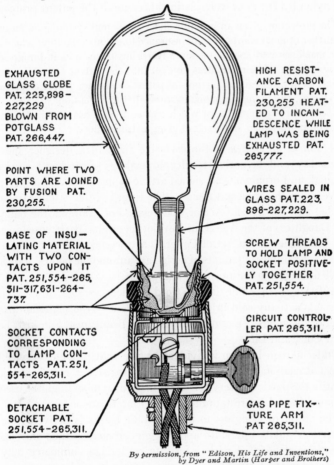

EXHAUSTED GLASS GLOBE PAT. 223,898 – 227,229 BLOWN FROM POTGLASS PAT. 266,447.

POINT WHERE TWO PARTS ARE JOINED BY FUSION PAT. 230,255.

BASE OF INSU — LATING MATERIAL WITH TWO CONTACTS UPON IT PAT. 251,554 – 265, 311 – 317,631 – 264 – 737.

SOCKET CONTACTS CORRESPONDING TO LAMP CONTACTS PAT. 251, 554 – 265,311.

DETACHABLE SOCKET PAT. 251,554 – 265,311.

HIGH RESIST-ANCE CARBON FILAMENT PAT. 230,255 HEATED TO INCANDESCENCE WHILE LAMP WAS BEING EXHAUSTED PAT. 265,777.

WIRES SEALED IN GLASS PAT.223, 898 – 227,229.

SCREW THREADS TO HOLD LAMP AND SOCKET POSITIVELY TOGETHER PAT. 251,554.

CIRCUIT CONTROL-LER PAT. 265,311.

GAS PIPE FIXTURE ARM PAT 265,311.

By permission, from " Edison, His Life and Inventions,"
by Dyer and Martin (Harper and Brothers)

NINETEEN OF EDISON'S PATENTS ON A SINGLE DEVICE

One of the most interesting new patents is for stainless steel stockings for women. They are still a laboratory curiosity, but it is claimed that steel threads can be woven into steel stockings as sheer as silk or nylon. The 2,500,000th patent was issued in 1950.

The Du Pont research organization comprises thirty-odd research laboratories with a technical and non-technical personnel of thousands of men and women. And the large expenditures involved in developing nylon by Du Pont were justified because of the patent protection.

The protection given an inventor under our patent system is an incentive to further original efforts, it is an insurance to the manufacturer who makes new machines and spends money advertising them, and it brings secret ideas to light. The more ideas you get into the Patent Office Gazette (a weekly publication giving pictures of patents and trade marks as currently registered), the more the public is stimulated to invention. It frequently happens that a patented idea which seemed foolish has germinated in the mind of another man and resulted in a great invention.

A Patent of Design is the exclusive right of a designer showing originality and inventive faculty to make, use, and sell any new, original, and ornamental designed article of manufacture for $3\frac{1}{2}$, 7, or 14 years, as the applicant elects. The length of the patent can be extended only by Special Act of Congress. For example, the badge of the Daughters of the American Revolution originally patented in 1891 has been renewed by Act of Congress at the end of each period of 14 years. Examples of patents of design are automobile bodies, fraternity emblems, lighting fixtures, and wall papers.

A Trade Mark is a distinctive word, emblem, symbol, or device used on goods actually sold in commerce, to identify the manufacturer or seller of the goods. Examples are Kodak, Beautyrest, Sun-kist, Ford, Coca Cola, and Life.

Under a 1946 law, an individual or firm that provides service but does not manufacture or sell goods can register a certain mark to identify the particular service. This mark or symbol might be used by a chain of hotels or restaurants with an interstate aspect.

The power of Congress to protect trade marks is derived from its power to regulate interstate and foreign commerce; thus only marks of articles associated with interstate or foreign commerce may be registered in the United States Patent Office. A trade mark is a common law property right and the courts will grant protection against encroachment even if it is not registered; but advantages of registration are (1) evidence of ownership, (2) right to bring suit in U. S. Courts, (3) right to register in many foreign countries, and (4) protection against the importation of articles bearing the same trade mark.

A trade mark is registered for 20 years, but it may be renewed any number of times.   There would be no object in an industry's spending large sums in advertising and using a distinctive trade mark if others could benefit by imitating advertising and trade marks.   A trade mark may be worth a million dollars, and it may be sold along with the business or the good name of the business.[1]

Courtesy "Look Magazine"

HOW MANY OF THE ABOVE TRADE MARKS DO YOU KNOW?

PATENT OFFICE REGISTRATIONS

IDEA	DURATION	RENEWAL	FEES
Patents of Invention	17 yrs.	{ Only by special	$60
Patents of Design .	3½, 7, 14 yrs.	{ Act of Congress	10, 15, 30
Trade Marks . . .	20 yrs.	20 yrs.	25

[1] Previous to 1940 labels and prints were registered in the Patent Office, but now they are registered in the Copyright Office.

A *Label* is attached to an article of commerce.   It is descriptive and often includes the trade mark with color scheme.   Examples are Del Monte canned fruits and Waterman's (Ideal) Ink.   Labels may be copyrighted for 28 years, and the cost is $6.

A *Print* is used for advertising merchandise in streetcars, magazines, etc. *Prints* may be copyrighted for 28 years, and the cost is $6.

The Bureau of Foreign and Domestic Commerce is charged with promoting the foreign and domestic commerce of the United States. It furnishes advice and aid to American businessmen at home and abroad and publishes periodic reports on business activities throughout the world. Businessmen bring many of their practical problems to the Bureau for solution. A cattleman from Texas, a lumberman from Oregon, a farmer from Iowa, an industrialist from Connecticut, all may benefit from the Bureau's detailed information on more than 800,000 foreign firms and individuals engaged in international trade and may secure accurate and up-to-date trade opportunity surveys from the Bureau.

The Civil Aeronautics Board (independent) and **Administration** (in the Department of Commerce) [1] regulate our interstate and foreign airlines. The Board or the Administration:

1. Provides basic pilot training.
2. Examines, inspects, or rates airmen and aircraft.
3. Licenses aircraft and records ownership.
4. Establishes rules to govern aircraft, and provides standards of safety and inspection.
5. Designates Federal airways and acquires, establishes, and operates air navigation facilities along such airways.
6. Regulates air rates charged for passengers and express; and sets rates paid by the Government for carrying air mail.
7. Prescribes maximum hours and minimum wages for aviators and other employees.
8. Co-operates with defense departments in promoting defense.
9. Gives conditional aid for building or improving airports.

The Weather Bureau receives reports of heat, cold, clouds, rain, snow, and the direction and velocity of the wind from stations on land and hundreds of ships at sea. From this information well-trained officials forecast weather conditions. Daily storm warnings are of especial value to aviators and they save millions of dollars invested in vessels, besides many lives. Frost warnings serve the growers of fruit and vegetables; flood forecasts, often a week in advance, enable farmers to save livestock and other property. Freezing forecasts en-

---

[1] The Board and Administration together are known as the Civil Aeronautics Authority.

able railroads to save perishables in transit, greenhouses to fire their boilers, gasoline engines to be drained, concrete work to be stopped, ice factories to reduce their output, and merchants to adjust their advertising.   Rain forecasts protect the raisin crop, enable fruit growers and farmers to harvest and shelter crops, and protect the manufacturer of lime, cement, and brick, as well as photographers.   During the war forecasts were restricted for military reasons.

The climatologist tells us, in terms of averages, what weather may be expected in a given locality for years to come, as based on past experience.   These statistics assist agriculture, engineering, transportation, and sanitation.   In the insurance business, information regarding lightning, tornadoes, hail storms, and rainfall is needed.

The following story illustrates the value of the Weather Service to aviation.

"Two passenger planes stood on the runways at Swan Island recently. One was to go north to Seattle and the other south to San Francisco.   From a doorway emerged a man carrying a sheet of paper with certain technical notations.   To one pilot he handed an order to gain an altitude of 7500 feet as he headed south, and to the other an order to travel north at a 4000-foot elevation.

"Propellers whirled and the planes skimmed the surface of the field, gained altitude, banked and headed in opposite directions.   When the control boards in front of the pilots indicated that they had gained their respective levels, both planes found strong tail winds and rode on the wings of the gales into port, making record time.

"This apparent aëronautical paradox was the result of careful studies of weather and air currents by attachés to the United States Weather Bureau. Without the information supplied by the observers, discovery of the favorable winds blowing in opposite directions high overhead would have been a matter of chance, with the probability that at least one of the planes would have bucked a head-wind instead of being helped on its journey by the great force of nature.

"By equipment of planes with radio sets it is possible to communicate weather data to pilots at regular intervals."

With the aid of daring pilots who fly into the very heart of hurricanes, the Weather Bureau is conducting extensive research into the nature of violent storms.   These investigations will enable the Bureau to forecast violent storms more accurately, warn people in its path, and provide greater safety for air travel.

The Federal Maritime Board and **The Maritime Administration** were created in 1950 to replace the independent United States Maritime Commission. New ship construction practically ceased in the United States during the depression, and we fell to ninth place as a ship builder. In wartime a country needs a vast supplemental naval tonnage for the transport of troops and supplies. So in 1936 the Maritime Commission was created to promote (and to some extent regulate) foreign shipping and provide a merchant marine adequate for national defense. In the interests of efficiency, the Commission has been replaced by a three-man Federal Maritime Board whose chairman is also the Maritime Administrator.

The duties of the Board and Administration are:

(1) To design model ships for commerce which are suitable for conversion to naval and military use.

(2) To encourage shipbuilding by lending money at low interest and paying the difference in cost of building here and abroad, which sometimes amounts to as much as 50 per cent.

(3) To grant subsidies to American lines to enable them to compete with foreign shippers despite higher American wages and other costs.

(4) To regulate rates and to prevent discriminations.

(5) To regulate working conditions on subsidized vessels.

(6) To build vessels. During World War II the Government constructed most of the shipyards and had them operated by private concerns, like the Kaiser yards on the Pacific Coast. These yards built thousands of Liberty ships, Victory ships, and other merchant and naval vessels.

(7) To preserve ships and yards needed for national defense; to scrap worthless vessels to reclaim critical materials for industry; and to requisition private ships for Government use in times of crisis.

The Bureau of Public Roads conducts research into highway design, construction, and economics; supervises the construction of National forest and other National roads; and administers Federal funds contributed towards State and local roads.

Federal-Aid Highways are built by State highway departments, subject to various restrictions administered by the Federal Commissioner of Public Roads. For instance, Congress has authorized a 40,000-mile interstate highway system; but before any State can receive Federal aid for its portion of this system the Federal Commissioner of Public Roads must approve the roads designated by the State highway department as its connecting links of the 40,000-mile system.

The Coast and Geodetic Survey is one of the oldest agencies of the National Government. In 1807 Congress created the Coast Survey. This bureau's task was to make an accurate survey of the coasts of the United States. In the 1870's Congress broadened its functions to include the entire country. The present name, Coast and Geodetic Survey, dates from a statute passed in 1878.

The Survey's charts, maps, and other reports are little known to the general public. But they are extremely useful to persons engaged in aviation, radio, engineering, fishing, navigation, construction, and related fields. For example, the Survey's seismological research is extremely valuable in the reduction of damage from earthquakes. Many of the larger buildings and dams in the United States have been designed and built on the basic of the bureau's earthquake data.

The Foreign-Trade Zones Board establishes and operates foreign trade zones in the United States. These zones (known as "free ports" in Europe) are located at or near various ports of entry. They are small enclosed and policed areas where foreign goods intended for trans-shipment to other countries may be stored and processed free of customs duties and regulations. Storage and processing facilities are also available for domestic goods destined for export. Of course, any foreign goods stored in these areas but later sold in the United States become subject to customs on the same basis as any other goods entering through normal commercial channels.

Six foreign trade zones, intended to promote foreign commerce, are now in operation: at New York, New Orleans, Los Angeles, San Francisco, Seattle, and San Antonio.

DEPARTMENT OF LABOR

The Secretary of Labor promotes the welfare of wage earners by improving working conditions and opportunities for employment.

The Bureau of Labor Statistics issues reports on employment and on the long range employment outlook in important occupations. It also reports on hours of work and wages. The Bureau maintains a file of current union contracts for the guidance of employers and employees. It publishes the indexes of wholesale and retail prices, rents, and consumer prices.

The Bureau of Labor Standards prepares reports on labor legislation, assists States and labor groups in drafting labor bills, and assists in preparing State industrial safety codes and bulletins dealing with industrial hazards.

The Division prepares pamphlets, bulletins, class outlines, and visual aids for use in schools. The Division also administers the child-labor provisions of the Fair Labor Standards Act which exclude children from employment in establishments producing goods for shipment in interstate commerce. (See page 307.)

The Public Contracts Division enforces maximum hour, minimum wage, child labor, convict labor, safety, and health stipulations for Government supply contracts exceeding $10,000. The contractor must pay at least the prevailing wages of the locality, and time and a half for overtime.

The Women's Bureau was established in 1920. Its functions are to formulate standards and policies to promote the welfare of wage-earning women, to improve their working conditions, increase their efficiency, and advance their opportunity for profitable employment.

The United States Employment Service was created in 1907 to find jobs for newly arrived aliens; during the First World War it was the recruiting agency for civilian workers in war work; after the war it found work for veterans; during the depression of the thirties it became a channel through which millions of unemployed were assigned to jobs on public works. During World War II the Service again recruited workers for war industries.

Now the Federal Government supplies the money, which the United States Employment Service turns over to the States subject to certain Federal restrictions, such as co-operation among the various State employment agencies. The State agencies commonly handle such additional matters as unemployment compensation.

Unemployment Compensation. — All States have unemployment compensation laws and pay weekly benefits to insured wage earners who become temporarily unemployed.[1] The benefits run about $20 to $25 per week in most States and are determined by the amount the worker has received in wages over a specified period. At least 20

---

[1] The law does not apply to agricultural laborers, domestic servants, children under 21, working for mother or father, or adults working for son or daughter or spouse, government employees, or employees of non-profit institutions.

weeks' employment during the year is usually required to make one eligible for the compensation. The payments begin after a two or three weeks' waiting period if the Employment Service has not found a suitable job for the unemployed; and they continue for not exceeding four months.

The Federal Government levies a tax on employers of eight or more persons in most industries; and the Social Security Board returns most of this to the States provided they conform to the standard regulations of the Board. The United States Treasury maintains the Unemployment Trust Fund and returns money to the States as they need it for the unemployed.

FAIR LABOR STANDARDS ACT OF 1938

Purpose. — This Act places a floor under wages and a ceiling over hours of work: that is, it provides minimum wages and maximum hours for employees engaged in interstate commerce or in the production of goods for interstate commerce. The Act also provides for the regulation of child labor in such industries.

Wages. — Until 1945 wages in these industries had to be not less than 30 cents an hour; from then until 1949, 40 cents; now 75 cents.

Hours.[1] — A workweek in these industries is limited to 40 hours.

Child Labor. — "Oppressive child labor" is forbidden in the production of goods to move in interstate commerce. Oppressive child labor means the employment of any child under 16 years, or under 18 years in hazardous occupations.[2]

Differential. — Local economic conditions and differences in freight rates must be taken into account, and exceptions to the above wages and hours may be allowed, *e.g.*, in Puerto Rico or the Virgin Islands.

---

[1] Extra hours are permissible if one and one-half times the regular rate of wages is paid. There is also an exception in favor of handling perishable goods, as for example in canneries. Likewise collective bargaining agreements certified by the National Labor Relations Board are exempted. Also persons physically or mentally incapable of doing a normal amount of work are permitted to receive less than the minimum wage prescribed. The Act does not apply to employees whose conditions of work and wages are already regulated by the Interstate Commerce Commission or a similar authority.

[2] This labor restriction does not apply to children in agriculture while not legally required to attend school, or to any child employed as an actor.

QUESTIONS ON THE TEXT

1. Name the services of the Department of Commerce.
2. What is the importance of the census?
3. What important facts were found by the 1950 census?
4. What valuable services are performed by the Bureau of Standards?
5. What is a patent? What kinds are there? How do you obtain one? What does one cost? Can it be renewed? Are you sure of protection when the application is granted?
6. What protection does a trade mark give? For what period?
7. What functions are performed by the Civil Aeronautics Board? The Weather Bureau? The Bureau of Public Roads? The Bureau of Labor Statistics? The Bureau of Labor Standards? The Public Contracts Division? The Women's Bureau? The Employment Service? and how is Unemployment Compensation handled?
8. Explain the Fair Labor Standards Act.

PROBLEMS FOR DISCUSSION

1. Money paid out by the Government to make new discoveries in the field of science has risen from $68,000,000 in 1938 to about $2,000,000,000. Should we continue thus to spend for labor-saving devices in industry and home, methods of combatting disease, and instruments of defense? Should we spend twice as much?

2. The following are typical of the two million patents granted by the patent office:

A featherweight insulating material called Santocel which will make possible blankets and sleeping bags weighing only a few ounces.

A photo-electric device which will dim headlights automatically when struck by rays from approaching headlights or street lights.

An alloy so magnetic (it can lift 4000 times its own weight) that the FBI plans to use it to fish in rivers and ponds for criminals' discarded weapons and other metallic clues.

A solar still now widely used on life rafts, which distills sea water by the sun's heat in a transparent plastic bag and produces a pint of fresh water on a sunny day.

What stimulates invention? Why do we invent more than China? Russia?

3. Population in the United States is increasing at the rate of more than 1,500,000 a year; in India, at the rate of 10,000,000. What social and economic factors might explain the difference?

4. Strikes are a wasteful and costly way of settling labor disputes. As a result of strikes in the United States, about 30,000,000 man-days of production are lost each year. Would you favor the compulsory arbitration of labor disputes? Would you favor creating a United States Court with power to settle labor disputes?

SELECT BIBLIOGRAPHY

CLIFFORD, C. "Government and Business." *Vital Speeches*, May 1, 1950.

HARRIS, H. "Trade — the Cure for Aid." *Nation's Business*. June, 1953.

LEEK, J. H. *Government and Labor in the United States.* Rinehart. New York, 1952.

LILIENTHAL, D. "Big Business for a Big Country." *Collier's.* May 31 through June 28, 1952.

NEUBERGER, R. L. "They Still Go West," *Reader's Digest*, November, 1950.

Newsweek, "The Census: More People and Problems," August 28, 1950.

U. S. News, "Political Power Moves West," August 4, 1950; "Still Enough Gasoline, But —," October 27, 1950; "Interview with the Chief, U. S. Weather Bureau." June 26, 1953; "Is U. S. Getting Too Crowded?" September 11, 1953.

CHAPTER XVII

TRANSPORTATION, COMMUNICATION, AND POWER

Independent Administrative Agencies

Introduction. — In addition to the ten administrative departments, whose heads are members of the President's cabinet, various independent agencies have been created. They have been established as separate agencies for a variety of reasons. For example, the work of an agency may be of such a nature that it does not fit readily into one of the Cabinet departments. Or, sometimes special interest groups may have persuaded Congress to create an agency outside any department. Or, because of the nature of its work, an agency may have been given independent status to protect it from partisan politics. Finally, if an agency has rule-making (quasi-legislative) powers and/ or decision-making (quasi-judicial) powers, it is, as a matter of course, made independent of the President.

Most of these bodies are *regulatory agencies*. That is, Congress created them to regulate particular activities, usually commercial.

There is much disagreement as to the merit and usefulness of these agencies. They are usually headed by a board or commission appointed by the President and Senate for a term of seven years. The long terms mean that the President cannot secure control of the commission's members in a single four-year period. And this means, on the one hand, that they are protected from the political whims of the Chief Executive. But it also means, on the other hand, that some commission members might remain in office for a long period even after their own views have been repudiated at the polls. The changes of administration in 1933 and again in 1953 illustrate this latter point.

Many people have described these commissions as a "headless fourth branch of the government." And the Hoover Commission recommended that most of these agencies be reorganized under a single head. President Truman began this work of reorganization and President Eisenhower is continuing it.

BALTIMORE AND OHIO PASSENGER CAR IN 1829

This horsecar, the first on rails, was pulled by the fastest trotters available between Baltimore and Ellicott's Mills, Maryland. It made a speed of 12 to 15 miles per hour.

In this Chapter we treat only the more important of these agencies concerned with transportation, communication, and power.[1]

INTERSTATE COMMERCE COMMISSION

When and Why Created. — After the Civil War, railroads combined into long and strong trunk lines. Some of them "watered their stock";[2] some gave preferential rates to cities that stockholders wanted to develop because they owned property there; some gave cut rates (in the form of rebates) to favored "big business"; some charged excessively high rates; and the public lost confidence in them. In the

---

[1] Note that the Federal Trade Commission, another of these independent regulatory commissions, is treated on pages 141–143; the Small Business Administration (successor to the Reconstruction Finance Corporation) on pages 331–333; the Securities and Exchange Commission on pages 333–336; etc.

[2] To "water stock" means to sell stock, or give it to existing stockholders, without putting the money into the railroad or other enterprise. For instance, a road earning 12 per cent profit might double its stock and earn only 6 per cent profit. Watered stock was sometimes sold to innocent purchasers, sometimes merely used to conceal the real profits earned.

Middle West the Grangers (organized farmers), who were financially pinched, gained control of State legislatures and legislated freight rates so low and made other restrictions so burdensome that the railroads were in danger of losing money. Therefore both the public and the railroads were willing to have Congress create a commission to secure just treatment for all; and in 1887 the Interstate Commerce Commission was established.

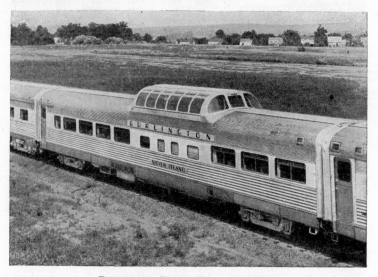

BURLINGTON ROUTE VISTA DOME CAR
The dome portion of the car is double decked.

Membership. — The membership of the Interstate Commerce Commission has gradually increased to eleven. The members are appointed by the President, with the consent of the Senate, for terms of seven years. But cases may be decided by as few as three members, so the Commission often sits in divisions.

Supervision over Interstate Carriers. — Congress enacts laws regulating interstate common carriers, and the Interstate Commerce Commission supervises the execution of laws which pertain to these interstate carriers: railroads; boats; express companies, sleeping-car companies; pipe lines carrying commodities other than water and artificial gas; and motor vehicles.

The Negative Duties of the Commission are to forbid common carriers:

(1) To charge unjust rates.

(2) To give rebates to individuals, or special rates to particular shippers or localities.

(3) To charge more for a short than for a longer haul, except when the Commission considers competition to justify it. (For instance, the rates from New York to the Rocky Mountain States may be higher than the rates from New York to the Pacific Coast. If the coast rates were not lower, the freight would go by way of the Panama Canal and the roads would lose this freight which the expensive roadbeds can carry without additional cost.)

(4) To grant free passes with certain specified exceptions.

(5) To build a new railroad in competition with another or to discontinue service without consent of the Commission.

(6) To issue capital stocks and bonds without the consent of the Commission.

(7) To prescribe rates between two points within a State so low as to put points outside the State at an unreasonable disadvantage.

The Positive Duties of the Commission are to require common carriers:

(1) To keep accounts uniformly as prescribed by the Commission; and to render annual reports to the Commission.

(2) To publish their rates and fares for public inspection.

(3) To require automatic train stops, etc., where needed.

(4) To co-operate in the interest of the shippers. (For instance, the Commission may transfer cars from one company to another in case of an emergency, may route traffic over other lines if the one receiving it is unable to handle it, may require co-operative use of terminal facilities, and may require convenient connections at junction points.)

(5) To provide reasonable service. (For example, the Commission may require railroads to build branch lines where they are reasonably necessary for shippers in a territory dependent upon a trunk line.)

How Complaints Are Made. — Any individual, corporation, board of trade, city, or other group of persons, may petition the Interstate Commerce Commission to redress grievances against a common carrier. The grievance may be an omission to perform a legal duty or it may be a violation of the law. Thousands of complaints are filed annually. For instance, a New England woman who shipped a couple of cans of milk each day once complained to the Commission. The Commission was impressed with the justice of the complaint and an extensive investigation of milk rates throughout New England resulted in more equitable rates.

The Right of Appeal. — Congress passes the laws pertaining to interstate carriers; the Interstate Commerce Commission administers them with the assistance of law-enforcing officers; but no decision of this Commission is final until there is an opportunity for a court hearing.

The Motor Vehicle Act. — *Reasons for the Act.* — Previous to 1935 truck and bus drivers were commonly underpaid and worked long hours, the vehicles used the public highways built at public expense, in cases of accident the truck and bus owners were commonly unable to pay damages, and the "cutthroat competition" was unfair to the drivers and especially so to the heavily taxed and regulated railroads.

In 1935, as a result of these conditions, Congress gave the Interstate Commerce Commission regulatory powers over motor vehicles which operate from State to State over public highways as common carriers or contract carriers. So far the Commission has not regulated farmers and factories hauling their own products or merchants hauling their merchandise.

Registration. — Common carrier buses or trucks which offer their services at a set price to anybody, and contract carriers who make individual contracts, to haul beyond a State's boundaries must now register with the Interstate Commerce Commission, show that they can comply with the Federal requirements, and obtain a permit plate to accompany the State license plate.

Insurance. — These interstate carriers must carry insurance against injury to others and to cover their damage obligations to passengers and shippers.

Qualifications of Employees. — Each year thirty-odd thousand persons are killed in motor-vehicle accidents, over a million are injured, and more than a billion dollars' worth of property is damaged. Therefore the Commission requires drivers to be twenty-one years of age, experienced and familiar with prescribed drivers' rules, of good physical and mental health, free from a drug addiction, and they must not drink

INTERSTATE CARRIERS IN CHICAGO STOCKYARDS

Trains and trucks are the mainstay of interstate commerce and therefore are subject to Federal regulation.

alcoholic liquor or beverage while on duty or otherwise make excessive use of it.

Safety of Operation and Equipment. — A driver must be well, must conform to an elaborate code of safeguards, and must not pick up "hitch hikers" or any persons except those authorized to ride. The motor vehicle must be equipped with lights and other traffic safeguards according to an elaborate code. There are regulations for the handling of explosives and other dangerous articles. The motto of the Commission is: "A safe driver on a safe vehicle."

Maximum Hours for Drivers. — Except in case of prescribed exceptions and prescribed cases of emergency, a driver is not permitted to work more than 10 hours a day and 60 hours a week. (Railroad employees work on a basic eight-hour day, but there are many exceptions.)

Regulation of Rates. — Common or contract carrier motor vehicle companies must file with the Commission a schedule of fares or rates charged, and these must be reasonable and available to all shippers. The carrier must not depart from these rates and discriminate between persons, or discriminate unreasonably between places.

Act Regulating Carriers by Water. — In 1940 Congress extended the powers of the Interstate Commerce Commission to include interstate carriers by water [1] as well as railroads and motor vehicles. It extended control over water carriers so as to bring them under regulation comparable to that exercised over railroads and motor vehicles. The water carriers had been allowed not only to offer lower rates but waterways had been dredged at public expense, whereas railroads had to keep up their own tracks, and motor vehicles had paid license taxes for the use of roads.

The Interstate Commerce Commission can now regulate fares and rates and prescribe conditions of service in interstate commerce for common carriers by rail, common or contract motor carriers, and common or contract water carriers. This regulation includes shipping on rivers, lakes, and seaports when the shipments begin and end in the United States (or incorporated territory). [2]

The 1940 Act enables the Commission to require the above three means of transportation to co-operate in joint hauls.

NATIONAL ADVISORY COMMITTEE FOR AERONAUTICS

Members. — The Committee is composed of 17 members appointed by the President, including two from the Air Force, two from the Navy,

---

[1] Certain powers granted to the United States Maritime Commission in 1936 were transferred to the Interstate Commerce Commission in 1940.

[2] The 1940 Act excludes from this regulation boats owned by a producing firm to carry its own products exclusively, certain tankers for liquid cargoes, and water carriers of commodities in bulk carrying not more than three commodities.

Congress Has Power to Regulate Interstate Commerce

Transportation
- Railroads, including shipments partly by rail, and partly by motor vehicle, and partly by water
- Express companies and sleeping car companies
- Pipe lines, except for water and illuminating gas
- Motor vehicles as common or contract carriers
- Interstate ships as common or contract carriers
- Airplanes: Regulated by the Civil Aeronautics Board, or Administration
- Electricity and Natural gas: Regulated by the Federal Power Commission

Regulation through the Interstate Commerce Commission

Communication
- Wire communication (telegraph, telephone, cable)
- Radio communication (messages, pictures, broadcasting, television)
- Radio transmission of energy

Regulation through the Federal Communications Commission

Persons
- Walking across State line } for business or pleasure
- Riding across State line

Labor
- Minimum wages, maximum hours, and safety standards for persons engaged in the manufacture of goods destined for interstate commerce
- Child labor in concerns manufacturing goods destined for interstate commerce

Commodities
- May be protected while in transit
- May be excluded from interstate commerce
- Protected against unreasonable State interference
- Protected against unreasonable restraint of trade by monopolies
- Unfair trade practices prohibited through Federal Trade Commission

Securities
- Original issuance of and subsequent trading in securities with an interstate aspect

Regulation through the Securities and Exchange Commission

Subject to incidental interference by States in the reasonable exercise of their "police powers" { health, morals, safety, welfare

317

two from the Civil Aeronautics Authority (see page 302), one each from the Smithsonian Institution, United States Weather Bureau, and Bureau of Standards, the office of the Secretary of Defense, and not more than seven additional civil and military aeronautical scientists and engineers. Members do not receive compensation for service on the Committee.

The Duties of the Committee are to determine the problems which should be experimentally attacked; to direct the scientific study of

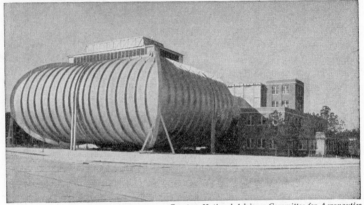

Courtesy National Advisory Committee for Aeronautics

HIGH-SPEED TUNNEL AT LANGLEY FIELD

The electric motor provides air currents up to 520 miles per hour.

these aeronautical problems; and to conduct experiments at the Langley Aeronautical Laboratory in Virginia, the Ames Aeronautical Laboratory at Moffett Field, California, and the Lewis Flight Propulsion Laboratory adjoining the Cleveland Airport. The Committee considers problems of both civil and military aviation.

Wind Tunnels. — For experimental work in the field of aeronautics wind tunnels are essential. In 1916 the Committee built its first tunnel at Langley Field. Since then it has constructed thirty-odd tunnels. (Universities and aircraft companies have built many others.) Most of these tunnels have been built at Langley Field, Moffett Field, and Cleveland.

The largest one, at Moffett Field, has a doughnut-shaped tunnel more than half a mile around. It is 80 feet in diameter at its narrowest point and is large enough to permit a two-engined plane to enter. The Cleveland laboratory has highly specialized equipment. The altitude tunnel can create temperatures down to 48° below zero, and can duplicate conditions from sea level to the stratosphere. To operate the tunnel at full capacity requires 52,000 horsepower, of which only 18,000 drives the fan; and the remainder is needed to drive the refrigeration and cooling systems. All tunnels must be cooled to counteract the heat produced by wind friction.

Some of the tunnels can produce winds up to 1500 miles per hour. The test object — whether it is an airplane, an airplane part, or a small scale model — is mounted on rigid streamlined supports, these supports are mounted on scales, and when the air stream is turned on, the scales "weight" the response of the object to the air flow.

Today most of the research conducted at the various laboratories is directly connected with military aviation; quite naturally, the results are extremely valuable for civilian aviation as well.

FEDERAL COMMUNICATIONS COMMISSION

Introduction. — In 1927 there were over 700 radio stations in the United States — twice as many as could operate at one time without serious interference. Some of these stations were described as little better than "electrostatic katydids." Thus government regulation was inevitable; and the Radio Act of 1927 was passed, providing for regulation through the Federal Radio Commission. This beginning evolved into the present Federal Communications Commission, which was created in 1934.

Powers of the Commission. — *Radio and Television.* — This Commission controls interstate [1] and foreign [2] broadcasting. It limits the number of stations by requiring licenses. Broadcasting stations are licensed for periods not exceeding three years and other classes of stations for periods not exceeding five years. Renewals may be granted for like periods; or a license may be revoked for proper cause.

The Commission also classifies stations, prescribes the nature of

---

[1] Any station that interferes with interstate communications comes under Federal control.

[2] Control over foreign transmissions applies only to outgoing communications. If objectionable communications are broadcast into the United States, diplomatic protest through the State Department would be the proper procedure.

service, assigns wave lengths, determines the power, the time during which the station may operate, and the kind of apparatus used. It classifies and licenses broadcasting operators, and makes regulations to prevent interference between stations.

The Commission apportions broadcasting licenses, wave lengths, periods of time for operation, and station power among the States and communities in a way that will provide a "fair, efficient, and equitable distribution of radio service to each."

, When paid matter is broadcast, it must be announced as such or the name of the sender given. If a station permits a candidate for public office to broadcast, it must afford opposing candidates equal opportunity at the same rates. In broadcasting, the use of obscene, indecent, or profane language is forbidden by Act of Congress, and giving information concerning lotteries is also prohibited. At one time or another the Commission has reprimanded broadcasting companies for broadcasting materials that were regarded as improper; and the courts have imposed prison sentences for profanity and vulgarity over the radio.

Telegraph and Telephone. — The Commission also supervises interstate and foreign telegraphic and telephonic communications by wire, cable, or wireless. The lines are "common carriers"; service must be adequate, rates just and reasonable, and rates can be changed only with notice given to the public and the Commission. Lines may be constructed or extended only with the consent of the Commission.

FEDERAL POWER COMMISSION

The Commission, as reorganized in 1930, is composed of five commissioners appointed by the President with the consent of the Senate for a term of five years. The Commission exercises administrative control over all power sites on navigable streams (or streams affecting navigable streams) and on public lands of the United States respecting the location, design, construction, maintenance, and operation of power projects. One desiring to develop power on such streams must obtain a license from the Commission.

Before the Federal Power Commission could regulate power transmitted across State lines, some holding companies owned the stock of a producing company in one State and a distributing company in an adjoining State. The State public-utility commission in the second State required the power to be sold at a reasonable rate on the basis of its cost to the distributing company; but the producing company in State one was not regulated as to the price charged across the State line.   Therefore the producing company could sell to the distributing company at a high price; and the unreasonable profits made by the producing company benefited all the stockholders through the holding company — but not the consumers.

BONNEVILLE DAM ON THE COLUMBIA

To the left is the spillway dam with flood gates; to the right the power house with 10 dynamos, each 40 feet in diameter; to the right of that the lock for ocean-going vessels; and on the island, fish ladders from below the dams.

Since 1935 the Commission has also had authority to regulate utilities engaged in the transmission of electric energy across State lines, including rates, services, business practices, and security issues. State public-utility commissions regulate the distribution of power after it enters the State.

POWER DEVELOPMENT PROJECTS

Although the Federal Power Commission does not construct power plants, it regulates them.   Some power plants are built through the Bureau of Reclamation, some through the Tennessee Valley Authority, and some through Army engineers. The Bonneville Dam, described below, was contracted for through Army engineers.

The Bonneville Dam across the Columbia River about 40 miles above Portland, Oregon, aids navigation and develops power. Power

SECTION OF BONNEVILLE FISH LADDER

Each of these pools is about a foot above the next lower; and here are six of about seventy that the fish must leap to get above the dam to spawning creeks.

lines, built through Washington and Oregon, connect Bonneville and Grand Coulee dams. (See page 268.) Power is sold to big industries, Rural Electrification Administration Co-operatives, cities and other public utility districts, and private electric companies.

This Bonneville plant is the greatest power plant ever built practically at tidewater; and a ship lock with massive gates 70 feet high provides passage for ocean-going vessels.

The Columbia River has a multi-million-dollar salmon industry, and this was safeguarded by a fishway winding around a hill to imitate a real creek, two fish locks to float the fish over the dam, and three fish ladders for the energetic fish to climb. In one day, salmon weighing a total of 500,000 pounds found their way over the dam. Their migration down stream is fraught with more danger. Many fingerlings wash over the spillways or through the ladders, but others are dashed to death at the power house.

QUESTIONS ON THE TEXT

1. Why have many administrative agencies been created independent of the President and his Cabinet?

2. Why was the Interstate Commerce Commission created? What are its duties? Is there an appeal from it to the courts?

3. What does the Motor Vehicle Act provide as to (1) Insurance, (2) Qualifications of employees, (3) Safety, (4) Hours, and (5) Rates?

4. Why were interstate carriers by water placed under the Interstate Commerce Commission?

5. What are the functions of the National Advisory Committee for Aeronautics?

6. What are the powers of the Federal Communications Commission?

7. What two kinds of powers has the Federal Power Commission?

PROBLEMS FOR DISCUSSION

1. The Interstate Commerce Commission regulates railroads, bus and truck lines, and interstate water carriers. Should it allow these to expand and compete; or should it encourage the carriage of slow bulk freight by boat (where there is water), fast freight by rail, long-trip passengers by air; and license trucks and buses for local traffic and as feeders to railroads and air carriers? Would competition or division of traffic be best?

2. Should the regulation of air transportation be assigned to the I.C.C.?

3. The Communications Commission can grant licenses for stations with favored wave lengths to religious organizations, to a city government, to a State University, to a news corporation, or to a corporation that reports prize fights and jazz music and receives $1000 for a very brief advertisement. If the Commission attempts to cancel a license, the friends of that station flood the Commission with petitions, and Congressmen, who could abolish the Commission, must fight for stations of their districts. Therefore, if licensing is not carefully handled, it may become a national issue. If you were on the Commission, how would you apportion the stations or time among the above interests?

4. Practically all of the standard broadcasting frequencies (in the centers of population where broadcasting is profitable) are now assigned; so anyone wanting a broadcasting license must buy a station that has a license. Broad-

casting time sales were $5 million in 1927, but now they are over $650 million. In one recent year 32 radio stations were sold — a small one in Washington City at a profit of $425,000 and another in Los Angeles at a profit of $730,000. The Communications Commission usually renews licenses, therefore station owners look upon broadcasting frequencies as monopolies — hence the enormous prices paid for them. Do you think Congress should restrict charges for broadcasting? Take over some stations for itself, for States, and for cities? Or how should it prevent practical private monopoly of government-owned radio frequencies?

5. Should the Government provide a constant superior program of valuable news, basic knowledge, clean humor, patriotic and character-building music, and popular music that appeals to the many — free from advertising break-ins? If so, why? If not, why?

6. The United States District Court of Oregon sentenced an anti-chain store radio broadcaster to serve six months in jail for using profane and indecent language over the radio. Should a young man use profanity to show emphasis and temper, or should he develop a vocabulary which will enable him to express himself emphatically within the law?

7. If the Government develops a few dams and scares private capital from this field, has it benefited or harmed the consumers? If the Government should develop all of the available water power to give employment should it sell power at the cost of production or should it sell all at whatever price it will bring? What effect would cheap power have on our ability to compete in foreign trade with other countries where wages are low?

SELECT BIBLIOGRAPHY

BORAH, L. A. "From Sagebrush to Roses on the Columbia." *National Geographic.* November, 1952.

COHN, DAVID L. "The Wild Missouri." *Holiday,* March, 1950.

FERGUSON, J. H., AND McHENRY, D. E. *The American System of Government.* McGraw-Hill. New York. 1953 ed. Chs. 26–28.

PETERSON, E. T. "Big-Dam Foolishness." *Reader's Digest.* July, 1952.

ROHLFING, C., *et al. Business and Government.* Foundation Press. Brooklyn. 1953 ed. Chs. 8 and 12.

CHAPTER XVIII

FINANCIAL AGENCIES OF THE GOVERNMENT

BANKING SYSTEMS IN THE UNITED STATES

Two Systems of Banks. — There are two principal systems of banks in our country — *State* and *National*. State banks are chartered by State authority; National banks, by Federal authority. Both kinds of bank are subject to the regulations of the State in which they operate and also to Federal regulations unless they are uninsured State banks that are not members of the Federal Reserve System. A National bank must have the word "national" in its corporate title.

Naturally, State laws and supervisory practices vary from State to State. This independence of the States permits, nevertheless, a sound mutual co-operation between State and Federal authorities in safeguarding the public interest without disturbing the American principle of free enterprise. In particular, the creation of the Federal

Reserve System in 1913 and of the Federal Deposit Insurance Corporation in 1933 has brought about considerable uniformity in the regulation and supervision of banks in general to protect the funds of depositors.

All National banks and the majority of State banks do the general business of a *commercial* bank, that is, they receive deposits for safekeeping, accept savings accounts, perform trust functions, employ their funds to make loans and investments, and render various other financial services. One group of State banks, however, the *mutual savings banks*, with one or two exceptions, restrict their business exclusively to the receipt and investment of small savings deposits. There are about 530 mutual savings banks, located chiefly in New

England and other eastern states. Although they comprise only a small portion of the some 14,675 banks in our country, they have impressive aggregate deposits of more than ten billion dollars.

Following the passage of the National Bank Act in 1863, State banks all but disappeared from the scene because most State banks at the time became National banks in order to retain the privilege of issuing currency. Then, as the use of checks increased, as mutual savings banks began to grow, and as trust companies began to do general banking, State banks began to increase in number again, until today there are more State banks (about 9700) than there are National banks (about 4970).

National banks came into being in order to provide a sound control of bank note currency. When currency-issuing Federal Reserve banks were set up in 1914, National banks lost this one distinctive feature (page 219), becoming merely Federally-controlled commercial banks that are much like State-chartered commercial banks.

Organizations and Functions of National Banks. — With the approval of the Comptroller of the Currency any five or more persons may secure from him a charter of incorporation for a National bank, if they can raise an amount of capital varying from $50,000 in places of less than 6000 inhabitants to $200,000 in cities of more than 50,000 inhabitants.

These banks receive deposits from individuals and corporations and lend money to individuals and corporations. They must be examined by a United States examiner at least twice a year, and must make reports to the Comptroller of the Currency at least three times a year — whenever called for.

Insurance of Deposits. — National banks, and State banks which are members of the Federal Reserve System, must insure their deposits up to $10,000; and non-member State banks may qualify to do so.[1] The insurance premium is paid by insured banks in proportion to their average deposits. The sign shown in the diagram on page 325 is displayed by insured banks.

The insurance fund is administered by the Federal Deposit Insurance Corporation, composed of the Comptroller of the Currency and two

---

[1] Unsound practices cause a non-member bank to lose its insurance privilege; a State bank to lose membership; and a National bank to be closed.

citizens appointed by the President and Senate. When a National bank is closed, the Corporation is appointed receiver. A new bank is organized and assumes the guarantee deposit liabilities of the closed bank. If stock in the new bank can be sold, the new bank will continue. If not, the assets may be sold to another bank. If neither of these arrangements is possible within two years, the bank will liquidate.

Branch Banks. — National banks may establish branches in their home cities if such cities have 25,000 or more inhabitants. They may establish branches in foreign countries. Those with $500,000 or more capital may, with the consent of the Comptroller of the Currency, establish branches within the State to the extent that State banks are allowed to create branches.

Courtesy Californians Inc.

SAVINGS UNION BRANCH OF SAN FRANCISCO'S AMERICAN TRUST COMPANY

Examinations. — In general, banks are subject to unannounced examinations by specially trained examiners whose work it is to see that the banks under their authority are in sound condition and soundly organized. Thus through improved regulation and supervision our banking system has been greatly strengthened in recent decades.

THE FEDERAL RESERVE SYSTEM — "BANKERS' BANKS"

Organization of Federal Reserve Banks. — To remedy certain defects, and to give National banks the strength of unity, the Federal Reserve System was established by Congress in 1913; and in 1935 it was brought decidedly more under the control of the National Government. The United States is divided into twelve Federal Reserve districts, and there is one Federal Reserve Bank located in the Federal Reserve Bank city of each district.

Each of these Federal Reserve Banks is in direct charge of a board of directors. There are also Federal Reserve branch banks.

Member Banks. — Every National Bank is a member of the Federal Reserve System and, as such, is required to subscribe to the stock of the Federal Reserve Bank of its district; and State banks and trust companies may become members by complying with certain conditions of membership.

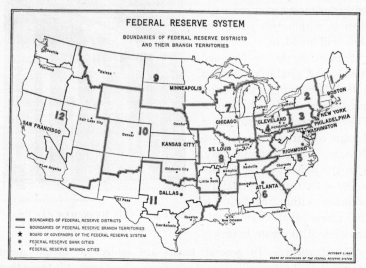

The Board of Governors of the Federal Reserve System is composed of seven members appointed by the President with the approval of the Senate for a single term of 14 years — one retiring every second year.

Powers of the Board of Governors. — *Reserves.* — The Board determines the percentage of deposits that member banks must deposit with the district Reserve Banks. If member banks are unwisely lending money for speculative purposes the Board will curb them by requiring them to place a larger proportion of their deposits on reserve; and conversely, if constructive business needs more loans the Board will return a portion of the reserves to the member banks to take care of these proper needs.

Issue of Federal Reserve Notes. — When more money is needed for legitimate purposes, the Board may issue any amount of Federal Reserve Notes through any of the Federal Reserve Banks; but the notes must be secured by 25% gold certificates and 75% Government bonds or 75% commercial paper.

Determination of Interest Rate. — When a business man borrows money from a National Bank or State bank he gives his note. If the bank needs money, it can get it from the Federal Reserve Bank by turning over these notes for security. The Board determines the interest rate charged the banks. If industry is slack, the interest rate will be low to encourage borrowing; but if a "boom" is on and speculation is raising prices unduly, the interest rate will be made high to discourage reckless borrowing.

Interest Rate on Deposits. — The Board limits the interest rate that member banks may pay on time and savings deposits. This is to prevent a reckless bank from paying more than a safely managed bank can afford to pay.

Supervision. — The Board supervises Federal Reserve Banks, and can even remove officers of recklessly managed member banks.[1]

SYSTEM OF FARM CREDIT BANKS

The **Farm Credit Administration** was created in 1933 to co-ordinate the various agricultural lending organizations which had been created by the Government to assist farmers during the depression. It is under an officer known as the Governor of the Farm Credit Administration, and he in turn is under the Secretary of Agriculture.[2] The Governor administers the Federal Land Banks and other banks of the Farm Credit system.[3] To make this possible the country is divided

---

[1] Also since 1935 the purchase and sale of bonds has become an important function of Federal Reserve Banks. The Board of Governors, plus 5 representatives of the Federal Reserve Banks, constitute the Federal Open-Market Committee. This Committee buys and sells United States bonds and other obligations. When money is scarce and U. S. bonds are falling in price, this Committee will require the Federal Reserve Banks to buy bonds and keep their price up to face value. This also puts money in circulation. Conversely, if money is plentiful and speculation is unduly raising the price of bonds, the Federal Reserve Banks are required to sell bonds and thus take money out of circulation and prevent a "run-away" market.

Originally Federal Reserve Banks lent only to member banks, but now they may also make loans to individuals and corporations under certain conditions.

[2] The Governor of the Farm Credit Administration is appointed by the President with the consent of the Senate.

[3] *Intermediate Credit Banks* make loans through various agricultural credit corporations instead of directly to the farmers. *Production Credit Corporations* make loans to production credit associations consisting of ten or more farmers. *Banks for Co-operatives* make loans to agricultural co-operative associations.

into twelve Farm Credit Administration Districts with an agricultural bank ("Federal Land Bank") in a centrally located city of each district.

Federal Land Banks were created in 1916 to give the farmer an opportunity to borrow money on his land at low rates of interest by giving a long-term mortgage. These banks borrow money by the sale of partially tax-exempt bonds on which they pay about 3% interest and then lend it to national farm loan associations at about 4% interest.[1]

Loans are made only for the purchase of land, for its improvement, or for purchase of livestock, equipment, fertilizers, or to provide buildings on a farm, or to pay off a debt under certain conditions. A loan must not exceed 65% of the normal agricultural value of the farm offered as security.

The amount borrowed must not be less than $100 or more than $100,000. No mortgage shall run for more than forty years, or for less than five except by special arrangement. The loan is repaid in annual or semi-annual installments.

Ten or more farmers who own land may form a national farm loan association, and through this association may borrow money from a Land Bank. The association is liable for the loan made to each of the members.

If direct loans are made to individuals, $\frac{1}{2}$ of 1 per cent more interest is charged.

FEDERAL HOME LOAN BANK SYSTEM

Regional Home Loan Banks, eleven in number, make loans to building and loan, savings and loan, and homestead associations, savings and co-operative banks, and insurance companies. These member institutions lend directly to borrowing home builders. Most of the member institutions are of the savings and loan type.

Federal Savings and Loan Associations can be organized by any responsible group of citizens by applying to the nearest Federal Home

---

[1] The *Federal Farm Mortgage Corporation* was created in 1934 as an emergency measure to assist farmers who were about to lose their farms because of the depression prices of farm products. The Corporation was authorized to issue partially tax-exempt Government guaranteed bonds, and to lend the proceeds to worthy farmers at a low rate of interest. Many a farm has been saved for its owner by this Government corporation.

Loan Bank. In these banks individuals may earn interest on their savings; or if they are good risks they can borrow for home-financing needs.

(Another agency for encouraging home ownership is the Federal Housing Administration treated in Chapter XXXVIII.)

Other Federal Loan Agencies

The Small Business Administration was created by Congress in 1953 to replace the Reconstruction Finance Corporation. This new lending agency is headed by an Administrator appointed by the President with the consent of the Senate. It is designed to encourage small businesses by making financial help available to them.

The S. B. A. has a lending authority of $275,000,000. Of this amount, $150,000,000 is available for loans to small businesses. Individual loans of as much as $150,000 may be made to small firms which cannot obtain suitable private financing. Another $25,000,000 of the total is available for the making of disaster loans (flood-damage loans, for instance); and the remaining $100,000,000 is available for governmental projects.

The Reconstruction Finance Corporation was ordered to begin a liquidation process intended to close it down by June 30, 1954. The R. F. C. was born in the depression year of 1932 at a time when, because of economic conditions, only the Government itself was able to borrow large sums of money. During its 22-year life it made public credit available to large and small commercial, industrial, and governmental borrowers. Of all the federal lending agencies it was the largest and the one most directly concerned with general business.

It lent over $2,000,000,000 to banks during the depression, practically all of which has been repaid. Without this aid a great many more banks than did fail would have had to close their doors. Without R. F. C. loans of some $500,000,000 a number of railroads would also have ceased operations in the depression years.

Many State and local governments received a total of about $2,000,000,000 in loans from the R. F. C. in the same period. And the R. F. C. helped to finance such agencies of the National Government as the Federal Deposit Insurance Corporation and the Export-Import Bank.

Loans were made for such projects as the Metropolitan Water District of Southern California (see Chapter XXXIV), San Francisco bridges, and New York tunnels.

In 1941 Arkansas refunded $136,000,000 of its outstanding 4.4% tax-exempt highway bonds to take advantage of lower prevailing interest rates. Private bankers offered to refinance the bonds at

Courtesy Bethlehem Steel Company

ENTRANCE OF BROOKLYN–BATTERY TUNNEL

This 1.73-mile-long tunnel was completed with a low-interest-rate R. F. C. loan. It is said to be the second longest vehicular tunnel in the world.

3.5% interest. The R. F. C. thought the private bank rates too high, bought the bonds at 3.2%, and then resold them at a slight profit. This one transaction will save Arkansas about $28,000,000 interest.

As World War II approached, the R. F. C. made loans to finance the expansion of war industries and bought large quantities of rubber, tin, and other raw materials for which we were dependent on overseas supply. During the war it actually owned and operated several war-born industries — for example, the Rubber Reserve Company which produced synthetic rubber, and the Metals Reserve Company which provided many scarce metals for wartime production needs. After the war it helped finance reconversion and made large loans to such concerns as Kaiser-Frazer and Northwest Airlines.

In recent years the agency had been severely criticized by private business and financial competitors; and there were disclosures of corruption among a very few R. F. C. employees. But, altogether, R. F. C. chalked up an impressive record in its lending operations. In addition to the industries and businesses it actually saved in the 1930's and its wartime work, it paid some $650,000,000 in interest into the United States Treasury.

Export-Import Bank. — This bank was created in 1934 during the depression to stimulate foreign trade. It is authorized to lend as much as $4,500,000,000. Originally its loans were made to foreign governments, but its banking powers were greatly extended in 1947.

During the depression, loans were made to enable other countries to buy in the United States. During the war, loans were made to China and to Latin-American governments to stabilize their money, and as a good-neighbor policy. Following the war, rehabilitation loans were made. For instance, the bank lent to large Italian industries, with the loans guaranteed by the Italian Government. These Italian loans had to be spent for United States equipment and machinery.

Typical loans in 1953 were those to Spain ($12,000,000) and Japan ($40,000,000) to help finance the importation of raw American cotton.

The International Bank and the International Monetary Fund, for which the United States is furnishing a large part of the capital, also makes similar loans. (See Chapter XL.)

THE SECURITIES AND EXCHANGE COMMISSION

Purpose. — In 1933 more than 16,000,000 of our people owned more than $100,000,000,000 worth of stocks and bonds. Along with the majority of honest dealers in stocks and bonds there are racketeers who exploit inexperienced and uninformed buyers of securities. Therefore the Securities and Exchange Commission was created by Congress in 1934 to give information and help to all investors.

Organization. — The Commission consists of five members appointed by the President and Senate for a term of five years.

Registration of Securities to Be Issued. — Prospectuses for mining stocks were once considered so misleading that Mark Twain defined a mine as a "hole in the ground owned by a liar." The Securities Act of 1933 provides for a fair and full disclosure of the character of securities sold in interstate or foreign commerce or by the use of the mails. This is acquired by means of registration statements required by law to be filed with the Commission. When satisfactory to the Commission, the more important statements are printed in a prospectus which must in general be given to all prospective purchasers. This does not insure a safe investment, but it insures some accurate knowledge of the security in which one is investing.

This Act also forbids fraudulent transactions in all securities through the mails or in interstate commerce.[1]

Registration of Outstanding and New Issues of Securities. — The 1934 Act of Congress requires the registration of securities listed on national security exchanges, such as the New York Stock Exchange. The Commission prepares elaborate forms with questions covering whatever the Commission thinks will help in an understanding of the real condition of a corporation. For instance, it required more than a hundred pages for the Standard Oil Company of New Jersey to answer all the questions the Commission asked. This information then becomes public property. Investors find the reports of corporations available in Washington, New York, and Chicago; or for a small fee they can have a photographic copy made.

Regulation of Security Exchanges and Over-the-Counter Markets. — The 1934 Act directs the Commission to set up machinery for the constant watching of security market activities. If the provisions of the Act are not conformed to, the Commission has power to close an exchange, to forbid trading in a security whose issuer has failed to comply with the requirements of the Act, to suspend or expel members of an exchange, and to make rules for an exchange if necessary.

It is the purpose of the Commission to prevent the manipulation of the price of securities, and to prevent unfair profits hitherto made by "corporate insiders" through the use of knowledge which had not been made available to the public.

Regulation or Elimination of Public Utility Holding Companies. — Very often, through the use of holding companies, complete control of a large operating unit could be maintained by actual ownership of

---

[1] For years unscrupulous persons and firms sold huge quantities of worthless stocks and bonds to a gullible public. The Government did little to interfere, and the losses resulting were about $25 billion as we passed from the boom of the twenties to the depression of the thirties.

only a fraction of 1 per cent of the property controlled. A financier would organize a small corporation with a small amount of voting stock and a large amount of nonvoting stock, and would retain the voting stock. Then he would float bonds. With the proceeds he would

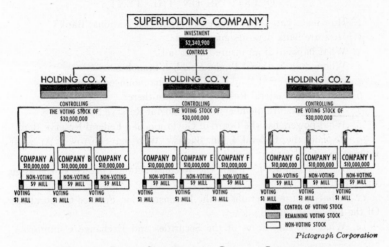

ELECTRIC POWER SUPERHOLDING COMPANY ILLUSTRATED

A financier organized an investment company with $2,340,900 capital, and he himself bought the majority of voting stock. He used this $2,340,900 to buy the majority of voting stock in companies X, Y, and Z. He then used the money obtained from the sale of stock in each of these to buy the majority of voting stock in three operating companies, or a total of nine companies (A to I). Thus with a small original investment, he controlled nine operating plants worth $90,000,000.

organize a larger company and retain the majority of voting stock in that second company. He could repeat this operation just as long as investors would buy the stocks and bonds.

This holding company procedure became extensively used in connection with electric power companies and gas companies. Financiers who controlled holding companies claimed that their holding companies were conducive to large-scale production and greater efficiency. Their opponents showed that their complexity made it possible for shrewd financiers to conceal their operations and produce undue personal gains which should be used to reduce the price of electricity and gas.

Therefore in 1935 Congress directed the Commission to require a full and fair disclosure of the corporate structure of holding company systems. The Commission was further directed to eliminate uneconomic holding company structures, and to supervise security transactions and other operations of *electric and gas* holding company systems.

QUESTIONS ON THE TEXT

1. How much capital is required to organize a National Bank?
2. How are bank deposits guaranteed?
3. What happens if an insured bank fails?
4. Where may National Banks establish branches?
5. Why are National Banks subject to unannounced examinations?
6. How many Federal Reserve Banks are there?
7. What banks are members of the Federal Reserve System?
8. What powers has the Board of Governors of a Federal Reserve Bank?
9. Explain the Federal Land Banks. Who may borrow? At what interest rate? For what period?
10. Explain conditions when the Reconstruction Finance Corporation was created.
11. What are the functions of the Reconstruction Finance Corporation? Of the Export-Import Bank?
12. What are the duties of the Securities and Exchange Commission?

PROBLEMS FOR DISCUSSION

1. How much money would be necessary to establish a National Bank in your town or city?
2. Of what Federal Reserve Bank are the National Banks in your town stockholders?
3. How will the Federal Reserve Act help to prevent "panics" like that of 1907, which resulted from a scarcity or rather a hoarding of money?
4. During "hard times" a merchant in a small city goes to the National Bank to borrow money by giving his note. Was he more likely to get this money before or after the Federal Reserve System was established? Why?
5. Deposits in insured banks are insured only to the extent of $10,000. This coverage gives full insurance to most depositors, so they do not care whether they deposit in banks well managed or in banks poorly managed. But depositors of amounts in excess of $10,000 still patronize banks that are well managed, so a poorly managed bank gets only the small deposits. This is a strong incentive for every bank to get the reputation of being well managed. Do you consider this limited coverage up to $10,000 a clever and admirable device, or would you favor no insurance, or would you favor full coverage?

6. In 1936 bankers wanted 5 per cent interest for money to refinance Great Northern Railway bonds coming due. The Reconstruction Finance Corporation agreed to refinance the bonds at 4 per cent. With this encouragement the Railroad Company was able to sell the bonds at 4 per cent to its own stockholders and bondholders, thus saving $1,000,000 annually. Why do you favor or oppose this Government competition with private banks?

7. Do you think the Government is justified in spending large sums of money through the Securities and Exchange Commission to protect the millions of investors; or should we merely "let the purchaser beware"?

SELECT BIBLIOGRAPHY

OGG, F., AND RAY, P. *Essentials of American Government.* Appleton-Century-Crofts. 1952. Chapters XXVI and XXVII.

SWARTHOUT, J., AND BARTLEY, E. *Principles and Problems of American National Government.* Oxford Univ. Press, 1954 ed. Chapter XXI.

———. *Materials on American Government.* Oxford Univ. Press, 1952. Chapter XXIII.

ROHLFING, C., *et al. Business and Government.* Foundation Press. Brooklyn. 1953 ed. Chapters VII, XVIII–XX.

CHAPTER XIX

DEPARTMENT OF HEALTH, EDUCATION AND WELFARE

The **Department of Health, Education, and Welfare** (H. E. W.) was created by Congress in 1953. It is the newest of the Cabinet Departments and was created as the first major reorganization step taken by the Eisenhower Administration.

This new Department was established to improve the administration of Government programs in the fields of education, health, and economic security. H. E. W. replaced the old Federal Security Administration and the Secretary assumed all of the functions of the Federal Security Administrator. Its principal agencies are the Office of Education, the Social Security Administration, the Public Health Service, and the Food and Drug Administration.[1]

The Office of Education. — The providing of public education is a function reserved to the States in the American federal system and it is usually regarded as a responsibility of local communities (see pages 62, 621–638). But the National Government does provide certain promotional services in this field.

Congress created the Office of Education in 1867 "for the purpose of collecting such statistics and facts as shall show the condition and progress of education in the several States and Territories, and of diffusing such information respecting the organization and management of schools and school systems, and methods of teaching, as shall aid the people of the United States in the establishment and maintenance of efficient school systems, and otherwise promote the cause of education throughout the country."

---

[1] H. E. W. also includes the Office of Vocational Rehabilitation, which works with the States in aiding the mentally and physically handicapped, and Saint Elizabeth's Hospital, the Government's mental hospital in the District of Columbia. Three corporations, in part supported by federal funds, are to a limited extent supervised by the Department: Howard University, an institution of higher education for Negroes, located in Washington, D. C.; Columbia Institution for the Deaf, Washington, D. C.; and the American Printing House for the Blind in Louisville, Ky.

The Office is headed by a Commissioner appointed by the President with the consent of the Senate. It administers funds appropriated by Congress for land-grant colleges and for vocational education in the States in such fields as agriculture and home economics. It also conducts extensive research programs in public education and generally assists State and local school authorities.

Need for Old-Age Security. — Modern science and hygiene have enabled an increasing number of people to reach old age. But as the average of man's life has been lengthened, his working years have been shortened in many industries because mass production requires speed and endurance — qualities of young men.

Because of sickness, accidents, or occasional unemployment, it may be impossible for one who has reared a large family to save for future security. In such cases, it seems reasonable to place the burden of support upon everybody instead of on some relative who may thus jeopardize his own future security. Also, an assured reasonable income for the old increases buying power and helps make jobs for the young.

OUR GROWING POPULATION OVER 65

Social Security Administration. — Many people lost their savings during the depression of the early thirties. Others lost their jobs because of man-saving machines. Moreover, most of these people live in cities in rented property and are dependent upon others for employment. In 1935 the Committee on Economic Security reported to the President that 18,000,000 people, including children and aged, were dependent upon emergency relief, and that 10,000,000 workers had no employment other than relief work.

Therefore in 1935 Congress passed the Social Security Act, creating an organization now known as the Social Security Administration.

The Administration's duties are to study and recommend methods of providing economic security; and to administer Federal grants to States for old-age benefits, unemployment compensation, old-age assistance, aid to the blind, and aid to dependent children, that is, children under sixteen who have been deprived of parental support and are living in private homes with near relatives.

FEDERAL INSURANCE BENEFICIARIES
Assured income may mean a happy old age.

Federal Old-Age and Survivors' Insurance. — Through the Social Security Administration, Congress provides for a retirement fund from which employees of most industries,[1] when 65 years of age, may stop work and receive a monthly benefit varying from $22.50 to $168.75 a month depending upon the average monthly earnings.

---

[1] In 1950 Congress amended the 1935 Act to broaden social security coverage. For example, most "self-employed" business men are now covered: grocers, filling station and barbershop operators, independent painters, carpenters, and plumbers. Lawyers and doctors are covered only if they receive a set salary. Agricultural laborers, domestics, and newsboys are now covered. State and local government and religious, charitable, and other non-profit organization employees may be covered by request. In all, 45,000,000 people are now covered.

The monthly benefit of a covered worker who reaches age 65 amounts to 55 per cent of the first $100 of his average monthly wage prior to retirement plus 15 per cent of the next $200 (or part thereof) of his average monthly wage.

If the beneficiary is married, his wife will receive, when she is 65, a monthly payment equal to 50 per cent of the husband's monthly benefit. Thus:[1]

AVERAGE MONTHLY EARNINGS	MONTHLY BENEFITS AT AND BEYOND AGE 65	
	Single Worker	Married Worker
$50	$27.50	$41.25
100	55.00	82.50
150	62.50	93.75
200	70.00	105.00
250	77.50	116.25
300	85.00	127.50

If the beneficiary dies before he is 65, his widow, if she has a child, will receive $\frac{3}{4}$ of the benefits he had earned up to that time, plus an additional amount for the support of the child or children, until the youngest child is 18. And when a widow becomes 65, whether or not she has had children, she may receive monthly $\frac{3}{4}$ of the benefits the husband had earned provided she has not remarried or is not entitled to a larger benefit on her own account.

To help provide the fund from which the benefits are paid each employee who comes under the Act must pay $1\frac{1}{2}\%$ of his wages[2] and the employer must pay a like amount for him. (Until 1950 employers and employees each paid only 1%; until 1954, $1\frac{1}{2}\%$; and at present 2%. As the law now stands, the rate goes up to $2\frac{1}{2}\%$ in 1960, to 3% in 1965, and reaches a maximum $3\frac{1}{4}\%$ in 1970.)

Until 1950, social security taxes were collected from employees and employers on only the first $3,000 of annual income. However, the

---

[1] Under the Social Security Act Amendments of 1952, Congress raised the benefits under the law for the fourth time since 1935.

[2] In the 1950 Act, Congress provided that the payroll tax on both employers and employees shall rise to 2% in 1954, $2\frac{1}{2}\%$ in 1960, 3% in 1965, and $3\frac{1}{4}\%$ in 1970.

tax is now collected on the first $3,600 of income of both wage-earners and most self-employed persons.

To benefit by the Social Security Act a wage-earner must register and receive a numbered account card. Then whenever he is employed

Courtesy Federal Security Agency

SOCIAL SECURITY ACCOUNT CARD

at an occupation covered by the Act the employer pays the tax quarterly with that number to the Director of Internal Revenue.

Benefits usually begin at 65, but if one works beyond that age wages will continue to count towards benefits. If one retires at 65 and later goes back to work on a job covered by Old Age and Survivor Insurance his benefits are suspended for any month in which he earns more than $75. Benefits begin again when he stops work. After retirement he may work on a job not covered by this insurance program, and continue to receive his insurance benefits, no matter how much he may earn.

Beginning in 1951, a self-employed person[1] (such as a taxi-cab driver who owns his own cab) who earns more than $400 a year pays his tax annually. It is collected with his income tax in March and the rate is $1\frac{1}{2}$ that of wage-earners (*i.e.*, now 3%) because the self-employed have no employers to match their contributions.

Federal Grants to States for Old-Age Assistance. — Between 1923 and 1935 three fourths of the States enacted some sort of old-age pension law. In 1935, to encourage this movement, Congress authorized an annual Federal appropriation of money to assist States in the payment of old-age pensions, under certain conditions. The Social Security Administration is to see that each State meets these conditions before it receives its grant.

The following conditions must be complied with by a State to receive the Federal grant:

1. State pension law must apply to needy of 65 and older.

_____

[1] Self-employed professionals (such as doctors, lawyers, engineers, architects, accountants, and funeral directors) are not covered by the Act. However, if these people are employed by others, they are covered by the Act.

2. Must not be granted to an inmate of a public institution.

3. Must be granted to all needy citizens applying, if resident of the State 5 years out of the last 9 years, and continuously for the last year.

4. If the pensioner dies with property and State law requires repayment of what he has received, the United States gets half.

Federal grants are determined by this complex 1952 formula: $\frac{3}{4}$ of the State's expenditures under the program up to an amount equal to the product of $20 times the number of persons covered, plus $\frac{1}{2}$ of any additional amount the State pays up to an over-all maximum of $55 per individual.   (This formula is also applied to Federal grants for State assistance to the blind.)

Courtesy U. S. Department of Labor

BOY WITH RHEUMATIC FEVER CONVALESCING AT HOME

The Children's Bureau matches State money and has developed special programs for rheumatic children.

The Children's Bureau investigates birth rate, infant mortality, orphanage, juvenile courts, dangerous occupations, employment, diseases, and legislation affecting children.

If the Social Security Administration approves a State plan for administering the fund, the Government will contribute up to $\frac{3}{4}$ of

State expenditures for needy children under 16 years (or 18 if in school) dependent by reason of death, absence, or incapacity of a parent, if the children live with certain relatives in residences maintained as homes. The Federal Government pays half up to a total of $27 per month for the first child and $18 for each additional child, plus one half of the amount a State grants above these sums.

Federal Aid Is Granted through the Children's Bureau for:
Crippled Children, if matched by the State.
Child Welfare — especially for neglected and near-delinquent children in rural areas. The State or locality pays part.
Mothers' and Children's Health. Part of the money is distributed among the States in proportion to live births and part according to need. The latter need not be matched by the State.

PUBLIC HEALTH SERVICE

United States Public Health Service. — A seventeenth-century English author incidentally mentions the fact that every fourth person in a large representative audience was horribly disfigured by smallpox. With our modern travel of persons and interchange of commodities in commerce we should never be safe from smallpox, cholera, yellow fever, and other dreaded diseases were it not for Uncle Sam's efficient family physician — the United States Public Health Service.

Protection against Communicable Diseases from Abroad. — Highly trained officers are sent to the foreign ports of the world to detect persons suffering from contagious diseases and keep them from embarking on vessels destined for the United States. American consuls stationed in hundreds of foreign cities make reports of health conditions. And physical examinations are given to immigrants. Also every airplane before departure from various foreign ports is inspected and fumigated. On arrival additional fumigation is done to prevent yellow fever.

Protection against Communicable Diseases from State to State. — Weekly telegraphic reports from State health officials and weekly mail reports from local health officials of all sizable cities enable the Service to establish interstate quarantines and other preventive measures. Water from about 3000 sources is tested to provide sanitary drinking water for trains and planes and boats.

The Domestic Quarantine Division controls the habitat of squirrels in the Pacific and Rocky Mountain States where they are known to be carriers of plague. Squirrel-free zones must be maintained around certain cities to prevent infected squirrels from coming in contact with city rats, which, in turn, could spread the plague. The Domestic Quarantine Division once tracked down an epidemic of typhoid fever caused by infected oysters, and then taught State health officers how to prevent the infection of oysters.

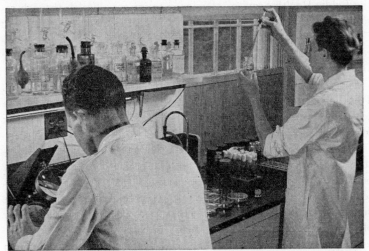

Courtesy United States Public Health Service

LABORATORY TECHNICIANS TESTING SAMPLES OF WATER

Local Health Departments and water purification plants generally are responsible for keeping drinking water safe for consumption.

Research. — Disease wasted more manpower in World War I than all the battle casualties. But research made it possible for more than 97 per cent of the wounded in World War II and the Korean War to recover. Research in other fields is important, too. Research in nutrition, for example, shows us how to make the best use of our available food supply.

The Public Health Service also discovered through research the cause and cure of pellagra, learned how to grind up ticks to make a vaccine against Rocky Mountain fever, and found that the cotton rat can carry infantile paralysis.

Venereal Disease Research and Treatment. — Thirty million Americans were found to be affected with varying degrees of venereal disease, but Norway and Sweden had freed themselves from it. During the First World War about 7,000,000 days of service were lost because of syphilis and gonorrhea. Now the Public Health Service is successfully spending millions of dollars annually to investigate, treat, and prevent these diseases.

The National Institutes of Health are the principal research arm of the Public Health Service. Designed to improve health through research and education, the following Institutes have been created: Cancer, Heart, Dental Research, Mental Health, Neurological Diseases and Blindness, Microbiological, and Arthritis and Metabolic Diseases.

The Clinical Center of the National Institutes was opened in 1953. This huge medical research center is a 14-story structure with a 500-patient capacity. It is located near Bethesda, Md., and took five years and $64,000,000 to build.

It is no ordinary hospital. As the Director of the National Institutes explains: "This is not a hospital. You don't get in just by being sick. You don't get in for medical care. You get in for research. . . . For the first time in history we shall be able to integrate laboratory and clinical research so that there can be a complete study of the chronic diseases that kill men."

All patients admitted (the first eight were women suffering from cancer) must be volunteers willing to lend themselves to research into their particular illness (cancer, heart diseases, arthritis, mental ailments, rheumatic fever, epilepsy, or dental diseases). Only patients recommended by physicians, hospitals, or medical schools may be admitted. Every step of the treatment is explained to the non-paying patient and he is free to call off the treatments and leave the Center at any time he pleases.

Marine Hospitals. — The Public Health Service maintains 18 hospitals, 23 outpatient clinics, and 100 outpatient offices where seamen of the Merchant Marine, Coast Guard personnel and their dependents may receive medical and dental care.

Freedmen's Hospital, in the District of Columbia, is also operated by the Service. This is a general hospital for the treatment of acute medical and surgical conditions, with an extensive system of clinics for outpatients. It also provides internship and clinical experience for medical students and graduates of Howard University.

Safe and Standardized Biologic Products. — Manufacturers of vaccines, serums, antitoxins, and the like are licensed by the Public Health Service, and their products are carefully examined.

The Division of Mental Health operates hospitals for narcotic addicts at Lexington, Kentucky, and Fort Worth, Texas, besides directing

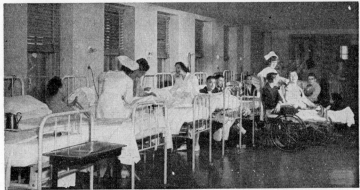

Courtesy United States Public Health Service

WARD IN A U. S. MARINE HOSPITAL

These Public Health Service hospitals give medical and hospital care to members of the United States Merchant Marine, the Coast Guard, and their families.

medical care of Federal prisoners, and furnishing psychiatric service in Federal courts.

The National Leper Home at Carville, Louisiana, cares for hundreds of quarantined patients, treats them, and carries on research for the prevention of the dreaded disease.

Sanitary Reports and Statistics are collected from everywhere, and information on the prevalence of disease is made available for the health officials of every county and city.

Health Education is encouraged by the Service through printed reports, bulletins, the press, radio, and moving pictures.

Flying Squadrons, consisting of especially trained physicians, engineers, and chemists, go anywhere in the country on short notice to provide technical consultation in co-operation with State or local health departments for assistance when epidemics need prompt attention.

Nutrition. — Even in normal times only about one fourth of the people of the United States are properly fed; and it is thought that the average active virile life-span could be increased by ten years through a perfect diet for everybody. Many families cannot afford adequate "protective foods" such as milk, meat, eggs, fresh vegetables, and fruits. The Food Stamp Plan enabled many a man and woman and child to live who had merely existed before; and the school lunch program has improved the capacity of underfed children to learn. In time of peace as well as when we are training soldiers for war, our motto should be "Food for Fitness."

Aid to States for Hospitals is granted by the Federal Government through the Public Health Service. Each State must submit its hospital plans, and when approved it receives not less than $100,000 annually.

FEDERAL PURE FOOD AND DRUG ADMINISTRATION

Introduction. — The Commissioner of Foods and Drugs administers the Pure Food and Drug Act of 1938 (strengthening the Act of 1906). This 1938 Act excludes from interstate commerce anything adulterated or misbranded, and many injurious drugs, devices, cosmetics, and foods and drinks for man or animal.

Drugs must meet the standards of official pharmacopoeias, or if changes are made the change must be clearly stated on the container. Dangerous drugs may be confiscated, and all new drugs are tested before the Administration authorizes their sale. A permit must be obtained before marketing a new drug, in order to prevent the repetition of the sulfanilamide disaster in which 105 people lost their lives.

Foods and Drinks are examined in numerous testing laboratories throughout the United States; and inspection services are likewise maintained. The Commissioner establishes definitions and standards of quality; and a reputable firm is now protected against competition by a "chiseling" competitor who would adulterate his product — *e.g.*, with clay in candy, peanut hulls in stock feeds, or tartaric acid in lemonade.

Confections must not contain alcohol except less than $\frac{1}{2}$ per cent from flavoring extracts.

Labels must give the significant ingredients and the quantity of a package, and must not misname them. For instance, veal must not be mislabeled as "canned chicken." Narcotic or hypnotic drugs must be labeled, "Warning: May be Habit-Forming." Poisonous or otherwise dangerous drugs must be plainly labeled and instructions given for use and for antidotes. For instance, coal tar dyes commonly used for dyeing hair must have a label which states that they are dangerous for some people and may cause blindness if used near the eyes.

Slack-filling and deceptive containers are forbidden.

The Act applies to interstate commerce and to imports, but not to all exports. States have their own local regulations.

The work of the Food and Drug Administration, together with that of the Federal Trade Commission (see pages 141–143) has saved untold thousands of lives and protected the health and well-being of all of our people.

A recent Federal court case presents an interesting illustration of the work of the Administration in protecting the public against unscrupulous racketeers. For nearly twenty years a man had been selling a device he called the "Spectro-Chrome." He claimed that it would cure practically any ailment known to medical science. His Spectro-Chrome was, in reality, nothing more than a box containing a strong electric light bulb and several different colored panes of glass. But he had sold over 9,000 of them at $90 each!

He claimed that when the light was passed through one of the panes and onto the "patient" it would cure cancer, when passed through another it would cure ulcers, and so on. One defense witness at his trial testified that the machine made calving easier for cows when they were faced to the north during treatment. Another claimed that the machine had actually cured a dachshund of constipation. But several Government witnesses told of many people suffering from serious illnesses who had died while being "treated" by the machine.

One defense witness who claimed that the Spectro-Chrome had cured him of epilepsy suffered an epileptic attack while testifying. He might have strangled to death had not a doctor (who was a Government witness) saved him.

Because the Food and Drug Administration and the Federal Trade Commission are understaffed and because of public indifference, it is estimated that for every criminal convicted for fraud of this kind two others are at large. Most of those who "get away with it" are petty crooks—selling fakes in a bottle for a dollar or two or such things as adulterated sugar or mislabeled horse meat. But they are still a real threat to the public health and safety.

QUESTIONS ON THE TEXT

1. Explain the increasing need for old-age security.

2. Explain: (*a*) the Office of Education; (*b*) Federal Old-Age and Survivors Insurance; (*c*) Old-Age Assistance; (*d*) Aid to Children and Mothers.

3. Explain: (*a*) Public Health Service; (*b*) Pure Food and Drug Administration.

SELECT BIBLIOGRAPHY

HOLEMAN, F. "They're Adding Years to Your Life." *Collier's*. August 30, 1952.

LOCKETT, E. "The Vanguard of Science." *Nation's Business*. November, 1952.

MERIAM, L. *Relief and Social Security*. Brookings Institution, Washington, D. C. (Pamphlet; 42 pp.)

Newsweek, "Pensions: What to Do about the Old Folks." March 20, 1950.

PRINGLE, H. AND K. "The Case for Federal Relief." *Saturday Evening Post*. July 19, 1952. (As seen by those who administer it.)

"Social Security Tax Increases." *U. S. News*. July 13, 1953.

"The Older Worker." *Time*. October 19, 1953.

CHAPTER XX

TERRITORIES AND OTHER DEPENDENCIES

Classification of Territories. — Except for Alaska all territories which the United States acquired before the Spanish-American War were adjacent and had been settled and developed by natives of this country and by European immigrants. The civilization and traditions of these people were not fundamentally different from our own, so Congress extended to them a large measure of self-government and all the civil rights secured by the National Constitution.

But the Spanish-American War brought under our control distant territory lying in the tropics and inhabited by peoples of different races who were inexperienced in self-government and unaccustomed to the same kind of civil and political rights enjoyed under our Constitution. Therefore in the famous "Insular Cases" the Supreme Court decided that the Constitution does not necessarily follow the flag, and that it bears three different relationships to (1) the Union of States, (2) incorporated territories, and (3) unincorporated territories.

All parts of the Constitution, of course, apply to the States; all parts, except such clauses as clearly and expressly apply only to admitted States, extend to incorporated territories. Hawaii and Alaska are the only incorporated territories because they are the only ones with all the guarantees of the Constitution. The territories or dependencies other than Alaska and Hawaii are classified as unincorporated. In them Congress does not have to grant guarantees of the Constitution such as indictment by grand jury and trial by jury; but Congress could not deprive their inhabitants of life, liberty, or property without due process of law, or take their property for public use without just compensation, because the courts have declared these to be fundamental rights which can be denied to none. That is, Congress can depart from procedural parts of the Constitution for unincorporated territories, but not from the fundamental substantive provisions. (See pages 70 and 71 on the admission of new States.)

351

HAWAII, LAND OF HAPPINESS AND BEAUTY

The wonderful climate and palm-fringed, surf-smoothed beaches vie with rich, fruitful plantations to attract the visitor's interest. Just as it is the center of the world's pineapple industry, so this Paradise of the Pacific may also be called the world's leading vacation land.

Hawaii. — In 1778 Captain Cook, an Englishman, explored the Hawaiian Group of Islands and named them "Sandwich Islands" in honor of his patron, the Earl of Sandwich. (The Earl of Sandwich was so fond of playing cards that he would not stop to eat. He had a servant bring him a slice of cold meat between two slices of bread so he could eat it while playing. This combination thus became known as a "sandwich.") However, the native name "Hawaii" has become the accepted name. When Captain Cook appeared the natives seem to have taken him for a god, but the outrageous conduct of his crew finally emboldened a native to kill him by stabbing him in the back with an iron dagger.

The foreign riffraff of explorers and whalers who visited the Islands during the next half century acted on the assumption that no laws, whether of God or man, were in force west of Cape Horn. But the coming of the missionaries in 1820 brought civilization to the natives. The missionaries brought the higher ideals of conduct, a written language (English), rules of health, impartial advice to the rulers, and monogamy. Descendants of the missionaries remained in Hawaii, and in 1893, after the forceful establishment of a republic, the Islands unsuccessfully sought annexation to the United States.

Upon the outbreak of hostilities with Spain in 1898 the value of island possessions as coaling stations and for other strategic purposes became very apparent. Therefore, the same year, the Republic was admitted as the Territory of Hawaii through a joint resolution of Congress.

The Hawaiian Islands are in the mid-Pacific between California and the Philippine Islands, and have a total area of 6449 square miles. According to the United States Census of 1950 their population was 499,794. This represents an increase of 76,464 persons since the 1940 Census. Of these the Japanese are about a third, the Filipinos a sixth, while native Hawaiians, Chinese, Portuguese, and Americans constitute most of the remaining half.[1]

---

[1] According to the 1940 Census the composition of the Hawaiian population was as follows:

Hawaiian and Part Hawaiian	64,310	Koreans	6,851
Caucasian	103,791	Filipinos	52,569
Japanese	157,905	Puerto Ricans	8,296
Chinese	28,774	Other races	834
		Total population	423,330

Any person born in Hawaii becomes an American citizen at birth and may enter and leave the continental United States on the same basis as any other citizen. Immigration is regulated under the same law that applies to the mainland.

YOUNG HAWAIIANS — AMERICAN CITIZENS ALL

In 1900 Congress framed laws for the government of Hawaii. These laws were very largely copied from those for the government of Oklahoma, New Mexico, and Arizona, which were then territories of the United States, and hence governed according to the wishes of Congress.[1] All the provisions of the Constitution and laws of the United States, except where special exception was made or where they were locally inapplicable, were extended to Hawaii.[2] Under this government American citizenship was extended to all Hawaiian citizens and Hawaiian citizenship to all resident American citizens.

The Hawaiian government is divided into three branches — the executive, the legislative, and the judicial. Members of both houses of the legislature are popularly elected, and because of this fact Hawaii is known as a *fully organized territory* of the United States.

[1] All of our forty-eight States were Territories before becoming States, except the thirteen original States and Maine, Vermont, Kentucky, West Virginia, Texas, and California.

[2] The Nineteenth Amendment to the United States Constitution brought woman suffrage to Hawaii.

The Chief Executive of the Territory of Hawaii is the *governor*. He is appointed by the President and Senate of the United States for a term of four years, and must be a citizen of the territory. He, in turn, appoints the chief administrative officers with the advice and consent of the territorial senate, and exercises the usual powers of a governor, including the veto of bills in their entirety or of separate items in appropriation bills.

The Legislature of the territory consists of a *senate* with fifteen members elected for the term of four years, and a *house of representatives* with thirty members elected for the term of two years. Regular sessions of the legislature are held biennially and are limited to sixty days. The legislature may enact any law which does not conflict with the Constitution, statutes, or treaties of the United States. Congress, however, has by statutes imposed restrictions upon the power of the legislature, especially in regard to financial matters.

The Judiciary is actually composed of two court systems: one federal and one territorial. One U. S. District Court handles all federal cases arising in the Territory. Its two judges are appointed by the President and Senate for six-year terms. The territorial courts, which hear all non-federal cases, consist of one supreme court, five circuit courts, and several local district courts.

A Territorial delegate to Washington is elected by the people for each term of Congress. He sits in the House of Representatives with the right to debate and serve on committees, but he cannot vote. His salary is the same as that of a Congressman.

Finances. — The Hawaiians pay Federal internal revenue taxes and customs on goods from countries other than the United States, just as they are paid by inhabitants of the 48 States. Of course there is no tariff on commodities from the United States to Hawaii or from the Islands to the United States.

The Coastwise Laws of the United States are applied to Hawaii; and in normal times only United States vessels or planes can carry freight or passengers between Hawaii and continental United States.

Education. — Hawaii is at the crossroads of the Pacific, and here the races meet without much racial prejudice. The public schools, using English exclusively, are merging Hawaiians, Americans, Japanese, Chinese, and Filipinos into loyal American citizens.

The Islands' Economy is largely based on the $230,000,000-a-year sugar and pineapple crops. World War II and the Korean War booms have expanded the economy, but there is still a wide excess of imports over exports.

James Sawders

THE HARBOR OF HONOLULU

Statehood. — Hawaii has been asking for Statehood since the turn of the century. Since 1937 various Congressional committees have investigated and recommended it. The House has passed statehood bills several times, but the Senate refused to do so until 1954. In 1954 the Senate passed a combined Hawaiian-Alaskan Statehood bill. Unless the House (which approved a Hawaiian bill in 1953) now accepts Alaskan Statehood, too, the issue is dead until 1955 at least. The people of Hawaii have voted more than 2 to 1 for Statehood and both major parties are on record in favor of Hawaiian Statehood.

With more than half a million people the Territory has a larger population than any of the States at the time of admission with the exception of Oklahoma. Her geographical importance, both commercial and military, make the "Crossroads of the Pacific" at least as important as some of our States. Her variously mixed races live harmoniously and democratically according to our Constitutional principles and customs.

During the Second World War her people demonstrated unquestionable loyalty to the United States.   Her men served with distinction in Europe and the Pacific.   Her people bought more war bonds per person than the people in any of the States.

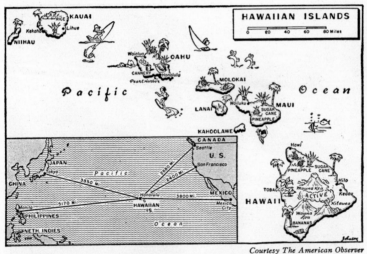

Courtesy The American Observer

AT THE CROSSROADS OF THE PACIFIC WHERE RACES MEET AND MIX

Hawaii has been a territory for more than 50 years.   During that time the people have demonstrated their ability for self-government. The Hawaiian educational system is at least on a par with the average in our States.

Alaska. — When Alaska was purchased from Russia in 1867 for only $7,200,000, very little was known about it, and one congressman called it "the refrigerator of the United States."   It was not realized that the parts of Alaska affected by the Japanese Current have more moderate winters than many of the northern States of our Union. The latitude is that of Norway and Sweden.

The area of Alaska is 586,400 square miles, and its population in 1950 was 128,643 [1] — about half Indians (Eskimos).   The inhabitants became citizens of the United States by treaty of cession, and in 1912 Congress created a *fully organized* territorial government.   Today

[1] Alaska's population has increased by 75 per cent in the last decade.   The 1940 population was 74,524.

the Territory of Alaska is governed in much the same manner as Hawaii. Its inhabitants pay taxes and come under the coastwise laws and the immigration laws of the United States like the inhabitants of our States.

ALASKA-JUNEAU GOLD MINING COMPANY   *James Sawders*

This is the largest quartz gold mine in the world.

The Governor is appointed by the President and Senate of the United States for a term of four years and has the usual powers. He does not have to be a citizen of Alaska.

The Legislature consists of a *senate* of sixteen members and a *house of representatives* of twenty-four members, — both houses popularly elected. It meets biennially for a period not exceeding sixty days and its powers are general except where specifically restricted. All Alaskan laws are valid until disapproved by an Act of Congress if they are originally passed within the limits of the organic act.

As an example of the restrictions imposed by Congress, neither the Hawaiian nor the Alaskan government may grant divorces to persons who have resided in the country less than two years.

Of course Alaska does not have power to interfere with the general laws of the United States. For instance, it cannot enact laws which in any way interfere with the customs, internal revenue, or postal laws of the United States; or with the general fish, game, and fur-seal laws of the United States.

SEAL ROOKERY ON ONE OF THE PRIBILOF ISLANDS

The seals come to these islands every year to breed, and here the surplus males are easily caught and killed.

The Judiciary of Alaska consists of four United States district courts with judges appointed by the President and Senate for a term of four years, and of minor local courts presided over by commissioners whom the district judges appoint.

A Territorial Delegate is elected every second November to represent Alaska in the Congress of the United States. Like the territorial delegate from Hawaii he has a seat in the House of Representatives, debates, and serves on committees, but has no vote. His salary is the same as that of a Congressman.

Resources. — The resources of Alaska are great. It has gold, coal, copper, timber, water power, reindeer, fish, and seals.

Alaska's Seal Industry. — The Pribilof Islands are the breeding grounds for the world's largest herd of furbearing seals.[1] Previous to

[1] In May the 500-pound bull seals arrive and fight over areas for their harems. In June when the 100-pound cows arrive the bulls drag as many as possible to their harems. And to protect their harems against would-be wife-thieves the bulls

1911 the seals were being rapidly exterminated because gasoline launches with rapid-fire guns from Canada, Japan, Russia, and the United States were taking them out of the sea. In 1911 these nations agreed to a system of dividing the take on the Russian, Japanese, and United States islands, so that an indiscriminate slaughter should not take place. The herd on the Pribilof Islands, under management of the Fish and Wild Life Service, has increased from 132,000 to nearly 3,000,000; and annually enough of 3-year-old surplus males are taken to produce furs worth between $2,000,000 and $3,000,000.

The Fishing Industry of Alaska ranks with that of Massachusetts and California, and above that of Oregon and Washington.

Alaska's Timber Industry is rapidly expanding and there is sufficient spruce and hemlock in her steep coastal forests to guarantee a sustained yield of a billion board feet a year. Cheap water power for producing wood pulp and cheap water transportation are readily available.

Alaska's Agricultural Resources in the millions of unbroken acres of grasslands and rich valleys present a challenge much like that which faced the pioneer settlers of our Far West.

Alaska's Potential Oil Resources are being explored. The Navy is drilling for oil and has found a promising source 180 miles from Point Barrow.

Alaska as a Military and Naval Outpost. — At the outbreak of World War II it was realized that it is only 700 miles from the nearest Japanese base to Attu, at the tip of the Aleutian Islands; and that an enemy in possession of Alaska would be within 750 miles of Seattle — less than three hours as the bomber flies. Therefore the United States rushed fortifications in Alaska. We now have various bases in the territory, and these are valuable for defensive warfare. Because of the shorter route to other parts of the Northern Hemisphere over the North Pole and the advances in aeronautical science, Alaska has become doubly important as an outpost of defense.

Any attack on this country by long-range planes and guided missiles is likely to come across the Arctic. Effective defenses require bases not only in Alaska, but in Northern Canada, Greenland, and Iceland

---

stand on guard without food, drink, or rest for weeks. In July, after a pregnancy of nearly a year the cows deliver their pups. Then follows the breeding season. About 50,000 young bachelors are annually slaughtered by our Government agents to provide skins for sealskin coats.

as well.   Alaska is separated only by the Bering Strait from Asia with
its immense resources and populations, and it might be used as a stepping stone to the United States.

During the Second World War a highway through Canada to Alaska
was built by the United States to reduce the submarine danger.   Since
the war the Canadian Government has maintained it.

Copyright 1946 United States News Publishing Company

Statehood for Alaska has long been advocated by Alaska's delegates
in Congress.   Hawaiian and Alaskan Statehood bills have been treated
together in Congress and have suffered a common fate.   Hawaii's
prospects appear much brighter than those of Alaska, however.

The Future of Alaska is bright because the country has great natural
resources, is no farther north than such progressive countries as Nor-

way and Sweden, is an important link in our chain of defenses, and is a convenient junction for the shortest air traffic route between Russia and the United States — the two richest countries in the world.

Puerto Rico. — The United States took possession of Puerto Rico in 1898 during the Spanish-American War, and acquired it by treaty the following year. Its area is 3435 square miles and its population in 1950 was 2,210,703, of whom three-fourths were whites and the rest mulattoes and Negroes.

The Puerto Rican Constitution. — A new constitution, drafted by the Puerto Ricans themselves, went into effect on July 25, 1952, fifty-four years to the day after American troops hauled down the Spanish flag and ran up the Stars and Stripes. Earlier in the year, the constitution had been approved by a popular majority of more than four to one and had then been approved by Congress. (From 1900 until 1952 the Island's basic charter was an Act of Congress.)

The convention which drafted the constitution made a careful study of the United States Constitution and of the constitutions of the various States. As a result, the new document contains many provisions common to constitutions adopted by the States, as well as other provisions which are designed primarily to meet local problems.

Under its new constitution, Puerto Rico is a "commonwealth . . . within our union with the United States of America." The basic relationships between Puerto Rico and the United States remain largely unchanged. Thus, Puerto Ricans are still American citizens. The Island remains within the American tariff system and continues to enjoy free trade with the mainland. Its citizens are still subject to Federal law, but they have control over their own internal affairs much as in the States of the Union. For example, Congress no longer has the power to repeal laws made by the Puerto Rican legislature.

The Governor is popularly elected for a term of four years.[1] He must be at least 35 years of age, and he must have been, for at least five years preceding his election, a citizen of the United States and a *bona fide* resident of Puerto Rico. The governor is vested with

---

[1] The system of voting in Puerto Rico is unique, and seems fraud-proof. Voters are required to be in their polling places before one o'clock. At that hour the doors are locked and the voting begins. Each registered voter's name is called in alphabetical order and he receives his ballot and casts his vote.

those powers usually lodged with a chief executive under our form of government, including the veto power. He appoints, with Senate consent, the heads of departments in the executive branch. Succession to the governorship falls to the Secretary of State.

The Legislative Assembly consists of a Senate and House of Representatives. The Senate has 27 members, two elected from each of the eight senatorial districts plus eleven chosen at large. The House contains 51 members, one elected from each of forty districts and eleven at large. Under a novel provision, whenever one political party gains more than two-thirds of the seats in either house the number of seats in that house may be increased to broaden the representation of the minority party or parties.[1]

Members of both houses are popularly elected for a term of four years and must be both United States and Puerto Rican citizens. A governor's veto may be overridden by a two-thirds vote of the total membership of each house. Although, as we have seen, Congress and the President no longer have the power to void laws passed by the Puerto Rican legislature, these laws must not be contrary to the Constitution, laws, or treaties of the United States, that is, to the Supreme Law of the Land.

The Judiciary has long since been almost completely Americanized in form, law, and procedure. The Supreme Court is the Commonwealth's highest court. It consists of a Chief Justice and four Associate Justices. They are appointed by the Governor and the Senate and hold office for life or good behavior. The number of justices cannot be changed unless at the direct request of the Supreme Court itself. The lower courts are established by the Legislative Assembly. There is also a United States District Court for Puerto Rico.

A Resident Commissioner, elected by the voters every four years, represents the Island in Washington. Unlike the delegates from

---

[1] This provision amounts in effect to a modified form of proportional representation (see pages 458–459). If one party gains more than two-thirds of the seats in either house, but does not gain more than two-thirds of the votes cast for governor, the number of seats at large is increased. This is done by declaring enough candidates of the minor party (or parties) elected to bring its total to 9 in the Senate or 17 in the House, as the case may be. If the dominant party obtains *more* than two-thirds of the votes for governor, enough additional minority candidates (but not exceeding 9 in the Senate and 17 in the House) are declared elected to bring the representation of minority parties as close as possible to the proportion of votes cast for each party in the gubernatorial election.

Hawaii and Alaska, he has no statute right to a seat in the House, but under the House rules he is given the privilege of debate and may serve on committees though he may not vote. He receives the same salary and allowances as a congressman.

The Bill of Rights in the Commonwealth's constitution includes provisions similar to those in the Constitution of the United States and those of the States. In addition, it contains express provisions regarding public education, the conditions of labor, and the protection of private property.

Constitutional Amendments may be proposed by two-thirds of the total membership of each house of the Legislative Assembly. They are ratified by a majority of the voters at a general or special election.

The Finances of Puerto Rico are not handled like those of the incorporated territories (Alaska and Hawaii). Instead of paying the internal revenue taxes levied by Congress, the local legislature levies these taxes for Puerto Rico, including the income tax. Commodities between Puerto Rico and the United States do not pay tariff duty, but articles entering the United States from Puerto Rico must pay the United States internal revenue tax, and articles from the United States entering Puerto Rico must pay the Puerto Rican internal revenue tax. Articles entering Puerto Rico from countries other than the United States pay the same tariff duties that they would pay if entering the United States. All of these taxes go into the treasury of the Puerto Rican Government.

Revenues and Federal grants-in-aid come to about $115,000,000 a year. Included in this total are: some $43,000,000 from excise taxes, $29,000,000 from local income taxes, refund of approximately $17,000,000 in U. S. internal revenue taxes on rum imported from Puerto Rico, and around $10,000,000 in grants-in-aid.

Economic Conditions. — Writing in 1897, a high official in Spanish-controlled Puerto Rico had this to say about the Puerto Rican laborer: "With a pale face, bare feet, lean body, ragged clothes, and feverish look, he walks indifferently, with the shadows of ignorance in his eyes, dreaming of the cock fight, the shuffle of the cards, or the prize in the provincial lottery."

The masses continue very poor in Puerto Rico but a definite improvement in their lot is developing, especially in the last few years. Yet the average annual income is only around $300, compared with more than \$1700 in the States.   Some 2,200,000 people live on the Island, averaging 641 people to the square mile, compared with 50 in the United States.   The total population is increasing at the rate of 70,000 each year.   Only half of the land is arable and there is little mineral wealth.

The migration of thousands of the Island's people to the continent and to neighboring Spanish-speaking countries seems to be at least one practical, although only a temporary, solution to Puerto Rico's economic plight.[1]

Wide World Photo

A COMMONWEALTH WITHIN THE UNION

July 4, 1952, was truly a day for celebration in Puerto Rico, for at long last it had its own Constitution, passed by its own people and signed the day before by President Truman.   Marching troops marked the day in San Juan by parading before the capitol.

Some of the facts just cited once led observers to call Puerto Rico "Uncle Sam's neglected stepchild."   Today, the child is coming of age.   The Island Government, with the backing of Washington, is bringing about a modern "industrial revolution," and a progressive, dynamic Commonwealth is in the making.

---

[1] As Puerto Ricans are citizens of the United States they may come here without restriction.   In recent years several thousands have come to New York by boat and plane each month.   Most of them settle in already overcrowded areas and get jobs in the needle trades, restaurants, as janitors, or in helping crews clean ships.

"Operation Bootstrap," as it is called, is a concerted effort to free the Island of its economic chains. Expanding American businesses are being encouraged to build their new plants in Puerto Rico. As one way of attracting these businesses, the Government grants acceptable businesses an almost complete exemption from Puerto Rican property and income taxes until 1959, with partial exemption from

A NATIVE HUT AND FAMILY IN PUERTO RICO

then until 1962. The large population provides a ready labor source and the Government is more than willing to co-operate in every way. Also a program of hydroelectric development is helping to bring in industry from the United States.

While taxes in the States are going up and regulations are becoming more stringent on the mainland, the Island becomes all the more attractive to American investors. When the Univis Lens Company dedicated its large new factory at Guayama in 1952, it became the 150th plant to be opened since the program began.

This recent and rapid expansion has been accompanied by related governmental efforts in other fields, such as education and social welfare. As one observer puts it, the program "has been like a sack of feed set in front of a starving chick." Ten years ago the Island's net income (total amount earned by residents and corporations after taxes and depreciation) was $359,000,000; now it has risen to about $800,000,000 a year. Employment has increased greatly. And the sharp lines between the many poor and the very few rich are being rubbed out by a rising middle class.

Vocational schools have been established and, amazing as it may seem, more than one-third of the Island's governmental budget is earmarked for education. A great many slums still exist, but a

R. I. Nesmith

THE DOCKS AT SAN JUAN, PUERTO RICO

The tall-masted ships are valuable for traffic with near-by islands. Note the capitol in upper left corner.

vigorous low-cost housing program is making inroads. Sugar is still the backbone of the Island's agricultural economy, but pineapple, tobacco, and coffee are becoming increasingly important.

The program still has a long way to go, but the goal for 1960 has been set at a $2,000,000,000 net income for the Island — well over twice what it is today. Puerto Rico still has a long way to go, yes. But the future is bright, and this proud Island promises to become, as did the Philippines, a model for other colonial domains around the world.

The Philippines. — The United States took possession of the Philippine Islands in 1898 during the Spanish-American War, and they were ceded to the United States the following year. This archipelago consists of thousands of islands with a total area of 114,400 square miles, which is slightly larger than the State of Oregon, or about the size of Great Britain.

Ewing Galloway

LOADING SUGAR ABOARD A STEAMER AT ILOILO, PANAY ISLAND

The Island of Panay produces sugar, tobacco, and rice in abundance, and Iloilo ranks next to Manila in commercial importance.

The Spaniards Christianized the natives and set up the only Christian nation in the Orient. According to the last census (1950) the population of the Philippines was 19,497,700, about twice the population of the Islands at the end of the Spanish regime. A decade ago it was 16,000,303. The dominant religion is Catholic, but there are about half a million Mohammedans (Moros, named after the Moors of Spain) and half a million pagans (Negritos and Hill Tribes).

There are 8 languages and 87 dialects spoken in the Islands, but all higher education was given in Spanish until the Islands were transferred to America. Then Spanish and English were made official languages; but the 1935 Philippine Constitution authorized the National Assembly to adopt a national language based on one of the existing native languages.

Toward Independence. — From the first occupation in 1898 the United States began working toward self-government and eventual independence for the Philippines.   For the first three years the Islands were controlled by a military government directed by the President. But in 1901 Congress authorized the creation of a temporary civil government.   And in 1902 an organic act was passed starting the Filipinos on the road to managing their own affairs.

The 1902 act was replaced by the Philippine Government Act in 1916.   This statute established a system of insular government, with a broadened suffrage and a popularly-elected legislature, which lasted until 1935.   Such strides were made toward self-government that by 1935 only a little over two per cent of all the Islands' public officials were not native Filipinos.

The Philippine Independence Act was passed by Congress in 1934. It authorized the Filipinos to set up their own government as the next step toward independence.   And the Act provided for independence in 1946.   The Filipinos drafted their own constitution and formed the Commonwealth Government which lasted until 1946.

The first President of the Philippine Commonwealth, Manuel Quezon, said in 1937: "The Philippines have been assisted economically and schooled politically by the United States for nearly forty years.   No people in history, coming under a foreign flag, have ever been treated so generously."

Japanese Invasion. — On December 7, 1941, when the Japanese made their treacherous attack upon Pearl Harbor they also were on their way to invade the Philippines.   For five long months a gallant handful of American and Filipino soldiers made a brave defense of the islands.   But it was impossible for the hard-pressed United States to send reinforcements and supplies, and in May, 1942, our forces had to surrender.   At almost the last minute, General Douglas MacArthur, the commander of the beleaguered troops, was ordered to escape.

The Filipinos were overwhelmingly loyal to us during the war; and with many Americans they fought a bitter guerilla war with the enemy all through the occupation.   When General MacArthur led our troops back to the Islands they met us with open arms.

The Philippine Republic. — Independence was proclaimed by the United States and the new Philippine Republic on July 4, 1946.   On that day the Philippines became a sovereign state in the family of nations.   Today she is recognized by practically all governments and is a member of the United Nations.

But with independence the United States could not just simply step out of the picture. The Republic could not be left to struggle along by herself. Three years of Japanese occupation and the fight to retake the Islands had left them shattered.

PRESIDENT RAMON MAGSAYSAY

Since the end of the war the United States has spent more than $2,000,000,000 to help in rehabilitation. This money has been used to bolster the economy and to build or rebuild hospitals, schools, highways, bridges, waterways, and the like. And much of this money went in the form of back pay to Filipinos who served against the enemy in the guerilla fighting.

In the Philippine Trade Act of 1946 Congress provided for free trade between our two countries until 1954. And now for the next 20 years, until 1974, tariff rates will increase at the rate of only 5 per cent annually.

Since 1947 we have had a 99-year treaty with the Philippines under which we maintain air, ground, and naval bases in the Islands. We also have a mutual defense treaty with them and our Army continues to train the Philippine Army. A large detachment of Filipino combat troops fought valiantly under the United Nations command in Korea.

All is not yet stable in the Philippines, however. They are still in economic and financial crises. And the communist-led *Hukbalahaps* (Huks) still cause trouble — but, as Defense Minister and now as new President, Ramon Magsaysay has done much to bring them under control.

All in all, the people of the Philippines can look back on eight years of notable achievements, however — and can look forward hopefully to much more progress in the years to come. And the rest of Asia has an object lesson in democracy and American intentions right on its doorstep.

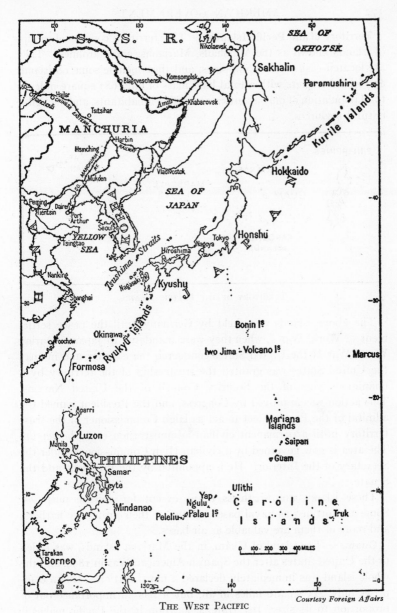

THE WEST PACIFIC

We need the friendship of all peoples in this area.

371

Territory of the Pacific Islands. — This territory consists of groups of islands known as the Marshalls, Marianas, and Carolines. They are located east of the Philippines, and they include some 98 islands and island clusters with a total land mass of only 687 square miles, a total population of only about 55,000 native inhabitants, and negligible natural resources.

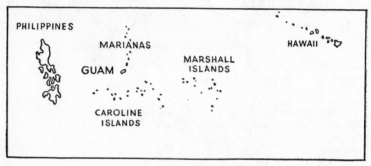

TERRITORY OF THE PACIFIC ISLANDS

The above islands were held by Germany until the peace settlement of World War I, when they were mandated to Japan. During World War II the United States conquered the islands; and in 1947 the United States was granted the trusteeship of the territory by a unanimous vote of the Security Council of the United Nations. This action was approved by Congress, and the President named the admiral of the Pacific Fleet to act as High Commissioner of the trust territory until a permanent civilian administration could be set up. The area is now governed by a civilian High Commissioner under the Secretary of the Interior. He is appointed by the President and the Senate.

These islands are worthless to us except for defense purposes. Some are fortified as naval bases because of their protective harbors, and more of them are valuable as air bases.

Guam. — The island of Guam, in the Mariana Islands, was ceded to the United States after the Spanish-American War in 1899, and the whole island was immediately declared a naval station. Guam comprises only 225 square miles in all, but it has an importance out of proportion to its size. Its strategic location in the Pacific makes it invaluable as a naval and air station.

Until 1950, with the exception of the two years that Japan occupied the island during World War II, Guam was governed by the Navy through an officer appointed by the Secretary of the Navy. But in 1950 Congress passed the Organic Act of Guam which makes all Guamanians U. S. citizens, establishes a Bill of Rights, and provides for a Governor appointed by the President and Senate, a popularly-elected single-house Legislature, and a United States District Court for Guam.

Naval and military installations are still maintained on the island, and Guam remains an unincorporated territory of the United States. It is administered for the United States through the Division of Territories and Island Possessions of the Department of the Interior.

Wake, Midway, Baker, and Howland Islands and Eastern Samoa in the mid-Pacific are valuable for aeronautic, naval, and radio use.

Panama Canal Zone. — The occupation, use, and control of a zone five miles wide on each side of the Panama Canal was granted by Panama to the United States by treaty in 1903. The Zone includes the Chagres River, where dams have been built to store water during the rainy season as a supply for operating the locks during the dry season; and it also includes all of the lake created by the Gatun Dam. It was necessary to include in the Zone the areas covered by the dams and the lake in order to insure a single, unified control over the water in the reservoir system. As a further precaution against the blocking of the canal by an enemy, Congress in 1939 authorized the construction of a new set of locks apart from the existing twin locks, with connecting laterals to the main channel so that a ship may detour if anything happens to one lock. Explosive deflector nets also have been constructed in each lock. All the way across the isthmus we constructed a military highway, also a double oil pipe line to use should a lock be destroyed, as well as searchlights which were concealed everywhere.

Shortage of manpower stopped work on the new set of locks in 1942; and the atomic bomb and guided missiles have necessitated a survey to determine whether we should complete the new set of locks or construct a sea-level canal.

The survey report backed by the Army and Navy and Joint Chiefs of Staff recommends a $2,483,000,000 sea-level canal. It would have only one lock to raise or lower ships over the 9-foot difference in Atlantic and Pacific tidal levels.

An ordinary bomb hitting a lock could close the present canal for

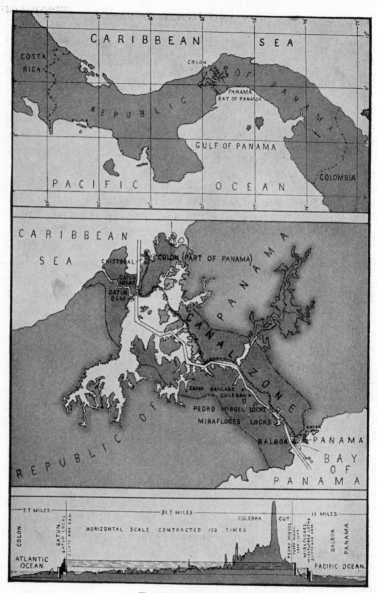

THE PANAMA CANAL

A new single channel is being constructed to parallel the existing twin channel.

months, and an atomic bomb for years. Should a bomb strike the tidal lock of a sea-level canal it would not stop traffic, and should an atomic bomb strike the canal and produce a slide the canal could be dredged in a few weeks.

The sea-level canal could carry about twice as much traffic because the time of passage would be reduced by one half.

The sea-level canal would be expensive — costing about five times as much as the Tennessee Valley Authority's 23 dams and vast power facilities. But during the last war 5300 combat vessels and 8500 military cargo and troopships used the canal, saving $1,500,000,000 in shipping costs, and even more in valuable time.

For the lease of the Canal Zone we shall pay the Panama Republic $430,000 a year forever. Privately-owned vessels pay the United States a toll of $1.20 a ton for passage. That means $12,000 toll on a 10,000-ton vessel. Tolls collected in the fiscal year 1953 amounted to $31,917,515.

During the construction of the Canal, the Zone was administered by a Commission appointed by the President. In 1913, with the work on the Canal nearly completed, Congress authorized the President to appoint a Governor and such other officers as he might find necessary.

Today the President and Senate appoint the Governor for a four-year term. He is usually an Army engineer and administers the affairs of the Zone under the Secretary of the Army. Because there is no local legislature, such laws as operate within the area are either enacted by Congress or take the form of Presidential orders. Because of the President's influence in the governing of the Canal Zone, it has been called a "crown colony." [1]

Organized towns (with no elective officials) and a system of courts have been provided by Congress. There is one District Court with several magistrates' courts (much like justice of the peace courts) under it. Congress has expressly provided for the extension of the Bill of Rights to the Canal Zone.

The Virgin Islands. — The Virgin Islands,[2] consisting of St. Croix,

---

[1] In 1930 the Canal Zone had a population of 39,467. By 1940 the total had increased to 51,827. In 1950 the Census Bureau reported a population of 52,822.

[2] Called "Virgin Islands" by Columbus after Saint Ursula and her eleven thousand virgins, because the islands were too numerous to name individually.

St. Thomas, St. John, and fifty-odd small and mostly uninhabited islands, were purchased from Denmark by treaty in 1917 for $25,000,-000. The inhabitants are governed by the President through the Department of the Interior, and in 1927 United States citizenship was extended to them. Their inhabitants are predominantly Negro; and in 1954 President Eisenhower appointed Archie Alexander, a Negro contractor from Des Moines, Iowa, as Governor of the Islands.

District of Columbia. — The Constitution of the United States gives Congress power to exercise exclusive legislation over the District of Columbia in all cases whatsoever. This means that Congress may act like a State Legislature and city council in the District of Columbia, and this it is now doing. Previous to 1871 Congress permitted the District to be governed in the main by elective officials, and regular elections were held. The so-called territorial government which existed from 1871 to 1874 was both zealous and high-handed in the use of power to develop the capital. It piled up an alarming deficit. In 1874 Congress placed the bankrupt District into a sort of receivership (under three commissioners) which was supposed to be temporary, but became permanent because Congress could not agree upon any substitute plan.

Since 1878 the District of Columbia has been administered by a three-man Board of Commissioners. Two of these are local residents appointed for three-year terms by the President and Senate. The third Commissioner is an engineer detailed by the President from the United States Army to serve for an indefinite period. Other officers are likewise appointed by the President. The three Commissioners direct most of the city departments, such as fire, traffic, police, and public health. They recommend needed legislation to Congress, but Congress is the only legislative body for the District. Thus the Commissioners may act only within the limits set by Congressional statute.

All bills relating to the governing of the District are considered by committees, usually by the House Committee and the Senate Committee on the District of Columbia, or by the House Committee and the Senate Committee on Appropriations. It is at public hearings of these committees that the people of the District make their views and wishes known. These committees have their hands full, but, unfortunately, most other members of Congress tend to shy away from the problems of the District.

Congress used to appropriate 50 per cent of the expenses of the District, but this proportion has been gradually reduced since 1920. For 1954 it was a lump sum of $12,000,000, which amounts to about 8 per cent of the District's expenditures. This appropriation is made because the Government owns so much tax-exempt property, makes much use of services rendered by District agencies (*e.g.*, water), and also wants an especially fine city as its capital. The balance of the revenues collected by the District come from local taxation.

Courtesy "Washington Star"

PROTEST OF RESIDENTS OF THE DISTRICT OF COLUMBIA AGAINST TAXATION WITHOUT SUFFRAGE

The Problem of Self-Government in the District. — Since 1874 the residents of the District have been denied the right to elect the officials of their local government. Because the District is not a State, they have never been permitted to vote for Presidential electors nor are they represented in Congress. It is paradoxical that a republic, proud of its system of representative government, should have "taxation without representation" in its very capital of 802,178 people.

Numerous proposals have been made to rectify this situation. Constitutional amendments and bills on the subject have been introduced in every recent Congress. An amendment would be needed to grant presidential suffrage in the District.[1] But, by statute, Congress could grant home rule and provide for representation by a District delegate (much like the Hawaiian and Alaskan delegates).

Various bills providing for municipal home rule have come close to final passage in recent years. The proposal with the most support today is one providing for a mayor-council form of government much like that found in many other large cities. Under it, a District Council, Mayor, Board of Education, and Delegate to Congress would be popularly elected. The Council would assume the powers of the present Board of Commissioners and, as well, have local legislative powers much like those of the Hawaiian and Alaskan legislatures.

At present, if any change is to be made, the plan for home rule appears to have the best possibilities for adoption by Congress. There are a number of municipal associations through which the citizens can express themselves on problems of local government.

QUESTIONS ON THE TEXT

1. Does the United States Constitution follow the flag?

2. What parts of the Constitution extend to incorporated territories? To unincorporated territories? Which territories are incorporated? What do you mean by incorporated?

3. What did the missionaries take to Hawaii?

4. What was the main reason for annexing Hawaii in 1898?

5. The government of Hawaii is somewhat similar to that of what former territories of the United States?

6. Are Hawaiians American citizens?

7. Into what three branches is the Hawaiian government divided?

8. How is the governor of Hawaii chosen? The senate? The house of representatives?

9. What laws may be enacted by the legislature of Hawaii?

10. By whom is the territory of Hawaii represented in Washington? May he vote?

11. What language is used in Hawaii?

12. Do Hawaiians pay Federal taxes as citizens of States do?

13. Do our immigration and coastwise laws apply to Hawaii?

[1] The United States Constitution provides that each *State* shall choose as many presidential electors as it has senators and representatives in Congress. The District of Columbia has no congressmen, therefore it would be unconstitutional for Congress to grant presidential suffrage to the District.

14. How and when did the United States acquire Alaska?
15. How is the governor of Alaska chosen? The senate? The house of representatives?
16. How is Alaska represented in Washington?
17. Of what importance is Alaska as a military and naval outpost?
18. How and when did the United States acquire Puerto Rico?
19. What are the major features of the new Puerto Rican constitution?
20. How is the governor of Puerto Rico chosen? The senate? The house of representatives?
21. How is Puerto Rico represented in Washington?
22. What factors have produced Puerto Rico's economic plight?
23. What is "Operation Bootstrap"?
24. What religion predominates in the Philippines?
25. How many languages are spoken in the Philippines?
26. Were the Filipinos loyal to the United States during the war?
27. How and when did the Philippines acquire independence?
28. What three groups of islands constitute our Territory of the Pacific Islands? How did we acquire them? How are they governed?
29. How and when did we acquire the Panama Canal Zone?
30. Explain the financial status of the Panama Canal.
31. How is the Panama Canal Zone governed?
32. Why is an international highway to the Panama Canal important?
33. Describe the government of the District of Columbia.

PROBLEMS FOR DISCUSSION

1. Because the English language was brought to Hawaii by missionaries from the United States there is less racial prejudice there than in most places where Orientals and Occidentals mingle. What does the Bible teach regarding the brotherhood of man?

2. What other reason for the fact that racial problems have been a minor matter in Hawaii can you suggest? Should Hawaii be made a State?

3. What arguments can you advance for or against Statehood for Hawaii? If in Congress would you vote for Statehood?

4. The latitude of Alaska is the same as that of Scandinavia, and because of this fact many say that it is possible for Alaska to attain as high a degree of development. What is your opinion?

5. Mr. Ickes, as a Secretary of the Interior, suggested legislation to help the transfer of surplus Puerto Rican population to South and Central America. How could this be done? Why not to the U.S.A.?

6. Another Secretary of the Interior, Julius A. Krug, stated to a Committee of Congress that Alaska could be satisfactorily defended in case of war

only if it is thickly populated, and that it will remain thinly populated unless it becomes a State. Do you agree that statehood would attract population? If not, by what means do you think it might be attracted?

7. Article 73 of the United Nations Charter provides, in part, that those nations with dependent peoples should guide them toward self-government. How did the United States train the Philippine Republic for self-government and independence? What are we doing to this end in Puerto Rico?

8. Why do you think Congress has denied the residents of the District of Columbia the right to elect local officers? And why do you think they have not submitted a Constitutional amendment to the States providing for Congressional and Presidential suffrage for the citizens of the District?

SELECT BIBLIOGRAPHY

American Observer, "Admitting States." March 6, 1950; "Washington's History and the City Today." March 27, 1950, pages 2–3.

COHN, H. "Operation Bootstrap." *Collier's*. March 29, 1952.

KIPLINGER, W. M. "Guide to Washington." *N. Y. Times Magazine*, April 16, 1950, pages 14 ff.

Life, "Alaska." October 2, 1950, pages 92–102.

MAGRUDER, F. A. *National Governments and International Relations*. Allyn and Bacon. 1950.

"Caribbean Dependencies of the United States," Chapter III.

"Hawaii, Alaska, and Our Outposts," Chapter XXV.

"The Philippines," Chapter XXVI.

MICHENER, J. A. "Hawaii: A State of Happiness." *Holiday*. May, 1953.

WHITMAN, H. "Can Eisenhower End Segregation in Washington?" *Collier's*. May 9, 1953.

GRUENING, A. "Statehood for Alaska." *Harper's*. May, 1953.

STEINBERG, A. "Let's Set Washington Free." *Reader's Digest*. July, 1953.

SHERROD, R. "Two Thousand Islands." *Saturday Evening Post*, November 8, 1952.

Time. "The Brown and White Mosaic (Hawaii)." February 18, 1952.

U. S. News. "Sun Never Sets on U. S. Frontiers." August 22, 1952.

CHAPTER XXI

THE JUDICIARY

Our Federal Courts. — By the Constitution the judicial power of the United States is vested in one Supreme Court and in such inferior courts as Congress may from time to time ordain and establish. Congress has established, and later abolished, various inferior courts, but at the present time the following Federal courts [1] exist:

Regular Courts

One Supreme Court
Eleven Courts of Appeals
About 227 District Judges
(84 districts)

Special Courts

One Court of Claims
One Customs Court
One Court of Customs and Patent Appeals

The Jurisdiction [2] *of Federal Courts.* — Cases are tried by Federal courts either because of (1) the character of the subject matter of the suit, or (2) the character of the parties to the suit.[3]

Depending upon the subject matter of the suit, the following cases may be tried in Federal courts: (1) cases in law or equity arising under the Constitution or statutes of the United States, or treaties made under their authority; (2) cases of admiralty and maritime [3] jurisdiction.

Depending upon the parties to the suit, the following cases may be tried in Federal courts: (1) cases affecting ambassadors, other public

---

[1] Territorial courts are treated under their respective territories.

[2] Jurisdiction means the legal right to hear and determine cases. A court is said to have jurisdiction over those cases which it has authority to try.

[3] See Article III, Section 2 of the Constitution; for meaning of "admiralty and maritime" see footnote on page 741.

381

ministers, and consuls; (2) controversies to which the United States is a party; (3) controversies between two or more States; (4) controversies between citizens of different States; (5) disputes between citizens of the same State claiming lands under grants from different States; (6) controversies between a State (or its citizens) and foreign states, citizens, or subjects.[1]

Regular Courts. — In order to show the proper relation of the different regular courts and how cases may be appealed from the lowest to the highest, the District Courts will be discussed first, the Courts of Appeals second, and third, the Supreme Court.

The District Courts. — The lowest regular Federal courts are known as District Courts. There are now 84 districts in the forty-eight States, each State forming at least one district. There is at least one judge for each district, but many important districts require more than one judge.[2] There are about two hundred judges in the various districts; and inasmuch as district court cases are usually conducted by a single judge,[3] several cases can be heard at the same time where there are several judges for one district.

A District Court has original jurisdiction[4] of all cases which come under the jurisdiction of the Federal courts[5] except cases to which a

---

[1] Under the Eleventh Amendment (1798), a State may not be sued by citizens of another State or by citizens or subjects of any foreign state. Thus a State may now be sued without its consent in Federal courts only by another State or a foreign state. If an alien, or a citizen of the same or another State wishes to sue a State, he may do so only with the latter's consent and only in State courts. However, a State may still bring suit in a Federal court against a citizen of another State or against an alien or even against a foreign state.

[2] Originally one judge to the district was the normal arrangement, but now nearly half of the districts have more than one judge, and the Southern District of New York has sixteen.

[3] When an effort is made to have a United States District Court enjoin (forbid) the enforcement of a State statute or an order of a State or Federal commission, the case is heard by three judges, at least one of whom must be a Court of Appeals judge or a justice of the Supreme Court.

[4] By "original jurisdiction" of a District Court is meant that a case is first brought in that court.

[5] The District Court has jurisdiction of (1) all civil suits brought by the United States or one of its officers authorized to sue; (2) cases arising under the Constitution, statutes, or treaties of the United States where the sum or value in controversy exceeds $3000; (3) cases between citizens of different States, or between a citizen of a State and a foreign state or citizen thereof, where the sum or value in controversy exceeds $3000; (4) all crimes and offenses recognized by the laws of the United States; (5) admiralty and maritime cases; (6) revenue cases, except tariff classifi-

State is a party, suits involving representatives of foreign governments, customs cases, and some claims against the United States. In most cases appeals may be taken from the decision of a District Court to a Court of Appeals, but in a few cases they may be taken directly to the Supreme Court.[1]

The Courts of Appeals[2] were created in 1891; and since 1929 the United States has been divided into ten judicial circuits and the District of Columbia, each having a Court of Appeals.

The reason for these courts was to relieve the Supreme Court of a large class of cases appealed from the District Courts. These cases had become too numerous for one court to hear, and as a result the Supreme Court was about three years in arrears with its business.

In 1925 Congress greatly limited the types of cases that may come to the Supreme Court as a matter of right; and the Supreme Court now reviews only the most important cases heard by the Courts of Appeals. This practice enables the Supreme Court to decide cases promptly and adds to the importance of the Courts of Appeals.

---

cations which come before the Court of Customs; (7) postal cases; (8) all suits arising under the patent, copyright, and trade-mark laws; (9) suits arising under the Federal laws regulating commerce; (10) damage suits brought by an officer against a person injuring him while protecting or collecting revenues of the United States; (11) suits against consuls and vice-consuls; (12) proceedings in bankruptcy; (13) claims not exceeding $10,000 against the United States (concurrent jurisdiction with Court of Claims); (14) immigration and contract labor cases; (15) suits againts monopolies (trusts); (16) suits brought by any person to redress the deprivation of any right, privilege, or immunity secured by the Constitution or statutes of the United States. But note that if the sum or value involved in cases enumerated under (2) and (3) is less than $3000 the action must be brought in a State court.

[1] The 1925 Amendment to the Judicial Code permits appeals directly from the District Court to the Supreme Court in the following cases only:

(1) Anti-trust cases prosecuted by the United States.

(2) Certain criminal cases where indictment depends upon the validity or construction of a statute, the United States may appeal.

(3) Injunctions forbidding the enforcement of

  a. State statutes upon the ground of unconstitutionality.

  b. Orders of the Interstate Commerce Commission.

  c. Provisions of 1921 Stock Yard Act by the Secretary of Agriculture.

[2] Previous to the establishment of the Courts of Appeals there existed nine Circuit Courts, but these courts have since been abolished (1911) and their jurisdiction transferred to the District Courts and to the Court of Customs and Patent Appeals.

Typical of the Courts of Appeals is the Court of Appeals, First Circuit, which comprises Rhode Island, Massachusetts, New Hampshire, Maine, and Puerto Rico. The judges hold court at least once a year at Boston.

The judges for each Court of Appeals include one justice of the Supreme Court assigned to the circuit, three to nine (68 in all) judges appointed for the circuit, and all the district judges within the circuit. The Supreme Court justice supervises his circuit (except that one supervises the 4th and D. C. and one supervises the 8th and 10th), but seldom finds time to sit in the court. Normally the court is held by three regular circuit judges, but a district judge may be assigned to sit on any case not appealed from his own district.

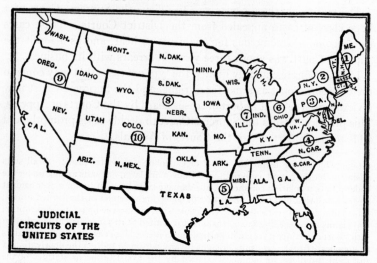

JUDICIAL
CIRCUITS OF THE
UNITED STATES

These Courts of Appeals have no original jurisdiction, but hear all cases appealed from the District Courts except the special classes of cases which may be appealed directly to the Supreme Court of the United States. These courts have final jurisdiction in some classes of cases, while in others appeals may be taken to the Supreme Court of the United States.

The Supreme Court is composed of one Chief Justice and eight associate justices. It sits from October to June. Its most important duty is to give final interpretation to the Constitution. Whenever anyone whose rights are legally involved thinks a clause of the Constitution has been violated by a law of Congress, a treaty, a provision of a State constitution, or a State statute, he may raise the question in any State or Federal court from the local justice of the peace to the highest judge, and in important cases may obtain the opinion of the Supreme Court.

The Supreme Court has both original and appellate jurisdiction. That is, some cases are brought directly to the Court and others are

Harris & Ewing

CHIEF JUSTICE EARL WARREN

The other members of the Supreme Court are Associate Justices Felix Frankfurter, Hugo L. Black, Stanley F. Reed, William O. Douglas, Tom C. Clark, Robert H. Jackson, Harold H. Burton, and Sherman Minton.

brought by appeal from the decisions of lower courts. In suits between States, the Supreme Court has original and exclusive [1] jurisdiction; in suits against ambassadors and other public ministers, it has original and exclusive jurisdiction; and in suits against consuls it has original but not exclusive jurisdiction.[2] A few types of cases may as a matter of right be appealed directly from a United States District

---

[1] When a court has exclusive jurisdiction over certain suits, they cannot be brought in any other courts. The Supreme Court also has original and exclusive jurisdiction in suits brought by the United States against one of our forty-eight States, and original but not exclusive jurisdiction in suits brought by a State against citizens of another State or against aliens.

The United States District Courts have original jurisdiction of suits brought by the United States against individuals, and they have original jurisdiction concurrently with the United States Court of Claims of suits or claims against the United States up to $10,000 in so far as the United States has consented to be sued.

[2] The U. S. District Courts also have jurisdiction of suits against consuls.

The exemption of ambassadors, ministers, and consuls from suit in State courts applies only to those of foreign governments accredited to the United States. It has no application to those sent to foreign countries by us.

Court, from the highest State court,[1] and from a Court of Appeals.[2] Other cases are brought to the Supreme Court from other courts only with its consent;[3] and its consent is hard to obtain, unless the lower court has departed from the usual course of judicial proceedings or there is conflict of opinion among the judges of the various circuits on the same subject matter.

In the Supreme Court, cases are decided by a majority vote.

Concurrent Jurisdiction. — Congress gives Federal and State courts concurrent jurisdiction in many cases, that is, it permits certain cases to be tried either in a Federal court or in a State court. Often a Federal question and a State question are included in the same controversy. Owing to the difficulty and expense of dividing a case for separate trials in different courts, both State and Federal questions are decided in the Federal court, or in some cases both questions may be tried in a State court. But if a plaintiff [4] brings a suit in a State court, over which the United States District Courts are given jurisdiction, the defendant [5] may have it transferred to the District Court.

Special Courts. — There are three special Federal courts: the Court of Claims, the Customs Court, and the Court of Customs and Patent Appeals. The first was established as a sort of investigating commission to advise Congress concerning claims against the United States Government, and the other two were established to insure a uniform interpretation of technical tariff laws, and to hear appeals from the Board of Appeals of the Patent Office.

The Court of Claims, established in 1855, consists of five judges who sit in Washington. It is a well-established principle of public law that

---

[1] Cases involving: (1) the validity of a statute or treaty of the United States; (2) the validity of a State statute on grounds of conflict with the Constitution, laws, or treaties of the United States; and, (3) a title, right, privilege, or immunity under the Constitution, laws, or treaties of the United States.

[2] A person relying on a State statute may appeal from a Court of Appeals if it declares a State statute unconstitutional.

[3] If the party losing his case in the Court of Appeals, let us say, petitions the Supreme Court for a review of his case, it will deny the review or will issue a writ of *certiorari* directing the Court of Appeals to certify to the Supreme Court the record of the proceedings for inspection and review. During one term of the Supreme Court, 680 petitions were submitted but only 95 were granted.

[4] A *plaintiff* is a person who commences a suit in law against another.

[5] A *defendant* is a person accused or summoned into court who defends himself against the charge.

THE SUPREME COURT BUILDING IN WASHINGTON

This classic main entrance with its Corinthian columns is one of the most beautiful in the world.

388   AMERICAN GOVERNMENT

a sovereign state cannot be sued against its will, and before the establishment of this court a person having claims against the United States Government could get no redress except by an Act of Congress.

The Court of Claims handles claims arising out of the Constitution, acts of Congress, regulations of the executive departments, and out of contracts entered into by the United States or its agents. Until 1946 all claims arising out of torts (wrongs) committed by Federal officers could be approved only by act of Congress. Since then, however, such claims (say, out of an auto accident) over $1,000 are handled by the District Courts and those under $1,000 by the Federal agency involved.

The awards of this court, unlike those of all other courts, cannot be paid until Congress appropriates the money to pay them. Upon the first day of each regular session of Congress the findings of the court for the year are sent to Congress, and the money is appropriated almost as a matter of course.

The Court of Claims may ask the Supreme Court for instructions on any definite and distinct question of law pertaining to a case, or the Supreme Court may require, by certiorari, that a cause be certified to it for review and determination.

Congress or any administrative department may refer claims to this court. The court will investigate the claims and report to Congress or to the department whether they ought to be paid. For instance, Congress will refer "war claims" which cannot be sued for in the courts; or a department will wish an opinion of the court which will enable it to settle claims in a practical way without the necessity of suit. No Federal court other than the Court of Claims will give an opinion unless suit is actually brought.

The Customs Court is the name applied by Congress in 1926 to the former Board of General Appraisers. The nine judges, who sit in divisions at the principal ports of entry, hear appeals from persons dissatisfied with the decisions of appraisers and collectors of customs affecting the valuation and classification of merchandise.[1]

The Court of Customs and Patent Appeals consists of five judges. Its headquarters is in Washington but many cases are heard in New York.

---

[1] The customs officials examine enough packages chosen at random to satisfy themselves that the contents are as represented. If there is any question as to the value of the goods, they are examined by experts. If the importer considers the appraisement wrong, he may appeal to the Customs Court.

Only court that will give an advisory opinion without suit being brought and than only to Congress or a dept of

It hears appeals from the Court of Customs, and has such questions as the following to decide: Are golf hose subject to the tariff duty imposed upon "wool half hose" or the lower duty imposed upon "equipment ordinarily used with golf balls in exercise or play"? Are ivory flowers dutiable as "artificial flowers"? Are jew's-harps dutiable as "musical instruments" or as "toys"? Are goose livers dutiable as "dressed poultry" or as "meats"? Also, does "manufactured furs" include fur skins whose holes have been sewed? This was decided affirmatively, hence the same rate had to be paid upon them as upon furs made into garments.

If an examiner of patents rejects an application for a patent, an appeal may be taken to the Board of Appeals of the Patent Office. If this board sustains the examiner in rejecting the application, an appeal may then be taken to the Court of Customs and Patent Appeals.[1]

The Tax Court of the United States, so called, is an independent agency of the Executive Branch, hence not treated as part of the Judicial Branch. It is composed of sixteen judges appointed by the President and Senate for twelve year terms. The principal office of the Court is in Washington, but the judges sit in divisions anywhere in the United States that the Secretary of the Treasury provides accommodations. It has jurisdiction of Internal Revenue cases only. For instance, if one thinks his income, estate, or gift tax is too high, he may appeal to this Tax Court.

Judges. — Federal judges are nominated by the President and appointed by and with the consent of the Senate. The salaries of these judges vary from $15,000 to $25,500 a year, and they hold their office during good behavior,[2] which means that they cannot be removed except through impeachment proceedings.[3] Any judge appointed to

---

[1] The Supreme Court may, upon the application of either party, require the Court of Customs and Patent Appeals to certify a case to it for review and determination. But in practice the Supreme Court refuses to review cases decided by the Court of Customs and Patent Appeals unless some important principle is involved.

[2] Judges for the District of Columbia and the territories and island possessions are appointed for only four, six, or eight years.

[3] Judge Pickering of the District Court for New Hampshire was removed for drunkenness in 1803; Judge Humphreys of a Tennessee District Court, for disloyalty in 1862; Judge Archibald of the Commerce Court, for improper business relations with persons having cases in court in 1913; and Judge Ritter of the southern District Court in Florida in 1936, for bringing his court into scandal and disrepute. Four other judges have been impeached by the House but acquitted by the

hold office for life who becomes disabled may retire on full salary if he has served 10 years or more, or half salary if he has served less. He may retire on full salary at age 65 if he has served at least 15 years on the bench, or at age 70 if he has served at least 10 years.

As all Federal courts, except the Supreme Court, are mere creations of Congress, they may be abolished by Congress at any time. In 1911 nine Circuit Courts were abolished but the judges were retained for service in the Courts of Appeals and other Federal courts.

CHIEF JUSTICE JOHN MARSHALL

Marshall was a great statesman, as well as an outstanding jurist who interpreted the Constitution to mold the States into a strong Union.

In September of each year the Chief Justice of the United States summons the senior circuit judge of each of the ten circuits and chief justice of the D. C. Court of Appeals to Washington for an annual conference. Preparatory to this conference the district judge of each district [1] submits a report to the senior circuit judge in August setting forth the number and character of cases on the docket. The conference makes a careful survey of the condition of the business of the courts and prepares for the temporary transfer of judges to circuits and districts where the condition of business indicates the greatest need. The senior circuit judge may temporarily transfer a district judge from one district to another within his circuit, and the Chief Justice of the United States may temporarily transfer a district judge to a district of another circuit.

Senate, the most famous one of whom was Associate Justice Chase of the Supreme Court, who was accused of expressing himself too freely in regard to politics. A number of District Court judges have resigned to avoid impeachment.

[1] The senior district judge reports in districts with more than one judge.

Court Officials. — *District Attorneys* are appointed by the President and Senate for a term of four years. There is one United States attorney for each judicial district. It is the attorney's duty to bring suit against all persons violating the Federal laws within the district, and to prosecute them — in short, to represent the Federal Government in any case arising within the district to which the Government is a party. Some districts have a number of Assistant United States Attorneys.

In addition to these district attorneys there are numerous Special Assistants to the Attorney-General stationed over the country and assigned to special classes of cases — *e.g.*, anti-trust, claims against the United States, taxation, narcotics, and land titles.

United States Marshals are appointed in the same manner as the district attorneys, one for each district. It is the marshal's [1] duty to make arrests and execute various court orders. If he meets with resistance in the performance of his duties, he may call upon the citizens for assistance; and if necessary, the President will send United States troops to assist him.

In the appointment of district attorneys and marshals the President consults with the Attorney-General, as the latter officer exercises general supervision over them.

Clerks are appointed by the courts, each court appointing one. The clerk has custody of the seal of the court and keeps a record of its proceedings, orders, judgments, etc. Each Court of Appeals and each District Court may have deputy clerks in cities where court is held away from the headquarters of the court.

District Court Commissioners are appointed in sufficient number by each district court. A commissioner issues warrants of arrest on criminal proceedings, takes bail, and determines whether the probability of guilt is sufficient to hold the accused to answer to the charge in court.[2]

(For State judicial system, see Chapters XXIX and XXX.)

---

[1] A United States marshal bears the same relation to the Federal court that a sheriff bears to the State court.

[2] A Federal district court commissioner discharges for the United States government such functions as are performed for a State government by a justice of the peace.

NAME	ESTABLISHED	NUMBER OF COURTS	NUMBER OF JUDGES	TERM OF JUDGES	JUDGES APPOINTED BY	SALARY OF JUDGES
(84 District Court districts)	1789	84	About 227	Life	President and Senate	$15,000
Court of Appeals . . .	1891	11	68	"	"	17,500[1]
Supreme Court . . .	1789	1	9	"	"	25,000
Court of Claims . . .	1855	1	5	"	"	17,500
Customs Court . . .	1926	1	9	"	"	15,000
Court of Customs and Patent Appeals . .	1909 &'29	1	5	"	"	17,500

QUESTIONS ON THE TEXT

1. Name the regular courts of the United States.   The special courts.

2. The Federal courts have jurisdiction over what two classes of cases because of the character of the subject matter?   Over what six classes because of the character of the parties?

3. How many District Judges are there and how many districts?

4. The District Courts have jurisdiction over what kind of cases?

5. To what higher courts may appeals be taken from the District Courts?

6. How many Courts of Appeals are there?   Who supervises each of the circuits?

7. How many judges has each of the Courts of Appeals?

8. From what court are cases appealed to the Courts of Appeals?   To what court are certain cases appealed from them?

9. Of how many judges does the Supreme Court of the United States consist?   When and where does the court sit?

10. From what courts are cases appealed to the Supreme Court of the United States?

11. In what two classes of cases does the Supreme Court have original jurisdiction?

12. May a question involving the interpretation of the Constitution of the United States be taken to the Supreme Court?

13. Of how many judges does the Court of Claims consist?   What cases are decided by this court?   In what respect does the Court of Claims differ from all other courts?

---

[1] The Chief Justice receives an additional $500.

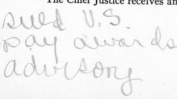

Presrdent with Senate.
elfe or good behavior

14. Of how many judges does the Court of Customs and Patent Appeals consist? Where does it sit? Over what cases does it have jurisdiction?

15. Who appoints all Federal judges? For what term? How may they be removed? Under what condition may they retire on full salary? *10 yrs at 70*

16. May Congress abolish Federal courts? *yes* *65 - 15 yr*

17. What is the duty of district attorneys? By whom are they appointed?

18. What is the duty of the United States marshals?

19. What is the duty of court clerks? By whom are they appointed?

20. What are the duties of district court commissioners? By whom are they appointed?

PROBLEMS FOR DISCUSSION

1. A woman attempted to pass a fifty-dollar note at Gimbel's store in New York City, but the clerk detected something peculiar about it. The floor detective discovered it to be a twenty-dollar bill with each figure two changed to five. The woman was arrested on the charge of attempting to pass counterfeit money. She was believed to be a "shover" for a band of counterfeiters. In what court was she tried?

2. At a "port of entry" along the Canadian border frog legs were appraised as dressed poultry, there being a tariff duty on poultry but not on frogs. Naturally the importer was dissatisfied with the decision of the appraiser. In what court could he bring suit?

3. The penalty for defacing a letter box is a fine not exceeding one thousand dollars or imprisonment for not more than three years, or both. In what court would a party accused of this offense be tried?

4. If Virginia should pass a law prohibiting farm hands from working more than six hours a day, the law would probably be unconstitutional. If a sheriff or constable should arrest a farmer for violating the State law and bring him before a justice of the peace for trial, he could claim that the law is unreasonable and contrary to the Fourteenth Amendment of the Constitution of the United States. If the lower courts should decide against the contention, how high could the farmer appeal the case?

5. In 1942, just after the beginning of World War II, all persons of Japanese ancestry — aliens and citizens — were compelled to leave their homes along the West coast. Those not leaving voluntarily were taken to relocation internment camps. The Federal courts declared this action to be constitutional during the war period of great national emergency. In what Federal court did a Japanese bring his case? Appealed how high?

6. When the Chicago Canal was dug, connecting Lake Michigan with the Illinois River, the sewage of Chicago was emptied into this Canal. The

outlet of the Canal is through the Illinois River into the Mississippi. St. Louis obtains its drinking water from the Mississippi; hence the State of Missouri sued the State of Illinois, demanding that Chicago be prohibited from polluting the accustomed supply of water of St. Louis. The counsel for Illinois had several hundred barrels of harmless bacteria emptied into the stream at Chicago and found that none survived until the water reached St. Louis. In what court did Missouri lose the suit?

7. The United States built a dam across a river in South Carolina to aid navigation, and thereby destroyed the value of rice lands. Mr. Hayward, the owner, claimed damages and won the suit. In what court did he win the suit?

8. In 1938 Congress authorized innocent persons convicted in United States courts to bring suit against the United States for damages not exceeding $5000. In what court would such a claim be brought?

9. What court of appeals decided that calf livers were dutiable as "meat" and not as "veal," and that a dollar horn is a "musical instrument" and not a "toy"?

10. Theodore Roosevelt once said: "A judge of the Supreme Court is not fitted for the position unless he is a constructive statesman, constantly keeping in mind his adherence to the principles and policies under which this nation has been built up and in accordance with which it must go on; and keeping in mind also his relations with his fellow statesmen who in other branches of the government are striving in co-operation with him to advance the ends of government. Marshall rendered invaluable service because he was a statesman of the national type, like Adams who appointed him, like Washington whose mantle fell upon him." Do you agree with Theodore Roosevelt? When the Court is interpreting the Act for minimum wages, maximum hours, and the exclusion of child-made goods from interstate commerce, is it merely explaining the words of the Constitution or is it performing the function of a statesman?

11. Just before appointing Oliver Wendell Holmes to the Supreme Court President Theodore Roosevelt said: "Judge Holmes' labor decisions, which have been criticized by some of the big railroad men and other members of large corporations, constitute to my mind a strong point in Judges Holmes' favor. The ablest lawyers and greatest judges are men whose past has naturally brought them into close relationship with the wealthiest and most powerful clients, and I am glad he preserves his aloofness of mind so as to keep his broad humanity of feeling and his sympathy for the class from which he has not drawn his clients. I think it eminently desirable that our Supreme Court should show in unmistakable fashion their entire sympathy with all proper effort to secure the most favorable possible consideration for

the men who most need that consideration." Why does the United States Senate feel free to refuse to ratify the appointment of judges?

12. The Supreme Court some time ago was called "The Nine Old Men." In retort, Henry Ford said: "Elderly persons are not as slow in taking up new things as young folks sometimes suppose. They are only a little more careful not to be fooled again by old fallacies that are masquerading as new truths." Is a judge who handles current problems in court daily as old at 70 as a reader of one partisan newspaper at 40? Is it better to appoint an untried man of 35 or a tried man of 55?

13. Which of the following quotations impresses you the more favorably, having in mind the power of the Supreme Court to declare Acts of legislative bodies unconstitutional?

"Those who zealously preach the religion of the Constitution want us to do the worshipping while they take up the collection." — Norman Thomas

"The combat between communism and fascism on the one hand, and democracy on the other, comes down to the simple question: What, if any, place shall be given to the average man and woman in government? Both communism and fascism would rob them of every right, every privilege, every guarantee given them in our Constitution. The first line of defense against a dictatorial government is the Constitution of the United States." — Senator Borah

14. "Democracy will survive only as long as the quick whims of the majority are held in check by the courts in favor of a dominant and lasting sense of justice. If democratic institutions are long to survive it will not be simply by maintaining majority rule and by the swift adaptation to the demands of the moment, but by the dominance of a sense of justice which will not long survive if judicial processes do not conserve it." — Charles Evans Hughes. Why do you agree or disagree?

SELECT BIBLIOGRAPHY

FERGUSON, J., AND MCHENRY, D. *The American System of Government.* McGraw-Hill. New York. 1953 ed. Ch. 16.

HUSTON, L. "How the Supreme Court Reaches a Decision." *New York Times Magazine.* May 24, 1953.

PUSEY, M. "Chief Protector of the Constitution." *New York Times Magazine.* September 20, 1953.

RODEBAUGH, E. "The Trials I've Seen!" *Saturday Evening Post.* July 25, 1953. (By an official court reporter.)

SWARTHOUT, J., AND BARTLEY, E. *Principles and Problems of American National Government.* Oxford Univ. Press. New York. 1954 ed. Ch. 16.

CHAPTER XXII

CIVIL RIGHTS AND LIBERTIES

Our Government. — Ours is a democratic government — a government of, by, and for the people. As we know, government in the United States is not all-powerful. It is limited; there are many things that government cannot do.

THE CONSTITUTION

The National Archives

Contrast this with the underlying principles of dictatorship. In a dictatorship the people exist for the state — the state is an end in itself. In a democracy the state exists for the people — the state is only a means to an end, and that end is the good life for all.

Chief among the things that government *cannot* do in the United States is to interfere with the basic liberties, the civil rights, of the American people. What are these civil rights? And where are they to be found?

The more precious rights are listed in the Constitution of the United States and in the constitutions of the States (especially in their Bills of Rights), and those in the U. S. Constitution cannot be restricted by Congress or the States, or those in State constitutions by legislatures.

CIVIL RIGHTS BEYOND THE CONTROL OF THE UNITED STATES AND THE STATES

The U. S. Constitution Restricts Both the U. S. and the States. —

(1) NEITHER THE UNITED STATES NOR THE STATES CAN ALLOW SLAVERY OR INVOLUNTARY SERVITUDE. (Thirteenth Amendment.) This means that no person is allowed to own another. It also insures a system of free and voluntary labor. For instance, in 1944 the United States Supreme Court declared unconstitutional a Florida "peonage" law enacted in 1919 under which a Negro laborer had been sent to jail for sixty days for lack of $100 to pay a fine imposed by a State court as penalty for not working off $5 his employer advanced to him.

(2) NEITHER THE UNITED STATES NOR THE STATES MAY PUNISH ANY PERSON BY A BILL OF ATTAINDER. (Art. I, Secs. 9 and 10).

A *bill of attainder* is a legislative act which inflicts punishment without a judicial trial. For example, in 1865 Congress passed a law providing that no person would be permitted to appear as an attorney before the Federal courts unless he would take an oath that he had not in any way aided the Confederate cause. The Supreme Court held this to be a bill of attainder, and hence unconstitutional.

(3) NEITHER THE UNITED STATES NOR THE STATES MAY PUNISH ANY PERSON BY AN EX POST FACTO LAW. (Art. I, Secs. 9 and 10.)

An *ex post facto* law is a *criminal law* which in any way works to the disadvantage of any person committing, or accused of committing, a crime before the law is enacted.[1] That means that a State law making it a crime to sell intoxicating liquors cannot penalize the selling of them before the law was passed; it means that a law increasing the penalty for first-degree murder from 20 years of imprisonment to death cannot be enforced against one who committed murder before this law was passed; and it means that a law providing for conviction by a unanimous decision of a jury of eight instead of twelve cannot apply to a crime committed before the passage of the law, because this new law works to the disadvantage of the accused.

Protection under the *ex post facto* clause applies to criminal cases only, and a retroactive *civil law* is not forbidden by the *ex post facto* clause. For example, an income tax law enacted in November can impose a tax upon one's income for the entire year including the preceding ten months.

---

[1] A California law made it illegal to possess metal knuckles. One man accused of possessing knuckles pleaded the *ex post facto* clause as defense because he had the knuckles before the law was enacted; but he was convicted for possessing them after the law was passed.

(4) Neither the United States Nor the States May Deprive Any Person of Life, Liberty,[1] or Property,[2] without Due Process of Law. (Fifth and Fourteenth Amendments.)

The Declaration of Independence spoke of the right to "life, liberty, and the pursuit of *happiness*." But before the Fifth and Fourteenth Amendments were added to the Constitution the country had become more conservative, so it provided constitutional protection for "life, liberty, or *property*."

Double Meaning of Due Process of Law. — When one reads the phrase "due process of law" he thinks of due, or proper, procedure in courts. But the phrase has come to mean much more. After the Civil War the Fourteenth Amendment was added to the Constitution primarily to insure justice to the freed slaves. But what good could proper procedure do them if they were tried under unjust laws? So the Supreme Court construed due process to mean not only a fair procedure but also a fair law. And if a fair law was good for the new freedman it was good for all individuals, and it was good for groups of individuals, or corporations.

So, judicially viewed, due process of law means a fair legal procedure; but legislatively viewed it means a law whose very substance is just and reasonable. Therefore we may view due process from the procedural side and from the substantive side.

From the Procedural Viewpoint the due process of law clauses forbid the taking of one's life, liberty, or property except by legal procedure in accordance with the fundamental ideas of fairness and regularity which exist in Anglo-Saxon countries. This includes due notice and an opportunity to be heard. A procedure may be in accordance with due process of law, however, without a jury trial,[3] provided judgment is rendered only after some sort of fair trial. If a trial is not fair, redress may be had in a higher court.

From the Substantive Viewpoint the due process clause of the Fifth

---

[1] *Liberty* means not only the right of freedom from imprisonment, but the right of one to use his faculties in all lawful ways, and to pursue any lawful trade or diversion.

[2] *Property* means more than mere physical property. It includes such things as stocks, bonds, good will, professional knowledge, and the income therefrom.

[3] The Sixth and Seventh Amendments of the United States Constitution guarantee jury trials in most Federal cases, and State constitutions usually guarantee jury trials in State cases of importance.

Amendment protects individuals or minority groups against Acts of Congress which are unjust, and the Fourteenth Amendment protects them against Acts of States and laws of local legislative bodies if unjust. The judges of the Supreme Court will declare unconstitutional any Act appealed to them if they consider it unjust.

If one considers legislation unreasonable, he may carry his contention to the Supreme Court. Thus the court becomes a third chamber above the two chambers of Congress or the State legislatures. In other words, the Supreme Court constitutes a house of censors to pass upon social and economic matters of public interest rather than mere legal technicalities. Therefore, when the President and Senate select a Supreme Court judge they should consider carefully his attitude on public problems as well as his legal knowledge.

The Fifth Amendment forbids only the National Government to deprive any person of life, liberty, or property without due process of law. As Congress was rather conservative the Supreme Court had little occasion to declare Acts unconstitutional under this clause. But after the Civil War the Fourteenth Amendment made this due process clause apply to the States, and there are 48 legislatures and thousands of city councils to pass acts or ordinances which may unreasonably deprive minority groups of their liberty or property. For example, in Oregon, Dirk De Jonge was sent to the penitentiary for seven years for making a speech in which he advocated communism for the United States. The Civil Liberties Union provided funds to carry his case to the United States Supreme Court. The court unanimously found that he had been deprived of liberty without due process of law because he had not advocated the use of force in establishing communism. A State cannot forbid speeches advocating a change in form of government by peaceful means, so the Oregon law was declared unconstitutional and De Jonge was freed.

Whenever the Supreme Court declares an act or ordinance in one State unconstitutional this decision henceforth restricts the legislatures and councils in all States. For example, when the Supreme Court declared unconstitutional the Oregon law requiring all children to attend *public schools*, it meant that no State could impose such a restriction.

Conflict of the Police Powers against the Due Process Clauses. — As soon as the Supreme Court judges used the Fourteenth Amendment due process clause to make themselves censors of State legislation, the States resented it and became jealous of their powers. The State lawyers, however, observed that the courts would allow legislation to interfere with property or money interests if it promoted health, good morals, safety, or welfare. So lawyers upholding State reforms would win their cases by showing that the legislation promoted health, morals, safety, or welfare; and the lawyers named these four defenses the Police Powers of a State. The Police Powers theory is that any State law [1] which promotes the health, morals, safety, or welfare of the people is reasonable and constitutional, and not in conflict with the due process clauses. So today, whenever an Act is attacked by an individual or corporation as depriving persons of life, liberty, or property without due process of law those defending the Act argue the Police Powers. If they persuade the Supreme Court that it promotes these ends, the Court will declare the Act constitutional.

This due process versus police powers situation can be illustrated by an 1887 case, *Mugler* v. *Kansas*. In 1881 Kansas had outlawed the manufacture or sale of intoxicating liquors, except for medicinal purposes. Mugler was convicted under the act for selling beer. His attorneys argued that he had invested his money in a brewing business when such activity was legal in Kansas. To deny him the right to operate his business now, they said, would be to deprive him of both liberty and property without due process of law. But the U. S. Supreme Court refused to accept this argument. It held that prohibition came within the State's power to regulate the public health, morals, safety, and welfare. One liberty after another has been restricted because legislators are inclined to consider health, morals, safety, or welfare of more importance than property. *Examples:*

To promote health States have been permitted to —

forbid or restrict the sale of intoxicants and opiates;
forbid unlicensed persons to practice medicine;
quarantine communicable diseases;
require residences to be connected with sewers; and
have their officers seize food unfit for consumption.

---

[1] The Federal Government has police powers over the District of Columbia and territories of the United States, and to a limited extent indirectly through the taxing and commerce powers. But police powers are usually thought of as reserved powers of the States.

To promote morals States have been permitted to —

forbid gambling or the sale of lottery tickets;
confiscate vehicles used in violating liquor laws;
forbid sale of obscene literature; and
forbid pool rooms in certain places.

To promote safety States have been permitted to —

forbid the carrying of concealed weapons;
require snow to be removed from sidewalks;
require weeds to be removed from city lots; and
require liability insurance for motor vehicles.

To promote welfare States have been permitted to —

reasonably restrict hours of labor;
reasonably prescribe minimum wages;
restrict public utilities to reasonable profits;
forbid oil and gas wells to operate in a wasteful way; and
require cedar trees to be cut to protect orchards.

By going through the decisions of the Supreme Court interpreting the Fifth or Fourteenth Amendment [1] we can get some idea as to whether or not the court will consider that a certain law deprives one unreasonably of life, liberty, or property; but we cannot be certain that an Act passed by Congress or a State legislature is a good, valid law until the Supreme Court of the United States has upheld the law after hearing an actual case in which the constitutionality of the law was questioned.[2]

---

[1] Some years ago a count was made of the Supreme Court decisions interpreting the "due process clause" of the Fourteenth Amendment for a period of ten years. The court was found to have made nearly four hundred decisions interpreting this clause. Fifty of these decisions declared State laws unconstitutional. For example, a State legislature enacted a law requiring railroads to carry passengers within the State at two cents a mile. The railroads showed that they would lose money carrying passengers at this rate, and the Supreme Court declared the law unconstitutional because its enforcement would be taking property unreasonably — "without due process of law."

Among the other three hundred and fifty laws which were tested in the Supreme Court but held to be constitutional were the following: (1) A Boston ordinance prohibited the holding of meetings on the Boston Common. (2) Tennessee prohibited the sale of cigarettes. (3) A Boston ordinance restricted the height of buildings. (4) Texas compelled railroads to cut wild (Johnson) grass from their right of way. (5) Massachusetts compelled people to be vaccinated.

[2] A Federal court will not tell one whether a certain Act will be lawful. It never acts until an individual or corporation accuses another of breaking the law and

State Due Process Clauses. — In addition to the due process clauses of the Fifth and Fourteenth Amendments to the United States Constitution, about half of the States have due process clauses in their State Constitutions. So if a State law is held to be constitutional under the United States Constitution, it may still be declared unconstitutional under the due process clause of the State constitution. For example, the Workmen's Compensation Law which compels employers to compensate employees injured in their employ was held by the United States Supreme Court to be constitutional according to the United States Constitution. But the Supreme Court of New York State declared the New York Workmen's Compensation Law contrary to the due process clause of the New York Constitution. Thus a law, which was considered according to due process of law in the other States, was unconstitutional in New York; and the New York Constitution had to be amended before New York could have a Workmen's Compensation Law.

CIVIL RIGHTS BEYOND THE CONTROL OF EITHER THE UNITED STATES OR THE STATES

Civil Rights beyond the Control of Congress. — The first ten amendments to the Constitution of the United States are known as the Bill of Rights because they contain so many guarantees of liberty that are set forth in the English Bill of Rights.[1] These amendments restrict Congress alone. This fact cannot be too strongly emphasized, because most people think that these restrictions apply to the States as well as to the United States. Congress may not take away any of the liberties set forth in these amendments, but through legislation the States may deprive their citizens of many of these liberties without violating the Constitution of the United States.

---

brings an actual case for its decision. There are two reasons for this practice: First, a judge could not possibly foresee all of the effects of a certain legislative act. Second, when an actual case comes to court, attorneys collect the law and arguments for each side of the contention, and the judge acts somewhat as a referee. If the judge did not have these arguments collected for him, it would be necessary for him to investigate the law as well as decide it, and for this he has not the time.

However, the Supreme Courts of some States will render an "advisory opinion" upon the request of the Governor or of the State Legislature.

[1] The English Bill of Rights is an Act of Parliament enumerating various liberties guaranteed to the subjects to which King William assented in 1689.

CONFLICT BETWEEN THE DUE PROCESS CLAUSES AND THE POLICE POWERS

	Judicial Liberty under the Due Process Clauses	*Legislative Restrictions under the Police Powers*	
U. S. Supreme Court	"No person shall be deprived of life, liberty, or property without due process of law," (Amendment V restricting Nat'l Gov't.)	The *Hawaiian Legislature* cannot compel children to complete third grade in public school before attending a foreign language school. The *Interstate Commerce Commission* cannot prescribe rates low enough to deprive a well-managed railroad of fair profits on reasonable valuation.	*Congress* may exercise police powers for the District of Columbia and territories, and indirectly under its tax and commerce powers. But police powers are primarily reserved powers of States. — **Congress**
Due Process of Law Clauses		*State Legislatures* may: require silver nitrate be dropped into eyes of newborn; compel quarantine, or vaccination; limit hours of work; and forbid child labor; — **Health**	
		forbid gambling; forbid sale of intoxicating liquors; forbid business on Sunday; — **Morals**	**State Legislatures**
U. S. Supreme Court	"No State shall deprive any person of life, liberty, or property without due process of law." (Amendment XIV.)	*A State Legislature* cannot require all children to attend *public schools*; nor forbid teaching foreign languages in private schools; nor forbid Negroes to move to a block where whites live; nor fix prices at which gasoline must be sold; nor prescribe rates for public utilities so low as to make a fair profit impossible.	enact traffic restrictions; forbid the carrying of firearms; require common carriers to employ safety devices; — **Safety**
		compel school attendance; regulate milk prices; restrict the use of property through zoning laws and impose rent controls. — **Welfare**	

Civil Rights beyond the Control of States. — The Constitution of the United States places upon the States three important restrictions involving civil rights which it does not place upon Congress.

(1) *No State may pass any law impairing the obligation of contracts.* (Art. I, Sec. 10.) This restriction means that a law enacted after a lawful contract has been made shall not affect the provisions of such contract. For example, Crowninshield of New York gave his note to Sturges of the same State on March 22, 1811. Shortly thereafter the State of New York passed a bankruptcy law [1] under which Crowninshield became a bankrupt. Paying Sturges the same per cent of the debt that he was able to pay other creditors, Crowninshield claimed that he was exempt from payment of the remainder. Application of this bankruptcy law of New York State to debts contracted before its passage was declared unconstitutional by the Supreme Court of the United States as impairing obligations of contract.[2]

---

[1] For meaning of "bankruptcy law" see page 100.

[2] A charter granted by a State to a *private corporation* is a contract which cannot be materially changed by the State, unless the charter itself, a State law, or the State Constitution reserves the right to change charters.

A charter granted to a *public corporation*, such as a city, can be changed because

(2) *No State may make anything but gold and silver coin a tender in payment of debts.* (Art. I, Sec. 10.) This restriction means that no State may enact a law requiring a creditor to accept anything but gold or silver when tendered in payment of a debt.

(3) *No State may deny to any person within its jurisdiction the equal protection of its laws.*[1] (Fourteenth Amendment.) This means that no State may enact laws which discriminate unreasonably between persons or classes of persons. For instance, Illinois could not prohibit all combinations to fix prices or restrict competition "except farmers and stock raisers." A State could not require railroads "alone" to pay court costs when defeated in a suit. In 1914 Arizona provided that any company or individual that employs more than five persons must employ not less than 80 per cent qualified voters or native-born citizens of the United States. This law was declared unconstitutional because its enforcement would have discriminated against aliens and thus would have deprived them of the equal protection of the State's laws. (Aliens may be excluded from government service.)

Civil Rights beyond the Control of State Legislatures. — Each State constitution contains a Bill of Rights placing restrictions upon the State legislature just as the Bill of Rights in the Constitution of the United States places restrictions upon Congress. The Bills of Rights of State constitutions contain such provisions as the following: guarantee of trial by jury, religious freedom, freedom of the press, writ of habeas corpus; prohibition of excessive bail, excessive fines, cruel and unusual punishment; and the guarantee that no person shall be deprived of life, liberty, or property without due process of law.

Religious Liberty. — Congress may neither make any law respecting the establishment of a religion, nor may it interfere with the free-

---

the city is merely a subdivision of the State. Such a charter is not a contract because one cannot contract with himself.

A charter, franchise, or license permitting business which adversely affects the health, morals, safety, or general welfare can be repealed, because the State cannot contract away its powers to regulate health, morals, safety, and welfare ("*police powers*"). For example, if a State granted a liquor license and then enacted a prohibition law, the license was construed to be legally canceled.

[1] Though this *equal protection of the laws* clause is a restriction upon the States only, a law of Congress depriving persons of equal protection might be declared unconstitutional as being in conflict with the Fifth Amendment, which prohibits Congress from depriving any person of life, liberty, or property without due process of law.

dom of religious worship. (First Amendment.) The Constitution of Virginia provides that "all men are equally entitled to the free exercise of religion, according to the dictates of conscience." (Art. I, Sec. 16.) However, if any of the various denominations have special peculiar religious observances which form a part of their beliefs, they are expected to make these conform to the general laws of the land. A person may believe whatever he pleases, but he must not, in the name of religious liberty, violate a statute enacted by the representatives of the people and approved by the courts. For example, students were expelled from the University of California because for conscientious reasons they refused to drill. The U. S. Supreme Court was appealed to and decided that a State does not have to require students to drill even in its "land grant" colleges; but if it does, it can reject or expel healthy students who refuse to drill.

But Jehovah's Witnesses cannot be required to salute the flag. In 1942 the West Virginia Board of Education ordered that the salute to the flag should become a "regular part of the program of activities in the public schools." Refusal to do so resulted in the expulsion of the

© *The Curtis Publishing Company*

FREEDOM OF SPEECH

son of one of the members of the Jehovah's Witnesses sect. The father was then prosecuted because his son was "unlawfully absent" from school. Holding that " a person gets from a symbol the meaning he puts into it, and what is one man's comfort and inspiration is another's jest and scorn," the Supreme Court declared that compelling one to salute the flag is in violation of the liberty clause of the Fourteenth Amendment (restricting the States) in the light of the purpose of the freedom of religion clause of the First Amendment.

The Freedom of Speech and of the Press. — Congress can make no law abridging the freedom of speech and of the press (First Amendment); and the Constitution of Virginia provides that "any citizen may freely speak, write, and publish his sentiments on all subjects, being responsible for the use of that right." (Art. I, Sec. 12.)

A person has the right to speak or publish what he chooses so long as he does not violate a statute law, violate public morality, create a disturbance calculated to result in bodily injury, or injure one's business or reputation. The *Saturday Evening Post* paid $1500 in an out-of-court settlement for calling a man a "Stalinist busybody." And later the same magazine paid $11,000 for calling another man "a Communist wrecker in American labor." One of the reasons for the difference in amounts was that one man had been damned in passing, while the other was dealt with at length. Officers of Government and candidates for office may be criticized if critics speak of what they know or believe, have only public interest in view, and speak without malice.

To illustrate, if John Smith is a candidate for the city treasurership, one could publish the fact that he had been a grafter during the World War II. But publishing the fact against Smith simply because one dislikes him would make such person subject to damage suit; or, if the publication results in a feud or a breach of the peace, such publication is also a crime which the State can punish, and proof that the statement is true will be no defense. If a person has lived as a good citizen for a number of years, he has a right not to have his past record made public by a person prompted by a spiteful or malicious motive.

Thomas in "Detroit News"

THE LIGHT OUR FOREFATHERS GAVE US

The prohibiting of addresses in public parks or thoroughfares and of profane language in certain places is not considered an abridgment of freedom of speech. For instance, it is a Federal crime to use profane or indecent language over the radio.

The Clear and Present Danger Rule. — In cases involving freedom of speech and press, the Supreme Court applies what is known as the "clear and present danger" rule. This standard was first enunciated by the great Justice Oliver Wendell Holmes in 1919: "The question in every case is whether the words used are used in such circumstances and are of such a nature as to create a clear and present danger."

In 1949, after a long and hectic trial, eleven leaders of the Communist Party in the United States were convicted of violating the Smith Act. This 1940 Act of Congress makes it unlawful for any one to teach and advocate the violent overthrow of ordered government in the United States. It also makes it a crime to "conspire to commit" these acts. The eleven appealed their conviction on the grounds that the Act violates the freedom of speech guarantee of the First Amendment; and that no act of theirs created a "clear and present danger" to the United States.

The conviction was upheld by the Court of Appeals in 1950. The noted Justice Learned Hand pointed out that the communists' conspiracy created a danger "of the utmost gravity and of enough probability to justify its suppression."

In 1951 the Supreme Court, upholding the conviction and the constitutionality of the Smith Act, said: "We reject any principle of governmental helplessness in the face of preparation for revolution, which principle, carried to its logical conclusion, must lead to anarchy." By 1954 some 60 Red leaders had been convicted by the Act.

The Right to Assemble and to Petition. — Congress may not prevent any peaceable assembling or any governmental petition, and a State may prevent neither a petition to the National Government nor a peaceful meeting for the purpose of preparing a petition to the National Government, but a State may prescribe where and when meetings may be held. To illustrate, a State could not prevent the meeting of reformers for the purpose of petitioning the National Government to propose a constitutional amendment prohibiting the use of intoxicating liquors; but if street meetings interfere with traffic, the city authorities may require the reformers to meet in halls or in the suburbs.

Constitutional Guarantees of Civil Rights Cannot Be Used as a Shield to Cover Criminal Activities. — The Supreme Court has said that freedom of religion does not cover actions "in violation of social duties or subversive of good order." Thus, the Court upheld the action of Kentucky authorities in prohibiting the use of live, poisonous snakes in the services of one religious cult. In another case, the

Court upheld the right of Congress to prohibit polygamy in the Federal territories. And, recently, the Court held the interstate transporting of plural wives by one sect practicing polygamy to be an "immoral act" punishable under the White Slave or Mann Act.

Picketing.[1] — The Supreme Court has said: "In the circumstances of our times, the dissemination of information concerning the facts of a labor dispute must be regarded as within the area of free discussion that is guaranteed by the Constitution." Thus, peaceful picketing is regarded as lawful, but a State may prevent any picketing "set in a background of violence." Further, a State may not lawfully prohibit the use of picketers who are not themselves employes or former employes of the picketed establishment. But the Court has also held that a union may not picket one employer not party to a dispute in order to force him to bring pressure upon a second employer who is involved in a dispute.

The Writ of Habeas Corpus. — The Constitution of the United States (Art. I, Sec. 9) provides that "the privilege of the writ of *habeas corpus* shall not be suspended, unless when, in cases of rebellion or invasion, the public safety may require it." [2] All State constitutions have similar provisions. This writ secures to any person who claims to be unlawfully detained by a public officer or a private person

---

[1] Picketing usually accompanies a strike, but is sometimes used against an employer who hires non-union workers or who hires members of one union to do work that another union claims should be done by its own members.

[2] Because of the grave situation in the Pacific in the early days of World War II, it was felt that the public safety was endangered by the presence of persons of Japanese ancestry on the Pacific Coast. In 1942 the United States Government removed 112,000 Japanese from the area to prevent possible sabotage and racial violence. At least two-thirds of these evacuees were United States citizens by birth.

The Supreme Court has not yet squarely faced the constitutionality of the evacuation and relocation program. In a 1944 case it unanimously held that citizens of Japanese ancestry could not be held once their loyalty had been established.

In 1949 a Court of Appeals severely criticized the entire program and upheld the District Court's restoration of citizenship to three women of Japanese ancestry who, like hundreds of others, had renounced their American citizenship while in a War Relocation Camp. The Court of Appeals held that the renunciation was caused by fear and coercion, not by free choice. It also criticized statements of the general who conducted the relocation program, comparing them to "the Nazi-like doctrine of inherited racial enmity."

Japanese-Americans fought heroically in the armed forces during the war and no evidence of *Nisei* disloyalty during the war has ever been found.

the right to have an immediate preliminary hearing before a civil court that he may learn the reason for his detention. This is in marked contrast with the conditions in countries under the control of dictators. There people are frequently thrown into jail and kept there for an indefinite length of time, without any possibility of learning the reason why they are confined.

This writ applies not only to persons who are imprisoned. It has been used by a husband to secure the return of his wife who was taken home by her parents, and by a mother to recover her infant who was through mistake exchanged for the infant of another woman.

Unreasonable Searches and Seizures. — "The right of the people to be secure in their persons, houses, papers, and effects against unreasonable searches and seizures" by Federal authorities is guaranteed by the Fourth Amendment, and State constitutions have like guarantees against State officers. A search warrant describing the place to be searched, the person or thing to be seized, and the reason for the seizure is required.

Thus a man's house is his castle. Authorities may not break into a man's home and gather evidence to be used against him without a warrant. And only such evidence as is described in a warrant may be seized.

Of course, no warrant is needed if an officer is in "hot pursuit" of a fugitive, or when a crime is being committed in his presence. In the latter case, though, no search and seizure may be made without a warrant if there is adequate time in which to secure one before the evidence of crime could disappear.

And an officer does not need a warrant to search an automobile he suspects of carrying something in violation of the law; and, likewise, he may seize evidence at the scene of a crime. The tapping of telephone wires and the use of a detectaphone by officers of the law have also been upheld by Federal courts and by some State courts; but other State courts have rejected evidence so obtained.

Evidence, the knowledge of which has been wrongfully gained by such methods as an illegal search, is not admissible in court unless and until it is rediscovered in a legal manner. For instance, officers searched a Chinese laundry with a warrant describing the laundry and specifying liquor. No liquor was found, but in an adjoining living room "dope" was found in the bottom of a baby's crib. This could not be used as evidence against the laundryman because the evidence was illegally obtained.

The Right of Trial by Jury. — The Constitutional guarantee of trial by jury applies only to Federal courts.[1] In civil cases at common law one is entitled to a jury trial if the value in controversy exceeds $20. In criminal prosecution one is entitled to a jury trial; and where the penalty is as much as six months' imprisonment or $500 fine, one cannot be tried unless indicted by the grand jury.

Double Jeopardy. — The Fifth Amendment provides, in part, that no person shall be "twice put in jeopardy of life or limb." In primitive times one could be penalized by taking his life or by cutting off his leg, arm, ear, or some other "limb" of the body. Hence the old English phrase "life or limb" was carried into our Constitution; and today the provision means, in plain language, that no person shall be twice put on trial for life or liberty for the same offense. However, the following explanations are needed.

A person may be tried for the same act under a Federal law in a Federal court and under a State law in a State court. An example of this would be one selling liquor without either a Federal or a State license. He could be tried and sentenced in a State court and again in a Federal court.

State Constitutions also forbid double jeopardy; but if one breaks into a store at night and steals liquor and later resells it without a license he can be tried for three offenses: illegal entry, theft, and selling liquor without a license.

A Speedy and Public Trial, guaranteed by the Sixth Amendment, means a trial within a reasonable time — not so soon as to prevent the accused from preparing his defense and not so long that he serves his sentence whether convicted or not.

Excessive Bails and Fines are prohibited by the Eighth Amendment; and if imposed the accused has the right of appeal.

Cruel and Unusual Punishments, also prohibited in the Eighth Amendment, are those which are unreasonably severe for the type of offense being dealt with.

Self-Incrimination. — According to the Fifth Amendment, no person accused of crime may be forced to testify against himself. Nor

---

[1] See Art. III, Sec. 2, Cl. 3, and Amendments V, VI, VII.

may an intimate member of his family be forced to provide information which might convict him. However, anyone may testify voluntarily against himself or against others. (The State Constitutions provide for jury trials in State cases. See Chapter **XXIX**.)

Injunction Proceedings. — An injunction is an order issued by a judge, which directs some individual or corporation to do or refrain from doing some particular act. Injunctions are either *mandatory* or *preventive.* They are mandatory when they compel a party to perform some particular duty, as, for instance, where a water company is compelled to turn on water which it has shut off without legal right. A preventive injunction is one which orders a party to desist from doing some act in which he is engaged, or proposing to do, in violation of the rights of others. For instance, if a property owner were attempting to build beyond his building line, the adjoining owners could restrain him by securing an injunction.

Injunctions are also classified according to the duration of the time that they are to be in effect. They may be issued for a temporary period only, or they may be permanent. Temporary injunctions are granted in order to stop a threatened injury, or to keep matters as they are until the controversy between the parties can be heard on its merits. If, after the case has been heard, the court thinks that the plaintiff is entitled to an injunction, the temporary order is made permanent.

When a court of equity is asked to issue an injunction, it will first determine whether the complainant has an adequate remedy at law (such as a damage suit), and whether an irreparable injury will result if the injunction is not issued. If he has such a remedy, or if the injury will not cause irreparable damage, the injunction will be denied. If an injunction is issued and violated, the judge may find the one who violates the order to be in contempt of court.

Contempt Proceedings. — Every court must have the power of self-preservation. It must have the power to quell any disturbance in or near the court room. It must have power to compel witnesses to attend and to give testimony, and to prevent their insulting the court. Every court must be able to enforce obedience outside of the court to certain writs and decrees. Therefore, to protect itself, the court has power to fine or imprison one who shows contempt for the person or the order of the court; and a judge may sentence one for contempt in most cases without trial by jury.

Injunctions in Labor Disputes. — Injunctions have frequently been issued to prevent picketing during a strike, to prevent parades by the strikers, or to prevent the holding of meetings. In fact, the injunction has sometimes been so broad in its prohibitions as to make the winning of a strike practically impossible. But in 1932 Congress enacted a law restricting the Federal courts in their use of injunctions in labor disputes.

This 1932 Act forbids a Federal court to issue an injunction in a labor dispute without hearing witnesses in open court for and against the request, except when a complainant persuades the court that delay in issuing a temporary injunction will result in substantial injury to the complainant's property. Then the injunction will be issued only when the complainant files adequate security to recompense those enjoined, in case of loss, expense, or damage to the strikers caused by an erroneous issue of such order. This injunction is void after five days.

In all cases arising under this Act in which the person shall be charged with contempt, the accused shall have a trial by jury unless the contempt was committed in the presence of or near a court or by an officer of the court.

Under the Taft-Hartley Act of 1947 the National Labor Relations Board is authorized to sue for an injunction to halt unfair labor practices by unions or employers. And if national health or security is involved the President may have the Attorney General petition a U. S. District Court to issue an injunction forbidding the threatened strike or lock-out for an 80-day period.

Equality before the Law. — Our legislators and judges endeavor to make all equal before the law, though there are instances where the ideal is not easy to realize.

(1) A poor man accused of a crime cannot afford able lawyers to plead his cause most advantageously; but often he has a sympathetic jury, and there are a number of "legal aid societies" to help him.

(2) When a poor man gets a final judgment against a man of means, the judgment must be paid, whereas a judgment against a poor man cannot be enforced unless within a limited period he acquires property. In America one cannot be imprisoned for a debt honestly contracted.

(3) When a fine is imposed, the rich man pays the fine — perhaps with no inconvenience; the poor man serves his time in jail. If the

offense is petty, why not give the poor man credit, release him, and allow him to pay the fine by installments?

(4) A rich man may appeal to the higher courts if the lower court decides against him and thus may drag out the case until the poor man is obliged to abandon his right for lack of lawyers' fees and court fees. The demand is for speedier justice.

This is a challenge to you — rich or poor — to remove the few remaining inequalities. In no other country are the inequalities so few. The rich pay high progressive income, estate, and inheritance taxes; and the poor have various social security laws, free education, equal suffrage, and can vote taxes upon the rich because they outnumber them. With free education a poor boy can become a Lincoln as readily as a rich boy.

QUESTIONS ON THE TEXT

1. What are *civil* rights? What are *political* rights?

2. In what documents are the more precious civil rights preserved?

3. What three civil rights are beyond the control of the United States and the States?

4. What is a *bill of attainder?*

5. What is an *ex post facto law?*

6. Explain fully the meaning of "due process of law." Give one illustration of a law which would be contrary to "due process of law" because of improper procedure; and another because of unreasonableness. How are the due process clauses and the police powers in constant conflict?

7. Will courts consider a moot point of law, or must actual cases be brought before them before they will explain the law?

8. What is a Bill of Rights? Why are the first ten amendments to the Constitution of the United States known as the Bill of Rights?

9. Do these amendments restrict State legislatures or only Congress?

10. The Second Amendment provides that the right of the people to keep and bear arms shall not be infringed. Could your State legislature pass a law restricting the carrying of arms?

11. What three important civil-right restrictions are placed upon the States which are not imposed upon Congress? Illustrate.

12. State Bills of Rights commonly prohibit State legislatures from interfering with what rights of the people?

13. May a person *believe* whatever he pleases regarding religious matters? May he *do* what he pleases, asserting that his deeds are a part of his religion?

14. May one person *say* what he chooses regarding another? May he *publish* it?

15. May the right to assemble and petition be denied?

16. What is the privilege of the writ of *habeas corpus?* Under what conditions may it be denied?

17. Explain the legal expression that "a man's home is his castle."

18. What guarantees are there in the Bill of Rights for a fair jury trial?

19. What kinds of injunctions are there and how are they used?

20. Upon whom does the responsibility rest to correct before the law such inequalities as do exist?

PROBLEMS FOR DISCUSSION

1. If the United States Congress should impose a death penalty for smuggling narcotics into the United States, could the Act of Congress apply to smugglers who had brought the narcotics in before the Act was passed?

2. Explain the meaning of the following statement of Professor Corwin: "The truth of the matter is that the modern concept of due process of law is not a legal concept at all; it comprises nothing more or less than a roving commission to judges to sink whatever legislative craft may appear to them to be, from the standpoint of vested interests, of a piratical character."

3. Referring to the Supreme Court, Mr. Coolidge said: "If its authority should be broken down and its powers lodged with the Congress, every minority body that may be weak in resources or unpopular in the public estimation, also nearly every race and religious belief, would find themselves practically without protection." Give illustrations of this fact.

4. Which of the following unconstitutional statutes interfering with liberty are in conflict with the Fifth, and which with the Fourteenth Amendment: Hawaiian statute compelling children to complete the third grade before attending a foreign-language school; Nebraska statute forbidding the teachings of foreign languages in private schools until the eighth grade is passed; Oregon statute requiring all normal children to attend *public* schools through the eighth grade.

5. Why could not the legislature of your State enact a law providing that no farm hand may work more than five hours a day?

6. Virginia permitted any county to vote for or against cedar trees which were responsible for cedar rust on apples. Shenandoah County voted to destroy cedar trees. The owner of a fine estate with beautiful old cedar trees in front of his house tested the constitutionality of the law; and the United States Supreme Court decided that the law did not deprive owners of cedar trees of their property without due process of law. Under what legislative power was this law upheld?

7. In England all important laws are prepared carefully and introduced to the House of Commons by the Cabinet composed of about 20 of England's great statesmen. In the United States some thirty-odd committees prepare bills for Congress and about three thousand committees prepare bills for the State legislatures, and in a third of the States any group may prepare initiative measures. Thus some laws passed by Congress and many passed by the legislatures or directly by the people are badly drawn, unreasonable, or unjust. Therefore nine of our outstanding statesmen forming the Supreme Court believe it necessary for them to declare unconstitutional Acts which seem dangerous to the welfare of the country. In other words, England has legislative centralization and the Cabinet gives careful attention to legislation; we have judicial centralization and declare unconstitutional unreasonable legislation after it has been enacted. What merits has each plan?

8. A West Virginia statute excluding Negroes from jury service was declared unconstitutional. What provision of the Constitution was violated by this law?

9. "We have learned that it is pent-up feelings that are dangerous, whispered purposes that are revolutionary, covert follies that warp and poison the mind; that the wisest thing to do with a fool is to encourage him to hire a hall and discourse to his fellow citizens. Nothing chills folly like exposure to the air; nothing dispels folly like its publication; nothing so eases the machine as the safety valve." — Woodrow Wilson. Do you agree or disagree with Mr. Wilson? Why?

10. A California law forbade the *possession* of metal knuckles. One was arrested for possessing such knuckles, and claimed that the law did not apply to him because he had them before the law was passed. The case was decided against him; but what law did he think would protect him?

11. If a grown daughter is not allowed to leave home, or a sane inmate at an asylum is detained, what writ would an attorney use in petitioning a judge to release the detained person?

12. Restrictions upon speech and the press increase during wars. During the Civil War speakers and editors who criticized the Government and advocated stoppage of the war were imprisoned. President Lincoln replied to critics that he had taken an oath to support the Constitution and therefore had the right to do all things necessary to sustain the Constitution and the Government founded upon it. He said, "Must I shoot a simple-minded soldier boy who deserts, while I must not touch a hair of the wily agitator who induces him to desert?"

The Espionage Act of 1917 and the Amending Sedition Act forbade speaking or printing anything that interfered with the success of our armed forces or intended to bring our military forces, flag, or form of government into contempt. These Acts were upheld by the courts, and many were imprisoned for such indirect thrusts as calling the war capitalistic, insisting that a referendum should have preceded war, and declaring conscription to be unconstitutional. Do you consider these restrictions justifiable? Give your reason for your answer.

13. Just to create excitement a man cried "Fire" in a theater. This resulted in a panic where persons were injured. In a State whose constitution provides for freedom of speech, is this party liable in a damage suit brought by the injured persons?

14. States may forbid speakers or writers to urge the overthrow of the Government by force. After President McKinley's assassination in 1901, New York enacted the criminal anarchy law. In 1920 the publisher of *The Revolutionary Age* in fervent language urged industrial disturbances and the overthrow of government through mass action. He was sent to the penitentiary, and in 1925 the United States Supreme Court upheld his conviction. What would probably have been the Court's decision if the publisher had advocated a change in the form of government through the ballot box?

15. By what *writ* could a husband have his wife released from a maternity hospital where she is detained because her bill is not paid?

16. A judge rejected evidence obtained by pumping the stomach of one who had swallowed narcotics to conceal them on the ground that one's stomach is as much his castle as his home. Would you have so decided?

17. "One man's liberty ends where the next man's liberty begins." Explain.

SELECT BIBLIOGRAPHY

DABNEY, V. "Crisis in the South: The Segregation Decisions." *Saturday Evening Post.* November 8, 1952.

FAIRMAN, C. *American Constitutional Decisions.* Henry Holt. 1950 ed. and 1952 supplement.

FRANK, J. *Cases on the Constitution.* McGraw-Hill. 1951.

SELBY, E. "The Smith Case." *Saturday Evening Post.* August 15, 1953.

SMITH, B. "I Refuse to Answer." *Saturday Evening Post.* July 25, 1953.

SWARTHOUT, J., AND BARTLEY, E. *Materials on American National Government.* Oxford University Press. 1952. Chapter VI.

To Secure These Rights. Report, President's Committee on Civil Rights. 1947.

WHITE, W. "How Detroit Fights Race Hatred." *Saturday Evening Post.* July 18, 1953.

CHAPTER XXIII

POLITICAL PARTIES AND POLITICS

Nature of Political Parties. — *Definition.* — A political party is a rather loosely knit organization of many people, united by common principles or a common policy, and having for its immediate end the control of government through the carrying of elections and the possession of public office. Its long goal, if it has one, is to put into effect its political, social, and economic philosophy.

If everyone agreed upon every public issue there would be no need for political parties. On the other hand, if no one could agree with anyone else political parties would be impossible. Actually, our parties are composed of individuals and groups holding *similar* (but not exactly the same) views on various public questions.

Importance. — The Constitution makes no provision for political parties; but because people have different views we need organizations to unify these views and to translate them into governmental action. Under governments in which power rests upon force there is no room for divergent opinions. Thus no opposition party is tolerated. The only manner in which popular will can be asserted is through revolution. In a democracy parties are substituted for revolution. Change is accomplished through ballots, not bullets.

Organization. — Lord Bryce observed that: "Organization is essential for the accomplishment of any purpose. To attempt to govern a country by the votes of the masses left without control would be like attempting to manage a railroad by the votes of uninformed shareholders, or to lay the course of a sailing ship by the votes of the passengers."

For these reasons each national party has a *National Committee* headed by a National Chairman, who is the real party manager. In each State the parties maintain a *State Committee* and a State Chairman who functions on the State level in much the same fashion that the national group functions on the national level. Within each State the party is organized into *county* and *city units* and finally into local *precincts* and *blocks*. (See pages 430–432.)

It is the duty of these party units to promote harmony, to arouse enthusiasm, to select candidates for public office, to instruct the voters on the merits of their own principles and leaders and the mistakes of their opponents, to enlist new voters, such as youth coming of age — in short, to capture the government.

Looking for an Issue. — An old party may have no principles differing

Courtesy Chicago Daily News

EACH PARTY'S ATTEMPT TO PROTECT ITSELF AGAINST ECONOMIC HURRICANES

from those held by the opposing party, and may be said to be "looking for an issue." In the words of Orman Ray: "A party may hold together long after its moral life is extinct. Parties go on contending because their members have formed habits of joint action, and have contracted hatreds and prejudices, and also because the leaders find advantage in using these habits and playing on these prejudices." As one cynic put it, politics has then become "the art of obtaining money from the rich and votes from the poor on the pretext of protecting each from the other." It has also been described as "the science of who gets what, when, and how."

Pressure Groups and Political Parties. — The primary distinction between pressure groups and political parties lies in the nomination of candidates. While both groups attempt to influence the course of government, parties do so by offering candidates to the voters at elections. Pressure groups, on the other hand, support favorable party candidates and exert influence on legislation and administration. Pressure groups usually support the candidates and program of the party which most nearly reflects its own views.

Functions. — Parties make democratic government function. Among the important functions of a party are:

1. To select issues and present a platform to voters.
2. To nominate candidates for election.
3. To inform the voters through speeches and literature.
4. To arouse interest in public issues.
5. To mold the party majority into a legislative unit through party loyalty.
6. To expose the shortcomings of the opposing party.
7. To elect a President and Congress of similar views to insure co-operation.

The Two-Party System. — There are two major parties in the United States: the Democratic and the Republican parties. And throughout all of our history there have been but two major parties, though they have gone under various names. The same is true of other English-speaking countries — as in England with the Conservative and Labour parties. In any two-party system each of the major parties must consist of many diverse groups because of the practical need for gaining a majority of the votes in order to win elections.

European countries have been plagued with too many political parties — racial groups, dynastic groups, economic groups, and what not. This results in unstable government. For nearly a century France has had a new government every nine months on the average. The many parties worked so badly in Italy and Germany that the people reacted in favor of a dictator who permitted only his one party.

At times the difference in principles of the two American parties is not great. In 1908 a wit remarked that the two great parties were like two bottles. Each bore a label denoting the kind of liquor it contained, but each was empty. This lack of basic difference is not a weakness but a strength in our political system. It is largely accounted for

because, to win votes, each party must appeal to the same voters.
Note, for example, there are no extremes of rich and poor in the
United States — economically, we are a middle-class nation.

A MODERN METHOD OF CAMPAIGNING

Modern campaign techniques range from television programs and one-minute
movies to this original means of reaching the voters, but there are still old-fashioned
torchlight parades to escort an office-seeker to his rally.

This necessity for appeal to the same great mass of voters in order to
win elections results in compromise as the essence of the two-party
system.   Neither party can long afford to direct its chief appeal to any
one particular group, such as labor, agriculture, or business.   Appeals
must be made, in effect, to all voters.

Adlai Stevenson, in congratulating Dwight Eisenhower on election
night in 1952, aptly illustrated our point when he said: "It is traditional for Americans to fight hard before an election.   It is traditional
also to close ranks after an election.   We vote as many, but we pray
as one."

One of the principal benefits of the two-party system is found in
the role of the party out of office.   Always eager to displace the party

in office, it acts as a watchdog, criticizing the "in" party and attempts to convince the voters that a change is needed. This competition generally results in a better performance by those in office — lest they find themselves the "outs" after the next election.

After his defeat in 1940 Wendell Willkie, in voicing the importance of the two-party system, said: "A vital element in the balanced operation of democracy is a strong, alert, and watchful opposition. Ours must not be an opposition against — it must be an opposition for — an opposition for a strong America, a productive America. For only the productive can be strong and only the strong can be free."

Political Parties in the United States. — *The Democratic Party* is over 150 years old. It arose during Washington's administration, under the leadership of Thomas Jefferson, and was known as the Anti-Federalist Party. It was next known as the Republican, then the Democratic-Republican, and now the Democratic Party.

In the Anti-Federalist days it stood for strict-construction of the Constitution, strong localized government, and private individual liberties. The party stood unopposed when Hamilton's Federalist Party died out in 1816. During Jackson's Democratic administration, however, a powerful Whig Party arose (1832).

The Civil War split the party and made the Democrats a minority group. From then until 1932 only two Democrats, Cleveland and Wilson, were in the White House. But the depression of 1929 brought Franklin Roosevelt into the White House for four terms.

Mr. Roosevelt's death on April 12, 1945, brought Vice-President Harry S. Truman into the White House to complete the fourth term. Mr. Truman was elected to a full term in 1948, but the 1952 Democratic candidate, Adlai Stevenson, was defeated in the landslide election of Dwight D. Eisenhower.

The Republican Party of today is the only minor party ever to displace a major party. It was formed in 1854 and elected its first President, Abraham Lincoln, in 1860.

Actually, it is the descendant of two earlier parties. The Federalist Party, led by Alexander Hamilton during the first years of the Republic, favored strong National Government, broad construction of the Constitution, and Government aid to business and commerce. When Aaron Burr killed Hamilton in a duel it was said that he had shot the brains out of the Federalist Party.

MAJOR POLITICAL PARTIES IN THE UNITED STATES

Year	(Left party)		(Right party)
1789		UNANIMOUS George Washington	
1793	REPUBLICAN		FEDERALISTS George Washington
1797			John Adams
1801	Thomas Jefferson		
1805	Thomas Jefferson		
1809	James Madison		
1813	James Madison		
1817	James Monroe		
1821		ERA OF GOOD FEELING James Monroe	
1825	DEM. REP.		NAT. REP. John Q. Adams
1829	Andrew Jackson		
1833	DEMOCRATS Andrew Jackson		
1837	Martin Van Buren		WHIGS
1841			William H. Harrison John Tyler
1845	James K. Polk		
1849			Zachary Taylor Millard Fillmore
1853	Franklin Pierce		
1857	James Buchanan		REPUBLICANS
1861			Abraham Lincoln
1865			Abraham Lincoln Andrew Johnson
1869			Ulysses S. Grant
1873			Ulysses S. Grant
1877			Rutherford B. Hayes
1881			James A. Garfield Chester A. Arthur
1885	Grover Cleveland		
1889			Benjamin Harrison
1893	Grover Cleveland		
1897			William McKinley
1901			William McKinley Theodore Roosevelt
1905			Theodore Roosevelt
1909			William H. Taft
1913	Woodrow Wilson		
1917	Woodrow Wilson		
1921			Warren G. Harding Calvin Coolidge
1925			Calvin Coolidge
1929			Herbert Hoover
1933	Franklin D. Roosevelt		
1937	Franklin D. Roosevelt		
1941	Franklin D. Roosevelt		
1945	Franklin D. Roosevelt Harry S. Truman		
1949	Harry S. Truman		
1953			Dwight D. Eisenhower

The opposition which rose up to challenge Jackson first called itself the National Republican and then the Whig Party. It was this Whig Party that gave way to the present Republican Party. The Republican Party dominated the national scene until the elections of 1930 and 1932. Except for a victory in the elections of 1946 (in which the G.O.P. won control of both houses of Congress), the Republicans served as the opposition party from 1933 until 1953. In the 1952 elections, Eisenhower not only won a smashing victory in the race for the White House, but led his party to control of both houses in the 83rd Congress as well.

Party Platforms. — A party platform is a statement of principles or policies on which the party stands. A National party platform is framed every four years by the Committee on Resolutions at the National Convention of the party. Each party platform contains a statement of its principles and policies; but if the delegates cannot agree upon specific problems, noncommittal planks are adopted to avoid offending any large faction of the party. · The value of a platform depends upon the party leaders and candidates who indorse it.

Because of the necessity for compromise within the party, the platform is generally intended to attract as many votes as possible while it alienates as few votes as possible. Thus both party platforms have long called for Statehood for Hawaii and Alaska and an Equal Rights for Women Amendment. Sometimes it seems as if some platform promises, like most of the bitter words of the campaign, are forgotten almost as soon as the votes are counted.

Party Membership. — The fact that the two parties must make their appeals to exactly the same group of voters is reflected in the heterogeneous membership of each. It is a cross-section of the American population. Catholics, Protestants, and Jews, workers, employers, professional men, farmers, white-collar workers, housewives — even "the butcher, the baker, the candle-stick maker" — all the many occupation groups that make up our society are to be found in both parties.

It is true that, for brief periods, the members of certain groups align themselves more solidly with one party than with the other. Thus, the Democratic successes from 1932 until 1952 can be explained in part because of an attraction for the big city-labor vote and the farm vote, together with the Solid South. But the three pillars of this uneasy alliance were convincingly shattered in 1952.

A person is a Democrat, a Republican, an Independent, or some other party member simply because he chooses so to regard himself. It is as simple as that (including, of course, the process of registration). Membership in either party is completely voluntary. It costs nothing — unless a person wishes to contribute to the party coffers. There are no dues to be paid and no chores to be done unless one wishes to work for the party. Both membership and participation are voluntary.

A variety of factors may cause one to say that he is a Republican or a Democrat. A great many people are one or the other simply because that is what their parents were. The section of the country (as, for example, the South) may have a lot to do with the choice. Material considerations (*e.g.*, "Which party is best for my own pocket?") determines the choice for many. But, whatever the reason, party allegiance can be changed almost at a snap of the fingers.

A Large Independent Voter Class. — The independent voters, those who feel bound to neither party, are extremely important in American politics. They come from every group and switch back and forth between the parties from election to election. For many, the switch is unfortunately made on the basis of mere whim. But for many others, it is the result of a decision made on the merits of the candidates and the issues.

All in all, there are probably about 12,000,000 straight-ticket or so-called "bullet" voters in each party. These are the hard-shell, rock-ribbed party members who will vote for any candidate so long as he bears the party label. (These people are sometimes criticized, but often they are thought of as the heart of party organization.)

The remaining 36,000,000 actual voters (based on some 60,000,000 votes cast in 1952) run the scale from the *almost*-always-straight-party voters to the true independents who go one way in one election and the other way in the next (or vote a split ticket in each election). It is this latter group that usually determines the outcome of elections in the United States. (It is not at all uncommon for one party to win the popular vote for President and the other to win the vote for United States senator in the same State at the same election — for example, Massachusetts, Missouri, and Washington in 1952.)

Minor Parties. — Third parties have flashed and faded across the American political scene. But only one, the Republican party, has ever replaced a major party. Some minor parties, like the Prohibition party since 1869, have been with us a long time.

Minor parties may be readily classified as either parties of the "great idea" or of the "great personality." Thus the Prohibition, the American Vegetarian, the Socialist, and the Socialist-Workers parties center on one theme; they live on one particular issue. The Bull Moose Progressive party of 1912, on the other hand, was built around a single dynamic personality: Theodore Roosevelt. These parties collapse or become impotent when their leader fades from the scene — as did the Bull Moose party when T. R. pulled out after the 1912 elections — or their issue loses its appeal or is taken over by one of the major parties.

The Republican party was originally one of the "great idea" minor parties. It was born in the cause of anti-slavery in 1854. The Whig party failed to embrace the new minor party's burning issue; and so the Whigs passed into oblivion as the Republicans replaced them in opposition to the Democrats.

In a few instances, minor parties have been successful on the State and local level. They have even elected a few members to Congress. They have never succeeded in capturing the Presidency, however.

Even so, minor parties have had a tremendous effect on American politics and the major parties. It was a minor party, the Anti-Masons in 1830, that first hit upon the idea of a national convention for nominating candidates for the Presidency. Woodrow Wilson won the election of 1912 largely because T. R.'s Bull Moose party took millions of votes that would otherwise have gone to William Howard Taft.

The main value of minor parties has been to introduce new ideas and sell them to the people; and it requires idealists to pay the price of bringing worthwhile new ideas to realization. Many times minor parties have promoted ideas to the point where the major parties could not ignore them. When this has happened the major parties have simply taken up the idea, presenting it as their own. Norman Thomas, six times the Socialist party candidate for President, more than once complained that "the major parties are stealing from my platform." So a minor party often pays the price of developing a promising idea only to have a major party appropriate it when it becomes popular.

A new party is usually more "liberal" or more radical than an older party. Occasionally, it becomes a vehicle for deception — as the 1948 Progressive Party whose leader, Henry Wallace, did not himself then understand the forces behind his party. Some cannot wait for evolution; they must have revolution. But if new ideas are imposed overnight, if radicals are not willing to wait for public opinion, then revolution, whether for good or evil, is the price.

In the 1952 elections, in addition to the Democrats and Republicans, seven minor parties had candidates for President and Vice-President on the ballots of at least some States: Progressive, Socialist, Socialist-Labor, Socialist Workers, Prohibition, Christian Nationalist, and Poor Man's parties. Four others were not on the ballot in any State but still had candidates: Greenback, Vegetarian, American, and American Rally.

The National Convention. — In the early summer of every fourth year each party holds a convention for the purpose of formulating its principles and policies into a party platform and for nominating candidates for President and Vice-President. Some months before a presidential election the National Committee of each of the National parties meets (usually in Washington) and decides upon the time and place to hold the convention. A number of the larger cities bid for the honor because it means more business for their merchants and helps to advertise their city. The one selected pays a large sum of money to the party treasury.

Both the Democratic and Republican parties chose Chicago for 1952 and the businessmen of the city gave $250,000, free use of a convention hall, free television, and numerous other inducements to each.

When the time and place are determined, the National Committee sends a call to each State Committee naming the time, place, and number of delegates to which the State is entitled. In 1952 the Republican National Committee assigned 1206 delegates to the States, and the Democrats 1230.[1]

---

[1] In 1952 the Republicans assigned two delegates for each U. S. senator, two for each representative-at-large, one for each congressional district, three additional for each State that went Republican in 1948, three additional for each State that elected a Republican U. S. senator in 1950, one additional for each congressional district casting more than 10,000 votes for a Republican in 1948 or 1950, five for Hawaii, three each for Alaska and the District of Columbia, and two for Puerto Rico. The Democrats assigned each State

When the call from the National Committee is received, the respective State committees see that their party delegates are duly elected for the National Convention.   In one third of the States delegates are elected by direct primary elections, while in the other States they

REPUBLICANS OPEN CONVENTION, 1952

This was the scene in Chicago's International Amphitheatre July 7 as Guy Gabrielson (lower left), Chairman of the Republican National Committee, called the Party's convention to order.

are chosen in district or State conventions — the delegates-at-large, of course, being chosen at State conventions.   The conventions or primary elections that choose these delegates frequently "instruct" them to support a certain candidate for the presidential nomination and to urge that certain policies be included in the party platform.

In the large auditorium decorated with flags, bunting, and pictures of candidates and statesmen of an earlier day, the convention is called

---

twice the number of senators and representatives it had in Congress, plus a bonus of four to each State that went Democratic in 1948, and six each for Alaska, the District of Columbia, Hawaii, and Puerto Rico, and two each for the Canal Zone and the Virgin Islands.

Each delegate usually has an alternate, and some States send more delegates than they have actual votes, which means that some delegates have only a fraction of a vote.

to order by the chairman of the National Committee. After the secretary reads the official call for the convention and prayer is offered, the National chairman names the temporary chairman and other officers whom the National Committee has nominated. Unless there is a factional fight, as there was in 1912 in both parties, these nominees are immediately elected by the convention. The temporary chairman is escorted to the chair and makes a lengthy speech in which he assails the record of the opposite party, eulogizes his own party, and pleads for harmony.

The Committees. — Four committees are now formed: (1) Committee on Permanent Organization; (2) Committee on Credentials; (3) Committee on Rules and Order of Business; and (4) Committee on Platform and Resolutions. Each State is entitled to one member on each committee. As the roll of the States is called, the chairman of each State delegation announces the members whom the delegation has chosen to represent that State on the respective committees. After these committees are named the first session generally ends.

The second session of the convention is usually devoted to receiving the reports of the committees. The Committee on Rules and Order of Business usually recommends the adoption of the rules of the preceding National Convention and of the House of Representatives so far as they are applicable, and recommends a program, or order of business, for the existing convention.

The Committee on Credentials recommends what delegates shall be seated when there is a split in the party and two sets of delegates claim to be the proper delegates.

The Committee on Permanent Organization nominates a permanent chairman and other permanent officers. When elected, the permanent chairman is escorted to the chair and delivers a long speech outlining the issues of the campaign.

Next, the Committee on Platform and Resolutions presents a platform of which a preliminary draft has been prepared by party leaders before the meeting of the convention. In committee a struggle may develop over the wording of the platform, and the debate may be continued on the floor of the convention.

The next duty of the convention is to nominate the President. The Secretary calls the roll of States alphabetically, beginning with Alabama; and as a State is called, its delegates have a right to propose candidates for nomination by long eulogistic speeches. Any number of delegates may second a nomination by similar speeches. After all candidates are placed in nomination, the balloting begins. The secretary again calls the roll of the States, and the chairman of each delegation announces the votes for the entire delegation.[1] The candidate who first receives a majority of all the delegates is nominated.

The Vice-President is then nominated in the same manner that the President has been nominated.

Notification of Candidates. — Having nominated the candidates, the convention authorizes its chairman to appoint two special committees, consisting of a representative from each State, to notify the candidates. The committees used to meet the candidates at their homes, or where large audiences could assemble, and each candidate delivered a "speech of acceptance."

In 1932 Franklin Roosevelt flew to the Convention and delivered his acceptance speech immediately; and other presidential nominees have followed this precedent, or attended the Convention.

Party Machinery.[2] — Between the nomination of candidates and election day a political campaign must be waged, and for this purpose party organizations are necessary. Party machinery in the form of a National Committee, National sub-committees, congressional campaign committees, State committees, and local committees is necessary for each party.

The National Committees of the Democratic and Republican parties consist of one man and one woman from each State and territory. In some States the committeemen are chosen by the direct primary method, in some by a State convention, while in others they are chosen by the State delegation at the National Convention. At the head of the National Committee is the National *chairman*,[3] nominally chosen

---

[1] Until 1912 the Democratic Party used what was known as the "Unit Rule," by which all the votes of a State went to the same candidate; but the 1912 Convention modified the rule by providing that the unit rule should not be enforced for the delegations from States whose laws provide for the nomination and election of delegates to the National Convention in congressional districts.

[2] The party machinery described in this section applies to both the Democratic and the Republican parties. That of other parties is very similar.

[3] Second in importance only to the National chairman is the National secretary, who is director at headquarters. He is more familiar with the details of the campaign than the chairman, who determines the policy.

by the National Committee, but really selected with the advice of the presidential candidate. He is the campaign manager, "the head master of the machine." For convenience and efficiency the National Committee is divided into subcommittees, such as an executive committee, a finance committee, a committee in charge of the bureau of speakers, a committee in charge of literary and press matters, and a committee in charge of distributing public documents.

ADLAI E. STEVENSON   *United Press Photo*
The Airport dedication in 1952 included a campaign speech by Mr. Stevenson.

Between campaigns the Chairman's main job is to keep the machine oiled by raising funds; he replenishes the party's ranks by recruiting new voters and keeping political fences mended.

The Congressional Campaign Committees are organized both in the House and in the Senate. In the House the Republican Committee consists of one representative from every State having party representation in Congress, and this member is chosen by the Republican representatives from his State. The Democratic Committee includes one representative from each State and territory. States not represented in Congress by a Democrat have a member chosen for them by the committee chairman. Women not members of Congress are often appointed to each committee on the suggestion of a member. The Senatorial Committee of each party is composed of about seven members, who are appointed for two-year terms by the party's leader in the Senate. These committees are very active, especially in the "off-year" elections, and are assisted by a party staff. They have no official connection with the other party groups but work in co-operation with them to secure the election of House and Senate party candidates.

The State Central Committees vary in composition and power from State to State. Members are chosen by State conventions or party primaries from congressional or legislative districts or from counties. Their functions are similar on the State level to those of the National Committee. Subordinate to State committees are county (or city) committees; and the door-to-door campaigning is done by block captains under a ward or precinct chairman. At this lowest level are found the majority of party workers, mostly voluntary and unpaid, but the party's life-blood.

Party Finance. — *Source of Funds.* — Unlike many European parties, major American parties do not collect dues from their members. Here party officials and candidates are expected to dig into their pockets. Persons of means may contribute because of devotion to the principles or candidates of a party. But most of it comes from people who have business interests at stake: those who get protective tariff or other favors from the government, those who want restrictions removed, and people of wealth who want lower taxes.

The major sources for party funds today are: (1) individual or family contributors; (2) State party committees; (3) independent "non-partisan" committees; (4) party social functions, such as Jefferson, Jackson, or Lincoln Day dinners and dances; and, (5) the officeholders or office-seekers.

Records of Expenditures. — Since 1910 the amounts of national campaign contributions and expenditures of the various parties have been filed with the Clerk of the House of Representatives.

Since 1940 the National Committees have been restricted to $3,000,000 each, and individual contributions to $5000; but these restrictions have been evaded by contributions to State and local committees, and by direct support of candidates by individuals and non-party organizations, such as the Political Action Committee of the C.I.O. About $75,000,000 was spent on the 1952 elections. In other words, about $1.25 was spent for each vote cast! Most of this huge amount was raised and spent by such "non-party" groups as the Volunteers for Stevenson, the Citizens for Eisenhower, the Republicans for Stevenson, and the Democrats for Eisenhower. Quite plainly, the costs of electioneering have gotten out of hand. The Congress is now considering measures to control such expenditures more effectively.

Restrictions on Corporations. — Laws enacted by Congress prohibit contributions by any corporation or labor organization to any campaign fund used to aid in the election of the President, Vice-President, a representative, or a senator. National banks and other corporations organized by authority of any law of Congress are forbidden to contribute to any campaign fund.[1]

Restrictions on Congressmen. — By the 1925 Corrupt Practices Act amending former acts, a candidate for representative in Congress may not expend more than $2500, and a senator not more than $10,000 [2] towards his election, or an amount equal to the amount obtained by multiplying three cents by the total number of votes cast at the last general election for all candidates for the office which the candidate seeks, but in no event exceeding $25,000 if a candidate for senator, or $5000 if a candidate for representative.[3] He must report the receipts

---

[1] Besides this Federal law prohibiting corporations from contributing, many States prohibit corporations from contributing to State and local elections. The different States have various laws limiting the amount of money a candidate may spend and also specifying for what purposes he may spend it.

[2] Postage and a few items such as those which members of Congress obtain free are not included in these limits.

[3] In 1921 in the Newberry case the Supreme Court of the United States declared that this Corrupt Practices Act did not apply to direct primaries because it did not consider primaries and conventions *elections* over which Congress has certain control. (In 1941 the Supreme Court reversed itself and brought direct primaries for the nomination of Federal officers under National control. See note on page 448.)

Friends of Mr. Truman Newberry lavishly but not fraudulently spent about $195,000 in behalf of his election in his primary and election contests in Michigan. Mr. Newberry was indicted under a Federal Act, but as that part of the Act under which he was indicted was declared void he was allowed to take his seat in the Senate.

However, the Senate resolved "that the expenditure of such excessive sums in behalf of a candidate, either with or without his knowledge and consent, being contrary to sound public policy, harmful to the honor and dignity of the Senate, and dangerous to the perpetuity of a free government, such excessive expenditures are hereby severely condemned and disapproved."

and expenditures for his campaign to the Secretary of the Senate or Clerk of the House within thirty days after an election.

The treasurer of a political committee, or an individual expending $50 or more in two or more states, must file a detailed report with the Clerk of the House annually, quarterly, ten days, and five days before a general election.

Restrictions on Pre-election Promises or Intimidation. — Under the 1939 Act, amended in 1940, it is unlawful in the election of the President, Vice-President, or Congressman, for any Federal, State, or local administrative official financed wholly or in part by United States funds to offer government work as a reward, or dismissal as a penalty, for a vote or for political activity; or to receive political contributions from persons on relief or on work relief; or to use their authority to affect Federal elections.

Restrictions on Activity in Political Campaigns. — The officials mentioned in the preceding paragraph (except elective State or local officers) and most Federal Civil Service employees are forbidden to take an active part in political campaigns. The U. S. Civil Service Commission tries to enforce the restrictions listed here and in the preceding paragraph.

Restrictions on Contributions to and Expenditures of Campaign Funds. — No person or firm entering into a contract with any agency of the Federal Government shall make or promise a contribution to a political party or candidate, nor shall anyone knowingly solicit such funds.

It is illegal for any individual to contribute more than $5000 towards a Federal election committee during a campaign or within a year.

No political committee shall receive contributions aggregating more than $3,000,000 or make expenditures aggregating more than $3,000,-000, during any calendar year.

Bribery, including gifts to influence voters, is illegal according to the laws of all States.

Newspapers and Other Periodicals must insert the word "Advertisement" at the end of political matter for which pay is received. Otherwise editors or papers would seem to be backing candidates or measures for money — a sort of bribe.

Circulars, and the like, concerning Presidential, Vice-Presidential, or Congressional candidates must be signed. Otherwise false statements could be made without anyone being liable.

QUESTIONS ON THE TEXT

1. What is a political party?
2. What is the National Committee? Of whom is it composed?
3. How is the National Chairman chosen? What is his position?
4. What makes new parties grow? What holds old ones together?
5. Why are political parties useful to a democratic government?
6. Is it better to have one, two, or a number of parties?
7. What is a political platform?
8. What is meant by a plank of a party platform?
9. Are minor parties of any value in American politics? Which ones offered candidates for President in 1952?
10. Describe a National Convention. When does it meet? Who, and what considerations, determine where it will meet?
11. What is accomplished by a National Convention?
12. How many votes of a convention are needed to nominate a candidate? *maj*
13. How are vice-presidential candidates nominated? *president*
14. Describe party machinery and methods of conducting a campaign.
15. What are the Congressional Campaign Committees?
16. Describe the political organization within a State.
17. Explain how funds are raised for campaign expenses.
18. Explain the following restrictions pertaining to political campaigns: On (1) corporations; (2) congressmen; (3) intimidation; *(two cong.?)* (4) active part by government officials; (5) contributions and expenditures; (6) bribery; (7) newspapers and periodicals; (8) circulars.   *N.C.   3 million dollars*

PROBLEMS FOR DISCUSSION

1. Is your State a one-party State? Would government be more efficient if there were two parties of about equal strength?
2. Political parties now function by counting heads. But when they originated in England they gained ascendancy by breaking heads — or cutting off those of the leaders. In Canada and England today the leader of the opposition party is paid. When your companions point out your faults in dress, language, and conduct, do you want to break their heads or compensate them for their interest in your welfare? In other words, do you act like a primitive man or like a modern man of thought?
3. Someone has said: "Every political party rests upon a foundation of fools." In other words, it must have a substructure firmly built on men and women who unthinkingly vote with the party no matter what the issues may be. Is this true in your community?
4. Which of the following political proposals do you consider to be

of most importance? (1) Pay the cost of political campaigns from government funds; (2) make party organizations illegal; (3) encourage a third party; (4) compel citizens to vote; (5) elect only a few officers at one time, and make the ballot short by appointing officers other than those who make the laws; (6) forbid the use of money in political campaigns; or (7) do away with the spoils system.

5. If one intends to take an active part in politics, should he join a party? If he does not intend to take an active part but is interested, should he join a party? Should he join a party if he is a preacher; if he is superintendent of schools or principal of a school?

6. In 1937 a stockholder of Swift & Co. sued its directors, asking that they be compelled to return $3000 to the Swift treasury because with corporation funds they had purchased $3000 worth of Democratic national campaign books (convention books — some of which were autographed by President Roosevelt). The stockholder claimed that this was really a gift in violation of the Corrupt Practices Act. What do you think? Corporations also paid large sums to advertise in these books.

7. James Freeman Clarke wrote: "A politician thinks of the next election; a statesman, the next generation." How do you think that a larger group of able men and women might be attracted to politics?

SELECT BIBLIOGRAPHY

ALSOP, J. AND S. "That's Politics for You." *Saturday Evening Post.* October 4, 1952. (Excellent historical materials on politics.)

BENDINER, R. "How Much Does Your Vote Cost?" *Collier's.* September 20, 1952.

BURNS, J. M. "The Case for the Smoke-Filled Room." *New York Times Magazine.* June 15, 1952.

KEFAUVER, E. "Indictment of the Political Convention." *New York Times Magazine.* March 16, 1952.

LUBELL, S. "Who Elected Eisenhower?" *Saturday Evening Post.* January 10, 1953.

PENNIMAN, H. *Sait's American Parties and Elections.* Appleton-Century-Crofts. New York. 5th ed., 1952.

THOMAS, N. "I'm Glad I'm Not Running This Time." *The American Magazine.* October, 1952. (Pointed observations on minor parties and campaigns.)

U. S. News. Full Text of Republican Platform and Major Speeches from 1952 Convention. July 18, 1952. Same for Democratic. August 1, 1952.

CHAPTER XXIV

SUFFRAGE

The Difference between Suffrage and Citizenship. — The word *suffrage* comes from the Latin word *suffragium,* meaning *a vote,* and is simply the privilege of voting at elections. *Citizenship* on the other hand means *membership* in a State. The Fourteenth Amendment to the Constitution defines citizenship: "All persons born or naturalized

Courtesy The American City Magazine

in the United States, and subject to the jurisdiction thereof, are citizens of the United States and of the State wherein they reside." Thus infants born in the United States are citizens and are entitled to the privileges of citizens at home and abroad, but they cannot vote till they reach the age prescribed by the laws of the State where they live.

Suffrage Determined by Each State. — So long as a State maintains a republican form of government [1] it may determine what persons are

_____
[1] A republican form of government is a representative government, or one in which the people elect their lawmakers and other public officers directly or indirectly.

to enjoy the political privilege of voting at both its own and national elections, with three exceptions: (1) that the same persons must be allowed to vote for United States senators and representatives that vote for members of the more numerous branch of the State legislature; and that no person may be deprived of the right to vote on account of (2) race, color, or previous condition of servitude, or (3) sex.[1]

The States commonly permit the same voters to participate in all elections. Today there are three restrictions on suffrage, or the right to vote, which apply to normal persons in every State and three additional ones in some States.

(1) *Citizenship.* — In no State may a person vote who is not a citizen of the United States. (States could allow aliens to vote if they chose to do so.)

(2) *Residence.* — In no State may a person vote who has not resided in the State for a period prescribed by law (6 mos.–2 yrs.).

(3) *Age.* — One must be 21 to vote in general elections in all States but Georgia, where the age is 18.

(4) *Registration.* — With the exception of Arkansas, every State requires registration, some States for all voters, other States for voters in urban areas.

(5) *Education.* — In nearly one half of the States a person may not vote who cannot read or write.

(6) *Taxation.* — In a few of the States a person may not vote who has not paid his poll tax.

Such abnormal persons as idiots or the insane, paupers permanently supported at public expense, and those guilty of certain crimes are, in nearly all states, denied the right to vote.

Suffrage Restrictions as to Citizenship. — Suffrage is now restricted to citizens of the United States in all the States.

Suffrage Restriction as to Residence. — When a citizen of the United States moves from one State to another, before he may vote in

---

[1] The Fourteenth Amendment to the Constitution of the United States (Sec. 2) provides that any State which denies male citizens twenty-one years of age the privilege of voting, except for crime, shall have its representation in Congress reduced in the proportion which the number of such male citizens shall bear to the whole number of male citizens twenty-one years of age in such State. This provision has never been enforced, but after each decennial census when a reapportionment of representatives is being made, some Congressman calls attention to the provision.

the latter State he is required to reside there for the period prescribed by the law of that State. This period of residence varies from six months in some States[1] to two years in others. If a citizen moves from one part of his State to another part, he must, in all States except Oregon, reside there for a brief period before he can vote.

Suffrage Restrictions as to Age. — In none of the States except Georgia may a person vote who is less than twenty-one years of age. Twenty-one years of age has no special significance. We have simply followed the English law which prescribed that age. In conservative pre-war Belgium the voting age was twenty-five; in Russia, eighteen.

"Old men for counsel and young men for war" is an old proverb. It means that those with experience should govern and the young with physical vigor should provide defense. With this theory we have had an older requirement for voting than for going to war.

Inasmuch as knowledge in certain fields is better preparation for voting than experience in other fields, the right to vote might be based on education as well as on experience. Would it be wise to allow youth to vote when they have satisfactorily completed certain courses in history, government, and social problems? Most youth, who complete high school, graduate at the age of eighteen; and the voting privilege extended to youth of eighteen who have completed these courses might be an incentive to qualify for intelligent voting throughout life.

Suffrage Restrictions as to Registration. — To find out whether all persons who claim the right to vote are really entitled to vote, and to identify individuals in communities where residents are not personally known to one another, most States require each voter to "register" his name, address, age, length of residence, and other facts. This is done before a registration officer provided for each county or voting-place. In some States registration is required only in cities. Reg-

---

[1] In Idaho, Indiana, Iowa, Kansas, Maine, Michigan, Minnesota, Nebraska, Nevada, New Hampshire, and Oregon a residence of six months is required; in Arizona, Arkansas, California, Colorado, Connecticut, Delaware, Florida, Georgia, Illinois, Kentucky, Maryland, Massachusetts, Missouri, Montana, New Jersey, New Mexico, New York, North Carolina, North Dakota, Ohio, Oklahoma, Pennsylvania, South Dakota, Tennessee, Texas, Utah, Vermont, Virginia, Washington, West Virginia, Wisconsin, and Wyoming, one year; and in Alabama, Louisiana, Mississippi, Rhode Island, and South Carolina, two years.

istration in a few States does not entitle one to vote unless he has paid the State poll tax.

In most States when one establishes his right to vote he remains a registered voter permanently unless he moves, is convicted of a crime or is committed to a mental institution, or dies; but if he fails to vote within a specified number of years or a specified number of elections some States require the voter to re-register.

Some States have periodic registration. For instance, in New York the voter must annually sign his name in the registration book, and on election day he must again sign his name so that the election officers may compare the two signatures and prevent "ghost" voting.

Both permanent and periodic registration have disadvantages. Under permanent registration votes are sometimes cast for people dead or removed. Under periodic registration political machines always make certain that their followers are registered, while many well-meaning citizens neglect to register.

Educational Restrictions on Suffrage. — Some sort of educational test is now required in nearly one half of the States.[1] In some it is merely ability to read; in others, to read and write; and in still others, to read, write, and understand a passage from the Constitution. The first educational test was adopted by Connecticut in 1855 during the "Know Nothing" agitation against foreign immigrants. Massachusetts followed in 1857, Wyoming in 1889, and Maine in 1891. Since that date most of the Southern States have adopted educational tests, and some include understanding clauses.[2] The "grandfather clauses"

---

[1] The following States have the educational test in some form: Connecticut (1855 and 1897), Massachusetts (1857), Wyoming (1889), Mississippi (1890), Maine (1891), California (1894), South Carolina (1895), Washington (1896), Delaware (1897), Louisiana (1898), Alabama (1901), Virginia (1902), North Carolina (1902), New Hampshire (1903), Georgia (1908), Arizona (1913), North Dakota (1896 Const. Amend. No legislation), New York (1922), and Oregon (1924).

[2] The Virginia educational test is as follows: Every person, unless physically unable, "makes application to register in his own handwriting, without aid, suggestions, or memorandum, in the presence of the registration officers, stating thereon his name, age, date, and place of birth, residence, and occupation at the time and for one year next preceding, and whether he has previously voted, and, if so, the State, county, and precinct in which he voted last; and . . . answers on oath any and all questions affecting his qualifications as an elector, submitted to him by the officers of registration, which questions and his answers thereto, shall be reduced to writing, certified by the said officers, and preserved as a part of their official records." This registration is permanent so long as the person registered remains in the same precinct.

which were inserted in the constitutions of most of the Southern States have been abolished.[1]

New York State Regents Literacy Test. — In 1921 an amendment was added to the New York State Constitution which reads: "After January 1, 1922, no person shall become entitled to vote . . . unless such person is . . . able, except for physical disability, to read and write English; and suitable laws shall be passed by the legislature to enforce this provision."

In 1922 the legislature left the administration of this literacy test to the election officials; and in New York, as in other States, the election officials did not administer it impartially. In some districts the law was not enforced at all.

In 1923 the legislature gave the power of determining literacy for voting to the State Board of Regents (State board of education); and since then the law has been administered with unusual success.

Under the Law of 1923 a new voter might present to the registration officials as evidence of literacy either a diploma showing that he has completed the eighth grade or its equivalent, or he might present a certificate of literacy issued under the rules of the Board of Regents. The Board of Regents has examinations prepared by educational psychologists and given through school superintendents. The following examination is typical:

NEW YORK STATE REGENTS LITERACY TEST

Read this and then write the answers. Read it as many times as you need to.

"Mary had been waiting for the Fourth of July. It was on this day that her father and mother were going to take her to the park. Because it was a holiday her father did not have to work. Mary had learned in school why we celebrate the Fourth of July. The Declaration of Independence was adopted on July 4, 1776. It was written by Thomas Jefferson. It is called the Declaration of Independence because it declared the thirteen American colonies free from England. The Fourth of July is celebrated as a national holiday by all of the forty-eight states."

---

[1] These clauses provided that persons who voted before the Civil War and their male descendants could vote without taking the educational tests. These exceptions, however, were all abolished by 1915 when the last, that of Oklahoma, was declared to be in conflict with Amendment XV of the Constitution of the United States.

(The answers to the following questions are to be taken from the paragraph at the bottom of page 441.)

1. For what day had Mary been waiting?
2. Where were her father and mother going to take her?
3. Why did Mary's father not have to work?
4. Where had Mary learned why we celebrate the Fourth of July?
5. When was the Declaration of Independence adopted?
6. Who wrote the Declaration of Independence?
7. From what country did the Declaration of Independence declare the thirteen American colonies free?
8. How many states celebrate the Fourth of July as a national holiday?

After all, a large turnout at the polls is of little value if many of the voters do not understand who or what they are voting for. And, for just this reason, many people advocate a much higher educational requirement for voting than any State now has.

Tax Restrictions on Suffrage. — In a number of Southern States suffrage is restricted to those who have paid a small annual poll tax. This tax varies from one to two dollars.

For instance, in Virginia one cannot vote unless he has personally paid his $1.50 poll tax six months previous to the regular election. Moreover, this tax must be paid for the past three years. That is, if one fails to pay this tax for three years, he must pay $4.50 (plus 5% annual penalty and 6% interest) six months before the regular election. The voter is required to pay this tax six months before the election so that the candidates for office will not have been nominated. Thus the politicians are not so likely to give voters money with which to pay this tax. The payment of this tax as a prerequisite to voting is strictly enforced.

A poll tax is not very just because the poor man must pay as much as the millionaire. In the South its purpose was to discourage voting by Negroes who had passed the educational test. In practice it also keeps a great many whites from voting, some worthy and some not so worthy.

Suffrage Restrictions as to Sex Removed. — Until the nineteenth amendment to the Constitution was ratified, States were allowed to grant suffrage to women or to withhold it. When the nineteenth amendment extended woman suffrage to all the States, full suffrage was already enjoyed by the women of fifteen States.

Non-Voters. — In 1952, at least 100,000,000 people were eligible to vote, about 80,000,000 were registered where registration is required, and yet only about 60,000,000 actually cast votes.

There are many reasons for this large non-voting group. Some were ill or otherwise handicapped on election day. But the chief cause for non-voting is indifference, not caring and not bothering to inform oneself. Perhaps the fact that these people stay away from the polls is to be counted among our blessings. Surely it is not a poll of ignorance we seek.

Some people do not vote because they oppose all candidates on the ballot and some are perfectly sincere when they say that they do not care who holds public office and guides the nation. But many more do not vote because they are confused by the long ballot found in so many places.

The long ballot is a serious problem in American elections. A recent Omaha ballot was over 13 feet long and contained as much fine print as half an average-size novel. A recent Georgia ballot contained over 70 constitutional amendments, many of them highly technical. And a recent Portland, Oregon, ballot listed 52 offices and 18 measures. The voter is justifiably confused under such conditions and many do not care to repeat the experience.

In situations like these, along with dozens of others, it seems harmful to good government to ask the voter to attempt to cast an intelligent ballot. Occasionally, a voter will pass up all but the top offices on such a ballot. Once in a while he purposely spoils his ballot — like the wag in Los Angeles who wrote the names of each of the seven dwarfs in for seven judgeships and then voted for Snow White for Assessor.

QUESTIONS ON THE TEXT

1. What is meant by the word *suffrage?* By the word *citizenship?*

2. Is suffrage determined by the United States or by the States?

3. May a Chinese woman born in the United States vote for presidential electors? (Amendment XIV, Sec. 1; Amendment XV.)

4. What three restrictions does every State place upon suffrage? What additional ones do some States impose?

5. What abnormal persons are excluded from suffrage in nearly all States?

6. Has the requirement in nearly all States that an American voter must be 21 years of age any special significance?

7. Do any States permit aliens to vote? Could they?

8. How many years must one reside in the State in which you live before he may vote?

9. Explain the sentence, Every right implies a duty; and tell why every mother who is eligible to vote should do so.

10. What kind of educational tests do a number of States have?

11. Explain the New York test; the Virginia test.

12. What tax restrictions do some States have on suffrage?

PROBLEMS FOR DISCUSSION

1. Should voting be viewed as a right, a privilege, or a duty?

2. What are the qualifications for voting in your State?

3. Does your State have an absentee voters' law? If so, make a summary of its provisions. What does it provide for soldiers?

4. Senator Capper suggested a penalty of 1 per cent of one's gross income for not voting. The St. Louis *Star* says that a valuable vote must be founded on a desire for decent government, created in the home, the school, and the church. Are these suggestions valuable? Why?

5. Do you favor universal suffrage? H. G. Wells says: "Before he can vote, he must hear the evidence. Before he can decide he must know. . . . Votes in themselves are useless things. Men had votes in Italy in the time of the Gracchi. Their votes did not help them. Until a man has an education, a vote is a useless and dangerous thing for him to possess." Should a legislator follow a universal suffrage "public opinion referendum" if contrary to his judgment?

6. The New York State Regents Literacy Test can be passed by fifth grade students. If you were preparing them, would you make them easier or more difficult? In the future, would you favor restricting suffrage to high school graduates, not having the law apply to persons already voting?

7. In a democracy is education a luxury, or is it a necessity?

8. Should our schools turn out citizens with a general education or a technical education? Should they be men of culture, of affairs, or cultured men of affairs? If a man is merely trained in a single trade, can he know much about complex society and help to manage a republic?

9. In a New England college town a group of college students attended a town meeting for fun and voted to build a town hall six feet wide and two hundred feet long. Because of this type of levity by young people the State constitutions have provisions like the following from the New York Constitu-

tion: "For the purpose of registering and voting no person shall be deemed to have gained or lost residence . . . while a student of any seminary of learning." If the student's family lives in the college town, or if he has no other home to which he intends to return, he may vote. In Latin America students play an important part in national politics. Do you think the practice in the United States or in Latin America is the better?

10. In the eighth assembly district of New York City it was once discovered that only 42 out of 13,662 families owned their own homes, and of these 42 homes all but 14 were mortgaged. Is this population likely to be conservative or radical in voting? Does this mean that all but the 14 families should be disfranchised?

11. It is the ideal of every good citizen to leave the world a little better than he found it. Intelligent voting is one way to attain this ideal. Are you preparing to be a good citizen? How?

SELECT BIBLIOGRAPHY

FERGUSON, J., AND MCHENRY, D. *The American System of Government.* McGraw-Hill. New York. 1953 ed. Chapters 9, 10, and 11.

OGG, F., AND RAY, P. *Essentials of American Government.* Appleton-Century-Crofts. New York. 1952 ed. Chapters 8 and 9.

PENNIMAN, H. *Sait's American Parties and Elections.* Appleton-Century-Crofts. New York. 5th ed., 1952. Chapters 25 and 26.

SWARTHOUT, J., AND BARTLEY, E. *Materials on American National Government.* Oxford University Press. New York. 1952. Chapters 7, 8, and 9.

Principles and Problems of American National Government. Oxford University Press. New York. 1954 ed. Chapters 7 and 8.

CHAPTER XXV

NOMINATIONS AND ELECTIONS

Nominating Methods. — Very soon after the establishment of the United States it became customary for political parties to nominate a candidate for their support at the election. In the United States there are at present five different methods of nominating candidates for elective offices.

(1) Self-announcement.

(2) Caucus or primary.

(3) Delegate convention.

(4) Direct primary election.

(5) Petition.

Self-announcement, or self-nomination, is very rare, and indicates either little competition within the party or a dissatisfied candidate whom the party has refused to indorse as its regular candidate. Some Southern and Western States provide for printing the names of self-announced candidates upon the ballots.

Caucus [1] is the New England name for a local mass-meeting of party voters, and *primary* [2] is the name used in the Middle or Western States. The caucus, or primary, selects candidates for town, ward, or precinct offices, and members of the town, ward, or precinct party committee. It also selects delegates to county and other nominating conventions.

The caucus has generally proved unsatisfactory because it is easily manipulated by machine politicians, especially in cities, and it is there that more than half the American population live. The unregulated caucus has often been called on short notice to meet in an inadequate

---

[1] The term "caucus" used in this sense must not be confused with the legislative caucus, which is a secret meeting of legislators of a particular party to decide upon united action against the opposing party on the floor of the legislative hall.

[2] The term "primary" as here used must not be confused with the term "direct primary," or "direct primary elections," which is a substitution for the delegate convention.

hall at an inconvenient time, and then "packed" with foreigners or "repeaters" hired by the "ring." As this uninviting caucus frequently ended in a "free for all" it is not strange that good citizens have considered it not only useless, but even dangerous, to attend.

The delegate convention has been in common use since 1840 for selecting county, State, and National candidates. The delegate convention for a county or city is a meeting of delegates from the various election districts of the county or wards of the city. These are chosen by caucuses or primaries, held in each district or ward.

The delegate convention for the State is a meeting of delegates from the counties and cities, commonly chosen at the county or city conventions. As the delegates have been selected directly or indirectly by caucuses, the evils of the caucus have also been the evils of the convention.[1] For this reason conventions rapidly gave way to direct primary elections.

The direct primary election is conducted with many of the safeguards accompanying a regular election, such as registration, secret voting, and penalties against bribery. Each party prints upon its ballot, or has printed at public expense, the members of its party who desire to be party candidates at the regular election, and the person receiving the greatest number of the party votes is nominated.

Nomination by petition means that candidates are placed in nomination by petitions signed by a certain number of voters and filed with some specified officer. This entitles the candidate to have his name printed upon the official ballot. This method practically eliminates national politics from local elections and is well suited to cities, where national political parties should play no part.

The Direct Primary. — In forty-odd States the direct primary method is used to nominate local, county, and State officers, as well as United States representatives and senators. The direct primary systems generally have the following points in common:

(1) Different parties hold primaries at the same time and place.

(2) Australian secret ballot is used.

---

[1] By controlling the pre-convention caucuses the machine politicians had the following candidates selected as delegates for a Cook County convention; held in Chicago in 1896: keepers of houses of ill fame, 2; ex-prize-fighters, 11; had been on trial for murder, 17; had served sentences in the penitentiary, 46; had been in jail, 84; no occupation, 71; political employees, 148; saloon keepers, 265. The total number of delegates was 723.

(3) Ballots are printed at public expense.

(4) Names are presented by petitions and are printed in alphabetical order, or are rotated.

(5) Regular election officials preside and are paid from public funds.

(6) Polls are open during specified hours.

(7) Plurality vote nominates.

(8) Corrupt practices acts for elections apply to primaries.[1]

(9) Members of party committees are selected at the primary.

Closed Primary. — Most of the States use the closed primary, which means that each voter may participate only in the nomination of candidates for the party with which he is registered or affiliated. At the precinct the voter is given a ballot of that party only.

The accompanying Republican primary ballot for Massachusetts was used for a closed primary. The main objection to closed primaries is that the voters must make known their party preference, which to some extent defeats the principle of the secret ballot.

Open Primary. — The other type, the open primary, is used by less than a fourth of the States. It allows the voter to decide at the voting place in which party's primary he wishes to vote.

Wisconsin has the "open primary," which is open to all voters without registering their party preference. The voter is given a separate primary ballot for each party. He votes one and deposits the other in a box for unmarked ballots. The open primary has one serious de-

---

[1] The National Government has the same authority over official direct primaries for Federal officials that it has over elections. In a 1941 case from Louisiana United States Supreme Court Justice Stone said: "We may assume that the framers of the Constitution did not have specifically in mind the selection and elimination of Candidates for Congress by the direct primary," but that a State was electing officials just the same when "it changed its mode of choice from a single step to two, of which the first is the choice of a primary." He pointed here to the fact that in Louisiana "the choice of candidates at the Democratic primary determines the choice of the elected representative."

In 1944 the United States Supreme Court held that a Negro in Texas could not legally be denied the right to vote in the Democratic primary which was regulated by the State and hence was an agency of the State. Such a denial would violate the Fifteenth Amendment. A State cannot practice racial discrimination indirectly through an official primary, the Court reasoned.

South Carolina Democrats thought they had a way out. Repealing all State primary laws, 157 of them, they reorganized the party into what they deemed a private club, with right to bar its membership to all but "white Democrats." But in 1948 the United States Supreme Court held this practice to violate the Fifteenth Amendment.

fect. It makes it possible for an unscrupulous boss of a party in which there is a "cinch-election" primary to direct some of his dishonest followers to vote the other party ticket in order to elect a weak opposing candidate, and thus insure victory for the boss.

The direct primary system has not proved a panacea for all the ills of the convention system, but it offers an *opportunity* to defeat a conspicuously unfit candidate or to nominate one conspicuously well fitted. No primary or election machinery takes the place of intelligence and public spirit, but the direct primary places the responsibility for good government upon the voter.

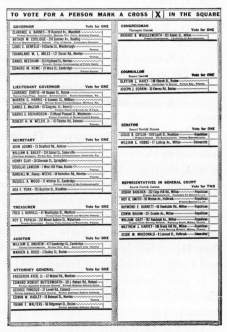

MASSACHUSETTS REPUBLICAN DIRECT PRIMARY
BALLOT, SEPTEMBER, 1950

Arguments for the Direct Primary. — (1) It has given every party member an equal chance to help nominate candidates and thereby encourages loyalty to the government.

(2) It has given aspirants for office an opportunity to appeal to the voters unrestricted by party action.

(3) It has allowed a vigorous candidate to conduct his campaign without having to pool his energy and money with weaker candidates on a party slate.

(4) It has prevented corrupt politicians from selling the party to selfish or corrupt interests.

(5) It necessitates a candidate's coming into close contact with the people and results in his more faithfully carrying out their will.

(6) It stimulates interest in problems of government by more frequent participation.

(7) In a one-party State the voter has no effective participation except at the primary.

Arguments against the Direct Primary. — (1) It entails extra expense.

(2) The voter often must choose between a great many more candidates than he can possibly evaluate intelligently.

(3) It ignores the necessity for consultation and conference in the selection of candidates.

(4) It affords no suitable opportunity for the formulation of party platforms.

(5) It increases the opportunities of self-advertisers and demagogues.

(6) Frequently desirable candidates will not enter primary contests because of the greater effort and expense.

(7) It develops bitterness which weakens the party in the ensuing campaign.

The Presidential Primary. — The direct primary is essentially a *nominating* election. It is used to select the party candidates for the general election. In seventeen of the States,[1] however, at least some of the delegates to the national conventions are *elected* at the primary. This method for popularly choosing national convention delegates is known as the *presidential primary*. Details of presidential primary laws vary from State to State. In the matter of dates, for example, New Hampshire held the first 1952 presidential primary on March 11, and California and South Dakota held the last ones on June 3.

In some States the party voters also express a preference among the party's possible nominees for President. This type of presidential primary is commonly known as the *presidential preference primary*.

Thus, in Oregon[2] in 1952 the Republican voters expressed a preference for Dwight Eisenhower, and all eighteen of the Republican delegates they selected were bound to support him in the convention. Oregon's Democratic voters expressed a preference for Estes Kefauver, and the twelve Democratic delegates were pledged to his support.

---

[1] In California, Massachusetts, Nebraska, New Hampshire, New Jersey, Ohio, Oregon, South Dakota, West Virginia, and Wisconsin, all the national convention delegates are chosen at the primaries. In Illinois, Maryland, Minnesota, New York, and Pennsylvania some delegates are also chosen by the State executive committee or by the State convention of each party. In Alabama and Florida all the Democratic delegates are selected at the primaries, while the Republican delegations are chosen by convention in Alabama and by the executive committee in Florida.

[2] Oregon was the first State to provide (1910) for a preferential primary. Its adoption came as a part of the famous Oregon System which was designed to accomplish more popular participation in and control of government. The Oregon System included the initiative and referendum, the recall, and the direct primary.

In some of these States only some of the national convention delegates are selected at the primaries while the rest are chosen at the State convention or by the State executive (central) committee. Thus, in New York in 1952 national convention delegates were selected by both the presidential primary and the convention method in each party; and in Pennsylvania they were selected by primary and committee.

Fitzpatrick—St. Louis Post-Dispatch

A great many people advocate the selection of all national convention delegates through presidential primaries. Others suggest that the conventions be done away with (except to draft platforms) and that the people nominate the major party candidates at a nation-wide presidential preference primary.

Elections. — *When Held.* — Most States hold their elections for the selection of State officers at the same time that presidential electors and United States senators and representatives are chosen — Tuesday after the first Monday in November of even-numbered years. However, Virginia, Kentucky, and Mississippi hold State elections in November of odd-numbered years.

Maine chooses its state officials on the second Monday of September in even-numbered years. For many years its election returns were regarded as fairly reliable forecasts of national trends in politics. In recent years this has not been the case. When State elections are held at a different time from the National elections, the voters pay more attention to State issues, and are not so likely to vote a straight Democratic or Republican ticket as they are during the excitement of a National campaign.

City and local election dates differ from state to state, occurring usually in the spring.

How Held. — For each voting district or precinct into which the county or city is divided, the county clerk, city clerk, board of election commissioners, or some designated officer provides a polling place, equipped with booths, a ballot-box, or voting machine, poll books. tickets, and in some States a flag. On election day the polls are open during prescribed hours — commonly from 8 A.M. to 8 P.M., but sometimes longer.

Each polling place is in charge of judges of election, whose duty it is to pass upon voters' qualifications. The judges have clerks to assist them. They open and close the polls, count the ballots, and certify the results to the proper officials (*e.g.*, county board of elections or county clerk). A "watcher" from each political party is permitted to be present at the voting place to challenge any person whom he does not believe to be qualified to vote, and to see that the votes are fairly counted.

Australian Method of Voting. — The Australians devised a secret method of voting, which found its way to the United States through England. In 1888 the Kentucky legislature adopted it for municipal elections in Louisville, and the following year Massachusetts adopted it for all elections. All States use this method today.

The Australian method of voting is as follows: The voter enters a room in which no one is allowed except election officers, "watchers," and perhaps a policeman. He gives his name, and if it is found on the registration book, he is given a ballot, which he carries into a booth about three feet square. After marking the ballot he folds it, comes from the booth, and goes to the ballot box where the ballot is deposited for counting. The ballots have been printed at public expense, and no official ballot may be taken from the voting place. Sample

MASSACHUSETTS BALLOT OF THE AUSTRALIAN TYPE FOR THE 1952 ELECTION

ELECTORS OF PRESIDENT AND VICE PRESIDENT.

To vote for Electors of President and Vice President under any one of the following Party Names or Political Designations, mark a Cross X in the Square at the right of each Party Name or Political Designation.

Vote for ONE

- EISENHOWER and NIXON — Republican
- HALLINAN and BASS — Peace Progressive
- HAMBLEN and HOLTWICK — Prohibition
- HASS and EMERY — Socialist Labor
- STEVENSON and SPARKMAN — Democratic

To vote for a Person, mark a Cross X in the Square at the right of the Party Name or Political Designation.

GOVERNOR — Vote for ONE
- PAUL A. DEVER — of Cambridge — Democratic
- CHRISTIAN A. HERTER — of Boston — Republican
- LAWRENCE GILFEDDER — of Boston — Socialist Labor
- FLORENCE H. LUSCOMB — of Cambridge — Peace Progressive
- GUY S. WILLIAMS — of Worcester — Prohibition

LIEUTENANT GOVERNOR — Vote for ONE
- CHARLES J. JEFF SULLIVAN — of Worcester — Democratic
- SUMNER G. WHITTIER — of Everett — Republican
- WILLIAM H. TERRY — of Boston — Prohibition
- FRANCIS M. VOTANO — of Lynn — Socialist Labor

SECRETARY — Vote for ONE
- EDWARD J. CRONIN — of Chelsea — Democratic
- BEATRICE HANCOCK MULLANEY — of Fall River — Republican
- ALICE M. FERRY — of Boston — Socialist Labor
- FRED M. INGERSOLL — of Lynn — Prohibition

TREASURER — Vote for ONE
- FOSTER FURCOLO — of Longmeadow — Democratic
- ROY CHARLES PAPALIA — of Watertown — Republican
- HENNING A. BLOMEN — of Boston — Socialist Labor
- HAROLD E. IRELAND — of Worcester — Prohibition

AUDITOR — Vote for ONE
- THOMAS J. BUCKLEY — of Boston — Democratic
- DAVID J. KAYE — of Boston — Republican
- ANTHONY MARTIN — of Boston — Socialist Labor
- ROBERT T. SIMMONS — of Boston — Prohibition

ATTORNEY GENERAL — Vote for ONE
- FRANCIS E. KELLY — of Boston — Democratic
- GEORGE FINGOLD — of Concord — Republican
- ARTHUR N. KLEMAN — of Malden — Socialist Labor
- EDWARD N. RAND — of Haverhill — Prohibition

SENATOR IN CONGRESS — Vote for ONE
- HENRY CABOT LODGE, Jr. — of Beverly — Republican
- JOHN F. KENNEDY — of Boston — Democratic
- THELMA INGERSOLL — of Lynn — Prohibition
- MARK R. SHAW — of Melrose — ——

CONGRESSMAN — Tenth District — Vote for ONE
- LAURENCE CURTIS — of Boston — Republican
- FREDERICK C. HAILER, Jr. — of Boston — Democratic
- KATHERINE E. GODDARD — of Boston — Prohibition

COUNCILLOR — Second District — Vote for ONE
- CHARLES I. GARDNER — of Hingham — Republican
- CHARLES L. McGRATH — of Boston — Democratic

SENATOR — First Suffolk District — Vote for ONE
- DANIEL RUDSTEN — of Boston — Democratic
- JEANNE BROOT WELBERG — of Boston — Republican

REPRESENTATIVES IN GENERAL COURT — Vote for TWO
- GEORGE GREENE — of Boston — Democratic
- EDWARD W. BROOKE — of Boston — Independent-Republican
- DWIGHT GATEWAY — of Boston — Republican
- LEO DONEAG — of Boston — Democratic

CLERK OF SUPREME JUDICIAL COURT — Suffolk County — Vote for ONE
- CHESTER E. DOLAN, Jr. — of Beverly — Democratic

CLERK OF SUPERIOR COURT (Civil Business) — Suffolk County — Vote for ONE
- THOMAS DORGAN — of Boston — Democratic
- ALEXANDER PLESS — of Boston — Republican

CLERK OF SUPERIOR COURT (Criminal Business) — Suffolk County — Vote for ONE
- WILLIAM MICHAEL PRENDIBLE — of Boston — Democratic

REGISTER OF DEEDS — Suffolk County — Vote for ONE
- LEO J. SULLIVAN — of Boston — Democratic
- EDWARD LOWELL DAVIS — of Boston — Republican

To vote on a Question, mark a Cross X in the Square at the right of YES or NO.

QUESTION NO. 1

A. Shall licenses be granted in this city (or town) for the sale therein of all alcoholic beverages (whisky, rum, gin, malt beverages, wines and all other alcoholic beverages)?
— YES / NO

B. Shall licenses be granted in this city (or town) for the sale therein of wines and malt beverages (wines and beer, do and all other malt beverages)?
— YES / NO

C. Shall licenses be granted in this city (or town) for the sale of all alcoholic beverages in packages, so called, not to be drunk on the premises?
— YES / NO

ballots printed on colored paper are commonly available; and in some States a "sample ballot" is mailed to each voter before the election day; but this, of course, cannot be used for voting.

Several States now permit the use of voting machines, which the voter manipulates by pulling a lever for the candidates or measures he favors. The machine automatically counts the votes, thus eliminating the long, expensive counting process. These machines are expensive, but soon pay for themselves in time and convenience. They reduce the possibility of "stuffed" ballot boxes and provide a permanent record of the votes cast. They have been extremely useful in cities where a great number of voters must be handled at the polls. The machines also eliminate "scratch" (improperly marked) ballots. The arrangement of levers does make voting a "straight ticket" easier, and some claim that the machines are too difficult to operate. But these latter objections are far outweighed by the many advantages.

Origin of Ballots in the States. — For many years our voting was oral in the presence of the public, and this encouraged vote-buying and intimidation. So the States gradually abandoned *viva voce* voting, but in the South it continued until after the Civil War.

Unofficial written ballots were at first substituted for the *viva voce* method, each voter preparing his own ballot. Then the candidates began to print their own ballots; and finally the political party had ballots printed — each party having ballots of a different color. Thus the new method was just as public as the old. A vote-buyer, friend, or employer could know how you voted from the color of your ballot or could see you deposit the ballot which he had prepared for you.

Ballots Now in Use. — While all forty-eight of the States now follow the general feature of the Australian plan and have made elections secret, less than half use the true Australian ballot, but the number is increasing. The Australian ballot places the names of the candidates of all parties for a given office in alphabetical order, giving each candidate's party affiliation after his name. Rotating the names of candidates is an improvement over the alphabetical arrangement. (See the Massachusetts ballot on page 453.)

In many States the Party Column ballot is still in use. On such a ballot all the names of the candidates of one party for the various offices are arranged in a vertical column under the party's name, usually with a circle at the top in which the voter by placing a cross mark

therein may vote for all of the candidates of that party — "a straight
ticket." This arrangement works in
the interest of a strongly organized
party because even an ignorant voter
can vote the ticket for all members
of the party. The accompanying top
of an Indiana ballot illustrates a Party
Column ballot.

The Short Ballot Movement. — *The
Usual American Ballot Is Too Long.* —
The classic recent example of an extra
long ballot is that voted in Omaha in
1946. The ballot was thirteen feet long
and contained 26,000 words. It would
have required four hours to read. Besides candidates, the ballot contained
57 questions — chiefly proposals for a
new auditorium, river terminal, civic
center, and the like, for Omaha City.
The appearance on the ballot of the
names of candidates for so many different offices is very confusing. It is next
to impossible for the average voter to
remember those for whom he wishes to
vote, much less to know their qualifications. (See pages 651–652.)

A Long Ballot Leads to Blind Voting.
— Instances of this confusion could be
cited in almost every district when an
election takes place. Some years ago
immediately after an election, figures
were collected from the most independent Assembly District in Brooklyn, New
York, which showed that 87 per cent of
the voters did not know the name of
the State treasurer just elected. When
the names of candidates for scores

TOP OF THE 1948 INDIANA
PARTY COLUMN BALLOT

of offices appear on a ballot, practically all voters cast a straight ticket.

Blind Voting Leads to Government by Politicians. — Because of the scores of officers to be voted for, about nine tenths of the voters vote

"FOR EXPERTS ONLY"

Conscientious citizens are unable to vote a long ballot intelligently and unwilling to put cross-mark at top and vote straight party ticket.

blindly, that is, vote a straight ticket. By so doing they practically ratify the "appointments" made by the other tenth — the politicians who nominate the men for office. Hence most of our officers are practically appointed by politicians.

The National Municipal League is promoting the short ballot movement through its monthly publication, *The National Municipal Review*. Its purpose is to educate the people to the fact that most officers are actually chosen by politicians, whereas the people imagine that they are electing them. This organization advocates the election of important officers for long terms. It would allow these few to appoint the others. For instance, the State governor, State legislator, county commissioner, city councilor or commissioner, and mayor could be elected. The other State officers could then be chosen by the governor, county officers by the county board of commissioners, and city officers by a small council or commission, or by the mayor or the manager. This would center the authority and responsibility in a few officers, who could be more easily watched by the voters.

The present method of electing officers is a puzzle, the intricacies of which are understood only by politicians. Those who favor the short ballot would make the election process so simple that even the voter might understand it and be able to know something about those for whom he is to vote. They claim this system would produce a democ-

VIRGINIA SCHEME OF ELECTIONS

1955	1956	1957	1958
Various County and District officials State Senator State Delegate	President and V. President U. S. Senator U. S. Representative	Governor Lieut. Governor Attorney General State Delegate	U. S. Senator U. S. Representative

City elections are held in June. County Clerks serve eight years.

racy *in fact* instead of a democracy *in theory:* that we now have a *democracy in theory — a politicians' oligarchy in fact.*

Short Ballot. — A few States have attained a short ballot. For example, Virginia has attained the short ballot by five methods:

1. Longer terms of office.

2. More appointive State and local officials.

3. City-manager government with appointive officials.

4. National, State, local elections separate years — November.

5. City elections in June.

The accompanying illustration is a good example of the short ballot.

In Virginia there are four elections (not including primaries) in four years (plus city elections), and this makes possible a more careful considera-

---

OFFICIAL BALLOT

GENERAL ELECTION

Shenandoah County, Virginia

Tuesday, November 8, 1949.

FOR GOVERNOR
(Vote For One)

☐ JOHN S. BATTLE
☐ WALTER JOHNSON
☐ CLARKE T. ROBB

FOR LIEUTENANT GOVERNOR
(Vote For One)

☐ LEWIS PRESTON COLLINS
☐ E. THOMAS McGUIRE

FOR ATTORNEY GENERAL
(Vote For One)

☐ J. LINDSAY ALMOND, JR.
☐ SIDNEY MOORE

FOR HOUSE OF DELEGATES
(Vote For One)

☐ V. S. SHAFFER

VIRGINIA SHORT BALLOT

tion of each set of candidates and issues. Neither are the more numerous elections expensive when so few names have to be printed, voted, and counted.

Proportional Representation seeks to give to parties, or groups of voters who have a common view on political questions, representation in proportion to their voting strength.

It has been used extensively in Europe because there a number of small parties can combine their strength in constitutional conventions and demand representation according to the number of votes cast by each party. But from the American standpoint it has caused endless bickering and instability of government.

In the United States under our two-party system the candidate getting the most votes is declared elected. Proportional representation is fairer to minority parties, but the method of counting the ballots is slow and complicated, and party responsibility is lost. For this reason and because of European experiences, none of our States, and less than a dozen small and medium-sized cities, together with Cincinnati, have the proportional representation system.

The main argument for the system is that you can elect from a large area, or city as a whole, and that the bigger the area from which you can choose, the better the representative is likely to be. The system also makes it possible for the voter to express successive preferences for the best men in several parties; and representation from different parties gives broader understanding in legislative sessions.

New York City inaugurated proportional representation for electing its city council in 1937, but in 1947 voted to abolish the system and at the next election(1949) to choose one member of the city council from each of the 25 senatorial districts within the city limits, under the common plurality system.

In the New York City elections of 1937, 1941, and 1945 under the system of proportional representation each of the five Boroughs was entitled to a councilman for every 75,000 valid votes cast therein. Any number of candidates could be nominated and get their names on the Borough ballot by having 2000 registered voters sign a petition. The voter wrote the figure 1 before the candidate he wanted most to elect, the figure 2 before his second choice, and consecutive numbers as far as he cared to continue. After the elections all ballots voted in a Borough were taken to a central place to be counted.

In Manhattan Borough in 1945 all ballots were first sorted into pigeonholes according to the first choice expressed on each ballot. The total number of valid ballots was divided by 75,000 and the result entitled the Borough to 4 Councilmen. Had any candidate received 75,000 votes he would have been declared elected. Candidates with fewer than 2000 votes were eliminated and their ballots awarded to second-choice candidates. When these second choices added to the first choices of another candidate totaled 75,000 he was declared elected. Next, the candidate receiving the least number of first choices was declared defeated, and his ballots were distributed according to the second choice expressed thereon. (Or if the second choice was for a candidate already declared elected it was distributed according to the third choice, or highest choice for a candidate not already declared elected.) Then the next lowest candidate was declared defeated, and his ballots were distributed in the same manner. The count continued by dropping the next low candidate until four candidates had obtained 75,000 votes or only four remained.

The Recall. — When the people elect very few officers and trust everything to them, it seems advisable to be able to remove those who do not give satisfaction. Therefore twelve States and several hundred cities, principally of the commission and commission-manager types, reserve the right to remove such officers.

Whenever a prescribed number of voters, the number varying from State to State, become sufficiently dissatisfied with an officer to petition for a new election, the officer whom they wish to remove must again stand for election. If the officer receives more votes than any other person who has offered himself as a candidate, he remains in office, but if any other candidate receives more than he, he is removed from office; that is, he is recalled by the people.

Direct Legislation. — The idea of the short ballot movement is to reduce the number of elective officers so that the voters may know the qualifications of those whom they elect. If these few officers refuse to enact laws desired by the people, the voters themselves may enact them by means of the *Initiative*. If they pass improper laws, the *Referendum* enables the voters to prevent the final enactment of such laws. Or if the officers prove incompetent or dishonest, they may be removed by the *Recall*. The chart on the next page further illustrates popular participation in legislation. (See also pages 487–8.)

Initiative is a political device whereby when 5 to 8 percent of the voters sign a petition a law that the people are interested must be voted upon by a) the people directly or 2) by the legislative body

POPULAR PARTICIPATION IN LEGISLATION[1]

Initiative	*Direct*. (Referred to the voters directly without being submitted to the legislative body.)	Constitutional Statutory
	Indirect. (Referred to the legislative body, and if enacted by this body, reference to the people is unnecessary.)	Statutory only

Referendum	*Mandatory by a constitutional provision* (also called compulsory or obligatory). Examples: State constitutional amendments; bond issues; amendment of home rule charters.	
	Optional with a legislative body (also called voluntary). Examples: A measure passed by a body with legislative power and submitted to the voters for ratification; a proposed law submitted to the voters for advice before action by the legislature.	Submitted for ratification. Submitted for advice.
	Appeal from a legislative body through popular petition. Example: An unpopular legislative Act voted on at special election called by petition of specified number of voters.	

Recall	Of legislative and executive officers. Of judicial officers also.

This direct action on the part of the people demands enlightenment on the part of the voters, and for this purpose many of the States which have adopted the Initiative and Referendum send a pamphlet to each voter before an election giving in condensed form the strongest arguments on each side of every question referred to them. Thus with this publicity the people may become better prepared to vote upon the various issues with a degree of enlightenment.

If too many measures are submitted to the people, the voters are just as burdened as when they have too many officers to elect. Woodrow Wilson argued that these safeguards should be considered merely as "a gun behind the door" to be used only in cases of emergency.

[1] The Initiative, Referendum, and Recall have been incorporated more or less completely in the charters of hundreds of cities and towns in the United States and are in successful operation. Many such municipalities are not in the Initiative and Referendum States listed on page 461. The Initiative, Referendum, and Recall were granted by the legislatures by means of general laws or special charters.

Voters or 10,000 sign a petition
a bill passed by the legislature
may be referred to the people at the
next election.

PROGRESS OF THE INITIATIVE, REFERENDUM, AND RECALL

Percentages in this table refer to voters required on petitions

Where Adopted	When	Statutory Initiative	Constitutional Initiative	Popular Petition Referendum	Recall
So. Dakota	1898	5% indirect[1]		5%	
Utah	1900	5% indirect 10% direct		10%	
Oregon	1902	8% direct	8% direct	5%	25%
Nevada	1904, 1912	10% 1912 indirect	10% 1912 indirect	10% 1904	25% 1912
Montana	1906	8% direct		5%	
Oklahoma	1907	8% direct	15% direct	5%	
Maine	1908	12,000 indirect		10,000	
Missouri	1908	8% direct	8% direct	5%	
Michigan	1908, 1913	8% 1913 indirect	10% 1913 direct	5%	25% 1913
Arkansas	1910	8% direct	10% direct	6%	Carried, but killed by Supreme Court
Colorado	1910	8% direct	8% direct	5%	25%
Arizona	1911	10% direct	15% direct	5%	25%
New Mexico	1911			25% in $\frac{3}{4}$ of counties	
California	1911	5% indirect 8% direct	8% direct	5%	12–25%
Ohio	1912	3% indirect 6% direct	10% direct	6%	
Nebraska	1912, 1920	7% direct	10% direct	5%	
Washington	1912	50,000 and indirect		30,000	25% State 35% local
Idaho	1933	10% direct		10%	10% State 20% county
No. Dakota	1914	10,000 direct	20,000 direct	7000	30% 1920
Kansas	1914				10, 15, 25%
Louisiana	1914				25%
Maryland	1915			10,000 voters[2]	
Massachusetts	1918	25,000 indirect	25,000 indirect	15,000	
Wisconsin	1933				25–33%

[1] "Indirect" means that opportunity must first be given for action by the legislature on initiated measures.

[2] Laws for any one county or Baltimore city may be referred to the voters thereof on a 10% petition.

QUESTIONS ON THE TEXT

1. Name five different methods of nominating candidates.
2. Describe a delegate convention.
3. Describe a direct primary election.
4. What is meant by nomination by petition?
5. Distinguish between the words *primary* and *direct primary.*
6. What is meant by the "closed" primary? By the "open" primary? What advantages and disadvantages has each?
7. Is the direct primary "an opportunity" or a "cure" of election evils? Explain.
8. Give arguments for the direct primary.
9. Give arguments against the direct primary.
10. When are most elections held for choosing State officers? Federal officers? City officers?
11. Explain just how an election is held — officers, place, equipment, ballots, booths, poll books, time of day, "watcher."
12. Explain the Australian method of voting and tell just how it was introduced into the United States.
13. Why do some people object to voting machines?
14. Explain why secret voting has come to take the place of the *viva voce* method.
15. Describe an Australian ballot.
16. Should the names of candidates be arranged on the ballot in party columns, or alphabetically, or rotated?
17. What is meant by the short ballot movement? Give the arguments in favor of short ballots.
18. Explain the Virginia method of obtaining the short ballot.
19. Explain proportional representation.
20. Explain the *Initiative;* the *Referendum.*
21. Explain the *Recall.*

PROBLEMS FOR DISCUSSION

1. What provision is made in your State constitution in regard to State elections?
2. Upon what date is your State election held? City election? National election? County election? Do you think that National, State, and local elections should be held on different dates?
3. Obtain a copy of the last ballot voted at your home and compare it with those printed in this chapter. Which do you consider to be the best? Why?

4. Have a member of your family make a list of the present National, State, county, and township, city or village officials voted on by the people in your community. If no one can do this, do you not think that it is a strong indication that more officers are being elected than the voters are capable of electing wisely? Which of them do you think should be appointed?

5. Explain the following quotation, which favors a "short ballot": "We cannot make the voters all go into politics, but by a drastic reduction in the number of elective officers we can make politics come to the voters."

6. As indicated by the name, proportional representation means apportioned according to party strength. Our usual system of plurality election results in the strongest party electing nearly all of the officers. In the New York proportional representation election in 1937 the Democrats elected 13 Councilmen and the minority parties or coalitions elected 13. Do you think a council dominated by one party or this mixed council is more likely to be efficient? Just to all groups?

7. Only one party is permitted in Russia. In the United States we usually have two strong parties and sometimes several other parties. Some countries, like France, have many parties. Do you think one, two, or many is best?

8. Prepare an argument on the subject, "Eternal vigilance is the price of liberty."

9. In 1896 the Municipal Voters' League of Chicago was organized to promote efficient government in Chicago. It investigates the records of candidates nominated by the regular party organizations and furnishes information pertaining to each candidate to the voters of the city. Its membership is never called together, its work being directed by an executive committee of nine members. This committee has the sole authority to commit the organization for or against any candidate or measure. Are the voters of your community informed as to the qualifications of candidates, or do you need such an organization?

10. Do you think the voters are more likely to elect the best candidates under the Chicago long ballot system or the Virginia short ballot system? Though Virginia holds more elections, the total cost over a four-year period is greater in Chicago than in Virginia, because the Virginia ballots cost so little and the time required to count them is so short. The number of ballots cast is greater where many officers are elected at one time, but do you suppose the quality is as good?

11. The legislature of each State determines the method of choosing its presidential electors every fourth year. Most States have allowed the people to vote for long lists of electors; but a newer and better method is to have

the party State committees or party State conventions nominate the requisite number of electors for each party and direct them to vote for the Presidential and Vice-Presidential candidates for whom the majority of voters express a preference at the November election. Study again the Wisconsin and Massachusetts ballots (pages 170 and 453) as examples of this simpler method. Would you favor having your State omit the names of electors from the ballot? Would you favor the direct popular election of the President?

12. In Nebraska each party holds an advisory nominating convention composed of 400 delegates elected in the preceding general election. In positions where two or more candidates offer themselves for party nomination the convention designates candidates for first and second place on the ballot. Additional candidates may follow these on the primary ballot. Why do you favor or oppose this modification of the direct primary system?

SELECT BIBLIOGRAPHY

Election Laws of Your State. (Usually free from the Secretary of State.) Sample ballots.

BENDINER, R. "Portrait of the Perfect Candidate." *New York Times Magazine.* May 18, 1952.

FRANK, S. "Campaigns Can Change Elections." *Nation's Business.* September, 1952.

KEY, V. O. *Politics, Parties, and Pressure Groups.* Crowell. New York. 1952 ed. Chapters 14, 15, and 22.

PENNIMAN, H. *Sait's American Parties and Elections.* Appleton-Century-Crofts. New York. 1952 ed. Chapters 19, 20, and 27.

STOKES, T. "Getting Nominated Is Intricate Business." *New York Times Magazine.* April 20, 1952.

Time. "And May the Best Man Win." Chicago. 1952.

GRAVES, W. *American State Government.* Heath. Boston. 1953 ed. Chapters 4 and 5.

BINKLEY, W., AND MOOS, A. *A Grammar of American Politics.* Knopf. New York. 1952 ed. Chapters 8–14.

SWARTHOUT, J., AND BARTLEY, E. *Principles and Problems of American National Government.* Oxford Univ. Press. New York. 1954 ed. Chapters 7 and 8.

CHAPTER XXVI

STATE CONSTITUTIONS

History. — When the Revolutionary War ended the thirteen colonies of North America became thirteen independent States. Each was faced with the problem of establishing its own government and making its own laws. And the only advice they had came from the Continental Congress on May 15, 1776, telling them "*to adopt such government as shall in the opinion of the representatives of the people, best conduce to the happiness and safety of their constituents in particular, and America in general.*"

There was no uniform type or pattern of government in the colonies. The charters granted them by England contained varying provisions according to the particular colony. Quite naturally the thirteen colonies turned to their charters for guidance in writing their new State constitutions; and quite naturally the results were not uniform.

Adoption of the State Constitutions. — The new Constitutions were to be *written* documents setting forth the fundamental principles by which the State would govern itself in the new Union. Between 1776 and 1780 every State adopted a new constitution except Connecticut and Rhode Island. These constitutions were very similar to the colonial charters. Connecticut and Rhode Island found their charters so liberal that they merely renounced their allegiance to the King of England and continued to be governed by the provisions of their charters until 1818 and 1842 respectively.

The first State constitutions were framed by conventions or congresses, some of which were composed of members of the State assemblies, while others were especially constituted for the purpose. The people were given scant opportunity to approve or reject these documents. Only in Massachusetts and New Hampshire was approval by the people thought essential. However, all the State constitutions in

465

existence today were framed by assemblies representing the people, and a large majority of them have been approved by the people.[1]

State Constitutions Analyzed. — State constitutions commonly consist of six parts:

(1) A *preamble* stating the general purpose for which the government is organized.

✓ (2) A *Bill of Rights* listing certain rights which must not be infringed upon even by enactments of the legislature.

✓ (3) *Provisions for the organization of the legislative, executive, and judicial departments*, and the powers and duties of each.

✓ (4) *Provisions of miscellaneous character* treating of such subjects as suffrage, elections, revenues, expenditures, local government, public education, and railroads and other corporations.

✓ (5) *Provisions for future changes* by partial amendment or total revision.

(6) A *schedule* providing for such matters as submitting the new constitution to the voters and putting it into operation without conflicting with the previous constitution.

Amendment and Revision of State Constitutions. — The wisest of constitution-makers cannot hope to build for all time. An essential part of any constitution is, therefore, the provision of methods whereby the fundamental law may be improved upon or altered to take account of social and economic change. When many changes are to be made, a *convention* is called to revise the old constitution or frame a new one. For only a few changes, the simpler procedure of *partial amendment* is used.

Constitutional Conventions. — A constitutional convention is an assembly of delegates chosen by the voters to revise an old constitution or to frame a new one. In all States the constitution may be changed by a convention, but in most States it must then be ratified by the voters.

There are usually three popular votes connected with a new or re-

---

[1] Congress never admits a new State into the Union until the territory desiring to be admitted has framed its constitution. On the admission of some States Congress has passed an Act empowering the people of a territory to hold a convention and frame a constitution; on the admission of other States Congress has accepted and confirmed the constitution previously drawn up by a territorial convention. No State may be divided or formed by the union of existing States without the consent of the legislatures of the States concerned and of Congress.

vised constitution: (1) the vote of the people authorizing a convention, (2) the election by the voters of delegates to the convention, and (3) the submission to the people for approval of the constitution framed by the convention.[1]

OPENING SESSION OF THE CONSTITUTIONAL CONVENTION AT ALBANY

Missouri Convention of 1943. — The Missouri Constitution requires a vote every 20 years as to whether a constitutional convention shall be held. In 1942 the people voted "yes"; in 1943 delegates were elected; and in 1945 an entirely new constitution only two thirds as long as the old one was ratified by a two to one majority of the State voters. The new constitution had cost about a million dollars, but it is worth it. The following are some changes in the new constitution:

Seventy-odd departments, boards, etc., reduced to fourteen.
Civil Service Merit System introduced in some State institutions.
Cities of 10,000 or more may frame their own charters — "home rule."
State required to support public libraries.
Legislature may give exceptional consent for white-colored schools.

---

[1] Some States dispense with one or more of these votes; and in 1890 the Mississippi Legislature provided for an election at which delegates were chosen, and when the delegates had framed the constitution they adopted it without consulting the people.

Intangibles (money, stocks, bonds) are taxed on yield instead of on market price and at a rate not to exceed 8 per cent of yield.

Legislature may reduce taxes for 25 years to encourage reconstruction of city slums or reforestation of lands not suitable for farming.

The New York Constitution of 1938 was submitted to the voters in nine parts to prevent unpopular changes from defeating the whole constitution. Only six parts were approved.

Partial Amendment. — The partial amendment procedure involves two steps: proposal and ratification. In New Hampshire, amendments as well as revision may be proposed only by a convention. But in the other forty-seven States amendments may be proposed by the legislature, and in thirteen States the people themselves may propose amendments.

Legislative Proposal. — The details of legislative proposal vary from State to State. In some States the process is fairly simple, while in a few it is extremely difficult. Both the California constitution of 1879 and the Louisiana constitution of 1921 have been altered some three hundred times. Tennessee's 1870 constitution was not amended until 1953. In both California and Louisiana the legislature may propose as many amendments as it cares to and ratification is secured by a simple majority of those voting thereon at the polls. In Tennessee, until 1953, amendments had to be proposed by a majority vote in each house at one session, and a two-thirds vote of each house in the next session, and then must be ratified by a majority of the people who vote for members of the legislature at the next election.

In thirty-four States amendments may be proposed by a single session, but the other thirteen [1] require proposal at two successive sessions. Only simple majority approval is required in each house in eighteen of the States,[2] but a two-thirds majority is needed in another eighteen,[3] while seven States require three-fifths.[4]

---

[1] Connecticut, Delaware, Indiana, Iowa, Massachusetts, Nevada, New York, Pennsylvania, Rhode Island, Tennessee, Vermont, Virginia, Wisconsin.

[2] Arizona, Arkansas, Indiana, Iowa, Massachusetts, Minnesota, Missouri, Nevada, New Mexico, New York, North Dakota, Oklahoma, Oregon, Pennsylvania, Rhode Island, South Dakota, Virginia, Wisconsin.

[3] California, Colorado, Delaware, Georgia, Idaho, Illinois, Kansas, Louisiana, Maine, Michigan, Mississippi, Montana, South Carolina, Texas, Utah, Washington, West Virginia, Wyoming.

[4] Alabama, Florida, Kentucky, Maryland, Nebraska, North Carolina, Ohio. New Jersey's 1947 constitution provides for either a three-fifths vote in one session

A few States limit the number of amendments that may be submitted to the voters at any one election; for example, in Kansas no more than three, and in Kentucky two. In Illinois, no single legislature may propose amendments to more than one article; in Colorado, to more than six articles. Various restrictions of this sort are found in other States.

Proposal by Popular Initiative. — Beginning with Oregon in 1902, thirteen States now provide for the proposal of constitutional amendments by the people themselves.[1] This procedure is known as the *initiative* because the amendments are initiated by the voters. Any individual or group may draft a proposal. If the required number of qualified voters signs an *initiative petition* the measure is then placed on the ballot. By this method the people take a direct part in the amending process.

In Massachusetts 25,000 and in North Dakota 20,000 qualified voters must sign the petition. The other eleven States each require a certain percentage, *e.g.*, eight per cent in Oregon and California, ten per cent in Ohio and Michigan, fifteen per cent in Arizona. As in the case of proposal by the legislature, the details of proposal by initiative petition vary from State to State.[2]

Ratification of Amendments. — In every State except Delaware, all amendments, whether proposed by the legislature or by initiative, must be ratified by the voters before they become effective.[3] Proposed amendments are usually placed before the voters at a regular election, but in some States special elections are also called for the purpose.

Generally, approval of a majority of those voting *on the amendment* makes it a part of the constitution. But again there are exceptions.

---

or a majority vote in two successive sessions. Connecticut requires a majority vote of the house of representatives in one session and a two-thirds vote of each house in the next; Tennessee a majority vote in each house in two successive legislative sessions; Vermont a majority of the house and two-thirds of the senate in one session and a majority of each house in the next.

[1] Arizona, Arkansas, California, Colorado, Massachusetts, Michigan, Missouri, Nebraska, Nevada, North Dakota, Ohio, Oklahoma, Oregon.

[2] For instance, in Massachusetts before an initiative proposal may be submitted to the voters it first must be approved by one-fourth of all the members of the legislature in joint session at two consecutive legislatures. In Arkansas, the petition must contain signatures of voters from each of fifteen counties; in Nebraska, from each of two-fifths of the State's counties, and in Ohio from each of one-half of that State's counties.

[3] In South Carolina and Mississippi *final* ratification, after a favorable popular vote, rests with the legislature.

Minnesota, Mississippi, Oklahoma, Tennessee, and Wyoming require a majority of all voting *in the election.* Many times amendments have been defeated in those States although they actually received more affirmative than negative votes.

Recent Trends. — (1) *Constitutions are becoming longer.* The Virginia constitution, written in 1776, was less than six pages in length; today it is ten times longer. The constitution of Rhode Island, which contains about 8000 words, is the shortest of them all, while California holds the record in length with over 75,000 words.

(2) *The newer constitutions provide more power for the government rather than less.* This partially accounts for the length of present constitutions. The government performs hundreds of functions that were once withheld from it; and the representatives of the people apparently have lost confidence in the ordinary legislator and hence include in the constitution itself many detailed laws which were originally left to be enacted by the legislature. Therefore, the newer constitutions carry specific provisions for the regulation of such phases of life as banking, insurance, labor, education, and charity.

(3) *Constitutions are easier to amend.* Laws which go into great detail need to be amended frequently, and for this reason many States have accepted the initiative, referendum, and legislative proposal as easy methods of amending their constitutions.

Authority of State Constitutions. — The constitution with its amendments constitutes the supreme law of the State, and it overrides any laws enacted by the legislature which conflict therewith. Whenever a legislature passes a law which conflicts with some provision of the constitution, the first person who is in any way inconvenienced by the law may refuse to abide by it, and permit some one to sue him because he knows that the court will or should declare the law null and void, that is, of no force.

For example, some years ago the legislature of New York State enacted a law providing that any employer whose workmen are injured in certain enumerated dangerous pursuits, such as stone quarrying, must compensate the workmen by a money payment, whether the employer was at fault or not. The first employee who was injured demanded his money. The employer refused to pay him, claiming that the law was contrary to the constitution of the State. The workman sued the employer, but the highest court of the State (Court of

Appeals) decided that the law did conflict with the constitution, was thus null and void, and could not be enforced.

The legislature still thought that there should be such a law; therefore two successive sessions proposed an amendment to the constitution and submitted it to the people. The majority of voters cast their ballots in favor of it, and thus changed the constitution so that the next legislature could enact the same workmen's compensation law, for it would no longer conflict with the constitution. The next legislature did pass the law, and today the courts enforce it.

Relative Rank of Laws in the United States. — By its very nature, the Constitution of the United States is the supreme law of the land, and every other law is subordinate to it. If Congress passes any statute which conflicts with the Constitution of the United States or if the President and Senate make any treaty which conflicts with the Constitution of the United States, such statute or treaty will not be enforced by the courts.

Likewise, if a State constitution contains any provision which is contrary to the Constitution of the United States or to a statute of Congress, it cannot be enforced. Furthermore, if a State legislature enacts a statute contrary to the Constitution of the United States, a statute of Congress, or a provision of the State constitution, it cannot be enforced. Or if a county board or town or city council passes a by-law contrary to any of these laws, it is void and the courts will not enforce it. In brief, our national, State, and local laws rank as follows:

United States Constitution.
    United States statutes, treaties, and executive orders.
        State constitutions.
            State statutes.
                County, town, or city statutes, called county "regulations" or "by-laws" and town or city "ordinances" or "by-laws."

It is impracticable to write definite laws regulating in detail all possible human actions; so in addition to the written laws we have a set of rules and principles which are not written in any definite form but are enforced by the government. These rules and principles grew out of custom and court decisions in England during a number of centuries, and because they were uniform throughout all England they were called *common law*. A similar branch of law, known as *equity*, will be discussed in Chapter XXX. When the American States became independent of England they retained the English common law to supplement their definite written laws.

As each American State has a distinct system of courts the common law rules and principles have undergone change in some details in the various States; but as decisions of the courts of each State are known to the judges of the courts of each of the other States these rules and principles remain very much the same throughout the country.[1]

If there is a case in court for which there is no definite written law or precedent, it must be decided according to the rules of common law or analogy. Occasionally a case arises which is unlike any previous case: for instance, a suit growing out of the collision of an airplane with a balloon. In the absence of an expressed law governing such a collision, the rules establishing a standard of care in the case of steamships and sailing vessels might be applied. The rules of the sea have long required the steamship to give the sailing vessel the right of way; likewise, by analogy, airplanes should be responsible for avoiding collisions with balloons because the latter are the less easily managed.

QUESTIONS ON THE TEXT

1. What is a State constitution?
2. Of what six parts does a State constitution commonly consist?
3. For what purpose is a constitutional convention assembled?
4. What part do the voters usually take in making a new constitution?
5. What is meant by *partial amendment* of a State constitution? Describe in detail how it is accomplished in the State in which you live.
6. What new way of amending constitutions has developed since 1902? Explain this method.
7. What are some of the present tendencies of State constitutions?
8. If you are in any way inconvenienced by an Act of the legislature which is contrary to the constitution, should you accept it or carry it to court?
9. If a law is declared unconstitutional, is there any possibility of making it constitutional?
10. Name the various kinds of laws in the United States according to their relative rank of importance.

---

[1] Louisiana, which State obtained its system of laws from France, is the only one that did not adopt the common law. But even there common law rules are gaining ascendancy.

PROBLEMS FOR DISCUSSION

1. Secure a copy of your State constitution from your Secretary of State. Study its contents and answer as many of the following questions as you can.

 a. When was it adopted? How many times has it been amended? By what process were the amendments made?

 b. How long is the document? Does it deal only with the framework of your State government or does it contain regulations of social and economic problems?

2. The average length of State constitutions is three times that of the Federal Constitution. The Model State Constitution prepared by the National Municipal League is 11,000 words in length. What has caused these constitutions to become so lengthy? Do you favor this trend?

3. The State constitution of Massachusetts requires a two-thirds vote in the House and a majority vote in the Senate in two consecutive General Courts before an amendment can be referred to the electorate. The Model State Constitution would require a simple majority vote of a unicameral (one-house) legislature. Which system would you prefer?

4. If State constitutions were abolished, would it make the governments more or less democratic?

5. In a number of State legislatures the cities are not represented in proportion to population because the legislators from the country who now dominate the legislature are unwilling to increase the legislative influence of cities. What effect would the introduction of the constitutional initiative have upon the representation of cities in a State where the city voters are in the majority?

6. How may new States be formed out of old States? (See U. S. Constitution, Art. IV, Sec. 3.) If the legislatures of New York and Illinois were willing to have New York City and Chicago become separate States, do you believe Congress would create new States of these cities? Would the House or Senate of Congress be more favorable?

SELECT BIBLIOGRAPHY

Constitution of Your State. (Usually free from the Secretary of State.)

GRAVES, W. B. *American State Government.* Heath. Boston. 1953 ed. Chs. 1 and 2.

Model State Constitution. National Municipal League. 1948. $1.

Modernizing State Constitutions. National Municipal League. 1948. 25¢.

SNIDER, C. *American State and Local Government.* Appleton-Century-Crofts. New York. 1951. Chapters 1–6.

CHAPTER XXVII

STATE LEGISLATURES

The Names of State Legislatures. — Every State has a legislative body. In twenty-four of the States this body is known as the "Legislature," in nineteen as the "General Assembly," in three as the "Legislative Assembly," and in New Hampshire and Massachusetts as the "General Court." In each State, except Nebraska, the legislative body is composed of two houses — the Senate and the House of Representatives.[1]

One House or Two? — Nebraska is the only State with a *unicameral* or one-house legislature today.[2] For the past several years the unicameral system has been widely recommended as the most practicable way to strengthen and improve our State legislatures. There is much to be said for both sides.

There were historical reasons for adopting bicameralism in the States. The two-house structure of Parliament influenced the original States, and the creation of a bicameral Congress had its effect.

Bicameralism's supporters claim that one house acts as a check on the other to prevent unwise legislation. Opponents cite numerous examples which show that the theory has not worked so well in practice. Although the second house fails to pass many bills from the first, the major reason is that they are never even considered. And those that do pass are seldom changed in any way by the second. The governor's veto power and popular opinion have proven a better check than has bicameralism on the State level.

---

[1] Instead of the term "House of Representatives," California, Nevada, New York, and Wisconsin call the more numerous branch "Assembly"; New Jersey calls it "General Assembly"; and Maryland, Virginia, and West Virginia call it "House of Delegates."

[2] Georgia until 1789, Pennsylvania until 1790, and Vermont until 1836 had unicameral bodies. In opposing the change to bicameralism in Pennsylvania, Benjamin Franklin quoted the fable of the snake with two heads and one body. "She was going to a brook to drink, and on her way was to pass through a hedge, a twig of which opposed her direct course; one head chose to go on the right side of the twig, and the other on the left; so that time was spent in the contest, and, before the decision was completed, the poor snake died with thirst."

Bicameralism in Congress reflects the federal character of the Union, but the States are not federal. In most States both houses represent exactly the same people and interests, one being but a mirror of the other. On the other hand, in a single house based on population, cities might so thoroughly dominate that rural interests would be virtually unrepresented. In some States, notably California, a balance of interests has been worked out. In California, the house is controlled by the urban population while the senate is in the hands of the rural population.

THE NEWEST OF OUR STATE CAPITOLS, SALEM, OREGON

In the complicated structure of a two-house system special interests have a better chance to block popular legislation. Furthermore, the two-house system makes it almost impossible to fix definitely the responsibility for some action.

The Nebraska experiment has not been a cure-all for all the ills of legislatures, but it has worked well thus far. The other States are watching with great interest, and several of them in recent years have been seriously considering making the change. In Nebraska costs have been reduced, greater efficiency of operation has resulted, and "unwise" legislation fears have proved to be unjustified.

Membership of State Legislatures. — The *Senates* vary in membership from 17 in Nevada to 67 in Minnesota. In some States one senator is elected from each county, but most States are divided into Senatorial Districts of about equal population. Senators are elected for terms of 4 years in 32 States, and 2 years in 16 States.

The membership of the *House of Representatives* varies from 35 in Delaware to about 400 in New Hampshire. In some States one or more representatives are elected from each county or each township, whereas other States are divided into House Districts of about equal population.

From time to time the legislatures create new Senate and House districts which correspond to the changed distribution of population. As the cities grow in population, the rural county representatives commonly refuse to increase city representation proportionately for fear that the counties will be controlled by the cities. An especially unfair apportionment is called a "gerrymander," as described on page 85.

In most States it is the constitutional duty of the legislature to reapportion the State, usually every ten years, to take account of population shifts and increases. Short of constitutional amendment or, in some States, the use of the initiative, there is no way to force the legislature to reapportion. And many States have not been reapportioned for several years. For instance, Oregon's legislature has ignored the constitutional requirement since 1910. Finally, the State's voters, through an initiative amendment in 1952, forced a reapportionment to take effect in the 1954 elections.

In some States the people have taken the job out of the hands of the legislature and given it to reapportionment boards, as in California, Maryland, and Ohio. In those States reapportionment is automatic and the problem no longer exists.

The rapid growth of cities has caused some States to fear the domination of the whole State by one city controlling the legislature. So in Pennsylvania no city is allowed to have more than one sixth of the senators; and in Rhode Island no town or city may have more than one fourth of the representatives.

In most States any qualified voter is eligible to membership in the Senate or House, but in some States the age qualification for the Senate is higher than that for the House. The members, either by law or custom, usually reside in the districts from which they are elected.

Legislative Sessions. — In ten of the States [1] the legislatures meet annually. In the other States, legislative sessions are held

---

[1] Arizona, California, Colorado, Maryland, Massachusetts, Michigan, New Jersey, New York, Rhode Island, South Carolina.

biennially. In forty-odd States the legislatures are elected at the November election of even-numbered years and take their seats in January following. But a few States elect their legislators in November of odd-numbered years when voters can center their attention upon State issues without being confused by presidential and other national issues.

A. Devaney Incorporated

THE STATE CAPITOL, AUSTIN, TEXAS

Many State constitutions absolutely limit the sessions to a definite number of days, others allow no compensation after the prescribed number of days. There is, however, a tendency to lighten this restriction because bills which are rushed through the last days of a session cannot receive the careful attention they deserve. The governor, and in thirteen states the legislature itself, may call an extra session for any special purpose.

Privileges, Immunities, and Compensation of Members. — State constitutions usually provide that for any speech or debate in either house a member may not be questioned in any other place; and that members are not subject to arrest under any civil process during any legislative session or coming thereto or going therefrom. This latter privilege amounts to scarcely anything today, for a member who commits treason, felony, or breach of the peace may be arrested like any other individual.

Each State pays members of both houses the same amount of salary. In some States the legislature determines the amount; in others the constitution prescribes it. Where the salary is restricted by the constitution some legislatures have allowed themselves a per diem for personal expenses in addition to the clerical allowance.

Powers of State Legislatures. — According to the Tenth Amendment to the Constitution of the United States "the powers not delegated to the United States by the Constitution, nor prohibited by it to the States, are reserved to the States, respectively, or to the people." State constitutions confer all of this reserved lawmaking power upon the legislatures, except as to certain specified matters reserved to the voters which may be altered only by changing the constitution.[1]

The legislatures do not attempt to exercise all of their powers, but delegate a portion of them to other local legislative bodies in counties, townships, school districts, cities, and towns or villages. The county board and the city council are examples of minor legislatures which derive all of their powers, except a few which are bestowed directly through the constitution, from general or special laws framed by a legislature.

Of course it is impossible to enumerate the powers of the State legislatures because they may enact any laws which are not in conflict with the Constitution or laws of the United States or the constitutions of the respective States. Examples of subjects concerning which they

---

[1] The following restrictions are commonly placed upon State legislatures by State constitutions:

1. The Bill of Rights guarantees freedom of the press and speech, religious liberty, jury trial, right to the writ of *habeas corpus*, etc., and prohibits the taking of private property for a public purpose without compensation.

2. Other parts of the constitution:

   (*a*) Prohibit special privileges to corporations.

   (*b*) Limit State debts and compel regular payment of interest and principal.

   (*c*) Prescribe qualifications for voters and define terms and duties of certain officers, or in several states, grant municipal "home rule."

   (*d*) Prescribe certain rules for local government, public education, and public institutions.

   (*e*) Place certain restrictions upon the passage of special or local laws, that is, laws applying to some particular person, corporation, or locality — township, county, or city. As an illustration of the need of such restrictions, some years ago the legislature of Pennsylvania compelled Philadelphia to build a city hall costing millions of dollars, which was larger and more extensive than the city needed or would have otherwise built.

State	Ann. or Bien.	Limit of Regular Session with Pay	No. of Members in Senate	No. of Members in House	Term of Senators (Years)	Term of Representatives (Years)	Salary of Members [1]
Alabama . . .	Bien.	36 days	35	106	4	4	$10 per diem
Arizona	Ann.	60 days	19	80	2	2	$8 per diem
Arkansas . . .	Bien.	60 days	35	100	4	2	$1200 bien.
California . . .	Ann.	120 days	40	80	4	2	$3600 ann.
Colorado . . .	Ann.	None	35	65	4	2	$2400 ann.
Connecticut . .	Bien.	Varies	36	279	2	2	$600 bien.
Delaware . . .	Bien.	None	17	35	4	2	$1000 ann.
Florida	Bien.	60 days	38	95	4	2	$10 per diem
Georgia	Bien.	70 days	54	205	2	2	$15 per diem
Idaho	Bien.	60 days	44	59	2	2	$10 per diem
Illinois	Bien.	6 mo.	51	153	4	2	$5000 ann.
Indiana	Bien.	61 days	50	100	4	2	$1200 ann.
Iowa	Bien.	None	50	108	4	2	$2000 bien.
Kansas	Bien.	None	40	125	4	2	$300 ses'n
Kentucky . . .	Bien.	60 days	38	100	4	2	$25 per diem
Louisiana . . .	Bien.	60 days	39	100	4	4	$5100 bien.
Maine	Bien.	None	33	151	2	2	$850 ses'n
Maryland . . .	Ann.	90 days	29	123	4	4	$1800 ann.
Massachusetts .	Ann.	None	40	240	2	2	$4500 ann.
Michigan . . .	Ann.	None	32	100	2	2	$2900 ann.
Minnesota . .	Bien.	90 days	67	131	4	2	$3000 bien.
Mississippi . . .	Bien.	None	49	140	4	4	$2000 ses'n
Missouri . . .	Bien.	5 mos.	34	157	4	2	$1500 ann.
Montana . . .	Bien.	60 days	56	94	4	2	$10 per diem
Nebraska . . .	Bien.	None	43	None	2	—	$872 ann.
Nevada	Bien.	60 days	17	47	4	2	$15 per diem
New Hampshire .	Bien.	None	24	400 [2]	2	2	$200 bien.
New Jersey . .	Ann.	None	21	60	4	2	$3000 ann.
New Mexico . .	Bien.	60 days	31	55	4	2	$20 per diem
New York . . .	Ann.	None	56	150	2	2	$5000 ann.
North Carolina .	Bien.	None	50	120	2	2	$15 per diem
North Dakota .	Bien.	60 days	49	113	4	2	$5 per diem
Ohio	Bien.	None	33	136	2	2	$3200 ann.
Oklahoma . . .	Bien.	None	44	119	4	2	$3275 bien.
Oregon	Bien.	None	30	60	4	2	$600 ann.
Pennsylvania . .	Bien.	None	50	210	4	2	$3000 ses'n
Rhode Island . .	Ann.	None	49	100	2	2	$300 ann.
South Carolina .	Ann.	None	46	124	4	2	$1000 ann.
South Dakota .	Bien.	60 days	35	75	2	2	$1050 bien.
Tennessee . . .	Bien.	75 days	33	99	2	2	$15 per diem
Texas	Bien.	120 days	31	150	4	2	$10 per diem
Utah	Bien.	60 days	23	60	4	2	$1000 bien.
Vermont . . .	Bien.	None	30	246	2	2	$1250 ses'n
Virginia	Bien.	60 days	40	100	4	2	$18 per diem
Washington . .	Bien.	60 days	46	99	4	2	$3000 bien.
West Virginia . .	Bien.	60 days	32	100	4	2	$500 ann.
Wisconsin . . .	Bien.	None	33	100	4	2	$2400 bien.
Wyoming . . .	Bien.	40 days	27	56	4	2	$18 per diem

[1] Most legislators receive additional payments in the form of expense money.
[2] Varies 350–400, as some small towns are not represented at all sessions.

legislate are taxation; civil matters, such as contracts, real and personal property, inheritances, mortgages, corporations, marriage, and divorce; crimes for which fines, imprisonment, or death are imposed; business or professional regulations; "police regulations," such as public health, morals, safety, or any general welfare rule which restricts a person's inclination to do as he pleases.

Organization of State Legislatures. — *The Houses.* — Each house commonly has power to select its own officers, except that 37 States elect a lieutenant-governor provided for in the constitution, and he presides over the upper chamber except in Massachusetts. Each house also determines its own rules of procedure and the qualifications of its members; and by a certain prescribed majority, usually two thirds, may expel members. Legally the speaker of the House and the president or chairman of the Senate, except in those cases where the constitution provides for a lieutenant-governor, are elected by the respective houses over which they preside, but practically they are chosen in a party caucus.

The officers of each house of the State legislatures are very similar to those of Congress and their duties are about the same. For instance, the speaker is presiding officer of the House and has power to refer bills to committees, but unlike the speaker of the United States House of Representatives he has, in all of the States,[1] power to appoint the committees.[2] Each house has a clerk and a sergeant-at-arms and numerous other officers varying in number from 21 in Delaware to 315 in Missouri.

The Committee System in State legislatures is very similar to that of Congress, discussed on pages 150–154. Most of the important work of a legislature is done through committees and sub-committees. Committees provide for specialization, and without them the legislature could not carry on its work. It would be impossible for all members to study all bills introduced. The wide variety and great number of bills presented for legislative action is suggested by the list on page 151.

---

[1] In Oklahoma the Speaker's appointments are subject to confirmation by a vote of the House membership.

[2] State senate committees are chosen in five different ways in the States: (1) by the Lieutenant-Governor, (2) by the President of the Senate, (3) by the President pro tem., (4) elected by the Senate, or (5) by a committee on committees.

Each committee usually deals with some particular subject, such as taxation, highways, health, appropriations, commerce, and local government. Members are usually assigned to those committees in which they express an interest and for which their training and experience equip them.

The number of standing committees varies in the House from six in Massachusetts to seventy-one in Kentucky; and in the Senate, from two in Maine to fifty-three in Arkansas. Most States seem to have far too many committees. For example, one State has 100 members of the House but 71 committees; another, with 100 members in the House, has 69 committees. The situation is even more pronounced in the Senates of some States. One State has 19 senators and 23 committees; another, 36 and 36; and still another, 35 and 51. Moreover, some committees seem far too large. For example, one State has 65 members on its House Ways and Means Committee and 66 members on another committee.

The practice of "pigeon-holing" bills is very common in State legislatures. For instance, a common method of preventing the passage of a bill is for the speaker to refer it to the Judiciary Committee, claiming it to be of doubtful constitutionality, but really desiring to prevent the bill from coming to a vote. The speaker can usually count on the majority of this committee to "pigeon-hole" the bill and fail to report on it. Thus it dies and is buried in the committee. Such a committee is often called "the graveyard committee."

Despite this and other abuses of the committee system, however, committee hearings and reports are an essential part of the legislative process. In Massachusetts, for example, notice of all hearings is given in the public press, and the committee hearings are well-attended, not only by people who have an ax to grind, but by citizens interested in legislative reforms. All testimony taken is carefully weighed; in fact, the legislature and its committees assume rather a judicial attitude. Petitions are brought before them, testimony given, arguments heard, and the committee generally decides the matter on the basis of all these considerations.

Joint Committees, composed of members from both houses, are being used more and more in several States. The savings made in time and duplication of effort are substantial.

How Bills Become State Laws. — *Preparation of Bills.* — Although
State legislators in general may have more than average intelligence,
few of them are trained to prepare bills in unmistakable language or in
accordance with superior law.[1] Nevertheless for some years the members of our legislatures drafted their own bills, the lawyer members
or some legislative clerk assisting the inexperienced.

After the development of large corporations their lobbyists, or legislative agents, often prepared bills free for members whose acquaintance
and good-will they desired. Today 42 of the States have trained
assistants whose duty it is to put in clear legal form the ideas that members wish to enact into statutes. The assistant is ordinarily connected
with a legislative reference bureau or the Attorney General's office.

A *Legislative Reference Bureau* is a library or division of a library
especially equipped to assist legislators. Such a bureau collects references, summaries, files, card indexes, court decisions, newspaper
clippings, magazine articles, reference books, government reports, bills
introduced into other legislative bodies, governors' messages, platforms
of political parties, and any other information available for legislators.
Since 1890 forty-odd States have undertaken this work on varying
scales, usually in co-operation with the State library; and more than
half of the States have a division devoted exclusively to legislative
reference service.

Legislative Councils. — In 1933 Kansas created a Legislative Council
to prepare a law-making program for each session of the legislature.
It is composed of 10 senators and 15 representatives appointed at each
legislative session by the presiding officers of the Senate and the House;
and the major political parties get representation approximately in
proportion to their numbers. Sessions of the Council must be held
at least four times a year, and are presided over by the president of the
Senate, or by the speaker of the House, who is vice chairman. The
Council may require the services of the legislative reference library and
may employ research assistants. Its recommended legislation must
be mailed to each member of the legislature and made public at least
30 days before the legislature meets. Each member of the council
receives the same pay per day as in the regular legislative session. A
number of other States have adopted the Legislative Council idea.

---

[1] *Superior law* means the Constitution of the United States, laws of Congress,
treaties, and the State constitution.

Introduction of Bills. — Any member of either house may introduce as many bills as he chooses; but important bills are commonly prepared by a committee and introduced by its chairman. In introducing bills the members merely file them with the clerk. Some legislatures prohibit the introduction of bills after the legislature has been

The State Capitol, Baton Rouge, Louisiana

in session a certain number of days; others require that bills of a local or private character must be announced in the locality to be affected; and others require that local bills receive a two-thirds vote of each house instead of a bare majority, which is sufficient for public bills.

The Passage of a Bill through the State legislature is outlined in the table on page 485.

On account of the large number of bills introduced at each session of the State legislature it would be impossible for the committees to give consideration to all of them. Therefore those bills which are not introduced by prominent members or backed by influential lobbyists are commonly not seriously considered and are said to be "pigeon-holed." Other bills which the committees do not favor, but feel obliged to report upon, are often intentionally reported too late to be considered by the houses.

Pressure Groups, or the Lobby. — State legislatures, like Congress, are also beset with lobbyists and pressure groups. Lobbyists are sometimes given the dignified names of legislative agents or public relations counsel. They make a practice of frequenting lobbies [1] or other convenient places for the purpose of persuading legislators to vote for or against certain bills.

As was suggested on page 161, lobbyists are sometimes former legislators who still have friends in the legislature, sometimes leaders of organizations, and sometimes high-pressure experts. These lobbyists form an important part of the "invisible government" and extra-legal legislative machinery. Their methods are not merely to button-hole legislators, but to put indirect influences to bear: friends, letters, telegrams, telephone calls, radio broadcasts, and newspapers and other periodicals. A lobbyist may represent big business, labor unions, farm organizations, reform groups, or groups like the liquor interests or gambling interests that are endeavoring to have legal restrictions removed.

Regulation of Lobbyists. — For many years, some States have controlled lobbying along the lines set up by Congress in its Reorganization Act of 1946 (page 163). For example, the State of Wisconsin requires all persons employed to lobby at a legislative session to be registered on a legislative docket which is kept by the Secretary of State. The names of the employer and employed must be entered with a statement of the legislation in which they are interested and the terms of employment. The lobbyist is not allowed to enter upon the floor of either house; and his lobbying must be restricted to committees or work properly incidental thereto, to newspaper publications, public addresses, or written briefs delivered to each member of the legislature and filed with the Secretary of State. A detailed statement of expenses must be filed within thirty days of the adjournment of the legislature.

---

[1] A *lobby* is an anteroom or corridor communicating with the main assembly room, or else a part of the room itself to which the public is admitted and which is usually railed off from the part used for the assembly.

THE COURSE OF A BILL

THE HOUSE OF REPRESENTATIVES

INTRODUCING MEMBER	CHIEF CLERK	SPEAKER OF HOUSE	HOUSE STANDING COMMITTEES	COMMITTEE ON RULES & ORDER "CALENDAR COMMITTEE"
FOR FILING		REFERRED TO STANDING COMMITTEE	CONSIDERED BY APPROPRIATE STANDING COMMITTEE	
	READ FIRST TIME BY TITLE			
	READING AND RECORD OF COMMITTEE REPORT	REFERRED TO		TO BE PLACED ON THE CALENDAR FOR SECOND READING
	READ SECOND TIME SECTION BY SECTION	REFERRED TO		TO BE PLACED ON THE CALENDAR FOR THIRD READING
	THIRD READING AND FINAL PASSAGE			
	CERTIFICATION			
			ENROLLING COMMITTEE	
	ENROLLED	SIGNED IN OPEN SESSION		

THE SENATE

SECRETARY OF SENATE	PRESIDENT OF SENATE	SENATE STANDING COMMITTEES	RULES AND JOINT RULES COMMITTEE "GENERAL FILE"
FOR FILING			
READ FIRST AND SECOND TIME	REFERRED TO	CONSIDERED BY APPROPRIATE COMMITTEE	
READING AND RECORD OF COMMITTEE REPORT	REFERRED TO		TO BE PLACED ON THE CALENDAR FOR THIRD READING
THIRD READING SECTION BY SECTION AND FINAL PASSAGE			
CERTIFICATION			
	SIGNED IN OPEN SESSION		

EXECUTIVE OFFICIALS

GOVERNOR	SECRETARY OF STATE
ORIGINAL SIGNED IF APPROVED	GIVES BILL CHAPTER NUMBER LAWS IN SESSION PERMANENTLY FILED

"THE ABOVE PROCEDURE FOR A NON-COMMITTEE BILL INTRODUCED IN THE HOUSE IS THE SIMPLEST POSSIBLE; NEITHER VETO NOR AMENDMENT HAS OCCURRED. IF SUCH A BILL IS INTRODUCED IN THE SENATE, THE SECRETARY OF THE SENATE WOULD PERFORM ESSENTIALLY THE SAME FUNCTIONS AS THE CHIEF CLERK OF THE HOUSE INDICATED ABOVE, AND THE ACTION OF THE HOUSE THEREON WOULD OCCUR AFTER PASSAGE THEREOF BY THE SENATE.

BUREAU OF GOVERNMENTAL RESEARCH AND SERVICES, UNIVERSITY OF WASHINGTON

Improving State Legislatures. — Following the lead of Congress, many of the States are now reorganizing and improving the organization and procedures of their legislative bodies. To aid these States, the private Council of State Governments has prepared a very valuable study entitled *Our State Legislatures.* In summarizing its findings, the report makes the following recommendations:

(1) Restrictions on the length of regular sessions should be removed. Legislatures should be permitted to meet as often and as long as conditions require.

(2) Adequate salaries, sufficient to permit competent persons to serve in the legislature, should be provided. Salaries should be determined by statute rather than by constitutional provision.

(3) Legislative terms of office should be lengthened and staggered to provide continuity in membership.

(4) Skilled and essential full-time legislative employees should be appointed on the basis of merit and should retain their positions regardless of changes in party majorities.

(5) Committees should be reduced in number wherever practicable; and they should be organized with regard to subject matter, equalization of work, and co-operation between the two houses. Permanent and public records of committee action should be kept.

(6) Committees should provide for public hearings on all major bills, with advance notice of time and place.

(7) Legislative councils or interim committees, with adequate clerical and research facilities, should be provided.

(8) Legislative reference services and similar organizations should be established and strengthened in each State.

(9) Legislative rules should limit the time period during which new bills may be introduced in order to prevent congestion at the end of the session.

(10) Legislative rules should be revised wherever necessary to expedite procedure, although with regard for full deliberation and minorities.

(11) The legislature should make suitable provision, by means of a budget, for all of its own expenditures.

(12) Special legislation should be avoided. Claims against the State should be handled by judicial or administrative agencies. Municipal affairs should be regulated by general or optional legislation, or by conferring home rule upon municipalities.

The Referendum. — *Mandatory.* — State constitutional amendments must be referred to the voters in all States except Delaware; and State constitutions require that such propositions as constitutional conventions and bond issues be referred to the people. For instance, in 1952 California voters approved one amendment barring from public office any person who advocates the forceful overthrow of ordered government in the United States, and another requiring a loyalty oath for most State officers and employees. Also in 1952, Oregon voters extended to Korean veterans the State's home- and farm-loan benefits for World War II veterans, and defeated a measure which would have made the State Superintendent of Public Instruction appointive.

Optional with the Legislature. — If a measure is voluntarily referred to the voters by a legislature, it is said to be an optional or legislative referendum. A State legislature is often willing to refer urged measures to the voters when it is unwilling itself to assume responsibility for them. Here are two examples:

Oregon (1938) Requiring physical and mental examination of men and women for marriage license. *Voted "Yes"; by majority of 2 to 1.*

Oregon (1947) Providing for a sales tax. *Voted "No" 3 to 1.*

Popular Petition. — In one third of the States the Governor is not the only authority that can prevent a bill which has passed the legislature from becoming law. In these States a petition signed by a prescribed per cent of voters may demand that any non-emergency measure [1] be referred to the people. Here are examples:

Oregon (1952) Imposing a 3¢ per pack sales tax on cigarettes and prohibiting sale of cigarettes below "fair trade" price. *Voted "No."*

Oregon (1952) Providing for sale of liquor by the drink in State-licensed restaurants, taverns, clubs, etc. *Voted "Yes."*

The Initiative. — All the States which have the popular petition referendum, except Maryland and New Mexico, also have the *initia-*

---

[1] In States with the popular petition referendum there are certain measures which need to become effective at once, without waiting the 90 days during which the people may have petitions signed for a referendum. These measures are called "emergency measures." If the legislature declares a measure to be an emergency measure, it may become effective immediately. The legislatures abused this privilege, and in some States declared half of the measures emergency measures. To prevent a legislature from declaring a measure an emergency measure just to avoid any possibility of its being referred to the people, some States gave the Governor the right to veto the emergency clause without vetoing the entire measure.

tive. The initiative, as we know from our study of constitutional amending procedures, is a device whereby a small percentage of voters may initiate a law and have it referred to all of the voters for their acceptance or rejection. Thus, if a legislature will not enact a law

Courtesy Washington State Advertising Commission

THE STATE CAPITOL, OLYMPIA, WASHINGTON

which a certain per cent of the voters think the majority favor, they can have the prescribed per cent sign a petition, and the measure will be referred to the voters at the next election. Here are examples:

Oregon (1952) approved measure reapportioning Legislature (takes effect for 1955 session) and providing for reapportionment by Secretary of State if Legislature fails to do so after each Federal census.

California (1950) defeated a proposal to legalize practically all forms of gambling in the State.

Arkansas (1950) defeated a statewide prohibition measure.

The initiative permits well-organized groups to go directly to voters.

QUESTIONS ON THE TEXT

1. By what name is the legislative body of the State in which you live known? The upper house? The lower house?

2. How many members are there in the upper house of the legislature of the State in which you live? The lower house?

3. How many senators are elected from the senatorial district in which you live? How many representatives?

4. How often does the legislature meet in the State in which you live? When? Is the length of the session restricted? How may an extra session be called?

5. What special privileges and immunities do State legislators enjoy?

6. What salary do legislators receive in the State in which you live?

7. What restrictions are there upon the legislative powers of the legislature of the State in which you live?

8. What legislative power may counties, townships, and cities exercise?

9. Mention a number of subjects which may be legislated upon by State legislatures.

10. How are the two houses of a State legislature organized and what control have they over their own members?

11. How are presiding officers chosen?

12. What powers have presiding officers?

13. How are committees chosen? Do all State legislatures have the same kind of committees?

14. What is the defect of our committee system, according to ex-Governor Sulzer of New York?

15. What is a joint committee?

16. Explain how committee hearings are conducted in Massachusetts.

17. How are bills proposed?

18. What is a legislative reference bureau? Does the State in which you live have one?

19. Who may introduce bills? What restrictions do some legislatures have regarding the introduction of bills?

20. What is meant by *lobbying?* How does Wisconsin regulate the practice of lobbying?

21. Explain the referendum. The initiative. Does the State in which you live have either or both?

22. Give arguments for and against unicameral legislatures.

PROBLEMS FOR DISCUSSION

1. Bound the senatorial district in which you live. Who is your State senator?

2. Bound the house district in which you live. Name your representative or your representatives.

3. If the salary of a State legislator is low it will not prevent candidates who have special interests from seeking election, but what effect does the low salary have upon one who is not backed by any special interests? Will a legislator who receives a low or a high salary be more likely to vote as the people desire?

4. Many State constitutions commonly restrict the session of State legislatures to a certain number of days, which means that bills must be passed or rejected because of the calendar rather than after due consideration. Would it not be well for all States to pay their legislators by the year and permit them to prolong the session as long as need be?

5. Some States now have voting machines for their legislatures. For instance, the Wisconsin Assembly has for some years saved about 125 hours a session by the use of a machine which records the votes of all members in less than a minute instead of ten minutes for a vocal roll call.

When an issue comes to a vote the Speaker turns a key on his desk and proclaims: "Roll call." Thereupon each legislator presses one of three buttons on his desk; and thereby registers either: "Yes," "No," or "Present but not voting." The Speaker inquires: "Has every one voted?" The Speaker then locks the machine, which produces a photostatic copy of the roll, showing the vote of each individual and the total recorded vote.

In the gallery, visible to each member, is the name of each member with a white light (yes) and a red one (no) which flash on at the touch of the button on the member's desk.

The machine cost $12,000 and one electrician is required to operate it during a session.

Do you think that your legislature should purchase such a machine? Give your reasons.

SELECT BIBLIOGRAPHY

Book of the States. Biennial. Council of State Governments. Chicago.

SNIDER, C. *American State and Local Government.* Appleton-Century-Crofts. New York. 1951. Chapters 7 and 8.

WALKER, H. *The Legislative Process: Lawmaking in the United States.* Ronald Press Co. New York. 1949.

GRAVES, W. *American State Government.* Heath. Boston. 1953 ed. Chapters 6, 7, and 8.

NEUBERGER, R. "Decline of State Governments." *Harper's.* October, 1953.

VELIE, L. Series of articles in *Reader's Digest.* January–May, 1953.

CHAPTER XXVIII

STATE GOVERNORS

The Office of Governor. — Every State has a governor as its chief executive officer, elected by the voters of the State.[1] In colonial days the royal governors did the bidding of the King and were often disliked by the people. But in many cases the legislatures were able to protect the colonists against despotic acts of the governors.

Thus when they gained their independence they naturally regarded governors with suspicion and looked upon the legislatures as guardians of their liberty. Therefore governors were granted little power in the early constitutions. In addressing the Federal Constitutional Convention of 1787 Madison said, "The executives of the States are in general little more than ciphers; the legislatures are omnipotent."

In recent times this prejudice against governors has disappeared. People seem to believe that it is easier to elect one honest and efficient leader who can be held responsible to the people than it is to elect numerous responsible legislators. And so in the last several years the powers of the governor have been greatly increased in nearly every State.

A Governor's Powers. — The powers of a governor are usually classified under three heads: (1) executive powers, such as appointing officers and seeing that the civil and criminal laws of the State are enforced; (2) legislative powers, such as sending messages to the legislature and vetoing objectionable laws; and (3) judicial powers such as pardoning persons convicted of crime.

Executive Powers of a Governor. — A State constitution almost invariably provides that the governor shall take care that the laws of the State are faithfully executed, but he is never given such power

---

[1] In Mississippi the governor must receive a majority of the popular votes of the State as in most States, but in addition to this requirement he must receive a majority of popular votes in more than half of the districts from which representatives are elected for the most numerous branch of the legislature.

for the performance of this duty as is given to the President of the United States.

In most of the States the more important State officers, such as the secretary of state, attorney-general, auditor, and treasurer, are still elected by the people. Judges also are elected by the people in most States. Sheriffs and state's attorneys are elected by the people with

THE GOVERNOR'S MANSION, RICHMOND, VIRGINIA

few exceptions. Thus, the governor is merely one of a number of officers whom the people elect to enforce the laws, and if the other officers do not perform their duties in an efficient and honest manner the governor is often helpless.

A story is told of a sheriff who permitted a prisoner to be taken from his jail and lynched. The governor wrote a letter to the sheriff reprimanding him for his neglect of duty. The sheriff promptly replied by telling the governor to mind his own business; that he was responsible to the people of his county who had elected him and to nobody else. According to the law of his State the sheriff was right. It may be said that a governor is the captain of a Ship of State which is navigated by a crew that he does not select, and over which he has few powers of command.

State	Capital	Term of Service (Years)	Annual Salary
Alabama	Montgomery	4	$12,000 and residence [1]
Arizona	Phoenix	2	15,000
Arkansas	Little Rock	2	10,000 and residence
California	Sacramento	4	25,000 and residence
Colorado	Denver	2	10,000
Connecticut	Hartford	4	12,000 and residence
Delaware	Dover	4	12,000
Florida	Tallahassee	4	15,000 and residence
Georgia	Atlanta	4	12,000 and residence
Idaho	Boise	4	7,500 and residence
Illinois	Springfield	4	25,000 and residence
Indiana	Indianapolis	4	15,000 and residence
Iowa	Des Moines	2	12,000 and residence
Kansas	Topeka	2	10,000 and residence
Kentucky	Frankfort	4	10,000 and residence
Louisiana	Baton Rouge	4	18,000 and residence
Maine	Augusta	2	10,000 and residence
Maryland	Annapolis	4	4,500 and residence
Massachusetts	Boston	2	20,000
Michigan	Lansing	2	22,500
Minnesota	St. Paul	2	15,000
Mississippi	Jackson	4	15,000 and residence
Missouri	Jefferson City	4	10,000 and residence
Montana	Helena	4	10,000 and residence
Nebraska	Lincoln	2	11,000 and residence
Nevada	Carson City	4	7,600 and residence
New Hampshire	Concord	2	10,000
New Jersey	Trenton	4	20,000 and residence
New Mexico	Santa Fe	2	15,000 and residence
New York	Albany	4	25,000 and residence
North Carolina	Raleigh	4	15,000 and residence
North Dakota	Bismarck	2	9,000 and residence
Ohio	Columbus	2	20,000 and residence
Oklahoma	Oklahoma City	4	15,000 and residence
Oregon	Salem	4	11,000
Pennsylvania	Harrisburg	4	25,000 and residence
Rhode Island	Providence	2	15,000
South Carolina	Columbia	4	12,000 and residence
South Dakota	Pierre	2	9,500 and residence
Tennessee	Nashville	4	12,000 and residence
Texas	Austin	4	12,000 and residence
Utah	Salt Lake City	4	10,000 and residence
Vermont	Montpelier	2	11,000
Virginia	Richmond	4	15,000 and residence
Washington	Olympia	4	15,000 and residence
West Virginia	Charleston	4	12,500 and residence
Wisconsin	Madison	2	14,000 and residence
Wyoming	Cheyenne	4	10,000 and residence

[1] The Governor also receives an expense account in most States — in New Mexico, $19,800; North Carolina, $10,000; Wisconsin, $3,000; etc.

As commander-in-chief of the State militia, the governor has a real power. When a riot occurs, when a prisoner is in danger of being lynched, or when a strike cannot be handled by local officers, the governor may call out the militia (National Guard).

State Police. — Several years ago the governor of Pennsylvania sarcastically remarked that he was charged with maintaining peace and order throughout the State — 45,000 square miles — with no one to assist him but his secretary and stenographer. Today every State has a State police force or highway patrol to aid the governor in the enforcement of State laws.

In most States the principal task of the State police is enforcement of motor vehicle laws. In some States, however, the State police have become the major arm of law enforcement. The State police in Massachusetts, New Jersey, and New York, and the Texas Rangers are widely known for their competence. In some States the State police systematically enforce law in rural areas, thus supplementing the work of local sheriffs and constables.

The Pennsylvania State Police Force, over 1300 strong, is divided into troops occupying barracks in different sections of the State, with numerous sub-stations in the region of each barracks. These police not only act upon the orders of the governor, but co-operate with peace officers of any community to prevent riots, lynchings, or unusual crimes. Disguised as civilians, they often detect serious crimes, where county detectives are not provided. They enforce motor-vehicle laws, quarantines, school laws, and dog laws. They raid disorderly resorts, gambling houses, and "bootlegger" joints; pursue criminals; act as game and fish wardens; and extinguish forest fires.

Members of this force are carefully selected and instructed in their duties. They are required to pass a mental and physical examination and to prove their honesty, moral character, and sobriety. They must also undergo a course of study given by the School Troop in the following subjects: cavalry drill, horsemanship, practical self-defense, and marksmanship; criminal law; fish, game, and forestry law; investigation of crimes and criminal procedure; methods of handling individuals, crowds, and mobs; geography and civil government.

Appointments. — In most States the outstanding officers are still elected by the voters. And even if these officers are appointed by the governor the Constitution often provides for terms over-lapping that

AN ELK IN THE SERVICE OF THE NEW YORK STATE POLICE

When snow is deep, Jargo takes a Policeman to otherwise inaccessible places.

Courtesy Pennsylvania State Police

MOUNTED PENNSYLVANIA STATE POLICEMAN

There are places where the Police cannot go in automobiles.

of the governor, on the theory that checks and balances are a necessary safeguard. Some progressive States, however, assume that the people will choose an honest and efficient governor and they allow him to appoint most State officials. If the governor can appoint the outstanding officers and can dismiss them, he is in a position similar to that of the President of the United States — he has a sort of Cabinet. (See New York organization on page 504.)

A good administration depends upon wise appointments; and the governor, because he is responsible for the administration, should have an opportunity to make good appointments. If he doesn't make good with this opportunity, his political future is doubtful.

Institutions. — State benevolent, educational, and penal institutions have commonly been administered by a great number of boards appointed by the governor. The system has proved inefficient and expensive, and many of the States have centralized the control of these institutions in an ex-officio or appointive board of control. An interesting example of this is the Board of Administration created in Kansas in 1917. This board is composed of four members, one of whom is the governor who also serves as chairman. The other three members are appointed by the governor and senate. This board takes the place of separate boards for the benevolent, educational, and penal institutions of the State. The law requires the board to employ a business manager for all the institutions under its control. This manager is expected to be the real administrative head of the institutions.

Legislative Powers of a Governor. — The governor is considered the head of the executive branch of government, yet he has three important legislative powers: (1) to send messages to the legislature, (2) to call an extra session of the legislature, and (3) to veto bills passed by the legislature.

Governors' Messages. — The message power has not been used by governors to the extent that the constitutions allow. A weak governor will send a formal message to the legislature when it meets, recommending legislation which the annual reports of the State officers bring to his attention. His message is read to the two houses sitting together, and the various recommendations are distributed to the appropriate legislative committees by the speaker of the House of Representatives. This is often the end of the matter.

A strong governor will send a number of short messages, and "get

back of them" — one at a time. In fact, in some States the governor
has the right to make his recommendation in the form of a bill if he
chooses, but it is wiser to take a number of members into his confidence and have a chairman of a legislative committee introduce a bill
containing his ideas.

Paul's Photos

MICHIGAN SCHOOL FOR THE DEAF

This fine building located at Flint, Michigan, typifies the warm interest which
Michigan, like all progressive States, shows in the welfare of her people.

In 1913 the Illinois House of Representatives adopted a rule providing that a bill which a governor has had introduced shall have precedence in the consideration of the House over all other measures except appropriation bills.

Extra Sessions. — For any reason that a governor thinks sufficient
he may call an extra session of the legislature. Several Governors
called special sessions of the legislature in 1953, each in addition to
regular sessions already held. For example, Utah's Governor Lee
called a special session to consider the financial problems of the
State school system. A special session was also called by Governor
White in Mississippi to consider increasing the State's cigarette, sales,
and severance taxes to provide more school revenues. Today more
and more States are finding that the short and biennial session is in-

adequate for the complex problems they face. That is why the annual session is becoming so widespread. Longer sessions and improved procedures would aid greatly. Fortunately, the need is being recognized in several States.

The Veto. — With the exception of North Carolina all States give the governor power to veto bills passed by the legislature, though such veto may be overridden by a subsequent vote of the legislature.[1] Originally most State governors did not have the veto power; but as suffrage expanded more rapidly than education, people attempted to safeguard themselves against unwise legislation by giving the veto power to their governors. Usually when a bill is sent to a governor for his signature, he is allowed from three to ten days in which to take action.[2] In case a governor does not approve a bill he may veto it in its entirety, and in nearly all States he is allowed to veto undesirable "items" in appropriation bills.

In order to check extravagance, most of the States allow the governor to veto specific items in a general appropriation bill. However, this power of the governor encourages legislators to vote appropriations in excess of the revenues in order to comply with the wishes of the various institutions seeking State aid, and thus "put it up to the governor" to veto numerous items so that the total amount appropriated will come within the revenues of the State.

In some States the veto is used quite freely — sometimes too freely and unwisely. On occasions more than half of the bills passed have been vetoed. In 1931 one governor vetoed 69 of the 208 bills passed, and eliminated a number of items from other bills. The vetoed bills included one creating a State income tax, one regulating marriage, a uniform traffic code passed in agreement with neighboring States, a bill to permit the city manager form of government, one permitting a district to develop irrigation, a reapportionment bill, and one requiring voters to declare their party preference when registering.

Judicial Powers of a Governor. — Nearly all of the governors have some power of mercy towards persons accused or convicted of crime.

---

[1] In two thirds of the States the legislatures are permitted to override the veto of the governor by the re-passage of a vetoed bill with a two-thirds vote in each house. In Delaware, Maryland, and Nebraska a majority of three fifths is required, and in a few States a bare majority is sufficient to overcome his veto.

[2] The period allowed the governor after adjournment is longer in some States. For instance, it is 20 days in Oregon and 45 in New Jersey.

It may be to remit fines, to shorten jail or penitentiary sentences, to pardon a prisoner conditionally or absolutely, to postpone the execution of a death sentence, or to change a death sentence to a penitentiary sentence. That is, a governor may have all or some of these powers, but these powers are commonly shared by a State board of pardons.

The primary purpose of the pardoning power is to release prisoners who have been proved innocent after being sentenced; but one governor pardoned some hundreds of prisoners because he thought the penitentiary as then conducted would do the convicted persons more harm than good, and another pardoned about a thousand because he thought the sentences were out of proportion to the offenses. This arbitrary use of the pardon power is dangerous because it encourages the so-called "lynch law." If one man can overturn the opinions of many jurors, there is danger that the people will take the enforcement of law into their own hands.

A good illustration of the wise use of the pardon occurred recently in New Jersey. The State law makes it a crime to kill rabbits out of season. A young boy, discovering a rabbit destroying his garden, got his gun and shot it. He was arrested and brought before a judge. The law was clear and the judge was forced to pronounce a jail sentence. However, the judge immediately wired the Governor requesting a pardon, and it was granted.

A pardon may be conditional. For instance, a governor of New York once pardoned a prisoner on condition that he would not make capital of his notoriety by posing for motion pictures or appearing on the vaudeville stage.

Miscellaneous Duties of a Governor are to serve on innumerable *ex-officio* boards, receive official visitors, attend official functions, hear persisting applicants for appointment, meet with party leaders, wade through stacks of documents, sign official papers, make a speech to every crossroads organization, and in some States dry the tears of mothers whose husbands are in the penitentiary. And, increasingly, governors are called upon to help settle labor disputes.

Removal of a Governor. — In most States the lower house of the Legislature may impeach a governor, and the senate sits as a court and may remove him by a two-thirds vote. In about a fourth of the States the governor may be removed by the recall. If a prescribed number of voters sign a petition for his recall, an election is held in which the majority of voters decide whether he shall be expelled from office.

Conference of Governors. — In 1908 Theodore Roosevelt called a Conference of Governors at the White House to confer in regard to the conservation of the natural resources of the country. Since then the governors have held an annual conference (this year in Seattle)

THE EXECUTIVE MANSION, BATON ROUGE, LOUISIANA

for the purpose of discussing uniform laws, interstate good will, and the interchange of State experience. Although few uniform laws have resulted from these gatherings, no doubt the conferences have encouraged a useful exchange of ideas and perhaps brought better co-operation in many interstate activities.

The Council of State Governments, *Cosgo* for short, is an organization which is attempting to facilitate co-operation among the States. It has headquarters in an "interstate capitol" building in Chicago with branch offices in New York and San Francisco. It arranges annual meetings of State officials called General Assemblies and is composed of Committees or Commissions on Interstate Co-operation in each of the forty-eight States. It is designed to promote uniform laws, reciprocal agreements, and interstate compacts.

A State Commission of Interstate Co-operation commonly consists of five *ex-officio* administrative officials, five senators, and five members of the lower house. Legislation establishing these commissions provides that "The Council of State Governments is hereby declared to be a joint governmental agency of this State and of the other States which co-operate through it."

HEADQUARTERS OF PUBLIC OFFICIALS ORGANIZATIONS

This building at 1313 East Sixtieth Street, Chicago, Illinois, is occupied by the secretariats of ten independent national associations of public officials, including Cosgo, the Council of State Government.

The Council is the secretariat for the Governors' Conference, the American Legislators' Association, the National Association of Attorneys General, the National Association of Secretaries of State, and the National Association of State Budget Officers. Some of the many projects promoted by Cosgo are flood control in New England; sanitation, power, and navigation in the Delaware River Basin; water conservation in the dry regions of the Northwest; transient relief and settlement laws; crime control; uniform taxation; milk control; liquor control; and conservation of wild life.

Executive Officers. — Most States have the following officers and, except in those States that have made progress in administrative consolidation, the officers are popularly elected and are more or less independent of the governor:

The Lieutenant-Governor. — There is a lieutenant-governor in thirty-seven of the States, and he is elected by the people. He serves when a governor is absent from his State or incapacitated for duty. He is *ex-officio* president of the Senate in all of these States except Massachusetts, but has a vote only in case of a tie. In most States he succeeds to the governorship if for any reason the office becomes vacant. In the eleven States which do not have a lieutenant-governor, and in Massachusetts, the Senate elects its own president.

The Secretary of State is the chief clerk and records the official acts of the governor and legislature, has charge of various State papers and documents, and performs other miscellaneous duties.

The Auditor or Comptroller (found in all but one State) [1] audits the accounts of State officers charged with the collection or disbursement of State funds. No money may be drawn from the State treasury without a warrant drawn by him; and he will not issue a warrant until he is satisfied that the expenditure is in all respects legal. In the different States he performs various other functions connected with the proper collection and disbursement of the public funds.

The State Treasurer receives the State moneys for safe keeping and pays them out only upon warrants (orders) from the comptroller, auditor, or other designated officer.

The Attorney-General is the principal law officer of the State. He gives legal advice to the governor and other executive officers, and represents the State in court if the case is of sufficient importance.

The Superintendent of Public Instruction [2] is the head of the public school system of the State, along with a school board which is found in most States. He issues regulations for the schools and sees that the school laws are enforced. He distributes school funds and collects school statistics for his regular reports.

Additional Officers and Boards or Commissions exist in great numbers but vary from State to State. A State function may be performed by

---

[1] The Secretary of State is *ex-officio* auditor in Oregon.
[2] In some States this school officer bears a different title.

a director or a superintendent or a commissioner or by a board or by a commission. The following are typical:

(1) *Boards for State Institutions* such as charitable, correctional, or educational institutions;

(2) *Boards to Supervise State Functions* such as board of health, board of agriculture, and highway commission;

(3) *Boards to Supervise Commercial Corporations* such as railway or public service commission, banking commission, and insurance commission; and

(4) *Examining Boards* such as board of medical examiners and civil service commission.

Administrative Consolidation. — As one function after another was added to the work of the State government, offices, boards, and commissions were established in a haphazard fashion, independent of one another, to care for the new tasks. Some States had over 100 such independent establishments, and their duties and functions often overlapped. Not only was there duplication of effort, but a lack of coordination between the separate agencies. The officers of the administration were usually elected by the people, thus making the governor responsible for persons he probably would never have chosen for his administration. All of these defects led to a general waste of funds in State government.

In the past 30 years about 40 of the States have undertaken steps to reorganize their systems of government. The general trends are (1) to consolidate into a few major departments the dozens of independent agencies existing heretofore; (2) to have a departmental head, appointed and removable by the governor, in full charge of each department; (3) to develop executive budget control and centralized purchasing power for the State. The chart on the following page illustrates how such consolidation was effected in New York State many years ago.

As a check on the administration and its use of funds, a State auditor is commonly elected by the voters, or, perhaps better, appointed by and responsible to the State legislature. He should audit all accounts kept by the administration and report on the financial condition of the State to the legislature and to the people.

Whenever there are functions of a legislative, judicial, advisory, or inspectional character within a department, a board or commission may

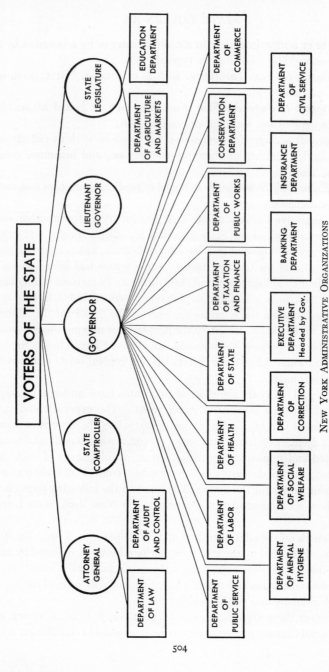

New York Administrative Organizations

Circles indicate elected officials; rectangles show those who are appointed.

advantageously be attached to the department to perform any one of these duties.

An Illustration of the Respective Responsibilities of Governor, Legislature, and a Commission. — Whether or not a State shall have a system of State highways is for its legislature to decide. Whether roads shall be State highways is also for the legislature to decide. Who shall construct the highways and how much money shall be expended are likewise questions for the legislature to decide. If the legislature prescribes a highway program, and creates a highway commission to be appointed by the governor to carry out the program, it is the commission's duty to build the highways, not the governor's.

The governor has nothing to do with how, when, and where the roads shall be built. His duty is to appoint the commissioners, and see that they carry out the program prescribed by the legislature. He should, however, have administrative power to see that the commission sets up an efficient organization and does not waste the State's money. He should therefore have the power of removal as well as the power of appointment.

QUESTIONS ON THE TEXT

1. By what title is the chief executive officer of each State known?

2. What did Madison mean when he said, "The executives of the States are in general little more than ciphers; the legislatures are omnipotent"? Does this condition remain true?

3. How do the powers of a governor compare with those of the President?

4. What executive powers has the governor?

5. What is meant by the statement that "a governor is the captain of a Ship of State, which is navigated by a crew that he does not select, and over which he has few powers of command"?

6. Describe the manner in which the State police in some States assist the governor in enforcing the laws.

7. Is the appointive power of the governor on the increase or decrease?

8. Name the three legislative powers of the governor.

9. Explain the use which a strong governor makes of messages.

10. Under what circumstances does a governor call an extra session of the legislature?

11. Under what condition may a bill become law in the State in which you live, if vetoed by the governor?

12. What advantage results from the power possessed by most governors to veto specific items in appropriation bills? What unpleasant duty is often shifted from the legislatures to the governor as a result of this power?

13. What judicial powers has a governor?

14. Under what conditions should a governor grant pardons?

15. Describe the Council of State Governments, and explain its purpose.

PROBLEMS FOR DISCUSSION

1. Who is the governor of the State in which you live? May he succeed himself as governor?

2. In New Jersey no executive officers of the State are elected by the people except the governor. With all the interest centered in the governor, it is easy to express intelligent opinions at the polls. Would you favor having the State executive officers appointed by the governor in your State?

3. Should a governor have power to remove sheriffs, prosecuting attorneys, and mayors when in his judgment they are guilty of neglect or inefficiency in the discharge of their duties?

4. Should a governor have power to grant pardons alone or only upon the recommendation of a State board of pardons?

5. The Michigan State Police have ingratiated themselves with the public through emergency services. For instance, every police car is equipped with a fire extinguisher, a respirator, and a first-aid kit. In an emergency, the car can be converted into an ambulance. For the troubled motorist they carry tire patches and extra gasoline. Should policemen assume the attitude of authority or of service? Should law-abiding individuals dread policemen, or realize that they are friends?

6. New York State keeps a small percentage of its employees' salaries each month and pensions them when they retire. When Governor Smith retired after serving the State in various capacities for a quarter of a century he was granted an annuity of $6100 for the rest of his life; and Senator Wagner $10,000 after 43 years' service. Does your State have such a pension system?

7. Employees in most cities and in nearly half of the States enter office through competitive examinations for permanent tenure; and in New York State it is a crime to discriminate even in private employment because of race, color, creed, or national origin. Five $10,000 commissioners enforce this law and promote friendly relations. Discuss.

8. New York State has a school for police which trains police for any locality. Do you consider that such schools should be made available for policemen in every State?

9. New York towns can have State police permanently by paying their salaries. Why may these State police be superior to police chosen locally?

10. Between the years 1870 and 1890 the State of Pennsylvania supplied the bulk of the lumber for the entire United States. Six million acres became desert because of unextinguished cigarettes and careless methods of logging. With the forests gone, the soil washed from the hillsides, springs dried up, water power declined, and in summer some regions had to be supplied with water by trains of tank cars. Gifford Pinchot, as a National Forest Commissioner and then as Governor of the State, had millions of seedling trees produced and planted in State forests or given to farmers to plant in their wood lots.

Pinchot's program was the forerunner of similar programs in other States. These programs require heavy expenditures of State and Federal funds. Pinchot predicted that an expenditure of $25,000,000 to purchase and replant five million acres of rough hillsides would yield, after forty years, an annual income equal to the entire appropriation. Give your reasons for approving or disapproving such a program for your State.

11. The 1947 Constitution of New Jersey increased from 5 to 45 days the period for the Governor to consider bills at the end of the legislative session. At the end of this period the legislature automatically re-convenes to consider vetoed measures. This gives the Governor time for careful consideration of the many bills that pile up at the end of a session; but it also prolongs his agony as pressure groups will harass him with requests to veto measures detrimental to particular interests. How long a period has the Governor of your State?

12. If a Governor is authorized to veto specific items in appropriation bills he can keep the budget balanced by vetoing all appropriations in excess of a State's revenue. It also enables a Governor to punish a legislator who opposes the Governor's measures by vetoing appropriations promoted by that legislator. Does your Governor have this power to veto items in appropriation bills? Do you favor the power?

SELECT BIBLIOGRAPHY

GRAVES, W. *American State Government.* Heath. Boston. 1953 ed. Chapters 9–12.

BOWLES, C. *Governor's Job as Seen by a Governor.* N. Y. Times Magazine. July 24, 1949, pages 8 ff.

Council of State Governments, *Reorganizing State Governments.* Chicago, 1950.

State Manual, Handbook, or Bluebook (perhaps different name). Usually free to a school from Secretary of State.

CHAPTER XXIX

STATE COURTS

A Court is a tribunal established by the State for the administration of justice according to law.[1] Courts settle disputes between private persons, and between private persons and government. They protect the rights of individuals as guaranteed in the Federal and State Constitutions. They determine the guilt or innocence of persons accused of crime. And they act as checks on the executive and legislative branches of the government.[2]

Organization of State Courts. — The constitution in each State provides for the judicial branch and usually leaves the detailed organization of the State court system to the legislature. Article VII, Section 1, of the Indiana Constitution is typical: "The judicial power of the State shall be vested in a Supreme Court, Circuit Courts, and such other courts as the General Assembly may establish."

Justice of the Peace. — At the base of the State judicial system, in rural areas and small towns, is the Justice of the Peace. He presides over what is commonly called the Justice Court, and he is usually elected for a short term, commonly two years.

The Justice of the Peace generally has jurisdiction[3] in most mis-

---

[1] Recall that in the American federal arrangement there are two separate and distinct court systems: the National judiciary and the 48 State judiciaries. The National court system (see Chapter XXI) has jurisdiction over a limited class of cases enumerated in the U. S. Constitution, Article III, Section 2 (see pages 381–2, 741–2). All other cases are States cases.

[2] In several States courts also perform a variety of non-judicial functions. School boards are judicially appointed in some States, for example; and in Tennessee the Supreme Court appoints the Attorney General. In various States courts also supervise elections, grant business licenses, administer estates, manage the properties of bankrupts, etc. These administrative functions consume much time and many feel that they interfere with the primary court function — to hear and decide cases.

[3] Jurisdiction (Latin *jus* and *dictio*) here refers to the authority of a court to hear and decide cases.

demeanor [1] cases and minor civil cases.[2] To illustrate, a Justice of the Peace often hears such misdemeanor cases as traffic violations, disregard of health ordinances, breaches of the peace, etc. He often hears such civil cases as those involving money demands (seldom over $50 or $100), the ownership of personal property, and wrongs or injuries to property. He generally does not have jurisdiction in such civil cases as those involving title to real estate, titles to office, torts (wrongs) to the person, and like matters of considerable importance.

A Justice of the Peace is often also empowered to hold preliminary hearings of serious complaints — as, for example, in a murder case. Here his function is much like that of a grand jury — to determine whether sufficient evidence exists to hold the accused for trial in a higher court.

Police or Magistrates' Courts. — The lowest courts in urban areas, especially in larger towns and cities, are known as Police or Magistrates' Courts. These courts are much like the Justice Courts, with almost identical jurisdiction. The judges are usually elected and salaries are generally quite low. Like the Justice Courts, the Municipal Courts are often criticized because the judges are seldom trained in the law [3] and corruption and political favoritism are not altogether unknown.

Municipal Courts. — In recent years so-called Municipal Courts have been created in practically every larger town and city. They usually have full jurisdiction over all civil and criminal cases arising within the municipality.

---

[1] Crimes are of two kinds: felonies and misdemeanors. A felony is the greater crime and may be punished by a heavier fine and/or imprisonment or death. A misdemeanor is the lesser crime involving a smaller fine and/or a short jail term.

[2] A *civil case* is a suit brought by one party against another for the enforcement or protection of a private right, or the prevention or redress of a tort (private wrong). It is distinguished from a *criminal case* which is brought by the State against one accused of committing a crime — a public wrong. The State is not often a party to a civil case, but it always is (as prosecutor) to a criminal case.

[3] Though a local lawyer sometimes does preside over these courts, this is not the common rule. A recent study in California showed that non-lawyer justices included carpenters, ministers, truck drivers, school teachers, real estate agents, contractors, bookkeepers, and druggists (not to mention a wife who held court when her husband went fishing). Several States, including California, have been attempting to remedy this situation. In Missouri, for instance, Justice Courts have been eliminated and replaced with Magistrates' Courts with judges selected from the legal profession.

In many of the largest cities the Municipal Courts have been organized into divisions — either on a geographic or on a functional basis. Thus among the five boroughs of New York City there are 28 Municipal Court districts. And in Philadelphia there are five divisions of the Municipal Court: civil, criminal, juvenile, domestic relations, and misdemeanor. Several cities also have other functional divisions such as traffic, small claims, probate, and the like.

More and more cities are organizing their Municipal Courts on this functional basis. They are doing so because the scheme provides for courts which specialize in the major types of controversies heard in Municipal Courts.

Take Small Claims Courts as an example. Many people cannot afford to pay the costs involved in suing for the collection of a small debt. A paper boy can hardly afford to hire an attorney and pay court costs in order to collect a month's subscription due from one of his customers. Or a widow who runs a lodging-house can hardly afford to sue for a month's room rent. Many small tradespeople have been forced to wipe such small debts off their books or sell them at about one half to collection agencies.

Small Claims Courts have been created to cover just such situations as these. In them a person can bring his claim at an extremely low cost or at no cost at all. The proceedings are quite informal, the judge usually handling matters without attorneys for either side.

The informality of these courts is illustrated by the court (known as the Conciliation Branch) in Cleveland, Ohio. In this court a landlady brought a claim against a boarder who had set fire to a mattress by smoking in bed. The defendant (the boarder) was willing to pay, but he disputed the amount demanded by the plaintiff (the landlady). The judge phoned a department store, learned the price of the mattress, and the matter was settled immediately.

The Small Claims Divisions of the Municipal Court in New York try cases involving less than $50. In one case a waiter in a spaghetti-house had spilled huckleberry pie and coffee on a customer's trousers. The judge believed the trousers were seersucker. But the customer's wife produced a receipt for $12.50 and said the trousers were "billed as flannel." "God help the dealer's soul," said the judge, as he gave judgment for $7 plus $1.25 costs.

As another of these functional divisions several cities now have

Juvenile Courts. These courts usually handle cases involving those under 18 years of age. And often they are (should be) presided over by judges especially trained and interested in minors and their problems. Depending on the facts in a given case, the judge may simply offer good advice, place a minor on probation, levy a fine, or if necessary sentence him to a reform school.

In a very short time one morning the judge of a Juvenile Court handled the following four cases. No. 1 was a fight between two small boys. The mother of the larger boy was present and was directed to go into an adjoining room and whip her boy in the presence of an officer. No. 2 was a young girl brought in by her parents. The girl, agreeing to do better, was directed to return to her home and to report weekly to a woman probation officer. No. 3, a girl who had previously been on probation, was accused of stealing. She was turned over to the State reformatory. No. 4 was a young man who accused a boy of annoying his "place of business," a shoe-shine stand. Their statements conflicted. When one referred to a reputable witness, they were ordered to return three days later with the witness.

General Trial Courts. — Above the courts so far considered are the general trial courts. They are variously known as County, Circuit, District, Superior, or Common Pleas courts. In over three fourths of the States the trial court judges are popularly elected, commonly serving a four-year term.

The jurisdiction of these trial courts is quite broad. They exercise both original and appellate (appeal) jurisdiction, and it is here that the major civil and criminal cases are begun. Many minor cases that may also be instituted in the Justice, Police or Magistrates', or Municipal Courts may be (and are) begun in the trial courts. And when appeals from the lower courts are heard in the trial court a completely new trial is often held.

Cases in the trial courts are usually heard by the judge and a petit jury (the trial jury which hears and decides the facts at issue in a case). Criminal cases are presented to the trial courts by grand jury indictments or by information on motion of district attorneys. (See pages 512–516.)

Intermediate Appellate Courts. — In over one third of the States there are courts of appeal between the trial courts and the highest State court. These intermediate appellate courts have been created in an effort to ease the load of the highest court. Besides their appellate jurisdiction these courts occasionally have original jurisdiction in such controversies as contested elections.

By Lady Stanley

HIS FIRST OFFENSE

This painting shows an English newsboy before the bar of justice.

Like the trial courts, these courts of appeal are known by a variety of names.[1] The judges are elected in some States and are appointed in others. In Illinois these appeals courts are composed of Circuit Court judges assigned by the State Supreme Court.

State Supreme Court. — As the capstone of the State judicial system stands a Supreme Court, the highest court in the State.[2] The justices, ranging from three in Arizona, Nevada, and Wyoming to sixteen in New Jersey, are most often elected by the people. In a few States the justices are appointed by the governor (as in Maine and Delaware) or by the legislature (as in Connecticut, Vermont, and South Carolina).

The State Supreme Court's primary function is to hear appeals from the decisions of the lower courts. It is the final interpreter of the State's constitution and laws.

Appeals may be taken from a State Supreme Court to the Supreme Court of the United States — *but only* when a "federal question" is involved, that is, when the case hinges upon the meaning of a provision of the United States Constitution or a Federal statute or treaty.

Juries. — A jury is a body of persons selected according to law, and sworn to declare the truth on the evidence laid before it. There are two kinds of juries [3] — the grand jury and the petit (trial) jury.

The Grand Jury. — A grand jury is a body of persons summoned into a court to consider the evidence against persons accused of crimes,

---

[1] In New York, for example, there is an Appellate Division of the Supreme Court. The highest court in the New York judicial system is known as the Court of Appeals.

[2] This court of last resort is known as the Supreme Court in 39 States. But in Connecticut it is styled the Supreme Court of Errors, in Maine the Supreme Judicial Court, in West Virginia the Supreme Court of Appeals, etc.

[3] The so-called coroner's jury is not a real jury.

and to determine whether the evidence is sufficient to justify a formal trial for such persons. This jury consists of twenty-three jurors or less, according to the State law and the importance of the charges to be investigated. In most States it consists of more than twelve jurors, of whom at least twelve must agree that an accused person is probably guilty, or he cannot be held for trial. In some States the grand jury may consist of as few as six. When it consists of as few as six jurors, five must agree or the accused cannot be held for trial. Sometimes one person is appointed to investigate for the prosecuting attorney.

When a grand jury is impaneled (selected) the judge instructs the jurors to find a *true bill of indictment* (charge) against all persons whom the prosecuting attorney brings to their attention and whom they think probably guilty. He further instructs them to bring a *presentment* (accusation) against any person whom they of their own knowledge believe to have violated the criminal laws of the State within their county. They swear or affirm that they will do so, and retire to the jury room, where they deliberate in secret. Their chairman, appointed by the judge or chosen by themselves, is known as the *foreman*.

The prosecuting attorney for the county brings into the jury room witnesses to testify against the accused and usually questions them himself, but after he retires the jurors may resummon the same witnesses and question them further or may have the court summon other witnesses to testify against the accused. Nobody is allowed in the room with the jurors except the witnesses, the prosecuting attorney, and, in some States, his stenographer. All are bound to secrecy.

After all witnesses have been summoned and questioned, the jurors are left entirely alone to deliberate, and when they have completed their finding they proceed to the court-room and their bill of indictment is read in their presence. The bill is recorded in the clerk's office and the jury is dismissed if the term has expired; or, if the term has not expired, the jury is adjourned until the court needs it again to investigate other accusations.[1]

---

[1] It is not uncommon for a State to impose upon the grand jury duties other than the consideration of evidence against accused persons. For instance, they may be required to approve the erection of public buildings and bridges in Pennsylvania, fix the tax rate in Georgia, investigate the sufficiency of the bonds of county officers in Alabama and Tennessee, arrest persons selling liquor contrary to law or arrest intoxicated persons in Vermont.

In a peace-abiding county one grand jury a year is often found to be sufficient, whereas in counties where large cities are located there must either be a number of grand juries during the year or else the same grand jury must sit from time to time during several months, unless the State permits persons to be brought to trial by "*information*."

As a substitute for the grand jury method of bringing persons to trial, more than half of our States permit the judge to proceed with the trial upon the accusation brought by the prosecuting officer. This is called an "*information*." In a rural community grand jurors often possess personal knowledge of crimes that have been committed, but in large cities they seldom have this knowledge and their principal function should be to act upon cases where the evidence is circumstantial or the accused an influential person, and to bring to trial persons whom the prosecuting attorney fails to bring forward for personal reasons.

The Petit Jury. — A petit or trial jury is a group of persons summoned into court to hear the evidence on both sides of a case and to decide the disputed points of fact, the judge in most States deciding the points of law. This jury tries both civil and criminal cases. Any one may usually demand a jury trial if the question of life, liberty, or property is at stake.

The number of petit jurors is usually twelve, but in a number of States a lesser number is sufficient in civil cases and minor criminal cases. In the court of the justice of the peace six jurors or less is the rule, though in several States this court, too, may have twelve jurors.

In nearly one third of the States an agreement of two thirds, three fourths, or five sixths of the jurors is sufficient for a verdict in civil cases or unimportant criminal cases. In the remaining States a unanimous verdict is required even in unimportant cases.

The Grand Jury and the Petit Jury Compared. — The same courts that have *grand* juries to *accuse* have *petit* juries to *try* the accused. But some courts which do not have grand juries do have petit juries. For instance, in most States Justices' Courts may use petit juries, though they nowhere have grand juries; and courts which have no criminal jurisdiction have no need of grand juries. Appellate courts of last resort do not use either grand or petit juries because they are concerned primarily with points of law which have been appealed to them from the lower courts. A grand jury investigates all indictable offenses committed during its existence, and usually hears only accusations, seldom defenses.

Selection of Jurors. — In scarcely any two States are jurors selected in exactly the same manner, but in all they are selected in a similar manner. Once a year, or oftener, some county official [1] or special

DRAWING NAMES FOR A JURY

The deputy county clerk, at the left, draws names one by one. As they are drawn, the clerk at the right enters them in the book for jury service.

jury commissioners, appointed or elected as the law prescribes, prepare a considerable list of persons who are eligible for jury service.

In some States any qualified voter of the county in which the court is sitting is eligible, while in others only tax-payers may serve. In the former States the names can be obtained from the poll books and in the latter from the tax assessors' books. Persons under twenty-one and those over sixty or seventy years of age, criminals, and illiterates are commonly ineligible. In most States other classes of persons,

---

[1] This official is usually the clerk of the court, the sheriff, the judge, or county board of commissioners. In the New England States and in Michigan names of jurors are selected by township ("town") officers and sent to a county officer.

such as State and Federal officials, professional men, foremen, firemen, and State militiamen, are not required to serve.

The chosen names are written on slips of paper and placed in a locked jury box,[1] which is usually kept in the custody of the clerk of the court. When the court needs a jury the names are drawn from the box by a designated official, and the sheriff is directed to summon such persons by a writ known as a *venire facias* (you must come). After eliminating the names of those who, for good reason, cannot serve, the judge makes a list of those who can serve and returns it to the clerk. This list is known as the *panel of veniremen.*

Grand jurors are commonly selected in the same manner as petit jurors, but in some States a separate list of names is prepared from which grand jurors are selected. Jurors for the justices' courts are commonly selected by the justice himself.

It is a serious mistake for any intelligent citizen to evade jury service. An accused person, who may be entirely innocent, can hardly expect justice from a jury whose members have been chosen from the least intelligent people of a community; nor can law be enforced if the best people evade jury service. Every citizen who feels that he has been endowed with sufficient intelligence to judge the facts of a case fairly, should feel it his duty to organized society to answer willingly the call for jury service.

Criticisms and Proposed Reforms of the Jury System. — No aspect of the administration of justice has come in for more criticism, by both lawyer and laymen alike, than the operation of the jury system. These criticisms are not so much directed at the system itself as at the *operation* of that system. All of the criticisms made do not apply to all juries everywhere, of course. And many times critics are inclined to forget this vital fact: the jury system is intended *first* to protect the innocent and only *second* to convict the guilty.

The jury system developed in medieval England on the theory that a man accused of crime, or involved in a dispute with his neighbor, could expect fairer treatment in his case if the facts were weighed

---

[1] In New Jersey the chancellor (highest judge) appoints for each county a jury commissioner of the party opposed to that of the county sheriff. These two are commissioners of juries and they select names of eligible persons as in other States, but instead of being put into the jury box the names are numbered consecutively and a piece of metal with a corresponding number is dropped into the box in place of the name.

and decided by a group of his neighbors. Thus jurors were selected because of their firsthand knowledge of local persons and events.

Today, however, the situation is completely reversed. Those with firsthand knowledge are excluded from service. In effect, as one student of the jury system has put it, in the attempt to get impartiality "ignorance [of the facts] is made virtually a prerequisite for jury service."

© A. R. Willett

JUSTICE AND MERCY

This symbolic painting, by A. R. Willett, suggests the importance of tempering justice with mercy. A trial of a man by his peers — the jury — safeguards his rights.

Other weaknesses are pointed to. The process of selecting jurymen is frequently long and tedious with the result that the judge falls far behind his docket of cases. Busy people engaged in important business or professional pursuits are often excused from service. Too often this may mean that better qualified jurors escape service while others less qualified serve. (The extreme here is the "professional juror" — a poisonous parasite in our judicial system.)

Another criticism stems from the fact that many jury verdicts are, in reality, compromises reached in the interest of a formal verdict. And at times a jury's verdict seems to be the result of emotional appeal rather than of unrefuted evidence. Jury tampering has occasionally been known, as has bribery of judges.

These and similar charges against the system have led most authorities to recommend various reforms and a few would even do away with juries. One proposal, already adopted in several States, involves reducing the size of juries from the usual twelve to five or six. A lesser number can, presumably, more readily reach agreement without any greater likelihood of injustice being done.

Another proposal, already adopted in several States, too, involves relaxing the unanimity requirement for jury verdicts. If a substantial majority, say three-fourths, is required, "hung" juries are largely eliminated.

Going to the very heart of the weaknesses charged to the jury system is the suggestion that persons accused of crime, or involved in civil suits, be allowed to waive their right to trial by jury and have their case heard only by the judge. This is now fact in nearly every State in civil suits and misdemeanor cases. About one-third of the States also allow for waiver in felony cases.

Some few critics propose complete elimination of the jury in all cases and the hearing of disputes by a single judge or a panel of three judges. This suggestion assumes, of course, complete impartiality from the bench.

Advisory Opinions. — Ten of the highest State courts render what are known as advisory opinions. In all ten, such opinions are made available to the governor and in seven of the ten to the legislature as well.[1]

These advisory opinions make it possible for the legislature, when considering passage of a bill, and for the governor, before signing a bill, to secure the justices' opinions as to its constitutionality. These opinions are advisory only. If the bill is passed and later challenged, the high court is free to construe the measure as it will. But at least some indication of the court's attitude may be had in advance.

Declaratory Judgments. — In nearly every State, the various courts will render declaratory judgments. These judgments are available *before* an acutal case is instituted and are designed to indicate the legal rights of parties to a controversy. Suppose that the owner of a glue factory wants to expand his plant and a neighboring property owner objects. Rather than the one expanding his plant and the other seeking damages in court, both parties may ask the

---

[1] To both the legislature and the governor in Alabama, Colorado, Maine, Massachusetts, New Hampshire, North Carolina, and Rhode Island; to the governor only in Delaware, Florida, and South Dakota. In other States the attorney general, as the State's chief legal officer, performs this task.

court for a declaratory judgment setting forth the rights of each. This practice has forestalled many actions that might have led to long and expensive legal entanglements.

Advisory opinions and declaratory judgments are often confused with one another. Advisory opinions are not given in disputes between parties; they are intended only as legal advice to the governor or the legislature. And an advisory opinion is in no sense binding, not even upon the judges who render it. But a declaratory judgment is binding between the parties involved.

Legalized Arbitration. — The crowded calendars of our courts and the delays and expense of law suits have encouraged the settlement of business disputes by arbitration. Courts are necessary in all criminal and domestic-relations cases because the general public is concerned, and in title-to-real-estate cases because the law is difficult. But simple cases and those where the facts turn upon expert knowledge can be decided by specialists in a particular trade more quickly, and probably with more justice, than by a judge and jury.

For a hundred years the New York Chamber of Commerce has continuously provided for arbitration, and arbitration boards in the motion picture industry annually settle thousands of disputes involving millions of dollars. The American Arbitration Association, with headquarters in New York City, arbitrated 184 disputes in one year at an average cost of one half of one per cent of the amount involved. This Association has a panel of about 500 experts in their respective fields who agree to act as arbitrators if called upon when matters are submitted to the Tribunal of the Association.

Trade or commercial organizations often incorporate in a contract provisions for arbitration in case any dispute or claim arises. The contract may (1) specify the number of arbitrators and the method of selecting them; (2) merely refer to the State statute; or (3) provide for following the Rules of the American Arbitration Association. Under these rules attorneys may appear as counsel, but in some trade organizations attorneys are barred from the proceedings.

According to statutes passed by New York, Massachusetts, New Jersey, Pennsylvania, Oregon, California, and Louisiana, an agreement to arbitrate civil disputes, except divorces and titles to real estate, is enforceable just like any other contract. If either party refuses to arbitrate, the courts will compel him to do so. Arbitrators may require the attendance of witnesses and demand that documents be submitted. The award of the arbitrators may be recorded in the same way as a court judgment, and can be collected by the officers of the court. The courts may set aside the award of the arbitrators if partiality, corruption, misconduct, or mistake is evident.

QUESTIONS ON THE TEXT

1. What are the duties of a court?
2. What two systems of courts are there in each State?
3. What classes of cases are brought into the Federal courts? into the State courts?
4. Distinguish a civil from a criminal case. A felony from a misdemeanor.
5. What are commonly the lowest courts in a State's judicial system?
6. What special courts do cities commonly have?
7. What is a juvenile court? Explain the need of small claims courts. Describe the different types.
8. What is meant by *appellate jurisdiction?*
9. Do judges have any duties other than interpreting law and deciding cases?
10. What is a grand jury? What is a petit jury? How many jurors commonly compose each? How does a grand jury differ from a petit jury?
11. Does the highest State court have jury trials?
12. Who serve on juries and how are they chosen?
13. What is meant by a *true bill of indictment? presentment? foreman?*
14. What is an advisory opinion? What is a declaratory judgment?

PROBLEMS FOR DISCUSSION

1. Describe your State's court system. What is the jurisdiction of each of the courts? How are the judges chosen for each? (Consult your State Constitution and, if there is one, the State Manual.)
2. If possible, invite a local judge or attorney to address the class.
3. Is it more important that a legislator, governor, or a judge be chosen for a long term?
4. Why are citizens never justified in resorting to lynch law?
5. "The Constitution of New Hampshire provides that when the governor cannot discharge the duties of his office, the president of the senate shall assume them. During the severe illness of a governor recently the president of the senate hesitated to act in his stead; it was not clear that the situation was grave enough to warrant such a course. Accordingly the attorney-general of the State brought an action against the president of the senate for

not doing his duty. The court considered the situation, decided against the president of the senate, and ordered him to become acting governor. Why was this necessary? Was it conducted in a hostile spirit? Wherein did the decision help the State? Wherein did it help the defendant? Wherein may it possibly prove helpful in the future history of the State?" — *Civil Government in the United States*, by John Fiske.

6. Most States elect their judges. Why do many students of government think it better to have them appointed by the governor or by the chief justice of the highest court in the State, or elected by the licensed lawyers in the territory in which they serve?

7. Jury service is so burdensome to business men of cities that some young men refuse to register for voting in order that their names may not be so easily obtained for jury service. Would you favor abolishing juries for civil cases and the less important criminal cases?

8. In Idaho a prisoner charged with threatening a man with a revolver was tried and found guilty by a jury composed wholly of women. Should men be tried by men, women by women?

9. A New Yorker kept account of 46 times that he put a penny in a subway vending machine for a penny chocolate and every time the machine failed to work; so he sued the company owning the machine and recovered 46¢ plus $1.25 advanced for a summons. In what court?

10. Does, or would, the presence of a small claims court in your community help to increase respect for law and government? Do you suppose the newsboy who won a 45-cent suit for a newspaper account became a more patriotic citizen because of the Small Claims Court?

11. In Virginia in each county the former Justices of the Peace are now replaced by one County Justice appointed by the Circuit Judge. As a practicing attorney, the appointee can hear these minor cases on the side. The appointee is usually an able lawyer very superior to the average Justice of the Peace. Should every State have such County Justices instead of township Justices of the Peace?

12. Give your arguments for or against a law, proposed or in existence, giving legal approval to arbitrated cases in your State. What disputes growing out of the industries of your community would lend themselves to arbitration?

SELECT BIBLIOGRAPHY

"Legal Log Jam in Chicago." *Life*, November 10, 1952.

State Manual. (Facts pertaining to courts of your State in State Constitution and State Manual.)

MACDONALD, A. *American State Government and Administration*. Crowell. N. Y. 1950 ed. Chapters 12 and 13.

CHAPTER XXX

CIVIL AND CRIMINAL PROCEDURE

Civil Procedure. — A civil suit is one between two persons [1] as distinguished from a criminal case, in which the State is the plaintiff against a person charged with a public offense. There are two kinds of civil procedure — *law* suits and *equity* [2] suits.

For instance, if one owes you a debt, does injury to your person or property, or violates a contract, you can sue him at law for money damages; but if you want to restrain persons from committing wrongs, you must get an injunction (an equity writ), which will direct the individuals to refrain from doing the wrong, or if you desire the specific performance of a contract instead of money damages, or if a person who has property in trust for you refuses to pay you the income, you can sue him in equity.

In cases at *law* the judge usually has a jury to decide the facts, and the witnesses usually testify in court; but in *equity* cases the judge usually decides the facts himself without a jury, and instead of having the witnesses in court he often appoints a "referee" to hear the evidence and report it to him in writing. In the following examples, the two kinds of suits are illustrated as they would proceed in Virginia. They would proceed in a similar manner in other States.

---

[1] One or both persons may be artificial, *i.e.*, a corporation, such as the Pennsylvania Railroad Company or the U. S. Steel Corporation.

[2] *Equity* is a branch of law which developed alongside of common law (page 472). Most of the early English law was developed by courts instead of by parliament. The judges of the courts in time became conservative and ceased to create means of obtaining justice as new conditions demanded. They had certain forms, called "court writs," upon which one had to state his case. If he could not state it on one of these forms, he could not bring suit in court. Aggrieved persons appealed directly to the king for justice. The appeals became so numerous that the king created a new court, called Chancery Court, to administer justice by deciding in a conscientious and equitable manner cases in which justice could not be obtained at common law. Hence grew up a branch of law known as *equity*, with a distinct set of principles and writs; and these two branches were brought over to our States.

Today 7 States have separate equity ("chancery") courts; in 12 others the same courts administer common law and equity; and the rest use the same procedure.

Suit at Law. — Suppose Mr. A., a passenger, has received bodily injury from a railroad wreck in Albemarle County, say on the Southern Railroad, and brings suit for $5000 damages. Here Mr. A. is the *plaintiff* and the Southern Railroad Company the *defendant.* Mr. A. will have his lawyer file his claim against the Southern Railroad Company with the clerk of the court in Albemarle County. The railroad company will deny A.'s right to $5000 damages, by a plea, and will have its lawyer represent it in court.

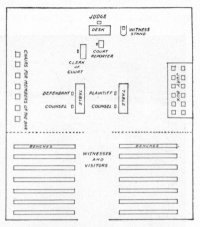

TYPICAL PLAN OF A COURTROOM

When the judge holds court in Albemarle County a jury will be impaneled unless the lawyers, known as the counsel for the plaintiff and defendant, are willing to dispense with a jury. The judge also must agree to decide the facts of the case, as well as the law, else the jury cannot be dispensed with. If a jury is impaneled it will decide all disputed facts, as, for example, whether Mr. A. was in fact injured, to what extent injured, and hence how much damages he should receive; whereas the judge will decide all points of law and instruct the jury as to the law.

After the counsel for each side argues the facts of the case, the judge instructs the jury as to the law and the jury retires to the jury room. After deliberation, if the jury can agree upon the amount of damage done Mr. A., it renders a decision, called a *verdict.* If the jurors cannot agree, it is a mistrial and the case may be tried again. The judge finally gives *judgment* in accordance with the verdict of the jury. In this case if the judgment is in favor of the plaintiff, the defendant may appeal the case to the Supreme Court of Appeals, because damages exceeding $300 are involved. Or suppose the defendant accepts the decision but fails to make prompt payment of the damages awarded; then the clerk will issue an execution to the sheriff or a constable directing him to levy execution and sell the personal property of the defendant. If there is no personal property the court may authorize the sale of real estate.

Suit in Equity. — Suppose X., a farmer, has a fresh stream of water running through his farm and by his house, which he uses to water his stock and which his wife uses for washing clothes. Y. establishes a

Harold M. Lambert

A LAWYER ADDRESSES THE JURY IN A SUIT AT LAW

large creamery on this stream above the farm of X. The creamery empties greasy water and acids into the stream to such an extent that it produces a stench at the farmer's home, his cattle refuse to drink the water, and the water can no longer be used for washing clothes.

X. will have his attorney file suit with the clerk of the court to enjoin (forbid) Y. from emptying the grease and acids into the water, and the clerk will have the sheriff notify Y. that suit has been brought. A jury is not needed to decide the facts, and witnesses need not appear in court.[1] A master in chancery, notary public, or justice of the peace gets the counsel for each side together at some convenient time and place to take *depositions* (testimony), which a stenographer records

---

[1] In some States the evidence would be taken in open court, the lawyers and judge asking questions of the witnesses.

word for word. These depositions are given to the judge, and the counsel for the plaintiff and for the defendant argue the points of law and evidence before the judge in court or in vacation (between terms).

If the judge is not satisfied as to the facts perhaps he will go to the scene, call witnesses before him, or order the master in chancery to make further investigation as to certain facts. With the facts and the law both presented, the judge is prepared to render a decision, which is called a *decree* in equity cases. If the judge decides that the injury to X. is as claimed, he will decree that Y. must cease emptying grease and acids into the stream.

The court costs of a civil suit such as witness fees, jury fees, and recording fees are usually placed by the court upon the party losing the case, and sometimes some costs are granted with which to pay lawyers, but each party usually pays his own lawyers.

Crimes. — A crime is an act or omission which is prohibited by law as injurious to the public and is punished by the State in a proceeding in its own name or in the name of the people thereof. Crimes may be immoral in themselves, such as murder or burglary, or they may be acts considered as crimes only because they have been prohibited by law, such as exceeding the speed limit in an automobile or failing to remove snow from the sidewalk. Crimes are of two degrees — felonies and misdemeanors.

Felonies are crimes of a more serious character than misdemeanors. They vary so much from State to State that no general definition of them can be given, but in many States all crimes which are punishable by confinement in a State penitentiary or by death are defined as felonies. The following crimes are almost universally classed as felonies.

(1) *Murder in the First Degree* generally means the unlawful, intentional, and premeditated killing of a human being, or such a killing resulting from the commission or the attempt to commit one of the graver crimes such as arson, burglary, or robbery. Such crimes are punished in about a fourth of the States by death, in about half by death or life imprisonment, and in the remaining States by long terms in the penitentiary — usually for life.

(2) *Murder in the Second Degree* generally means the unlawful, intentional killing without premeditation, or such killing as a result of an attempt to commit some lesser crime. It is punished by imprisonment

varying from a minimum of one year in a few States to a maximum of life in many States, and even death in several.

(3) *Manslaughter* is the unlawful killing of another without malice. The killing may be voluntary, upon a sudden heat of passion; or it may be involuntary, in the commission of some unlawful act or a lawful act without due caution. Many States divide manslaughter into two degrees. It is punished by imprisonment for a term ordinarily shorter than that for murder in the second degree. Great discretion is given to the jury or judge.

(4) *Arson* is the act of unlawfully and maliciously burning a building or other property. It is more serious if done at night and most serious if an inhabited dwelling is burned at night.

(5) *Burglary* is the breaking and entering of a dwelling house during the night, with the intent to commit a felony therein, whether the felony be actually committed or not. The same offense is called housebreaking if committed during the day. In some States, the charge of burglary covers illegal entry into other buildings besides dwelling houses.

(6) *Robbery* is the theft of property from the person or in the immediate presence of the victim, accompanied by force or fear.

(7) *Larceny* is simply theft, and *grand larceny* is the theft of property above a fixed value, generally from $25 to $50. In a number of States to steal any amount from the person of another without force or fear is considered grand larceny.

Arson, burglary, robbery, grand larceny, assault with intent to kill, bigamy, perjury, forgery, and embezzlement are commonly punished by a considerable term of imprisonment. Burglary may be punished by death in one State, robbery by death in two States, and arson by death in six States.

Misdemeanors are crimes of a less serious character than felonies and, like felonies, cannot be defined by any general definition which will apply to all States. For instance, in Virginia offenses which are punishable with death or confinement in the penitentiary are felonies; all other offenses are misdemeanors. In the same State the following crimes are misdemeanors and, in general, would be so classed in other States: violation of town or city ordinances, carrying concealed weapons, cruelty to animals, attempting to defraud a hotel-keeper, petit larceny, which is a theft less than a grand larceny, non-support of wife and minor children, permitting a gambling house on one's premises, libel, assault and battery. These misdemeanors are punishable by confinement in jail or by fine. But such misdemeanors as drunkenness without disorder or profanity are punishable by fine only. In such cases if the person who has been fined cannot or will not pay his fine, he may be sent to jail according to the law of many States.

Criminal Procedure. — *Arrest of Felons.* — A private individual may arrest a person to prevent the commission of a felony in his presence, or may, without a warrant, arrest a felon whom he has seen commit a felony, or may even arrest one without a warrant on reasonable suspicion of his having committed a felony, provided a felony has been committed.

An officer of the peace (sheriff, constable, police) may do anything a private person may do. He should furthermore pursue a felon who is making his escape though he has not actually seen the crime committed. If the police, constable, or sheriff does not attempt to arrest a felon, the prosecuting attorney will usually take the initiative and have the suspected felon arrested.

The injured party or anyone knowing of the crime may go to a justice of the peace or some other magistrate who has power to issue a warrant and, by taking oath as to the crime, have a warrant issued for the arrest of some designated person, provided the magistrate is satisfied as to the truth of the complaint. The *warrant* is a written document describing the felon, setting forth the offense, and directing that he be brought before some specified magistrate, usually the one who has issued the warrant. A policeman, constable, sheriff, or any other peace officer may make the arrest ("serve the warrant") and bring the felon before the proper magistrate for trial. In making the arrest the officer may call upon any persons to assist him, may break into a building, or may kill the felon *if necessary*. By "necessary" is meant self-defense or preventing the escape of one who has committed a felony.

Arrest of Misdemeanants. — A private person may arrest another without a warrant to quell a breach of the peace in his presence, but he may not arrest one to prevent any other misdemeanor; nor may he arrest one for any misdemeanor already committed. A peace officer may arrest without a warrant for a breach of the peace or any other misdemeanor committed in his presence. If the misdemeanor was not committed in his presence he can arrest only on a warrant. The same magistrates who issue warrants for felons may issue them for misdemeanants, and arrests are made by the same officers in the same manner except that an officer is never justified in killing a misdemeanant fugitive, though of course he has the right of self-defense.

The Commitment. — After the accused is arrested he is brought before the magistrate, usually the justice of the peace, except in cities where there is a special police justice, or in towns in which the mayor has the powers of a justice. If the crime is a misdemeanor the accused is probably tried at once. If the crime is a felony the magistrate gives the accused a preliminary hearing: and when the evidence indicates a probability of guilt, the accused is held for the grand jury, or brought to trial by *information.* If the crime is murder the accused is usually committed to jail, but otherwise, unless his being at large is considered especially dangerous, he is released until the grand jury meets, provided he can give bail.[1]

The Indictment. — The *prosecuting attorney,* called state's attorney or district attorney in some States, investigates the evidence against such persons as the committing magistrates have held for the grand jury, or against any other persons whose probable guilt has been brought to his attention. If he thinks there is sufficient evidence to convict, he draws up a *bill of indictment,* a written document stating the charge, and has witnesses summoned for the grand jury.

If a certain majority of the grand jury, which majority varies from State to State, thinks there is sufficient evidence to warrant a court trial, the foreman writes across the face of the indictment the words, "a true bill" (of indictment), and the indicted person must stand trial in court. If the prescribed majority does not think that the evidence justifies a trial the words "not a true bill" are used, and the accused is discharged, if he has already been committed.

---

[1] Furnishing bail (Old French *bail* = a guardian) is theoretically putting a man in charge of a private jailer and in effect is the guarantee that an accused person will appear for trial if allowed to go at large. It is usually a sum of money, depending upon the character of the charge, and is determined by a judge or special bail officer. The cash, or other security, may be furnished by a friend or by the accused himself if he possesses the amount required.

Professional criminals often secure bail through one who makes a business of going bail for a fee. And too often the criminal commits another crime while out on bail to secure money with which to pay his bail fee.

The Trial. — The justice's court usually has original jurisdiction in misdemeanor cases, and here the trial is very informal because justices of the peace are not always lawyers and must depend upon what untrained minds can glean from a volume of laws compiled for their use. With few exceptions an appeal may be taken to the county or superior court in criminal cases.

In felony cases sent to the county or superior trial court by the grand jury the prisoner appears in the custody of the sheriff, deputy-sheriff, or some like officer who perhaps bears a different title. In misdemeanor cases sent from the grand jury or appealed from a justice of the peace the prisoner need not appear in person. He often prefers to leave his case to an attorney. But a felony case cannot proceed unless the accused is present.

The prisoner is charged with committing a crime against the State [1] and is prosecuted by the prosecuting (state's) attorney of the county. The clerk of the court reads the indictment or presentment to the prisoner, who pleads "guilty" or "not guilty." If he pleads guilty, and is of a sound mind, the judge usually pronounces the sentence according to the State law, and the case ends. But if he pleads not guilty he is entitled to a trial by jury if he desires it, and in some States one accused of a felony is obliged to stand trial by jury. If the prisoner cannot afford an attorney the judge appoints a lawyer, commonly a young inexperienced one, to defend him. In most States this attorney is paid a small fee by the State.

There are usually about twice as many persons summoned as are needed for the jury, but when the court meets, the counsel may challenge a certain number, which is limited by law, without giving any cause, and the judge will excuse such veniremen. Then the counsel may challenge any other veniremen for cause, such as relationship to the parties to the suit or some other reason why they might not give an

---

[1] For a great many acts a person may be proceeded against criminally by the State because he has disturbed the peace of the community generally, and also in a civil action by a person because the latter has been injured individually. If a man libels you by an unlawful malicious publication and thereby injures your good name, you can sue him for money damages; if his libeling you causes a breach of the peace, he has also committed a crime and may be punished by the officers of the State in the name of the State, because the entire State is injured by lawless people who break the peace.

impartial decision; if it is a murder trial, because they do not believe in capital punishment.[1]

If others are challenged, the judge, in some States, may have the sheriff summon bystanders (*talesmen*), whereas in other States a new

THE ACCUSED IN THE WITNESS STAND

list must be prepared as the former one was and this procedure must continue until the prescribed number of suitable men are *impaneled*, that is, secured to serve.[2]

After the case is opened the witnesses for the State and for the prisoner are examined and cross-examined, arguments are delivered by the attorneys for each side, and the judge gives the *instructions* to the jury explaining the law governing the case. (In Virginia the instructions precede the arguments.)

---

[1] In some States unsatisfactory laws or inefficient judges often permit the lawyers to ask every conceivable question in order to determine whether the jurors hold any opinions which would cause them to be prejudiced in the case. For example, after the Iroquois Theatre fire in Chicago, in which so many people lost their lives, the Theatre Company was being sued, and the counsel for the company asked the prospective jurors such questions as these: "What paper do you read? Do you believe in card playing? Dancing? Theatre going? Have you any prejudices against city people? Have you ever had a friend killed in a fire?"

[2] In the famous Gillooley murder case (1878) in Indiana, 4150 veniremen were summoned and nine and a half weeks were required to complete the jury. More recently 91 days were required to select a jury in a certain California case.

The jury then retires to consider the evidence of the case and arrive at a decision. If the jury cannot agree, the foreman reports "no agreement"; if the requisite number agree, usually all in an important criminal case, he reports "guilty" or "not guilty." If guilty, the jury usually determines the punishment in its verdict,[1] which is read by the clerk of the court, and the judge pronounces the sentence. If the

THE OBSTINATE JUROR AND A HUNG JURY

penalty is merely a fine, this is paid to the clerk; if more than a fine, the sheriff takes charge of the prisoner, who is taken to jail to serve his term, or until he can be transferred to the penitentiary, executed, or disposed of according to the sentence. If there has been a disagreement ("a hung jury"), the case is either set for a new trial or dismissed.

If the verdict has been "guilty," the prisoner may petition for an appeal to a higher court on the grounds that the verdict is not according to the law, or to the evidence, or that some error has been committed in the trial. If the appeal is granted and is sustained the higher court will order the lower court to hold a new trial; but if no error is found the appeal is dismissed and the order of the lower court stands.

Recommended Improvements in Criminal Procedure. — In the administration of justice in criminal cases we have come a long way from the Middle Ages when an accused was submitted to physical torture, and if he emerged uninjured, he was judged innocent of the crime.

---

[1] In many States the judge determines the punishment after the jury has determined the guilt.

Our present penalties may not be a true measurement of guilt if we take into account the surroundings of the accused; but if we have penalties, they should be efficiently administered.

The following summary of the National Crime Commission report contains recommendations of our leading jurists for improvements in State legislation concerning criminal procedure. (Some States have already adopted one or more of these recommendations.)

Bring persons charged with a felony before a magistrate when arrested, for an opportunity to make a public statement and to answer questions.

Permit prosecution either by indictment or by information.

If bail is granted, the bondsman should submit a full statement of what, if any, collateral he has received from the defendant. If the defendant fails to appear, after ten days the forfeited bond should become a final judgment.

The fact that the juror has heard of the case and has formed an opinion should not disqualify him if he is satisfactory to the judge.

The State should have as many challenges as the defendant.

If the accused fails to testify as a witness, his failure may be commented upon by the judge or by the counsel.

The defendant or the State should be permitted to take depositions within or outside the State under conditions fixed by the court (judge); also to take depositions of a witness likely to leave the court's jurisdiction.

The judge should instruct the jury as to the law and should make comments on the evidence and character of any witness.

A five-sixths verdict should be sufficient to convict except where the penalty is death.

The jury should determine guilt and the judge fix the punishment as authorized by law.

On appeal a judgment of conviction should not be reversed unless an error complained of has resulted in a miscarriage of justice.

A pardon or parole should not be granted until notice has been given to the prosecuting officer and judge who tried the accused, and the reasons should be made public five days before taking effect.

A defendant asking for an appeal should remain in jail at least until the appeal is granted.

An insanity plea should be required ten days before the trial begins except with the consent of the judge.

When the plea for the defendant is insanity, the judge should summon an expert and the county should pay him.

The prosecuting attorney should not be allowed to drop a case against an indicted person without the consent of the judge.

QUESTIONS ON THE TEXT

1. What is the difference between a civil suit and a criminal suit?

2. If you sue for a sum of money do you sue *at law* or *in equity?*

3. If you want to prevent the commission of a wrong which cannot be remedied after once committed, would you bring suit *at law* or *in equity?*

4. Explain just how a suit *at law* proceeds. What do you mean by *plaintiff? defendant? verdict? judgment?*

5. Explain just how a suit *in equity* proceeds. What is a *decree?* What are *depositions?*

6. What is a crime? Are all crimes wrong in themselves? If not, why are they considered crimes?

7. Crimes are of what two degrees? What distinguishes them in many States?

8. What is Murder in the First Degree? Murder in the Second Degree? Manslaughter? Arson? Burglary? Robbery? Larceny? Grand Larceny?

9. Who may arrest felons?

10. What is a *warrant?* Is it necessary to have a warrant to arrest a felon? Who serves a warrant? May he call upon bystanders to assist him?

11. May a peace officer without a warrant arrest one who has committed a misdemeanor?

12. Who usually tries a criminal and commits him to jail when he is first arrested?

13. What do you mean by *giving bail?*

14. Who draws up bills of indictment to present to the grand jury?

15. Describe a jury trial.

16. What do you mean by *instructions?*

17. By whom is the law governing a case decided? the facts?

18. What is meant by a "hung jury"?

19. Describe a court in session.

20. On what grounds may one petititon for an appeal?

21. What legislation is recommended by the National Crime Commission?

PROBLEMS FOR DISCUSSION

1. In New York City a thief stole a plume worth $57, but proved that it was marked down to $49.50 the day he stole it; hence his offense was merely a misdemeanor, whereas it would have been a felony if he had stolen goods valued for as much as $50. What crime did this thief commit?

2. In the eighteenth century nearly 200 crimes were punishable by death in England. A death penalty was prescribed for stealing a handkerchief. The people and even the judges ceased believing in the justice of such laws and did not enforce them. For instance, in one case a man was accused of stealing a sheep. Because it was a ewe that had been stolen, the judge threw the case out of court so that he might not have to pronounce a death sentence. Have any of these technicalities of the law come down to us today even though we do not need them? Why do we not need them today?

3. Are crimes prevented more by the severity of punishment or by the certainty of punishment? Would you consider it extravagant for the government to spend $100,000 in order to detect and bring a murderer to justice?

4. In Oregon a boy charged with violating the cigarette ordinance was sentenced by the judge to wheel eight tiers of wood from the street into the City Hall. Do you consider that the judge showed wisdom in his sentence?

5. You cannot compel a person accused of a crime to testify against himself according to law. You cannot so much as ask him where he was when the crime was committed. What do you think of this old legal rule? Would you favor compelling the accused to make a statement as to his whereabouts to the justice of the peace before whom he is brought — else assume that he is guilty?

6. In some States persons convicted of murder are put to death by the gallows, in others by the electric chair, in others by lethal gas, in Utah by a firing squad, and in some there is no capital punishment. Which sentence do you think is most likely to reduce crime?

7. Learn from some lawyer which of the National Crime Commission's recommendations are already the law of your State. Do you favor adopting the remaining ones?

8. The late Judge George Shaughnessy of the Municipal Court of Milwaukee heard about 150 criminal cases a month — principally felonies. He was efficient and gave prompt *justice*. One morning a man murdered his wife, and in less than eight hours he was serving his life sentence in the penitentiary.

In Milwaukee the accused are brought to trial by "information" instead of the slow grand jury process; there is no easy bail, so there are no professional bondsmen there; a juror is not disqualified merely because he has formed a tentative opinion about the case; with the consent of the accused, the trial is without jury; and dilatory tactics are not permitted.

Criminals know about Milwaukee. A visiting burglar was caught there at midnight. By noon the next day he was on his way to the penitentiary to begin an eight-year sentence, and he thus voiced his disgust to an inquiring reporter: "Tell my pals in Chicago," he said, "to stay out of this man's town!" It is not surprising that the murder rate in Milwaukee was found to be less than that of any other city as large or larger.

If under this system of "prompt justice" it should be discovered that an injustice has been done, is there any redress for the one thus imprisoned? What?

9. Do you agree with the following statement of Judge Shaughnessy? "Speedy trials reduce the upkeep of prisoners in tax-supported county jails. And delay ought to be avoided if only because in our day it has become the refuge of the caught criminal: he realizes far too shrewdly that if his case is continued often enough and long enough, witnesses may disappear or die, important papers and exhibits can be 'lost,' public interest will certainly wear out — and there is a strong chance that the verdict will finally be 'Not guilty!'"

10. A Federal-State-Municipal Co-operative Police Force has been proposed, with the Federal Government paying 50 per cent of the cost of local police that measure up to a standard set by the Federal Government. Annually the State police and city police would be inspected to determine whether the 50 per cent annual grant should be made. The standard might include a force of adequate numbers, of education and police training, of up-to-date equipment, with retirement pension sufficient to encourage a life career of efficient honest service, with an able secret service division, and with complete up-to-date criminal records. Do you favor this proposal?

If this system were adopted should there be a Police Academy (comparable to the Military Academy) for the training of higher police officers?

What are the qualifications for appointment to the police force in your town?

In your community what is the proportion of policemen to population? Do you consider that your police force is adequate?

SELECT BIBLIOGRAPHY

Copies of warrants of arrest, indictments, subpoenas, summons, etc.
GRAVES, W. *American State Government*. Heath. Boston. 1953 ed. Chapters 16–18.

CHAPTER XXXI

STATE FINANCE

Limitations on the Taxing Power of States. — Taxes are charges imposed by a legislative body upon persons or property to raise money for public purposes. A State legislature may impose taxes of any kind

Courtesy Port of New York Authority

THE LINCOLN TUNNEL

This interstate tunnel built by the Port of New York Authority is being paid for by tolls; but the highways that funnel their traffic through the tunnel are paid for by taxes. (See page 538.)

and any amount, or may give permission to the legislative bodies of counties, townships, towns, or cities to do the same, subject to the State constitution and the following Federal restrictions.

(1) *Taxes must be for a public purpose.* Exactly what is meant by a "public purpose" cannot be defined, but must be decided by the courts whenever taxpayers feel that they are being taxed for a private purpose and carry their complaints into court.

Some years ago Topeka, with the permission of the legislature of Kansas, agreed to pay a sum of money to a manufacturing concern if it would locate its iron works in that city. The factory was so located, but when

taxes were assessed for the payment of this sum of money, certain taxpayers brought their complaint to court, and, after several appeals, the Supreme Court of the United States decided that taxes could not be collected for this private purpose.

(2) *Taxes must operate uniformly upon those subject to them.* The assessment of all persons and property within a class or district se-

536

lected for taxation must be according to a uniform rule. For instance, when a citizen of New York State inherits a certain amount of property he must pay a State tax varying from one per cent to twenty per cent, depending upon the amount inherited and the degree of relationship. This tax operates uniformly because all who fall within the same class are taxed alike.

(3) *The classification of property for taxation must be reasonable.* For instance, it was declared reasonable for Louisiana to impose a license tax upon manufacturers of sugar, at the same time exempting from its operation those who refined the products of their own plantations. But you could not thus tax Jews, Germans, Negroes, Republicans, or Catholics who manufacture sugar and exempt all others, because the classification would be unreasonable.

(4) *Either the person or the property taxed must be within the jurisdiction of the government levying the tax.*[1] Double, or even triple, taxation, however, is not forbidden. For example, a person working in one State and living in another might have to pay an income tax both in the State where he earns his money and in the State of his residence. And if he has invested his savings in a third State, that State also may tax the income from the investment.

(5) *In the assessment and collection of a tax, certain guarantees against injustice to individuals must be provided.* For instance, if property worth $10,000 is assessed for $15,000, the owner has the right to go before some tax revision board or court and have the mistake corrected.

(6) *A State can tax neither Federal Government property, nor Federal Government bonds or the income therefrom.* The Constitution does not expressly forbid this, but in the case of McCulloch v. Maryland the State was denied the right to tax a branch of the Bank of the United States because "the power to tax is the power to destroy."

---

[1] The city of Charleston, South Carolina, borrowed money by issuing bonds which paid 6 per cent interest. Afterward it attempted to tax these bonds whether they were held by citizens of Charleston or persons living outside the State, the city treasurer being directed to deduct 5 per cent of the interest before sending it to the owners of the bonds. Those living outside the State went to court, and the Supreme Court of the United States decided that the city could not thus tax persons living outside the State. The city government did not have jurisdiction either of the persons or the bonds (property); hence to keep back a part of the interest was breaking the contract with the persons who lent money from outside the State.

(U. S. Constitution, Art. I, Sec. 10.)

(7) *A State may not, without the consent of Congress, tax imports or exports to or from the United States.*[1] Nearly half of the imports of the United States come through the port of New York. If New York State could tax these imports, most of which are intended for other States, she would really be levying a tax upon other States.

Courtesy Port of New York Authority

New Jersey Portals of the Lincoln Tunnel

This twin-tube vehicular tunnel under the Hudson River runs between midtown New York City and Weehawken, New Jersey. The tolls collected are not construed to be a tax on interstate commerce, but merely a service charge.

The same would be true if she could tax Western wheat which is shipped abroad from the port of New York.

(8) *A State may not tax interstate commerce as such.* If a State could tax interstate commerce, it might interfere with the right of the United States to regulate it. For instance, logs owned by one Coe were floating down a river from Maine to New Hampshire. When the river froze they were within the town of Errol, which town attempted

---

[1] ". . . and the net produce of all duties and imports, laid by any State on imports or exports, shall be for the use of the treasury of the United States."

to tax them. The Supreme Court of the United States prohibited it, as it would have been a tax upon interstate commerce.

A State may not place a license tax on traveling salesmen who sell commodities to be sent from another State, but may tax peddlers who carry the commodities with them or get their supplies from commodities already in the State, provided, of course, that they are not discriminated against because of the fact that they also sell goods brought from without the State.

(9) *A State may not, without the consent of Congress, lay any duty on tonnage.* Tonnage means the internal cubic capacity of a vessel in tons of one hundred cubic feet each. A State may tax a vessel as ordinary property, but may not tax it on the basis of tonnage.

(10) *State constitutions place a few restrictions upon their legislative bodies.* For instance, a constitution may limit the tax rate to a prescribed number of mills on the dollar; or may exempt from taxation such property as churches, schools, and burial grounds.

Kinds of State and Local Taxes. — Aside from the restrictions of the Federal Constitution, which we have considered, each State may levy taxes as it sees fit. And subject to a few varying restrictions in State Constitutions, the legislatures determine what taxes will be imposed, and what taxes the counties, towns, and cities may levy. The following are those commonly used.

The General Property Tax. — There are two kinds of property: (1) *real property*, which is land, buildings, and improvements that go with the property if sold, and (2) *personal property*, which is either tangible or intangible. Tangible personal property consists of all movable wealth which is visible and the value of which can easily be assessed. Farm implements, live stock, pianos, refrigerators, and watches are examples of tangible property. Examples of intangibles are stocks, bonds, mortgages, money, and bank accounts. Because intangibles can be hidden from tax assessors more easily than tangibles, some States do not attempt to tax them — or tax them at a lower rate than real property or tangibles.

When wealth consisted mainly of land, the property tax was a fair measure of one's ability to pay taxes. But today dishonest persons, who own only intangible wealth, can often evade taxes by not declaring their intangibles. And professional men and those of the high-salaried class often own very little tangible property. For these reasons States have largely given up the property tax as a source of State revenue; but the property tax is still the principal revenue producer for counties, towns, and cities.

The Sales Tax is now the largest producer of State revenue. It is a tax on each sale, measured by the amount of the sale. Some States have this tax on commodities in general, some on tobacco and cigarettes or intoxicating beverages, and all have it on gasoline.

The sales tax alone would be as unfair as the property tax alone because it takes a larger portion of the poor man's income than it does of the rich man's. The sales tax applied to luxuries only, like tobacco and cigarettes and gasoline for pleasure cars, is more popular. And the tax on intoxicating beverages is levied partly to discourage their use.

The Income Tax has become an important source of revenue for more than half of the States. It is a tax on net income (gross income less allowed deductions) and is progressive; that is, the larger the income the higher the rate.

The income tax is, in general, a good tax because it is in proportion to ability to pay; but if used alone, it would be so high that it would discourage business enterprise.

Some cities levy a small income tax. So in some cities of some States residents must pay three income taxes: the city tax, the State tax, and of course the Federal tax. Even if the rates are not high, having three sets of reports to file is a nuisance. Some advocate a Constitutional Amendment allocating certain kinds of taxes to the Federal Government, others to State governments, and still others to local governments. (See pages 113–116 for Federal Income Taxes.)

The Business Taxes are used in various forms in all States. The best producers are taxes on corporations, in general, and public utilities. Insurance companies, railroads, bus and truck companies, and gas and electric companies are examples of the corporations that are taxed. Merchants usually pay license taxes, and professional men are increasingly being taxed.

Share of Local Governments in State Taxes. — The various sources of revenue tapped by State governments are shown in the chart on page 541. Since it is not practical for local governments to levy many of these taxes, the States themselves are increasingly distributing among the local governments a percentage of the State taxes

State Tax Collections by Type of Tax

Type of Tax	Fiscal 1953	Fiscal 1952
General and Selective Property Taxes	$365,000,000	$370,000,000
Sales Taxes:		
General Sales	2,433,000,000	2,229,000,000
Alcoholic beverages	465,000,000	442,000,000
Tobacco	467,000,000	449,000,000
Motor vehicle fuel	2,017,000,000	1,870,000,000
Other	817,000,000	740,000,000
Licenses:		
Motor vehicles and operators . . .	1,012,000,000	924,000,000
Corporations	266,000,000	226,000,000
Alcoholic beverages	79,000,000	77,000,000
Hunting, fishing	76,000,000	70,000,000
Other	196,000,000	178,000,000
Net Income Taxes:		
On individuals	969,000,000	913,000,000
On corporations	810,000,000	838,000,000
Death and Gift Taxes	222,000,000	211,000,000
Severance Taxes	286,000,000	272,000,000
Miscellaneous	62,000,000	48,000,000
Total State Tax Collections . .	$10,542,000,000	$9,857,000,000

collected, or else appropriating money to the local governments from the general State funds. When this is done, the State has a good opportunity to apportion the money on condition that the local government maintain the service — schools, roads, and similar undertakings — according to standards required by the State.

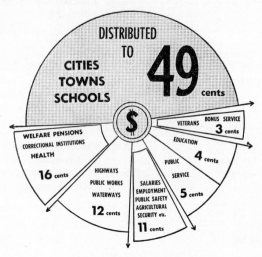

SPENDING THE STATE TAX DOLLAR

This is one way in which tax dollars collected by a State might be spent. Notice how much is used for local purposes. How are taxes allocated in your state?

The General Property Tax. — *Assessment.* — Counties in 29 States have tax assessors to determine the value of property which is subject to taxation. In the States from New England to the Dakotas it is done by township assessors; but New York, Illinois, and Missouri have a mixed county-township system. Where personal taxes are levied, assessments are made each year, but in some States, although realty is taxed each year, assessments are made at longer intervals. Assessors are expected to visit property and have the owner fill in a tax form. In practice they are likely to assess one's real property as it was assessed the previous year, and thus avoid the trouble and duty of visiting the property, unless a building permit has been granted during the year. The valuation put upon property by these assessors is usually accepted as the basis for State, county, and local taxation.

In most States property is assessed at less than its true market value. Property owners are better satisfied if the assessment is at say one half its real value; therefore assessors not infrequently have an understanding that the assessment will be made on this basis.[1] Thus, a city house assessed at $5000 may be worth $10,000. If the tax rate is 4% the tax will be $200. In reality it is a 2% tax on $10,000 property.

Equalization. — If your property is assessed higher than a neighbor's property of equal value, usually there is a means of having the injustice corrected. You may complain to an appeal tax court, to the county board of commissioners, or to a local board of equalization, as the law provides. Many States have county boards of equalization to come into a township and raise or lower the assessment on all real estate in that township if it has been improperly assessed.

In most States there is also a State board of equalization to see that the property is assessed alike in the different counties. States without such boards often have property in one part of the State — *e.g.*, in a large city — assessed at its full value, whereas in another part of the State — *e.g.*, rural counties — it is assessed at only half of its value. This means that the city people are paying twice as much State property tax as justice demands.

Collection. — State, county, and local taxes are usually collected by the same officials. After the taxes are assessed tax bills are prepared. In some States they are mailed to the taxpayers; but in others the taxpayer must go to the county treasurer or township officer who collects taxes, to learn the amount of his taxes.

Delinquency. — If taxes are not paid on a prescribed date, a certain per cent is added. The owner of the property upon which the tax is levied is then said to be *delinquent*, and if the tax remains unpaid for a certain length of time, the property is sold, perhaps at auction. If it brings more than enough to pay the taxes, added per cent, and costs, the former owner receives what is left.

Exemption. — State constitutions commonly enumerate certain kinds of property which the legislative body may not tax. Schools,

---

[1] Several reasons are advanced for assessing property at a fraction of its actual market value — none of them valid: one is the belief that full assessments mean exorbitant taxes; another is the wish to lessen the share of State or county taxes paid by an assessed area; third, political considerations such as the desire of county or other assessors to be re-elected; fourth, difficulty of making a fair, full-value assessment.

free libraries, churches, and government property are good examples of property usually exempt from taxation.

The General Sales Tax, in the form of a flat-rate general retail sales tax, is levied by over half of the States. The rate is usually 1 per cent, 2 per cent, or 3 per cent of the sale price. States having the tax

THE ARTS BUILDING AT THE UNIVERSITY OF COLORADO

State-supported educational institutions like this are tax exempt as a matter of course, but so are private non-profit institutions of learning.

usually apply it only to tangible personal property; and some of them exclude some such items as bread, milk, all food, produce sold by the farmer direct to the consumer, newspapers, sales under a certain amount, or something bearing a special selective tax such as gasoline.[1]

In some States the sales tax applies to the sale of all commodities, wholesale as well as retail; and even to the sale of real estate, and to personal services.

---

[1] Illinois, for example, collects only on the last transaction prior to ultimate use or consumption. For instance, there is no tax on cream sold to an ice-cream manufacturer, but there is one on the ice or ammonia consumed in freezing the cream. The ultimate dispenser of ice cream also pays the sales tax.

Purchases Made Outside the State. — To prevent the avoidance of the tax by making purchases outside the State, the States impose a "use" tax on the use of articles upon which the tax has not been paid. For instance, Washington State imposes a tax on articles valued at $20 or more brought into the State. If one buys an automobile outside the State, a license will not be granted until the use tax is paid. Iowa holds mail-order houses outside the State, as well as within, responsible for the collection of the sales tax on goods sold to residents of Iowa.

How Tax Is Collected. — In Illinois each retailer pays the tax on his total gross taxable sales, and then usually adds the tax to the price of the goods. In some States where the tax on small purchases may be less than a cent, the State sells small metal tax tokens to merchants who sell and resell them to customers. Another State, with a 3% tax, issues a tax card for three cents, which has places to punch for small purchases until the total reaches a dollar. Thus, instead of paying a penny tax on each of ten ten-cent purchases, you pay only three cents.

In Ohio retailers are required to collect the tax from the purchasers at the time of sale. The purchasers receive from the retailers tax receipts that the retailers have purchased from the State. As an incentive for the purchasers to take the receipts, the State will redeem them at 3% of their face value. Churches, lodges, and charitable organizations have boxes into which the receipts can be dropped.

The sales tax is an excellent producer; but it is often opposed because it is felt more by those with a small income than by the rich.

The Gasoline Tax is levied by every State. The rate ranges from 2 to 9 cents a gallon. Gasoline revenue was originally used for State roads; but now many States use part of it for education or otherwise.

Other Selective Sales Taxes on such commodities as tobacco, cigars, cigarettes, playing-cards, alcoholic drinks, oleomargarine, automobiles, tickets of admission, electrical energy, gas, and telephones are levied by this or that State. And a 1949 U.S. law requires a seller of cigarettes across a State border to a non-licensed purchaser in a State taxing them to report names of purchasers to the State tax collector.

Income Taxes. — In addition to the Federal income tax which applies to all States (see pages 111–115), thirty-one States levy a State income tax. In a few of the States only income from intangibles, or from investments, is taxed; but most of the States tax all net income other than a small personal exemption for each member of the family.

The rates of the tax vary from State to State; and they are all progressive. The rates begin at 1% in most States and reach a maximum of 10% in a few.

The above paragraph applies to taxation of the income of individuals. The net income of corporations is also taxed by States. The rates vary from 1% to about 10%.

Inheritance Taxes.[1] — With the exception of the State of Nevada all of the States now have the inheritance tax; but in many States the amount is very small because they exempt from the tax a certain amount of property inherited by lineal ancestors, lineal descendants, husband or wife, and brother or sister.

In New York an exemption of $20,000 is allowed on property inherited by husband or wife. To descendants or ancestors it is $5000. The inheritance tax on the net estate, after allowing for the exemptions, varies from one per cent on a valuation up to $150,000 to 20 per cent of the amount by which the net estate exceeds $10,000,000.

The method of assessing higher rates on large estates than on small ones is known as *progressive* taxation; and where higher rates are assessed on distant relatives the method is known as *collateral* taxation.

Severance Taxes on natural resources severed from the earth can be levied by States which contain such natural resources as coal, oil, iron, or timber. For instance, the State of Minnesota with rich iron deposits has profited by this tax.

Graduated Tax for Chain Stores. — Many of the States have protected small businesses against large ones by a progressive tax on chain stores. The more stores in the State under one ownership the more tax per store is levied. The highest tax is in Louisiana where the tax is $10 per store for the first ten, and increases to $550 per store in Louisiana if a company operates as many as five hundred anywhere in the United States.

State Budget Systems. — Until 1913 most State incomes were expended in a very haphazard manner. The various spending departments and institutions of the State would send in their estimated needs, which were merely compiled by some State officer or perhaps sent directly to the legislatures. After the appropriation committees of the

---

[1] As pointed out on page 118, the term "estate tax" should be used instead of "inheritance tax" if the tax is figured on the entire net estate instead of the separate bequests.

houses had framed the general appropriation bills which were based on these estimates, and the houses had passed them, a large number of petty appropriation bills were introduced.

Proposals to spend money came forward every year by the thousand, and their chance of adoption was not in proportion to their merits, but rather to the political influences behind them. When the legislature adjourned, no one knew definitely how much money had been appropriated. With the pressure of local interests and logrolling methods of legislation, waste, extravagance, and deficits were inevitable.

The governors of many States were given the power to veto specific items in appropriation bills, and some legislatures, to satisfy all interests asking appropriations, voted millions more than there was revenue to meet, and thus placed upon the governor the disagreeable task of offending many interests by vetoing this and that item.

Now all States have devised some method of preparing a budget before the legislature meets, but because there is a wide variation in the location of responsibility for the preparation of the budget the systems fall into three fairly distinct classes.

(1) *Legislative Budget.* — Arkansas continues to have its budget prepared and submitted to the legislature by a committee of the legislature. This system makes it difficult to fix responsibility.

(2) *Board or Commission Budget.* — Nearly a fourth of the States prepare their budgets through boards or commissions, of which the governor is usually a member. These commissions are constituted either of members of the legislature and ex-officio administrative officers or of ex-officio administrative officers alone.

(3) *Executive Budget.* — Three fourths of the States make the governor responsible for the preparation of the budget — usually with the assistance of a director. This system is best for locating responsibility, and the methods used in the following States illustrate how responsibility may be fixed.

In Maryland the governor prepares a budget divided into two parts: one deals with the appropriations for the legislative, executive, and judicial departments, state debt, and other expenditures required by the constitution; and the other part deals with the general appropriations for State institutions, etc. The legislature is permitted to increase or decrease items relating to the legislature, to increase items relating to the judiciary, but otherwise may not alter the bill except to strike out or reduce items. Supplementary appropriations may be considered by the legislature after the budget bill has been finally acted upon, but every supplementary appropriation must be embodied in a separate bill limited to some single work, object, or purpose; and each supplementary appropriation bill must provide the revenue necessary to pay the appropriation so made. The governor may veto any item of such bills.

In Nebraska, where the governor also prepares the budget, the legislature cannot make appropriations in excess of his recommendations except by a three-fifths vote.

The governor of Massachusetts also bears the responsibility for the preparation of the budget, but the legislature may increase, decrease, or add items or omit items. However, after the budget is passed the governor can veto or reduce items or parts of items.

How Revenue Is Expended. — After revenue is collected, and the State, the county, and the city or other local division has each received its proper share, the respective treasurers are not permitted to pay it out until a proper warrant is presented.

After the State legislature appropriates its revenue, the State comptroller or auditor issues warrants to persons entitled to the money, as he is directed to do by the legislative Acts appropriating the money. After the county board appropriates the county money, the county treasurer pays it out when a warrant signed by the county auditor, or some other designated person, is presented. In cities and towns the council appropriates the revenue, and some designated officer or officers sign the warrants to be cashed by the treasurer.

QUESTIONS ON THE TEXT

1. What are taxes?
2. What restrictions are there upon a State's power to impose taxes?
3. Name the principal sources of State revenue.
4. What is the general property tax?
5. How are general property taxes assessed?
6. What do you mean by a board of equalization?
7. How are taxes collected?
8. What is meant by delinquent taxes?
9. What classes of property are usually exempt from taxation?

10. How are sales taxes collected?
11. What is an inheritance tax?
12. What is meant by progressive inheritance taxes?
13. Explain how each of the three types of State budgets operates.
14. Explain the use of warrants in the expenditure of revenue.
15. Give the principal sources of State revenue.
16. What taxes have grown in importance in recent years?

PROBLEMS FOR DISCUSSION

1. What provisions are made in your State constitution regarding taxation?

2. How many mills on the dollar is property taxed for State purposes in your State? For county purposes? For village or city purposes?

3. Does your State have a poll tax? If so, how much is it and who must pay it?

4. Does your State have an inheritance tax? If so, what would be the inheritance tax on $100,000 left by a husband to his wife?

5. How much does your State contribute towards the support of the National Government, assuming that it contributes in proportion to its population?

6. If your property is assessed higher than your neighbor's, what redress do you have?

7. Until a gambling crackdown by State police in mid-1953, 95 slot machines in the town of Tallulah, La., provided the bulk of the revenues for the town and for Madison Parish (county). This income for the town and parish ran at about $150,000 a year. And with this source Tallulah was able to levy property taxes as low as 70¢ for each $100 valuation. (In New Orleans the rate runs about $10 a $100 for city and parish taxes.)

With this revenue Tallulah (pop. 3,000) has been able to cover practically all of its operating expenses. And in recent years the slot machines also provided funds for 19 new school busses, resurfacing of all Tallulah streets at a cost of $110,000, a $26,000 bridge, two football fields each costing about $50,000, a health building, several fire trucks, and a library.

Why would you favor or oppose permitting local governments to finance themselves in this manner?

8. Give arguments for and against a general sales tax.

9. A State is not allowed to tax goods imported from a foreign country until the original package is once sold, broken open, or used. A State may, however, tax goods shipped in from another State as soon as they come to

rest — that is as soon as they are delivered to the person to whom they are shipped.[1]

When Tennessee legislated against the sale of cigarettes, a dealer attempted to evade the law by having the cigarettes delivered from outside the State in small retail packages. Why did the court hold that the sale of these packages was illegal? Could Tennessee have confiscated cigarettes brought from without the State in regular size commercial cartons? Could she have taxed them?

Can boxes of silk from France be taxed by the State in a New York warehouse? Boxes of silk from Paterson, New Jersey, in a Chicago warehouse?

10. Both the United States and many States tax incomes, inheritances, gasoline, motor vehicles, other commodities, chain stores, and various industries at different rates, which annoys and disturbs business.

Moreover, the collection of these taxes by both State and Federal governments is costly to the governments and troublesome to the persons taxed who have to make two reports instead of one.

Do you think the United States Government alone should collect these taxes and refund to the States an agreed portion of the amount collected according to population? Should the rates be the same throughout the country?

11. There is no express provision in the United States Constitution forbidding the taxation of the income of Federal and State bonds; but there are Supreme Court decisions forbidding the States to tax the income from Federal bonds and forbidding the Federal Government to tax the income from State bonds. Therefore neither may tax the income from the bonds of the other unless the Supreme Court reverses itself or its decisions are overruled by a constitutional amendment.

The income from Federal bonds now being issued is taxed by Congress. State bonds (including those issued by local governments) are usually made exempt from State or local taxation by State constitution or statute.

Do you think the income from all public bonds should be made taxable by both governments? If so, would the rate of interest on new issues in-

---

[1] As suggested on page 138, a State may not exercise its *police powers* for protecting health, morals, safety, and general welfare until the original package or article imported from abroad or from another State is once sold, opened, or used, unless permitted to do so by the Constitution or by act of Congress. The original package, however, must be one ordinarily used for the shipment of goods.

Originally States could not regulate alcoholic liquors until the original package or jug was open, but now both the Constitution and Congress allow States to exclude intoxicating liquors from their borders or to regulate them as soon as they enter the State for consumption. Congress also permits States to exclude plants or materials likely to spread pests or disease within the State.

crease or decrease? What interest rate does your city now pay? Is this higher or lower than the rate paid by the Federal Government? Why?

12. In 1952 the per capita State taxes collected (meaning the average amount for every man, woman, and child in the State) ranged from $107 in Washington and $102 in Louisiana down to $37 in New Jersey. For the ten most populous States the per capita tax was as follows:

New York $73
California 100
Pennsylvania 56
Illinois 58
Ohio 60
Texas 55
Michigan 86
New Jersey 37
Massachusetts 67
North Carolina 69

What explanations can you give for the great variations in State taxes per capita?

SELECT BIBLIOGRAPHY

ANDERSON, W., AND WEIDNER, E. *State and Local Government.* Holt. New York, 1951. Chapters 24 and 25.

MACDONALD, A. F. *American State Government and Administration.* Crowell, New York, 1950. Chapters 18, 19, 20.

OGG, F., AND RAY, P. *Essentials of American Government.* Appleton-Century-Crofts. New York. 1952 ed. Chapter 41.

State Tax Collections — issued annually. Bureau of the Census, Washington 25, D. C. 10 pages. Free.

"Where Your Tax Rises Next — States, Cities." *U. S. News.* February 6, 1953.

GRAVES, W. *American State and Local Government.* Heath. Boston. 1953 ed. Chapters 14 and 15.

KOETHER, G. "Tax Road . . . or . . . Toll Road." *Look.* June 16, 1953.

CHAPTER XXXII

COUNTY AND TOWNSHIP GOVERNMENT

I. County System

History. — The Southern colonists were agriculturalists living far apart on plantations. A small class of well-educated aristocrats owned most of the property, but illiterate slaves formed the masses. Under these conditions the people did not develop local self-government as they did in New England, where there was a substantial middle class of townspeople.

Therefore it was necessary to divide the colonies into counties[1] so that the laws might be properly enforced. Thus the county became the most important governmental division of the colony. After the colonies became States the importance of county government continued, and the new States in the Southwest and extreme West copied the Southern county system.[2]

Chaotic Structure. — County government in the United States has often been described as "the dark continent of American politics." Despite the importance of county government, the average person knows little and cares less about the government of his own county.

It has often been said, also, that if county governments in the United States have any one principle of organization in common, it is that of confusion. In practically every county, no one person corresponds to a State governor or a city mayor; thus it is extremely difficult to fix the responsibility for lax or inefficient county government. Authority is usually scattered among several elective officers, boards, and commissions. Executive, legislative, and judicial powers are often concentrated in the hands of the same individual or board.

In short, county government is in serious need of reform all over

---

[1] The divisions were called *counties* because the divisions of England were so called.

[2] In Louisiana the divisions corresponding to counties are named *parishes*.

the country. Fortunately, recent years have seen a slight trend in this direction. The reforms accomplished in such counties as San Mateo in California, McMinn in Tennessee, and Montgomery in Maryland, are notable. But much remains to be done.

Number, Size, and Population of Counties. — There are now 3049 counties in the United States. They vary in number from 3 in Delaware to 254 in Texas. San Bernardino County, California, is the largest, embracing 20,131 square miles. The smallest county in the United States is New York County (one of the five within New York City), 22 square miles in area. Counties also vary widely from the standpoint of population. Loving County, Texas, with its 227 residents has the least population, while there are more than 4,500,000 people living in Cook County, Illinois.

Legal Status of Counties. — "While the county is an agency of the State, it is likewise a creature of the State." Thus in 1924 the Supreme Court of Illinois stated a rule common to all forty-eight of the States. Counties are created by the State, are at all times subject to its control, and may be abolished by it. For example, the latest county to be created in the United States is Los Alamos County, New Mexico, created by the State legislature in 1949. In the early period of State history this absolute control was largely exercised by State legislatures; but abuses of this legislative power have long since brought about many State constitutional provisions relating to counties. For example, many State constitutions now provide for definite county boundaries, fix the duties of county officials, and designate county seats. But, again, counties are merely administrative subdivisions of the State and have no existence apart from the State.

Functions of Counties. — Because of the legal status of counties as creatures of the State, they are responsible for administering State laws and such county laws as the legislature or the constitution permits them to enact.

In most States it is the duty of the county to preserve peace; administer justice; distribute the property of a deceased person; register titles to land; maintain schools; build and repair roads and bridges; care for the poor; protect the health of the community; collect local, county, and State taxes, and expend the county portion of these taxes in the performance of the county functions just enumerated.

The increasing demand for governmental services has brought a

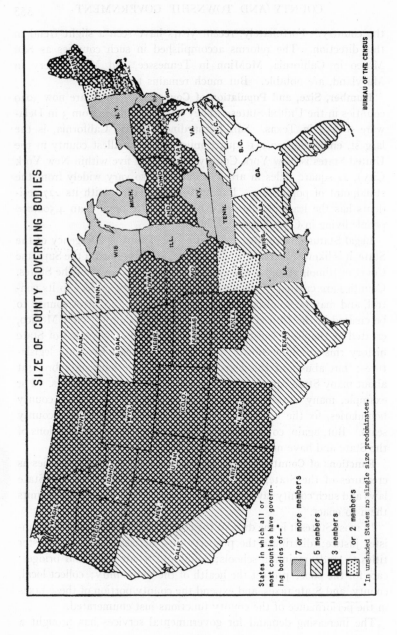

SIZE OF COUNTY GOVERNING BODIES

BUREAU OF THE CENSUS

States in which all or
most counties have governing bodies of—*

7 or more members

5 members

3 members

1 or 2 members

*In unshaded States no single size predominates.

554

trend toward State administrative control of nearly every county function — schools, roads, welfare, health, taxation, etc.

AREAS WITHIN CONTINENTAL UNITED STATES LACKING COUNTY GOVERNMENT [1]

A. "Independent" cities located outside of designated counties and administering functions elsewhere performed by counties 29
  1. Maryland: Baltimore city (distinct from Baltimore county).
  2. Missouri: St. Louis city (distinct from St. Louis county).
  3. Virginia: Alexandria, Bristol, Buena Vista, Charlottesville, Clifton Forge, Colonial Heights, Danville, Falls Church, Fredericksburg, Hampton, Harrisonburg, Hopewell, Lynchburg, Martinsville, Newport News, Norfolk, Petersburg, Portsmouth, Radford, Richmond, Roanoke, South Norfolk, Staunton, Suffolk, Waynesboro, Williamsburg, and Winchester.
B. Unorganized areas bearing county designations 8
  1. Rhode Island: (county areas with no county government) Bristol, Kent, Newport, Providence, and Washington.
  2. South Dakota: (county areas attached to other counties for governmental purposes) Shannon, Todd, and Washabaugh.
C. Federal areas 4
  1. District of Columbia (without county government and operating primarily as a city).
  2. Yellowstone Park (not organized for local government).

Area in Idaho 1
Area in Montana 1
Area in Wyoming 1

How County Functions Are Performed. Most county officers are chosen by an election conducted at various voting places throughout the county for short terms — commonly two or four years — but in some States a few officers are chosen by the county board, the State legislature, the governor, the judge, or otherwise appointed. The officers are not exactly the same in all States, but only in the State of Rhode Island is some type of county board (usually called "board of commissioners" or "board of supervisors") unknown.

---

[1] Based on U. S. Census Bureau data.

The County Board. — In England the counties were administered by the Quarter Sessions Court of the justice of the peace of the county. Naturally this system was copied in America. In Kentucky, Tennessee, and Arkansas the justices of the peace continue to administer the counties, but since they are elected for definite terms the system is not unlike the most recent systems to be described in the next paragraph.

"THE COUNTY ELECTION"

In the early days of our country, few legal restraints controlled the voting. This painting shows the second voter in line refusing a bribe as the first voter gives his oath to the election judge. Nowadays the privilege of voting is increasingly recognized as an important responsibility, and voting is secret.

Board of Supervisors. — New York early departed from the system described in the last paragraph by establishing a county board consisting of one supervisor elected from each township, and called "board of supervisors." This system, with certain changes, has been adopted by many States in all parts of the country. But in 1936 the New York Legislature provided for five optional plans of county government within the State.

Board of Commissioners. — Pennsylvania also departed from the system described above, and provided that each county should elect three commissioners at large, that is, from the whole county, to be known as the "board of commissioners." This system has been adopted by most of the States which have not accepted the New York plan. It must be remembered that all of these plans have been greatly modified by the various States, and in a few States the practices of one system have been adopted with the name of the other.

The county board, under whatever name, has often been called the "county legislature" because in nearly all States it has power to determine the county tax rate and to appropriate the money for county purposes when collected. In some States it has power to enact certain ordinances, such as fish and game laws and the granting of bounties for the destruction of certain wild animals; but its duties are primarily to administer State laws within the county. It has charge of county buildings at the county seat (courthouse and jail) and the poorhouse, hospital, workhouse, and pesthouse, if the county owns such institutions; and it determines the location of all or certain roads and bridges and provides for their maintenance.

Courtesy Santa Barbara Chamber of Commerce

THE COUNTY COURT HOUSE AT SANTA BARBARA, CALIFORNIA

In the South and West the county board commonly establishes polling places and provides ballots, and in some States it acts as a county board for declaring the results of elections. In most of the States the board appoints a superintendent of the poor, but the other officers whom the board appoints in one State or another are, as a rule, very few.

Judicial Officers. — In all parts of the country, even in the New England States, the county is an important unit for judicial purposes. There is a courthouse in every county and a clerk of the court, unless the county clerk acts as clerk of the court, who keeps records of suits brought in the county and of judgments and decrees of the court when the judge has disposed of the cases; but less than half of the States have a judge for each county. Instead of a county judge it is more common to have a "district" or "circuit" judge, who holds court in several counties according to their individual requirements.

The counties of nearly half the States have probate judges, whose duty it is to probate (prove) wills; whereas in the other States the regular county judge, county clerk, clerk of the court, or some other officer probates wills.

Courtesy Portland Cement Association

A CENTER OF LOCAL GOVERNMENT

The county courthouse is an important feature of county administration. Its importance is well recognized by the dignity and beauty of buildings like this one at Bagley, Minnesota, the county seat of Clearwater County.

Every county, except the five in Rhode Island, has a prosecuting attorney to see that criminals are brought to justice, though in a few States he, like the judge, serves for two or more counties and is called the district attorney. If he serves for one county he is called the county attorney, State's attorney, commonwealth's attorney, or merely prosecuting attorney. In fact, he is sometimes called district attorney though his district consists of only one large county; and in some States he is called "solicitor."

The Sheriff. — Every State has county sheriffs, and in all except Rhode Island (where he is appointed for an unlimited term) he is

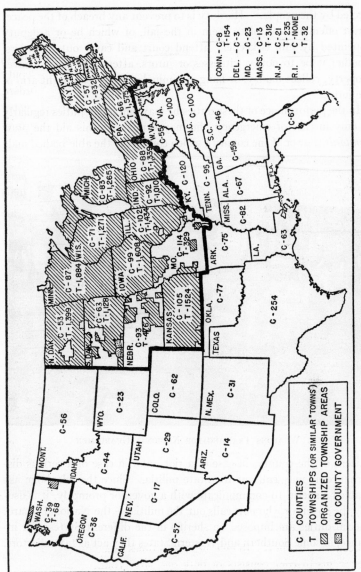

TYPE OF GOVERNMENT IN RURAL AREAS

C – COUNTIES
T – TOWNSHIPS (OR SIMILAR "TOWNS")
ORGANIZED TOWNSHIP AREAS
NO COUNTY GOVERNMENT

elected by the people.[1]   His duty is to prevent any breach of the peace;
arrest offenders and place them in the jail, of which he or a deputy
appointed by him is keeper; attend court and carry out its orders,
whether it be to notify witnesses or jurors, attend the jury, recover
property, collect money, or hang a criminal. He is "the right arm of
the judge."

In the performance of these duties he may employ deputies regularly
or only in case of emergency; he may summon to his aid the *posse
comitatus* (power of the county), which consists of the able-bodied male

WEAPONS TRAINING FOR NATIONAL GUARDSMEN

citizens of the county, in case of a riot; and in case of a serious disturbance he may call out the State militia. Since the telephone has
enabled a sheriff to communicate with a governor promptly, it is usually the governor who now calls out the militia — the National Guard.
Special duties are imposed on sheriffs in the different States; for instance, in some Southern and Western States they act as tax collectors.

---

[1] The word "sheriff" comes from *shire-reeve*, which means "peace officer of the
shire," shire being the Anglo-Saxon name for a division of England which became
known as county (district of a count) after the Norman Conquest of 1066.

The Coroner. — In nearly all States the coroner [1] is an officer of the county who holds inquests upon the bodies of persons who are believed to have died from violent or other unlawful means. He empanels a jury, usually of six bystanders, who inquire from witnesses, or even physicians, chemists, and detectives, as to the probable cause of a death which is known to have resulted or is supposed to have resulted from an illegal act.

If the jury decides that the deceased person has probably met death unlawfully at the hands of a certain person, the coroner may issue a warrant for the arrest of the accused and commit him to jail to await trial, or he may report the facts to a committing magistrate or the prosecuting attorney as the State law may provide. As a knowledge of medicine and pathology is desirable in the office, several States have replaced the coroner with county medical examiners. Some States have retained the office but prescribed specific qualifications. A study of coroners' reports some years ago did much to prompt the change. Many coroners' verdicts were found to be almost meaningless and, occasionally, even illiterate. Some of the "verdicts": "Found dead"; "Diabetes, tuberculosis, or nervous indigestion"; "I lerned the man while under the Enfluence of Whiskey or white mule Just willfully drowned himself."

The County Clerk. — In half of the States there is a county clerk. He acts as clerk of the court in some States; prepares election ballots and receives election returns, and issues marriage licenses in others; and audits the county accounts, acts as clerk of the county board, and records documents such as deeds, wills, and mortgages in others. In short, he is assigned various functions of a clerical nature for which there is no specialized officer in the county.

The Register of Deeds. — In the more populous States it has been thought expedient to have a special officer to keep the records of such legal documents as deeds and mortgages. It is the duty of the register of deeds to make exact copies of instruments to be recorded and enter them in indexed books where they may easily be found. As one's title to property often depends upon these records it is very important that no mistakes be made.

---

[1] "Coroner" is the modern spelling of the older form *crowner*, who in the time of King Alfred was appointed by the king and was especially the crown officer in the shire (county).

The County Auditor. — Nearly half of the States have a county auditor, whose business it is to go over the accounts of the other officers of the county, prepare statements of county finances, and issue warrants on the treasurer for the expenditure of county money according to the appropriations made by the county board. Until recently the duties of this office were performed in a very slack manner, but the States are gradually enacting laws for State supervision of local finances. For example, many States require a uniform method of accounting, so that the records can be examined easily by a State accountant or even by a citizen of the county.

The County Treasurer. — In every State except Rhode Island, where township officers have charge of local funds, and in several Southern States, where the sheriffs or banks perform the duties of county treasurers, there is a county officer to receive and safeguard the county taxes. In a few States there are tax collectors in addition to the treasurer, and in several Southern and Western States collections are made by the sheriff. The treasurer is always placed under bond to insure the State and county against loss from dishonesty or carelessness. He is usually paid a definite salary, but some are paid wholly by commissions on the money handled by them.

The Superintendent of Schools. — In nearly every county outside of New England (where public education is administered locally) there is a county superintendent of schools. In most States he is elected by the people, but in some he is chosen by the county school board, the State school board, appointed by the governor, or otherwise selected. In most States his duty is to conduct teachers' examinations, visit schools to observe and advise teachers, assist district trustees in the selection of teachers and with other advice, and collect school statistics; and in many States he acts as assistant to the State commissioner of education in a general campaign against illiteracy and indifference to education.

According to a report of the Association of American School Administrators, few people realize the magnitude of the county superintendent's responsibilities. On the average, he has around 150 teachers under his supervision, much of his time must be spent in traveling from place to place, and his best efforts are constantly challenged by problems of finance, buildings and equipment, improvement of the curriculum, school transportation, and the like.

Minor County Officers. — Most counties have a surveyor who surveys land for private owners at their own expense, or upon the direction of the court when a dispute in court over a land boundary necessitates it. In some of the more progressive States there is a county engineer instead of a county surveyor, who performs those duties formerly done by the county surveyor; but in addition to this he acts as engineer in the construction of roads, bridges, drains, and like improvements.

Southern and Western counties have assessors to determine the value of property to be taxed, but in New England and the Central States this function is usually performed by local assessors. Other usual county officers are a health officer or board and a superintendent or overseer of the poor who has charge of the almshouse, poor farm, or hospital of the county, unless the county has substituted cash relief for institutional care.

County-City Duplication. — With county and city governments operating over the same area, there is a duplication of functions resulting in unnecessary governmental expenditures and conflict in authority. To remedy this duplication, where the city covers a large part of the county, the boundaries of the city should be made to coincide with the county. The city of San Francisco and the county of San Francisco now cover the same area, and the board of supervisors is the city council.[1]

When a county and city are thus merged, many advantages result. In the first place, only one set of administrative officers is necessary. This makes for efficiency of administration as well as economy in government. In the same way, various municipal employees, such as the police, carry on and complete duties which under the dual system must be handled by two sets of employees. Likewise, responsibility for such matters as good roads, zoning, park systems, and the like, become undertakings of a single administration, rather than the divided responsiblity of a dual organization.

In a large county the rural population is usually unwilling to be taxed and governed by the urban population, and it will oppose a union when the matter comes up in the legislature. So instead of ex-

---

[1] While the county board and city council of San Francisco have merged, unfortunately several of the county and city offices still duplicate one another.

tending the city bounds, a number of cities have become independent counties. For example, Denver was made independent of the original county and now constitutes a county in itself.[1] It retained only two of the former 17 elective county officers, the city officers performing the other county functions. For instance, the duties formerly performed by the sheriff are now cared for by the police department.

Courtesy Board of State Harbor Commissioners

SAN FRANCISCO, CALIFORNIA

This famous city is also a county. Its city and county governments have been merged, producing excellent results in economy and unity of administration.

Separating a city from the rest of the county is not so satisfactory as extending the city bounds to coincide with the county bounds. As the city population spreads you soon have a surrounding county thickly settled, usually inefficiently governed, and often corruptly governed. It may plague the city by permitting badly-policed roadhouses just beyond the city bounds as well as other nuisances against which the city is zoned.

---

[1] St. Louis, Baltimore, Philadelphia, and all of class one cities of Virginia are other good examples of cities which are independent of the surrounding counties.

Re-organization of County Government. — Franklin D. Roosevelt made the statement that "county government is no more fit for its purpose today than an ox-cart would be fit for the task of supplying modern transportation between New York and Chicago." And indeed there are many criticisms of county government, among them being the following:

1. There is no one to take full responsibility because of so many elected and independent officers.
2. This means that local politics, instead of the merit system, too often control.
3. The management of funds and finances is so poor that nearly 2000 local governments went into bankruptcy in the United States in 1933–1934.
4. The county as a unit is so small, as a rule, that it does not correspond to the social and economic problems of today.
5. There is much confusion as to the proper functions of the county; its relation to the State; and its relation to the city.

Many movements are under way for county government reform, and the leading one is the proposal of the county manager plan.

The County Manager Plan. — In order to eliminate waste, duplication, and corruption, a few counties in the nation have adopted the county manager plan. The county plan is similar to the city manager plan to be discussed in the next chapter.

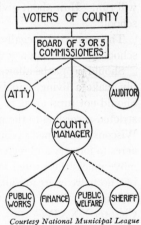

Courtesy National Municipal League

THE COUNTY MANAGER PLAN

Under this plan the voters of the county elect the county board which usually consists of 3 or 5 members. The board in turn appoints a county manager. It is desirable that the board should appoint a professional public administrator or someone equally well qualified to fill the position.

The county manager then appoints his assistants to handle such matters as finance, welfare, public works, and police. As an experienced administrator appointed for a definite term, receiving an adequate salary and remaining above local politics, he is in a better position than the county board to make wise appointments and to carry on impartially the business of county government.

The county manager system locates responsibility in one person. When something goes wrong the appointed official is definitely responsible and something may be done to correct the matter.

With more appointive and fewer elective officers under the county manager system the voters are more likely to know something about the candidates for whom they are voting in county elections.

The Need for County Zoning. — A man bought some poor land and settled on it with his wife and two children. The unproductive soil yielded him only an aching back and a broken heart. Stranded on the so-called "farm" in which his hopes and meager fortune had been invested, he turned to whatever other source of income he could find. His home was twelve miles from the nearest school, so he wrote to the county school superintendent:

"My wife still has her teaching certificate. Couldn't you give her a job teaching the children at home rather than have them travel 24 miles a day to and from school? If you can't, well, I have a Ford that will run. How about giving me a job driving them back and forth to school?"

The county was legally bound to see that the settler's children had schooling, so the county was saddled with a new expense.

Should people be allowed to move onto land where they can't possibly make a living, and burden the county for schooling and roads? Should not rural areas be *zoned*, that is, have the use of each area restricted according to the most suitable use of the area? For example, Wisconsin has zoned 24 counties and restricted the use of some 5,000,000 acres to forestry and recreation. People already there are not forced to move unless the United States or the local government buys the land, but no newcomers are allowed to move to this low-grade zoned land. Zoning as a feature of city planning will be discussed more fully in Chapter XXXIV.

Centralizing Tendencies. — *State Centralization.* — The States are gradually taking over many of the county functions that lend themselves to more efficient centralized administration. School systems and roads are two good examples of this. For example, in most States we still find county roads which are built and maintained by each individual county. But, beginning with Virginia and North Carolina, the States are assuming responsibility for all roads, and former county roads are now more efficiently maintained as a part of the larger State system.

In the field of education, States are now requiring teachers to have more advanced training, are prescribing minimum wages for teachers, and are increasingly supporting county and district schools.

Federal Centralization. — Originally, the Federal Government had practically no direct contacts with the local government units. But today, chiefly through grants-in-aid, the Federal Government contributes toward the maintenance of county and township roads; in agriculture it maintains county agents and 4-H Club leaders; in education it has introduced industrial arts, home economics, and ROTC in high schools; and it has largely replaced the county poorhouse with Social Security.

II. TOWNSHIP SYSTEM

In the study of the township system it is important to know that counties are relatively unimportant in New England except as districts for the administration of justice.

Origin of Town Government in New England. — The Pilgrims came to Plymouth, Massachusetts, as a congregation, and very soon (1622) they erected on Burial Hill a "meeting-house," which was used both for public worship and for town meetings. The church and the government were practically one: sermons were preached on the inside to save souls from perdition and a cannon was mounted on the outside to save bodies from the Indians. It was at the meeting-house that the voters met and made their laws directly.

Other congregations from England settled along the coast and established similar governments. As the population of these coast settlements increased, pastors led congregations from them and established towns. The desire to be near the church, the hostility of the savages, the severe climate, and the unsuitableness of the country for large plantations caused the immigrants to settle in compact communities, called "towns."

Terms "Town" and "Township" Distinguished. — These communities were called "towns" [1] because they had been so called in

---

[1] When a clan of our ancestors in northern Europe or England fixed upon some spot for a permanent residence and built a wall around it, the wall was known as a

England. When it became necessary to survey boundaries between the various towns the small irregular patches of land which resulted were properly known as "townships" (townshapes),[1] but frontier communities are not very discriminating in their terms, and the term "town" was used not only for the cluster of buildings but for the entire township.

THE FIRST MEETING-HOUSE AT PLYMOUTH

"The best school of democracy the world ever saw" found deep roots in the early meeting places of the Pilgrim settlers.

In New England today "town" means a political subdivision of a county which in other parts of the country is called "township." For the sake of uniformity we shall use the word township when referring to what is called "town" in New England. The early townships were very irregular in shape and contained an average of not more than twenty square miles.

---

tun; in time the space within the wall was known as a *tun*, or *town*. The settlers were called by the clan name, as for example "the Boerings" or "the Cressings"; and the town would be called *Barrington*, "town of the Boerings," or Cressingham, "home of the Cressings."

[1] The word *ship*, as here used, comes from the Anglo-Saxon word *scip*, which means shape, hence township means the shape of the town or the entire bounds of the town.

Powers of New England Townships. — For many years the New England townships were undisturbed by the king or parliament of England and exercised such powers of government as are now exercised by a State. They waged war against the Indians, established schools, and as late as the Revolutionary War they appropriated money for war supplies; in fact, they created the States which now control them.

Today they exercise only such powers as the States permit. They have control of most roads, bridges, schools, libraries, poor relief, and taxation for most local purposes. Some townships have charge of such public works and institutions as street pavements, sewers, water-works, electric light plants, public baths, parks, and hospitals. They also have certain powers to enact police ordinances, such as determining traffic speed restrictions.

The Town Meeting. — Township laws have always been made in the town meeting. During the first few years the colonists attempted to hold monthly meetings, but this was found to be a cumbersome way to transact business and, as early as 1635, *selectmen* (officers selected by the people) were chosen to administer the affairs of the township during the interval between the assemblies. Thus the government became less democratic (direct rule of the people) and more republican (indirect rule of the people through representatives).

Today the regular meetings are usually held in the town hall once a year, but the selectmen may call special meetings. The first Monday in March is a favorite time to have the meetings, but some are held as early as February or as late as April, and Connecticut prefers October. The general nature of the business to be transacted at a meeting must be announced in a *warrant* which is posted in the various parts of the township.

The town clerk calls the meeting to order, usually at nine o'clock, and acts as secretary of the meeting. The first business is the election of the presiding officer, called the *moderator*. In many townships some well-respected citizen is elected year after year as a matter of course. The organization being perfected, the principal township officers are nominated from the floor, but the nominations have frequently been arranged by preliminary party meetings, called *caucuses*. Election is by ballot, and the polls remain open several hours, depending upon the population of the township.

The interesting session of a town meeting occurs after the balloting — usually in the afternoon, but in a few larger towns not until evening. Each voter has been furnished a printed report of the expenditures for the previous year, and the selectmen make an oral report of what has been done during the year. It is then that the policy for the next year is to be discussed — the real interest of the meeting.

TOWN HALL, GEORGIA, VERMONT   *James Sawders*

Standing in marked contrast to the meeting place of the Pilgrims, this town hall of today still symbolizes the simple precepts of free men who keep democracy strong.

Nahum Smith may rise and say, "I should like to be informed why the selectmen took the stone from Red Hill quarry instead of Cross Roads quarry, which is nearer." If there is "a rooster in the bag," he is rather certain to crow. It is difficult for a political boss or ring to prosper under this system because any bag containing a rooster must annually or oftener be brought into the presence of the interested parties, and a Nahum Smith is pretty certain to bring at least one crow from the rooster.

Perhaps the cross-questioning of the chairman of the school committee by Jeremy Jones will bring discomfort to the chairman, much to the delight of the boys seated in the rear of the hall. Or the younger blood may advocate a consolidated school or a new high school, which is probably opposed by those farmers living a distance from the proposed location.

In 1947 two towns without a doctor guaranteed a young doctor an income of $5000 a year to settle in their midst and charge $2 for office calls and $4 per home call no matter how far.

Township Officers. — *Selectmen*, of whom there are three, five, seven, or nine, three being the more usual number, are the principal officers of the township. They are elected by the town meeting, annually as a rule, but in some Massachusetts townships they are elected for three years, one being elected each year.

They issue warrants for holding regular or special town meetings, specifying in a general way the subjects which the citizens desire to have acted upon; lay out highways; grant licenses; arrange for elections; have charge of township property; appoint some of the minor officers; and may act as assessors, overseers of the poor, and health officers. It should be borne in mind that they have no power to determine the tax rate or appropriate money, these functions being performed by the town meeting, and that they have no powers except those conferred by the State or the town meeting.

The Town Clerk is just as important as the selectmen, and performs many duties which are imposed upon the county clerk outside of New England. He keeps minutes of town meetings, of meetings of the selectmen, and other town records; he records the vote for State and county officers and issues marriage licenses; and he records births, marriages, and deaths. He is elected by the town meeting for only a year at a time, but is usually re-elected for a number of years.

Other Township Officers are the town treasurer, assessors of taxes, overseers of the poor, justices of the peace (township officers in some States), constables, commissioner of roads (under various titles), a school committee (board), and numerous other less important officers. Most of these officers are elected at the annual town meeting. Some years ago the township of Middlefield, Massachusetts, had eighty-two voters and eighteen officers.

Difficulties of Township Government. — Township government in New England has a noble heritage, but today there are many conditions unfavorable to the town meeting type of government. Ease of transportation and communication is centralizing financial, highway, police, health, and educational powers in the State. The influx of French Canadians and Europeans who are unaccustomed to local self-government adds discord to the town meeting. The growth of factories increased the diversity of interests between the settlement and the surrounding farms. In some places the town meeting has been undermined by the caucus, held beforehand, to nominate candidates for office.

The increase in the population of many towns has left the town hall too small for a town meeting. Some of the larger towns are remedying this by a limited town meeting. Brookline, Massachusetts, with a population of fifty-odd thousand, was first to adopt this plan. An Act of 1915 divided the town into nine voting precincts and provided for election of twenty-seven members of the limited town meeting from each. Some settlements that have reached an unwieldy size have been incorporated into municipalities, like cities of other sections of the country; and the city council takes the place of the popular assembly.

Absence of Townships in the South and West. — In the Southern and Western States townships cannot be said to exist. In some States the counties are subdivided into one or more sets of districts for one or more purposes. They have no township meetings, and districts other than school districts usually have no power of taxation or of owning property, and few, if any, officers independent of county officers. They are simply convenient divisions for performing county functions. Different districts exist for various purposes, such as schools, roads, justice, and elections; and one kind of district commonly overlaps another kind. The name for the more important of these districts varies from State to State.[1]

---

[1] In North Carolina, South Carolina, Missouri, Arkansas, Montana, and Nevada these districts are called *townships;* in California, *judicial townships;* in Virginia, West Virginia, and Kentucky, *magisterial districts;* in Tennessee, *civil districts;* in Mississippi, *supervisors' districts;* in Georgia, *militia districts;* in Texas, *commissioners' precincts;* in Delaware, *hundreds;* and in the remaining Southern and Western States, *election districts* or *precincts*, except in Louisiana, where the parishes (counties) are subdivided into *wards*.

III. County-Township System

Imitation of New England Township Government. — Nowhere outside of New England is township government so important as in those six States, but in the tier of States extending from New York to Nebraska it is of considerable importance. The northern portions of these States were settled largely by emigrants from New England, who were accustomed to township government; but those who settled the southern portions were from Pennsylvania and the States to the south of the Ohio River and were accustomed to county government. Those accustomed to county government had never attended town meetings but preferred to elect county officers and trust them with all functions of local government.

The result was a compromise. Some functions were assigned to the county and some to the township. In this tier of States the State government preceded the township government and created it; hence those democratic elements did not develop as they were found in New England, where the township existed first and created the States.

County-Township Conflict in Illinois. — When Illinois was admitted to the Union in 1818, the greater number of her citizens were emigrants from the South, who had settled in the southern part of the State; so the State was divided into counties, which were governed by a small board of county commissioners elected at large according to the Pennsylvania plan.

By 1848 when the second State constitution was framed, New England settlers, or emigrants with New England ideas, had settled in large numbers in the northern part of the State; so in this constitution we find a local option provision which permitted the voters of each county to divide the county into townships whenever the majority should vote in favor thereof. Today 85 of the 102 counties of the State have townships.

Township Officers in the Central States. — The New England title of *selectmen* is nowhere found in the Central States. In Pennsylvania, Ohio, Iowa, Minnesota, and the Dakotas their place is taken by a "board of supervisors" or "trustees." In other States there is a well-defined head officer who is assisted, and checked in some matters, by a township board. In New York, Michigan, and Illinois, where this officer is called "supervisor," he is also a member of the county board of supervisors. In Indiana, Missouri, Kansas, and Oklahoma the title of "township trustee" is applied to this officer. The other usual township officers are the clerk, assessor, treasurer, overseer of the poor, overseer of roads, justices of the peace, and constables.

Village Government Weakens Township Government. — Townships of the Central States are not only under greater State and county control than New England townships, but as soon as a considerable settlement develops it will obtain a "village" or "town" charter from the State and then exist as a separate government, performing all or certain functions within its boundaries that were formerly performed by the township. In New England many compactly settled communities which would be incorporated cities in other States and absolutely independent of the township are there a part of the township.

IV. Geographical Townships

The Terms "Governmental Township" and "Geographical Township" Distinguished. — In the preceding sections we discussed townships merely as divisions of territory for the purpose of government, and these are known as governmental or political townships. Divisions of territory for the purpose of surveys are another kind of township, and are known as geographical or congressional townships because they are merely bounded by imaginary lines drawn upon the earth in accordance with Acts of Congress.

In States where the geographical townships were surveyed before settlements were made, they were generally used also as governmental townships; but in some localities natural obstacles, such as rivers and mountains, made them unsuitable for purposes of government, and separate areas were created for governmental townships.

Conditions Preceding Geographical Townships. — During the colonial period New England and the Southern States developed two very different land systems. In the South as the settlers pushed from Virginia and North Carolina into Kentucky and Tennessee the pioneer selected a fertile piece of land and occupied it. A rude survey was made by a public surveyor or by his inexperienced deputy. The several boundaries or limits of the property were marked by "blazing" the trees with a hatchet, and the survey was put on record in the State land office.

Conflicting patents [1] were not infrequently given for the same tracts, and this confusion produced countless lawsuits. Some of the feuds for which the mountains of eastern Kentucky were once famous are said to have grown out of these disputed land patents and the irregularly shaped pieces of land which lay between the patents. This Southern system, which encouraged initiative and resourcefulness, has been called "indiscriminate location."

In New England the laying out of geographical townships preceded the settlement made during the eighteenth century, and there could be no title to land outside of townships. Square townships were easier to survey in a systematic way than those of any other shape; hence when the land north of the Ohio River, known as the Northwest Territory, was to be surveyed, Thomas Jefferson suggested that it be surveyed into square townships for convenience of description when sold by the government, and to prevent disputes as to title. He also had in mind that they would be of convenient size for governmental townships.

Geographical Townships in the West. — When Congress was preparing for the government and settlement of this Northwest Territory, the National Government decided that it should be laid out into townships six miles square.[2] A law of Congress passed in 1785 applied this system of rectangular surveys to all lands belonging to our public domain. This "Ordinance of 1785" was the foundation of the American land system, and its leading principles have continued in operation to the present day.

According to the system gradually perfected, north-and-south and east-and-west lines are established. As starting points certain meridians have been designated as *prime meridians*. There are twenty-four of these, the first being the dividing line between Ohio and Indiana, and the last running a little west of Portland, Oregon.

On each side of the prime meridian are subordinate meridians known as *range lines*. These lines are six miles apart and are numbered east and west from the prime meridian. There must also be a *base line* for each survey following a parallel of latitude, and this crosses the

---

[1] "Patent" as here used means a written title to land granted by the proper State authority.

[2] The fact that a six-mile square rather than any other size square was adopted by Congress has no special significance.

meridians at right angles. There are numerous base lines for surveys in different parts of the country. For example, eleven of them cross the State of Oregon.

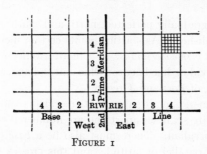

MERIDIANS AND BASE LINES

On each side of a base line are subordinate parallels called *township lines*, six miles apart, and numbered north and south from the base line. Thus these range lines and township lines divide the land into townships six miles square.

The map on this page shows the prime meridians and base lines in Ohio, Indiana, and Illinois; that is, in the area between the Ohio and Mississippi rivers. From any prime meridian the tier of townships directly east is called range 1 east (R. 1 E. in Figure 1) and of course other ranges are numbered east and west of that meridian. They are likewise numbered 1, 2, 3, etc. both north and south of the base line. Thus the sectioned township in Figure 1 is township 4 north, range 4 east of the 2d Prime Meridian in the State of Indiana.

6	5	4	3	2	
7	8	9	10	11	12
18	17	16	15	14	13
19	20	21	22	23	24
30	29	28	27	26	25
31	32	33	34	35	36

Six Miles Square

FIGURE 1   FIGURE 2

This township six miles square is surveyed into thirty-six square miles, which are numbered as shown in Figure 2, and each square mile is called a *section*. Each section is subdivided into rectangular tracts known as halves, quarters, half quarters, and quarter quarters, as shown in Figure 3. Thus if we consider this square mile (Figure 3) as section 1 of Figure 2, we should describe the forty-acre tract starred in Figure 3 as follows: SW¼, NE¼, Sec. 1, T. 4 N., R. 4 E., which means the southwest one quarter of the northeast one quarter of section 1, township 4 north of the base line in range 4 east of the 2d Prime Meridian in

One Square Mile
FIGURE 3

the State of Indiana. So you can readily see that if this tract is to be sold, it is very easy to describe it in the deed of conveyance [1] without the costly aid of private surveyors.

QUESTIONS ON THE TEXT

1. Explain how county government originated in America.

2. What functions are performed by county governments?

3. What State first established county "boards of supervisors"? "Boards of commissioners"? How did they differ originally?

4. What legislative powers have the county boards? What administrative powers?

5. What judicial officers has a county?

6. What other county officers are there in the State in which you live? For what terms are they selected? What are their duties?

7. What is meant by *posse comitatus?* Of whom does it consist?

8. What officer does Massachusetts have instead of a coroner? Why is the Massachusetts plan preferable to that of most other States?

9. Explain how county government should be reorganized. Explain the county manager plan. Explain the need for county zoning.

10. How may county-city duplication be remedied?

11. Explain how the New England town or township originated.

12. What does "town" mean in New England? What does it mean in the South and West?

13. What powers do New England towns possess?

14. Explain the work done by a town meeting. What is a town "warrant"? What is a moderator? What are the duties of the selectmen?

15. What are the benefits of a New England town meeting?

16. How are the various town or township officers selected in New England? For what term?

17. What are some of the difficulties of township government in New England?

---

[1] A deed of conveyance is a contract giving the boundaries of real estate transferred from one person to another.

18. What name is given to the districts into which the counties of your State are divided?

19. Explain to what extent the Central States imitated New England township government.

20. Why are townships less important in States having numerous villages than in New England?

21. Describe the county-township conflict in Illinois. In what division of States are counties least important?

22. In your State, if you have townships, what title is applied to township officers, such as the "selectmen" in New England?

23. Distinguish governmental townships and geographic townships. How did geographic townships come into existence, and why are they useful?

24. Explain how a survey of land is described where geographical townships exist.

PROBLEMS FOR DISCUSSION

1. Give the names of as many county officers as you know.

2. Bound the county in which you live.

3. If you had a vote, would you vote for a member of the county board of commissioners or supervisors who favors low taxes or high taxes?

4. Could your county board enact an ordinance requiring all heavy vehicles to have wide tires? If not, what body could give it authority to do so?

5. In Virginia each city of the first class forms a separate county. The San Francisco government embraces the whole county. Which method of avoiding overlapping powers do you consider best?

6. Some Southern counties have dispensed with a county treasurer and the taxes are collected and warrants paid by a designated bank for about half the usual cost. Do you favor the new plan?

7. In the United States there are about 3000 counties. If this was enough when one traveled to the county seat on horseback, is it too many when we have automobiles and telephones? If an attempt is made to consolidate counties why do office holders oppose it? Who else oppose it? Would it be easier to agree to consolidate at a future designated date?

8. There is no county official corresponding to the President of the United States, the governor of the State, or the mayor of a city. Responsibility is scattered into too many hands. Would you favor centralizing it in a county manager? How should the manager be chosen? Would you have him take the place of other county officers and appoint such assistants as he needs? In that event, the people would elect the county board or commissioners, the board would choose the manager, and he would hire and fire his assistants.

9. Should the prosecuting attorneys for counties be elected by the voters or appointed by the Attorney General of the State?

10. Should each county elect an auditor or should the State Auditor appoint district auditors to safeguard the finances of several counties?

11. Should the State Governor appoint county sheriffs?

12. If you do not like the above proposals, would you favor having the county board or commission appoint all county officers?

13. Oregon permits counties as well as cities to vote bonds for water districts and electric power districts. Is this power as logical for counties as for individual cities?

14. The Chamber of Commerce persuaded the farmers of Kent County, Maryland, to pave 51 miles of secondary road in one year. The county had paved roads for tourists and the larger cities, but some of the by-ways were almost impassable in winter. The farmers were shown that paved roads would save them two cents on every mile traveled by motor vehicles, so they voted a bond issue. The bonds are cared for largely by the county's share of the State gasoline tax.

In order to have the benefits of paving reach all the farmers, a nine-foot strip along the center of each roadway was paved and crushed rock was used for the shoulders. If an 18-foot, two-way paving had been used, only half of the farmers who were taxed for the improvement would have received its benefits. Now the pavement can be widened as funds are available. Would you favor a nine-foot pavement for the by-ways of your county?

SELECT BIBLIOGRAPHY

American County — Patchwork of Boards. National Municipal League, New York, 1946. 24 pages. 35¢.

The County Manager Plan. National Municipal League, New York, 1950. 20¢.

LANCASTER, L. *Government in Rural America.* Van Nostrand. New York. 1952 ed.

SNIDER, CLYDE F. *American State and Local Government.* Appleton-Century-Crofts, New York, 1950. Chapters 13, 15, 16.

WEIDNER, E. *The American County.* (Survey of antiquated systems and need for modernization.) National Municipal League. 1946. 35¢.

GRAVES, W. *American State Government and Administration.* Heath. Boston. 1953 ed. Chapters 21–23.

CHAPTER XXXIII

VILLAGE AND CITY GOVERNMENT

VILLAGE GOVERNMENT

"Village" Defined. — A village is an organized community whose population is less and whose government is more simple than that of cities in the same State. When enough people collect in a district sufficiently compact to justify such public improvements as sidewalks, street lights, and a public supply of water, a State permits them to form a government separate from that of the township or county in order that they may select officers, collect taxes, and provide these public conveniences within the defined area.

In the New England States, villages have not been created, except in a few cases, because in New England the township itself is sufficiently organized to collect taxes and provide these public conveniences that villages provide elsewhere.

In the West and South the small incorporated centers of population are called "towns," but in the States east of the Mississippi River which border on Canada they are more generally known as "villages," and in Pennsylvania, New Jersey, and Connecticut the English term "borough" is commonly used. However, for the sake of uniformity, the term "village" will be used to include towns and small boroughs.

How Villages Are Incorporated. — Each State prescribes under what conditions and in what manner a community may become incorporated as a village. In Alabama 100 inhabitants are all that are necessary, but a minimum of 200 or 300 is a more common requirement. Some States further specify that the required number of inhabitants must reside within a prescribed area — a square mile in New York State.

In some States a community may become an incorporated village by a charter enacted by the State legislature, but the usual procedure is for the inhabitants to present to a designated public officer a petition with a prescribed number of signatures. When this officer (usually a judge) is satisfied that the required conditions are fulfilled, he will declare that the people living within a certain surveyed area are incorporated [1] as the village of X and have such powers of self-government as the State has granted to villages. In most States the officer may not declare a village incorporated until the inhabitants have voted in favor of it at an election called by the officer when petitioned to do so by a prescribed number of the inhabitants.

Raymond E. Hanson

VILLAGE STREET IN ROCKPORT, MASSACHUSETTS

What can be more inviting on a summer day than a New England village with white houses and green blinds, shaded by stately elms!

Powers of Villages. — The few incorporated villages of New England continue a part of the township for many important purposes, such as roads and schools, but may provide for sidewalks, water, lights, sewers, fire protection, and police protection, independently of the township. In those States which adopted the New England township system the villages remain a part of the township for certain purposes, but are more independent of the township than those in New England.

In certain other States, including New Jersey, Pennsylvania, Wis-

---

[1] "Incorporated" means created into a legal body (artificial person) by the State. This body may then bring suit in court, borrow money, or enter into other contracts as a natural person may do. The word "incorporate" comes through French from Latin *in* = into, and Latin *corpus* = body.

consin, Minnesota, and the Dakotas, the villages are entirely independent of the township and have power to perform township functions in addition to the usual village functions. In the South and West, villages, called "towns," are usually included in the township, or county district known by some other name, but as these districts are unimportant the village has power to deal with practically all local problems except those attended to directly by the county.

The Organization of Village Government. — *The Council.* — Every village has a legislative body usually known as the council or the board of trustees. This body varies in number from three to nine, and is usually elected at large for terms of one or two years. In all States the council has power to determine the tax rate, within certain limits prescribed by the State, and to appropriate the money for the various needs of the village.

Generally it can levy special assessments against persons whose property borders streets which have been especially favored by sidewalks or other improvements; but villages have rather limited power to borrow money, and most villages must submit the question of a bond issue to the voters. The power to pass ordinances differs from State to State and often from village to village as provided by the State. Commonly a council may choose certain officers and regulate their duties; pass health and police ordinances on special subjects within certain limits; determine the license taxes of movies, peddlers, public vehicles, and other businesses that are licensed; control streets, bridges, and public grounds; maintain police and firemen; and control any public services owned by the village.

The Mayor. — The principal executive officer of a village is usually called "mayor" or "president," and is ordinarily elected for one or two years. He presides over council meetings, and usually has the rights of a member, but in some villages he merely casts the deciding vote in case of a tie, and in very few villages does he have the veto power. He enforces the village ordinances enacted by the council, and in a number of States he acts as police justice.

Every village has a clerk or recorder, a treasurer or collector, and a police officer ("constable," "marshal," "sergeant," or "bailiff"). There are in many places a street commissioner, an assessor, and an attorney or solicitor. In the West these officers are usually elected by the voters; in other sections they are commonly selected by the council or appointed. Some villages have a justice of the peace, and if the village forms a separate school district it, of course, has school officers. Larger villages have such officers as health, fire, lighting, sewer, and cemetery commissioners.

CITY GOVERNMENT

Meaning of the Term "City." — A city is a governmental unit created by the State, with more population and more powers than a town or village. Each State determines how many inhabitants a town or community must have to become a city, and what governmental powers it will permit its cities to exercise.

SYMBOLS OF CITY GOVERNMENT

This mural in the City Hall of Gloucester, Massachusetts, symbolizes the many roles which city government must play. Education, social welfare, trade, commerce, engineering, fire and police protection, law, the city seal, and the flags of State and Nation, all are depicted.

In Kansas a community with as few as 200 inhabitants may become a city, but in New York State 10,000 inhabitants are required. There are about as many of our forty-eight States which create city governments with less than 2500 inhabitants as there are which require a greater population, but the United States census classifies as cities all incorporated places with as many as 2500 inhabitants.

Rapid Growth of Cities. — When the first United States census was taken in 1790 only 123,475 people, or about 3 per cent of the population, dwelt in cities with as many as 8000 inhabitants. New York,

Philadelphia, Boston, Baltimore, and Charleston were then the only cities of that size.

Just nine years previous to the taking of this first census, Watt had taken out a patent for his double-acting steam engine, which made large-scale manufacturing possible. Fulton's steamboat (patented 1809) and Stephenson's locomotive (1829) made easy the transportation of raw materials to the factories and the distribution of the manufactured products from the factories. Thus factories were erected where there was transportation, and workmen had to move to the factory town for employment.

As a result of the invention of various farming implements, less labor was needed for the production of food and other raw materials; therefore the excess labor was employed in turning the raw products into finished goods — grains into breakfast cereals, wool and cotton into fine clothes, and iron ore into automobiles. So long as improved machinery and fertilizers continue to reduce the amount of labor necessary to produce the world's food supply, so long will cities probably continue to grow.

The growth of cities over 2500 by decades has been as follows:

DATE	TOTAL POPULATION	URBAN POPULATION	PER CENT URBAN
1790	3,929,214	201,655	5.1
1800	5,308,483	322,371	6.1
1810	7,239,881	525,459	7.3
1820	9,638,453	693,255	7.2
1830	12,866,020	1,127,247	8.8
1840	17,069,453	1,845,055	10.8
1850	23,191,876	3,543,716	15.3
1860	31,443,321	6,216,518	19.8
1870	38,558,371	9,902,361	25.7
1880	50,155,783	14,129,735	28.2
1890	62,047,714	22,106,265	35.1
1900	75,994,575	30,159,921	39.7
1910	91,972,266	41,998,932	45.7
1920	105,710,620	54,157,973	51.2
1930	122,775,046	68,954,823	56.2
1940	131,669,275	74,423,702	56.5
1950	150,697,361	95,892,000	63.7

This rapid growth of cities is not peculiar to the United States, but is world-wide, and is due to industrial conditions. City growth in England and Germany has been even greater than in the United States.

New York City, with 8,000,000 population, competes with London for first place among the cities of the world. It has a foreign-born population exceeding 2,000,000, including more than 400,000 Russians; more than 400,000 Italians; and Irish, Germans, and Poles exceeding 200,000 each. There are 2,000,000 Jews in New York City — more than in all Palestine. It has an annual expenditure greatly exceeding one billion dollars, and a debt exceeding two billion dollars.

Mayor-Council Type of City Government. — There are three types of city government in the United States: the mayor-council, commission, and city manager. Of these the mayor-council type is the oldest

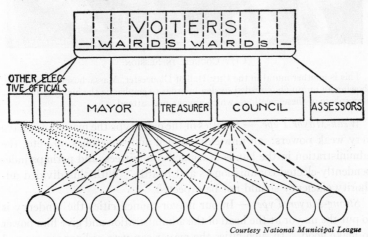

Courtesy National Municipal League

MAYOR-COUNCIL FORM OF GOVERNMENT

Functions overlap; and when things go wrong, the voter cannot know who is responsible.

and as yet the most prevalent. It consists of a council — usually composed of one chamber — to make the laws, and a mayor with more or less power to enforce them.

The council, elected by the voters of the city for terms varying from one to four years, enacts city ordinances, determines the tax rate, and appropriates the revenue for city purposes.

The mayor, too, is elected by the voters — usually for the same term as the council. He is the social and legal head of the city, in some cities he presides at council meetings, and in nearly all cities he can veto ordinances passed by the council, which can then become law only by a larger vote of the council — usually two thirds.

CITY COUNCIL IN SESSION

This is another mural in the City Hall of Gloucester, Massachusetts (page 583), showing an unusually crowded session in order to emphasize the highly democratic atmosphere of these meetings, which anyone may attend.

Weak-Mayor Type. — In cities of the older type the mayor may have very weak powers: an unwieldy council and sometimes no veto, the administration in the hands of council committees, and perhaps independently-elected commissioners and boards. With this divided authority efficiency should not be expected.

Strong-Mayor Type. — In our mayor-council cities the tendency is to put the mayor at the head of the administration and give him power to make good. In such cities the mayor can veto ordinances enacted by the council, usually prepares the budget, and has power to appoint heads of departments and to dismiss them if they are not efficient.[1] The strong-mayor type is better than the weak-mayor type, but it too has its defects.

Criticism of the Mayor-Council Type. — The mayor-council type of city government has been criticized because no one person is responsible. The government is so complex that the citizens do not understand the working of it; therefore some shrewd person, usually a

---

[1] The school affairs of a city are usually intrusted to an independent school board.

corrupt politician, by making a practical study of it, often makes himself political boss. He receives no salary as boss, but by controlling the elections and filling the offices with his friends he can compel them to spend large amounts of money in a manner which will yield "graft" for him. For instance, in 1868, when Tweed was boss of New York, a courthouse was designed which was to cost $250,000. Three years later more than $8,000,000 had been expended upon the building and it was still unfinished. For thermometers, $7500 was charged. Contractors for various parts of the building presented enormous bills and then divided with the boss. Even if a city avoids a boss there is likely to be a lack of harmony between the mayor and council — especially in the *weak* mayor-council type.

Commission Type of City Government. — A commission government is one in which a few elective officers (usually five) exercise all legislative and executive powers and are held responsible to the voters for their proper use. This form of city government was first tried with success at Galveston, Texas, in 1901, after a tidal wave swept over the island city and left it in partial ruins — drowning about 6000 of its then 37,000 inhabitants. The city had been extravagantly managed under its mayor-council type of government, and it was unable to cope with the terrible conditions resulting from the flood.

The Texas Legislature granted the city a new charter providing for the government of the city by five commissioners [1] with power to make laws and enforce them. The plan was intended to be temporary, but it proved so efficient that it was the beginning of a new type of city government, known as the Commission Plan; and publicity concerning it made Galveston famous. The plan spread rapidly to other Texas cities; and soon after, it was adopted in Des Moines, Iowa, with some new features.

The Typical Commission Government consists of five popularly-elected commissioners. In some cities the voters, and in others the commissioners themselves, designate one of these five as mayor. All executive and legislative powers are centered in this body, and the mayor seldom possesses any more authority than his fellow-commissioners. He does represent the city on ceremonial occasions, but rarely does he have the veto power.

---

[1] These five "commissioners" were so named because part of them were originally appointive.

The commission is the city government. As a group the commissioners enact local legislation (city ordinances). Individually they head the several administrative departments and supervise the enforcement of ordinances passed by the whole commission. Usually there are as many departments as commissioners, and each commissioner is responsible for the work of his own department. The names of the various departments may differ from city to city, but in general their work covers the following activities: public affairs, accounts and finance, public safety, streets and public improvements, and parks and public property. Unlike the councilmen under the mayor-council form, the commissioners serve full-time.

Various plans are used to determine which department each commissioner is to head. In most cities the commission itself assigns its members to particular posts. In some cities the voters elect commissioners to head specific departments, while in others the assignments are made by the mayor. The mayor is commissioner of public affairs in nearly all cases.

Following the lead of Des Moines, Iowa, many commission-type cities have the initiative, referendum, and recall. (Des Moines now has a city manager government.) Commissioners are usually nominated in non-partisan primaries and elected in non-partisan general ("run-off") elections. Some cities have independently chosen auditors and many have attempted to defeat machine politics by providing a civil service committee appointed by the commission.

The advantages of the commission government are: (1) the number to elect is small; (2) they can act promptly; (3) they have full power to act, and cannot shirk their responsibility by referring an aggrieved citizen to someone else; and (4) they are easier to watch than if they were many.

The way to get good government is to give power to a few people and watch those few in order to hold them responsible. A city boss does not steal when he is being watched. The commissioners meet in public, record their votes for the inspection of the public, publish their ordinances in the papers, and issue frequent financial reports.

If they refuse to enact an ordinance which the majority of voters desire, the voters themselves may initiate and pass it (initiative); if the commission passes one which the voters do not want, they may

have it referred to them and reject it (referendum); if the commissioners are believed to be dishonest or are inefficient, a new election may be
called and one or all of the commissioners recalled by electing others to
take their places (recall). Thus we get government for the people by a
few who are responsible directly to the people.

In one sense, however, the Commission Plan violates the basic
principle of government that legislators should be elected by the people

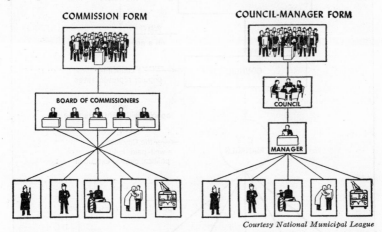

COMMISSION FORM   COUNCIL-MANAGER FORM

BOARD OF COMMISSIONERS

COUNCIL

MANAGER

Courtesy National Municipal League

GRAPHIC COMPARISON OF THE COMMISSION AND THE COUNCIL-MANAGER FORMS
OF CITY GOVERNMENT

Note how the Board of Commissioners both legislates and administers the departments — and sometimes at cross purposes. Under the council-manager form, the
council legislates and chooses a manager who appoints the heads of departments.
This clearly locates responsibility.

but administrators should be appointed. In the Commission Plan,
the people should and do elect their representatives as councilmen to
make the city laws. These same councilmen also administer the laws.
But efficient experts to enforce laws and administer a city should not
be subject to those political influences and residential restrictions which
control elective positions. That is why such experts are usually best
secured through executive appointment.

Moreover, the Commission Plan does not locate responsibility as well
as the Manager Type. It often creates five little governments as each
commissioner attempts to draw all the money and authority he can to
his department, to make himself important.

The City-Manager Type of Government. — The manager type of government is really a modification of the commission type. Except in very large cities, it usually consists of a council of three or five members, who determine the policy, but select a manager to administer the

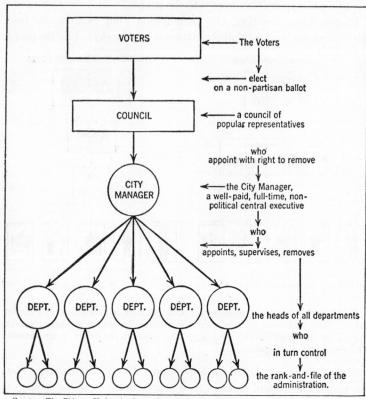

VOTERS ◄——— The Voters

◄——— elect
on a non-partisan ballot

COUNCIL ◄——— a council of
popular representatives

who
appoint with right to remove

CITY MANAGER ◄——— the City Manager,
a well-paid, full-time, non-political central executive

who

appoints, supervises, removes

DEPT.   DEPT.   DEPT.   DEPT.   DEPT.   the heads of all departments

who

in turn control

the rank-and-file of the administration.

Courtesy The Chicago University Press, from Ridley and Nolting's "The City-Manager Profession."

THE CITY-MANAGER PLAN

Compare this chart with the others. Note the simplicity of this form of government, and how responsibility is centralized so the voters can exercise control.

government of the city. The council of five who represent the people are like the directors of a commercial corporation who are selected by the stockholders to determine the business policies, and the city manager selected by the council is like the general manager of a commercial corporation.

In 1907 Staunton, Virginia, wanted a more efficient city government. Its charter permitted the council to appoint new officers and so, early in 1908, it appointed a "city manager." He was given full charge of the administration of the city, and was allowed to appoint and dismiss heads of departments and other city employees.

The manager of Staunton for the first three years was Mr. Ashburner of Richmond, formerly construction engineer for the Chesapeake and Ohio Railroad Company. Through businesslike methods he brought about efficient administration for the city. For example, by purchasing supplies for all of the departments he saved a neat sum for the city; he laid granolithic walks at about half their cost when put out at contract under the old system; and by putting meters in all houses the usual shortage of water was overcome. Many other cities have added a manager to their existing form of government.

The first real manager government was organized by Sumter, South Carolina, in 1912, after obtaining permission from the State legislature. The first three councilmen were exceptionally capable men, one being a planter, one a banker, and the third a lawyer. They advertised for a manager and chose one from another State. He brought about a number of economies.

An interesting incident is told of how this manager got rid of mistletoe which was killing miles of trees in the city streets. It had not been removed previously because of the great cost. The manager knew that mistletoe has a time and place value, so he had the mistletoe cut from the trees and sold it in the North for enough to cover the entire cost of cleaning the trees.

An amendment added to the Constitution of Ohio in 1912 permits cities to draft their own charters, and after the flood in the spring of 1913 Dayton elected a charter committee pledged to the manager plan, and their charter was accepted by the voters. Dayton was the first city with more than 100,000 inhabitants to adopt the manager plan.

The Dayton Type of Manager Government is as follows:

(1) A Commission of five elected from the city at large for a term of four years, partial renewal biennially, on a salary of $1200 (Mayor $1800). Duties: enact ordinances, determine policy, make appropriations, and elect a manager and a civil service board.

(2) A Mayor who is the commissioner receiving the greatest vote the year that three are elected. Merely first among equals. Duties: presides

at meetings of the commission, is ceremonial head of the city, stands for the city in actions at law, is agent of the governor in carrying out the State militia law, but has no veto.

ORGANIZE TO GET MANAGER PLAN

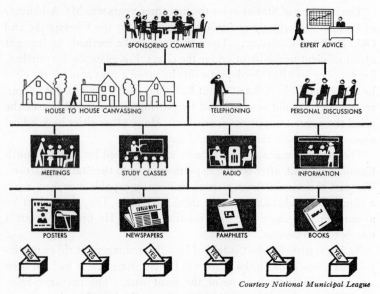

Courtesy National Municipal League

CITIZENS ORGANIZE TO GET MANAGER PLAN

(3) A Manager chosen by the commission for an indefinite term. Removed either by commission or by recall of the voters. Salary determined by the commission. Duties: enforces the city ordinances, employs and dismisses department heads, dismisses even civil service employees subject to appeal, advises commission as to needs of city.

(4) Nonpartisan primaries and elections.

(5) Initiative.

(6) Referendum.

(7) Recall of commissioners or manager.

(8) Publicity provisions as in the regular commission plan.

The manager type of government has given satisfaction to the majority of people in Dayton, but minority groups do occasionally complain that they have no representation because all five commissioners are elected at large.

Over 1200 cities and towns have adopted the manager type of gov-- ernment either by charter amendments or by ordinances where the city councils have added a manager to their old type of government; and many others have adopted a modified manager plan.

The advantages of the manager plan are: (1) The burdensome duties are performed by the manager, therefore a prominent business man can afford to serve as commissioner because he can continue with his regular business. (2) The manager may be chosen from within or without the city. (3) The manager may be chosen without political considerations. (4) Powers and responsibility are centered in one man. "If anything goes wrong you know whom to hang." Either the manager or three of the five commissioners are to blame. Commissioners give the manager great latitude. (5) It makes city governing a profession instead of political "graft." For instance, the manager of Staunton received $2500 a year, but was successful and became manager of Springfield, Ohio, on a salary of $6000, and then of Norfolk, Virginia, at $12,000, and then of Stockton, California, at $20,000. (6) It is efficient. For instance, the Saginaw Manager found 42 full-time bridge tenders who did nothing but raise drawbridges an average of twice a week when barges passed through. He reduced the number to 7 by having police cars speed to bridges when they needed to be raised.

City Charters. — A city government has only such powers as the State grants it. These powers are usually enumerated in a charter which contains the name of the city, a description of its boundaries, the form of its organization, and an enumeration of its powers. In colonial days the Colonial Governor granted city charters. After the Revolution, State legislatures took over this function because of the unpopularity of Colonial Governors; and in some States they still grant them. However, this practice of a State legislature's granting a separate charter to each city resulted in favoritism to those cities which were loyal to the majority party machine. In order to overcome this defect, many State legislatures grouped their cities into classes according to population and enacted general uniform laws for the government of all cities of a given class. In home rule States the people of a community prepare their own city charter.

Home Rule for Cities. — City inhabitants felt that they should have more control over their own government, and "home rule" provisions were placed in the constitutions of a number of States. These provisions allow the people of a city (and in some States a village), under certain restrictions,[1] to frame their own charter. Of course these charters must not contain provisions inconsistent with the State laws.

Of the States permitting cities to draft their own "home rule" charter none is more liberal than Ohio.[2] The Ohio Constitutional Convention of 1912 gave cities the power either to frame their own charters or to adopt by local referendum any general or special charter laws which the State legislature might pass. The legislature promptly prepared three model charters: one of the council-mayor type, one of the commission type, and one of the manager type. However, most of the larger cities of Ohio prepared their own charters and are now enjoying self-made or "home rule" charters.

A home rule charter may be framed by the city council, by a group of interested citizens, or by a charter convention composed of elective delegates. It is then submitted to the voters for ratification or rejection. Amendments are submitted by the council or else initiated by petition, but must be submitted to the voters.

---

[1] The restriction may be a four-sevenths majority of the city voters, the approval of the governor, or the approval of the legislature.

[2] The following States have constitutional municipal home rule:

STATE	YEAR OF ADOPTION	APPLICABLE TO
Missouri	1875	Cities of over 10,000
California	1879	Cities of over 3500
Washington	1889	Cities of 20,000 or over
Minnesota	1896	Any city or village
Colorado	1902	Cities of 2000 or over
Oregon	1906	Any city or town
Oklahoma	1907	Cities of over 2000
Michigan	1908	Any city or village
Arizona	1912	Cities of over 3500
Ohio	1912	Any city or village
Nebraska	1912	Cities of over 5000
Texas	1912	Cities of over 5000
Maryland	1915	Baltimore and any county
Indiana	1921	Cities of over 2000
Pennsylvania	1922	Cities of over 10,000
New York	1923	Any city
Nevada	1924	Any city or town
Wisconsin	1924	Any city or village
Utah	1933	Any city or town
W. Virginia	1937	Cities of over 2000
Louisiana	1947	Any city (governor's consent)

Changing Municipal Boundaries. — Population continues to move city-ward; but the family car has also enabled it to move from city centers to the suburbs where it can still have many of the city advantages plus lower taxes. This area beyond the city bounds creates many problems. So-called "septic tanks" bring pollution; old car lots come because they are not excluded by zoning; and immoral road houses spring up unregulated by city laws.

Methods of annexation are determined by the State legislature unless restricted by the State constitution. Originally the legislature handled each city petition separately. Today legislative statutes usually provide that municipal boundaries shall be extended only upon the consent of a majority of the inhabitants of a district sought to be annexed. And an authorized court may call an election when properly petitioned.

As suburbs tend to resist annexation, some State legislatures have given cities regulatory powers over thickly settled areas beyond the city's boundaries.

Cities sometimes induce suburbs to accept annexation by agreeing not to raise the taxes of the annexed area for a certain number of years; or to raise them gradually over a long period according to an agreed schedule.

Legal Liability of Cities and Towns. — *Liability for Breach of Contract.* — The city or town is liable to the same extent and in the same manner as a private corporation for contracts legally made in the exercise of powers granted it by the State.

Liability for Torts (Wrongs) of Employees When Engaged in Undertakings of a Private or Corporate Character. — If a city or town operates a water system, a lighting plant, a street railway, or other income-producing properties, the city or town is engaged in business and is liable for the wrongful acts of its officials and employees very much as a private corporation is liable for its officers, employees, and other agents.

Not Usually Liable for Torts of Employees When Engaged in Purely Governmental Functions. — "The King can do no wrong" is an adage handed down to us through the ages. After our separation from England we associated the same idea with the State: "The State can do no wrong." The birth of counties, townships, cities, and villages as offspring of the State carried with it this heritage of governmental immunity. Thus a city is not usually held liable for wrongs committed by such city employees as police, firemen, public school teachers, or employees of the health service, because these functions are performed for the general good and not for profit.

Tendency to Increase Liability of Cities. — According to common law inherited by our States from England, a city is not liable for the wrongful acts of its employees engaged in governmental functions. But the State courts (*e.g.*, in Ohio) have increasingly construed common law so as to increase the liability of cities.

Also State legislatures have here and there enacted statutes specifically increasing the liability of cities. For example, in 1929 the California Legislature removed all governmental immunity of the State and its subdivisions respecting damage caused through the negligent operation of any motor vehicle by its employees.

According to this California Act, the city is liable for damages if a traffic officer or a driver of a fire engine negligently injures another car or a person. But we must not let this exception mislead us. Outside of California, or a State with similar legislation, the general common law rule would not hold the city liable under these circumstances.

QUESTIONS ON THE TEXT

1. What is meant by incorporating a community?
2. What is a *village?* Where are incorporated places so named?
3. Where are small incorporated centers called *towns? Boroughs?*
4. What is meant by the term *town* in the New England States?
5. What are the usual powers of towns or villages?
6. By what name is the legislative body of a town or village commonly known? What character of ordinances may it enact?
7. By what title is the principal executive officer of a town usually known?
8. What other officers do towns or villages commonly have?
9. How does a city differ from a town or village?
10. How many inhabitants are necessary for city government?
11. What per cent of the American people lived in cities in 1790? Now?
12. What has been the cause of such rapid growth of cities? Is this rapid growth of cities peculiar to the United States?
13. What three types of city government are there in the United States?
14. Is the tendency toward a council of two branches or of one branch?

15. Explain the present organization of the mayor-council government for cities.

16. How is the mayor selected and what are his duties?

17. How is the council selected and what are its duties?

18. Explain why the mayor-council type of city government does not work well and why it is favored by political bosses.

19. Describe the commission type of city government. Explain how it originated in Galveston.

20. Why is it called "commission government"?

21. What do you mean by *city charter?* What are the provisions of the Des Moines charter?

22. Name the advantages of the commission type of government.

23. Describe the city-manager type of government. Explain how the idea originated in Staunton, Virginia.

24. Explain the working of this type of government in Sumter, South Carolina.

25. Why and when was the manager type adopted in Dayton, Ohio?

26. Explain the Dayton type of manager government.

27. What are the advantages of the manager type of government?

28. What is meant by "home rule" for cities? Why is it important? Which State has the most liberal "home rule" provisions?

29. Explain to what extent a city is liable for breaking a contract; for wrongs resulting from negligence of its employees.

PROBLEMS FOR DISCUSSION

1. How are towns or villages incorporated in your State? How many inhabitants are necessary?

2. If you live in a town or village name its important officers and tell how they are chosen.

3. If you live in a town or village tell about where the boundaries run.

4. How can the boundaries of towns, villages, and cities be extended?

5. What is the population of your town or village or city?

6. Why does it need a government distinct from that of your county?

7. Would you favor an annual town meeting at which your principal public officials would explain their duties and problems?

8. What determines the location of cities?

9. Does your State constitution contain any provisions in regard to cities? What are they? Could some town that you know become a city? How?

10. What is the population of the largest city of your State?

11. Name the principal officers of some city with which you are acquainted. How are they selected? For what term?

12. The cities of Ohio are allowed to draft their own charters. Do you think every city should be allowed to prepare its own charter?

13. States may enact any laws which do not conflict with Federal laws. Why not allow all cities to enact any laws which do not conflict with State laws or Federal laws?

14. Is the city likely to get the best results by electing only a few officers or many?

15. Other things being equal, should a city manager be an old resident of the town or an experienced manager from another town?

16. Would you advocate paying a manager of a city of 100,000 population ten or twenty thousand dollars?

17. A city charter authorized the city to "construct and operate an airport." The city constructed an airport, but leased it to an individual instead of operating it. Why did the court decide that the city did not have power to lease the airport?

18. According to the common law rules would a *city* be liable for damages in most States under the following circumstances?

(1) A policeman lost his temper when arresting a drunken driver and broke the latter's arm.

(2) The motorman of a city-owned and city-operated street railway started his car too soon and injury resulted to a passenger boarding the car.

(3) The city ambulance carrying a patient to a quarantine station drove recklessly and smashed a private car.

(4) Typhoid fever was contracted from city water because of carelessness on the part of the city employee in charge of the reservoir.

(5) A Chinese restaurant was destroyed by a gang of ruffians because the police were sympathetic with the gang and did not give vigorous protection.

19. Would you vote to make your city liable for all damage to individuals or their property through negligence on the part of your city employees? For malicious acts on the part of the employees? For accidents which they cannot avoid? Is your city or the individual better able to bear the loss?

20. If your city were liable for damages under all circumstances, would it be more or less careful in the selection of its officers? Would it be likely to pay higher salaries?

21. If you should choose city managership for a profession, what kind of educational preparation would you make?

22. Should the United States establish academies similar to West Point and Annapolis for the training of city officials?

23. In San Francisco as soon as a street accident is reported a white police car speeds to the scene so that evidence may be collected while it is "hot." Eye witnesses are interviewed on the spot, a map is made of the accident scene, and the wreckage is photographed. Does this police "Traffic Court on Wheels" work to the advantage of the more innocent party or of the reckless driver? Do most cities have as good a method?

24. Since 1925 Cincinnati has had the Manager Form of Government. A council of nine is elected by proportional representation; and the council chooses the mayor and the manager. Col. C. O. Sherrill, honor graduate of West Point, army engineer, etc., was manager until he resigned in 1930. Then Clarence Dykstra was manager until he resigned in 1937 to become President of the University of Wisconsin. Then Col. Sherrill resigned a $50,000 position in private life to again become Manager of Cincinnati for a salary of $25,000. What do these facts imply as to the value of manager government and the type of managers attracted to Cincinnati?

SELECT BIBLIOGRAPHY

The Charter of your own City or Village.

Forms of Municipal Government. National Municipal League, New York, 1951. 20 pages. 25¢.

BROMAGE, A. *A Councilman Speaks.* George Wahr Publishers. Ann Arbor. 1951.

BUTTERFIELD, R. "Revolt in Philadelphia." *Saturday Evening Post.* November 8, 15, 22, 1952.

League of Women Voters. *Know Your Town Government.* 726 Jackson Place. Washington, D. C. 25¢.

"A Mayor and His City." *Life.* April 21, 1952.

Story of the Council-Manager Plan. National Municipal League, New York, 1952. 36 pages. 20¢.

CHILDS, R. *Civic Victories.* Harpers. New York. 1952.

KNEIER, C., and FOX, G. *Readings in Municipal Government.* Rinehart. New York. 1953.

"Ex-Mayor." "Are You *Sure* You Want an Honest Mayor?" *Collier's.* October 30, 1953.

CAMERON, F. "He Hunts Firebugs." *Saturday Evening Post.* Sept. 19, 1953.

CHAPTER XXXIV

CITY AND VILLAGE PROBLEMS

City Planning. — Washington City was planned by L'Enfant before it was built. It has beautiful circles, adequate parks, parallel streets systematically named according to the alphabet with those at right angles numbered, houses numbered 100 to the block, and wide avenues cutting diagonally through the city as the shortest distance between two points. Paris was remade on a grand scale a century ago by Napoleon III, who was unhampered by legal restrictions for the protection of private property which have made large-scale city improvements in America difficult. Many early American cities just grew without plan, like the narrow crooked streets of the original Boston which are said to have followed cow paths. Fortunately, more and more cities are recognizing the problems of unplanned expansion, congestion, and the like, and are meeting the challenge with systematic planning.

Philadelphia began as a "planned" city. It was first laid out by William Penn in 1682 much in the fashion of a checkerboard. Penn's simple scheme called for two main thoroughfares crossing one another at right angles, with an open place at the point of intersection, and with other lesser streets crisscrossing the pattern at regular intervals. This "gridiron plan" has since been followed by most American cities. In Penn's plan, the City of Brotherly Love was to cover approximately two square miles.

The city has long since outgrown its founder's plan. It now sprawls over 130 square miles with a population of more than 2,000,000. Much of this growth has been haphazard, without plan, and inevitably has resulted in congestion. The city's problem was compounded by the fact that for 75 years it lay in the grip of a corrupt political machine only recently thrown out by the voters.

But now Philadelphia is engaged in a vast and popular campaign of self-improvement. Whole blocks of aged buildings are being torn down to be replaced by beautiful parks, modern highways, and business projects. As part of this program, the Pennsylvania Railroad's ancient Broad Street Station, in the heart of the city, has been razed. To celebrate the razing, the 103-piece Philadelphia Orchestra played a requiem in the train shed and Conductor Eugene Ormandy led a large and enthusiastic crowd in the singing of Auld Lang Syne.

Courtesy Public Housing Administration

AN UP-TO-DATE LOW-RENT HOUSING PROJECT
IN NEW ORLEANS

St. Thomas Street Extension consists of 540 attractive, low-rent homes, built, owned, and operated by the New Orleans, Louisiana, Housing Authority under the provisions of the United States Housing Act.

Radburn, New Jersey, was built as a model town by its planners. It was planned to provide the utmost in health, safety, convenience, and happiness. Its homes are clustered about short closed-end streets — not facing busy thoroughfares with their steady streams of smelly, noisy cars, buses, and trucks. These closed-end streets lead from traffic arteries which bound the residential sections. Underpasses provide safe pedestrian crossing of the busy-trafficked streets. The attractive houses sit in park-like landscapes and each large block has a park, playground, school, or some other civic or benevolent institution at its center.

The larger insurance companies have lent cities a hand in recent years. They have replaced slums with vast and modern housing projects — "cities within cities" in such communities as New York, Los Angeles, and Newark. Parkchester, Peter Cooper Village, and Stuyvesant Town in New York City and the smaller Parklabrea in Los Angeles and Parkfairfax in Alexandria, Virginia, for example, all are creations of the Metropolitan Life Insurance Co.

Metropolitan Districts. — Most major American cities are afflicted with "suburbanitis." Congestion and industrial growth plus rapid means of transportation have led millions of city dwellers to seek the open air around their cities. Thus, between 1940 and 1950 the suburbs of each of the nation's twelve largest cities grew at a faster rate than the cities themselves. Los Angeles' population grew only about 30 per cent while that of many of its suburbs grew over 100 per cent. Chicago gained only 7 per cent while its suburbs increased 32 per cent. And, in some places, this spreading out has meant that neighboring cities have grown together like Siamese twins.

The residents of these populated areas face many common problems — such as water supply, sewage disposal, police and fire protection, transportation, and city planning. Duplication of functions by city and city or city and county is wasteful and at times even dangerous. More than one fire has burned on while neighboring fire departments quibbled over which was responsible for fighting it.

To meet these problems, various States have taken the control of certain functions away from the cities and counties and vested them in specially created *metropolitan districts*. Over 150 of these districts are now in existence; their boundaries commonly include all of the area involved without regard to city and county lines.

These metropolitan districts are most often established for a single purpose — for example, sewage in the case of the Chicago Sanitary District and park development in the Cleveland Metropolitan Park District.

But there is no reason why a district's authority cannot be expanded to include other functions. Thus the Boston Metropolitan District began as a sewage district in 1889. Today it controls sewage, water supply, park development, and also has duties in connection with planning the development of the District as a whole. There is also a rapid transit commission for the District. Boston itself accounts for only about one third of the District's total population and the District now includes some forty municipalities.

Zoning. — *Introduction.* — One would be surprised to find a cook stove in a parlor or a piano in a kitchen. Yet it was just as absurd for

BOSTON METROPOLITAN DISTRICT

American cities to allow stores to crowd in at random among private dwellings, or factories and public garages to come elbowing in among neat retail stores or well-kept apartment houses, or tall and bulky office buildings to rise so closely crowded that the lower floors become dungeon-like and unsatisfactory for human use. Such conditions also added to the always present fire hazards of congested communities.

The courts would not allow city councils to restrict the use of private property except in case of such well-recognized nuisances as pig pens, glue factories, tanneries, slaughterhouses, forges, gas works, oil tanks, powder magazines, and the like.   We inherited the right to regulate the location of these nuisances in the common law of England.

The developing science of sanitation taught us that there were many nuisances which we had not formerly recognized; and with the spread of culture, ugliness hurt the eyes as noise had hurt the ears or odors the nose.   So judges recognizing new nuisances gradually permitted more and more regulation of private property as a proper exercise of the police powers.   For example, Boston was allowed to limit the height of buildings.   Then Los Angeles was allowed to exclude brick yards from residential districts.   And Roanoke, Virginia, was allowed to require buildings to be erected a specified distance back from the street.

It has long been the practice of real estate dealers in establishing suburban plots to sell the lots subject to certain restrictions as to their use.   These restrictions are incorporated in each deed of conveyance. But it is only since a Supreme Court Decision rendered in 1926 that the cities have definitely known that it is legal to plot a whole city into districts, or zones, in which there are restrictions as to the height and size of buildings, the percentage of the lot that may be occupied, the size of yards and courts, the location and use of buildings, and the use of land for trade, industry, residence, or other purposes.

The Purpose of Zoning is well stated in the following ten points set forth by the Boston City Planning Board:

1. Zoning divides the city into districts, according to the most suitable and valuable uses for each district, based on existing conditions and future needs, and regulates the location and use of new buildings.

2. Zoning makes provision for *general business districts* in suitable locations in which industrial plants may not impair the business environment.

3. Zoning chooses suitable land for *industrial districts* where the best of transportation facilities by rail, water, and highway may be secured and factories may easily expand without tearing down expensive buildings.

4. Zoning provides *unrestricted districts*, suitable places for those heavy industries such as stockyards, boiler works, coke manufacture, and other industries that would be objectionable elsewhere.

5. Zoning regulates the *heights of buildings* appropriate to their use, so as to provide an equitable distribution of light and air for all, minimizes overcrowding of people, and relieves traffic congestion.

6. Zoning provides *local business districts*, conveniently located near residential neighborhoods, where stores will be concentrated instead of being scattered everywhere.

7. Zoning protects the comfort, convenience, and quietness of *residential districts* by excluding stores, public garages, laundries, factories, and other business and industrial uses.

8. Zoning establishes *uniform building lines* in residential districts to assure an equal amount of light and air and access for all residences.

9. Zoning provides adequate light and air by *side and rear yards* around every building in the suburban residential districts and establishes the *percentage of area of a lot* that may be occupied by buildings.

10. Zoning preserves the home character of single and two-family *residence districts* by segregating types of residences into districts where they are appropriate.

A Zoning Law Must Reasonably Promote Health, Morals, Safety, or the Welfare of the Citizens. — States, or cities with the consent of States, have power to protect the health, morals, safety, and general welfare of the community. These powers are called the "police powers" of the States; and unless the restrictions in the use of property can be justified in the courts as a proper exercise of the police powers, they will be declared void as depriving one of liberty or property without due process of law (unreasonably). (Amendments V and XIV.)

A Zoning Law Must Provide for the Issuance of Permits under Circumstances Where the Law Would Cause an Unreasonable Hardship. — Under a Zoning Law there must be an appeal to the city council or some board of adjustment where citizens consider the application of the law to work unreasonable hardship in their cases. For instance in Portland, Oregon, a residence district was zoned against various things, including churches. A congregation petitioned and obtained a permit to build a church there. It agreed to build a beautiful structure on a half block — 150 feet from the nearest residence. It would have been a hardship on the congregation to have to build the church in another part of the city.

A Zoning Law Must Not Apply to Structures Already Erected, Except As Applied to General Nuisances. — For example, a zoning law cannot require buildings higher than the specified height to be torn down, nor apartment houses in a restricted zone to be abandoned, nor residences moved farther back from the street. The law applies to future building.

However, as a city grows, it can require such nuisances as slaughter houses, powder magazines, glue factories, or stables to be removed.

Excess Condemnation. — In America, if land is needed for public use, the city may have it condemned through the right of eminent domain. To take land for streets, parks, public-building sites, bridge heads, and the like, is clearly to take it for public purposes. But it may be desirable, in connection with a public improvement, for a city to acquire more land than is actually needed for the immediate purpose.

LAKE WASHINGTON FLOATING BRIDGE, SEATTLE, WASHINGTON

For example, if land for a new city hall is acquired in a congested district, it may be desirable that the city should take some unsightly property near by in order to have the new structure set in favorable surroundings. It may also be desirable to resell the excess land under such restrictions as will insure the attractiveness of the district. This is the regular procedure in Europe, but in many American cities, the constitutions, laws, and courts stand in the way. However, some States have amended their constitutions, and their courts now permit "excess condemnation." Hence, city planning with an eye to the beautiful as well as the serviceable is becoming possible.

Billboards. — Nothing mars the beauty of city streets more than billboards. City laws prohibiting billboards on private property have usually been declared unconstitutional; but the Vermont Supreme Court holds that a State or municipality may prohibit highway advertising without depriving the property holder or billboard owner of any Constitutional rights. And the Massachusetts and New York courts are tending to hold that billboards may be regulated if they depreciate property values.

Billboards which might conceal thugs, produce disease, set fire to adjoining property, blow down and destroy life, or obstruct the vision and endanger traffic may be prohibited.

For instance, New York requires fireproof billboards with secure wind braces and prohibits electric signs which unduly interfere with sleep. Chicago requires billboards to have an open space below them and at the sides. St. Louis limits the area of billboards to 500 square feet, some cities tax them as real estate, and others impose a license tax of so much a square foot.

Public Utilities. — A public utility is an enterprise which, though under private ownership, makes use of public property and is a natural monopoly. Street railways, telephone lines, gas plants, and electric power plants are good examples of city public utilities.

In past years many cities tried the plan of setting two public service companies at rivalry with one another, but this involved public inconvenience, and soon competition proved unprofitable and a resulting combination would raise rates enough to recover former losses.

There can be no economic competition between public utilities operating in the same area. Therefore, as public utilities are monopolies by nature, there must be public authorities over them to prevent any abuse of their power.

A public utility must obtain a *franchise* (right to use public streets or other property), which is commonly granted by the city council. This franchise specifies the duration of the privilege and contains many provisions as to the rates and quality of service.

In order to make the regulation of public utilities elastic it is usually provided that differences of opinion regarding rates and service shall be determined by a *public service commission*. The larger cities sometimes have a public service commission of their own, but more often a State commission regulates rates in the cities as well as in other parts of the State because:

(1) the public utility often extends beyond the city boundaries;
(2) the commissions are expensive;
(3) a State commission is less likely to be prejudiced.

Fairchild Aerial Surveys, Inc.

MANHATTAN

New York City has five boroughs or municipal centers. They are Manhattan, The Bronx, Queens, Brooklyn, and Richmond.

Manhattan, shown at the center of the picture, includes all of Manhattan Island. It is the smallest of the boroughs. The sturdy little island with its towering skyscrapers built firmly on its rocky base is one of the world's great industrial and cultural centers. It is the "home town" of almost 2,000,000 people and the seat of government for the metropolis to which it belongs. The tiny island in the foreground is Governors Island.

Municipal Ownership. If public utilities are owned by the city, the council or a designated body regulates rates and services.

Public Ownership is increasing steadily in the United States and we accept it as a matter of course in most instances. Public roads, bridges, water systems, and sewers are excellent examples, which are taken for granted. The public school systems have been publicly-owned for so long that no one thinks twice about them now.

There are over 2000 publicly-owned power and light systems in the United States, though they serve principally the smaller municipalities. More than two-thirds of all our cities with over 100,000 population own their own airports, including the new $200,000,000 New York International Airport financed by the New York Port Authority. While most city transportation systems are privately-owned, outstanding cities like New York, Cleveland, Chicago, Detroit, San Francisco, and Seattle own their own transportation systems. New York now collects 7,000,000 ten-cent fares each day from subway passengers.

Those favoring public ownership claim that private ownership of public utilities results in political graft and in inflated or untrue values on which rates are based.

Those opposing public ownership claim that public ownership of public utilities results in political corruption and the loss of individual initiative.

The truth of the matter seems to be that cities with capable public-spirited citizens who are willing to donate valuable services usually make a good showing with public ownership where all profit is for public benefit. But if such capable public-spirited citizens are lacking, private ownership is probably the best solution where the stockholders demand efficient management and the public regulatory commissions safeguard the people.

Slum Clearance. — City slums, to say nothing of rural slums, have become a national disgrace, so the National Government is in a variety of ways co-operating with local governments and corporations in low-rent housing projects. The re-building of our cities should be a major project. Slum clearance will be more fully discussed in Chapter XXXIX.

ONE CAUSE OF TRAFFIC CONGESTION

Traffic Congestion, accentuated by motor transportation, has been studied by planning commissions; and the following accomplishments may be suggestive for your city:

The old Erie Canal was abandoned and the city of Rochester turned the bed into a subway for passengers and freight.   It built an avenue over it.

San Francisco relieved congestion in front of the Municipal Ferry, where the electric cars from all parts of the city converge and circle, by digging a tunnel for through traffic under the circle.   It has built two enormous bridges to span the harbor and the Golden Gate.   Los Angeles has pedestrian tunnels under dangerous streets adjacent to school houses.

San Francisco made a garage under Union Square (see page 694); and now Boston, when and if financial arrangements can be made, is planning for a garage for 2000 cars under the historic Common in the very center of the shopping district.

Also, the Metropolitan Transit Authority for greater Boston is establishing parking areas at terminal rapid transit stations — privately conducted at a moderate fee.   This will allow people from the numerous towns surrounding Boston to shop in the city's center without the inconvenience of downtown traffic jams.   One can park his car at any one of several terminals (see accompanying drawing and picture) and go by elevated-subway trains to any part of the downtown shopping center.

Seattle has constructed a two-level viaduct to allow through traffic to skirt the downtown business area.   One-way traffic on each level may travel as fast as 45 miles per hour and the downtown congestion caused by through traffic is relieved.

In Chicago, between Wacker Street and Chicago River, the commission houses were removed and a wide drive built.   This drive has two levels and communicates with the two-level Michigan Avenue bridge and approaches — in all, a dozen blocks of wide two-level street.

Chicago also pointed the way for relieving automobile-choked streets by utilizing the interiors of high buildings for garages.   In this type of garage, motor cars are automatically stored in record time, and as briskly roll forth at the touch of a button.

From forty seconds to two minutes is delivery time in these garages. The owner drives his car upon a loading platform before one of the elevators.   An attendant takes a key from a master board, numbered to correspond with a vacant stall.   The withdrawal of the key makes electrical connections which set in motion a sliding platform above, and the vacant stall comes to rest directly in front of the elevator shaft.

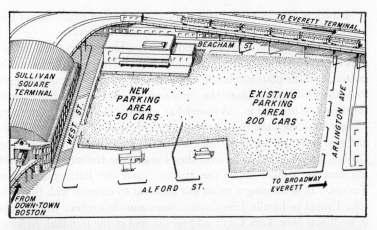

PARKING AREA PROVIDED BY THE METROPOLITAN TRANSIT AUTHORITY
AT SULLIVAN SQUARE, BOSTON

Meantime the elevator operator punches a button which causes the loading platform to tilt, and the car slides into the elevator.

The operator dials a number and the elevator rises to the floor assigned, where the door opens automatically. The operator presses a button, and the platform in the elevator tilts, letting the car slide into its stall. Bumpers engage the tires and hold the car in place until the owner returns for it. A somewhat similar process returns the car.

New York elevated the downtown continuation of Riverside Drive; and also provided for fast traffic along the East River. It built the George Washington Bridge over the Hudson, the Holland Tunnel and the Lincoln Tunnel under the Hudson, and the Battery-Brooklyn Tunnel. It is building a union bus terminal to connect with the Lincoln Tunnel to handle Jersey commuters and thus relieve traffic jams in midtown New York City; and on the roof of the terminal, parking is provided for 500 cars. Private capital has just built on the old Hippodrome site a parking garage for several thousand cars. The site is said to have cost $3,500,000. The city has been experimenting with parking out from the city center. It reopened the old World's Fair parking field for 3000 cars (25 cents for 12 hours). From there commuters can come to the city's center on fast trains or by subway.

Simple arithmetic proves that cities cannot provide downtown parking, or even driving space, on its streets for every individual in an 18-foot car. Why not speed mid-town traffic by restricting it to public officials, trucks, public conveyances, cars whose owners have permanent off-street parking space, and those granted emergency plates like doctors and service men?

Traffic Accidents. — In the United States, street or highway accidents result annually in about thirty-odd thousand deaths, a million personal injuries, and nearly a billion dollars in economic loss. Many cities are endeavoring to reduce these losses through better traffic engineering, traffic regulation, and traffic education. When Barron Collier was deputy commissioner in charge of the bureau of public safety of the New York Police, he reduced fatalities fifty per cent through an educational campaign. He said that accidents are caused by carelessness; therefore the work of his bureau was to make people think.

The first form of carelessness as revealed by his records is carelessness in crossing streets — " jaywalking." This one cause alone

AN AIRVIEW OF LONG ISLAND PARKWAYS

This remarkable group of highways, which eliminate grade intersections, speeds
traffic and effectively reduces the number of accidents.

accounted for practically fifty per cent of street accidents. Through newspapers, posters in buses and in garages, billboards, pamphlets, lectures in schools and theaters, and millions of small cards handed out by boy scouts, Mr. Collier persuaded people to cross streets at the right places and in the right manner.

To assist him in reaching the public consciousness he created a new character, "Aunty J. Walker," a smiling old lady in uniform, armed with a club and a benevolent smile which would attract attention anywhere. Aunty J. Walker would advise you to "Cross streets at crossings, not in the middle of the block. Go straight across, not diagonally. Look both ways."

Water Systems. — In 1907, when Los Angeles had a population of only 200,000, the city had sufficient vision to spend $25,000,000 on a water system. It brought water 250 miles — 54 miles through mountains and 150 miles across deserts. The gravity of the water supplied 120,000 horse power of electrical energy through five power plants, and reclaimed 150 square miles of arid lands near the city. Each year this watered garden yielded products of a value equal to the cost of the entire water system. Also this water controlled by Los Angeles forced most of the surrounding suburbs to become a part of the city. Hence the water has made possible the growth of the city from 200,000 to more than 2,000,000 population.

In Los Angeles there is almost a car for every two people. This expansion in transportation has enabled the population to spread over a wide area. This necessitates an enormous quantity of water to maintain green lawns and grow shubbery and shade trees in such a dry climate. It is estimated that it requires about 125 gallons of water per day for a tree — as much as the average per capita consumption.

To keep the water supply ahead of the population, the city has built a series of dams at the mouths of the great canyon basins along the way. In these, water is stored during the wet season and allowed to pass through the power plants uniformly. If a break occurs along the pipe line, no waste results. The water is stored in the reservoir just above, and the lower reservoirs keep the power plants running and supply the city. One reservoir, completed in 1925, is about 300 feet in height, and another beautiful one completed the same year overhangs the very edge of Hollywood. Therefore, there is a canyon full of water right at the edge of the city which will take care of any emergency.

Still looking ahead, Los Angeles, with other cities forming the Metropolitan Water District of Southern California, voted a $220,000,000 bond issue for a billion-gallon-a-day water supply from the Colorado River. The Reconstruction Finance Corporation helped finance this project by buying part of these bonds.

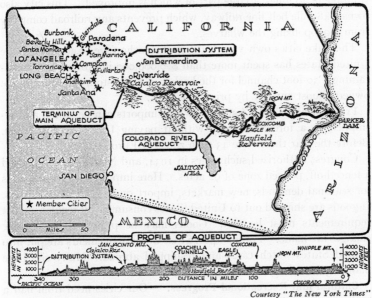

Courtesy "The New York Times"

THE COURSE OF THE COLORADO RIVER AQUEDUCT

Power from Hoover Dam pumps water through a 16-foot tunnel. Some power is regained by dynamos at falls along the aqueduct.

Sewage Disposal. — Most cities no longer contaminate streams by sewage. For instance, in Baltimore sewage is siphoned from one tank to another, then flows through a revolving screen, is sprayed into the air by thousands of small fountains, and is filtered through stone and sand. The filtrate flows into Chesapeake Bay as pure as the water in the city reservoirs. As the water falls from the filtration beds into the bay, it is used to generate electricity by which the disposal plant is operated. Pasadena uses the filtrate of its treated sewage to water a city farm which produces oranges, English walnuts, grain, and hay.

Wharves. — New Orleans, gateway to the Panama Canal, owns practically all of its water front, and the State of California has long been developing the water front of San Francisco. Greater New York now owns 349 of its 577 miles of water front.

Los Angeles, whose center is 21 miles from the coast, has a water frontage of 40 miles, a large part of which is improved. This city also owns a 48-mile belt line railway, which prevents any railroad company from monopolizing the wharves.

The Lake cities own very little of their wharfage; and though the United States has spent more than $20,000,000 improving and maintaining a 30-foot channel for the harbor of Galveston, the wharves are owned almost entirely by private persons.

Free Foreign Trade Zones are where imports can be stored and reshipped to a foreign country without paying United States tariffs. Before the war there were 43 such zones in Europe.

Congress authorized such zones in 1934, and New York established a fenced-off, policed zone of 92 acres. Here importers can hold goods for seasonal demands, new markets, import quotas, or other reasons. If goods are shipped out to United States consumers all regular import requirements must be met. Goods may be processed if no basic changes are made. For instance, Swiss watch movements are put into United States watch cases and reshipped abroad. Many cities are planning free zones. (See page 305.)

Cultural and Recreational Progress. — Our cities need from half a million to a million more teachers to give all children the educational advantages that some have; and at least a million children are without safe places to play. However, many cities are making progress along cultural and recreational lines. A report of the Berkeley, California, Chamber of Commerce, made the following appeal to its members: "Berkeley today is growing fast enough. Let us bend our energies to supply schools and playgrounds, parks and boulevards, enlarge our library, start a civic center, maintain our symphony orchestra, start an art gallery and a museum of natural history, and, indeed, provide those things which will make us stand out in the eyes of the world as a really enlightened and superior community. The right kind of people will want to live in such a place and will come here automatically, just as fast as we can make provision for them."

The New York City Radio Broadcasting Station enables the public officials to tell the people what their departments are doing. For instance, summaries of the proceedings of the city boards are broadcast the evening of the meeting. In addition, entertaining and instructive programs are rendered through this municipal station.

Health Protection. — Most cities have a health board to look after the general health conditions of the city. School children are inspected in nearly all American cities, and in many, free treatment is given to the eyes and teeth. Free medical dispensaries are commonly maintained to supply the needs of the poor; and many of the cities maintain hospitals.

In 1906 a group of 24 of our largest American cities had a typhoid fever death rate of 35 per 100,000. Now the rate for these same cities is 3 per 100,000 — less than in the rural communities around them. This reduced death rate is due to such steps as protection of water supplies, pasteurization of milk, supervision of food markets and restaurants, and widespread anti-typhoid inoculation.

Civilian Defense. — Atomic bombs and long-range bombers have made American cities prime targets in any future war. New York's Civilian Defense Commission predicts that an atomic explosion a half-mile above Union Square would lay waste to the city for two miles in every direction. The Empire State and Metropolitan Life Buildings, Peter Cooper Village and Stuyvesant Town, Rockefeller Center and Times Square, the Holland and Queens Tunnels, Pennsylvania and Grand Central Stations, the Metropolitan Opera House, and many schools, universities, and hospitals — all would lie among the wreckage.

Fire, explosions, flying debris, and broken gas and water mains and telephone and electric wires would add to the confusion, chaos, and devastation.

New York City has made great strides in preparing for such an attack. Police and firemen, medical teams and rescue squads, and maintenance and evacuation crews are being trained and equipped for possible action. Mobile aid stations and kitchens, river fire pumps and heavy clearing equipment, temporary shelters and other facilities are being readied.

Many other cities and States are following New York's lead. The task is tremendous, but given the frightful possibilities, it is a task that no city can afford to ignore.

Radio and Police Protection. — Nowadays, police cars carry first-aid equipment, riot guns, tear bombs, and two-way radio equipment. If someone phones police headquarters of crime or attempted crime, the cars cruising in that part of the city reach the scene in a few minutes. If someone observes the number of the car used by bandits, the fact is broadcast to police cars throughout the city. The progress of a fleeing car may also be broadcast to police cars from police headquarters.

QUESTIONS ON THE TEXT

1. What good features has the Washington City plan? Radburn, New Jersey.

2. What is "suburbanitis"? Why is it a problem? What is a metropolitan district?

3. How was the use of land limited previous to zoning laws?

4. What are the purposes of zoning cities?

5. Explain how zoning aids health, morals, safety, and social welfare in general.

6. What is meant by a zoning Board of Adjustment?

7. Does zoning apply to past developments, future, or both?

8. What is "excess condemnation," and to what extent is it legal in the United States? Should it be legal?

9. May a city forbid billboards on private property? May it discourage them?

10. What is a public utility corporation? Are these corporations usually regulated by a city commission or a State commission? Why?

11. Give suggestions for remedying traffic congestion.

12. How many traffic accidents occur in the United States? How might the number be reduced?

13. Describe the Los Angeles water system.

14. Should cities own the docks? Name some cities that do.

15. Describe the Baltimore sewage disposal system.

16. How has the typhoid fever death rate been reduced?

17. How does radio contribute to police protection?

18. Is New York of the manager, commission, weak-mayor, or strong-mayor type?

PROBLEMS FOR DISCUSSION

1. If you were zoning your city, where would you permit residences only? Apartment houses? Schools? Churches? Hospitals? Retail stores?

Garages? Filling stations? Factories? Stockyards? Moving pictures? Pool rooms? Dancing halls?

2. One half of a block is zoned for residences only; the other half facing another street permits garages. The latter street is widened and cuts off so large a portion of the front of the garage that the owner cannot make it pay. He asks to extend the garage from the rear a hundred feet into the half of the block in which garages are forbidden. The residents protest; one resident claiming that the sale of his property at a nice profit would be called off if the garage is permitted to extend. If you were on the board of adjustment, how would you vote?

3. Do you favor private ownership of electric power? City ownership? County ownership? State ownership? National ownership?

4. Congress authorized a survey to determine the feasibility of a subway for the District of Columbia. Would one be feasible in some city you know which does not have a subway?

5. Cities of New York State are allowed to levy a sales tax up to 2 per cent. Should your city have such a tax to raise revenue for schools?

6. Zurich, Switzerland, built houses on the four sides of large city blocks with playgrounds in the centers of the blocks. These houses are rented only to families with children. Do you think the American cities should do this?

7. Practically all of our larger and many of our smaller cities face acute parking problems. Suburban branch stores have been established by many large department stores — in order to reach more customers *and also* because many people refuse to shop in downtown stores because of the severe parking problem. In Los Angeles a number of stores have parking lots in the rear and have placed main customers' entrances there. Drive-in banks, restaurants, laundries, theaters, and even post offices are becoming more and more common every day. Office buildings with inside parking lots and large municipally-owned parking lots are also common. Does your city have a parking problem? If so, what steps are being taken to meet it?

8. Do billboards add or subtract from the value of property? Do they usually advertise anything that the people need to know about?

9. Automobiles have created a new park problem. The city parks are no longer sufficient for city people. From 1933 to 1937 thirty-seven States acquired 350 new parks for autoists, to which city dwellers have access. New York State has at least 62 such parks. One of them, the Adirondack, contains 1,700,000 acres, and the Palisades Interstate Park of 35,000 acres is visited by more than 10,000,000 people annually. Should these parks be supported by the nearest cities, by the State, or by the National Government?

10. What is your city or the city nearest to you doing to relieve traffic congestion? What do you think it should do?

11. The more important causes of traffic accidents follow:

Narrow streets	Excessive speed	Jaywalking
Bad curves	Road hogs	Walking on wrong side
Bad hills	Drinking	Driver-lover
Dirty windshields	Four in front seat	Asleep at the wheel
Glaring headlights	Failing to signal	Daydreamer
Grade crossings	Ignoring stopsigns	Lighting cigarette

Divide these dangers into three groups: those that may be removed (1) by better traffic engineering, (2) by law enforcement, (3) by education.

12. The Port of New York Authority has financed and built a $20,000,000 bus terminal — the most modern, spacious, and comfortable in the world — to accommodate 2500 intercity buses daily (page 66). It extends from 8th to 9th Avenues between 41st and 42nd Streets. This four-level brick and steel structure has interior roadways, a roof parking area for 500 cars, shops, restaurants and other concessions, including a bank and a news-reel theater.

Does your city need parking areas that could be financed by a similar organization: self-liquidating projects without additional taxes? Or could downtown property owners finance them as was done in San Francisco (page 694), and thus make it possible for customers to come to their stores in the center which is becoming too congested and is driving people to the suburbs to shop?

SELECT BIBLIOGRAPHY

BROMAGE, A. *Municipal Government and Administration*. Appleton-Century-Crofts. New York, 1950. Chapters 3–5, 7, 24–30.

BUTTERFIELD, R. "Revolt in Philadelphia." *Saturday Evening Post.* November 8, 15, 22, 1952.

DINNEEN, J. "Safer Highways — the Massachusetts Way." *Collier's.* August 23, 1952.

MARTIN, J. "Death on M–24." *Saturday Evening Post.* April 5, 1952.

McGAVIN, C. "Solving That . . . Parking Problem." *Collier's.* November 1, 1952.

REED, T. H. AND D. "Does Your City Suffer from Suburbanitis?" *Collier's.* October 11, 1952.

DRAKE, W. "The Truth About Traffic Jams." *American Magazine.* February, 1953.

FRANK, S. "The Motorist's Maddest Mile." *Saturday Evening Post.* July 18, 1953.

CHAPTER XXXV

PUBLIC EDUCATION

Education as a Governmental Function. — To be successful, a representative democracy must be based on an enlightened citizenry, and so we have long since realized that the provision of "free" but tax-supported schools is a proper function of government. In a republic, it is essential that educational opportunities be made available to all the people.

The United States Constitution makes no mention of education. It is, therefore, within the scope of the reserved powers of the States. The National Government does aid the States in the field of education through such programs as the land-grant colleges, high school vocational education, and the G.I. Bill. Many private schools also exist, but over ninety per cent of the nation's school pupils attend public schools.

Early Education. — Free public schools were established in several of the New England States as early as the seventeenth century, shortly after their settlement; but even there interest in education declined during the next century.

It is doubtful whether previous to the Revolutionary War as many as one half of all the white persons throughout the thirteen colonies could read and write. Most children depended upon the little instruction that their parents could give them at home, and the boys were given the preference because it was not considered that girls needed much schooling to prepare them for household duties. It was not until the nineteenth century that a systematic effort was made to educate the masses of people throughout the country.

In 1838 Horace Mann, first secretary of the Massachusetts State Board of Education, aroused great interest in public school education throughout the North. In the South there were no successful efforts to establish systems of public free schools until after the Civil War. As late as 1880, 17 per cent of the individuals over ten years of age in the United States were illiterate — that is, could not write. By 1930 the number had been reduced to 4.3%; but the 1940 Census showed that 13.5% of those over 25 years old (10,104,000 adults) could not read a newspaper.

Compulsory Education. — Most States compel youth up to sixteen years of age to attend school unless excused for physical, mental, or a

Courtesy The American Seating Company

EDUCATION TODAY

Healthful surroundings and modern equipment typify today's classrooms. So, too, do modern courses of study seek to insure healthy minds in healthy bodies.

few other reasons.[1] A few States require the complete high school course if a high school is maintained by the local school district. In other States some cities have compulsory high school education.

Growth of Secondary Education. — Public high schools began to spring up about 1850 in most of the large Northern cities, and gradually spread to the Southern cities following the Civil War. By 1900 most towns had high schools; and today there are over 6,000,000 students in public high schools and nearly 500,000 in our private and parochial high schools. Also there has been a rapid consolidation movement which has brought real high schools to a great many rural communities.

Transportation. — Millions of pupils are now being transported to public schools. Without transportation most rural high schools would not be practicable. The free transportation of students insures more

---

[1] In many States the compulsory attendance law is not strictly enforced.

QUEEN OF A RECENT ROSE FESTIVAL AND HER RETINUE, PORTLAND, OREGON

Each high school elects a Princess and each Princess addresses a large audience in the City Auditorium. Then a committee of distinguished persons selects as Queen the one who ranks highest in beauty, personality, scholarship, and character.

regular attendance, reduces tardiness, protects children from wet and cold weather, and moreover, a well-supervised school bus provides a wholesome moral atmosphere.

THE EIGHT BRANCHES OF THE UNIVERSITY OF CALIFORNIA

The University, consisting of seven "Campuses" and Lick Observatory, has about 40,000 students.

Junior High Schools. — About 5000 junior high schools are organized. They usually embrace grades 7, 8, and 9. These schools are organized into departments, and this arrangement gives the pupils the advantage of teachers specially trained for the courses they offer. The junior high school tends to hold pupils in school for a year longer, and to give them some insight into social and civic activities.

Nearly all of our larger cities and many smaller communities have special vocational schools offering training in electrical installation, plumbing, carpentry, sewing, cooking, stenography, and a host of other trades and callings. In the regular high schools preparation for college is still a primary purpose, but also more and more emphasis is on courses designed to fit students to become breadwinners. Despite this evergrowing provision for "practical" courses, good schools continue to recognize the importance of training in the fine arts and other so-called cultural subjects.

Growth of Higher Education. — Nine colleges which continue to exist[1] were established under church influence before the Revolutionary War and were assisted by the colonial treasuries. Since the Revolutionary War schools of higher education have increased to about 1750 colleges, junior colleges, universities, and technical schools. More than 600 of these are supported by States and municipalities.

[1] Harvard (1636), William and Mary (1693), Yale (1701), Princeton (1746), Kings, now Columbia (1754), University of Pennsylvania (1759, reorganized 1779), Brown (1764), Rutgers (1766), and Dartmouth (1769).

"... And As You Leave These Tranquil, Ivied Walls to Face the Stern Realities of Life ..."

The State University of New York is not one institution, but a unified system consisting of several smaller State-supported schools. Pennsylvania has arrangements with three private universities (Temple, Pennsylvania, and Pittsburgh) under which they operate in some respects as State Universities. New Jersey maintains a similar arrangement with Rutgers.

Land Grant Colleges are maintained in every State. These State Colleges receive Federal aid under the Morrill Act of 1862 and subsequent legislation. The States have been granted some 11,000,000 acres of land for the support of these schools which specialize in mechanical and agricultural education.

Higher Educational Aid to Veterans. — From the discovery of America until World War I, less than 1,000,000 students had graduated from all of our colleges. Today more than 2,000,000 are enrolled in institutions of higher education.

In the last few years hundreds of thousands of World War II veterans were helped through college by the G.I. Bill and now Korean veterans are being similarly aided by the Government.

Junior Colleges are gradually increasing. There are about 450, including about 45 in California. They offer locally the first two college years of liberal arts, pre-professional, or completion work, and enable many students to extend their education two years because they can remain at home, being supported by city, State, or private endowment.

Adult Education is becoming more widespread in the United States. Classes in vocational and cultural subjects are being offered for adults by both public and private schools and colleges. Some of these classes are taught in the school buildings at night while others are offered by correspondence. The extension divisions of many State Universities are especially active in adult education, offering courses in a great many subjects in communities across the State. The people who take these courses do so for a variety of reasons — many to gain a high school or college diploma, some to learn a particular skill, and others merely to improve themselves.

Administration of Public Schools. — Each State has its own system of public schools. Certain central control is reserved by the State governments, but the regulation of school affairs is left chiefly to the local governments — districts, townships, counties, and cities.

The District System, which originated in New England, places each school under the control of the patrons residing in the district from which the school is attended. This system is considered inefficient and is being replaced by a much larger unit, such as the township.

The Township System places all the schools within its limits under one authority, usually a small board chosen by the voters. This system makes possible the establishment of consolidated schools.

Courtesy Jackson, Mississippi, Chamber of Commerce

BAILEY JUNIOR HIGH SCHOOL, JACKSON, MISSISSIPPI

Modern buildings are an important part of modern school systems. Jackson may well be proud of this fine school.

The County System originated in the South, but has spread northward and westward. In all States except New York and the New England States an elective or appointive county superintendent supervises schools outside of independent cities, but he is more or less subordinate to an elective or appointive county school board.

The City System exists independent of the township or county in nearly all large cities and most small ones. Usually there is a small school board elected from the city at large, but in some cities the board is appointed by the mayor, the city council, or the courts. For the administration of the schools the board selects a city superintendent.

The Trend toward Larger Units. — In the past several years, most States have considered and many have passed school district reorganization laws. The result has been a sharp decrease in the number of local units and a gradual shift to fewer and larger districts. The total number of school districts in the United States has decreased from 108,579 in 1942 to about 70,000 today.

State Supervision. — Each State has a superintendent of education,[1] and about three fourths of them have State Boards of Education. In about thirty States the superintendents are elected, but the boards are selected by various methods.[2] The superintendent, or the board working through a superintendent, supervises the State system in accordance with the general school laws of the State.

Courtesy Detroit Public Schools

TRAINING FOR SUCCESS

"Nothing succeeds like success," and success is more likely when young people receive basic training in the practical skills for which they are naturally fitted. This young man is getting first-hand practice in wiring a motor at a technical high school in one of our largest cities.

Thus far only one State, Delaware, has reorganized its school system to provide a single, centralized Statewide unit. There the powers that are usually vested in local units in other States are found in the State Board of Education. The local school districts exist only for administrative purposes and school finance is a State function. (Wilmington and a few other larger communities do retain local school boards subject to general State supervision.)

In most States the current trend is in the direction of more and more State control and supervision. This can be seen especially in such

---

[1] He is commonly called Superintendent of Public Instruction or Commissioner of Education.

[2] In a number of States the State board is ex officio — the governor, secretary of state, treasurer, attorney general, and superintendent of public instruction usually being members. Since most school boards have technical functions these boards are not very logical. The members are too busy in their own special fields.

matters as the setting of minimum standards for teachers, salary scales, and standards for school building construction.

School Revenue spent on public grade schools, high schools, and colleges is only about $4,000,000,000 yearly — less than for tobacco, and only half as much as for alcoholic drinks. It is derived principally from local taxes, to a less, but increasing, extent from State taxes, and to a very small extent from the income of permanent school funds and school lands. In some States the local school taxes are levied by the county or city school board, while in others they are levied by the county commissioners or the city council. In about half of the large cities the school board submits to the city council for approval or disapproval an estimate of school needs. In the other half, the school board either has full power to fix the annual school rate or to decide the amount of money needed and to require the council to levy the taxes necessary to produce that amount, subject to State restrictions.

Proposed Federal Aid to Education. — The educational opportunities found in some areas of the country are far superior to those found in others. This variation in quality occurs both within each and among the several States. In large part, it is caused by the uneven geographic distribution of wealth (tax sources). A recent study by the Council of State Governments shows that income per school pupil in some States is as much as four to five times as high as it is in some other states.

This general picture has led various groups, such as the National Education Association, to recommend Federal aid to education in the States. The proponents contend that, through such aid, children in the poorer areas will be given educational opportunities similar to those found in the more well-to-do areas. Those who oppose the plan fear it may result in Federal control of education.

Apportionment of School Funds. — After school taxes have been collected by the State or county the money must be distributed among the townships or other school districts to supplement their local taxes in the support of their schools. There are various bases for the distribution of these funds,[1] and most States attach certain conditions to

---

[1] These various bases are: (1) Taxes-Where-Paid Basis, (2) Total Population Basis, (3) School Population Basis, (4) Average Daily Attendance Basis, (5) Aggregate Days Attendance Basis, (6) Teachers Employed Basis, (7) Combined Basis of Apportionment, and (8) Discretion of Board.

a grant to a local school system. In Massachusetts, for example, the amount granted is geared to the quality of the system's teaching staff. Unfortunately, the wealthier systems, which least need the money, are best able to meet the State's requirements.

J. C. Allen & Son

PRIZE-WINNERS

Stock raising is a primary interest in 4-H Clubs. This girl from Indiana, like many other 4-H Club girls throughout the nation, proves that the interest is not limited exclusively to boys.

Two Critical School Problems. — There are now more than 34,000,000 students enrolled in the nation's public and private schools and colleges — over one fifth of our entire national population. Approximately 26,000,000 are enrolled in the elementary schools and over 6,000,000 are in the secondary schools. Hence, among the many problems facing the schools today none are more critical than (1) the need for additional and more adequate school buildings and (2) the need for more teachers.

According to the United States Office of Education, sixty-one per cent of the nation's classrooms are overcrowded and one out of every five pupils attends school in a building that does not meet even minimum fire safety requirements. The need for more and better school buildings is accompanied by the need for more teachers. There are now some 1,000,000 public school teachers in the United States. Yet, for the 1953–1954 school year, the nation's elementary schools alone opened their doors more than 50,000 teachers short of the *minimum* felt necessary for adequate instruction and supervision.

The need for new teachers is created only in part by the rising school population. The attraction of better salaries and working conditions in other fields has lured many away from the teaching profession.

Suggestions from New York Times National School Survey. —

1. Expenditure of 5% of national income for education instead of the 2% now expended.

2. Minimum salary of $2400 for all public school instructors.

3. Systematic advancement, tenure, and adequate retirement pay.

4. Minimum of 5 years of college required of all new elementary and high school teachers.

5. Federal aid to education, divorced from Federal control.

6. Smaller classes and less extra-curricular or clerical duties.

7. More teacher participation in planning school program.

Courtesy "Washington Star"

A NATIONAL PROBLEM

Schools from Maine to the Gulf and across the country are overcrowded.

8. Teachers should be selected for moral character as well as for scholarship and personality; they should be respected as leaders in the community; but there should be less petty meddling by the community in the way teachers live their own lives.

9. Adequate up-to-date textbooks, periodicals, libraries, and laboratories in comfortable, sanitary buildings.

10. The public should show greater interest in the nation's schools, and appreciate their importance in a democracy.

RELIGION AND EDUCATION

Separation of Church and State. — As we have seen, the First Amendment to the Constitution of the United States provides: "Congress shall make no law respecting an establishment of religion, or prohibiting the free exercise thereof." And this provision is ex-

VISUAL EDUCATION

Moving pictures and lantern slides are essential for teaching the natural sciences and vocational subjects to large classes. Here a tiny insect can be seen by a hundred students at the same time because of the magnification on the screen.

tended to the States through the Fourteenth Amendment and the various State constitutions.

The prohibition of laws respecting "an establishment of religion" thus creates what is commonly called a "wall of separation between church and state" in the United States. But this wall of separation does not, as the Supreme Court has said, make religion and the state opposed or indifferent to each other. It means, rather, that neither the States nor the National Government may establish or actively promote any church.

The close relationship between education and religion, both of which are directed toward the betterment of man, can be illustrated with a brief reference to Thomas Jefferson and Horace Mann. Jefferson was especially responsible for the First Amendment and he had previously been the author of the Statute for Religious Freedom in Virginia by which the Church of England was disestablished, thus

Three Lions

TOMORROW'S LEADERS

Our nation's future is bright with promise because throughout our land there are thousands of young people working towards a better world for people everywhere. Their assurance of success springs from the freedom of action and thought which education in a democracy alone makes possible.

separating church and state. However, Jefferson was not disinterested in religion and he once compiled the sayings of Jesus from the Bible. He thought that they should be taught in every school in the land. This collection was later published as a Congressional document popularly known as *Jefferson's Bible*.

Horace Mann, father of the American public school system, also favored the separation of church and state. But, like Jefferson, he too appreciated the value of religion. In judging the value of school systems he wrote: "Do they cultivate the highest faculties in the nature of childhood — its conscience, its benevolence, a reverence for what is true and sacred? Or are they only developing upon a grander scale the lower instincts and selfish tendencies of the race."

The problem of church-state separation and education are made doubly complex by the existence of numerous parochial schools, that is, schools maintained by various church organizations.

The Supreme Court, Religion, and the Schools. — The direct application of the separation of church and state to the field of education did not come before the Court until quite recently, 1947. A few prior cases had bearing on the problem, but not directly.

In 1925 the Court declared unconstitutional an Oregon law which compelled all children between the ages 8 and 16 to attend *public* schools, thus forestalling attendance at private and parochial schools. This, said the Court, was a deprivation of property without due process of law and thus in violation of the Fourteenth Amendment.

In 1930 a Louisiana law authorizing the use of public funds to supply "school books to the school children of the State," including not only public school children but private and parochial school children, too, was upheld. The Court said that "the school children and the State alone are the beneficiaries," and not the schools they attend.

A 1934 case involved two students who had been suspended by the University of California because of their refusal to take part in the compulsory R.O.T.C. program. They had refused on religious grounds. They claimed that the suspension deprived them of their "liberty" as guaranteed in the Fourteenth Amendment. The Court was not sympathetic to their argument. It held that while their liberty "undoubtedly" included the right to object to military training on religious grounds, "California has not drafted or called them to attend the University."

In 1947 the Court faced the first clear-cut case involving education and "an establishment of religion" — the issue: State aid for a church-supported school. A New Jersey law providing public (tax-provided) school bus transportation for parochial school students was challenged as "an establishment of religion." In a 5–4 decision the Court held that the New Jersey law was not an aid to religion. Rather, the law was held to be a safety measure much like the posting of a policeman at school crosswalks.

The so-called "released time" programs have been the subject of the latest important church-state-school cases. This program involves the release of students on school time to attend classes in religious instruction. The classes are taught by private teachers employed by religious groups — not by the State, of course. The student may attend these religious classes or remain in school, as he chooses.

In the first released-time case, in 1948, the Court held invalid the Illinois released-time statute. It was, said the Court, "an establishment of religion" because the public school classrooms were used for the purpose of religious instruction.

But in a 1952 case, a New York released-time law was upheld on grounds that the instruction was held off school grounds and, hence, no school (tax-provided) properties were used for the purpose.

Moral Training Is Essential to Good Character Building. — The little red schoolhouse lacked about every material and academic tool. But it had one thing for which neither money nor degrees can compensate — moral purpose.

Because the Supreme Court has outlawed the conduct of formal religious instruction in public school buildings and because courses in ethics are now seldom given, it becomes doubly important that high moral character be brought to the student through the teaching of such courses as literature and the social studies.

QUESTIONS ON THE TEXT

1. More than a hundred years ago, who aroused great interest in public school education in the North?

2. When were systems of public free schools established in the South?

3. Most States require youth to attend school until what age?

4. What are the arguments in favor of free transportation of pupils in rural areas?

5. What is the main argument for junior colleges?

6. Explain the four common types of public school administration in the United States.

7. How much is spent on our schools annually? How does this compare with the amount spent on tobacco and on alcoholic drinks?

8. Does most revenue for schools come from local, State, or Federal taxes? Are States contributing more or less than formerly?

9. By what different bodies are school taxes levied?

10. Advance arguments in favor of the Federal Government's contributing to the States for education. Give arguments against.

11. On what different bases are school funds distributed by States or counties to the schools?

12. How many pupils are enrolled in the elementary schools in the United States? In the secondary schools?

13. Why are the problems of overcrowded classrooms and school buildings and the shortage of teachers so closely related?

14. Why do we have a teacher shortage? What solutions can you see? Explain how your solution would help meet the problem?

15. What does the New York Times National Survey suggest as to:
    (1) The amount of national income that should be spent on education?
    (2) The minimum annual salary that should be paid public school teachers?
    (3) College preparation for new teachers?
    (4) Federal aid with Federal control or State control?
    (5) Size of classes?
    (6) What should the general public do?

16. What is meant by separation of church and state in the United States?

17. Why are education and religion so closely related?

18. May States require children to attend only public schools? Why?

19. May States provide textbooks for private and parochial as well as public school students? Why?

20. May a State provide school bus transportation for parochial school students? Why?

21. What is a "released time" program? Is it constitutional?

PROBLEMS FOR DISCUSSION

1. What provisions does the constitution of your State make regarding education?

2. Is the compulsory education law enforced in your community? If not, by what means do you think it could be enforced?

3. During the depression, half a billion dollars were given or lent the States to assist public education. An annual appropriation is now urged. If granted would you favor distributing it on the basis of population, or conditionally? What conditions?

4. The Policies Commission of the American Association of School Administrators has recommended the operation of elementary schools on a year-round basis. Schools would be open six days a week with attendance on Saturdays for extra-classroom activities being optional. Proportionately better pay and a month off for vacations would be provided for teachers. Each school would operate a camp to supplement classroom work, and pupils would be promoted at any time that their teacher found them qualified. By operating the schools three additional months each year the youth would get through sooner and thus make the buildings available for the now-increasing grade-school population. Why do you favor or oppose this recommendation?

5. With more people living to old age, is more adult education necessary to keep alive the spirit of progress?

6. Henry Adams wrote: "They know enough who know how to learn." The poet Milton: "As good almost kill a man as kill a good book: who kills a man kills a reasonable creature, God's image; but he who destroys a good book kills reason itself." About 300 B.C., Ptolemy I, King of Egypt, wanted to study geometry without first mastering the thirteen parts of Euclid's *Elements*. He asked for a short cut, but Euclid replied, "There is no royal road to geometry." (Often misquoted: "There is no royal road to learning.") Discuss each of these in turn.

7. Prepare a constitution for the government of your school, or discuss the one already in force.

8. In many high schools it is customary for either the class in government or the graduating class to go to Washington to see Congress in session and visit the various departments, the Library of Congress, Mount Vernon, and other places of interest. The cost is usually defrayed by a school entertainment. Could the graduates of the several high schools in your county arrange to take this trip together? If they already do so, discuss the arrangements.

9. "There is a vociferous enthusiasm for what is called progressive education, than which, in its extreme forms, nothing could be more reactionary or damaging to youth. By progressive education appears to be meant the turning loose of youth in the world in which they live, to express themselves, as the saying is, and to form such habits and tastes as they from time to time choose or which appear to be natural with them. . . . To call any such process education contradicts all human experience." — *Nicholas Murray Butler*. What do you think?

10. In 1953 about 4 billion dollars were spent on public education, but 8 billions were spent on alcoholic liquors. Is this a reasonable measure of our relative interest in education and luxuries?

11. "At a public meeting called to discuss school taxes the following argument is advanced in an effort to reduce school taxes: (a) The State and local governments are overburdened with school charges, — 'schooling' is a matter for those who can afford it, — let every one take as much as he can pay for in private institutions; (b) there are too many 'fads' in education. Let every one be given the good old-fashioned 'three R's' without the many additional 'trimmings' that have been loaded on to our school system, — if the old system were maintained, school expenses would be materially reduced. What would be your attitude toward each of these arguments and how would you express it?" — *The New American Government and Its Work*, by James T. Young.

12. Some years ago, a Dean of a College of Business Administration found the average maximum income of the untrained man to be $1200, of the high school graduate $2200, and of the college graduate $6000. The total individual earnings in each group up to the age of sixty were $45,000, $78,000, and $150,000 respectively. The untrained man at the age of fifty begins to drop towards dependence, while the college man reaches his maximum capacity at sixty. What is the value of a college education? Are the present higher incomes temporary or permanent?

SELECT BIBLIOGRAPHY

DABNEY, V. "Southern Crisis: The Segregation Decision." *Saturday Evening Post*. November 8, 1952.

"Law and the Schools." *Newsweek*. April 11, 1952.

Livingstone, R. "Essentials of Education." *Atlantic Monthly*. January, 1952.

Pope, L. "Religion and Our Schools." *American Magazine*. May, 1952.

"School Jamming: Worst Ever." *U. S. News*. September 12, 1952.

Pringle, H. F. and K. "Mississippi Gives her Colored Kids a Break." *Saturday Evening Post*. November 22, 1952.

Teaching As a Career. Government Printing Office, Washington 25, D. C. 15¢.

U. S. Schools. Life, Special Edition. October 16, 1950.

GRAVES, W. *American State Government*. Heath. Boston. 1953 Ed. Chs. 12 and 23.

JAMESON, R. "So You Want to Go to College." *Saturday Evening Post*. October 17, 1953.

WORDEN, W. "Nothing's Too Good for Their School." *Saturday Evening Post*. September 5, 1953.

Text of Senate Internal Security Subcommittee Report: How Communists Try to Influence American Teachers. *U. S. News*. July 31, 1953.

CHAPTER XXXVI

MAKING DEMOCRACY WORK

Too often we Americans take the existence of our democratic system of government for granted. Too often we forget that others before us established our democracy — a democracy in a republic. We have inherited from them a working system. Our job is to *keep* that system working. And in order to keep it working we must understand it.

Democracy Defined. — As we read on page 33, a democratic government is one in which the people rule.[1] It is that form of government in which the sovereign power is in the hands of all of the people and is exercised by them either directly, or through elected representatives who are responsible to the people.

A democracy is, in Abraham Lincoln's words, a "government of the people, by the people, for the people." But notice that it is the second of the three phrases that distinguishes a democracy from other forms of government. All governments are *of* the people. Even dictatorships are sometimes *for* the people. But a democracy is not only a government of and for the people, it is also a government *by the people.*

In a democracy any and all authority for governmental action *must* come from the people. Thus a democratic government may exercise only those powers which the people permit it to exercise.

The Fundamental Equality of All Men. — Democracy is based upon the belief that "all men are created equal." This does not mean that all men are physically or mentally equal. Nor does it mean that all men shall share equally in the material things of life. It does mean that all men possess the same rights to "life, liberty, and the pursuit of happiness" without regard to race, color, religion, or economic or social status. It means that no man is privileged over another before the law. It means that each man is free to develop himself to the fullest extent of his abilities.

The Peoples' Capacity for Self-Government. — Democracy is based upon the belief that the people as a whole can govern more wisely than

---

[1] The word "democratic" comes from the Greek *demos*, the people, and *kratos*, authority — authority in the people. See pages 30-33.

can one or a few. When the government is popularly controlled the rights and interests of individuals are more jealously guarded than they are under a dictatorship. Benevolent despots, who claim to know what is best for the people, do not feel acts of misgovernment as immediately as do the people. When governmental power is held by all of the people no few can benefit at the expense of the many. This is what Lincoln had in mind when he said: "You can fool all of the people some of the time and some of the people all of the time, but you can't fool all of the people all of the time."

Good Sportsmanship Essential to the Success of Democracy. — If a democracy is to be a success, its citizens must have a sense of good sportsmanship. This means that they should be good losers and generous winners.

Adlai Stevenson demonstrated fine sportsmanship in conceding his defeat by Dwight Eisenhower in the 1952 presidential election. The following words are from his concession speech:

"The people have rendered their verdict and I gladly accept it. It is traditionally American to fight hard before an election. It is equally traditional to close ranks as soon as the people have spoken. That which unites us as Americans is far greater than that which divides us as political parties. We vote as many but we pray as one. With a united people, with faith in democracy, with common concern for others less fortunate around the globe, we shall move forward with God's guidance toward the time when his children shall grow in freedom and dignity in a world at peace."

The Fruits of a Democracy Ripen Slowly, but Their Roots Grow Deep. — True, our democratic government with its checks and balances cannot act as promptly as twenty-four-hour dictatorships, but it has compensating advantages. The fruits of a democracy ripen slowly and are not spectacular, but their roots grow deep and promote contentment and permanency. A dictatorship goes up like a rocket, but comes down like the stick.

Democracy is a Challenge. — Our forefathers have given us our democracy — a system of government under which we may govern ourselves through representatives of our own choosing. It is a system which depends upon us — upon us, the people — for its very life. Because it is government by the people, government by us, it can be no better than we, the people, are willing to make it.

Democracy then is a challenge. It is a challenge to *all* of us, not just to "the other fellow," and not just to all of us *some* of the time. If we are to maintain and enjoy and develop our democratic system we must meet this challenge. We must work to make democracy work, to make democracy live.

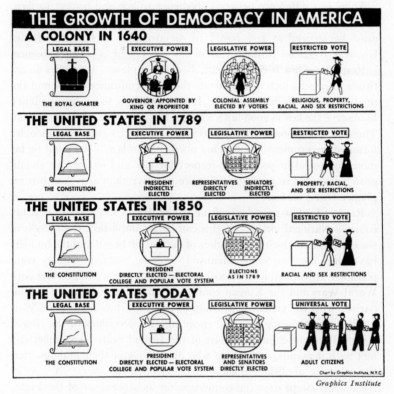

Graphics Institute

Certainly we may agree with James Bryce that "No government demands so much from the citizens as Democracy and none gives back so much."

Citizenship in a Democracy. — Our citizenship in a democracy carries with it many privileges. It guarantees to us liberty to live our lives without burdensome, arbitrary restrictions. We may speak our thoughts freely, worship as we please, and hold our property free from fear of confiscation or invasion.

The liberty we enjoy, however, is a liberty under law. Like any form of government, democracy is dependent upon law and law enforcement for its life. We all pride ourselves on the part we have in the making of the laws under which we live. Are we as ready to accept our responsibility for law enforcement?

There is a difference between obedience to law and respect for law. No government can endure unless there is obedience to law. This must be secured at any cost. In dictatorships such as the Soviet Union it is gained through fear of the consequences of disobedience.

Respect for law is deeper than obedience to law. It implies an attitude of mind which comprehends the full significance of law and the relation of each individual to it. It acknowledges, too, a responsibility to observe the law in good faith whether it is approved or not approved. There is a question whether democracy can be as successful as older forms of government in enforcing obedience to law. It should be far more successful in promoting respect for law and out of this should grow an obedience to law much more effective than any slavish compliance based on fear.

Respect for law must be built up in the American people until it becomes a National virtue. If this can be accomplished, the success of the experiment which the founders of our nation began and the builders have thus far "so nobly advanced" will be assured. Ready compliance with the requirements of the Selective Service Act during both World Wars and the Korean conflict is indicative of progress in comparison with the violent opposition to the draft during the Civil War.

There are some signs not so encouraging. Decisions of the courts, especially of the Supreme Court of the United States, are sometimes met with demands, from those who disapprove of their findings, that the courts be abolished or shorn of many of their powers. A wave of lawlessness swept over the country as far as observance of the Eighteenth Amendment to the Constitution was concerned. No matter what the differences of opinion on prohibition are, the fact remains that the prohibition amendment was written into the Constitution in the regular way by a two-thirds majority vote in Congress and ratification by three fourths of the States. It was law and as long as it was law the duty of an American citizen was to obey it. In a democracy, we have freedom of choice in the making of laws, not in the observance of laws after they are made.

Personal Liberty. — Our whole concept of democracy rests squarely on a recognition of the dignity and worth of the individual. We believe that "*all* men are created equal." No one man or group of men stands above the rest.

If *all* men are equal and all enjoy the same rights, it is obvious that each man cannot enjoy *absolute* or *complete* freedom. In his actions, each man must take account of the rights of all other men. Each man may do as he pleases only so long as he does not infringe upon the rights of others to do as they please. If each man could do absolutely as he pleased, first chaotic anarchy and, finally, rule by the strong would result. In other words, each man's liberty is relative to the liberty of the whole.

Liberty can be absolute only in a state of complete anarchy. On the other hand, the *control* of liberty can be absolute only in a totalitarian state where all individual liberty has been done away with.

Drawing the line between what an individual may or may not do is an extremely difficult task. Yet, the problem lies at the very core of the meaning of liberty in a democracy. Man desires both authority and freedom. The authority of a government must be adequate to the needs of society, but it must not be such as to restrain the individual beyond the minimum necessary to the general welfare of all.

The true meaning of liberty in a democracy is found in the old saying: "Personal liberty ends where public injury begins."

Law and Order. — A recent President of the United States made the following clear statement as to the importance of law enforcement and law observance:

"Laws, of course, represent restrictions upon *individual* liberty, and in these very restrictions make liberty more secure. For the common good, the individual surrenders something of his privilege to do as he pleases, and so organized society is possible. It is successful just about in proportion as laws are wise, as they represent deliberate and intelligent public opinion, and as they are obeyed. Civilization had to travel a long way before it came to be commonly accepted that even an unwise law ought to be enforced in orderly fashion, because such enforcement would insure its repeal or modification, also in orderly fashion, if that were found desirable.

"I do not see how any citizen who cherishes the protection of law in organized society may feel himself secure when he himself is the example of contempt for law. Clearly there is call for awakened conscience and awakened realization of true self-interest on the part of the few who will themselves suffer most when reverence for law is forgotten and passion is expressed in destructive lawlessness. Ours must be a law-abiding republic, and reverence and obedience must spring from the influential and the leaders among men, as well as obedience from the humbler citizen, else the temple will collapse."

Crime a Major Problem. — Democracy is clearly dependent in part on the extent to which its citizens obey the law of the land. Yet crime is on the increase in the United States. J. Edgar Hoover, chief of the "G-men," estimates the cost of crime in the United States at about $20,000,000,000 a year. Our tax bill because of crime amounts to more than $130 a year for every man, woman, and child in the country. We have some 12,000 murders annually, and 600,000 persons are sent to jail each year.

In one recent year, the Federal Bureau of Investigation reported 1,686,670 major crimes committed in the United States. This means that an average of 4621 major crimes were committed each day during that year. On an average day, 247 persons were killed or assaulted, 150 persons were robbed, 467 cars were stolen, 1034 places were burglarized, and 2679 thefts were committed. Or, to put it another way, the F.B.I. says that a major crime was committed every 18.7 seconds during the year. Over 2,000,000 major crimes were committed in the year 1952 alone, an increase of more than 8 per cent over 1951.

The crime tide has been swelling in the United States since the beginning of this century. And the most discouraging feature is the fact that an increasing per cent of crimes are committed by the young — in many cases mere children.

F.B.I. Director Hoover recently said: "The nation is facing a potential army of 6,000,000 criminals and an ever-increasing wave of lawlessness which is feeding the criminal ranks with a never ending supply of recruits. Our homes and our lives are daily threatened by this vast army. Law enforcement today is facing one of its most gigantic tasks. The army of criminals is ten times greater in number than the students in our colleges and universities. And for every school teacher in America, there are more than seven criminals."

Juvenile Crime has increased at an alarming rate in recent years. In one recent year alone 115,940 persons below the age of 21 were arrested:

Age	Number Arrested
15 and younger	7,223
16	9,311
17	15,216
18	25,926
19	28,912
20	29,352
	115,940

To list the major causes of crime is a relatively simple matter. They include: poverty; broken homes; physical and mental defects; such unhealthy influences as obscene and sordid pulp magazines; the desire for "adventure"; the illegal and indiscriminate sale of narcotics, liquor, and firearms; antiquated laws and lax enforcement; corruption in public office; and all too often the lack of adequate religious, educational, or parental training.

But recognizing these causes is only the first step toward their elimination.

In his inaugural address President Hoover said, "Our whole system of self-government will crumble either if officials elect what laws they will enforce or citizens elect what laws they will support."

In a speech to representatives of the press President Hoover pointed out that the press plays a dominant part in creating the attitude of the individual to the law. "It is almost final in its potency to arouse the interest and consciousness of our people. It can destroy their finer sensibilities or it can invigorate them. If instead of the glamour of romance and heroism which our American imaginative minds too frequently throw around those who break the law, we would invest with a little romance and heroism those thousands of our officers who are endeavoring to enforce the law, it would itself decrease crime. Praise and respect for those who properly enforce the laws would help."

Speaking to a Law Enforcement Officers' Conference, President Truman called for local, State, and Federal co-operation in the war against crime, and added: "Above all, we must recognize that human misery breeds most of our crime. We must wipe out our slums, improve the health of our citizens, and eliminate the inequalities of opportunities which embitter men and women, and then turn them toward lawlessness.   In the long run these programs represent the greatest of all anti-crime measures."

Organized Crime. — The investigations of the special Senate Crime (Kefauver) Committee brought into sharp public focus the widespread

JOHN EDGAR HOOVER

This famous lawyer and criminologist has constantly urged the importance of crime prevention through social betterment even as he waged unceasing warfare against organized crime. He has made the Federal Bureau of Investigation one of the most efficient law-enforcement agencies in the world.

existence of organized crime in the United States. The gambling syndicates, organized traffic in narcotics, prostitution, tax evasion, and other organized criminal activities exposed by the Committee could not exist without public indifference and official laxity or complicity.

Many States have now created so-called "Little Kefauver Committees" and reform movements have accomplished much in several cities. The vermin of crime abhor the light of public scrutiny.

But much remains to be done. J. Edgar Hoover has said that organized crime could be eliminated in the United States within forty-eight hours by vigorous law enforcement at the local level. Through perjury, tax-evasion, and deportation proceedings the Federal Government is acting against many criminals clever enough to escape State action for other illegal activities.

In its report to the Senate, the Kefauver Committee made several recommendations for combating crime. It proposed giving the Securities and Exchange Commission more authority to expose the infiltration of legitimate business by criminal elements, and the placing of all wire services transmitting racing and other gambling information under the supervision of the Federal Communications Commission.

The Committee favored requiring all who admittedly profit from locally-outlawed activities (such as gambling) to file complete financial statements along with their tax returns each year. This would enable the Internal Revenue Bureau to collect millions in taxes that now go unpaid.

The Committee also favored the creation of a permanent Federal Crime Commission. This body would carry on a continuing in-

Hungerford in "The Pittsburgh Post-Gazette"

DEMOCRACY'S GREATEST CHALLENGE

Substandard conditions of living are inexcusable in a land of opportunity like ours. The national situation may not be as sorry as the cartoon suggests, but it is bad enough. The remedy speaks for itself.

vestigation of organized criminal activities. It would report directly to Congress and provide information to all National, State, and local law enforcement agencies.

But, again, as Senator Estes Kefauver emphasized, this "filth on America's doorstep" can be effectively eliminated only with the active backing of citizens at the local level across the nation.

An Informed Citizenry Essential. — Democracy in the United States involves more than government by the people through elected representatives. In a very real sense, our democracy is government by public opinion. Indeed, the major task of our elected representatives is the translation of the popular will into public policy.

It is obvious that government by public opinion, democracy, works best when the opinions held by the public are *informed* opinions. And, clearly, it is the duty of each and every citizen to keep himself informed on public affairs.

Keeping informed may not always be an easy task, but it is an essential one. Corrupt political machines and selfish interests breed on public apathy. Democracy flourishes on citizen interest and enlightenment.

In keeping informed, it is important to distinguish propaganda from fact and partisan argument from objective analysis, even though the propaganda or the partisan argument may happen to support one's own point of view.

Unfortunate though it may seem, there is seldom any clear-cut yes-or-no, black-or-white, right-or-wrong solution to public questions. Usually there are good features to every side of an argument. The proper solution to most public problems lies somewhere in between the extremes of argument. And this fact makes it necessary for the conscientious citizen to examine all sides of an issue.

There are a great many sources of information available. Newspapers, magazines, books, and radio and television commentaries are ready at hand. (Naturally, they should be used with care to insure the closest possible approach to unbiased fact.) And there are many non-partisan groups formed exclusively to provide citizens with objective information on public affairs. Among these groups are outstanding organizations like the National League of Women Voters and the National Municipal League. Several local groups around the country, for example, the Seattle Municipal League, the City Club of Chicago, the Citizens League of Cleveland, and the Citizens Union of New York City are worthy of mention, too.

We can surely agree with the late H. G. Wells: "Before he can vote, he must hear the evidence. Before he can decide he must know. . . . Votes in themselves are useless things."

Active Participation in Public Affairs. — Citizenship in a democracy carries with it certain definite and important obligations. Some of these duties are obvious — paying taxes and serving in the Nation's defense, for example. Other obligations are not nearly so obvious.

But they are, in the long run, just as important for they go to the very heart of the democratic process. We have just noted one of these less obvious duties — that of keeping informed on public affairs.

Another of these obligations is *active participation* in public affairs. It does little or no good for a person to keep himself informed only to do

Three Lions

TRAINING FOR CITIZENSHIP

Schools and clubs have always been important factors in training young people for the responsibilities of adult citizenship. These boys are learning at first hand through club activities how voting is carried on in real elections.

nothing with his information. He might better have spent his time and effort at something else. All too many people are inclined to be scornful of politics and politicians. But there is a positive, constructive point of view to be taken here. Politics, like water, can rise no higher than its source, and in the United States that source is the people.

Certainly there have been and there are corrupt political machines in some places in the United States. But there never has been a corrupt machine that could succeed in the face of an informed *and an active* citizenry.

How can a citizen participate? In a variety of ways. He can make his influence felt by intelligent voting. He can join and work with groups working for better government. He can participate in public meetings and forum discussions. He can write to his elected representatives and other public servants and call on them in person. He can work with the political party of his choice. He can run for and serve in public office. And each of these suggestions in turn suggests other ways in which the average citizen can make his influence felt — that is, make democracy work. Multiply the one citizen by the many and you have an extremely potent force for good in American politics.

Philadelphia's "Gripe Office." — Under its new city charter, Philadelphia is conducting a unique experiment. One department in the city government, the Mayor's Office for Information and Complaints, has been established solely for the purpose of answering questions and handling complaints from the city's 2,000,000 residents.

This office is no politician's trick to influence the voter. It handles some 700 problems a day. When it first began operating, it was widely publicized in the city newspapers and some 400,000 taxpayers received "invitations-to-complain" along with their monthly sewer and water bills.

Questions and complaints are phoned in, mailed in, or brought in in person. All sorts and kinds of problems have been handled promptly. Their variety is interesting and astonishing, covering such items as a complaint that a traffic light was obscured by the branches of a tree; a request for a bit of soil from Independence Square for a soil map of the United States; a complaint that trucks were driving on and breaking sidewalks along a narrow street; a request for advice on where to go with a marital problem; complaints about firetraps, dirty alleys and broken fences, gambling, street brawls, and irregular trash collections. Thus Philadelphia is bringing City Hall closer to the people — and giving them a real, down-to-earth opportunity to participate in public affairs.

The Over-Burdened Voter. — The most obvious way that a citizen can participate directly in public affairs is at the ballot box. Hence, except on the score of his ignorance or indifference, we need not shed too many tears for the uninformed non-voter (see page 443). As long as he remains uninformed, he is doing a service by staying away from the polls.

But the uninformed citizen who *does* vote presents a much more serious problem. He is rendering a distinct disservice to himself and to our democracy. He, like the non-voter, is failing in the performance of one of his duties as a citizen. Still, his ballot counts for just as much as one cast by a conscientious and informed citizen.[1] Making these people see the error of their ways is one of the most concrete steps that can be taken in helping to make democracy work more effectively.

The Long Ballot. — Intelligent voting is a "must" in making democracy work. Yet, all too often, even the conscientious citizen finds this a well-nigh impossible task, as pointed out on pages 443 and 455. The task seems impossible because he finds that he must mark a ballot containing so many offices that he cannot even name the candidates, let alone decide intelligently among them.

Woodrow Wilson once pointed to this situation when he said:

I vote a ticket of some thirty names, I suppose. I never counted them but there must be quite that number. Now I am a slightly busy person, and I have never known anything about half the men I was voting for on the ticket that I voted. I attend diligently, so far as I have light, to my political duties in the borough of Princeton — and yet I have no personal knowledge of one half of the persons I am voting for. I couldn't tell you even what business they are engaged in — and to say in such circumstances that I am taking part in the government of the borough of Princeton is an absurdity. I am not taking part in it at all. I am going through the motions that I am expected to go through by the persons who think that attending primaries and voting at the polls is performing your whole political duty.

The voter can perhaps vote intelligently for president, congressmen, governor, legislators, mayor, and a few other offices. But when he is asked to decide between candidates for a welter of such offices as county coroner, treasurer, surveyor, clerk, animal hides inspector, public weigher, prosecuting attorney, registrar of elections, registrar of deeds, and dog catcher, he is at a loss.

Twenty, forty, even sixty offices are regularly filled at elections in the United States. Is it any wonder, then, that sometimes fictitious

---

[1] As amazing as it may seem, a former governor of Oregon bought space in several newspapers in the State just before the 1952 elections to advise voters to vote "no" on any and all ballot measures on which they were uninformed.

characters are elected to office? Or that party machines are able to elect men to office simply because their names happen to be similar to those of prominent people? Or that one city treasurer was recently re-elected even though he had run off with several thousands of dollars in city funds six weeks before the election?

There seems to be no valid reason for the popular election of so many public officials. The number of elective offices can probably be cut down with no harm whatever to the democratic process. Indeed, the end result would seem to be only improvement, for the voter can then become the master of his ballot. As matters now stand, most voters either do not vote for the minor offices or simply vote a straight ticket blindly hoping that the party has put up a good slate of candidates.

A few States, like New Jersey, New York, and Virginia, have come to the rescue of the over-burdened voter. And so have a great many cities, especially those with council-manager government. They have done it by providing for the appointment rather than the election of non-policy making officials.[1] But in most State and county elections the ballot is still overloaded with far too many elective offices.

QUESTIONS ON THE TEXT

1. What does the word *democracy* mean? Why is it so difficult to define?
2. What kind of equality does the true democrat believe in?
3. Why can the people govern themselves more wisely and justly than one or a few can?
4. Why must personal liberty in a democracy be relative rather than absolute?
5. What are the major causes for crime in the United States?
6. Why is an informed citizenry so essential in a democracy?
7. How may the average citizen take an active part in public affairs? Why is this one of the most important of the obligations of citizenship?
8. What is the long ballot? Why is it a problem?

---

[1] They have followed the general rule that policy-making officials should be elected and thus held responsible to the voters for their acts while those who do not *make* but only *execute* policies as determined by elected officials should be appointed. For example, a county registrar of deeds does not make public policy, he simply carries out policies as laid down by State law and the county board. He should be appointed, then, by the county board and be responsible to it for his performance. The county board, in turn, should be responsible to the voters for the actions of the registrar of deeds and all other officers of the county administration

PROBLEMS FOR DISCUSSION

1. Comment on this statement by Judge Learned Hand:

"What then is the spirit of liberty? I cannot define it; I can only tell you my own faith. The spirit of liberty is the spirit which is not too sure that it is right; the spirit of liberty is the spirit which seeks to understand the minds of other men and women; the spirit of liberty is the spirit which weighs their interests alongside its own without bias; the spirit of liberty is the spirit of Him, who nearly 2000 years ago, taught mankind that lesson it has never learned, but never quite forgotten: that there may be a kingdom where the least shall be heard and considered side by side with the greatest."

2. President Truman's Committee on Civil Rights puts the argument for freedom as we know it in these words:

"In a free society there is faith in the ability of the people to make sound, rational judgments. But such judgments are possible only where the people have access to all relevant facts and to all prevailing interpretations of the facts. How can such judgments be formed on a sound basis if arguments, viewpoints, or opinions are arbitrarily suppressed? How can the concept of the marketplace of thought in which truth ultimately prevails retain its validity if the thought of certain individuals is denied the right of circulation?"

How would you apply this statement in the current problems of communism and loyalty?

3. Explain the following quotation from Abraham Lincoln:

"Let every man remember that to violate the law is to tear up the charter of his own and his children's liberty."

4. From the Bluebook or Official Manual of your State or some other source, secure the returns for the various offices in the 1952 elections in your State. What conclusions can be drawn from the number of people who voted, the number who voted for the various offices, the indications of straight- and split-ticket voting, etc.? What efforts are being made or have been made to shorten the ballot? What elective offices in your State do you think should be made appointive, if any?

5. "The law of loyalty is simpler than the law of gravitation. It is this: We love not those who do most for us, but those for whom we do most. Not gratitude but sacrifice begets loyalty. God never did a better thing for the children of men than when he threw Adam and Eve out of the Garden of Eden and told them to hustle for themselves." — Dr. George Barton Cutten, President of Colgate University.

Do you agree that loyalty comes from sacrifice rather than from gratitude?

SELECT BIBLIOGRAPHY

BUTTERFIELD, R. "Revolt in Philadelphia." *Saturday Evening Post.* November 8, 15, 22, 1952.

DILLARD, I. (ed.). *The Spirit of Liberty.* Knopf. New York. 1952. (The non-legal papers and addresses of Justice Learned Hand.)

DOUGLAS, WM. O. "The Black Silence of Fear." *New York Times Magazine.* January 13, 1952. (Justice Douglas on the fear of ideas.)

HOUSEMAN, W. "Are U. S. Teenagers Rejecting Freedom?" *Look.* February 26, 1952.

KEFAUVER, E. "Kefauver on Crime in the United States." *Reader's Digest.* July, 1951. (Also in *Saturday Evening Post.* April 7, 14, 21, and 28, 1951.)

McCARTHY, E. J. "Who Says the Majority Rules?" *The Reporter.* March 18, 1952. (A Congressman on representation.)

MORSE, A. D. "Invitation to Gripe." *Collier's.* November 21, 1952.

NEVINS, A. "A New Ray of Light on Lincoln." *Saturday Evening Post.* February 16, 1952.

RIKER, W. *Democracy in the United States.* Macmillan. New York. 1953.

SEVAREID, E. "Why Did They Fight?" *Harper's.* October, 1953.

CHAPTER XXXVII

THE GOVERNMENT SERVICE AS A CAREER

Today the National Government's payrolls list more than 2,000,000 civilian employees, and the States and local governments employ another 4,000,000. Only a relative handful of these are elected to office. Most of them are appointed.

It is upon these appointees that the burden of day-to-day government rests. They are the administrators, the postmen, the police, the firemen, the tax officials, the secretaries, etc. They are the "civil servants."

The quality of these persons in large measure determines the quality of government. No matter how wisely legislators may have determined policy the people cannot benefit unless this policy is properly and successfully executed. In effect, the administration of policy is, as Woodrow Wilson once noted, "government in action."

The best of governmental machinery is useless unless it is staffed with competent and qualified personnel. Few people would go so far as to agree with Alexander Pope that "For forms of government let fools contest — That which is best administered is best." But most would agree with Alexander Hamilton "that the true test of good government is its aptitude and tendency to produce a good administration."

Public service, especially in the National Government, is becoming more attractive to young people. This is true because of job security, promotion according to merit, and relatively good starting salaries. And many times public service is its own reward.

The Civil Service of the United States. — The Constitution of the United States provides that Congress may by law vest the appointment of such inferior officers as they think proper in the President alone, in the courts of law, or in the heads of departments. Congress vested the appointment of most inferior officers in the President or in the heads of departments. For half a century following Andrew Jackson's administration the President and heads of departments appointed members of their own political parties, giving little consideration to qualifications, and turning out of office those of the opposing party. This practice was known as the "spoils system." [1]

Modern Government Services Complex. — When our nation was in its infancy it was a comparatively simple matter to select the personnel for the various activities of the government. Much of the appointment of civil service was done directly by the President with the advice of members of Congress. But each year more employees were added, until Lincoln, during the Civil War, likened his task as personnel appointer to a landlord so busy showing the office seekers what was to be had in one wing that he didn't have time to put out the raging fire in the other wing of the national structure.

The appointment of supporting party members to political positions became not only a terrible burden on our Presidents, but even became a dangerous thing that culminated in the death of President Garfield, who was shot by a disappointed office seeker. Following this tragedy a Civil Service Commission was established, and now more than two thirds of the civilian employees of the National Government, except department heads and key diplomats, are chosen through Civil Service examinations.

Opportunities in Government Service. — There are scarcely any skills or professions that are not needed in some branch or service of the Government, ranging from janitors, typists, and mechanics, to the most skilled and highest trained scientists. Doctors, lawyers, merchants, fire chiefs, and practically every other category of modern activity are included on the Government's pay roll.

Before World War II called for a sudden and temporary expansion of personnel there were about a million and a half men and women working for the various agencies of the Federal Government, and almost as many, not counting public school teachers, who were engaged in work for city, county, and State governments. The war made it necessary to expand the civilian activities of the War, Navy, and other Defense Agencies by another million and a half. This made a total of over three million, and today there are over two million civilians employed by the Federal Government.

---

[1] In 1832 when President Jackson was criticized for removing political opponents from office, William L. Marcy in defending the action of the President said, "To the victors belong the spoils of the enemy."

The Pentagon, Headquarters of Our Military Services and the World's Largest Office Building

There is a constant opportunity for capable young men and women to enter the numerous branches of Government service in the type of work for which each is best suited.   There are more than 1700 different positions for which competitive examinations are given at frequent intervals, and other highly skilled positions are open for classification through educational training and experience.

How to Get a Civil Service Appointment. — When a vacancy occurs in a Civil Service position it may be filled in four ways: (1) by *promotion* of an employee in a lower position who is already in classified civil service; (2) by *transfer* of a person who is employed by the Government in another position; (3) by *re-employment* of a person who has a classified status and was formerly employed by the Government; or (4) by the *entrance appointment* of a person who has qualified for the position in an open competitive examination held by the Commission for the type of work to be performed.

Notices of Examination. — A young person who is interested in Civil Service work can obtain information concerning the many examinations at each first- or second-class post office, or at any one of the thirteen district offices.   Frequently notices concerning positions that are to be filled are posted in the post office or other Government buildings. If a person is interested in a particular examination, he may have his name put on the mailing file in the district and National offices, and when that examination is next given he will be notified.

Application for Examination. — When an examination is announced for a type of work in which the young person is interested, he should secure the necessary application blanks from the nearest first- or second-class post office, or from the district office.   The applications ordinarily must be in at a set deadline, and all proof of qualifications and other requested records must be included.

If the applicant is eligible to take the examination, he will be sent an admittance card which entitles him to take the tests which are prepared and given by the Civil Service Commission without charge.

Examinations. — Many examinations for Civil Service positions have been scientifically prepared to test the abilities of each applicant for the particular kind of work covered by each test.   Some of these tests, such as typing, require that the applicant actually type and be rated for speed and accuracy.   Mechanical skills have specialized mechanic tests.   The grading is also scientifically checked and rechecked, and the person is rated by standardized scales — always by number and never by the person's name.

Name on the Register. — The names of the persons who have passed the examination are placed in a file, known as the register, and kept for several years.   When there occurs a vacancy which must be filled by a person who meets the qualifications covered by the test, the personnel director of the department having the vacancy sends a requisition to the Civil Service office and asks for the names of three qualified applicants.   These names, together with the rating, personal records, and other information, are sent to the personnel director who then selects one of the three for the position.   Usually the person with the highest rating on the register is offered the position, but if he does not accept, the next name on the list is given an opportunity.

Probationary Appointment. — When the person accepts the job with the department or agency, he is given a temporary appointment that becomes permanent after a few months of satisfactory work.   The employee must pass a rigid physical examination and be of good character in order to be eligible for most civil service positions.

Reclassification and Promotion. — From time to time after the individual has received his final appointment to civil service, his duties and work are investigated to see if his responsibilities have increased and if his work has improved sufficiently to warrant a new classification with the accompanying raise.   If the work is of a better rating than that which was originally required, then the worker is "reclassified" and the raise is given.   If a vacancy occurs for which the worker is qualified, he may be given a direct promotion.

Pensions and Retirement for Government Workers. — Each employee of the Classified Civil Service pays 6 per cent of his salary into a retirement fund.   The retirement age varies from 50 to 70, depending upon the work and the location of the job as well as the length of service.   If the employee has reached the retirement age and has been in the service for at least fifteen years, he is automatically retired. Congress annually appropriates additional sums to supplement the retirement fund so that each employee who has served his nation long and well can have a moderate pension on which to retire and under certain conditions the surviving widow of a Government employee may be pensioned.   The amount is determined by the salary he has received and the length of his service.   If the employee leaves the service before the retirement age is reached, he receives the amount he has paid to the retirement fund with interest.

Veteran's Preference. — Men who have undergone the hardships of military service for their country have been given a preferential rating through Acts of Congress. Believing that those who have given much

VETERANS' PREFERENCE

Veterans of wars and campaigns for which campaign ribbons are authorized are entitled to certain preference in the Federal Civil Service.

to their country and who return to civilian life at times when the economic hardship may be great deserve special consideration, the Government gives all veterans of the military services five points additional to their civil service rating. Those who have had a disability because of their military service, or widows of veterans, are given ten points. This often places them in a higher rank than the top civilians and their names are considered for appointment at an earlier date.

Temporary Appointments. — In normal times temporary jobs in the Federal service may be filled without examinations; or if there is an opening in a field which has no waiting list on the Civil Service Register, someone may be appointed until he or somebody else qualifies by examination.

During World War II, when hundreds of thousands of extra stenographers, filing clerks, etc., were needed, positions were filled through the Civil Service on a temporary basis. The temporary rolls were expanded again during the Korean War, but are now being reduced.

Federal, State, and City Civil Service. — More than two thirds of all permanent Federal employees are under the Civil Service merit system. About half of the States provide for employment under the competitive merit system, and other States have civil service laws applying to certain departments; but "temporary" appointments without examinations too often become permanent fixtures. The merit system is accepted, at least in part, by practically all cities with a population in excess of 100,000; and by many smaller cities.

QUESTIONS ON THE TEXT

1. How should our Government personnel be chosen for different kinds of offices? What is the spoils system?

2. Why should young people be chosen for the Government service?

3. What types of positions are covered by the Civil Service?

4. How many different kinds of examinations are given through the Civil Service Commission?

5. Where may anyone obtain information concerning Civil Service positions and examinations?

6. How may one obtain a Civil Service appointment?

7. How do Federal employees under Civil Service become eligible for retirement pensions? On what is the amount based?

8. What is meant by veteran's preference?

9. Explain the temporary appointments for Federal positions.

PROBLEMS FOR DISCUSSION

1. In the Civil Service should promotions be based on length of service, efficiency ratings, or periodic examinations; or the combination of all three?

2. In recent years we have created well over a thousand new Government jobs that pay as much as $10,000 a year. Give arguments for or against the Government's paying more attractive salaries than formerly.

3. Should examinations for young men or women entering the Government services be based upon the work they will immediately have to do; or

on their general education, ability, and character, as is done in England? Would your answer be different if middle-aged persons are admitted to the service?

4. Why do we have pensions for Government employees?

5. Civil employees contribute towards their pensions. Military employees do not. Do you see any reason for the distinction?

SELECT BIBLIOGRAPHY

BINKLEY, W., AND MOOS, M. *A Grammar of American Politics.* Knopf. New York. 1952 ed. Chapters XIX and XX.

BRUCE, H. *American National Government.* Holt. New York. 1952. Chapter XXII.

BURNS, J., AND PELTASON, J. *Government by the People.* Prentice-Hall. New York. 1952. Chapter XVII.

FERGUSON, J., AND MCHENRY, D. *The American System of Government.* McGraw-Hill. New York. 1953 ed. Chapters XVII and XVIII.

OGG, F., AND RAY, P. *Essentials of American Government.* Appleton-Century-Crofts. New York. 1952 ed.

SWARTHOUT, J. M., AND BARTLEY, E. *Materials on American Government.* Oxford Univ. Press. New York. 1952. Nos. 118–120.

SWARTHOUT, J. M., AND BARTLEY, E. *Principles and Problems of American National Government.* Oxford Univ. Press. New York. 1954. Chapter XXI.

CHAPTER XXXVIII

SOCIAL LEGISLATION

Conservation of Health

Introduction. — The general health of the American people has improved steadily over the past half century. Where white male children born in 1900 could expect to live, on the average, 48 years, those born today have an average life expectancy of over 68 years. The infant death rate now stands at an all-time low in the United States: 29 deaths under one year of age for every 1000 live births.

This marked improvement in the nation's health can also be seen in these statistics: In 1900 some 3,000,000 people (4.1 per cent of the total population) were over 65 years of age; in 1953 over 13,000,000 people (8.4 per cent of the total population) were over 65.

Tremendous strides in medical and scientific research have been and are constantly being made. The once-great killers, like typhoid fever, scarlet fever, and smallpox, are now largely conquered. The new "wonder drugs" and new methods of treating and preventing diseases have done much to lengthen the life span. The fact that scientists are now able to nurture human skin in a bottle is just one indication of the amazing advances that have been made in medical research.

But, while the nation's health is steadily improving, it is quite obvious that much still remains to be done. During World War II about 5,000,000 men were rejected for selective service because of physical or mental defects, and nearly one out of every three is likewise being rejected today.

Approximately 1,400,000 persons die in the United States each year.[1] According to Federal health authorities, 325,000 of these deaths could be prevented each year through the medical knowledge and skill we now possess. Sickness and accidents take a terrific economic toll: today it is estimated that the nation loses 4,300,000 man-years of work each year through bad health and $27,000,000,000 in national wealth annually because of sickness and partial or total disability.

---

[1] There are more than 3,500,000 live births registered each year.

663

Two Serious Problems. — Scientific progress has made available new drugs and advanced techniques which have sharply reduced the number of cases and the severity of many illnesses. Still many cases of preventable or curable diseases go unattended. Why? The individual, through indifference, negligence or ignorance may be partly responsible. But there are some reasons beyond the individual's control. These include in addition to possible financial limitations, such factors as:

Shortage of Medical Personnel. — There is a very serious shortage of doctors, nurses, dentists and other trained personnel. There was one doctor for every 636 persons in 1900. Today the ratio is one for every 750. It is estimated that we shall need 254,000 doctors by 1960; yet, as matters now stand, we shall have only 212,000. Today we have only 80 per cent of the number of doctors needed.

The problem is further complicated by the fact that the nation's doctors are not evenly distributed. For example, New York has one doctor for every 500 persons, but Mississippi has only one for every 1500. Doctors, like anyone else, prefer to settle in the wealthier and more comfortable areas. As a result, there is a marked shortage of doctors in the poorer and in the rural areas.

Because of the general population increase (and especially the increased number of older persons), the demands of the armed forces and other governmental agencies, and the increase in the number of families who can now afford at least some medical care, the shortage of doctors and other trained medical personnel is alarming. More doctors must be trained and they must be persuaded to practice in the rural and the poorer areas.

Several possible solutions have been advanced. The medical schools (both State and private) might well be expanded, and many are expanding. Many suggest a government scholarship program for medical students who agree to practice for a certain number of years in areas where doctors are urgently needed. It has also been suggested that medical students' expenses could be met through loans, either by the State or National Government or privately; these could be repaid on a long-term installment basis. Some form of health insurance (see pages 668–670) would go a long way toward solving the problems of the number and the distribution of doctors, too.

Shortage of Hospitals. — About 1000 of the counties in the United

States possess no adequate hospital facilities. There is a severe shortage of general, mental, and tuberculosis hospitals that meet approved standards. Many of our hospitals are overcrowded as well as understaffed. As with doctors, hospitals are generally concentrated in the higher-income sections of the country.

To help meet this problem, Congress passed the Hospital Survey and Construction Act in 1946. It established a grant-in-aid system for the construction and expansion of hospitals and public health facilities. Under this law the National Government puts up one dollar for every two from the State. In many communities the necessary State money has been raised through private fund campaigns. By 1954 some 1500 projects, costing over $1,000,000,000 were under way or had been completed. This program has furnished a wonderful example of what people, acting locally, can do to solve civic problems.

Mental Diseases. — About a half million persons are now patients in State-operated mental hospitals. Untold thousands more suffer from mental disorders. Mental and nervous diseases are the largest single reason for selective service rejections and by far the most important cause for medical discharges from the armed forces.

Every State maintains at least one mental hospital. But many of these mental institutions are aptly described as "snake pits." Overcrowded and understaffed, they too often treat their patients as prisoners. Inadequate and even cruel treatment and neglect are not uncommon. The rate of recovery in many of these hospitals is little higher than it was fifty years ago.

These revolting conditions were brought to light all over the country a few years ago. The resulting wave of public indignation forced much-needed reforms. But, here again, much still remains to be done.

Prevention of Disease. — When people believed that disease was a "humor" in the blood, they waited until the malady appeared and cured it with medicines — or at least tried to cure it. But now that we know most of our prevalent diseases to be caused by bacilli (germs), we know it is possible to prevent them if the bacilli are kept from our systems.

For instance, if the parasites causing the hookworm disease had been understood in the United States before Doctor Stiles of the United States Public Health Service identified them in 1902, and not allowed to spread, the millions of victims of the disease would have escaped.

Fortunately this disease can now be easily prevented or cured, and State and county health boards are co-operating with public schools to eradicate it. Again, if we have the water and milk supply free from typhoid bacilli, and screen against the flies which carry these germs, we are not likely to contract typhoid fever. But individuals living in cities, especially, cannot know whether the water and milk supplies are pure or whether the hotels are sanitary. So States and cities must have officers to inspect the milk supply, water supply, food supplies, hotels, and restaurants. While the major purpose of private medicine is the treatment and cure of diseases, the major purpose of public health officers and agencies is the prevention and eradication of diseases and their causes.

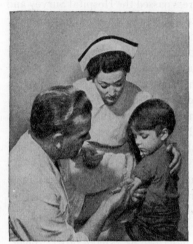

Courtesy E. R. Squibb & Sons

"AN OUNCE OF PREVENTION"

Periodic inoculation is an established safeguard of health in all up-to-date communities. Nowadays youngsters take this important preventive measure for granted as part of their health program.

Today, States and cities maintain laboratories for the examination of water, milk, and other foods; they conduct annual examinations of school children and even of adults; they regulate vaccination; they inspect meat shops, soda fountains, hotels, tenements, factories, and the premises of residences; they disinfect places where contagious diseases have existed; and they maintain health stations, hospitals, pest houses, sanatoriums for consumptives, and recreation grounds for all persons.

Citizens were at one time slow to realize that it is cheaper to pay taxes for the prevention of disease than to pay doctors' bills and hospital bills for their care. National, State, and local governments are co-operating in public health work today. More than $70,000,000 in Federal grants-in-aid go to State and local health agencies each year. And everyone agrees that this amount is still far below what is badly needed.

Sanitation to be of any great value in a community must be practiced throughout the entire community. When Mr. Preston was Mayor of Baltimore he waged a war on the mosquito. Inspectors were employed to go from house to house to locate places where mosquitoes might breed. Behold, in the Mayor's own yard was found

Courtesy Automobile Manufacturers Association

CLEAN CITIES

Clean cities are healthy cities. One task in keeping them clean is to pump out and dispose of the refuse and debris which accumulates in street drains and storm sewers. These men are using up-to-date equipment for this task.

a jar containing water in which mosquitoes could multiply. He paid his fine cheerfully, but the incident goes to show that the sanitation of a city, or State, cannot be left to individuals. It is too natural for one to be negligent — to be absorbed in his own pressing duties. We need specialists, whose duty it is to promote sanitation by concentrating on the annihilation of mosquitoes.

The United States Public Health Service discovered that on any winter day there are 6,000,000 people in the United States who are kept away from school or work by illness. It also found that there is almost twice as much illness among families with less than $2000 a year income as among families with more than $6000 income. Illness usually strikes those least able to afford adequate medical care. Today many doctors, public officials, and interested private groups are seeking a fair method to provide adequate care to all on the basis of need.

HEALTH INSURANCE

Public Clinics and Hospitals are supported by all large cities or counties. For instance, New York has a master plan providing for 63 public clinics. And New York recently built a $15,000,000 hospital on Welfare Island in East River with 2000 beds to care for ambulant and bed-ridden cases.

While cities and counties may take care of the poor in clinics and hospitals for the under-privileged; and while privately conducted hospitals may care for the well-to-do; the low-income middle class is especially pinched when a member of the household suffers from a prolonged illness. For this reason there has been an increasing demand for group medicine.

The Group Clinic Plan is one in which the clinical staff is composed of several physicians on a full-time basis. Subscribers pay a small monthly fee. The Stowe-Lipsett Clinic in Oakland, California, is an example of this type and it provides its subscribers with hospitalization for 45 days, with physicians' and surgeons' services, a clinical psychologist, X-ray and laboratory tests, and ambulance service. Subscribers' dependents receive reduced rates on services if they are not themselves members.

The Closed-Staff Plan is one in which all the subscribers living within a certain area are treated by one physician. The Transport Workers Union of New York City operates a plan of this sort. The city is divided into districts. Within each district there is a general practitioner who treats union members who reside in his district and also carries on his private practice as well. The union pays the doctors a salary. Specialists, druggists, and opticians are also available within the plan.

The Free-Choice, Private Practice Plan is one in which the subscriber may choose his doctor from a large panel of doctors who have agreed to participate in the plan. Doctors are paid according to the type and amount of services rendered and they retain their private practice as well. Under this plan, as in the two above, the subscriber makes a small monthly payment. The various medical societies favor this plan, if any.

The Blue Cross Hospital Plan is by far the most popular of all the forms of voluntary health insurance. The American Hospital Association passes on all organizations wishing to use the name Blue Cross. Associated Hospital Service of Philadelphia illustrates the general pattern. It is incorporated as a nonprofit corporation under the supervision of the State Insurance Department. The governing board is composed of an equal number of representatives of the hospitals, the medical society, and the general public. The subscribers pay a small fee and the Hospital Service pays the hospitals within the plan a flat rate per day which covers bed and board for a limited number of days, as well as the special hospital services.

Many insurance companies also operate pre-paid health and accident insurance programs.

State Medicine. — President Truman advocated Federal aid for more hospitals, more doctors, more research, and compulsory medical insurance. In 1948 Great Britain inaugurated a National Health Service Program to provide free medical and dental care for all "from the cradle to the grave."

Our Veterans Administration, which employs more than 15,000 doctors and provides free medical care to all the more than 20,000,000 veterans if they have service-connected disabilities or cannot afford to pay for treatment (liberally interpreted), is an outstanding example of state medicine.

Those in favor of a plan of state medicine advance the following arguments:

1. Almost one third of all those examined for military service in the Second World War were rejected because of physical disabilities.

2. On any winter day there are 6,000,000 people kept away from school or work by illness.

3. The nation is short of doctors and nurses and hospital facilities — and many rural areas have no medical facilities other than the family medicine chest.

4. Many people cannot afford to pay the high cost of medical services today, and thus their health, and the nation's health in the event of contagious diseases, is endangered.

Those who oppose a plan of state medicine advance these arguments:

1. It would destroy medical free enterprise, and therefore the incentive to maximum efficiency of doctors would be lost.

2. Political bureaucrats would probably administer such a system.

3. It would standardize medical service at a low level.

4. With free care those with imaginary ailments would pester the doctor.

While a great many people favor some form of Government health insurance program, many others are opposed to any such arrangement. We do not disagree as to the existence of a need for more and better medical care; the evidence of the need is overwhelming. And we know that the physical health and well-being of all our people is absolutely essential to the over-all strength of the nation. But many of us disagree as to the proper *method* to be used in meeting the need.

Whether the solution finally reached takes the form of a compulsory or a voluntary health insurance plan or is governmentally or privately administered remains to be seen. No matter what decision is reached we must take care to see that individual initiative within the medical profession is preserved. Individual initiative is the mainspring of progress in our civilization, and, in this, the medical profession is no exception.

PUBLIC HOUSING

Why Low-Rent Housing Is a Government Problem. — When mechanical inventions and immigration flooded our cities with laborers from the farm or from European cities, investors built solid blocks of houses to rent to them. Profit was the prime consideration. Open-air spaces, sanitary plumbing, and conveniences were neglected. Now these slum dwellings breed disease, immorality, and crime. How slums encourage crime is well illustrated by the following extract from a pamphlet called "Crime," published by the University of Chicago Press:

Slum conditions of themselves might not create grumbling and dissatisfaction if the slum families had no means of knowing how differently other people lived. But only a few blocks away from the miserable tenements, shop windows blaze with their tempting displays of jewelry, furs, and expensive clothes. Only a few blocks away are the homes of the rich, who can afford all the good things of life. All this contrasts sharply with the grime and sweat and filth of the cheap, dingy rooms of the poor and with their strenuous efforts to keep body and soul together. . . . We shouldn't be surprised at the number of youngsters in the slums who become lawbreakers. The marvel is that slums don't produce many more criminals.

Harris & Ewing

A SLUM IN SIGHT OF OUR NATIONAL CAPITOL

Private enterprise, with government backing, is doing a great deal to remedy situations like this. There is still much more to do.

Where private capital is not sufficient to build homes for low-income groups, the Government can and does aid in such undertakings.

THE FEDERAL GOVERNMENT AND HOUSING

According to the 1950 census, 95,892,000 people, or 63.7 per cent of the total population, now live in urban communities. The city-dwelling population has increased by more than 20,000,000 since 1940. All of these people have housing of some sort or other, of course; but in many cases this housing is far from adequate.

Home building fell off drastically during the Depression of the 1930's and so the Federal Government assumed an active role in the promotion of adequate housing facilities. Congress passed several laws to help home owners with the maintenance and mortgages on homes built before the Depression. Then the Government began to encourage the building of new homes. This was done mainly by guaranteeing loans for new home construction and by making grants-in-aid to local communities for the elimination of slum areas.

The Second World War aggravated the housing problem, particularly in defense production centers. To help relieve the pressures of housing war workers, the Government financed and built several housing projects all over the country. Some of these were permanent housing projects, but many of the temporary ones are still in use.

At the end of the war it was estimated that some 12,000,000 new homes were needed to meet the pent-up demand. Even at the high rate of 1,000,000 new homes a year, the demand could not be satisfied until sometime late in the 1950's. And the current remobilization has made the housing situation even more critical.

The greatest need is for adequate housing within the reach of low- and middle-income families. It is estimated that the average family can afford to buy a house costing about twice the family's annual income. Under present conditions, then, a family with an income of, say, $2000 a year does not face a too-happy home-owning prospect.

The Federal Housing Administration is the best-known of the Government's housing agencies. The F.H.A. itself does not build homes, nor does it lend money for home construction. It guarantees home mortgages and home improvement loans on one- to four-family dwellings built by private persons or companies. The actual loans are made by banks or other private lending institutions. The F.H.A. guarantees loans up to 90 per cent of the appraised value of the property.

Let us illustrate how your home-town bank will lend money at a low interest rate because the loan is insured through the Federal Housing Administration. Any person of good reputation and sufficient income to justify building, let us say, a house of 5000 dollars value, including lot, can borrow from his local bank 90 per cent of the cost and pay it back in monthly installments over a period of as long as 20 years. The maximum interest rate is $4\frac{1}{2}$ per cent plus $\frac{1}{2}$ per cent for insuring that the loan will be paid. The F.H.A. requires that fire insurance be carried on all homes constructed with its aid.

The location and plans of the house must be approved and the construction inspected from time to time, and a mortgage must be given on the house for the amount of the loan to be granted.

The F.H.A. also insures $4\frac{1}{2}$ per cent loans for re-financing existing homes up to 80 per cent of their value. These loans must be repaid in monthly installments over a period of not longer than 15 years.

The work of the F.H.A. in encouraging home building is supplemented by that of the Federal Home Loan Banks (see pages 330–331), which make credit available to local institutions engaged in home financing. The Veterans Administration guarantees GI loans up to $4000 to veterans of World War II and the present emergency.

The Public Housing Administration is the other principal housing agency of the Federal Government. While the F.H.A. is intended to encourage private building and home ownership by helping people to help themselves, the P.H.A. is directly engaged in the providing of public housing.

The basic task of the Public Housing Authority is the administration of a low-rent housing program. Under this program the P.H.A. makes direct loans to city, county, and State governments for the construction of low-rent housing projects. The Government pays annual subsidies to these local housing authorities in order to provide below-cost rents. Tenants in these projects are limited to citizens with low incomes.

To illustrate, a city housing authority (with the approval of the city council) prepares a plan for a low-rent housing project near a large defense plant. It then applies to the Public Housing Administration for an annual subsidy (not exceeding 40 years) so that the city can build and rent dwellings to the needy for 20 per cent less than the prevailing rents in the area. If the P.H.A. approves the details of the plan, the actual construction begins.

The housing project is financed by issuing low interest rate tax-exempt bonds, which are paid off with the rents and the annual Government subsidy. Veterans and those moved out of slum clearance areas (provided they have only low incomes) are given a priority.

The P.H.A. is also engaged in the management and sale of wartime housing projects, many of which have been sold to cities at a very low price. It also administers various veterans housing projects, and it now administers farm-labor camps previously under the supervision of the Department of Agriculture.

A General View of Greenbelt, Maryland

This model town was built during the depression of the 'thirties to provide labor for the unemployed and to furnish homes for persons of limited income. The government began selling all land, buildings, and other facilities to private owners in 1952.

As in the case of many of the other services provided by the Government today, the question of private enterprise versus Government subsidization arises here! But one interesting aspect of all of this is often overlooked in the housing field. As matters now stand, the Government, in many cases, assumes practically all of the financial risks involved and private lending agencies and construction companies are able to make whatever profit there may be in the situation.

We are still quite a distance from solving the housing problem in the United States. Much remains to be done by both the Government and private housing interests.

LIQUOR

Alcoholic Drinks through the Ages:

The Mosaic Law provided that a glutton and a drunkard should be stoned to death.

Solomon said: "Wine is a mocker, strong drink a brawler; and whoever erreth thereby is not wise."

Isaiah told how "even the judges reel with wine, and stagger with strong drink; . . ."

Paul said: "Be not deceived: . . . drunkards shall not inherit the kingdom of God."

Emperor Vitellius gave a bacchanalian banquet which cost a million dollars but allowed his own mother to die in want because she rebuked him.

Shakespeare said: "Oh God, that men should put an enemy in their mouths to steal away their brains!"

The colonial *Virginia House of Burgesses* enacted a law providing that "ministers shall not give themselves to excess in drinking."

Abraham Lincoln said: "Liquor might have defenders, but no defense. Whether or not the world would be vastly benefited by a total and final banishment from it of all intoxicating drinks, seems to me not an open question."

Dr. Charles Mayo, noted physician and surgeon, said: "You can get along with a wooden leg, but you can't get along with a wooden head. The physical value of a man is not so much. Man as analyzed in our laboratories is worth about ninety-eight cents.[1] Seven bars of soap,

---

[1] Dr. Mayo's figure is based on pre-war prices.

lime enough to whitewash a chicken coop, phosphorus enough to cover the heads of a thousand matches, is not very much, you see. It is the brain that counts, but in order that your brain may be kept clear you must keep your body fit and well. That cannot be done if one drinks liquor."

Liquor Laws. — Since the repeal of nation-wide prohibition the sale of liquor has been regulated by the States. The 21st Amendment to the U. S. Constitution provides that "the transportation or importation into any State, Territory, or possession of the United States for delivery or use therein of intoxicating liquors, in violation of the laws thereof, is hereby prohibited." The United States Government has done very little to enforce this provision; but the provision does make it legal for prohibition States to exclude liquor coming from other States, which they could not do without a constitutional provision or an Act of Congress.

Courtesy "Christian Advocate"

A DEAD-END STREET

This street of wrecked lives and lost hopes knows no turning for those who follow it to its bitter end.

In the United States liquor is legally sold in nearly half a million licensed places, and twice as much is expended for alcoholic drinks as for education. In some States saloons are wide-open for the sale of intoxicants to men and women. In some States liquor may be legally sold only at government dispensaries in the original package; and in others hard liquor may be sold only in Government dispensaries while light wines and beer may be sold at eating places, candy stores, filling stations, and other places, where licensed. Other States permit cities, counties, or other localities to vote themselves dry ("local option"). Still other States have prohibition against the sale of hard liquor but not of light wines and beer. Mississippi and Oklahoma have statewide prohibition.

The Organized Labor Movement

Outstanding Labor Unions. — *The American Federation of Labor* was formed in 1881 by the affiliation of unions of skilled workmen of the various crafts or trades, so the A. F. of L. has been known as the parent organization of trade unions. It now has about 9,500,000 members, including carpenters and teamsters. The late William Green was succeeded by George Meany as president in 1952.

The Congress of Industrial Organizations broke away from the A. F. of L. in 1935 under the leadership of John L. Lewis. It is an industrial union of all the workers (skilled and unskilled) in a particular branch of industry, such as steel, automobile, textile, and clothing industries. In 1940 the late Philip Murray became president, followed by Walter Reuther in 1952. The C. I. O. membership is about 6,000,000.

Independent (Unaffiliated) Unions. — The United Mine Workers, with a membership of about 600,000, have John L. Lewis as president. Besides mine workers, there are unassociated with A. F. of L. or C. I. O. such unions as The International Association of Mechanics; and a dozen railway unions such as the brotherhoods of Railway Trainmen, Locomotive Engineers, and Locomotive Firemen and Engineers.

Even Federal Government employees (*e.g.*, postal clerks) may organize, and may even become members of one of the federations; but they are not allowed to declare strikes. The Taft-Hartley Act provides that a Government employee striker cannot be re-employed in any Federal agency for three years. Many State governments, such as New York, have similar laws. But, as pointed out some years ago by the New York State Joint Legislative Committee on Industrial and Labor Relations: "Though we may legislate to the end of time, there will never be industrial peace and harmony without good faith, integrity, a high degree of responsibility and a real desire to co-operate on the part of all parties concerned. Without this spirit of good will, all of the social, economic and labor laws of man will prove eventually to be in vain."

Aims. — A labor unionist would state his aims about like this: "Labor is entitled to reasonable pay, a reasonable work day, and human conditions of labor." [1]

---

[1] Employers often accuse laborers of demanding unreasonable pay, hours, or conditions; and the unorganized purchasing public sometimes thinks that it is

Collective Bargaining. — The means employed by labor to attain its aims is called "collective bargaining" whereby representatives of union labor arrange with the employer terms and conditions of work to be performed. The need for such an arrangement springs from the corporate form of modern industry. Instead of a few laborers bargaining directly with a few employers whom they know, we now have thousands of employees bargaining with one employer, the corporation manager, whom they do not know and who represents thousands of investors owning stock in the corporation.

COLLECTIVE BARGAINING

Representatives of the General Motors Corporation and the United Automobile Workers (C. I. O.) averted a strike of 225,000 employees. The settlement climaxed eighteen hours of almost continuous bargaining.

Industrial Revolution Cause of Union Evolution. — Let us now inquire into the reasons for two large labor organizations whereas only one existed before 1935. The American Federation of Labor is organized as a craft union in which each craft of skilled employees, or group of allied crafts, makes a separate bargain with the employer, and has certain items of work assigned to it to perform, called its jurisdiction.

Change in technique and in materials, due to modern invention, causes these jurisdictions to overlap continually, which results in much internal friction among crafts, and annoyance to employers. For in-

squeezed between the upper and nether millstones of monopolistic capital and organized labor.

stance, during the depression there were unemployed in practically all crafts and each wanted all the work that it could get, so while the plumber and the steam-fitters, let us say, were deciding which should make repairs on a steamship the ship was unable to sail.[1]

A MEETING OF NEW YORK INTERBOROUGH RAPID TRANSIT COMPANY
EMPLOYEES

About a thousand shop workers halted work to attend a rally and listen to a C. I. O. representative. He demanded that the Board of Transportation cease conferring with leaders of the Civil Service Forum, a group not affiliated with the C. I. O.

The Congress of Industrial Organizations is an industrial union of all workers in a particular branch of industry. As the development of mass production, with its conveyor belts and machine methods, largely supplanted the individual skill on which craft unionism was formed, there were millions of workers without a very definite craft or trade. The C. I. O. promises special protection to such groups. The C. I. O. claims a reduction in jurisdictional disputes, increased bargaining power, fuller co-operation of employees, and equal protection for un-skilled laborers.

---

[1] The A. F. of L. is gradually eliminating the worst of these jurisdictional annoy-ances.

On the other hand, the A. F. of L. feels that the C. I. O. movement created a rift in the ranks of labor with ill-feeling and conflict; that with the inclusion of unskilled labor a larger proportion of radicals were inducted into organized labor; and that an organization that gives an equal vote to unskilled labor will tend to secure the same pay for unskilled labor as for those workers who have spent more time and money making themselves efficient craftsmen.

Need of Increased Annual Income Rather Than Hourly Income. — On a few occasions, some producers have restricted the output of a commodity to increase the unit price; organized laborers have restricted the supply of labor to increase hourly wages. Naturally, when output is small and the unit price is high, the general public is unable to buy a large quantity of the output. As a result, in normal times the organized laborer has work only part of the year, and invested capital is employed only part of the year.

From a long-range point of view, it might be well if capital would accustom itself to smaller profits and if organized labor would accustom itself to working all the year for what it now receives for the hours it works. Then, perhaps, output would be increased and the prices lowered. Thus in normal peace times both capitalists and laborers could buy and enjoy more products.

FEDERAL MEDIATION AND CONCILIATION SERVICE

The Federal Mediation and Conciliation Service seeks to bring about peaceful settlements of disputes arising between employers and employees.

The Mediation and Conciliation Services are furnished at the request of either party or proposed by the Service itself. If accepted, the mediator or conciliator meets representatives of employers and employees and tries to bring them to an agreement.

The Arbitration Branch may act if mediation or conciliation fails, but only if requested by both parties in the dispute. It appoints arbitrators agreed to by the parties; and their decision is binding on the parties.

The Technical Service Branch may assist efforts at settlement by studying plant problems such as wage incentive and piece-rate plans, wage classification, or merit systems.

NATIONAL LABOR RELATIONS BOARD

Organization and Purpose. — In 1935 the Wagner Act was passed, creating the National Labor Relations Board; and in 1947 the Taft-Hartley Act expanded it. The Board consists of 5 members appointed by the President and Senate. Its duty is to promote collective bargaining and to prevent specified unfair employer-labor practices that affect interstate or foreign commerce. This means the regulation of employer-labor controversies in practically all big industries — except railroads, which are regulated under the Railway Labor Act.

Courtesy "Chicago Daily News"

WHY NOT PULL TOGETHER?

The General Counsel of the Board supervises attorneys and other employees of the Board, investigates charges of illegal practices by employers and employees, and prosecutes these complaints before the Board. The Board may use the Federal courts to prevent illegal acts by the use of injunctions, or other means of enforcing decisions; but employees have the right of appeal.

Employers cannot discharge workers, except foremen, for joining a union; and are required to bargain with union leaders. Employers can discharge workers who strike in violation of a contract, for sit-down strikes, and other waste of time or work not done ("featherbedding"). They can sue unions for breaking contracts, or losses caused by a strike called by a union in a jurisdictional dispute with another union, or for losses caused by a union boycott of the products of an employer who is on the union's blacklist ("secondary boycotting"). And they may ask the N. L. R. B. to seek an injunction against certain unfair labor practices.

Employees, through their union leaders, can sue employers who break contracts; but they cannot strike during a 60-day waiting period, and Government workers may organize but are not allowed to strike under any circumstances.

The closed shop (in which only union members may be employed) is outlawed; and a union shop (in which workers must join the union within thirty days after being hired) requires the assent of the employer and a majority of employees. The Board may call an election.

A union shop contract cannot be signed until a detailed financial report of the union is made public through the Department of Labor; and union officers must swear that they are not Communists before they are permitted to bring their grievances to the Board.

Board of Inquiry. — Whenever a threatened or actual strike or lock-out imperils the national health or safety, the President may appoint a board of inquiry. Upon receiving a report from this board the President may have the Attorney General petition a District Court to enjoin (forbid) such strike or lock-out or the continuance thereof.

When an injunction is issued the President reconvenes the board of inquiry; and by the end of 60 days the board reports to the President the current position of each party and of the employer's last offer. The President makes this report available to the public; and within 15 days the National Labor Relations Board takes a secret ballot of the employees of each employer as to whether they accept the final offer. The results are certified within 5 days, and then the injunction ends. If the offer is not accepted and the strike continues, the President submits a report to Congress "together with such recommendations as he may see fit to make for consideration and appropriate action."

VOLUNTARY CO-OPERATION BETWEEN LABOR AND MANAGEMENT

Profit-Sharing. — Many companies, like chain stores, pay their managers a salary plus a percentage of profits. And many firms pay their sales force a salary plus a commission on all sales above a specified amount. Others distribute a share of their profits among their employees. For instance, the Procter and Gamble Company with plants all the way across the country distribute to their employees half of the firm's profits — that is, in addition to their regular wages employees receive in profits the same amount that is paid in dividends to those furnishing the capital.

Guaranteed Job Throughout the Year. — For more than a quarter of a century Procter and Gamble have guaranteed regular work to their employees. Their employees are guaranteed 48 weeks of work during a year, provided they have been with the firm for two years, and provided they will accept work available at the rate of pay for the job available, and provided the company may reduce the regular work-week as much as 25%. (But this latter was done only for a short time one year in three plants during a quarter of a century.)

United Press Photo

LABOR AND MANAGEMENT MEET

After an all-night conference in Detroit, officials of the CIO Communication Workers Union and of the Michigan Bell Telephone Company announced a "basic agreement" for ending a five-day strike. This agreement may provide a pattern for avoiding such differences in the future.

This regular work necessitated storage warehouses; but to compensate the factories need only 105% capacity of probable sales. Under the old system 140% capacity was needed to take care of peaks. The employer profits by having a small turnover of workmen, and as a result more efficient work and a uniform and better product. The employee can assume regular income, can buy a home on the installment plan, and can plan education for his children.

A Promising Experiment. — In times of prosperity and rising prices, employers generally urge that wages must be stabilized to curb rising prices. Workers, on the other hand, usually argue that prices must be stabilized in order to make higher wages unnecessary. In times of recession and falling prices, employers tend to reduce wages and try to maintain them or slow the decline. In both situations the consumer is caught in the squeeze between the contending forces.

A new and promising experiment in adjusting wages to the rise and fall of prices is being conducted by several companies and their employees — especially under the contract between the General Motors Corporation and the United Auto Workers. Under the scheme wages are automatically adapted to the rise or fall of the Bureau of Labor Statistics' consumers' price index.

This "escalator" or "sliding scale" plan has worked successfully for over five years now. Many of the new union-management contracts are now incorporating the idea.

QUESTIONS ON THE TEXT

1. What is the life expectancy of a white male child born today? What was it 50 years ago?

2. How many people are over age 65 in the United States today? How many were there in 1900?

3. What is the rate of selective service rejection for physical and mental causes?

4. How many people die in the United States each year?

5. Why is the shortage of doctors and hospitals so serious a problem?

6. Give arguments for and against government health insurance.

7. Why do governments assist private capital in building houses?

8. What is the F. H. A.? The P. H. A.? Explain the functions of each.

9. Explain how the Federal Housing Administration makes more private capital available for the building of private homes and apartment projects.

10. Explain Procter and Gamble's system of profit sharing and guaranteed job.

PROBLEMS FOR DISCUSSION

1. Doctor Carl Kelsey has grouped the causes of poverty into three main classes:

(1) *Environmental:*

    a. Adverse physical environment: polar regions, tropics, deserts, swamps.

    b. Disasters: flood, earthquake, fire, famine.

(2) *Personal:*

    a. Physical defects: feeble-mindedness, insanity, blindness.

    b. Moral defects: dishonesty, laziness, shiftlessness, etc.

    c. Intemperance.

    d. Licentiousness.

    e. Sickness.

    f. Accident.

(3) *Social:*

    a. Industrial changes affecting the worker: changes of location of trade, inventions, strikes.

    b. Exploitation.

    c. Race prejudice.

    d. Sickness, death, desertion, crime of natural supporter.

    e. Defective sanitation.

    f. Defective educational system.

    g. Bad social environment.

    h. War.

    i. Unwise philanthropy.

What are the chief causes of poverty in your immediate neighborhood? Which of these various causes enumerated are secondary to some primary trait of character or habit; for instance, lack of foresight and frugality? Drunkenness? Lack of religious or moral training?

2. How many of the conditions mentioned below have you observed? Discuss them.

"Intemperance cuts down youth in its vigor, manhood in its strength, and age in its weakness. It breaks the father's heart, bereaves the doting mother, extinguishes natural affections, erases conjugal love, blots out filial attachments, blights parental hope, and brings down mourning age in sorrow to the grave. It produces weakness, not strength; sickness, not health; death, not life. It makes wives widows, children orphans, fathers fiends, and all of them paupers and beggars. It feeds rheumatism, nurses gout, welcomes epidemics, invites cholera, imports pestilence, and embraces consumption. It covers the land with idleness, misery, and crime. It fills your jails, supplies your almshouses, and demands your asylums. It engenders controversies, fosters quarrels, and cherishes riots. It crowds your penitentiaries, and furnishes victims to your scaffolds. It is the life-blood of the gambler, the element of the burglar, the prop of the highwayman, and the support of the midnight incendiary. It countenances the liar, respects the thief, esteems the blasphemer. It violates obligations, reverences frauds, and honors infamy. It defames benevolence, hates love, scorns virtue, and slanders innocence. It incites the father to butcher his helpless offspring, and helps the husband to massacre his wife, and the child to grind the parricidal axe. It burns up men, consumes women, detests life, curses God, and despises heaven. It suborns witnesses, nurses perjury, defiles the jury-box, and stains the judicial ermine. It degrades the citizen, debases the legislator, dishonors the statesman, and disarms the patriot. It brings shame, not honor; terror, not safety; despair, not hope; misery, not happiness. And with the malevolence of a fiend, it calmly surveys its frightful desolation, and unsatisfied with its havoc, it poisons felicity, kills peace, ruins morals, blights confidence, slays reputation, and wipes out national honors." — Robert Ingersoll.

3. There is an old proverb to the effect that a democracy will eat itself up: that the improvident majority will confiscate the wealth of the provident minority by taxation and consume the wealth. Is this as likely in this day of surpluses as in past ages when there was a scarcity?

4. Do you agree with the following statement? "Property is the fruit of labor; property is desirable, is a positive good in the world. That some should be rich shows that others may become rich, and hence is just encouragement to industry and enterprise. Let not him who is houseless pull down the house of another, but let him work diligently and build one for himself, thus by example assuring that his own shall be safe from violence when built." — Abraham Lincoln.

5. Profit sharing is an incentive for loyalty and for a greater output by employees. Can you give an example where it is now being practiced? Should investors taking the risk of a new industry be entitled to more than the average rate of interest? If a company loses money one year, should it make that up before sharing profits in subsequent years?

6. "Featherbedding" is a "make-work" practice requiring pay for work not actually done. Some unions have succeeded in writing the plan into contracts with employers. A good example is a contract with a musicians' union which required a radio station to pay full-scale wages to "stand-by" members of the union who did nothing whenever the station presented a program of amateur musicians. Do members of the class know other examples?

7. The United Mine Workers, under John L. Lewis, may retire on a $100-a-month pension at age 62 provided they have been working in the mines at least 20 years. The money is paid by employers who add the necessary amount to each ton of coal sold. Employees in other industries contribute to their smaller Social Security pensions. Is it a dangerous precedent to allow an industry to tax the consumers as this plan does?

8. Why do you favor or oppose the following proposed Truman Plan for compulsory health insurance?

Health insurance, compulsory for nearly everybody. Workers, employers each pay $1\frac{1}{2}$ per cent pay-roll tax on first $4800 of wages; self-employed pay up to 3 per cent on net income up to $4800.

Medical care, at no additional cost, to include: examinations, doctors' visits; limited dental treatment; 60 days' hospitalization; home-nursing, laboratory, X-ray, ambulance service; expensive medicines, hearing aids, wheel chairs, eye-glasses, crutches and other special appliances.

Federal subsidies for medical schools, students, local health units, hospital construction, rural doctors, etc. Estimated cost of health-insurance benefits: about $6,000,000,000 a year.

SELECT BIBLIOGRAPHY

American Observer, "Rival Medical Plans," January 9, 1950.

BACON, S. "The Facts about Alcoholism." *U. S. News.* October 2, 1953.

CUTLER, A. "Dilemma in the Hospitals." *Nation's Business.* October, 1952.

DIMOCK, M. *Business and Government.* Holt. New York. 1953 ed. Chapters IX, X.

DUBINSKY, D. "How I Handled the Reds in My Union." *Saturday Evening Post.* May 9, 1953.

HARRIS, A. "The Labor Vote: Myth or Margin?" *Nation's Business.* October, 1952.

HOLMAN, F. "They're Adding Years to Your Life." *Collier's.* August 30, 1952. (The National Institutes of Health.)

LANDIS, P. H. "The Changing Family." *Current History*, September, 1950. Pages 151–153.

LEEK, JOHN. *Government and Labor in the United States.* Rinehart. New York. 1952.

MEANY, G. "What Labor Wants." *U. S. News.* November 6, 1953.

OGG, F., AND RAY, P. *Essentials of American Government.* Appleton-Century-Crofts. New York. 1952 ed. Chapters XXIX, XXX.

SWARTHOUT, J., AND BARTLEY, E. *Materials on American National Government.* Oxford Univ. Press. New York. 1952. Nos. 139–143.

THOMPSON, C. L. "Labor's Problem: Real Wages." *Current History*, January, March, April, 1950.

Annual Reports of Federal Security Agency and State Department of Health.

VELIE, L. *"Supermarket Medicine." Saturday Evening Post.* June 20, 1953.

CHAPTER XXXIX

PROGRESSIVE PLANNING

America at Work. — A busy America is a prosperous America. To-day we are a busy people. Our standard of living is the highest in the world's history. We have the technical equipment, the skilled workers, and the natural resources to lift that standard still higher, but to do so, we must plan on a national scale to keep those workers busy.

Progressive planning both in private enterprise and in governmental undertakings is our best insurance against the tremendous loss of income through unemployment and non-production such as marked the depression thirties. We must not waste our resources of men and materials through failure to heed the lessons of those dark years.

The United States has suddenly become the spearhead of the democracies in a world-wide struggle for liberty. It is the only democracy with sufficient population and resources to accept the responsibilities of leadership. Unselfish leadership is costly; and our country must plan not only for itself, but for much of the world as well. We must plan not only for food and clothes and houses, but for an international understanding that will enable us to divert our man-power from defense to a higher standard of living.

Today our problems of planning are complicated by our huge program of defense production. Yet labor and industry, with typical American initiative, are taking this new burden in stride to push total production (military and civilian) to an amazingly high level.

Wartime needs and defense production goals are not necessarily basic to continuing prosperity. That is why our Government has planned and must continue to plan for the years when man-power and natural resources are devoted entirely to peacetime goals.

In all of this planning, every good citizen will keep in mind his duties as well as his rights of citizenship. Our belief in the system of free enterprise as a basic element of our democracy must lead us all to work for that balance of rights and responsibilities without which there is no liberty.

The Council of Economic Advisers, in the Executive Office of the President, is a three-man body appointed by the President and the Senate. It reports periodically to the President on the state of the nation's economy, and assists him in the preparation of his annual Economic Message to Congress. This message, delivered in January of each year, deals with such matters as the levels of employment, taxes, production, and purchasing power, current and possible future economic trends, the Government's economic program, and recommended legislation. The Joint Committee on the Economic Report then considers and reports on the message for possible congressional action.

Federal Grants-in-Aid. — Each year the National Government grants large sums of money to the States and to local governments to assist them in carrying out various public programs. For the fiscal year 1954, these grants-in-aid amounted to about $3,000,000,000 or 4 per cent of the total Federal budget and about 15 per cent of all State and local expenditures.

These funds are usually, but not always, granted on a matching and conditional basis. That is, the National Government agrees to put up so much money provided the States will match that amount with so much and also agree to meet certain conditions in use of the funds.

Take Federal aid for highway construction as an example. As early as 1916 Congress passed the Federal Aid Road Act. That Act directed the Secretary of Agriculture to co-operate with the States in the spending of $75,000,000, over a five-year period, on roads over which the mails were carried. From that rather modest beginning, the grant-aided highway program has grown tremendously.

Grants are now made for major interstate highways and connecting links, for important secondary and feeder roads (farm-to-market roads, school-bus routes, and mail routes), for city highway projects, for the elimination of railroad grade crossings, and for highways on public lands of the United States. Congress authorized the appropriation of $550,000,000 for highway construction aid in fiscal year 1953 and a like amount for 1954.

To be eligible for a grant under this program a State must have a highway department with enough authority and adequate equipment to co-operate with the Public Roads Administration (see pages 304–305). A State must match a Federal grant dollar for dollar. The

States plan the construction and maintenance of the roads, but these plans must be approved by the Public Roads Administration.

This program, with its pooling of Federal and State funds, knowledge, and experience, is providing us with a nationwide network of good highways. And this is of untold importance both to commerce and national defense.

Similarly, under the Federal Airport Act, Congress has authorized the appropriation of $100,000,000 a year to aid State and local governments in the construction of public airports. States' and cities' plans must be approved by the Civil Aeronautics Administration (see page 302) and they must match the Federal grants dollar for dollar. As another example, see the mention of hospital construction grants on page 665.

Planning by Private Industry. — The research laboratories of industry are an outstanding example of free enterprise at work for the common good. All over our land, they are making invaluable contributions to the development of "better things for better living."

Nor does the service of industry limit itself merely to the roles of research and production. It educates the public in the knowledge and use of its products. Colorful advertisements tell the stories of steel, rubber, glass, metals, medicines, and a hundred and one other products that make for a happier, healthier America.

Many other examples of progressive planning by industry will suggest themselves to the thoughtful reader. Some are mentioned in the following pages, and still others may be recalled from their mention in previous chapters. Surely, business and industry are in the forefront of progressive planners for a prosperous America.

Better Cities. — Large portions of our cities need to be rebuilt — not by the square block, but by the square mile. In replanning the cities there is an opportunity to locate schools, libraries, churches, medical clinics, hospitals, and playgrounds appropriately in each community. Convenient spaces may be allotted to local markets and shops. The larger stores, offices, and even factories, with parking spaces in basements, on roofs, and in the interior of office buildings, may be located in the city center. In brief, the city should be zoned.

These great clearance projects are too much for cities to handle alone. Therefore, States may well give cities the right to acquire all property over a wide area at a fair price by right of eminent domain. In the District of Columbia this right exists now. Cities can borrow money at interest rates as low as the National Government because the interest from city bonds is exempt from the United States income tax. Moreover, the National Government now insures loans for slum-clearance and low-rent housing projects.

Naturally, when a city decides to rebuild certain areas, it takes title to the land. After any section needed for public purposes is segre-

PART OF A CITY PARK

This is a view of the swimming pool in Oglebay Park, Wheeling, West Virginia. This park contains seven hundred and fifty acres of natural woodland with zoological gardens and picnic grounds — a pleasant place for rest and recreation, free from the rush of the city.

gated, the remainder could be sold for residential purposes and for business, but only after the area is zoned as to use. The city might retain ownership of the land and lease it for long terms if direct sale is not practicable. (See Chapter XXIV.)

How Cities Can Clear Slums. — The New York City Housing Authority is building low-cost housing projects. The Housing Authority sells bonds secured by a city guarantee, and grants an annual cash subsidy from the city occupation tax. It rents apartments at relatively low prices. (See pages 600–602.)

How States Can Assist Private Industry in Clearing Slums. — In 1941 the New York legislature enacted the Urban Development Law allowing cities to trade with private corporations in encouraging them to rebuild slum areas. With this authority New York City induced the Metropolitan Life Insurance Company to clear 72 acres of slums in

BEFORE

Closely crowded, poorly ventilated, poorly lighted houses like these invite disease and misery. The transformation of the area speaks for itself in the accompanying picture.

the lower East Side between 14th and 20th Streets and to build Stuyvesant Town for about 24,000 people. Nearly three fourths of the area is airy, open space. Main thoroughfares curve around the town. There are no back yards. It is like a big park. Curving access roads will not cross the project, so there is no through traffic. Garages are underground and are approached from the bordering avenues. Rentals average about $17 a room monthly. Compensation will permit the replacement of schools and churches.

The old property was taken by right of eminent domain, under the city's authority to condemn property in substandard unsanitary areas on behalf of a private business. Also the city agreed that for twenty-five years the insurance company will pay taxes on the valuation of the slum property destroyed instead of on the new property. And the city surrendered streets needed for the project in exchange for wider avenues surrounding it. With similar encouragement, the Equitable Life Assurance Society built the Clinton Hill project in Brooklyn. (See also pages 601–602.)

AFTER

The once dirty, unattractive neighborhood is now an area of neat, healthy homes. Slums are surely on the way out, now that good housing has become a national concern.

How the Federal Government Can Assist Private Industry in Clearing Slums. — Colonial Village in Harlem, New York City, with rooms originally estimated to rent at about $12.50 a month, is being financed by seven New York savings banks. In addition to the privileges granted the insurance company projects, the Federal Housing Administration was willing to insure the bank investments to the extent of 80%.

Local Business Men Can Co-operate in Creating Work and Improving the City with Reconstruction Finance Corporation Assistance. — A good illustration of helping the city by this method is the building of

the Union Square Garage in San Francisco. Lack of parking space
was hurting business near Union Square Park, so business men and
professional men formed the Union Square Garage Corporation and
built an immense garage beneath the park. The four underground
levels provide space for 1700 cars. To build the garage it was necessary to make a 50-foot excavation, but the park was restored to its
former beauty, with monument and trees as before.

UNION SQUARE GARAGE, SAN FRANCISCO

Traffic congestion hurts business. This underground garage with space for 1700
cars on four levels, located in the center of downtown San Francisco, suggests one
way of solving the traffic problem in city business areas.

The directors of the corporation sold $680,000 worth of 6% cumula-
tive preferred stock, at $100 a share, to merchants, hotels, theaters, and
professional people within three blocks of the square, and to conces-
sionaires. The Reconstruction Finance Corporation then lent $850,-
000 on a first mortgage. One hundred shares of common stock were
issued and given to San Francisco, which receives a token rental of
$5000 a year plus $15,000 in taxes. When the RFC loan is paid off in
21 years and the preferred stock is retired, ownership of the garage re-
verts to the city — at no cost.

Better Education. — A true democracy cannot rise above the level of its citizenry. The success of a democracy depends upon the intelligence, education, moral stamina, and patriotism of its people. For much of this we depend upon our schools; and yet we spend only half as much on education as for alcoholic drinks, and less than for tobacco. In our public schools we assign, on the average, thirty-five pupils to the teacher. A playground director might handle this number efficiently for group play, but how can one teacher give needed individual attention to thirty-five youngsters, some of whom are in school because the law requires it, and some in underprivileged areas who come from homes that do little to supplement the teacher's efforts?

According to the United States Office of Education, there are just over 1,000,000 public school teachers in the United States. Yet, in the fall of 1953, elementary schools, as we have read, were more than 50,000 teachers short of the minimum felt necessary for adequate instruction and supervision. Dr. Earl J. McGrath, former U.S. Commissioner of Education, commented: "We just haven't been graduating enough teachers to fill the many thousands of positions which record elementary school enrollments are creating." Higher salaries, comparable to those available in other fields, would help to raise the standard of teaching and persuade many to remain in the teaching profession.

All normal youth should have a high school education, or its equivalent in a church school or private school. This should include a thorough grounding in English composition for lifetime utility; a well-rounded course in the social sciences so they can vote intelligently; and an appreciation of good literature and periodicals to insure a wholesome lifetime enjoyment for leisure hours. Other courses might be more or less elective according to vocational abilities and interests, preparing some for college and the professions and others for nonprofessional vocations.

Every first-class city should have a vocational school above high school for those not going to college. A youth should not specialize unduly in high school, but should have that special training available after having had his basic work in high school.

Conservation and Reclamation Projects. — Conservation of our natural resources is an important consideration in any long-range planning for the nation's welfare. Consider, as an example, the pressing problem of southern California. The Los Angeles area is forced to bring huge quantities of water from reservoirs in the Sierra Nevadas (170 miles away) and the Colorado River (270 miles distant). Still, as population and industry continue to grow, the level of the local water table sinks. Indeed, the problem is so serious that the City of Los Angeles is said to have a standing offer of a $1,000,000 reward

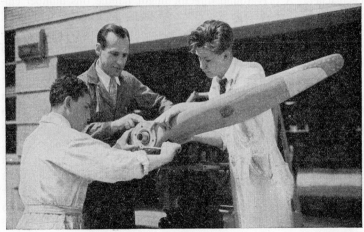

Courtesy New York Board of Education

INDIVIDUAL INSTRUCTION

to anyone who can provide a practical and economic method for providing fresh water from the abundant salt water of the Pacific. (In 1952 Congress appropriated $2,000,000 for a five-year study of the problem of converting salt to fresh water.)

The work of the Bureau of Reclamation (pages 265–270) shows what excellent results can be had by careful planning in this field. But our basic problem in the field of natural resources is actually a double-barrelled one: we must continue our efforts to make new resources available and at the same time we must preserve those that we now have and use.

On the other hand, whenever Government projects encroach or seem to encroach on undertakings which private enterprise regards as its own field, there is always controversy. Arguments pro and con may sooner or later reach the stage of legal decision, but the question is always an open one as to how far the Government should go in exploiting natural resources in competition with private enterprise. This controversy is particularly pronounced in the case of power projects. There are those who maintain that the Government should not engage in power projects because to do so stifles private initiative; others assert that Government power means cheaper power, with the resulting development of many new industries and thousands of new jobs.

The Tennessee Valley Authority is the best example of a regional development financed by the National Government through a publicly-owned corporation. This T. V. A. is administered by three appointees of the President known as the Authority. It developed all the water power of the Tennessee River, building dams at planned locations to install locks which extended navigation six hundred miles. It also built storage dams which reduced floods at Chattanooga by ten feet and Mississippi floods by two feet, and supplied water for power and navigation during the summer. Also the Government planted trees and shrubs and grasses to prevent the rain from running off as gulley washers, which produce barren hills. It is the well-rounded program that makes this project outstanding.

The Missouri Valley Project, like the T. V. A., has to do with power plants, navigation, and flood control; and also with irrigation. It is difficult to co-ordinate the use of a river for irrigation, power, and navigation during the dry season.

The Missouri project is not handled by a single authority, as the T. V. A. is, but by the Reclamation Service and by Army Engineers. These two branches of the Government do not always agree, for the Reclamation Service is especially interested in irrigation and the Army Engineers are more interested in power, navigation, and flood control. Also as the project touches ten states, there are many governors and congressmen to please.

The St. Lawrence Seaway and Power Project has been a dream for more than fifty years. It involves the construction of a series of locks that would link the Great Lakes to the Atlantic Ocean and a power project that would provide more energy than Boulder or Grand Coulee.

The seaway would open an artery to the heart of the Continent for ocean-going vessels up to 20,000 tons. Seventeen locks are required to overcome the 600-foot drop in the water level between Lake Superior and the Atlantic. Nine of these already exist. Deep-draft

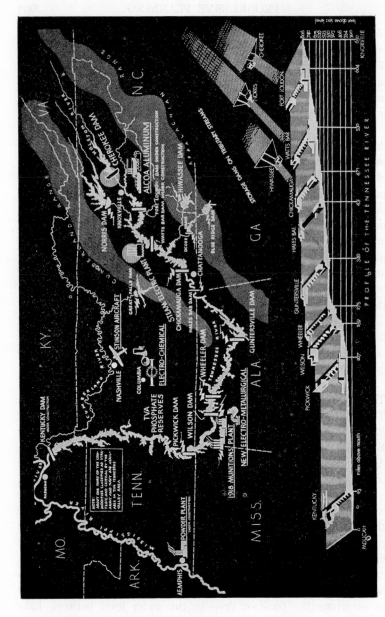

GOVERNMENT POWER AND INDUSTRIAL DEVELOPMENTS OF THE TENNESSEE VALLEY AUTHORITY

ocean-going vessels now navigate the 1000 miles up the St. Lawrence River to Montreal. And similar ships ply the Great Lakes from Ogdensburg, New York, to Duluth, Minnesota. Thus the only major construction required is in the 120-mile stretch of the river between Ogdensburg and Montreal.

The power project involves the construction of a dam and hydro-electric power plant at the International Rapids between Massena, New York, and Cornwall, Ontario. In late 1953 President Eisenhower authorized the New York State Power Authority to act as the official agent of the United States in constructing the project in cooperation with the Ontario Hydro-Electric Power Commission.

The project will produce more than 12 billion kilowatt-hours of energy a year. This energy is to be divided equally between New York and Ontario; and New York must make a "fair share" of the power available to neighboring States within economical transmission distances. New York's half of the energy produced will add 10 per cent to the power supply now available to practically all of New England and the eastern two-thirds of New York.

The total cost of this power project is estimated at $600,000,000. New York plans to finance its share of the construction through the sale of $135,000,000 in revenue bonds to be retired within 50 years.

Proposals for joint United States-Canadian development of the seaway and power projects have been before Congress for the past several years, in fact through most of the present century. All recent Presidents have favored the plan. It has enthusiastic favor through-out most of the Midwest. It is favored by both the C. I. O. and the A. F. of L. On the other hand, the railroads, fearing loss of business to the seaway, private power companies, the coal industry and the United Mine Workers, and the port interests of the Atlantic and Gulf Coasts are generally opposed to the plan.

Congress in 1953 again failed to approve joint United States-Canadian development of the St. Lawrence. Now, as noted above, New York and the Province of Ontario are going ahead with the con-struction of the power project. Congressional leaders hope to secure approval for the seaway in 1954. Under present plans, if Congress does not act, Canada plans to construct the seaway by herself and in her own territory. If this happens, proponents in this country claim that tolls paid by Americans will, in effect, pay for the seaway.

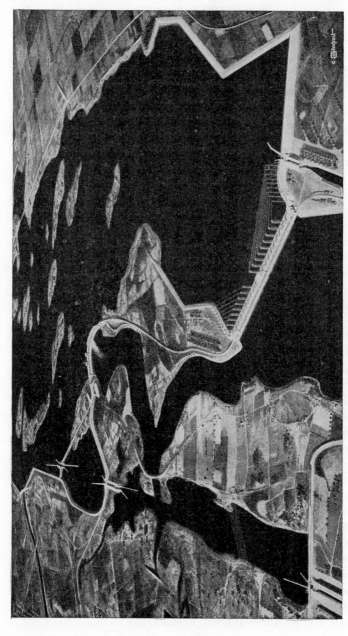

PROPOSED ST. LAWRENCE HYDROELECTRIC PROJECT

Plans include construction of a hydroelectric plant (center foreground), a dam (white curve, center), and locks (left background).

A Sound National Economy. — Our national economy weathered the storms of World War II and the post-war period of readjustment. But the economic seas are still rough. Once again we are in the midst of a defense boom.

This boom is a result of vast governmental defense spending. We must be prepared to defend ourselves against any possible military attack from abroad. But, at the same time, we must be prepared to defend ourselves against an economic attack at home. Radical movements thrive upon discontent and poverty; therefore, inflationary pressures must be held in check. If prices and profits outstrip wages, or if prices, profits, and wages rise unchecked, economic chaos may follow.

Two dependable safeguards are available to check inflation (page 220); one is America's amazing ability to increase production; the second is the use of certain economic controls such as credit restrictions and price ceilings, excess profits taxes, and wage controls. On the other hand, economic controls destroy the incentive to production if they become so restrictive that they stifle the exercise of private initiative and free enterprise. Yet in times of national emergency our nation readily accepts such restrictions, as was shown by the prompt passage of the heavy excess profits tax in December, 1950.

In general, the American idea is for governmental controls and projects to aid private industry, not to compete with it. Wherever possible, the contract system should be used for Government projects, with the employees hired by the contractor. The United States should become a nation of skilled workers rather than a nation of unskilled "reliefers."

QUESTIONS ON THE TEXT

1. What is the Council of Economic Advisers? The President's Economic Message? The Joint Committee on the Economic Report?
2. What is meant by "grants-in-aid"? Give examples.
3. Give examples of planning by private industry.
4. How can the Federal Government assist in the rebuilding of our cities? The States? Private industry and groups?
5. How can education be improved through better salaries for teachers?
6. What is the double-barrelled problem in the field of natural resources?
7. Explain the St. Lawrence Seaway and Power Project.

PROBLEMS FOR DISCUSSION

1. What arguments can you give for and against Federal grants-in-aid to the States and local governments?

2. Why is it desirable for private industry to solve as much of the unemployment problem as possible?

3. What worthwhile problems could your State undertake?

4. Is your city modern and well planned? How could it be improved?

5. What kinds of Federal projects do you consider the most desirable? Explain.

6. Why is a high wage standard necessary to maintain our American way of life?

SELECT BIBLIOGRAPHY

BEETLE, D. "What a Highway They're Building!" *Saturday Evening Post*, March 7, 1953. (New York's $500,000,000 Thruway.)

DINNEEN, J. "Safer Highways." *Collier's*, August 23, 1952.

EMERSON, W. "The New New Orleans." *Collier's*, November 29, 1952.

FERGUSON, J. AND McHENRY, D. *The American System of Government*. McGraw-Hill. N.Y. 1953 ed. Chapter 28.

MERSON, B. "Insurance Companies: What Do They Do with All That Money?" *Collier's*, August 2, 1952.

SLICHTER, S. H. "No More Big Depressions!" *Coronet*, July, 1950, pages 28–31.

SWISHER, C. *The Theory and Practice of American National Government*. Houghton Mifflin. Boston. 1951. Chapters 25–29, 36–38.

Tennessee Valley Resources: Their Development and Use. Tennessee Valley Authority. Knoxville, Tenn. 1947.

THRUELSEN, R. "New York's Deepest Tunnel." *Sat. Eve. Post*, March 25, 1950.

WELLS, G. "Ice-Age Reservoir on the Columbia." *New York Times Magazine*, May 4, 1952.

U. S. News. "Next Quarter Century in U. S." July 4, 1952.

CHAPTER XL

THE UNITED NATIONS AND BASES FOR A LASTING PEACE

The United Nations. — Physically, this is "one world" whether we like it or not. It took the *Mayflower* sixty days to make its difficult way across the Atlantic: today the trip is less than one day's com-

UNATIONS

UNITED NATIONS HEADQUARTERS AND MIDTOWN MANHATTAN SKYLINE

The UN buildings are, left to right, the Secretariat, the Conference Area, and the General Assembly Hall. This is the view from the East River.

fortable air journey. Politically, however, the world has not caught up with this physical fact.

We know that political upheaval or military aggression anywhere in the world threatens our own national security. The unsettled world of today makes it essential that we and our friends maintain armed forces adequate to our defense and to the preservation of world peace.

But the only sure way to prevent war is to eliminate the causes for war. To this end, we and most of the other nations of the world created the United Nations at the close of the Second World War.

The San Francisco Conference, attended by delegates from fifty Allied Nations, met in 1945 and drafted the United Nations Charter. The United States was the first nation to ratify and by 1954 there were sixty member states. The organization established its permanent headquarters in New York City when John D. Rockefeller, Jr., gave it an $8,500,000 six-block tract on the East River. The Congress authorized a loan of $65,000,000 for construction and the new headquarters opened in 1951.

United Nations Charter

Purpose: To promote international peace and the general welfare of all peoples.

Membership: The General Assembly, upon recommendation of the Security Council, may admit any "peace-loving" state.

General Assembly: It consists of not exceeding 5 representatives chosen by the government of each member state; but each state has only one vote. The General Assembly has power to:

Discuss international peace problems, and make recommendations to the Security Council or to the governments of the member states.

Initiate studies and make recommendations regarding international law and its codification.

Initiate studies and make recommendations regarding cultural, health, social, educational, and economic welfare.

Consider and approve the budget; and apportion the expenses among the member states. (U.S. share: about one-third.)

Elect non-permanent members of the Security Council.

Decisions of the General Assembly on important questions are made by a two-thirds majority of those present and voting.

Security Council: It consists of 11 members — 5 permanent members (Great Britain, France, Russia, China, and the United States) and 6 other members elected by the General Assembly for terms of two years.

Decisions on procedural matters are made by an affirmative vote of 7 members; and on other matters by an affirmative vote of 7 members

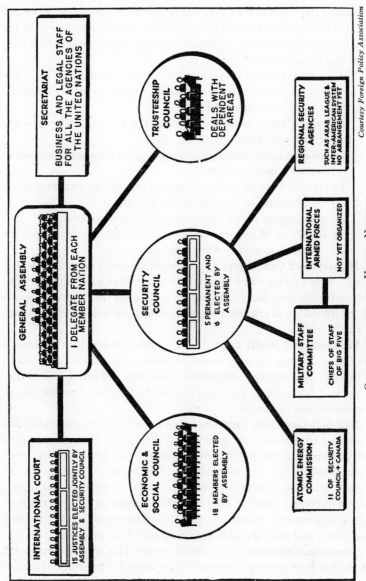

ORGANIZATION OF THE UNITED NATIONS

Courtesy Foreign Policy Association

including the votes of the 5 permanent members. Thus on important actions the Security Council must have the unanimous consent of the Big Five; and the success of the organization depends upon the friendship and co-operation of these 5 powers.

The Security Council is organized to function continuously. Each member must be represented at all times at the seat of the organization. The Security Council has power:

To submit plans to the members of the United Nations for the regulation of armaments.

To consider international disputes on which the states themselves have been unable to agree.

To take such action as is necessary to prevent international wars:

(a) by severance of international relations;

(b) by stoppage of transportation and communication; or

(c) by action of air, sea, or land forces, that the members have agreed to supply when needed.

Military Staff Committee: It consists of the chiefs of staff of the Big Five. Other states asked to supply force are associated with the committee for the time being. It advises and assists the Security Council in the regulation of armament or disarmament, or in the use of military force.

Economic and Social Council: This body, chosen by the General Assembly, studies cultural, social, economic, educational, and health problems; may set up commissions; and may call international conferences. Its findings are reported to the General Assembly or to member states for action.

Non-Self-Governing Territories: Self-governing commonwealths like Canada and Australia are members of the United Nations; but non-self-governing territories like Wake Island and Bermuda are given some consideration by the Charter. The governing states, like the United States and Great Britain, are required to make regular reports to the Secretary-General regarding the progress of these territories. These reports may constitute a basis for discussion in the General Assembly, and resulting public opinion may force progress.

Trusteeship Council: This council consists of a member from each of the Big Five and one from each of the other United Nations administering "trust territories" with an equal number of members elected by the General Assembly from other member states.

"Trust Territories" may be one of three kinds: (1) those held under mandate (created by the League of Nations), (2) those that were detached from enemy states at the end of World War II, and (3) others voluntarily placed under the system. None of these territories become "trust territories" except through agreement with the governing state.

UNATIONS

KITCHENS AT UNITED NATIONS HEADQUARTERS

Some members of the UN Secretariat Staff visit the newly-opened kitchens serving the Headquarters' cafeteria.

The purpose of the Trusteeship Council is to promote justice and welfare for natives and equal trade opportunities for members of the United Nations. It prepares questionnaires and considers reports from the administering states; and provides for periodic inspection trips to the respective trust territories at times agreed upon with the administering authority.

The Secretariat: This branch consists of a Secretary-General, the chief administrative officer, and his staff. The Secretary-General is appointed by the General Assembly on the recommendation of the Security Council, and he appoints his own staff.

The Secretary-General is a sort of executive secretary for the General Assembly, Security Council, Economic and Social Council, and the Trusteeship Council. His chief duty is to bring to the attention of the Security Council any matter that threatens peace.

Every international agreement entered by a member state must be published by the Secretariat. If not reported it does not have international standing.

International Court of Justice: The court consists of 15 members elected by the General Assembly and the Security Council (voting separately) for terms of 9 years (and may be re-elected). The seat of

the Court is at The Hague, but the Court may divide and sit elsewhere. Salaries are fixed by the General Assembly, are paid by the United Nations, and are not taxable.

Only states (members of the United Nations or non-members) may be parties in cases before the Court. The jurisdiction of the Court comprises all cases which the parties voluntarily refer to it and all matters specially provided for in the Charter of the United Nations or in treaties in force.

UNATIONS

DAG HAMMARSKJOLD, SECRETARY-GENERAL OF THE UNITED NATIONS

The official languages of the Court are French and English, but a party to a suit may use another language if it so requests. Decisions are made by majority vote.

The Court may give an advisory opinion on any legal question when requested by the General Assembly or the Security Council, or by other organs of the United Nations with the consent of the General Assembly.

Amendments: Amendments to the Charter are proposed by two thirds of the members of the General Assembly (or two thirds of an international conference) and ratified by two thirds of the member states, including all of the Big Five.

If a general conference is not held to revise the Charter before the tenth session (1955) of the General Assembly, this session must vote on the holding of such a conference; and the conference must be held if so decided by a majority of the members of the General Assembly and any seven members of the Security Council.

Charter Not Applicable to Action against World War II Enemies: The enemy states in World War II were not invited to membership in the United Nations by the fifty Allied Nations that met at San Francisco; and the Charter expressly places no restrictions on the actions taken by Allied Nations concerning Germany, Japan, and the other recent enemy nations.

Courtesy Royal Dutch Air Lines

THE PEACE PALACE AT THE HAGUE

This courthouse was built half a century ago by Andrew Carnegie for the settlement of international disputes voluntarily submitted to a so-called court set up by a peace conference held at The Hague. Inside is a beautiful reproduction of the Christ of the Andes.

The Charter Gives Very Limited Powers to the United Nations. — The organization is not a federation of states. It is more like the League of Nations; more like the American Confederation (1777–1789) which failed for lack of adequate powers, and was replaced by our strong central federation of states.

The most immediate problem facing the world today is the creation of a just and lasting peace. Current American foreign policy centers on the United Nations because, weak as it is, it offers the best hope for realizing that peace.

THE UNITED NATIONS IN ACTION

Not Perfect but Helpful. — The church hasn't eliminated all sin, the schools haven't eliminated all ignorance, and the United Nations hasn't eliminated all war. But all three of these institutions are more than worth what little money we have put into them. The United Nations was formed to promote world peace — yet the whole world spends less on the United Nations each year than the United States alone spent in one day on World War II.

In its short life thus far the U.N. has not brought an end to world tensions and the threat of a World War III. Because of this, many believe that the U.N. is a failure. But these people may be overlooking one important fact. The U.N. is *not* a world government. Like water which can rise no higher than its source, the U.N. can be no more effective than its members make it.

It is easy to overlook the many accomplishments of the U.N. in its brief existence. Among other things, the U.N. prevented the Soviet Union from seizing the oil fields in northern Iran; it settled an Arab-Jewish war in Palestine and helped to establish the new state of Israel. It helped settle the Dutch-Indonesian war and establish the new United States of Indonesia. It was instrumental in settling the Berlin blockade dispute and stopped the fighting between India and Pakistan over Kashmir. Through the International Court it settled a dispute which arose when a British ship was sunk by an Albanian mine.

Through several specialized agencies (international organizations outside of the U.N. but supervised by it) a great deal has also been accomplished. For example, the World Health Organization stopped a cholera plague in Egypt; the Food and Agriculture Organization defeated a chestnut tree blight in Italy; and the International Refugee Organization has aided more than 1,500,000 displaced persons.

The mere fact that nations face one another in open forum before the world is significant in itself. World public opinion can be a powerful force in international relations. When one nation is in the wrong, the rest are already united to defend the right — as in Korea.

To date the United Nations has not banished war and brought lasting peace to the world, but neither has it been a failure.

A United Nations Military Force. — The United Nations Charter provides for a police force to consist of air, land, and sea forces to be furnished by the member states, and subject to call by the Security Council with the unanimous consent of the Big Five. The Council's Military Staff Committee, composed of representatives of the Big Five, has been unable to agree upon a workable plan. So, to date, the United Nations has no military force.

On June 25, 1950, the Security Council (with the Soviet Union absent) called upon "all members to render every assistance" in meeting North Korean aggression. The response demonstrated the effect with which a United Nations military force could operate.

Then, on November 3, 1950, the General Assembly, virtually ignoring the Security Council and overriding the Soviet Union, adopted a resolution placing an international force at its own disposal.

This historic resolution provides that, in cases of aggression in which the Security Council fails to act, the General Assembly may meet within 24 hours. It also calls upon all member states to maintain, within their own armed forces, fully-equipped units available for immediate action at the Assembly's call. *Remember, there is no veto power in the General Assembly.*

The United Nations and Atomic Energy. — For the past eight years the United Nations has wrestled with the problem of the international control of atomic energy. The need for such control is obvious. Man, as Dr. Albert Einstein has observed, now has the knowledge with which to wipe himself off the face of the earth.

In August, 1945, in order to end the Second World War, the United States dropped the first atomic bombs on Japan. The first bomb fell on Hiroshima August 6; a second bomb hit Nagasaki three days later. The Hiroshima bomb caused an explosion equal to that of 20,000 tons of TNT. The blast, flash burn, fires, and falling debris killed 78,150 people, injured 37,425, and left 13,083 missing. Many of the injured later died of radiation sickness. At least 170,000 others were reported ill, homeless, hungry, or indigent. The bombing levelled some five square miles of Hiroshima. The Nagasaki blast was equally severe, leaving 73,884 dead.

Since then, and because of the threat of a third World War, the United States has been stockpiling bombs and other atomic weapons much more destructive than the bombs dropped on Japan. Late in 1953, President Eisenhower declared that today "the United States stockpile of atomic weapons, which, of course, increases daily, exceeds by many times the explosive equivalent of the total of all bombs and all shells that came from every plane and every gun in every theater of war through all the years of World War II."

Since 1949 the Soviet Union also has been producing and stockpiling atomic bonds. In 1952 we completed the first explosion tests of a hydrogen bomb. And in 1953 the Russians claimed to have produced an H-bomb. Atomic scientists have told us that a single H-bomb could destroy New York or any other of the world's great cities.

Soon after the end of the war with Japan, the United States announced its willingness to share its atomic secrets with the rest of the world — *provided* adequate and enforceable international safeguards against destructive use could be established.

Early in 1946 the U.N. created an Atomic Energy Commission, now known as the Disarmament Commission, to work out such safeguards. Bernard Baruch presented the American plan for international control. The Baruch Plan called for an International Atomic Development Authority with broad powers to own and control all atomic production and materials. But the Russians refused to agree to its provisions for strict international inspection and enforcement. Instead, they proposed a plan calling for only limited supervision and inspection.

After two years of deadlock and 220 meetings, and noting that the Soviet bloc would not agree "to even those elements of effective control considered essential from the technical point of view," the Commission adjourned indefinitely. But late in 1953 the General Assembly instructed the Disarmament Commission to make another attempt — this time by having "the powers principally involved . . . seek, in private, an acceptable solution."

Then, on December 8, 1953, President Eisenhower made a dramatic speech to the Assembly. In order to "lead the world out of fear and into peace," he called for the creation of an international atomic energy agency. He proposed that all nations possessing atomic materials make continually increasing contributions from their stockpiles to this agency, a sort of "bank of fissionable materials."

Through these contributions the destructive power of the world's atomic stockpiles would be gradually cut down. And, as a result, the prospects for peace would be considerably improved. Of equal importance, the international agency would use its stockpiles to encourage worldwide scientific investigations into the apparently limitless peacetime uses of atomic energy.

As 1954 opened, even the U.S.S.R. was giving the plan close study.

The United Nations Operates under the Handicap of the Veto. — When the United Nations Charter was written in 1945, our Government insisted upon the veto. At the San Francisco Conference it proposed the present wording of the veto provision to the Soviet Government as a means of securing adherence by that country to the United Nations Charter — and as a means of assuring ratification by the United States Senate.

The veto provision, contrary to the spirit of compromise which gave it birth, has proved an insurmountable road block to effective action by the Security Council. In the first eight years the Russians have used the veto over sixty times in the Security Council. It was originally intended for use only in substantive matters (*e.g.*, sanctions), but the Russians have used it in procedural matters as well.

Courtesy "The New York Times"
THE ROAD BLOCK

INTERNATIONAL BANK

International Bank for Reconstruction and Development, with fifty-four member nations, has an authorized capital of $10,000,000,000, provided chiefly by the United States. The Bank's powers are vested in a Board of Governors and a Director with headquarters in Washington, D. C.

The Bank makes loans to member governments for productive enterprises, including materials for reconstruction, power plants, transportation systems or repairs, and irrigation systems. The first loan was $250,000,000 to France towards her four-year plan for reconstruction and industrialization; and the second was $195,000,000 to the Netherlands to repair war damage and restore production. The Bank may also insure loans to member governments if made through private banks or other investment channels, for which an annual fee is charged. By 1954 over $1,500,000,000 had been loaned to 26 nations.

To obtain funds to lend governments, in addition to the capital stock provided by the members, the Bank issues bonds. By 1954, the Bank had issued $556,000,000 in bonds. Most of these — about $500,000,000 worth — were issued in the United States.

The International Bank for Reconstruction and Development has to make loans on a businesslike basis, because if loans are made on a large scale the funds will have to come from the sale of bonds to American investors; and naturally investors will not buy the Bank bonds unless they expect to get their money back.

For instance, Poland applied for a loan of $600,000,000 with which to buy equipment for her coal mines so she could trade coal for machinery from the west. The loan was withheld. Had this risk been taken by the Bank, American investors, fearing that political influence in Poland might result in the cancellation of debts, would not buy the next bonds offered by the Bank.

International Monetary Fund. — Following the world-wide panic of 1929, Japan lowered the value of its money (yen) so that prices would be low and other parts of the world would buy in Japan. Then the British lowered the value of the pound, the United States created the 60-cent dollar, the French lowered the franc, and the Germans created special marks for trade that outsiders could buy cheap.

To maintain orderly exchange rates member countries agree not to change the value of their money without permission of the International Bank; and loans are made from the Fund to help them maintain the exchange value of their money. In 1949 the Bank allowed countries to devalue their currencies (*e.g.*, Br. pound to $2.80) so that we will buy more from them with dollars which they can use to buy from us.

Loans Made to Foreign Governments Cannot Be Repaid except by Gold, Commodities, or Services. — During the depression of the thirties the *Export-Import Bank* was created by the United States Government (1934) to advance credit to foreign governments for the purchase of our commodities. During the war, the Bank made loans to China and Latin America to stabilize their money, and as a good-neighbor policy. Today loans are made rather cautiously.

Congress made a loan direct to Great Britain of $3,750,000,000 for fifty years at 2% to enable the British to have dollars with which to buy food, equipment for rehabilitation, and similar basic needs.

But no matter to whom the money is lent, it can be repaid only in gold (to be stored at Fort Knox), in commodities, or in services such as water transportation. Inasmuch as our exports have been twice as much as our imports since the war, it is difficult to see how our foreign loans can be repaid. However, we continue to give or lend money to foreign nations for the following reasons:

(1) So their people won't starve and thus become easy prey to our foes.

(2) So they can recover from a war that they helped us to win.

(3) To retain them as friends should a war be waged against the United States.

(4) To build up credits for the day when we have to import most of our oil and certain other raw materials.

(5) Against the day when world competition may be keener and our needs greater.

More exports than imports used to be called "a favorable balance of trade" (especially when we were indebted to Europe); but that procedure now when they are indebted to us may be merely depleting our natural resources. Our fifty-odd billions in lend-lease during the war, and excess exports since the war, have drawn heavily on our timber, oil, iron, high-grade coal easiest to mine, and various other minerals.

AN EDITORIAL COMMENT ON THE EFFECTIVENESS AND VALUE OF THE UNITED NATIONS [1]

On October 24, 1945, governments representing a majority of the world's peoples launched the most ambitious undertaking in recorded history — the United Nations.

In the fall of 1945, hopes were high. The most horrible of wars had just come to a victorious end, and the victors had demonstrated what then appeared to be a desire to work together to prevent future conflicts and to promote economic and social advancement through international cooperation. Today, few are so sanguine. The U.N. itself is at war. On the one side the United States carries the burden of the forces of peace and order. On the other, another U.N. charter member, Russia, is the scarcely concealed aggressor. And at the council table, too, there have been disappointments. Some U.N. undertakings — e.g., the draft convention on freedom of information — seem actually farther from their goal than in 1945.

Naturally, the bright hopes of 1945 have become tarnished as do all such hopes when exposed to the harsh realities of a far-from-perfect world. Many set their sights too high, still have them too high. Such are bound

---

[1] From *The Oregonian* (Portland, Oregon), October 23, 1952. This editorial, under the title "The U.N. Seven Years Old," first appeared the day before the seventh anniversary of the first meeting of the United Nations General Assembly, held October 24, 1945. It is reprinted here with the kind permission of *The Oregonian* because we believe it to be one of the clearest, most concise statements of the value and the true nature of the United Nations as an instrument for promoting international co-operation, peace, and security.

to be disillusioned by U.N. performance. The U.N. is not a world government. It has no means of enforcing the collective will. It has no power
other than that represented separately in its 60 individual member states.
And in each of these — as in the United States — the national interest is
patriotically considered as paramount to the collective interest except where
the two coincide.

It is more productive [now] to take stock of what the U.N. is and what it
has done, rather than what it is not and what it has not done and cannot do.
A few brief references will illustrate our point. The U.N. has been a primary
instrument in preventing or stopping postwar armed strife between the
Dutch and Indonesians in the South Pacific, between India and Pakistan
over Kashmir, between communists and loyal government troops in Greece
and between Israel and the Arab states. In Korea the U.N. cause is a
symbol of resistance to aggression the world over. Meanwhile U.N.
agencies work quietly in less spectacular fields. Dependent children aid
has been extended to 64 countries. U.N. organizations have sparked life-
giving projects in all parts of the world: a penicillin plant near Bombay;
public health compaigns to wipe out malaria, tuberculosis, venereal disease,
plague; the application of science to the improvement of the world's basic
food supplies. . . .

No new vehicle is ever again quite so clean and shining as the day it leaves
the assembly line. But we hazard the suggestion that the U.N. today is a
more serviceable vehicle than when it was new. . . . It has had its shake-
down runs, and its operators are familiar with its capabilities. It should
not be encumbered and weakened by a load it was not designed to carry.
Its mechanism should have solicitous attention, for it is the most adequate
conveyance at hand headed in the direction of international understanding
and amity.

QUESTIONS ON THE TEXT

1. Why is international co-operation more important now than ever
before?

2. When and where was the United Nations Charter drafted?

3. What is the U.N.'s basic purpose? Describe the organization and the
duties of the General Assembly. The Security Council. The Military
Staff Committee. The Economic and Social Council. The Trusteeship
Council, The Secretariat.

4. Has the United Nations been a failure? Explain.

5. What progress has been made toward the international control of
atomic energy? What has been the major stumbling block?

6. Does the United Nations possess a military force?

7. Explain how the veto power works.

8. Distinguish between the International Bank and the International Monetary Fund.

PROBLEMS FOR DISCUSSION

1. Article 109 of the United Nations Charter provides that a conference to review the Charter and propose amendments to it may be called at any time by a two-thirds vote in the Assembly and any seven members of the Security Council. If no such conference is called within ten years (by 1955), the question of calling one must be considered by the tenth annual session (1955) of the General Assembly. One may then be called by a majority vote in the Assembly and a vote of any seven members of the Security Council. Amendments to the Charter must be proposed by a two-thirds vote of the conference and ratified by two-thirds of the member-states, including all of the Big Five.

If, as now appears likely, such a conference is called in 1955 or 1956, what changes would you suggest be made?

2. Why do you agree or disagree with the following statement: The United Nations is a failure. It is falling apart — let it. No rational person really expected it to work anyway. If it fails, then we can put our effort and our money into pursuing our own national interests.

3. In presenting the American plan for international control of atomic energy, Bernard M. Baruch made the following remarks. Discuss them in class.

"We are here to make a choice between the quick and the dead. That is our business. Behind the black portent of the new atomic age lies a hope which, seized upon with faith, can work our salvation. If we fail, then we have damned every man to be the slave of fear. Let us not deceive ourselves. We must elect World Peace or World Destruction.

"Science has torn from nature a secret so vast in its potentialities that our minds cower from the terror it creates. Yet terror is not enough to inhibit the use of the atomic bomb. The terror created by weapons has never stopped man from applying them. For each new weapon a defense has been produced, in time. But now we face a condition in which adequate defense does not exist.

"Science, which gave us this dread power, shows that it *can* be made a giant to help humanity, but science does *not* show us how to prevent its baleful use. . . . We must provide the mechanism to assure that atomic energy is used for peaceful purposes and preclude its use in war."

4. For years it has been proposed that the strategic straits and canals of the world be placed under international control. Such waterways as the

Straits of the Bosporus and Dardanelles, the Kiel Canal, the Panama Canal, the Straits of Gibraltar, and the Suez Canal are involved in such proposals. Locate each of these on a map of the world and explain why they are "strategic." What do you think of the internationalization proposals?

SELECT BIBLIOGRAPHY

BERLE, A. "Our Self-Interest in the United Nations." *Reader's Digest.* July, 1953.

CHASE, E. *The United Nations in Action.* McGraw-Hill. New York. 1950.

DULLES, J. F. "The U.N. Charter." *U. S. News.* September 4, 1953.

GROSS, E. "Answer to the Critics of the U.N." *New York Times Magazine.* April 27, 1952.

"Guide to World Agencies." *U. S. News.* October 24, 1952.

STRATEGIC STRAITS

Courtesy "The New York Times"

Under our international system of "dog eat dog," straits have become terribly expensive. It costs Turkey an army of half a million men to defend the Bosporus-Dardanelles. The British need a fleet to protect the Suez Canal, and Uncle Sam is counting his money to see whether he can afford a $2,000,000,000 bomb-proof Panama Canal.

HAMILTON, T. "U.S. and U.N., the Choices Before Us." *New York Times Magazine*. March 22, 1953.

HARTMAN, F. *Basic Documents in International Relations*. McGraw-Hill. New York. 1950.

KIHSS, P. *The UN: How and When It Works*. Headline Series. Foreign Policy Association. New York. 1951. 35¢.

LAWSON, R. "United Nations: Dilemmas and Discords." *Current History*. April, 1953.

LEONARD, L. *International Organization*. McGraw-Hill. New York. 1951.

LODGE, H. "Don't Sell the U.N. Short." *Newsweek*. October 12, 1953.

LODGE, H. "Why We Need Russia in the U.N." *American Magazine*. August, 1953.

MANGONE, G. *A Short History of International Relations*. McGraw-Hill. New York. 1954.

ROSS, A. Constitution of the United Nations. Rinehart. New York. 1950.

Rotary International. "From Here On!" (The U.N. Charter and analysis.) Rotary International. 15 East Wacker Drive, Chicago. 1952 ed. 35¢.

"Should the U.S.A. Continue to Support the United Nations?" Pro and Con. *Congressional Digest*. August, 1952.

"Should U.S. Policy be Moral?" *Life*. September 29, 1953.

SWARTHOUT, J., AND BARTLEY, E. *Materials on American Government*. Oxford Univ. Press. New York. 1952. Nos. 95–99, 103, 108.

"The National Interest — Alone or With Others?" *Annals* of the American Academy of Political and Social Science. July, 1952.

The United Nations Today. U. S. State Department. Washington, D. C. 1952.

VANDERBOSCH, A., AND HOGAN, W. *The United Nations*. McGraw-Hill. New York. 1952.

World (United Nations monthly). 510 Madison Avenue, N. Y. $4 a year.

Which Way to World Government? Headline Series. Foreign Policy Association. New York. 1950. 35¢.

CHAPTER XLI

THE UNITED STATES IN WORLD AFFAIRS

Our World Today. — Our world today is truly one world when seen through the eyes of science. Radio waves span it with the speed of light. Radar pierces its fogs and storms to guide airplanes in their global flight, and television reaches to its far horizons. New miracles of healing mark the progress of its peoples while new weapons of destruction threaten its civilization. Science has, indeed, made a geographic neighborhood of the world where no nation may live to itself alone or safely usurp the rights of other nations.

Politically, however, we live in a world composed of seventy-odd sovereign states. It is a world still torn with strife, and one in which vast numbers of people still live in abject poverty. It has not yet created an international organization truly capable of "securing and maintaining international peace and security." The members of the "family of nations" have not yet learned to live in harmony with each other. But, it is plain to all that these conditions must be overcome, or civilization itself seems doomed to the awesomely destructive war that science has made possible.

The World Is Divided into Two Armed Camps. — The United States and the Soviet Union, the two most powerful nations in the world, lead the opposing sides in a world-wide struggle, the Cold War. The nations of Western Europe and most other nations are on one side with the United States, while the Soviet Union and her communist satellites are on the other side.

Actually, the struggle between East and West is not between communism and capitalism, as such. It is between the totalitarian communist bloc, headed by the Soviet Union, and the free nations who wish to remain free and democratic.

Since 1945 the Soviet Union has brought more than 500,000,000 people and 7,500,000 square miles of new territory under its control. Some of this vast empire was taken by the Red Army during and immediately after World War II. But most of it has been taken by native Communist parties trained, controlled, and directed by Moscow. These parties and other Communist parties throughout the world are banded together in an organization known as the *Cominform* (Communist Information Bureau) "to co-ordinate the activities of Communist parties on a foundation of mutual agreement."

American foreign policy, opposed to communism and Russian expansion, is based upon collective action through the United Nations. We hold that the U.N. is our best hope for establishing a just and lasting world peace. (See the discussion of American Foreign Policy Today, pages 205–208.)

The United States Has Spent More Than $200,000,000,000 in the East-West Cold War. — Well over eighty per cent of our annual budget of some $65,000,000,000 is due to foreign relations — including world wars and national defense. The Second World War cost the world more than $1,000,000,000,000 — and that figure does not include the tragic cost in lives, human suffering, and property. The cost to civilized progress and in natural resources is beyond calculation.

We Keep Our Powder Dry. — As the President has said: "Our economic and our military strength are our nation's shields — without which peace could never be preserved, nor freedom defended." We sincerely want lasting peace and are working for it; but, at the same time, we realize that we must be able to defend ourselves. In effect, we have taken a leaf from the pages of our own Revolutionary history: "Put your trust in God, my boys, but keep your powder dry."

We have expanded our Army, Navy, Marines, and Air Force. We have stockpiles of critical materials essential to defense; and we now spend more than a hundred times as much on military research as before the last war. On our defense forces alone we spend four times the amount spent on all the branches of the National Government a little over a decade ago.

In providing for security, we have come to the realization that we can no longer "wrap our two oceans around us" in isolation. Of necessity, the world's business has become our business. In halting the march of aggression, we have undertaken the tremendous task of building up our friends and allies in all parts of the world — both economically and militarily.

The Mutual Security Program. — The strengthening of our Allies, both militarily and economically, is the purpose of the Mutual Security

Program. Under its forerunner, the Marshall Plan, the United States helped the democracies of Western Europe to rebuild and strengthen their economies. That program's amazing success has enabled us to shift the major emphasis in our foreign aid program to the military strength of our Allies. But economic aid continues, too, because we realize that economic and military strength are two sides of the same coin. The President has stated the case for foreign aid in these very practical terms: "We need allies, and these allies must be bound to us in terms of their own enlightened self-interest, just as in like terms we are bound to them."

The Point Four Program. — While millions of people are still suffering from the effect of World War II, many millions more are poverty-stricken because they live in backward and underdeveloped areas of the world. Poverty, disease, and ignorance provide fertile soil for the growth of communism with its promises of quick remedies for economic and social ills by change of government.

The Point Four Program is aimed at helping the peoples of these backward and underdeveloped areas to help themselves through the use of the knowledge and technical skills that we now possess.

Essentially, this program takes two forms. One is technical co-operation, the use of American "know-how" and scientific knowledge to help these peoples raise their standard of living. The other is large-scale development of regional resources, involving sizable investments of American capital, both public and private. The Government is guaranteeing private capital against loss, and is also encouraging other nations to invest in this great project.

The North Atlantic Treaty Organization. — Under the North Atlantic Treaty, we have joined with thirteen other nations to form the North Atlantic Treaty Organization. The other NATO members are: Canada, Great Britain, France, the Netherlands, Belgium, Luxembourg, Iceland, Norway, Denmark, Italy, Portugal, Greece, and Turkey. The purpose of the alliance is the mutual defense of its members against possible aggression from *any* source, but particularly from Russia, of course. Should any member be attacked each of the other nations agrees to take "forthwith, individually and in concert with the other parties, such action as it deems necessary, including the use of armed force, to restore and maintain the security of the North Atlantic area." Each member, then, is to take whatever action it deems suitable and in accord with its own constitutional processes.

NATO is a purely defensive alliance. It warns a potential aggressor that an attack will be met with force. (Note that NATO does not bypass the U.N.; it accords with the Charter's recognition of each nation's right of "individual and collective self-defense.")

Under NATO's executive body, the North Atlantic Council, a unified defense force is being built. This force is composed of military, naval and air units drawn from each of the 14 member-nations. The United States is making the largest material contribution to NATO and, as a part of our armed forces contribution, we began sending atomic artillery units to Europe in late 1953 and early 1954.

To supplement the NATO alliance, the United States entered a defense pact with Spain in 1953. Under it, we are granted strategic sea and air bases in Spain in return for economic and military aid.

Germany, the Buffer Between Totalitarianism and Democracy. — At the end of the Second World War, Germany was divided into five parts. Poland incorporated the eastern part; and the other four zones were occupied by Russia, Great Britain, the United States, and France. The city of Berlin is now divided into two zones — one governed by Russia, and the other by the three Western Powers.

Because the Western Allies and Russia were unable to agree on a plan for creating a new, democratic, and unified Germany, each side now has a German government in its own sector. The immediate prospects for a unified Germany are remote, but Germany's geographic location and physical resources make her the key to Europe's future.

In order to bring at least a democratic West Germany back into the family of nations, the Western Powers concluded a peace contract with the German Federal Republic in 1952. Under it, the government at Bonn gained almost complete control over West German affairs.

The West is now attempting to bring a strictly-controlled German army into the NATO defense force. But our basic problem remains: How to create a strong, productive Germany on the side of freedom.

The Schuman Plan, for the pooling of Western Europe's coal and steel industries, became a reality in 1952. France, West Germany, the Netherlands, Belgium, Luxembourg, and Italy joined to create a common market in coal and steel. In effect, they have erased national boundaries insofar as these industries are concerned. This may prove to be the first major step in the creation of a West European federation.

Yugoslavia, a New Buffer State. — In mid-1948, declaring that Yugoslavia was no longer an "economic colony" of Russia, Tito broke with Moscow and the Cominform.   Though still Communist, Yugoslavia has followed a nationalistic policy of independence from Moscow

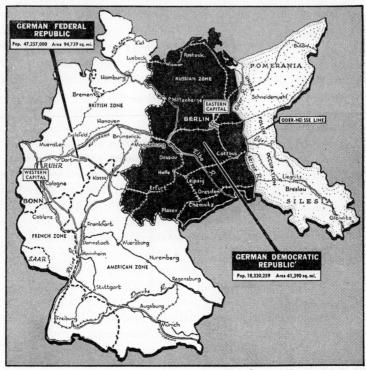

Courtesy "The New York Times"

The Two Germanys of Today

control.   Since the break, Moscow and the Cominform have bitterly opposed the Tito regime.   But the Yugoslavs have shown that a communist state can defy the Kremlin and yet continue to exist.

We and our Allies are making the most of this split.   By extending economic and military aid, stepping up trade, and generally encouraging Yugoslavia we hope to keep her friendly to the West.   We hope, also, that her experience will help encourage opposition to communist oppression in the remaining satellite countries of Eastern Europe.

Greece, Turkey, and the Truman Doctrine. — A glance at the map will readily show the strategic importance of Greece and Turkey. They lie to the south of Russian-dominated Eastern Europe and block direct Soviet access to the Mediterranean. From either one, the Mediterranean, the Suez Canal, and the oil-rich Middle East can be controlled.

Shortly after World War II a civil war broke out in Greece. Communist guerrillas, supplied and given refuge by Albania, Bulgaria, and Yugoslavia, attempted to overthrow the Greek Government. At the same time, Great Britain announced that she could no longer afford to maintain troops in Greece, even though the Greeks had requested them.

Meanwhile Turkey was in danger of attack. Russia was demanding, among other things, that she be given a share in the control and defense of the Turkish Straits — a long-time Russian ambition. Russia also revived an old claim to portions of Turkish territory and launched a propaganda campaign against the Turkish Government.

This was the situation when, in March, 1947, President Truman went before a joint session of Congress and announced what has come to be known as the Truman Doctrine, a proposal to send economic and military aid to Greece and Turkey. But, more than that, it was the announcing of an American policy of supporting "free peoples who are resisting attempted subjugation by armed minorities or by outside pressures."

Since then we have provided economic and military assistance to both nations. At a cost of less than $3,000,000,000 Greece and Turkey have been saved to the West. Greece has long since beaten the Communist guerrillas, and her economy has improved tremendously. And Turkey is now our strongest ally in the Middle East.

Oil Makes the Middle East Important to the Great Powers. — Oil is essential to a modern industrial society — in peace or war. In the United States we are rapidly exhausting our supplies. The oil fields of Iran, Iraq, and Saudi-Arabia contain over two-fifths of the world's proved oil reserves. In a normal year these fields provide 80 per cent of Europe's needs.

Until Iran nationalized her oil fields in 1951, Britain held important concessions there. American companies have gained important concessions in Saudi-Arabia by paying a high royalty to King Ibn Saud

on each barrel pumped. Russia has consistently demanded concessions from Iran. In addition to oil, the Middle East is a vital stake
because of its strategic location in respect to air bases and shipping,
and as a Mediterranean outlet for Russia.

Israel. — When the British withdrew from Palestine in 1948, the new
Jewish state of Israel was born. In the midst of Arab states this new
republic has been receiving American aid and support.

The United States, Great Britain, and France are working to set up
a Middle East Defense Command somewhat similar to NATO, but
progress has been slight to date.

The Far East in Ferment. — The peoples of the Far East make up
more than half of the total population of the world. And most of
these people are in the throes of political, economic, and ideological
unrest — a revolution against poverty and against centuries of foreign
domination. The populations of already overpopulated India,
China, Japan, and other areas are still increasing at the rate of tens of
millions a year. The United States is providing economic aid to many
of the countries of the Far East. But the problems of the Orient are
so vast that stable conditions there cannot be expected for years to
come — a fact the Communists well know and play upon.

China. — Until recent years, we had always maintained close ties
of friendship and trade with China. When Japan attacked China we
sent help for this reason and also because we did not want a strong
Japan in the Far East. After World War II, we attempted to concili-
ate the Nationalist-Communist civil war. But to no avail. The
former Nationalist Government under Chiang Kai-shek now occupies
Formosa off the Chinese mainland. The Chinese Communists, under
Mao Tse-tung, now rule China, working closely with the Soviets.

The fact that the Chinese Reds fought against us in the Korean
War and that they continue to obstruct a peaceful solution to Asia's
problems has stiffened American opposition. We oppose the Communists' claim to membership in the United Nations and continue to
recognize the Nationalists as the legal Government of China.

Japan. — The seven-year Allied occupation of Japan, which ended
in 1952, was largely conducted by the United States. During the
period of occupation the Japanese people complied fully with the
terms of surrender and established a truly democratic government.

The United States ratified a treaty with Japan, in 1952, as did most of the other Allies.   The treaty legally ended the war against Japan and re-admitted her to a place among the family of nations.   Japan has pledged never to wage aggressive war again, to settle her international disputes peacefully, and to support the United Nations in its efforts to maintain peace.   A mutual defense pact grants us air, land, and sea bases in the Japanese home islands, and we are working for a re-armed Japan as our strongest ally in the Far East.

The Pacific Mutual Defense Treaties. — In 1952 the United States ratified a mutual defense treaty with the Philippines, and another with Australia and New Zealand.   These treaties simply underscore an already existing friendship and pledge each of the parties to a program of collective security in the Pacific.   Our obligation to the Philippines is clear.   And certainly any attack on Australia or on New Zealand would immediately involve the United States.

India. — The great sub-continent of India and Pakistan is of critical importance to us in the Far East today.   The area, with its teeming millions, vast resources, and huge market, is today the strategic "balance wheel" for all Asia.   We are working very hard to help these new nations achieve their rightful place in the forefront of the world's peace-loving nations.

Korea. — The Korean War, begun by the North Koreans in June, 1950, ended with the signing of a truce on July 27, 1953.   The war pitted the United Nations Command (composed largely of U.S. and South Korean forces, but with troops from 16 nations altogether) against the Russian-trained and -equipped North Korean and Chinese Red armies.

A $2\frac{1}{2}$-mile-wide buffer zone, mostly north of the old boundary of the 38th parallel, separates the armies during the truce.   A Neutral Nations Supervisory Commission polices the truce and manages the disposition of the few U.N. and thousands of communist prisoners who refuse to return to their homelands.

Under the terms of the armistice, a political conference is to be held in an attempt to reach a permanent settlement in Korea.   The negotiations for the actual holding of the conference stalled along through late 1953; but it is fair to observe that stalemated talks in Korea are a far better thing than was stalemated fighting there.

The 37 months and 2 days of bitter fighting did not end in a clear-cut U.N. victory in the sense that the communists were beaten to their knees.   The war cost the United States alone more than 140,000 casualties, including some 28,000 dead or missing, and over $20,000,-000,000.   The South Koreans suffered untold thousands of civilian casualties and practically all of Korea, North and South, was laid waste.

But, despite this, much was accomplished.   The aggressors were repulsed and with much heavier losses.   For the first time in history an international army fought under a common flag to resist aggression. In the hope of preventing World War III communist aggression had to be halted with force somewhere; and there is no way of knowing how far it might have gone had South Korea not been defended.

The Korean War with its tremendous cost to the communists told them, in the most forceful of terms, that the free world, led by the United States, is ready to fight for peace and security.   They know that we most earnestly want a just and lasting peace; but they also know that we prize our freedom far above mere peace.

The war aroused and united the free world.   Only history can judge how effective Korea was in preventing another global conflict. But the free world is strong today and growing stronger all the time.

The United States began its life with the Declaration of Independence.   Today, as then: "We hold these truths to be self-evident: that all men are created equal; that they are endowed by their Creator with certain unalienable Rights; that among these are Life, Liberty, and the pursuit of Happiness.   That to secure these rights, Governments are instituted among Men, deriving their just powers from the consent of the governed. . . ."

We have become a leader among nations and we have accepted the responsibilities that this position has thrust upon us.   We are firmly committed to the cause of world peace and the brotherhood of man. We face the future secure in the knowledge that our cause is just.

QUESTIONS ON THE TEXT

1. What have international relations cost the United States?

2. How much territory and how many people have been brought under the domination of Communist Russia since the end of World War II?

3. What is the "keynote" of U. S. aid programs?   Why?   Why are these programs so necessary today?

4. What two nations are rivals for world leadership?

5. What is (1) the Mutual Security Program, (2) the Cominform, (3) the North Atlantic Pact?

6. How is Germany now organized?

7. Describe Yugoslavia as a buffer state.

8. What is the United States doing for Greece, Turkey, and Israel?

9. Explain the present situation, and what we might do for: (1) China, (2) Japan, (3) Korea, and (4) India.

PROBLEMS FOR DISCUSSION

1. Russian Communists are working for an extreme materialistic form of socialism throughout the world — by revolution if necessary. Leaders in the United States are working for the retention of private industry. Each side is endeavoring to retain and to gain as many governments as possible with its point of view. Is the United States justified in supporting other governments in their fight against Communism or should it return to isolationism and attempt to settle the problem here only?

2. In what ways has the United States promoted social justice without communism or radical socialism?

SELECT BIBLIOGRAPHY

BRADLEY, O. "A Soldier's Farewell." *Saturday Evening Post.* August 22, 29, 1953.

"Dulles Outlines U.S. Policy." *U. S. News.* September 25, 1953.

O'DONNELL, J. "Our Two Toughest Allies." *Saturday Evening Post.* August 29, 1953.

RIDGWAY, M. "How Europe's Defenses Look to Me." *Saturday Evening Post.* October 10, 1953.

SHERROD, R. "The Inside Story of the Korean Truce." *Saturday Evening Post.* October 17, 1953.

"The Truce." *Time.* August 3, 1953.

U.S. Department of State. *Foreign Policy Briefs.* Bi-weekly. $1 a year.

"United States Diplomacy." *Current History.* October, 1953.

LEONARD, L. *Elements of American Foreign Policy.* McGraw-Hill. New York. 1953.

PALMER, N., AND PERKINS, C. *International Relations.* Houghton Mifflin. Boston. 1953.

"Long May Our Land Be Bright
With Freedom's Holy Light."

APPENDIX I

THE CONSTITUTION OF THE UNITED STATES

[Recommended by the Philadelphia Convention, September 17, 1787; ratified by the ninth State (Article VII) June 21, 1788; in effect, April 30, 1789]

PREAMBLE [1]

We, the people of the United States, in order to form a more perfect Union, establish justice, insure domestic tranquillity, provide for the common defence, promote the general welfare, and secure the blessings of liberty to ourselves and our posterity, do ordain and establish this Constitution for the United States of America.

ARTICLE I

LEGISLATIVE DEPARTMENT

Section 1. Two Houses

All legislative powers herein granted shall be vested in a Congress of the United States, which shall consist of a Senate and House of Representatives.

Section 2. House of Representatives

1. The House of Representatives shall be composed of members chosen every second year by the people of the several states, and the electors in each state shall have the qualifications requisite for electors of the most numerous branch of the state legislature.[2]

2. No person shall be a Representative who shall not have attained to the age of twenty-five years, and been seven years a citizen of the United States, and who shall not, when elected, be an inhabitant of that state in which he shall be chosen.[3]

3. Representatives and direct taxes shall be apportioned among the several states which may be included within this Union, according to their

---

[1] The Preamble is an introduction to the main subject and assists in interpreting the various clauses that follow by indicating the intentions of the framers of the Constitution.

[2] "Electors" means voters.

[3] The first woman representative, Miss Jeanette Rankin, was elected from Montana in 1916.

731

respective numbers, which shall be determined by adding to the whole number of free persons, including those bound to service for a term of years, and excluding Indians not taxed, *three-fifths of all other persons*.[1] The actual enumeration shall be made within three years after the first meeting of the Congress of the United States, and within every subsequent term of ten years, in such manner as they shall by law direct. The number of Representatives shall not exceed one for every thirty thousand, but each state shall have at least one Representative; and, until such enumeration shall be made, the state of New Hampshire shall be entitled to choose three, Massachusetts eight, Rhode Island and Providence Plantations one, Connecticut five, New York six, New Jersey four, Pennsylvania eight, Delaware one, Maryland six, Virginia ten, North Carolina five, South Carolina five, and Georgia three.

4. When vacancies happen in the representation from any state, the executive authority thereof shall issue writs of election to fill such vacancies.

5. The House of Representatives shall choose their Speaker and other officers; and shall have the sole power of impeachment.

Section 3. Senate

1. The Senate of the United States shall be composed of two Senators from each state [chosen by the legislature thereof] [2] for six years; and each Senator shall have one vote.

2. Immediately after they shall be assembled in consequence of the first election, they shall be divided, as equally as may be, into three classes. The seats of the senators of the first class shall be vacated at the expiration of the second year; of the second class, at the expiration of the fourth year; and of the third class, at the expiration of the sixth year; so that one-third may be chosen every second year; [and if vacancies happen by resignation, or otherwise, during the recess of the legislature of any state, the executive thereof may make temporary appointments until the next meeting of the legislature, which shall then fill such vacancies].[2]

3. No person shall be a Senator who shall not have attained to the age of thirty years, and been nine years a citizen of the United States, who shall not, when elected, be an inhabitant of that state for which he shall be chosen.

4. The Vice-President of the United States shall be President of the Senate, but shall have no vote, unless they be equally divided.

5. The Senate shall choose their other officers, and also a President *pro tempore*, in the absence of the Vice-President, or when he shall exercise the office of President of the United States.

---

[1] The clause in italics, referring to slaves, is superseded by the Thirteenth and Fourteenth Amendments. [2] See Seventeenth Amendment.

6. The Senate shall have the sole power to try all impeachments. When sitting for that purpose, they shall be on oath or affirmation. When the President of the United States is tried, the Chief Justice shall preside; and no person shall be convicted without the concurrence of two-thirds of the members present.[1]

7. Judgment in cases of impeachment shall not extend further than to removal from office, and disqualification to hold and enjoy any office of honor, trust, or profit, under the United States; but the party convicted shall, nevertheless, be liable and subject to indictment, trial, judgment, and punishment, according to law.

Section 4. Elections and Meetings of Congress

1. The times, places, and manner of holding elections for Senators and Representatives, shall be prescribed in each state by the legislature thereof: but the Congress may at any time, by law, make or alter such regulations, except as to the places of choosing Senators.[2]

2. The Congress shall assemble at least once in every year, and such meeting shall be on the first Monday in December,[3] unless they shall by law appoint a different day.

Section 5. Powers and Duties of the Houses

1. Each House shall be the judge of the elections, returns, and qualifications of its own members,[4] and a majority of each shall constitute a quorum to do business; but a smaller number may adjourn from day to day, and may be authorized to compel the attendance of absent members, in such manner, and under such penalties, as each House may provide.

2. Each House may determine the rules of its proceedings, punish its members for disorderly behavior, and, with the concurrence of two-thirds, expel a member.

3. Each House shall keep a journal of its proceedings, and, from time to time, publish the same, excepting such parts as may, in their judgment, require secrecy; and the yeas and nays of the members of either House, on

---

[1] "Two-thirds of the members present" must be at least two thirds of a quorum. There are now 96 senators; 49 is a quorum, hence 33 could convict.

[2] In 1842 Congress provided that representatives should be elected from districts. In 1872 Congress provided that representatives should be elected on the Tuesday after the first Monday in November of every even year. Maine, the only exception to this rule, elects in the late summer, and its election is viewed by some as a political barometer.

[3] Changed to January 3d by Amendment XX.

[4] This provision permits either House to exclude a member-elect by a majority vote.

any question, shall, at the desire of one-fifth of those present, be entered on the journal.

4. Neither House, during the session of Congress, shall, without the consent of the other, adjourn for more than three days, nor to any other place than that in which the two Houses shall be sitting.

Section 6. Privileges of and Prohibitions upon Members

1. The Senators and Representatives shall receive a compensation for their services, to be ascertained by law, and paid out of the treasury of the United States. They shall, in all cases, except treason, felony, and breach of the peace,[1] be privileged from arrest during their attendance at the session of their respective Houses, and in going to, and returning from, the same; and for any speech or debate in either House, they shall not be questioned in any other place.[2]

2. No Senator or Representative shall, during the time for which he was elected, be appointed to any civil office under the authority of the United States, which shall have been created, or the emoluments whereof shall have been increased during such time;[3] and no person, holding any office under the United States, shall be a member of either House during his continuance in office.

Section 7. Revenue Bills: President's Veto

1. All bills for raising revenue shall originate in the House of Representatives; but the Senate may propose or concur with amendments as on other bills.

2. Every bill which shall have passed the House of Representatives and the Senate, shall, before it become a law, be presented to the President of the United States; if he approve, he shall sign it, but if not, he shall return it, with his objections, to that House in which it shall have originated, who shall enter the objections at large on their journal, and proceed to reconsider it.[4]

---

[1] *Treason* is defined in Art. III, Sec. 3.

Felony is any serious crime.

Breach of the peace means any indictable offence less than treason or felony; hence the exemption from arrest is now of little importance.

[2] The privilege of speech or debate does not extend to the outside publication of libelous matter spoken in Congress.

[3] After President Taft had selected Senator Knox to be Secretary of State it was discovered that during the latter's term as senator the salaries of cabinet officers had been increased. The objection was removed by an Act of Congress reducing the salary of the Secretary of State to its former figure.

[4] Particular items of bills cannot be vetoed by the President, which fact is very unfortunate.

If, after such reconsideration, two-thirds of that House shall agree to pass the bill, it shall be sent, together with the objections, to the other House, by which it shall likewise be reconsidered, and, if approved by two-thirds of that House, it shall become a law. But in all such cases the votes of both Houses shall be determined by yeas and nays, and the names of the persons voting for and against the bill shall be entered on the journal of each House respectively. If any bill shall not be returned by the President within ten days (Sundays excepted) after it shall have been presented to him, the same shall be a law, in like manner as if he had signed it, unless the Congress, by their adjournment, prevent its return, in which case it shall not be a law.

3. Every order, resolution,[1] or vote, to which the concurrence of the Senate and House of Representatives may be necessary (except on a question of adjournment), shall be presented to the President of the United States; and before the same shall take effect, shall be approved by him, or, being disapproved by him, shall be repassed by two-thirds of the Senate and House of Representatives, according to the rules and limitations prescribed in the case of a bill.

Section 8. Legislative Powers of Congress

The Congress shall have power:

1. To lay and collect taxes, duties, imposts, and excises,[2] to pay the debts, and provide for the common defence and general welfare, of the United States; but all duties, imposts, and excises, shall be uniform throughout the United States;

2. To borrow money on the credit of the United States;

3. To regulate commerce with foreign nations, and among the several states, and with the Indian tribes;

4. To establish a uniform rule of naturalization, and uniform laws on the subject of bankruptcies,[3] throughout the United States;

---

[1] "Every . . . resolution . . . to which the concurrence of the Senate and the House of Representatives may be necessary," means every resolution which has the effect and force of law. There are two kinds of resolution, "joint" and "concurrent."

A joint resolution is, in general, the same as a bill with the exception of the different wording of the enacting clause; hence must be signed by the President, except that an amendment to the Constitution is proposed by a joint resolution which need not be signed by the President because it has not the effect of law; it is merely a proposal of a law to the States.

A concurrent resolution does not have the effect of law; it is merely an expression of the will of Congress on some particular subject, such as adjournment beyond three days, or an expression of sympathy, so does not need the approval of the President.

[2] For the meaning of these terms see pages 111–119 of the text.

[3] For explanation of bankruptcy see page 100.

5. To coin money, regulate the value thereof, and of foreign coin, and fix the standard of weights and measures;

6. To provide for the punishment of counterfeiting the securities and current coin of the United States;

7. To establish post offices and post roads;[1]

8. To promote the progress of science and useful arts,[2] by securing, for limited times, to authors and inventors, the exclusive right to their respective writings and discoveries;

9. To constitute tribunals inferior to the Supreme Court;

10. To define and punish piracies and felonies, committed on the high seas, and offences against the law of nations;

11. To declare war, grant letters of marque and reprisal,[3] and make rules concerning captures on land and water;

12. To raise and support armies; but no appropriation of money to that use shall be for a longer term than two years;

13. To provide and maintain a navy;

14. To make rules for the government and regulation of the land and naval forces;

15. To provide for calling forth the militia to execute the laws of the Union, suppress insurrections, and repel invasions;

16. To provide for organizing, arming, and disciplining the militia, and for governing such part of them as may be employed in the service of the United States, reserving to the states respectively the appointment of the officers, and the authority of training the militia, according to the discipline prescribed by Congress;

17. To exercise exclusive legislation in all cases whatsoever, over such district (not exceeding ten miles square) as may, by cession of particular states, and the acceptance of Congress, become the seat of the government of the United States, and to exercise like authority over all places, purchased by the consent of the legislature of the state in which the same shall be, for the erection of forts, magazines, arsenals, dock-yards, and other needful buildings; — And

---

[1] "Post" is the French word *poste* meaning "mail"; and "post roads" mean mail routes, such as turnpikes, railroads, rivers, city streets, mountain paths, etc.

[2] This clause refers to copyrights and patents.

[3] *Marque* is a French word meaning "boundary." "Reprisal" is from the French word *représaille*, which means retaliation. Hence, originally letters of "marque and reprisal" were licenses to cross the boundaries into the enemies' country, and to capture or destroy goods. As used here it means a commission authorizing private citizens to fit out vessels (privateers) to capture or destroy in time of war. No privateers were commissioned during the Civil War, during the Spanish-American War, or during the two World Wars. See page 105, note 1.

18. To make all laws which shall be necessary and proper [1] for carrying into execution the foregoing powers, and all other powers vested by this Constitution in the government of the United States, or in any department or officer thereof.

Section 9.   Prohibitions upon the United States

1. The migration or importation of such persons, as any of the states, now existing, shall think proper to admit, shall not be prohibited by the Congress prior to the year one thousand eight hundred and eight; but a tax or duty may be imposed on such importation, not exceeding ten dollars for each person.

2. The privilege of the writ of *habeas corpus* [2] shall not be suspended, unless when, in cases of rebellion or invasion, the public safety may require it.

3. No bill of attainder, or *ex post facto* law, [3] shall be passed.

4. No capitation, or other direct tax, shall be laid, unless in proportion to the *census* or enumeration hereinbefore directed to be taken. [4]

5. No tax or duty shall be laid on articles exported from any state.

6. No preference shall be given by any regulation of commerce or revenue to the ports of one state over those of another; nor shall vessels bound to, or from, one state, be obliged to enter, clear, or pay duties, in another.

7. No money shall be drawn from the treasury, but in consequence of appropriations made by law; and a regular statement and account of the receipts and expenditures of all public money shall be published from time to time.

8. No title of nobility shall be granted by the United States; and no person holding any office of profit or trust under them shall, without the consent of the Congress, accept of any present, emolument, office, or title, of any kind whatever, from any king, prince, or foreign state.

---

[1] *Necessary* does not mean absolutely or indispensably necessary, but merely appropriate.   This so-called *necessary and proper clause* is also known as the elastic clause, because it has made it possible for the courts to stretch the meaning of other clauses of the Constitution.

[2] A *writ of habeas corpus* is directed by a judge to any person detaining another, demanding that person to produce the body of the person detained in order to determine whether such person is rightfully or wrongfully detained.   Such person may be a prisoner in jail, an inmate of an insane asylum, or any person detained contrary to law.

[3] A *bill of attainder* is a legislative act which inflicts punishment without a judicial trial.   See Art. I, Sec. 10; see also Art. III, Sec. 3, Cl. 2.

For the meaning of *ex post facto* see page 397 of the text.

[4] See Amendment XVI.   Also see pages 113 and 115 of the text.

Section 10. Prohibitions upon the States

1. No state shall enter into any treaty, alliance, or confederation; grant letters of marque and reprisal; coin money; emit bills of credit;[1] make anything but gold and silver coin a tender in payment of debts; pass any bill of attainder, *ex post facto* law, or law impairing the obligation of contracts, or grant any title of nobility.

2. No state shall, without the consent of the Congress, lay any imposts or duties on imports or exports, except what may be absolutely necessary for executing its inspection laws; and the net produce of all duties and imposts, laid by any state on imports or exports, shall be for the use of the treasury of the United States; and all such laws shall be subject to the revision and control of the Congress.

3. No state shall, without the consent of Congress, lay any duty of tonnage,[2] keep troops, or ships of war, in time of peace, enter into any agreement or compact with another state, or with a foreign power, or engage in war, unless actually invaded, or in such imminent danger as will not admit of delay.

ARTICLE II

EXECUTIVE DEPARTMENT: THE PRESIDENT AND VICE-PRESIDENT

Section 1. Term: Election: Qualifications: Salary: Oath of Office

1. The Executive power shall be vested in a President of the United States of America. He shall hold his office during the term of four years, and together with the Vice-President, chosen for the same term, be elected as follows:

2. Each state shall appoint, in such manner as the legislature thereof may direct, a number of Electors, equal to the whole number of Senators and Representatives, to which the state may be entitled in the Congress; but no Senator or Representative, or person holding an office of trust or profit, under the United States, shall be appointed an Elector.

3. [The Electors shall meet in their respective states, and vote by ballot for two persons, of whom one, at least, shall not be an inhabitant of the same state with themselves. And they shall make a list of all the persons voted for, and of the number of votes for each; which list they shall sign

---

[1] *Bills of credit* mean paper money.

[2] *Tonnage* is a vessel's internal cubical capacity in tons of one hundred cubic feet each. *Tonnage duties* are duties upon vessels in proportion to their capacity.

and certify, and transmit, sealed, to the seat of the Government of the United States, directed to the President of the Senate.   The President of the Senate shall, in the presence of the Senate and House of Representatives, open all the certificates, and the votes shall then be counted.   The person having the greatest number of votes shall be the President, if such number be a majority of the whole number of Electors appointed; and if there be more than one, who have such majority, and have an equal number of votes, then, the House of Representatives shall immediately choose, by ballot, one of them for President; and if no person have a majority, then, from the five highest on the list, the said House shall, in like manner, choose the President.   But in choosing the President, the votes shall be taken by states, the representation from each state having one vote; a quorum for this purpose shall consist of a member or members from two-thirds of the states, and a majority of all the states shall be necessary to a choice.   In every case, after the choice of the President, the person having the greatest number of votes of the Electors shall be the Vice-President.   But if there should remain two or more who have equal votes, the Senate shall choose from them, by ballot, the Vice-President.] [1]

4. The Congress may determine the time of choosing the Electors, and the day on which they shall give their votes; which day shall be the same throughout the United States.

5. No person, except a natural-born citizen, or a citizen of the United States at the time of the adoption of this Constitution, shall be eligible to the office of President; neither shall any person be eligible to that office, who shall not have attained to the age of thirty-five years, and been fourteen years a resident within the United States.

6. In case of the removal of the President from office, or of his death, resignation, or inability to discharge the powers and duties of the said office, the same shall devolve on the Vice-President, and the Congress may by law provide for the case of removal, death, resignation or inability, both of the President and Vice-President, declaring what officer shall then act as President, and such officer shall act accordingly, until the disability be removed, or a President shall be elected. [2]

7. The President shall, at stated times, receive for his services a compensation, which shall neither be increased nor diminished during the period for which he shall have been elected, and he shall not receive, within that period, any other emolument from the United States, or any of them.

8. Before he enter on the execution of his office, he shall take the following oath or affirmation:

---

[1] This paragraph has been superseded by Amendment XII.

[2] For the order of succession to the presidency see page 172 and Amendment XX.

"I do solemnly swear (or affirm), that I will faithfully execute the office of President of the United States, and will, to the best of my ability, preserve, protect, and defend the Constitution of the United States."

Section 2. President's Executive Powers

1. The President shall be Commander-in-Chief of the army and navy of the United States, and of the militia of the several states, when called into the actual service of the United States; he may require the opinion, in writing, of the principal officer in each of the executive departments upon any subject relating to the duties of their respective offices,[1] and he shall have power to grant reprieves and pardons [2] for offenses against the United States, except in cases of impeachment.

2. He shall have power, by and with the advice and consent of the Senate, to make treaties, provided two-thirds of the Senators present concur; and he shall nominate, and, by and with the advice and consent of the Senate, shall appoint ambassadors, other public ministers, and consuls, judges of the Supreme Court, and all other officers of the United States whose appointments are not herein otherwise provided for, and which shall be established by law; [3] but the Congress may by law vest the appointment of such inferior officers, as they think proper, in the President alone, in the courts of law, or in the heads of departments.

3. The President shall have power to fill up all vacancies that may happen during the recess of the Senate, by granting commissions which shall expire at the end of their next session.

Section 3. President's Executive Powers (continued)

He shall, from time to time, give to the Congress information of the state of the Union, and recommend to their consideration such measures as he shall judge necessary and expedient; he may, on extraordinary occasions, convene both Houses, or either of them, and in case of disagreement between them, with respect to the time of adjournment, he may adjourn them to such time as he shall think proper; he shall receive ambassadors and other public ministers; he shall take care that the laws be faithfully executed, and shall commission all the officers of the United States.

---

[1] This clause is the only authority for the President's Cabinet. There is no law of Congress that makes a department head a member of the Cabinet.

[2] For the pardoning power of the President see page 185 of the text.

[3] For the President's power to remove officers see page 177 of the text.

Section 4. Impeachment

The President, Vice-President, and all civil officers [1] of the United States, shall be removed from office on impeachment for, and conviction of, treason, bribery, or other high crimes and misdemeanors.[2]

ARTICLE III

JUDICIAL DEPARTMENT

Section 1. Courts: Terms of Office

The judicial power of the United States shall be vested in one Supreme Court, and in such inferior courts as the Congress may from time to time ordain and establish. The judges, both of the Supreme and inferior courts shall hold their offices during good behavior, and shall, at stated times, receive for their services a compensation which shall not be diminished during their continuance in office.

Section 2. Jurisdiction

1. The judicial power shall extend to all cases, in law and equity,[3] arising under this Constitution, the laws of the United States, and treaties made, or which shall be made, under their authority; to all cases affecting ambassadors, other public ministers, and consuls; to all cases of admiralty and maritime jurisdiction; [4] to controversies to which the United States shall be a party; to controversies between two or more states, between a state and citizens of another state,[5] between citizens of different states, between citizens of the same state claiming lands under grants of different states, and between a state, or the citizens thereof, and foreign states, citizens, or subjects.

---

[1] *Civil officers* subject to impeachment include all officers of the United States who hold their appointments from the National government, high or low, whose duties are executive or judicial. Officers in the army or navy are not civil officers; neither are senators and representatives officers in this sense, nor can they be impeached, but this would be useless as either House can expel a member by a two-thirds vote.

[2] A majority of the House of Representatives may impeach any civil officer of the United States whom they consider morally unfit for his position.

[3] For the meaning of *Equity* see page 525, note 2, and pages 524–525.

[4] *Admiralty jurisdiction* includes cases of prizes seized in time of war, and crimes, torts, etc. in time of peace, which occur on the high seas or navigable waters. *Maritime jurisdiction* has reference to contracts, claims, etc. that are connected with maritime operations — *e.g.*, a contract on land for ship supplies. Admiralty jurisdiction is given by the locality of the act; maritime, by the character of the act.

[5] This clause was modified by the Eleventh Amendment.

2. In all cases affecting ambassadors, other public ministers and consuls, and those in which a state shall be a party, the Supreme Court shall have original jurisdiction.[1] In all the other cases before mentioned, the Supreme Court shall have appellate jurisdiction, both as to law and fact, with such exceptions and under such regulations as the Congress shall make.

3. The trial of all crimes, except in cases of impeachment, shall be by jury;[2] and such trial shall be held in the state where the said crimes shall have been committed;[3] but when not committed within any state the trial shall be at such place or places as the Congress may by law have directed.

Section 3. Treason

1. Treason against the United States shall consist only in levying war against them, or in adhering to their enemies, giving them aid and comfort. No person shall be convicted of treason unless on the testimony of two witnesses to the same overt act, or on confession in open court.

2. The Congress shall have power to declare the punishment of treason, but no attainder of treason shall work corruption of blood, or forfeiture except during the life of the person attainted.[4]

ARTICLE IV

RELATIONS OF STATES

Section 1. Public Records

Full faith and credit shall be given in each state to the public acts, records, and judicial proceedings of every other state. And the Congress may, by general laws, prescribe the manner in which such acts, records, and proceedings shall be proved, and the effect thereof.

---

[1] *Original jurisdiction* means the right of hearing and determining a case in the first instance. *Appellate jurisdiction* means the right to hear cases appealed from inferior courts.

[2] Jury trials are guaranteed in federal courts only. States could abolish jury trials if they should desire to do so.

[3] If a crime is committed on the sea, the accused is tried by the United States District Court of the district where the prisoner is landed.

[4] During the Civil War an act was passed by Congress according to which all Confederate army or navy officers should forfeit their property. A certain piece of real estate in Virginia belonging to a Confederate naval officer, Forrest by name, was seized by the government and sold by legal proceedings to one Buntley. Buntley sold it to Bigelow. After the death of Forrest his son and rightful heir claimed it, and obtained it because treason cannot "work corruption of blood or forfeiture except during the life of the person attainted." See Art. I, Sec. 9, Cl. 3.

Section 2. Rights in One State of Citizens of Another

1. The citizens of each state shall be entitled to all privileges and immunities [1] of citizens in the several states.

2. A person charged in any state with treason, felony, or other crime, who shall flee from justice, and be found in another state, shall, on demand of the executive authority of the state from which he fled, be delivered up, to be removed to the state having jurisdiction of the crime.

3. No person held to service [2] or labor in one state, under the laws thereof, escaping into another, shall, in consequence of any law or regulation therein, be discharged from such service or labor, but shall be delivered up on claim of the party to whom such service or labor may be due.

Section 3. New States: Territories

1. New states may be admitted by the Congress into this Union; but no new state shall be formed or erected within the jurisdiction of any other state, nor any state be formed by the junction of two or more states, or parts of states, without the consent of the legislatures of the states concerned as well as of the Congress.

2. The Congress shall have power to dispose of and make all needful rules and regulations respecting the territory or other property belonging to the United States; and nothing in this Constitution shall be so construed as to prejudice any claims of the United States, or of any particular state.

Section 4. Protection Afforded to States by the Nation

The United States shall guarantee to every state in this Union a republican form of government, and shall protect each of them against invasion; and on application of the legislature, or of the executive (when the legislature cannot be convened), against domestic violence.

ARTICLE V

PROVISIONS FOR AMENDMENT

The Congress, whenever two-thirds of both Houses shall deem it necessary, shall propose amendments to this Constitution, or, on the application of the legislatures of two-thirds of the several states, shall call a convention for proposing amendments, which, in either case, shall be valid, to all intents and purposes, as part of this Constitution, when ratified by the legislatures of three-fourths of the several states, or by conventions in three-fourths

---

[1] For *privileges* and *immunities* see note 2 on Fourteenth Amendment.

[2] *Person held to service* means slave; hence this clause has no significance now.

thereof, as the one or the other mode of ratification may be proposed by the Congress: provided that no amendment which may be made prior to the year one thousand eight hundred and eight shall in any manner affect the first and fourth clauses in the ninth section of the first Article; and that no state, without its consent, shall be deprived of its equal suffrage in the Senate.

ARTICLE VI

NATIONAL DEBTS: SUPREMACY OF NATIONAL LAW: OATH

1. All debts contracted and engagements entered into, before the adoption of this Constitution, shall be as valid against the United States under this Constitution, as under the Confederation.

2. This Constitution, and the laws of the United States which shall be made in pursuance thereof, and all treaties made, or which shall be made, under the authority of the United States, shall be the supreme law of the land; [1] and the judges in every state shall be bound thereby, anything in the constitution or laws of any state to the contrary notwithstanding.

3. The Senators and Representatives before mentioned, and the members of the several state legislatures, and all executive and judicial officers, both of the United States and of the several states, shall be bound, by oath or affirmation, to support this Constitution; but no religious test shall ever be required as a qualification to any office or public trust under the United States.

ARTICLE VII

ESTABLISHMENT OF CONSTITUTION

The ratification of the conventions of nine states shall be sufficient for the establishment of this Constitution between the states so ratifying the same.

Done in Convention, by the unanimous consent of the States present, the seventeenth day of September, in the year of our Lord one thousand seven hundred and eighty-seven, and of the Independence of the United States of America the twelfth. *In Witness* whereof we have hereunto subscribed our names.

Attest: WILLIAM JACKSON, *Secretary*

G°: WASHINGTON,
Presidt. and Deputy from Virginia
[Followed by the signatures of thirty-eight other delegates]

---

[1] If a federal law and treaty conflict, the courts accept the one most recently passed or ratified. A State law always yields to a treaty.

AMENDMENTS

ARTICLE I [1]

FREEDOM OF RELIGION, OF SPEECH, AND OF THE PRESS: RIGHT OF PETITION

Congress shall make no law respecting an establishment of religion, or prohibiting the free exercise thereof; of abridging the freedom of speech, or of the press; or the right of the people peaceably to assemble, and to petition the government for a redress of grievances.

ARTICLE II

RIGHT TO KEEP ARMS

A well-regulated militia being necessary to the security of a free state, the right of the people to keep and bear arms shall not be infringed.[2]

ARTICLE III

QUARTERING OF SOLDIERS IN PRIVATE HOUSES

No soldier shall, in time of peace, be quartered in any house, without the consent of the owner; nor, in time of war, but in a manner to be prescribed by law.

ARTICLE IV

SEARCH WARRANTS

The right of the people to be secure in their persons, houses, papers, and effects, against unreasonable searches and seizures, shall not be violated; and no warrants shall issue, but upon probable cause, supported by oath or affirmation, and particularly describing the place to be searched, and the persons or things to be seized.[3]

---

[1] The first ten amendments, the cherished "Bill of Rights," were adopted in 1791. They were originally considered restrictions upon Congress or the Federal Government only; but more recently the Supreme Court has cited them in increasing its control over States through Amendment XIV. The Court uses such phrases as "violating the purpose [or spirit] of Amendment 1."

[2] As this amendment restricts Congress only, a State may restrict the use of arms as it sees fit — e.g., to militia authorized by it. A State may prohibit the carrying of arms by such organizations as the Knights of Columbus or the Masons. Many States prohibit the carrying of concealed weapons, or even the possession of pistols, dirks, etc.

[3] Congress cannot authorize the opening of first class mail except by a warrant issued by a court. The warrant must describe the mail to be opened.

ARTICLE V

CRIMINAL PROCEEDINGS

No person shall be held to answer for a capital, or otherwise infamous, crime, unless on a presentment or indictment of a grand jury, except in cases arising in the land or naval forces, or in the militia, when in actual service, in time of war, or public danger; nor shall any person be subject, for the same offence, to be twice put in jeopardy of life or limb; nor shall be compelled, in any criminal case, to be a witness against himself; nor be deprived of life, liberty, or property, without due process of law;[1] nor shall private property be taken for public use, without just compensation.[2]

ARTICLE VI

CRIMINAL PROCEEDINGS (*continued*)

In all criminal prosecutions, the accused shall enjoy the right to a speedy and public trial, by an impartial jury of the state and district wherein the crime shall have been committed, which district shall have been previously ascertained by law; and to be informed of the nature and cause of the accusation; to be confronted with the witnesses against him; to have compulsory process for obtaining witnesses in his favor; and to have the assistance of counsel for his defence.

ARTICLE VII

JURY TRIAL IN CIVIL CASES

In suits at common law, where the value in controversy shall exceed twenty dollars, the right of trial by jury shall be preserved; and no fact, tried by a jury, shall be otherwise re-examined in any court of the United States than according to the rules of the common law.

ARTICLE VIII

EXCESSIVE PUNISHMENTS

Excessive bail shall not be required, nor excessive fines imposed, nor cruel and unusual punishments inflicted.

---

[1] *Due process of law* means the law of the land, both written and unwritten (principles known to courts). In brief, *due process of law* is what the majority of the Supreme Court of the United States thinks the law of the land to be.

[2] While this restriction applies only to the National government, the Fourteenth Amendment extends a portion of it to the States. See Amendment XIV, Sec. 1.

ARTICLE IX

UNENUMERATED RIGHTS OF THE PEOPLE

The enumeration in the Constitution of certain rights shall not be construed to deny or disparage others retained by the people.

ARTICLE X

POWERS RESERVED TO STATES

The powers not delegated to the United States by the Constitution, nor prohibited by it to the states, are reserved to the states respectively, or to the people.

ARTICLE XI [1]

SUITS AGAINST STATES

The judicial power of the United States shall not be construed to extend to any suit in law or equity, commenced or prosecuted against one of the United States by citizens of another state, or by citizens or subjects of any foreign state.[2]

ARTICLE XII [3]

ELECTION OF PRESIDENT AND VICE-PRESIDENT

1. The Electors shall meet in their respective states, and vote by ballot for President and Vice-President, one of whom, at least, shall not be an inhabitant of the same state with themselves; they shall name in their ballots the person voted for as President, and in distinct ballots the person voted for as Vice-President; and they shall make distinct lists of all persons voted for as President, and of all persons voted for as Vice-President, and of the number of votes for each, which lists they shall sign, and certify, and transmit, sealed, to the seat of the Government of the United States, directed to the President of the Senate; the President of the Senate shall, in the presence of the Senate and the House of Representatives, open all the certificates, and the votes shall then be counted; the person having the greatest number of votes for President shall be the President, if such number be a majority of the whole number of Electors appointed; and if no person have such a majority, then, from the persons having the highest numbers, not exceeding

[1] This amendment was adopted in 1798.

[2] Officers of a State can be sued in some cases, which practically amounts to a suit against a State.

[3] This amendment was adopted in 1804 and supersedes Art. II, Sec. 1.

three, on the list of those voted for as President, the House of Representatives shall choose immediately, by ballot, the President. But in choosing the President, the votes shall be taken by states, the representation from each state having one vote; a quorum for this purpose shall consist of a member or members from two-thirds of the states, and a majority of all the states shall be necessary to a choice. And if the House of Representatives shall not choose a President, whenever the right of choice shall devolve upon them, before the fourth day of March next following, then the Vice-President shall act as President, as in case of the death, or other constitutional disability, of the President.

2. The person having the greatest number of votes as Vice-President, shall be the Vice-President, if such number be a majority of the whole number of Electors appointed; and if no person have a majority, then, from the two highest numbers on the list, the Senate shall choose the Vice-President; a quorum for the purpose shall consist of two-thirds of the whole number of Senators; a majority of the whole number shall be necessary to a choice.

3. But no person constitutionally ineligible to the office of President shall be eligible to that of Vice-President of the United States.

ARTICLE XIII [1]

SLAVERY

Section 1. Abolition of Slavery

Neither slavery nor involuntary servitude, except as a punishment for crime, whereof the party shall have been duly convicted, shall exist within the United States, or any place subject to their jurisdiction.

Section 2. Power of Congress

Congress shall have power to enforce this article by appropriate legislation.

ARTICLE XIV [2]

CIVIL RIGHTS: APPORTIONMENT OF REPRESENTATIVES: POLITICAL DISABILITIES: PUBLIC DEBT

Section 1. Civil Rights

All persons born or naturalized in the United States, and subject to the jurisdiction thereof, are citizens of the United States and of the state wherein

[1] This amendment was adopted in 1865.
[2] This amendment was adopted in 1868.

they reside.[1] No state shall make or enforce any law which shall abridge the privileges or immunities of citizens [2] of the United States; nor shall any state deprive any person of life, liberty, or property, without due process of law, nor deny to any person within its jurisdiction the equal protection of the laws.

Section 2.[3] Apportionment of Representatives

Representatives shall be apportioned among the several states according to their respective numbers, counting the whole number of persons in each state, excluding Indians not taxed.   But when the right to vote at any election for the choice of electors for President and Vice-President of the United States, Representatives in Congress, the executive and judicial officers of a state, or the members of the legislature thereof, is denied to any of the male inhabitants of such state, being twenty-one years of age, and citizens of the United States, or in any way abridged, except for participation in rebellion or other crime, the basis of representation therein shall be reduced in the proportion which the number of such male citizens shall bear to the whole number of male citizens twenty-one years of age in such state.

Section 3.   Political Disabilities

No person shall be a Senator or Representative in Congress, or elector of President and Vice-President, or hold any office, civil or military, under the United States, or under any state, who, having previously taken an oath, as a member of Congress, or as an officer of the United States, or as a member of any state legislature, or as an executive or judical officer of any state, to support the Constitution of the United States, shall have engaged in insurrection or rebellion against the same, or given aid or comfort to the enemies thereof.   But Congress may, by a vote of two-thirds of each House, remove such disability.

---

[1] By defining *citizenship* it is made clear that Negroes are citizens.

And subject to the jurisdiction thereof would exclude children of diplomatic representatives of a foreign state and children born to alien enemies in hostile occupation.

[2] *Privileges and immunities* have never been defined, but the courts have named many things which are and are not a denial of such privileges and immunities. For example, it is not a denial to prohibit marriage between whites and blacks; nor to provide separate schools for these races; nor to provide separate coaches for the races; nor to close business places during certain hours or on Sunday.   It is a denial for a State to prohibit the employment of a particular nationality; or to pass an Act excluding persons from jury service because of their color or race.

[3] This section has never been enforced; and some jurists argue that it has been superseded by Amendment XV.

Section 4. Public Debt

The validity of the public debt of the United States, authorized by law, including debts incurred for payment of pensions and bounties for services in suppressing insurrection or rebellion, shall not be questioned. But neither the United States nor any state shall assume or pay any debt or obligation incurred in aid of insurrection or rebellion against the United States, or any claim for the loss or emancipation of any slave; but all such debts, obligations, and claims shall be held illegal and void.

Section 5. Power of Congress

The Congress shall have power to enforce, by appropriate legislation, the provisions of this article.

ARTICLE XV [1]

RIGHT OF SUFFRAGE

Section 1. Right of Negro to Vote

The right of citizens of the United States to vote shall not be denied or abridged by the United States or by any state on account of race, color, or previous condition of servitude.

Section 2. Power of Congress

The Congress shall have power to enforce this article by appropriate legislation.

ARTICLE XVI [2]

INCOME TAX

The Congress shall have power to lay and collect taxes on incomes, from whatever source derived, without apportionment among the several states, and without regard to any census or enumeration.

ARTICLE XVII [3]

SENATE: ELECTION: VACANCIES

The Senate of the United States shall be composed of two Senators from each state, elected by the people thereof, for six years; and each Senator

---

[1] This amendment was adopted in 1870. It was passed to secure Negro suffrage and to prevent Negroes from being disfranchised.

[2] Amendment XVI was adopted in 1913. It modifies Art. I, Sec. 9, Cl. 4.

[3] This amendment was adopted in 1913. It modifies Art. I, Sec. 3, Cls. 1 and 2.

shall have one vote.   The electors in each state shall have the qualifications requisite for electors of the most numerous branch of the state legislatures.

When vacancies happen in the representation of any state in the Senate, the executive authority of such state shall issue writs of election to fill such vacancies: Provided, That the legislature of any state may empower the executive thereof to make temporary appointment until the people fill the vacancies by election as the legislature may direct.

This amendment shall not be so construed as to affect the election or term of any Senator chosen before it becomes valid as part of the Constitution.

ARTICLE XVIII [1]

NATIONAL PROHIBITION

Section 1.   Prohibition of Intoxicating Liquors

After one year from the ratification of this article the manufacture, sale or transportation of intoxicating liquors within, the importation thereof into, or the exportation thereof from the United States and all territory subject to the jurisdiction thereof for beverage purposes is hereby prohibited.

Section 2.   Concurrent Enforcement

The Congress and the several States shall have concurrent power to enforce this article by appropriate legislation.

Section 3. Conditions of Ratification

This article shall be inoperative unless it shall have been ratified as an amendment to the Constitution by the legislatures of the several States, as provided in the Constitution, within seven years of the date of the submission hereof to the States by Congress.

ARTICLE XIX [2]

WOMAN SUFFRAGE

The right of citizens of the United States to vote shall not be denied or abridged by the United States or by any State on account of sex.

Congress shall have power to enforce this article by appropriate legislation.

---

[1] This amendment was adopted in 1919 and repealed in 1933 by Amendment XXI.

[2] This amendment was adopted in 1920.

ARTICLE XX [1]

CHANGING THE TIME OF CONVENING CONGRESS AND OF IN-AUGURATING THE PRESIDENT AND VICE PRESIDENT

Section 1. Terms of President and Vice-President

The terms of the President and Vice-President shall end at noon on the 20th day of January, and the terms of Senators and Representatives at noon on the 3d day of January, of the years in which such terms would have ended if this article had not been ratified; and the terms of their successors shall then begin.

Section 2. Meetings of Congress

The Congress shall assemble at least once in every year, and such meeting shall begin at noon on the 3d day of January, unless they shall by law appoint a different day.

Section 3. Interim Succession

If, at the time fixed for the beginning of the term of the President, the President elect shall have died, the Vice-President elect shall become President. If a President shall not have been chosen before the time fixed for the beginning of his term, or if the President elect shall have failed to qualify, then the Vice-President elect shall act as President until a President shall have qualified; and the Congress may by law provide for the case wherein neither a President elect nor a Vice-President elect shall have qualified, declaring who shall then act as President, or the manner in which one who is to act shall be selected, and such person shall act accordingly until a President or Vice-President shall have qualified.

Section 4. Congressional Choice

The Congress may by law provide for the case of the death of any of the persons from whom the House of Representatives may choose a President whenever the right of choice shall have devolved upon them, and for the case of the death of any of the persons from whom the Senate may choose a Vice-President whenever the right of choice shall have devolved upon them.

Section 5. Time of Effect

Sections 1 and 2 shall take effect on the 15th day of October following the ratification of this article.

---

[1] This amendment was adopted in 1933.

Section 6. Conditions of Ratification

This article shall be inoperative unless it shall have been ratified as an amendment to the Constitution by the legislatures of three-fourths of the several States within seven years from the date of its submission.

ARTICLE XXI [1]

REPEALING NATIONAL PROHIBITION, AND PROHIBITING THE IMPORTATION OF INTOXICATING LIQUOR INTO STATES IN VIOLATION OF THEIR LAWS

Section 1. Statement of Repeal

The eighteenth article of amendment to the Constitution of the United States is hereby repealed.

Section 2. Conditions of Transportation or Importation

The transportation or importation into any State, Territory, or possession of the United States for delivery or use therein of intoxicating liquors, in violation of the laws thereof, is hereby prohibited.

Section 3. Conditions of Ratification

This article shall be inoperative unless it shall have been ratified as an amendment to the Constitution by conventions in the several States, as provided in the Constitution, within seven years from the date of the submission hereof to the States by Congress.

ARTICLE XXII [2]

LIMITING PRESIDENTIAL TENURE TO TWO FULL TERMS AND NOT MORE THAN TEN YEARS

Section 1. Limiting Presidential Tenure and Exception

No person shall be elected to the office of the President more than twice, and no person who has held the office of President, or acted as President,

---

[1] This twenty-first amendment was referred to the States by Congress in February, 1933, and was ratified by the thirty-sixth State in December of the same year. This is the first amendment ever submitted to conventions of the States for ratification.   The previous twenty were referred to State legislatures.

In referring this amendment to the States, Congress did not give any instructions as to how the conventions should be called, when, or where.   Each State legislature provided for the details of its convention and paid the expenses thereof.

[2] This amendment was adopted in 1951 after referral to State legislatures.

for more than two years of a term to which some other person was elected President shall be elected to the office of the President more than once. But this Article shall not apply to any person holding the office of President when this Article was proposed by the Congress, and shall not prevent any person who may be holding the office of President, or acting as President, during the term within which this Article becomes operative from holding the office of President or acting as President during the remainder of such term.

Section 2.　Conditions of Ratification

This Article shall be inoperative unless it shall have been ratified as an amendment to the Constitution by the legislatures of three-fourths of the several States within seven years from the date of its submission to the States by the Congress.

APPENDIX II

POPULATION OF STATES

RANK			STATE	POPULATION		PER CENT OF CHANGE
1930	1940	1950		1940	1950	
1	1	1	New York	13,479,142	14,830,192	10.0
6	5	2	California	6,907,387	10,586,223	53.3
2	2	3	Pennsylvania	9,900,180	10,498,012	6.0
3	3	4	Illinois	7,897,241	8,712,176	10.3
4	4	5	Ohio	6,907,612	7,946,627	15.0
5	6	6	Texas	6,414,824	7,711,194	20.2
7	7	7	Michigan	5,256,106	6,371,766	21.2
9	9	8	New Jersey	4,160,165	4,835,329	16.2
8	8	9	Massachusetts . . .	4,316,721	4,690,514	8.7
12	11	10	North Carolina . . .	3,571,623	4,061,929	13.7
10	10	11	Missouri	3,784,664	3,954,653	4.5
11	12	12	Indiana	3,427,796	3,934,224	14.8
14	14	13	Georgia	3,123,723	3,444,578	10.3
13	13	14	Wisconsin	3,137,587	3,434,575	9.5
20	19	15	Virginia	2,677,773	3,318,680	23.9
16	15	16	Tennessee	2,915,841	3,291,718	12.9
15	17	17	Alabama	2,832,961	3,061,743	8.1
18	18	18	Minnesota	2,792,300	2,982,483	6.8
17	16	19	Kentucky	2,845,627	2,944,806	3.5
31	27	20	Florida	1,897,414	2,771,305	46.1
22	21	21	Louisiana	2,363,880	2,683,516	13.5
19	20	22	Iowa	2,538,268	2,621,073	3.3
30	30	23	Washington	1,736,191	2,378,963	37.0
28	28	24	Maryland	1,821,244	2,343,001	28.6
21	22	25	Oklahoma	2,336,434	2,233,351	− 4.4
23	23	26	Mississippi	2,183,796	2,178,914	− 0.2
26	26	27	South Carolina . . .	1,899,804	2,117,027	11.4
29	31	28	Connecticut	1,709,242	2,007,280	17.4
27	25	29	West Virginia . . .	1,901,074	2,005,552	5.4
25	24	30	Arkansas	1,949,387	1,909,511	− 2.0
24	29	31	Kansas	1,801,028	1,905,299	5.8
34	34	32	Oregon	1,089,684	1,521,341	39.6
32	32	33	Nebraska	1,315,834	1,325,510	0.7
33	33	34	Colorado	1,123,296	1,325,089	18.0
35	35	35	Maine	847,227	913,774	7.9
41	37	36	District of Columbia . .	663,091	802,178	21.0
37	36	37	Rhode Island . . .	713,346	791,896	11.0
44	44	38	Arizona	499,261	749,587	50.0
40	41	39	Utah	550,310	688,862	25.2
45	42	40	New Mexico	531,818	681,187	28.1
36	38	41	South Dakota . . .	642,961	652,740	1.5
38	39	42	North Dakota . . .	641,935	619,636	− 3.5
39	40	43	Montana	559,456	591,024	5.6
43	43	44	Idaho	524,873	588,637	12.1
42	45	45	New Hampshire . . .	491,524	533,242	8.5
46	46	46	Vermont	359,231	377,747	5.2
47	47	47	Delaware	266,505	318,085	19.4
48	48	48	Wyoming	250,742	290,529	15.9
49	49	49	Nevada	110,247	160,083	45.2
			Total	131,669,275	150,697,361	14.5

APPENDIX III

GENERAL BIBLIOGRAPHY

This general bibliography is for those students and teachers who desire more comprehensive or more specific references on the chapter topics than given in the Select Bibliography at the end of chapters. Many of the pamphlets listed in the select bibliographies at the ends of chapters may be purchased from the following organizations. They should be ordered in advance.

Foreign Policy Association, 22 East 38th Street, New York 16. Single copy 35¢.

National Education Association, 1201 Sixteenth Street, Washington 6, D. C. Free or inexpensive.

National League of Women Voters, 1026 Seventeenth Street, N. W., Washington 6, D. C.

REFERENCE BOOKS FOR THE SCHOOL LIBRARY

United States Code, containing the general and permanent laws of the United States in force January 3, 1953 (latest printing).
(To order Government publications, please see Appendix IV.)

The Congressional Directory, containing a short biography of each congressman, a list of congressional committees, maps of States showing congressional districts, a list of the administrative departments and bureaus and the duties of the officers thereof. — Published twice a year.

House Manual, contains the rules of the House of Representatives and the United States Constitution. — Government Printing Office.

The Manual, Legislative Handbook, or *Blue Book* of your State. This document contains the State Constitution, list of State and local officers, election returns, and various other interesting information. — It can usually be obtained free through the Secretary of your State.

The Statistical Abstract of the United States. — Issued annually by the Department of Commerce.

The World Almanac. — Published by the *New York World-Telegram*. An annual encyclopedia for $1.10 (paper).

Book of the States. Biennially. Council of State Governments, 1313 East 60th Street, Chicago.

The following books are also good books for the school library, if funds and space permit their purchase.

Annual U. S. Government Reports such as the *Yearbook of Agriculture*.
Reader's Guide to Periodical Literature.
State Code and Session Laws or *Legislative Acts*.

The American Year Book.
The New York Times. Index.
The Statesman's Yearbook. — Facts about governments of the world.
United States Census.

PERIODICALS, PAMPHLETS, AND NEWSPAPERS

The American Observer. Weekly review of current history for high schools.
   Civic Education Service, 1733 Case St., N. W., Washington 6, D. C.
American Political Science Review. Quarterly.
Annals of the American Academy of Political and Social Science. Bi-monthly.
Congressional Digest. Monthly.
Foreign Policy Reports. Foreign Policy Association.
Headline Series. Bi-monthly. Foreign Policy Association.
New York Times. Daily, with index.
State Government. Monthly.
The National Municipal Review. Monthly.
Time. Newsweek. U. S. News & World Report. Weekly.
U. S. Government Organization Manual. Treats all agencies of the Government. $1. Government Printing Office, Washington, D. C.
Vital Speeches of the Day. Bi-monthly.

ADVANCED GOVERNMENT TEXTBOOKS FOR REFERENCE

All publishers cited have New York addresses unless another address is given. Prices may usually be obtained through local libraries, county superintendents' offices, or direct from the publishers. In ordering, please specify "latest edition."

BONE, H. *American Politics and the Party System.* McGraw-Hill.
BURNS and PELTASON. *Government by the People.* Prentice-Hall.
CARR, R., *et al. American Democracy in Theory and Practice.* Rinehart.
CORWIN, E. S. *The Constitution and What It Means Today.* Princeton Univ. Press (Princeton, N. J.).
FAIRMAN, C. *American Constitutional Decisions.* Holt.
FERGUSON, J., and McHENRY, D. *The American System of Government.* McGraw-Hill.
GRAVES, W. B. *American State Government.* D. C. Heath (Boston).
JOHNSON, C. *Government of the United States.* Crowell.
KELLY, A. H., and HARRISON. *The American Constitution.* Norton.
KNEIER, CHAS. *City Government in the United States.* Harper.
MACDONALD, A. F. *American City Government and Administration.* Crowell.
   American State Government and Administration. Crowell.
MACDONALD, H., *et al. Outside Readings in American Government.* Crowell.
MAGRUDER, F. A. *National Governments and International Relations.* Allyn and Bacon (Boston).
MAXEY, C. *The American Problem of Government.* Appleton-Century-Crofts.
MUNRO, W. B. *The Government of the United States.* Macmillan.

O<small>GG</small> and R<small>AY</small>. *Essentials of American Government.* Appleton-Century-Crofts.
P<small>ATTERSON</small>, C., and W<small>ALKER</small>. *American National Government.* D. C. Heath (Boston).
S<small>CHULTZ</small>, E. *American City Government.* Stackpole and Heck.
S<small>TUBBS</small>, W., and G<small>OSNELL</small>. *Select Readings in American Government.* Charles Scribner's Sons.
S<small>WARTHOUT</small>, J., and B<small>ARTLEY</small>. *Principles and Problems of American National Government.* Also, *Materials on American National Government.* Oxford University Press.
S<small>WISHER</small>, C. *American National Government.* Houghton-Mifflin (Boston).

CHAPTER I. — STRENGTH THROUGH UNION

C<small>HASE</small>, S<small>TUART</small>. *For This We Fought.* Twentieth Century Fund. 1946.
D<small>AVENPORT</small>, R. *USA, The Permanent Revolution.* Prentice-Hall. 1952.
D<small>ULLES</small>, J<small>OHN</small> F. *War or Peace.* Macmillan. 1950.
E<small>ZEKIEL</small>, M. (editor). *Towards World Prosperity.* Harper. 1947.
G<small>UNTHER</small>, J. *Inside U. S. A.* Harper. 1947.
L<small>ASSWELL</small>, H. *National Security and Individual Freedom.* McGraw-Hill. 1950.
L<small>INDLEY</small>, E. K. *Atomic Challenge.* Headline Series No. 63. Foreign Policy Association. May–June, 1947.
M<small>OULTON</small>, H. *America's Wealth.* Brookings Institution (Washington, D. C.). 1952.
R<small>IKER</small>, W. *Democracy in the United States.* Macmillan. 1953.

CHAPTER II. — THE DEVELOPMENT OF THE STATE

B<small>ISHOP</small>, H. M., and H<small>ENDEL</small>, S. (eds.). *Basic Issues of American Democracy: A Book of Readings.* Appleton-Century-Crofts. 1952 (2nd ed.).
C<small>ARTER</small>, G., *et al. Major Foreign Powers.* Harcourt, Brace (New York). 1952.
C<small>HANDLER</small>, A. *The Clash of Political Ideals.* Appleton-Century-Crofts. 1950.
C<small>OLE</small>, T. *European Political Systems.* Knopf. 1953.
E<small>BEN</small>, M<small>ARTIN</small>. *World Communism Today.* Whittlesey House. 1948.
E<small>BENSTEIN</small>, W. *Great Political Thinkers.* Rinehart. 1951.
———. *Introduction to Political Philosophy.* Rinehart (New York). 1952.
F<small>ISHER</small>, M. *Communist Doctrine and the Free World.* Syracuse University Press. 1952.
G<small>URIAN</small>, W. *Bolshevism: An Introduction to Soviet Communism.* University of Notre Dame Press. Notre Dame, Ind. 1953.
H<small>OOVER</small>, H. C. *Challenge to Liberty.* Charles Scribner's Sons. 1934.
K<small>ALIJARVI</small>, T., *et al. Modern World Politics.* Crowell. 1953 ed.
L<small>INCOLN</small>, G., *et al. Economics of National Security.* Prentice-Hall. 1950.
M<small>AGRUDER</small>, F. A. *National Governments and International Relations.* Allyn and Bacon. 1950.

MARX, F. *Foreign Governments.* Prentice-Hall. 1952.
MAXEY, C. *Political Philosophies.* Macmillan. 1949.
NEUMANN, R. *European and Comparative Government.* McGraw. 1951.
SHOTWELL, J., *et al. Governments of Continental Europe.* Macmillan. 1952.
STOUT, H. *British Government.* Oxford Univ. Press. 1953.

CHAPTER III. — ORIGIN OF OUR FEDERAL CONSTITUTION

AGAR, H. *The Price of Union.* Houghton-Mifflin. 1950.
BEARD, CHARLES A. *An Economic Interpretation of the Constitution of the United States.* Macmillan. 1935.
COMMAGER, H. S., and NEVINS. *The Heritage of America.* Heath. 1949.
CRAVEN, A., *et al. A Documentary History of the American People.* Ginn (Boston). 1951.
FARRAND, M. *The Framing of the Constitution.* Yale Univ. Press (New Haven). 1913.
The Fathers of the Constitution. Yale Univ. Press. 1922.
FISKE, JOHN. *The Critical Period of American History.* Houghton-Mifflin. 1888, and subsequent editions.
LANE, R. *Problems in American Government.* Prentice-Hall. 1952.
LATHAM, E. (ed.). *The Declaration of Independence and the Constitution.* Heath. 1950.
LEOPOLD, R., and LINK. *Problems in American History.* Prentice-Hall. 1952.
MORRISON, S., and COMMAGER. *The Growth of the American Republic.* (2 vols.) Oxford. 1950 (4th ed.).
PADOVER, S. *The Living U.S. Constitution.* Praeger. 1953.
RIKER, W. *Democracy in the United States.* Macmillan. 1953.
SWISHER, C. *American Constitutional Development.* Houghton-Mifflin.
VAN DOREN, C. *The Great Rehearsal.* Viking. 1948.

CHAPTER IV. — OUR FEDERAL SYSTEM OF GOVERNMENT

CHATTERS, C. *The Crossword Puzzle of Government Relations.* Municipal Forum of New York. 57 William St., N.Y.C. 1953.
CROSSKEY, W. *Politics and the Constitution in the History of the United States.* Univ. of Chicago Press. Chicago. 1953.
FAIRMAN, C. *American Constitutional Decisions.* Henry Holt & Co. (New York). 1950.
FELLMAN, D. *Readings in American National Government.* Rinehart. 1950.
RIEMER, N. *Problems of American Government.* McGraw. 1952.

CHAPTER V. — THE LEGISLATIVE DEPARTMENT

BAILEY, S. *Congress at Work.* Holt. 1952.
CHAMBERLAIN, JOSEPH. *Legislative Processes.* Appleton-Century-Crofts.
GALLOWAY, G. *The Legislative Process in Congress.* Crowell. 1953.
GRIFFITH, E. *Congress.* New York University Press. 1951.
HAYNES, G. H. *Senate of the United States.* Houghton-Mifflin. 1938.

KEFAUVER and LEVIN. *20th Century Congress.* Duell, Sloan & Pearce.
WILSON, H. H. *Congress: Business as Usual.* Rinehart. 1951.

CHAPTER VI. — POWERS OF CONGRESS — EXPRESSED AND IMPLIED

CORWIN, E. S. *The Constitution and What It Means Today.* Princeton
Univ. Press (Princeton, N. J.). 1948.
CUSHMAN, R. E. *Leading Constitutional Decisions.* Appleton-Century-
Crofts. 1950.
DODD, W. F. *Cases on Constitutional Law.* West Publishing Co. (St.
Paul). 1950. (Annual Supplement also.)
FENN, P. *The Development of the Constitution.* Appleton-Century-Crofts.
FRANK, J. *Cases on the Constitution.* McGraw. 1952.
HELLER, F. *American Constitutional Law.* Harper. 1952.
HURST, J. W. *The Growth of American Law.* Little, Brown. 1950.
MATHEWS, J. M. *The American Constitutional System.* McGraw. 1940.
ROTTSCHAFER, HENRY. *Cases on Constitutional Law.* West Publishing Co.
(St. Paul). 1948.

CHAPTER VII. — THE POWERS OF CONGRESS TO TAX

ANDERSON, W. *Taxation and the American Economy.* Prentice-Hall.
1951.
BLOUGH, R. *The Federal Taxing Process.* Prentice-Hall. 1952.
FAINSOD, M. *Government and the American Economy.* Norton. 1950.
ROHLFING, C., *et al. Business and Government.* Foundation Press
(Brooklyn). 1953.

CHAPTER VIII. — COMMERCIAL POWERS OF CONGRESS

COOK, F. *Principles of Business and the Federal Law.* Macmillan. 1951.
DAHL, R., and LINDBLOM, C. *Politics, Economics, and Welfare.* Harper.
1953.
DIMOCK, M. *Business and Government.* Holt. 1953.
LILIENTHAL, D. *Big Business: A New Era.* Harper. 1953.
NOURSE, E. *Economics in the Public Service.* Harcourt, Brace. 1953.
OXENFELDT, A. *Economics for the Citizen.* Rinehart. 1953.
PIQUET, H. *Aid, Trade, and the Tariff.* Crowell. 1953.
RIBBLE, F. D. *State and National Power over Commerce.* Columbia Univ.
Press. 1937.
ROHLFING, C., *et al. Business and Government.* Foundation Press
(Brooklyn). 1953.
Tax Institute. *Tax Barriers to Trade.* The Institute. 1941.
"War and Inflation." *Current History.* May, 1953. Entire Issue.

CHAPTER IX. — CONGRESS IN ACTION

BAILEY, S. *Congress at Work.* Holt. 1953.

BURDETTE, F. L. *Filibustering in the Senate.* 1940.

BURNS, J. *Congress on Trial.* Harper. 1949.

DOOB, L. W. *Public Opinion and Propaganda.* Henry Holt & Co. 1948.

FINLETTER, T. *Can Representative Government Do the Job?* Harcourt, Brace & Co. 1945.

GALLOWAY, G. *The Legislative Process in Congress.* Crowell. 1953.

GROSS, B. *The Legislative Struggle: A Study in Social Combat.* McGraw-Hill. 1953.

HELLER, R. *Strengthening the Congress.* (Pamphlet No. 39. National Planning Association. 25¢.) 1945.

House Rules, Senate Rules, Congressional Record.

KEFAUVER, ESTES. *Twentieth Century Congress.* Essential Books. 1947.

KEY, V. O. *Politics, Parties, and Pressure Groups.* Crowell. 1952. (3d ed.).

RIDDICK, F. *The United States Congress: Organization and Procedure.* National Capital Publishers, Washington, D. C. 1949.

RIGGS, F. W. *Pressures on Congress.* Columbia Univ. Press. 1950.

VOORHIS, J. *Confessions of a Congressman.* Garden City Publishing Co.

WALKER, H. *The Legislative Process.* Ronald. 1948.

WILMERDING, L. *The Spending Power.* Yale Univ. Press. 1944.

WILSON, H. *Congress: Corruption and Compromise.* Rinehart. 1951.

YOUNG, R. *This Is Congress.* Knopf. 1943.

CHAPTER X. — THE EXECUTIVE DEPARTMENT

BINKLEY, W. E. *President and Congress.* Knopf. 1947.

BROWNLOW, L. *The President and the Presidency.* Public Administration Service (Chicago). 1949.

CORWIN, E. *The President: Office and Powers.* N. Y. Univ. Press. 1948 ed.

EWING, C. *Presidential Elections from Lincoln to Roosevelt.* Univ. of Oklahoma Press (Norman, Okla.). 1941.

GERVASI, FRANK. *The Meaning and Purpose of the Hoover Commission Report.* McGraw-Hill. 1949.

LASKI, HAROLD. *The American Presidency.* Harper. 1940.

LAZERSFELD, P. F. *The People's Choice: How a Voter Makes Up His Mind in a Presidential Campaign.* Columbia Univ. Press. 1948.

LEVIN, P. *Seven by Chance: The Accidental Presidents.* Farrar. 1948.

LORANT, S. *The Presidency.* Macmillan. 1951.

MOOS, M. *Politics, Presidents, and Coattails.* Johns Hopkins Press (Baltimore). 1953.

PATTERSON, C. PERRY. *Presidential Government in the United States.* Univ. of North Carolina Press (Chapel Hill, N. C.). 1948.

RANKIN, R. (ed.). *The Presidency in Transition.* Kallman, Gainsville, Florida. 1949.

STODDARD, H. L. *Presidential Sweepstakes: The Story of Political Conventions and Campaigns.* G. P. Putnam's Sons. 1948.

TORPEY, W. *Public Personnel Management.* Van Nostrand. 1953.

CHAPTER XI. — THE DEPARTMENT OF STATE

BAILEY, T. A. *A Diplomatic History of the American People.* Appleton-Century-Crofts. 1950.

BENTWICH, N., and MARTIN, A. *The Charter of the United Nations.* Macmillan. 1950.

BOLLES, B. *The Armed Road to Peace: NATO.* Foreign Policy Assoc. 1952.

CAMPBELL, J. C. *The United States in World Affairs.* Harper. Annual.

CHAMBERLAIN, L. (ed.). *American Foreign Policy.* Rinehart & Co. 1948.

CHILDS, J. RIVES. *American Foreign Service.* Henry Holt & Co. 1948.

Foreign Affairs. Quarterly.

Foreign Policy Reports. Bi-weekly.

GRAHAM, STUART. *The State Department.* Macmillan. 1949.

HULL, CORDELL. *The Memoirs of Cordell Hull.* Macmillan. 1948.

HUTCHINS, ROBERT. *The Atomic Bomb versus Civilization.* Human Events, Inc. 1946.

LEONARD, L. *Elements of American Foreign Policy.* McGraw-Hill. 1953.

LONDON, K. *How Foreign Policy Is Made.* D. Van Nostrand. 1949.

MANGONE, G. *A Short History of International Relations.* McGraw-Hill. 1953.

Massachusetts Institute of Technology. *Publications in International Affairs Twice a Year.*

MORGENTHAU, H. *Principles and Problems of International Politics.* Knopf. 1950.

PERKINS, D. *Evolution of American Foreign Policy.* Oxford Univ. Press. 1948.

PLISCHKE, E. *Conduct of American Diplomacy.* D. Van Nostrand. 1950.

SPROUT, H. *Foundations of National Power.* D. Van Nostrand. 1952. (2d ed.)

STIMSON, H. L., and BUNDY, M. *On Active Service: In Peace and War.* Harper. 1948.

STRAUSZ-HUPE, R., and POSSONY, S. *International Relations.* McGraw-Hill. 1950.

VAN ALSTYNE, R. *American Diplomacy in Action.* Stanford Univ. Press (Stanford, Calif.). 1946.

VANDENBOSCH, A., and HOGAN, W. *The United Nations.* McGraw. 1952.

CHAPTER XII. — THE TREASURY DEPARTMENT

Annual Report of the Secretary of the Treasury.

BACKMAN, J., et al. *War and Defense Economics.* Rinehart. 1952.

CLOUGH, S. *The American Way: The Economic Basis of Our Civilization.* Crowell. 1953.

Committee on Public Debt Policy. *Our National Debt, Its History and Meaning Today.* Harcourt, Brace. 1949.

DIMOCK, M. *Government and Business.* Holt. 1953.

DWINELL, O. C. *The Story of Our Money.* Meador Publishing Co. 1946.

FILLEY, H. *The Wealth of the Nation.* Univ. of Nebraska Press (Lincoln).

KENDRICK, M. *Public Finance.* Houghton-Mifflin. 1950.

KENT, R. *Money and Banking.* Rinehart. 1951.

MAZUR, P. *The Standards We Raise.* Harper. 1953.

PENROSE, E. *Economic Planning for the Peace.* Princeton Univ. Press. (Princeton, N.J.). 1953.

RITTER, L. *Money and Economic Activity.* Houghton-Mifflin. 1952.

STEINER, G. *Government's Role in Economic Life.* McGraw-Hill. 1953.

CHAPTER XIII. — THE DEPARTMENTS OF DEFENSE AND OF JUSTICE

Defense:

Annual reports of the Secretary of Defense and of the Attorney-General.
Information Pamphlet, U. S. Military Academy (West Point, N. Y.).
LASSWELL, H. *National Security and Individual Freedom.* McGraw-Hill.
1953.
LAWRENCE, D. *Atomic Attack.* New York Times. 1950.
METCALF, C. H. *A History of the United States Marine Corps.* Putnam.
NORMAN, R. *Operation Overlord: The Allied Invasion of Western Europe.*
Military Service Publishing Co. (Harrisburg, Pa.). 1952.
PAYNE, R. *The Marshall Story.* Prentice-Hall. 1952.

Justice:

KONVITZ, MILTON. *The Alien and Asiatic in American Law.* Cornell
Univ. Press (Ithaca, N. Y.). 1947.
LYSING, H. *Men Against Crime.* David Kemp & Co. 1938.
THOMPSON, W. *Population Problems.* McGraw-Hill. 1953.
WITTKE, C. *We Who Built America.* Prentice-Hall. 1940.
ZIEGLER, B. *Immigration: An American Dilemma.* Heath (Boston).
1953.

CHAPTER XIV. — THE POST OFFICE AND INTERIOR DEPARTMENTS

CLAWSON, M. *Uncle Sam's Acres.* Dodd, Mead. 1951.
Fortune. "Decline of the Forests," February, 1945. Page 169. "Triumph
of the Empire Builders," February, 1952. Page 111.
PINCHOT, G. *Breaking New Ground.* Harcourt. 1947.
RAUSHENBUSH, S. "The Future of Our Natural Resources." *Annals of
the American Academy.* May, 1952.
SMITH, G. *Conservation of Natural Resources.* Wiley. 1951.

CHAPTER XV. — THE DEPARTMENT OF AGRICULTURE

Annals. *Rural Electrification in the United States.* January, 1939.
BANFIELD, E. *Government Project.* Free Press (Glencoe, Illinois). 1951.
BLAISDELL, D. C. *Government and Agriculture.* Rinehart & Co. 1940.
HARDIN, C. *The Politics of Agriculture.* Free Press (Glencoe, Illinois).
1952.
HICKMAN, C. *Our Farm Program and Foreign Trade.* Council on Foreign
Relations. 58 East 68th Street, New York 21. 1949.
KOLB, J., and BRUNNER. *A Study of Rural Society.* Houghton-Mifflin. 1952.
McCUNE, WESLEY. *The Farm Bloc.* Doubleday. 1943.
McWILLIAMS, C. *Factories in the Fields.* Little, Brown (Boston). 1939.
ROSS, R. *Introduction to Agricultural Economics.* McGraw-Hill. 1951.
STEELE, E. M. *How to Be a Forest Ranger.* R. M. McBride & Co. 1943.
STEVENS, JAMES. *Timber.* Row, Peterson & Co. 1942.
U. S. Report of the Secretary of Agriculture. (Annual.) Government Print-
ing Office (Washington, D. C.).

U. S. What Is Soil Erosion? Government Printing Office (Washington, D. C.). 1938.
U. S. Yearbook of the Dept. of Agriculture. Government Printing Office (Washington, D. C.).
VAN DERSAL, W. R. *The American Land.* Oxford Univ. Press. 1943.

CHAPTER XVI. — COMMERCE AND LABOR DEPARTMENTS

CLOUGH, S. *The American Way: The Economic Basis of Our Civilization.* Crowell. 1953.
DIMOCK, M. *Business and Government.* Holt. 1953.
Domestic Commerce (Monthly) Commerce Department. Government Printing Office (Washington, D. C.).
Foreign Commerce (Weekly) Commerce Department. Government Printing Office (Washington, D. C.).
GALBRAITH, J. *American Capitalism.* Houghton-Mifflin. 1952.
McCRANE, R. *The Economic Development of the American Nation.* Ginn (Boston). 1950.
METZ, H. W., and JACOBSTEIN, M. *The National Labor Policy.* Brookings Institution (Washington, D. C.). 1947.
STOCKING, G., and WATKINS. *Monopoly and Free Enterprise.* Twentieth Century Fund. 1951.
U. S. Report of the Secretary of Commerce. (Annual.) Government Printing Office (Washington, D. C.).
WHELPTON, P. K. *Forecasts of the Population of the United States: 1945–1975.* U. S. Census Bureau. Government Printing Office. 1948.
See Chapters XXXVIII and XXXIX of this list for bibliographies on Labor Problems.

CHAPTER XVII. — TRANSPORTATION, COMMUNICATION,
AND POWER

APPLEBY, P. *Big Democracy.* (Defense of bureaucrats.) Knopf. 1945.
BIGHAM, T. C. *Transportation: Principles and Problems.* McGraw. 1952.
CLARK, W. H. *Railroads and Rivers.* L. C. Page & Co. (Boston). 1939.
CUSHMAN, R. E. *The Independent Regulatory Commissions.* Oxford Univ. Press. 1941.
Electric Power and Government Policy: A Survey of the Relations Between the Government and the Electric Power Industry. The Twentieth Century Fund. 1948.
Foreign Affairs. *Radio as a Political Instrument.* January, 1938.
Fortune. "The Zealous Men of F.T.C.," February, 1952.
MACDOUGALL, C. *Understanding Public Opinion.* Macmillan. 1953.
McKINLEY, C. *Uncle Sam in the Pacific Northwest.* Univ. of California Press (Berkeley). 1952.
SUMMERS, H. B. *The Railroad Problem.* Wilson. 1939.
Twentieth Century Fund. *Power Industry and Public Interest.* The Fund (New York 36).

CHAPTER XVIII. — FINANCIAL AGENCIES OF THE GOVERNMENT

ATKINS, W. E., and OTHERS. *Regulation of the Security Markets.* Brookings Institution (Washington, D. C.). 1946.
BEATY, J. Y. *How to Understand Banks.* Business Publications, Inc.
BROWN, F., and ROUCEK. *One American.* Prentice-Hall. 1952.
CHANDLER, L. V. *The Economics of Money and Banking.* Harper. 1948.
CLOUGH, S. *The Rise and Fall of Civilization.* McGraw. 1951.
DULLES, E. *The Export-Import Bank.* (Dept. of State Publication 2234. Commercial Policy Series 75. 10¢.) (Washington, D. C.)
KENT, R. *Money and Banking.* Rinehart. 1950.
KREPS, C. *Federal Taxes.* Wilson. 1952.
LEEK, J. *Government and Labor in the United States.* Rinehart. 1952.
LEVI, W. *Fundamentals of World Organization.* Univ. of Minnesota Press (Minneapolis). 1952.
MIKESELL, R. *United States Economic Policy and International Relations.* McGraw. 1952.
MOULTON, H. *America's Wealth.* Brookings Institution. 1952.
OXENFELDT, A. *Economics for the Citizen.* Rinehart. 1953.
ROHLFING, C. *et al. Business and Government.* Foundation Press (Brooklyn). 1953.
STEIN, H. *Public Administration and Policy Development.* Harcourt, Brace. 1952.

CHAPTER XIX. — DEPARTMENT OF HEALTH, EDUCATION AND WELFARE

DOUGLAS, PAUL. *Social Security in the United States.* McGraw. 1939.
GAER, J. *What Uncle Sam Owes You.* Wilfred Funk, Inc. 1943.
General Motors. *How to Plan and Pay for Better Highways.* (Detroit). 1953.
HOHMAN, H. F. *Old Age in Sweden.* 1940.
MERIAM, L. *Relief and Social Security.* Brookings Institution (Washington, D. C.). 1946.
SERBEIN, O. *Paying for Medical Care in the United States.* Columbia Univ. Press. 1953.

CHAPTER XX. — TERRITORIES AND OTHER DEPENDENCIES

ABELARDE, P. *American Tariff Policy Towards the Philippines.* Kings Crown Press. 1947.
BARBEAU, M. *Alaska Beckons.* Caxton Printers. 1947.
BERNSTEIN, DAVID. *The Philippine Story.* Farrar, Strauss. 1947.
Fortune. "The Philippines," June, 1940. "Hawaii," August, 1940. "Panama," January, 1941. "Puerto Rico," February, 1941.
GRIFFENHAGEN and ASSOCIATES. *The Organization of Government for the District of Columbia.* 1939.

Hawaii Bureau of Research. *Our Territorial Government.* The Bureau (Hawaii). 1949.
HERRON, E. A. *Alaska, Land of Tomorrow.* Whittlesey House. 1947.
HILSCHER, H. H. *Alaska Now.* Little, Brown (Boston). 1948.
JONES, G., and OTHERS. *Washington — Yesterday and Today.* Ginn. 1943.
LIND, A. W. *Hawaii's Japanese, An Experiment in Democracy.* 1946.
MAGRUDER, F. A. *National Governments and International Relations.* Allyn & Bacon. 1950. "Caribbean Dependencies of the United States," Chapter III. "Hawaii, Alaska, and Our Outposts," Chapter XXV. "The Philippines," Chapter XXVI.
OLIVER, D. *The Pacific Islands.* Harvard Univ. Press (Cambridge). 1951.
PETRULLO, VINCENZO. *Puerto Rican Paradox.* Univ. of Pennsylvania (Philadelphia). 1947.

CHAPTER XXI. — THE JUDICIARY

ANGELL, E. *Supreme Court Primer.* Reynal & Hitchcock. 1937.
CALLENDER, C. N. *American Courts.* McGraw. 1927.
CARR, ROBERT. *The Supreme Court and Judicial Review.* Rinehart & Co.
HUGHES, CHAS. E. *The Supreme Court of the United States.* Columbia University Press. 1928.
JOHNSON, J. E. *Power of Court to Declare Acts Unconstitutional.* 1936.
MCCUNE, WESLEY. *Nine Young Men.* 1947.
SHOLLEY, J. *Cases on Constitutional Law.* Bobbs-Merrill (Indianapolis). 1951.

CHAPTER XXII. — CIVIL RIGHTS AND LIBERTIES

Annals of the American Academy of Political and Social Science. *Constitutional Rights.* The Academy. January, 1938.
BECKER, CARL, and OTHERS. *Safeguarding Civil Liberty Today.* 1947.
CARR, ROBERT. *Federal Protection of Civil Rights.* Cornell Univ. Press (Ithaca, N. Y.). 1948.
CHAFFEE, Z. *Free Speech in the United States.* Harvard Univ. Press (Cambridge, Mass.). 1941.
EMERSON, T., and HABER, D. *Political and Civil Rights in the United States.* Dennis. (Buffalo). 1953.
FRAENKEL, O. *Our Civil Liberties.* The Viking Press. 1944.
HOCKING, W. E. *Freedom of the Press.* Univ. of Chicago Press (Chicago).
HURST, J. W. *The Growth of American Law.* Little, Brown (Boston). 1950.
KONVITZ, MILTON. *The Constitution and Civil Rights.* Columbia Univ. Press. 1947.
NEWMAN, E. *The Law of Civil Rights and Civil Liberties.* Oceana Publications (New York 11). 1949.
PATTERSON, G. J. *Free Speech and a Free Press.* Little, Brown (Boston).
WORMAER, R. *The Law.* Simon and Schuster. 1949.

CHAPTER XXIII. — POLITICAL PARTIES AND POLITICS

BONE, H. *American Politics and the Party System.* McGraw-Hill. 1949.

BUCHANAN, L. *People and Politics.* Stephen-Paul. 1949.

EWING, C. A. M. *Presidential Elections.* Univ. of Oklahoma Press (Norman, Okla.). 1940.

GALLUP, G. H. *A Guide to Public Opinion Polls.* Princeton Univ. Press (Princeton, N. J.). 1944.

GOSNELL, H. F., and MERRIAM, C. E. *Grass Roots Politics.* American Council on Public Affairs. 1942.

HERRING, E. P. *The Politics of Democracy; Parties in Action.* W. W. Norton & Co. 1940.

HESSELTINE, W. B. *The Rise and Fall of Third Parties.* Public Affairs Press (Washington, D. C.). 1948.

IRION, F. C. *Public Opinion and Propaganda.* Crowell. 1950.

KEY, V. O. *Politics, Parties and Pressure Groups.* Crowell. 1952.

McKEAN, D. D. *Party and Pressure Politics.* Houghton-Mifflin (Boston).

MERRIAM, C., and GOSNELL. *An Introduction to the Study of Political Parties in the United States.* Macmillan. 1949 ed.

ODEGARD, PETER. *American Politics.* Harper. 1947.

PENNIMAN, H. R. *Sait's American Parties and Elections.* Appleton-Century-Crofts. 1952.

SCOTT, H. *How to Go Into Politics.* John Day Co. 1949.

CHAPTER XXIV. — SUFFRAGE

BEAN, L. H. *Ballot Behavior.* American Council on Public Affairs. 1940.

CHRISTENSEN, A., and KIRKPATRICK, E. *The People, Politics, and the Politician.* Holt. 1953.

GALLUP, G. H. *The Pulse of Democracy.* Simon & Schuster. 1940.

PORTER, K. H. *History of Suffrage in the United States.* Univ. of Chicago Press (Chicago). 1918.

CHAPTER XXV. — NOMINATIONS AND ELECTIONS

ALBRIGHT, S. D. *The American Ballot.* American Council on Public Affairs. 1942.

BEAN, L. H. *Ballot Behavior.* American Council on Public Affairs. 1940.

BONE, H. *American Politics and the Party System.* McGraw-Hill. 1954.

BROOKS, R. C. *Political Parties and Electoral Problems.* Harper. 1933.

CHILDS, R. S. *Short Ballot.* National Municipal League. 1930.

DANIELS, W. (ed.). *Presidential Election Reforms.* Wilson. 1953.

HALLETT, GEO. *Proportional Representation.* National Municipal League. 1940. 25¢.

HARRIS, J. P. *Election Administration in the United States.* Brookings Institution (Washington, D. C.). 1934.

KEY, V. *Politics, Parties and Pressure Groups.* Crowell. 1952.

LEWIS, S. *Party Principles and Party Practices.* Prentice-Hall. 1928.

MERRIAM, C. E., and OVERACKER. *Primary Elections.* Univ. of Chicago Press (Chicago). 1928.

Election Laws of your State.
Sample Ballots.

CHAPTER XXVI. — STATE CONSTITUTIONS

ANDERSON, W., and WEIDNER, E. *State and Local Government.* Holt. 1951.

Council of State Governments. *Book of the States.* The Council (Chicago). Biennial.

GRAVES, W. *American State Government.* Heath (Boston). 1953.

LANCASTER, L., and BRECKENRIDGE, A. *Readings in American State Government.* Rinehart. 1950.

McLEAN, J. *American Democracy in Theory and Practice: State and Local Government.* Rinehart. 1953.

National Municipal League. *Model State Constitution.* The League. 1948.

SNIDER, C. *American State and Local Government.* Appleton-Century-Crofts. 1951.

A copy of the State constitution can usually be obtained gratis from the Secretary of State.

CHAPTER XXVII. — STATE LEGISLATURES

Annals of the American Academy of Political and Social Science. *Our State Legislators.* The Academy. January, 1938.

BUCK, A. E. *Modernizing Our State Legislatures.* American Academy of Political and Social Science. 1936.

GRAVES, W. B. *American State Government.* D. C. Heath (Boston). 1953.

JOHNSON, A. W. *The Unicameral Legislature.* Univ. of Minnesota (Minneapolis). 1938. (In 1937 books appeared under practically the same title by Aly, B.; Buehler, E. C.; Senning, J.; Smith, E. P.; Summers, H. B.; and Walch, J. W.)

JOHNSON, C. *State and Local Government.* Crowell. 1950.

KEY, V. O., and CROUCH, W. W. *The Initiative and Referendum in California.* University of California (Berkeley). 1939.

LUCE, R. *Legislative Assemblies.* Houghton-Mifflin. 1924.

Legislative Problems. Houghton-Mifflin. 1935.

MACDONALD, A. F. *American State Government and Administration.* Chaps. 7–9. Crowell. 1950.

McLEAN, J. *American Democracy in Theory and Practice: State and Local Government.* Rinehart. 1953.

WALKER, H. *The Legislative Process.* The Ronald Press Co. 1948.

WINSLOW, C. I. *State Legislative Committees.* Johns Hopkins Press (Baltimore). 1931.

CHAPTER XXVIII. — STATE GOVERNORS

BATES, *et al.* *State Government.* Chaps. 11–12. Harper. 1950.

GRAVES, W. B. *American State Government.* Chaps. 9–12. D. C. Heath (Boston). 1953.

JOHNSON, C. *State and Local Government.* Chaps. 3, 6, 8. Crowell. 1950.

MACDONALD, A. F. *American State Government and Administration.* Chaps. 10 and 15. Crowell. 1950.

MATHEWS, J. M. *American State Government.* Appleton-Century-Crofts.

OGG and RAY. *Essentials of American Government.* Chaps. 32–33. Appleton-Century-Crofts. 1950.

SNIDER, C. *American State and Local Government.* Chaps. 9–10. Appleton-Century-Crofts. 1951.

CHAPTER XXIX. — STATE COURTS

ANDERSON, W., and WEIDNER, E. *State and Local Government.* Chaps. 18, 26. Holt. 1951.

GOSNELL, C., and HOLLAND, L. *State and Local Government in the United States.* Chaps. 13–14. Prentice-Hall. 1951.

GRAVES, W. *American State Government.* Chaps. 16–20. Heath. (Boston). 1953.

POUND, R. *Organization of Courts.* Little, Brown (Boston). 1940.

CHAPTER XXX. — CIVIL AND CRIMINAL PROCEDURE

American Academy of Political and Social Science. *Murder and the Penalty of Death.* The Academy. 1952.

American Academy of Political and Social Science. *Administration of Justice.* The Academy. 1933.

GRAVES, W. *American State Government.* Chaps. 16–20. Heath (Boston). 1953.

JACKSON, P. E. *Look at the Law.* Dutton & Co., Inc. 1940.

ORFIELD, L. B. *Criminal Procedure from Arrest to Appeal.* New York University Press. 1947.

Copies of warrants of arrest, indictments, subpoenas, summonses, etc.

CHAPTER XXXI. — STATE FINANCE

Annual Report of the State Tax Commission.

Annual Report of the State Treasurer.

BLAKEY, R. G. and G. C. *Sales Taxes and Other Excises.* Public Administration Service. 1945.

GRAHAM, F. P., and OTHERS. *The Poll Tax.* American Council on Public Affairs. 1940.

GRAVES, W. B. *American State Government.* Chaps. 13–14. D. C. Heath (Boston). 1953.

MACDONALD, A. F. *American State Government and Administration.* Chaps. 17–19. Crowell. 1950.

Public Administration Service. *Grants-in-Aid and Other Federal Expenditures within the States.* The Service. 1947.

Public Administration Service. *Postwar State Taxation and Finance.* The Service. 1947.

CHAPTER XXXII. — COUNTY AND TOWNSHIP GOVERNMENT

BISHOP, D. G. *The Structure of Local Government.* National Council for the Social Studies. 1945.

CARPENTER, W. *State and Local Government in the U. S.* Crofts. 1936.
FAIRLIE, J. A. *County Government and Administration.* Appleton-Century-Crofts. 1930.
FISHER, M., and BISHOP, D. *Municipal and Other Local Governments.* Chaps. 2, 27, 28. Prentice-Hall. 1950.
GOULD, JOHN. *New England Town Meeting.* Steven Daye Press, Inc.
LANCASTER, L. W. *Government in Rural America.* Van Nostrand. 1953.
LONG, H. C. *County Library Service.* American Library Association.
MULLER, HELEN. *County Manager Government.* H. W. Wilson Co. 1930.
National Municipal League. *County Manager Plan.* The League. 1948.
PONTIUS, D. *State Supervision of Local Government.* American Council on Public Affairs. 1942.
WELLS, R. H. *American Local Government.* McGraw. 1939.
The Manual or Legislative Handbook of your State.

CHAPTER XXXIII. — VILLAGE AND CITY GOVERNMENT

ANDERSON, W., and WEIDNER, E. *American City Government.* Holt. 1950.
CHILDS, R. S. *Best Practice under City Manager Plan.* National Municipal League. 1953. 15¢.
Forms of Municipal Government: How Have They Worked? National Municipal League. 1953. 25¢.
International City Managers' Association. *Municipal Year Book.* The Association (Chicago).
KNEIER, C., and FOX, G. *Readings in Municipal Government.* Rinehart. 1953.
MACCORKLE, STUART A. *American Municipal Government and Administration.* D. C. Heath (Boston). 1948.
MACDONALD, A. F. *American City Government and Administration.* Crowell. 1951.
MOTT, R. L. *Home Rule for American Cities.* American Municipal Association. Chicago. 1949.
National Municipal Review (Monthly).
NEVANS, A. (editor). *The Greater City: New York.* Columbia Univ. Press. 1948.
SCHULZ, E. *American City Government.* Stackpole and Heck. Philadelphia, 1949.
ZINK, H. *City Government in the United States.* Macmillan. 1947. The City Charter of your city.

CHAPTER XXXIV. — VILLAGE AND CITY PROBLEMS

ADAMS, T. *Outline of Town and City Planning.* Russell Sage Foundation.
BARD, E. W. *The Port of New York Authority.* Columbia Univ. Press.
CHILDS, R. *Civic Victories: The Story of an Unfinished Revolution.* Harper. 1953.
FABRICANT, S. *The Trend of Government Activity in the United States Since 1900.* National Bureau of Economic Research, 1952.
GREER, GUY. *Your City Tomorrow.* Macmillan. 1947.
Holiday. "San Francisco." September, 1953. (Entire Issue.)

Illinois Legislative Council. *Structure of Governments in Metropolitan Areas.* Univ. of Illinois (Urbana). 1952.

MUMFORD, L. *City Development.* Harcourt, Brace & Co. 1945.

Municipal Year Book. International City Managers' Association (Chicago).

MUNRO, W. B. *Municipal Administration.* Macmillan. 1934.

National Municipal League. *City Growing Pains.* The League. 1941.

National Municipal Review (Monthly).

Newark Bureau of Municipal Research. *The Development of Newark Government* (Newark, N.J.). 1953.

PFIFFNER, J. M. *Municipal Administration.* The Ronald Press Co. 1946.

QUEEN, S., and CARPENTER, D. *The American City.* McGraw-Hill. 1953.

SAARINEN, E. *The City — Its Growth — Its Decay — Its Future.* Reinhold Publishing Corp. 1943.

SANDERS, I. *Making Good Communities Better.* University of Kentucky Press (Lexington). 1953.

SEARS, P. *Los Alamos — Boom Town Under Control.* University of New Mexico (Albuquerque). 1953.

The American City (Monthly) (470 Fourth Ave., New York).

THORNDIKE, E. L. *Your City.* Harcourt, Brace & Co. 1939.

WILSON, NORMAN. *Municipal Health Services.* Macmillan. 1947.

CHAPTER XXXV. — PUBLIC EDUCATION

BOGUE, JESSE P. (ed.). *American Junior Colleges.* American Council on Education (Washington, D. C.). 1948.

BRUMBAUGH, A. J. *American Universities and Colleges.* American Council on Education (Washington, D. C.). 1948.

Citizens Research Council of Michigan. *Schools and the Modern Community.* Detroit 26. 1953.

Congressional Digest. "Federal Funds for Public Schools." Feb. 1946.

Council of State Governments (Chicago). *The Forty-Eight State School Systems.* 1949.

DOUGLASS, H. *American Public Education.* The Ronald Press. 1948.

HAVEMANN, E., and WEST, P. *They Went to College: The College Graduate in America Today.* Harcourt, Brace. 1952.

MULHERN, JAMES. *A History of Education.* The Ronald Press. 1946.

POSTON, R. *Democracy Is You.* Harper. 1953.

QUATTLEBAUM, C. A. *Federal Aid to Elementary and Secondary Education.* Public Administration Service (Chicago). 1948.

RESTOR, A. *Educational Wastelands.* University of Illinois (Urbana). 1953.

SUMPTION, M. *How to Conduct a Citizen School Survey.* Prentice-Hall. 1952.

THURSTON, HENRY. *The Education of Youth as Citizens.* Richard K. Smith. 1947.

WYMAN, L. K. *Character and Citizenship through Student Government.* John C. Winston Co. 1935.

Annual Report of the State Superintendent of Education.
Annual Report of the United States Commissioner of Education.
A Summary of School Laws. (Usually distributed by the State Superintendent.)
Biennial Survey of Education issued by the U. S. Office of Education (Washington, D. C.).

CHAPTER XXXVI. — MAKING DEMOCRACY WORK

American Citizens Handbook (United Nations Ed.) National Educational Association, Washington 6, D. C. 1948.
CHILDS, R. *Civic Victories: The Story of an Unfinished Revolution.* Harper, 1953.
Final Report of the American Bar Association Commission on Organized Crime. American Bar Association (Washington). 1952.
GALLUP, G. H. *The Pulse of Democracy.* Simon & Schuster. 1940.
GOSNELL, H. *Democracy: The Threshold of Freedom.* Ronald. 1949.
HAYS, A. G. *Democracy Works.* Random House. 1939.
HOOTEN, E. A. *Crime and the Man.* Harvard Univ. Press (Cambridge, Mass.). 1939.
MIMS, E., JR. *The Majority of the People.* Geo. J. McLeod, Ltd. (Toronto). 1941.
MOSHER, W. E. *An Introduction to a Responsible Citizenship.* Henry Holt & Co. 1942.
POSTON, R. *Democracy Is You.* Harper. 1953.
RIKER, W. *Democracy in the United States.* Macmillan. 1953.
STAPLETON, L. *The Design of Democracy.* Oxford Univ. Press. 1949.
VON HENTIG, HANS. *Crime: Causes and Conditions.* McGraw. 1947.
WRIGHT, D. M. *Democracy and Progress.* Macmillan. 1948.

CHAPTER XXXVII. — THE GOVERNMENT SERVICE AS A CAREER

DIMOCK, M., and DIMOCK, G. *Public Administration.* Rinehart. 1953.
GRAVES, W. B. *Public Administration.* Heath. 1950.
HYNEMAN, C. *Bureaucracy in a Democracy.* Harper. 1950.
MARX, F. M. *Elements of Public Administration.* Prentice-Hall. 1946.
MOSHER, W. E. *Public Personnel Administration.* Harper. 1941.
NIGRO, F. *Public Administration: Readings and Documents.* Rinehart. 1953.
SIMON, H., *et al. Public Administration.* Knopf. 1950.
SPERO, STERLING. *Government as Employer.* Remsen Press. 1948.
WHITE, L. D. *Introduction to the Study of Public Administration.* Macmillan. 1948.
U. S. Civil Service Commission. *Civil Service Act* (regulations, etc.). Government Printing Office (Washington, D. C.).
U. S. History of the Federal Civil Service. Government Printing Office.

CHAPTER XXXVIII. — SOCIAL LEGISLATION

ABRAMS, C. *The Future of Housing.* Harper. 1947.

BACHMAN, G. W., and MERIAM, L. *The Issuance of Compulsory Health Insurance.* Brookings Institution (Washington, D. C.). 1948.

BAUER, L. H. *Private Enterprise or Government in Medicine.* Charles C. Thomas (Springfield, Ill.). 1948.

BURNS, E. *American Social Security System.* Houghton-Mifflin, Boston. 1949.

CHERNICK, JACK. *Guaranteed Annual Wages.* Univ. of Minn. 1945.

DE SCHWEINTIZ, K., *et al.* *Man and Modern Society.* Holt. 1953.

DULLES, J. FOSTER. *Labor in America.* Thomas Y. Crowell Co. 1949.

KAPLAN, A. D. H. *The Guarantee of Annual Wages.* Brookings Institution (Washington, D. C.). 1947.

LEVENSTEIN, A. *Labor Today and Tomorrow.* Knopf. 1946.

METZ, H. W. *Is There Enough Manpower?* Brookings Institution. 1948.
Labor Policy of the Federal Government. Brookings Institution (Washington, D. C.). 1945.

METZ, H. W., and JACOBSTEIN, M. *International Labor Policy.* Brookings Institution (Washington, D. C.). 1948.

MILLER, B. F. *You and Your Doctor.* McGraw. 1948.

MILLER, G. *American Labor and the Government.* Prentice-Hall. 1949.

MUSTARD, H. S. *Government in Public Health.* Commonwealth Fund.

PETERSON, F. *American Labor Unions.* Harper. 1946.

SERBEIN, O. *Paying for Medical Care in the United States.* Columbia Univ. Press. 1953.

SPIEGEL, H. *Current Economic Problems.* Blakiston Co. Phila. 1949.

DE VYVER, T. F., and CUMMINS, E. E. *Labor Problems in the United States.* Van Nostrand. 1947.

CHAPTER XXXIX. — PROGRESSIVE PLANNING

BEVERIDGE, W. *Full Employment in a Free Society.* Norton. 1945.

BROOKS, B. *Peace, Plenty, and Petroleum.* Jaques Cattell Press. 1944.

CHASE, STUART. *Democracy Under Pressure.* Twentieth Century Fund.

DIMOCK, M. *Business and Government.* Holt. 1953.

GOLDMAN, E. *Rendezvous with Destiny.* Knopf. 1953.

GOODMAN, P. *Communitas* (Community planning). Univ. of Chicago Press (Chicago). 1947.

HANSEN, A. *Economic Policy and Full Employment.* McGraw. 1947.

INFIELD, H. *Cooperative Communities at Work* [here and abroad]. The Dryden Press. 1945.

LILIENTHAL, D. *Big Business: A New Era.* Harper. 1953.

McWILLIAMS, C. *Ill Fares the Land.* Little, Brown (Boston). 1942.

PENROSE, E. *Economic Planning for the Peace.* Princeton Univ. Press. (Princeton, N.J.). 1953.

PRITCHETT, C. H. *The Tennessee Valley Authority.* University of North Carolina Press (Chapel Hill, N. C.). 1943.

RODGERS, CLEVELAND. *American Planning* [past, present, future]. Harper. 1947.

ROHLFING, C., *et al. Business and Government.* Foundation Press (Brooklyn). 1953.

SELZNICK, P. *TVA and the Grass Roots.* University of California Press (Berkeley). 1949.

CHAPTER XL. — THE UNITED NATIONS AND BASES FOR A LASTING PEACE

ARNE, SIGRID. *United Nations Primer.* Rinehart. 1948.

BENTWICH, N., and MARTIN, A. *The Charter of the United Nations.* Macmillan. 1950.

BERNARD, L. *War and Its Causes.* 1945.

BRIGGS, H. *Law of Nations.* Appleton. 1952.

BROWN, S. (ed.). *Great Issues.* Harper. 1951.

CARR, W. G. *One World in the Making.* Ginn and Co. 1947.

CHASE, E. *The United Nations in Action.* McGraw. 1950.

CORNELL, JULIEN. *New World Primer.* New Directions Books. 1948.

EVATT, H. V. *The United Nations.* Harvard Univ. Press. 1948.

Everybody's United Nations. Funk and Wagnalls. 1948. $1.00.

GALT, TOM. *How the United Nations Works.* Crowell. 1947.

HARTMAN, H. *Readings in International Relations.* McGraw. 1952.

JOHNSON, J. E. (Comp.). *United Nations or World Government.* H. W. Wilson. 1947.

MAGRUDER, F. A. *National Governments and International Relations.* Allyn and Bacon (Boston). 1950.

MANDER, LINDEN. *Foundations of Modern World Society.* Stanford Univ. Press (Palo Alto, Calif.). 1947.

MORGENTHAU, H. *Principles and Problems of International Politics.* Knopf. 1950.

OSGOOD, R. *Ideals and Self-Interest in America's Foreign Relations.* Univ. of Chicago Press (Chicago). 1953.

PALMER, N., and PERKINS, H. *International Relations.* Houghton-Mifflin (Boston). 1953.

PLISCHKE, E. *International Relations: Basic Documents.* Van Nostrand. 1953.

SCHUMAN, F. *International Organization.* McGraw. 1953.

STRAUSZ-HUPE, R., and POSSONY, S. *International Relations.* McGraw-Hill. 1950.

THEIMER, W. *An Encyclopedia of Modern World Politics.* Rinehart. 1950.

"The United Nations." *Current History.* January, 1952. (Entire Issue.)

United Nations. *Yearbook of the United Nations.* Department of Public Information, United Nations (Lake Success, N. Y.).

WILLKIE, WENDELL L. *One World.* Simon & Schuster. 1943.

WRIGHT, QUINCY. *A Study of War.* Cambridge Univ. Press (London).

CHAPTER XLI. — THE UNITED STATES IN WORLD AFFAIRS

BAILEY, T. A. *Diplomatic History of the American People.* Appleton-Century-Crofts. 1950.

BEMIS, S. F. *Diplomatic History of the United States.* Holt. 1950.

BEUKEMA, H. *Contemporary Foreign Governments.* 1950.

BRINTON, C. C. *From Many One.* (Problems of World Federation.) Harvard Univ. Press. 1948.

BROWDER, R. *The Origin of Soviet-American Diplomacy.* Princeton Univ. Press (Princeton, N.J.). 1953.

BUCK, P., and MASLAND, J. *The Governments of Foreign Powers.* Holt. 1950.

CARR, E. H. *The Soviet Impact on the Western World.* Macmillan. 1947.

DEAN, VERA M. *The United States and Russia.* Harvard Univ. Press (Cambridge, Mass.). 1948.

North Atlantic Defense Pact. Foreign Policy Reports. February 15, 1949.

DULLES, JOHN FOSTER. *War or Peace.* Macmillan. 1950.

FEIS, H. *The China Tangle.* Princeton Univ. Press (Princeton, N.J.). 1953.

FRYE, R. *Iran.* Holt. 1953.

HARPER, S. *Government of the Soviet Union.* D. Van Nostrand. 1949.

JACK, E. (ed.). *Background of the Middle East.* Cornell Univ. Press (Ithaca). 1952.

LEONARD, L. *Elements of American Foreign Policy.* McGraw-Hill. 1953.

MANGONE, G. *A Short History of International Relations.* McGraw-Hill. 1954.

LEVI, W. *Free India in Asia.* Univ. of Minnesota Press (Minneapolis). 1952.

McCLOY, J. *The Challenge to American Foreign Policy.* Harvard Univ. Press (Cambridge). 1953.

MIKESELL, R. *Arabian Oil: America's Stake in the Middle East.* Univ. of N. C. Press (Raleigh). 1949.

PADELFORD, N. (ed.). *Contemporary International Relations.* Massachusetts Institute of Technology (Cambridge, Mass.). 1953.

RANNEY and CARTER. *The Major Foreign Powers.* Harcourt, Brace & Co. 1952.

REISCHAUER, E. *Japan and America Today.* Stanford Univ. Press. (Stanford, Calif.). 1953.

THAYER, P. (Ed.). *Southeast Asia in the Coming World.* The Johns Hopkins Press. (Baltimore). 1953.

U. S. DEPARTMENT OF STATE. *Our Foreign Policy.* Pub. No. 3972. 1952.

U. S. SENATE COMMITTEE ON FOREIGN RELATIONS. *A Decade of American Foreign Policy.* Washington, D. C. 1950.

WELLES, SUMNER. *We Need Not Fail.* Houghton (Boston). 1948.

WHITAKER, A. P. *The United States and South America: Northern Republics.* Harvard Univ. Press (Cambridge, Mass.). 1948.

WILCOX, F., and KALIJARVI. *Recent American Foreign Policy.* Appleton. 1951.

APPENDIX IV

GOVERNMENT PUBLICATIONS

SUPERINTENDENT OF DOCUMENTS
GOVERNMENT PRINTING OFFICE
WASHINGTON, D. C.

EVERY American should be interested in the publications issued by the Government, for public documents are the history of the country. While a small proportion of the issues might be obtained without cost through the friendship of public men, by far the larger part must be purchased, and nearly everyone interested in the literature of the United States prefers to pay for what he desires, rather than to be under obligation for small favors. Because of this it may be desirable to give the widest possible publicity to the fact that public documents can be purchased from the Superintendent of Documents, Government Printing Office, at a nominal cost.

Price lists, like those on the following page, indicate the subjects covered, and may be obtained free, upon application in person or by mail. The character of the price lists may be better understood by an illustration. Price List 45, entitled Public Roads Office, lists several hundred reports, bulletins, and circulars, which sell for five or ten cents each. The following titles are typical: Sand-clay and earth roads in the Middle West; Dust prevention and road preservation; Bitumens and their essential constituents for road construction and maintenance; Examination and classification of rocks for road building; Road-making material in Arkansas; Public roads of Alabama (and each of the other states); Federal aid; Highway signs; Roadside improvements; Inter-American Highway; Traffic and taxation of motor vehicles.

The *Monthly Catalog of U. S. Public Documents* is available at $3.00 a year. Send order with remittance to Superintendent of Documents, United States Government Printing Office, Washington 25, D. C.

A biweekly list of *Selected U. S. Government Publications*, arranged alphabetically by subjects, with prices and annotations, may be obtained free upon application.

The rules of the Government Printing Office require that remittances be made in advance of shipment of publications, either by coupons, sold in sets of 20 for $1 and good until used, or by check or money order, payable to the Superintendent of Documents. Currency may be sent at sender's risk. Foreign money or defaced or smooth coins are not acceptable. Do not send postage stamps.

(Lists 1 to 9, 12 to 14, etc. are out of print)

10. **Laws.** Federal statutes and compilations of laws on various subjects.
11. **Foods and Cooking.** Home economics, household recipes, canning, cold storage.
15. **Geological Survey.** Covers geology and water supply.
18. **Engineering and Surveying.** Leveling, tides, magnetism, triangulation, and earthquakes.
19. **Army and Militia.** National defense, veterans' affairs.
20. **Public Domain.** Public lands, conservation, National Resources Planning Board.
21. **Fish and Wildlife Service,** and other publications relating to fish and wildlife.
24. **Indians.** Publications pertaining to Indians, anthropology, and archeology.
25. **Transportation and Panama Canal.** Railroad and shipping problems, postal service, communications, Coast Guard, Panama Canal.
28. **Finance.** Banking, securities, loans.
31. **Education.** Includes agriculture and vocational education and libraries.
32. **Insular Possessions.** (Philippines, Puerto Rico, Guam, American Samoa, Virgin Islands.)
33. **Labor.** Child labor, women workers, wages, workmen's insurance and compensation.
35. **Geography and Explorations.** National parks, guidebooks.
36. **Government Periodicals,** for which subscriptions are taken.
37. **Tariff.** Compilation of acts, decisions, and regulations, relating to tariff, taxation, and income tax.
38. **Animal Industry.** Domestic animals, poultry, and dairy industries.
41. **Insects.** Bees and honey, and insects harmful to man, animals, and plants.
42. **Irrigation, Drainage, Water Power.** Federal Power Commission, water resources.
43. **Forestry.** National forests, ranges, lumber and timber.
44. **Plants.** Culture of fruits, vegetables, cereals, grasses, grain.
45. **Roads.** Construction, improvement, and maintenance.
46. **Agricultural Chemistry and Soils and Fertilizers.** Chemistry of foods, soil surveys, soil erosion, and conservation.
48. **Weather, Astronomy, and Meteorology.** Climate, floods, aerological observations.

49. **Proceedings of Congress.** Bound volumes of Congressional Record and Congressional Globe.
50. **American History and Biography.** The Revolution, Civil War, World War.
51. **Health.** Diseases, drugs, sanitation, water pollution.
53. **Maps.** Government maps, and directions for obtaining them.
54. **Political Science.** Government, crime, District of Columbia, Supreme Court, un-American activities.
55. **National Museum.** Contributions from National Herbarium, National Academy of Sciences, and Smithsonian reports.
58. **Mines.** Explosives, fuel, gas, gasoline, petroleum, minerals.
59. **Interstate Commerce.** Steam railways, motor carriers, carriers by water.
60. **Alaska and Hawaii.** Mineral and agricultural resources, coal lands, geology, water supply, seal fisheries.
62. **Commerce and Manufactures.** Foreign trade patents, trusts, public utilities.
63. **Navy.** Publications relating to Navy and Marine Corps.
64. **Standards of Weight and Measures.** Tests of metals, building materials, electricity, photography.
65. **Foreign Relations.** Executive agreements, treaties, neutrality, international conferences.
67. **Immigration.** Aliens, citizenship, naturalization, races.
68. **Farm Management.** Agricultural credit, farm products, marketing, agricultural statistics.
69. **Pacific States:** California, Oregon, Washington. All material relating to these States.
70. **Census.** Statistics of population, manufactures, agriculture, occupations.
71. **Children's Bureau,** and other publications relating to children.
72. **Suburbanites.** Publications of interest to suburbanites and home builders.
75. **Federal Specifications.** Federal standard stock catalog.
77. **World War II.** National defense, postwar planning.

List of Field Manuals and Technical Manuals.

List of Radio Publications.

The foregoing by no means embrace all the subjects treated in public documents. If you fail to see here what you want, send your inquiries to the —

SUPERINTENDENT OF DOCUMENTS,
GOVERNMENT PRINTING OFFICE,
WASHINGTON, D. C.

"PROCLAIM LIBERTY THROUGHOUT ALL THE LAND UNTO ALL THE INHABITANTS THEREOF."

INDEX

Accidents, traffic, 612, 620.
Acreage allotments, 288.
Adult education, 626.
Aeronautics Committee, 316–319.
Agricultural Conservation and Adjustment, 283–290.
Agriculture, Department of, 277–292.
Air Force, 227, 228, 238–240.
Air Transportation, 316–319.
Alaska, 357–362.
Alcoholic drinks, 212, 675–676.
Aliens, admission of, 249; deportation of, 250; exclusion of undesirable, 246–247; naturalization of, 251–254; quotas, 247–248.
Ambassadors, 195–198.
Amendments, Federal, 73–78, 743–744, 745–754; State, 466–470.
American Arbitration Association, 519.
American Federation of Labor, 677–680.
American Heritage, 1, 5, 12.
Amnesty, 185.
Animal Industry, Bureau of, 277–278.
Anti-Federalists, 52, 55.
Anti-trust laws, 139–141.
Arab States, 725.
Arbitration, to settle disputes, 519–520.
Archivist of the U.S., 169 note, 194.
Army, 736, 740, branches of, 230–231; duties of, 228; federal powers, 60; National Guard, 232; organization of, 228–232; Secretary of, 228.
Articles of Confederation, 47–49.
Assemble, right to, 408–409.
Atomic bomb, 9, 10, 15, 128, 237–239, 617.
Atomic Energy, Commission, 242–243; international control of, 711–712.
Attachés, 198–199.
Attainder, Bill of, 397, 737, 738.
Attorney-General, State, 502; U.S., 243; Auditor, county, 562; State, 502.

Bail, 528 note.
Ballots, 170, 449, 452–458.
Bankruptcy, 63 note, 100–101, 735.
Banks, National, 325–333; State, 325–327.
Bicameralism, 80–82, 474–475.
Bill of attainder, 397, 737, 738.
Bill of Rights, 5, 55, 74, 402–414, 466, 745–747.
Billboards, 606–607.
Bills, public and private, 160, 734–735, 737, 738; congressional, 154–160; State legislatures, 481–485.
Blue Cross, 669.

Bonds, Government, 100, 216–217, 261–262.
Bonneville Dam, 268, 322, 501.
Boulder Project, 267.
Bribery, in elections, 434.
Budget, National, 160–161, 183; State, 546–548.
Bureau of, the Budget, 160; Foreign and Domestic Commerce, 302; Internal Revenue, 210–211; Investigation, 243; Labor Statistics, 305; Labor Standards, 306; Land Management, 263–265; Mines, 272; Prisons, 243–245; Reclamation, 265–267; Standards, 103–104, 295–296.

Cabinet, presidential, 77, 89, 175, 186–188.
Canals, power to build, 108.
Canal Zone, 373–375.
Capital and Labor, co-operation, 682–684.
Capitalism, defined, 34–35.
Caroline Islands. See Pacific Islands.
Caucus, congressional, 149–150; party, 446–447; town, 569.
Ceiling prices, 220.
Census, Bureau of, 293–295.
Central Valley Project, 268–270.
Chain Store taxes, 546.
Charters, city, 593.
Check and Balance System, 72–73.
Chemistry, agricultural and industrial chemistry, 280–281.
Child Labor, 121, 307; Act void, 121.
Children's Bureau, 343–344.
China, 726, 727.
Circuit Courts, 511.
Citizenship, distinguished from suffrage, 437; extended to Chinese, 245 and note, 247 note; extended to Indians, 273; how acquired, 101, 251–255; in a democracy, 641–642, 647–652.
City Government, 583–596, 600–620.
City-Manager Government, 590–593.
City Populations, growth of, 583–585.
Civil Aeronautics Administration, 302.
Civil Aeronautics Board, 302.
Civil case, defined, 509 note.
Civil procedure, 522–525.
Civil rights, 396–417, 745–749.
Civil Service, 177 and note, 655–661.
Civilian Defense, 617.
Clayton Act, 140.
Clerk, county, 561; town, 571.
Coast and Geodetic Survey, 305.
Coast Guard, 222–223, 238.
Collective bargaining, 16, 678.

779

ALABAMA   ARIZONA   ARKANSAS   CALIFORNIA

GEORGIA   IDAHO   ILLINOIS   INDIANA

MAINE   MARYLAND   MASSACHUSETTS   MICHIGAN

NEBRASKA   NEVADA   NEW HAMPSHIRE   NEW JERSEY

OHIO   OKLAHOMA   OREGON   PENNSYLVANIA

TEXAS   UTAH   VERMONT   VIRGINIA